MW01033835

The Architecture of Law

The Architecture
of Law

REBUILDING LAW
IN THE CLASSICAL TRADITION

BRIAN M. McCALL

UNIVERSITY OF NOTRE DAME PRESS
NOTRE DAME, INDIANA

University of Notre Dame Press
Notre Dame, Indiana 46556
www.undpress.nd.edu

Published in the United States of America

Library of Congress Cataloging-in-Publication Data

Names: McCall, Brian M., author.
Title: The architecture of law : rebuilding law in the classical tradition /
Brian M. McCall.
Description: Notre Dame, Indiana : University of Notre Dame Press, [2018] |
Includes bibliographical references and index. |
Identifiers: LCCN 2018011741 (print) | LCCN 2018011923 (ebook) |
ISBN 9780268103354 (pdf) | ISBN 9780268103361 (epub) | ISBN 9780268103330
(hardcover : alk. paper) | ISBN 026810333X (hardcover : alk. paper)
Subjects: LCSH: Law—Philosophy. | Natural law. | Christianity and law. |
Thomas, Aquinas, Saint, 1225?–1274. Summa theologica.
Prima secundae. Quaestio 90–97.
Classification: LCC K235 (ebook) | LCC K235 . M389 2018 (print) |
DDC 340/.112—dc23
LC record available at https://lccn.loc.gov/2018011741

∞This paper meets the requirements of ANSI/NISO Z39.48-1992
(Permanence of Paper).

Archbishop Lefebvre
Tradidi quod et accepi

CONTENTS

A C K N O W L E D G M E N T S

An earlier draft of chapter 5 first appeared as "Consulting the Architect When Problems Arise: The Divine Law," *Georgetown Journal of Law and Public Policy* 9, no. 1 (2011): 103–30. An earlier draft of chapter 6 first appeared as "Decorating the Structure: The Art of Making Human Law," *Journal of Catholic Legal Studies* 53, no. 1 (2014): 23–91. Earlier drafts of some sections of chapter 7 first appeared as "Why It Is Good to Stop at a Red Light: The Basis of Legal Authority," *Journal of Catholic Legal Studies* 55 (2016): 83–139. Parts of chapters 2, 3, and 4 previously appeared as "The Architecture of Law: Building Law on a Solid Foundation, the Eternal and Natural Law," *Vera Lex* 10 (2009): 47–101. I am grateful to each of these journals for publishing these articles and permitting me to use them as a foundation for parts of this book.

I am grateful to Selby Brown, Leah Bruce, and Drew McNeil for their work as research assistants, to Leslee Roybal for her outstanding editing, and to Elaine Bradshaw for indexing.

I also wish to thank C. G. Bateman, Patrick Brennan, J. Budziszewski, Bradley Lewis, Fr. John McFarland, John Rziha, Kenneth Pennington, Steven Smith, and Jean Porter for their advice and guidance and for reading and commenting on drafts of my work.

I am indebted to the University of Oklahoma College of Law for supporting my research for so many years by providing summer research and travel grants and for permitting my sabbatical semester, during which much of the underlying research was conducted. I am indebted to both Dean Coats and Dean Harroz. I particularly wish to thank the outstanding Law Library staff of the College of Law (especially Lauren Bardgett, Lisa Bowles, Darin Fox, and Joel Wegemer), who worked hard to locate and obtain all the sources necessary for my work, many of which were out of the ordinary for typical law library requests.

I am grateful for the opportunity to present and discuss my research at conferences sponsored by the following organizations: Angelus Press, Institute for the American Constitutional Heritage at the University of Oklahoma, International Society for MacIntyrean Enquiry, Roman Forum Gardone Symposium, and York University Osgoode Hall Law School. Comments and questions elicited at these presentations have greatly improved this work.

Finally, I must thank my wife and children for all of their support.

ONE

Introducing
the Building Project

Summum jus, summa injuria.
The greater the law the higher the injury.[1]

With these words the great Roman orator Cicero warned against the dangers of an exaggerated exaltation of human law. His words take on a new poignancy in light of much contemporary jurisprudence. Not only have human positive laws grown exponentially in their number and scope, but the dominant theory of legal positivism has exalted the place of human positive law by building an entire system of law upon it alone. Human-made law has come to be viewed as self-referential, self-justified, and essentially self-restrained. Classical natural law jurisprudence understood human law to be merely one part within a grand hierarchical edifice of laws. Human-made positive law is the detailed and varied decoration that brings into clearer view the lines, structure, and foundation of a larger legal edifice. This structure is organized and held together by a frame, or universal principles, and erected on a firm ontological foundation. This book explores the various components of the legal architecture of the universe. Great jurists and philosophers from Aristotle and Cicero to Gratian and Aquinas, to varying degrees of clarity, saw this cosmological edifice and wrote of its grandeur. The tradition to which they contributed was for centuries the foundation of all legal studies. Yet, in recent times the tradition has all but faded into obscurity. We have lost sight of the legal architecture because of our myopic focus on the decorations. The primary aim of the book is to understand the importance of human law within its proper context, not reducing it to insignificance or elevating it beyond its rightful limits. Putting positive law in its place requires a full exploration of the architecture of the classical natural law tradition and an examination of both the craftsmen who labor on its erection and preservation and the architect who designed it.

Various general themes are woven through the discussion of these components of the architecture of law. In the first theme, the hierarchical frame of natural law will be shown to be anchored to its foundation, the eternal law, by two equal pillars, reason and volition. Outside this structure, law balances precariously either on the sole pillar of abstract rationalism or on that of antirational willfulness. The second theme centers on the interdependence of each level of the structure—natural law cannot survive if severed from its source and foundation, the eternal law. Otherwise it becomes a nonobligatory element floating by itself. Human law severed from the eternal and natural law becomes a sconce detached from its wall. It becomes lost and unrestrained. It has become disconnected from its purpose and wanders about with greater danger of oppressing the people the law is meant to guide toward virtue. The metaphor of a building exemplifies the third theme of this book, namely, that law is something real, possessing deep ontological properties and a clear form and purpose. Although human beings have a role in guiding the decoration of this cosmological building, it is not solely a product of human ingenuity or desire. Law has an existence and an essence independent of human understanding of it or human desires for it. By examining these themes, the book binds together an overall schematic for the erection of the complete legal edifice, which will encase and thereby reduce the greatness of human-made law and thereby reduce the injury.

SURVEYING THE BUILDING SITE: CONTEMPORARY
LEGAL THEORY AND LAW AS POWER POLITICS

The term "classical natural law jurisprudence" or the "classical natural law tradition" is used to distinguish this type of jurisprudence from three other categories of contemporary jurisprudence identified by Philip Soper: classical positivism, modern positivism, and modern natural law.[2] Classical natural law refers to the jurisprudential and philosophical tradition shared among Aristotle, Cicero, Augustine, Gratian, and Aquinas (notwithstanding the important differences among them). Contemporary examples of scholars with a close affinity to the classical natural law tradition are Stephen D. Smith, J. Budziszewski, Jean Porter, and Philip Soper. Classical positivism, exemplified by John Austin, understood law as pure command backed by force. Modern positivists, such as Hans Kelsen, H. L. A. Hart, and Joseph Raz, accept the idea of law as command backed by threat, but add the claims that, at least from the internal point of view of a posited legal system, law is normative. Modern natural law scholars, such as Ronald Dworkin, John Finnis, and Michael S. Moore, attempt to salvage normative criteria for evaluating what is binding as positive law but do so by abandoning the philosophical and theological commitments integral to the classical natural law tradition. My summations here of these schools are obviously oversimplified and incomplete, but more of their details will be flushed out throughout this book as I advocate for the superiority (both descriptively and normatively) of classical natural law jurisprudence over the other three schools. Although many points of agreement exist between classical natural law jurisprudence and modern (or new) natural law scholarship, this book will argue that modern natural law cannot prevail as a compelling system without the philosophical and theological commitments of classical natural law jurisprudence. Since positivism, of the classical or modern form, dominates most academic discourse on law, the main focus of the following chapters is to use classical natural law jurisprudence to critique it; however, I do note points of important differences with new natural law scholarship.

Much of what is erroneous about contemporary jurisprudence can be summarized in a misunderstanding of the ancient legal aphorisms: "What pleases the prince has the force of law,"[3] and "The prince is not bound by the law."[4] In the nonregal American political context, the principle has been abstracted to a more generalized one: "The intention of the lawgiver is the law."[5] The aphorism has become politically ambivalent. Whatever political system happens to be the reigning system for making law (a monarchy, an oligarchy, republic, democracy, totalitarian regime, etc.) is irrelevant. All that matters is that whatever the designated lawgiver decrees to be the law is the law, without any other justification as long as the correct lawgivers comply with the reigning procedures for making and promulgating law. No higher legal criteria or foundation exists to make or judge or legally criticize human-made laws. In fact, this very procedure for making law itself is merely a creature of positive law. Lawmakers only have to comply with the "rule of law," meaning they comply with the way laws are made, until that rule of law itself is changed. Law has come to resemble the satiric remark of the English poet Alexander Pope: "One truth is clear, 'Whatever IS, is RIGHT.'"[6]

A common thread running between both classical and modern positivism is the premise that law is in the end a product solely of human will (of either an individual or a society). Like cars and airplanes and computers, law does not exist by nature; it is fabricated by men to help organize their common life. Although the concept might be helpful to coordinate activities, law is not, in the words of philosophers, a naturally occurring real being—it is merely a human construct. Although difficult to imagine, the world could exist without law. The pessimists view this world as possible but unpleasant (the Hobbesian state of nature), and the optimists dream of a natural paradise in which all people are good and law unnecessary.

If law is merely an artificial fabrication of men, then it can be whatever men want it to be. There are no universal intrinsic principles of law that enable us to identify any purported command to be law. It is simply a rule of behavior that, once posited by someone in a position of power, becomes law. John Austin, the father of the various forms of legal positivism, argued that any command to guide the behavior of persons that is given by one with power to back up his command is a law.[7] In Austin's own words, the idea of a command is "the key to the sciences of jurisprudence."[8] According to Austin, "If you express or intimate a wish that I shall do or forbear from some act, and if you will visit me with an evil in case I comply not with your wish, the *expression* or *intimation* of your wish is a *command*."[9] This understanding places law solely within the power of the will. It is a verbal manifestation of a desire or wish. For Austin, the source of our duty or obligation to obey this wish or desire of another is that the one uttering it can inflict harm on us if we do not comply.[10] The only requirements necessary for some statement to become a law are that (1) it is the wish of someone (2) who can inflict harm on one who fails to comply. Law is located in the will of one person to move the will of another by threat of harm. Jeremy Bentham, a disciple of Austin, defined law as "an assemblage of signs declarative of a volition conceived or adopted by the sovereign in a state."[11] Bentham's formulation ("or adopted by") indicates that politics has been transformed into the game of "capturing" the will of the sovereign (the levers of power). The sovereign need not even "conceive" of the new law or in fact desire it. If the sovereign can be made to "adopt" it, the new command becomes law. Lawmaking is the art of persuading the sovereign to adopt one's particular desire. Thomas Hobbes expands this notion of human control over law to the very idea of justice itself. Hobbes argues: "We ourselves make the principles—that is; the causes of justice (namely laws and covenants)—whereby it is known what *justice* and *equity*, and their opposites *injustice* and *inequity*, are. For before covenants and laws were drawn up, neither justice nor injustice . . . was natural among men."[12] Even positivists who have developed more nuanced positions beyond this blunt Austinian variety, such as H. L. A. Hart and Joseph Raz, are still faced with this strong dependence on the will to legitimize law. Although attempting to tone down the raw power element of this system by explaining how the sovereign (the dispute resolver) is bound by rules as to the way disputes are settled,[13] they never offer criteria for establishing, evaluating, and changing these primary or system rules, which ultimately rest on the will of the sovereign.[14] The will of the personal sovereign has been abstracted into impersonal concepts or systems (Hart's "Rule of Recognition" or Kelsen's "Basic Norm"), but even if the collective will of a society over time replaces Austin's personal sovereign, the basis of the system is still unrestrained volition. The offspring of these theories is law as power politics. Pope Benedict XVI summarized the contemporary effect of the raw conception of power at the heart of modern law thus: "Today, a positivist conception of law seems to dominate many thinkers.

They claim that humanity or society or indeed the majority of citizens is becoming the ultimate source of civil law. The problem that arises is not, therefore, the search for good but the search for power, or rather, how to balance powers."[15]

For our purposes, two consequences follow from this concept of law. First, it does not contain a requirement that this wish or desire be reasonable to become law. There is no quality other than the desire itself being expressed by the right person or persons to conclude that the utterance is a law. A more refined positivist might insist that an unreasonable law is a bad law but it is a law nonetheless. Second, if one having power to use force utters the wish, it is law regardless of the command's content. Hart attempted to soften this brute positivism by arguing that not everybody has the power to issue commands backed by force. To have this power, the one speaking must be authorized to do so through some other law (Hart's Rule of Recognition, which tells us who has the power to command us to obey their wishes).[16] Yet, this refinement only obscures the problem. It leads to an infinite regress. Who gave the one who commanded the Rule of Recognition the power to do so? Who gave that person the power to command, and so on and on? To avoid infinite regress, Hart merely assumes that a Rule of Recognition exists within every legal system, and whatever one or more people it designates as having the power to command can make law. We find this assumed Rule of Recognition by identifying whomever we would recognize as the one holding the power viewed from within that legal system.[17] More importantly, any restraint the Rule of Recognition places on whose command counts as law does not restrict the content of the command. Even for Hart, law is a closed system that is caught within the internal point of view.

In his attempt to return normativity to law and transform classical positivism into modern positivism, Hart struggles to distinguish three things from law properly speaking.[18] First, Hart is haunted by the need to distinguish law from the command of an armed gunman. We may comply with a gunman's command, but we would not consider it law or normatively binding. Hart eventually uses procedure to distinguish the two: the posited Rule of Recognition tells us the gunman's order is not law (until the Rule of Recognition is changed to declare the gunman capable of making law). (In contrast, classical natural law uses the concept of authority flowing from the eternal law to provide a clear distinction between the gunman's order and law.)To remain faithful to positivism, Hart struggles to maintain law's normative claims while arguing that law is separate from morality. At one point, Hart claims that "law is best understood as a 'branch' of morality."[19] This branch theory understands law and morality as two separate normative systems. Normativity returns to a positivist conception of law, but law is kept completely separate from morality, which is only analogous to law as a different normative system. Throughout this book, I will argue that morality and positive law are not two independent normative systems but, rather, they are both particular determinations of general principles of natural law. They are both part of the same normative system founded on eternal law. The distinction between law and morality (as opposed to separation) lies merely in the identity of the person entrusted with making the determination and the jurisdictional scope of that determination: individuals or personal superiors, as opposed to governors of political communities. Finally, Hart seeks to distinguish law from rules, particularly developing customary rules of a community. Hart struggles to define rules in a way that distinguishes rules of law from rules as predictions of future behavior (i.e., as a rule people go to the cinema once a week), rules of games, rules of etiquette, and rules of morality.[20] Hart experiences a problem defining the concept of a rule. He explains that definitions are usually a statement of a *genus* and the *differentiae* distinguishing the thing defined. Yet, for Hart, this method does not work because it is not clear to which genus these different types of rules belong.[21] Once the full architecture of the cosmological legal system is explored in future chapters in this book, this difficulty will be solved. Rules as a principle of human action will emerge as a *genus* to which different types of rules belong. Legal rules are a species of rules demonstrated or determined from the precepts of the natural law. All rules in some way are related to natural law. Even rules of a game are particular determinations of just treatment of people's interaction in a social context. They are not legal rules, because they are determined by those devising the game and not political authorities.

Having severed the ontological connections between law and morality, even modern positivism places the origin and meaning of law solely within human control. Legal systems are self-referential and closed within the will of whoever, from the internal point of view, is recognized as having the power to command and harm. Utterances that purport to be obligatory as law can only be judged to be such on the basis of other commands within that same closed system. Purported laws can only be denied legal validity on the basis of procedural flaws or inconsistency with other commands. The substantive content of a command is irrelevant to it being law. Using our human reason, we might judge a particular law to be harmful or unjust. It may command something we know to be unacceptable. Yet, it is still a law we are legally obligated to obey (even if we are compelled in fact to break the law sometimes). Hart and Kelsen solve the ontological problem by simply avoiding the question and pushing it outside of the internal point of view of the legal system. Hart's Rule of Recognition or Kelsen's Basic Norm are merely assumed to exist without any explanation of their origin.

Legal positivism deeply affects how people think about law. First, we tend to shut down our reason when considering the law. The law simply is; it does not have to be reasonable. It simply exists, and we must unquestionably obey even if we disagree with its content—unquestionably because there is no purpose to questioning it. The only questions we entertain are these: Was the law made by the correct person? Can we persuade the correct person to change the law in the future? Did it come from Congress? Was it signed by the president? Is it permitted by the Constitution? If there is no procedural flaw, we stop questioning the legally obligatory nature of the utterance. Our only option is to lobby those in power to change the law to something else. In the interim, if we find the law to order something unjust, we may disobey but we accept that we have "broken the law" and must accept the consequences of doing so as oxymoronically unjust but legally justified.

Most people have come to understand law as only the specific rules promulgated by the recognized authority. The law is confined to the texts produced by the correct persons. The only contexts for a law are other promulgated texts. Law has become synonymous with texts. This has led to an explosion of particular laws. Since nothing can supplement the law, the legislator is tempted to say everything. Legislatures try to write texts to cover every conceivable situation. To make certain a law is written for every scenario, we write more and more laws. The understanding of law as text has resulted in the depersonalization of law. Law, although seen as a product of human volition, is not understood as the product of any actual person. This tendency is exacerbated by prevalent forms of government that disperse lawmaking power throughout many populated institutions, parliaments, congresses, or administrative agencies.

These consequences have produced a dangerous legalism in our culture. We focus on the strict letter of the promulgated text, shutting down our reason or at least limiting its purview. We can also become acculturated to living with contradiction. In a legal positivist world, the law can, and does on occasions, contradict reason and what we perceive to be just. We can be presented with conflicting obligations, legal and moral. The two are not necessarily reconcilable. Even if the pull of our conscience requires we disobey a particular law (that commands something wrong, for example), we accept that we have broken the law and deserve any legal consequences. We do not conclude that the text purporting to be law is not binding as law and that it would be unjust to punish our apparent disobedience. As long as it is written in a book and we can prove its legal genealogy, its obligatory force is unquestioned.

Politicians should not be surprised at the lack of "bipartisanship" or "cooperation" in our political system. Under positivism, politics is merely the combat to see who can control the "intention of the legislator." Lawmaking and politics are about power, not justification. Democrats or Republicans, as the case may be, can pass whatever laws they want because they have a "mandate" to do so in conquering the will of the legislature by winning an election. This is no different from the victorious prince claiming the right to revise the laws of the vanquished territory according to "his" will. The principles of legal positivism apply equally to the "rule of law," the procedural system for controlling the will of the legislator. Thus, when a desired result is not obtained, the power seekers need only change the rules of the game or the existing "rule of law" so that they can effect their will. Thus, when the proposed EU constitution was voted down in France and the Netherlands,[22] "the will of the people" was not allowed to stand as the rule of law. The will of the governments of the member states simply dismissed the need for a popular referendum to enact the constitution and simply amended existing treaties to accomplish the same changes voted down in France and the Netherlands. According to a UK Parliament research report: "Under the Lisbon Treaty most of the text of the *Treaty Establishing a Constitution for Europe* concluded in 2004 (referred to here as the EU Constitution) will be incorporated as amendments to the existing Treaties."[23] A document with essentially the same provisions was reproposed as amendments to existing treaties, thus avoiding a vote in all countries except Ireland.[24] When elections produce an undesired result, the rules of the game are simply changed. As Pope Benedict XVI has remarked: "*It is necessary to go back to the natural moral norm as the basis of the juridic norm*; otherwise the latter constantly remains at the mercy of a fragile and provisional consensus."[25]

This paradigm of law as power is not the only available paradigm. Other structures have and can be utilized. Classical natural law jurisprudence encapsulates the act of making human law within a broader and more complex system. For thousands of years, from ancient Greek philosophers through Roman and medieval jurists, understanding of this vast system developed, and the interaction, relationship, and interdependence of the components of its structure have been elucidated. This book seeks to rediscover these lost threads of the tradition and weave them back into a richer, deeper, broader, and ultimately more accurate understanding of the thing we call "the law."

THE DEFINITION OF LAW AS A DIALECTIC AMONG REASON, COMMAND, AND CUSTOM

Harold Berman once described three modes of jurisprudence: *positivist* (will of lawgiver), *natural law* (expression of moral principles as understood by reason), and *historicist* (law as a development of custom).[26] For Berman, all three are necessary elements of law, as all three are intrinsic to all being. He explains:

> Will, reason, memory—these are three interlocking qualities, St. Augustine wrote, in the mind of the triune God, who implanted them in the human psyche when He made man and woman in His own image and likeness. Like the persons of the Trinity itself, St. Augustine wrote, the three are inseparable and yet distinct. He identified will (*voluntas*) with purpose and choice, reason (*intelligentia*) with knowledge and

understanding, and memory (*memoria*) with being—that is, the experience of time. . . . Their applicability to law is particularly striking, for law is indeed a product of will, reason, and memory—of politics, morality, and history—all three.[27]

Three of the schools identified by Philip Soper[28] can be understood as disproportionately emphasizing one of these three modes. Classical positivism embraces commands to the exclusion of the other two. Modern positivism reintroduces the historically situated (custom) Rule of Recognition of a particular legal system to restore normativity to positivism, but excludes reasoning from universal principles. Finally, the "new" natural law school relies almost exclusively on abstract rationality (or, in the vocabulary of John Finnis, practical reason) to the displacement of the other two modes. The following chapters will demonstrate that classical natural law jurisprudence advocates the integration of all three elements of jurisprudence—universal principles understood by reason, commands of the legislator, and developing historical customs—into a harmonious, although dialectical, definition of law. The three components, though part of a unified system, have been considered distinct parts of the legal order. As Berman has observed, medieval jurists not only divided law by jurisdiction and subject but also among reason, custom, and command.[29] Advocates of new natural law jurisprudence, reacting to both forms of positivism, often reduce it to universal moral principles accessible by reason. For example, Lloyd L. Weinreb defines the point of natural law jurisprudence: "The task of natural law is to identify, in a form acceptable to the modern mind, some aspect of human existence that validates moral principles themselves as part of the description of reality."[30]

In contrast to this more abstract new natural law, the classical definition of law, best formulated by St. Thomas Aquinas, combines all three elements. Aquinas defines law as "an ordinance of reason for the common good, made by him who has care of the community, and promulgated."[31] The first element, "ordinance of reason for the common good," incorporates within the concept of law universal principles of reason concerning the common ends of human nature. Second, "made" and "promulgated" refer to an act of the will—a command of a specific authority whose command binds as a rule and measure. Finally, laws are made by one who "has care of the community." Lawmaking must be historically situated within a developing community and not be a mere abstraction of reason or disembodied commands. Classical natural law jurisprudence considers all three elements as necessary components of law. A proper definition and explanation of these three elements is contained in the remainder of the book. In this introductory chapter, I will merely attempt to sketch their terms and highlight some of the tensions and difficulties that will emerge during lengthier considerations.

Ordinance of Reason: Reasoning from Nature

Aquinas's definition of law begins by clarifying that anything which does not possess the qualities enumerated in his definition is not in fact a law—"nothing is [law] other than that which . . ."[32] There are definitional criteria, beyond the volition of the lawgiver, necessary to make an utterance or command a law. Although the ultimate answer is more complex, a primary reply to Hart's question of what distinguishes the command of a gunman from a law[33] is that a law must be an ordinance of reason (*ordinatio rationis*).[34] Law is a product of reason. The primary criteria for something to be a law is that it must be "of reason" or reasonable. The great medieval jurist Gratian notes this requirement of law when he says that law "*ratione consistat*,"[35] which can be translated "consists in reason" or "stands with or agrees with reason." In the same section, Gratian points out that reason designates (with a connotation of entrusting) the law (*legem ratio commendat*), and that if law consists in reason, then it will be all that may have already stood (or agreed) by reason (*si ratione lex constat lex erit omne iam, quod ratione constiterit*).[36] The use of the perfect subjunctive (*constiterit*) in this last phrase is interesting. It expresses the temporal potentiality of law. Law arises after truths may have been constituted in reason. The grammatical mood of the verb *constiterit* acknowledges the uncertainty of success in this first step—"may have stood by reason." There is no certainty of complete success in deriving law from truths known from reason. This uncertainty underlines one of the tensions of natural law jurisprudence: objective truths of reality are accessible to human reason, but we may fail to access them fully.

This relationship between law and reason is clearly distinguished from positivism, which accepts as law anything that meets the currently reigning procedural requirements for making a law. For the natural law system, such is not sufficient; to be a law, the rule and measure must agree with or stand in the faculty of reason, not merely the will.

As Aquinas's and Gratian's definitions highlight, law is first an ordinance formulated by the rational power. Yet, as Gratian indicates, the rationality of human law flows from prelegal truths known by reason, with which law must agree. Classical philosophy distinguished different types of reasoning—the speculative and practical intellect. As the Thomist Henri Grenier explains, the two types of intellect are not two different powers but one single power distinguished by the two different types of ends to which the power can be directed.[37] According to Grenier, "The *speculative intellect* is the name given to the intellect as it knows truth for the sake of the knowledge of truth. The *practical intellect* is the name given to the intellect as it directs knowledge to work, i.e., it directs its knowledge to some practical end."[38] The speculative intellect is directed at knowledge of things as they are. It seeks to know the truth of things for what they are. The practical intellect is directed to action. The former seeks to know what something is and the latter seeks to know what someone should do. Law is a practical discipline. Its end is action. A law is at its core a rule directing one to act. Yet, jurisprudence is rooted in both the speculative and practical intellect because one must first know things for what they are before one can know how to act. As Grenier explains, the practical intellect, although aimed at knowing the right action to attain an end, presupposes the speculative intellect has come to know the end to which the practical intellect tends:

> An act of the practical intellect presupposes an act of the will: v.g. an act of the intellect concerning means presupposes the act of willing an end. An act of the speculative intellect does not presuppose an act of the will: v.g. an act of intellect concerning an end. Since an end is proposed to the will by the speculative intellect, and since an end is the first principle of action, the speculative intellect is called the first rule of all action. Thus we understand how everything practical is radicated, i.e., has its foundation in the speculative.[39]

Law directs action, and therefore in order to know how to make good law, we must understand to what end it directs human action. We must know what is the nature and end of human action. The classical natural law tradition refuses to accept the segregation of such practical enquiry from speculative knowledge about universals. Cicero (whose influence on the natural law tradition is significant) explains how speculative knowledge is essential for knowing how to live: "He who is to live in accordance with nature must base his principles upon the system and government of the entire world. Nor again can anyone judge truly of things good and evil, save by a knowledge of the whole plan of nature and also of the life of the gods, and of the answer to the question whether the nature of man is or is not in harmony with that of the universe."[40] The breadth of speculative knowledge essential to living well is not only natural but even touches knowledge of things divine. Throughout this book we will return to the question of whether speculative knowledge of not only natural things but also supernatural things is necessary to perfect practical reason. From Cicero's quotation, we can see that for him knowledge of things divine was essential.

Putting aside this issue of the necessity of knowledge of things divine, we can establish for now that at least some speculative knowledge is essential to natural law jurisprudence. As philosopher Ralph McInerny indicates, some forms of intellectual activity require the engagement of both speculative and practical knowledge.[41] When one is making a law, one is engaging the practical intellect—what law in this particular set of circumstances conforms action to the good? Yet, to engage in this reasoning, the lawmaker must know what is truly good. Analogically, a housebuilder uses the practical intellect in knowing how to build a house, but his intellect must know what it means to be a house. He must understand the universal "house" before he can know how to build this house.

Alasdair MacIntyre explains that two interrelated questions must be asked in any craft, including the craft of philosophy (and I would add law): What is good and best for me within the context and limitations in which I find myself? and What is good and best *per se*?[42] The answers to these questions are inherently interdependent. For the natural law tradition of Aquinas, and for the Augustinian and Aristotelian strands upon which it drew, "there is then no form of philosophical inquiry ... which is not practical in its implications, just as there is no practical enquiry which is not philosophical [i.e., speculative] in its presuppositions."[43]

Modern philosophy forces a cleavage between speculative and practical knowledge, because they are seen as incompatible. The theories of Descartes, Rousseau, Hobbes, and Locke choose the speculative. Knowledge about ourselves or society comes from speculative contemplation of a mythical disembodied self or a mythical state of nature. The other extreme, represented by Edmund Burke, disparages speculative knowledge and contends that politics and law must be purely practical.[44] Burke maintains, "Whereas theory rejects error, prejudice, or superstition, the statesman puts them to use."[45] It is a myopic focus of modern conceptual jurisprudence on practical knowledge that lies at the heart of Aaron Rappaport's critique of how it has obscured the big questions that must be addressed to make jurisprudence meaningful and useful.[46] John Finnis is a good example. He presents his concept of law as practical knowledge, and although he believes there is a sound speculative foundation for it, that speculative knowledge is not essential to his presentation of practical reason. Speculative knowledge, for Finnis, is literally an appendix rather than a foundation. This separation of speculative and practical intellect is a break with classical, and particularly Aristotelian, thought.[47]

Law is a practical discipline because law involves knowing what to do. Yet, law is dependent on speculative knowledge. As the Thomist Charles De Koninck explains, "Political science and prudence are practical in that they direct towards an end in conformity with right reason. But that presupposes that we know in some way the nature of the thing to direct and of the end; which is to say that the rectitude of practical rule presupposes the rectification of the speculative intellect."[48] The speculative must come first. We must know what the goal is, and then law, practical knowledge, can tell us how to attain it. De Koninck further compares speculative and practical knowledge and shows the dependence of the latter on the former: "In speculative knowledge the intellect is measured by the object, and in speculative wisdom we are principally concerned with things better than ourselves. . . . In practical knowledge, insofar as it is practical, the intellect is itself measure."[49] Law can direct actions but it must first know the end to which it is directing in order to formulate its content.

A simple example can illustrate this primacy of the speculative. If I am lost and stop to ask for directions, I cannot simply ask, "Which way should I turn?" The person I ask cannot answer this question. If he just formulates a practical rule "turn left" without knowing my ultimate end, the practical rule is of no value. If he happens to choose the direction that will take me to my goal, it is only accidentally a good rule. To formulate a rule for my action, the end must be known. The proper question to ask in this situation is this: "I am trying to reach place X, which way should I turn?" The speculative knowledge, where I am going, must come before the practical question.

But the relationship is in fact more complex. Not only is practical knowledge dependent upon speculative knowledge, as we shall see in chapter 3, but we come to know the universal nature of things through our knowledge of particulars. We come to understand the universal truths of the speculative intellect in the context of making practical decisions in contingent situations. Speculative truths are learned through encounters with particulars. This conclusion is a corollary of the general principle that sense knowledge is the material cause of intellectual knowledge.[50] Aquinas, relying on Aristotle, argues that classical jurisprudence understood the principles of natural law to be general rules not made by human reason but rather discovered through reflecting on human nature in a process that is both inductive and deductive. These principles of natural law must be known both for their own sake (because they define the good of human existence) and for the sake of directing human lawmaking. Human-made positive laws, on the other hand, are formulated by human reason to add greater specificity to the general principles of natural law to direct people to specific action in particular circumstances and to help them to know the principles of natural law that they should see in particular laws. We can see in this simplified description of the natural law legal order (which will be developed throughout the book) the interconnectedness of speculative and practical knowledge.

It is time to make explicit what has been implied thus far in the consideration of the role of reason in natural law jurisprudence. A law is not just any ordinance. It is an ordinance of reason, by which is meant a particular type of reasoning from nature. This concept is at the heart of the importance of speculative knowledge to natural law jurisprudence. An ordinance of reason is a rule that is consonant with the way things truly are. In short, legal rules are rationally discovered from considering the nature of things.

To introduce the term "nature" raises a host of issues. As Finnis remarks, as far back as the Stoics this term has possessed a variety of meanings: "Being scholastics, interested in establishing a technical vocabulary, the Stoics were aware that *natura* was a word with a variety of meanings and shifting references."[51] Confusion over the meaning of the claim that rules of action can be discovered from rightly understanding nature has led to a widespread rejection of classical natural law reasoning as a fallacy. Since the Enlightenment, this ancient epistemological approach has been dismissed as the "naturalist fallacy." The simplified version of the argument is that it is not possible to demonstrate from what something is what it ought to do, or one cannot derive an "ought" statement from an "is" statement.

MacIntyre explains that the key to recognizing the legitimacy of classical reasoning from nature is that classical authors clearly understood that the word "nature" had two related meanings. MacIntyre explains that for Aristotle, ethics is the science of the transition of "man-as-he-happens-to-be" to "man-as-he-could-be-if-he-realized-his-essential-nature."[52] Those who decry natural law reasoning as fallacious would be correct if it merely argued that man-as-he-happens-to-be at a moment in history tells us what man-ought-to-be. This would be an unsupported mere rationalization of whatever man-happens-to-be at any point in time. It would provide no universally valid rules of action other than justifying the ever changing status quo. In contrast, for Aristotelian and hence natural law jurisprudence, one critically considers what man-happens-to-be in light of the potential for what man-could-be if he perfected the elements of what makes him what he happens to be. Aristotle's central concept of potency and act is at the heart of MacIntyre's insight. We consider man-as-he-happens-to-be in order to discover the potencies for what man-could-be-if-he-realized-his-essential-nature. Likewise, by considering water as it happens to be we can discover that it has the potency to become steam under the right conditions. When those grounded in the naturalist fallacy argument encounter the term "man-as-he-happens-to-be," they understand it only to encompass current acts. Yet, for Aristotelians the term also includes the unrealized potentialities within what man-happens-to-be. Man-as-he-happens-to-be encompasses both what man is in act at the moment plus all the potencies for perfection contained within man. Identification of natural law precepts involves, at its heart, identifying these potentialities contained within man-as-he-happens-to-be and then specifying rules directing action toward actualizing these potencies.

The closer one comes to attaining the state of man-as-he-ought-to-be the closer one comes not only to goodness or perfection but to the fullness of being. The more good or perfect something is, the more real it is or the more being it possesses.[53] Many modern authors who have an aversion to understanding rules in light of human nature are really arguing against basing laws on man-as-he-happens-to-be in act rather than the position of classical natural lawyers that it should be based on man-as-he-could-be-if-he-realized-his-essential-nature as evidenced in the potencies for perfection. The transition from the former to the latter involves an interconnected examination in light of reason and experience of (1) man-as-he-happens-to-be, (2) the precepts of the natural law (or "rational ethics"), and (3) man-as-he-could-be-if-he-realized-his-essential-nature.[54] Rather than deriving the precepts from man-as-he-happens-to-be as conclusions from premises, there is a more nuanced dialectic among all three perspectives. Their relationship involves a movement from man-as-he-happens-to-be to man-as-he-could-be-if-he-realized-his-essential-nature by means of the principles of natural law.[55] But it is only through the process of attempting this movement from one to the other that we discover those principles of natural law. The process is not a simple movement of one to the other through the third. It is dialectical. The Christian synthesis expands (in a paradoxical way that simplifies rather than complicates matters) the notion of man-as-he-could-be-if-he-realized-his-essential-nature to include not only a natural component but a supernatural component, and also an expanding notion of rules of rational ethics that includes precepts of divine law.[56]

Jean Porter similarly highlights the tension between facts about things as we find them and their underlying order and intelligibility in natural law jurisprudence. Nature as we find it must be understood in terms of its preordained intelligibility. She explains that natural law reasoning involves rational evaluations of natural facts in light of the intelligibility of nature. She begins by distinguishing between

> nature seen as the ordered totality of all creatures, and nature seen as the intrinsic characteristics of a given kind of creature. It can also refer to the human capacity for rational judgment, which gives rise to

moral norms, or to God's will as revealed in Scripture, since the divine will certainly exists prior to all human enactments and provides their ultimate norm. At the same time, while this interpretation of the natural can be extended widely, it does not encompass every possible sense in which nature can be understood. In order to be incorporated into the concept of the natural law, a given idea of nature has to carry connotations of order and intelligibility. Nature in the sense of sheer facticity is not incorporated into the scholastic concept of the natural law, because nature taken in this sense cannot offer a basis for understanding the regularities of the non-human or social world.[57]

Reasoning from nature involves rational consideration of the facts as we find them throughout history. The facts of human experience of living in society and living with laws are the matter necessary for speculative reflection on the underlying order and purpose of human existence that imperfectly shows itself through these facts. If we can define it by a negative, reasoning from nature is not merely accepting facts about human experience as we find them. It is about discerning the underlying intelligibility hidden beneath often contradictory facts.

Aristotle likewise mentions two competing understandings of nature as either the matter of something or its substantial form: "Some identify the nature or substance of a natural object with that immediate constituent of it which taken by itself is without arrangement, e.g., the wood is the 'nature' of the bed, and the bronze the 'nature' of the statue. . . . Another account is that 'nature' is the shape or form which is specified in the definition of the thing."[58] He concludes that the "form indeed is 'nature' rather than the matter; for a thing is more properly said to be what it is when it has attained to fulfilment than when it exists potentially."[59] The form of something contains the definition of that which constitutes its fulfillment. Thus, another way to define nature is "the end or 'that for the sake of which'" of a thing.[60] Even in saying that the form is the proper meaning of nature, Aristotle argues that we need knowledge of both particular matter and the universal form to know something, whether in the discipline of medicine, physics, housebuilding, or law. He concludes:

> But if on the other hand art imitates nature, and it is the part of the same discipline to know the form and the matter up to a point (e.g.,

the doctor has a knowledge of health and also of bile and phlegm, in which health is realized, and the builder both of the form of the house and of the matter, namely that it is bricks and beams, and so forth): if this is so, it would be the part of physics also to know nature in both its senses.[61]

Yet, although the end of something is properly its nature, the end "belongs to the same department of knowledge as the means."[62] As we have seen throughout this discussion, Aristotle also argues that practical knowledge of the means is related to speculative knowledge of the end, or "that for the sake of which." Law is about human actions. The matter of the jurisprudential reasoning is actual human actions; jurisprudence requires the discovery of the forms that transcend individual human acts.

Thus, returning to the alleged naturalist fallacy, as MacIntyre points out, the question of what something "is" and what it "ought" to do are not distinct questions but rather the same question. What I ought to do is a function of what I am. As MacIntyre notes: "So 'such and such is the good of all human beings by nature' is always a factual judgment, which when recognized as true by someone moves that person toward that good. Evaluative judgments are a species of factual judgments concerning the final and formal causes of activity of members of a particular species."[63] Elsewhere, MacIntyre argues that evaluative and factual judgments are commonly encountered together. The claim of those who decry of the "naturalist fallacy" is itself a fallacy, for the rule that an "ought" judgment cannot be derived from an "is" statement is not universally true. For example, MacIntyre observes when we state that this is a watch, we can and do conclude that it ought to display the correct time, because the reason we identify it as being a watch is that it is a being that ought to keep time. This conclusion is true even if we find as a fact that it has been keeping incorrect time. Notwithstanding this fact, it ought to be keeping accurate time. The more accurate time it keeps, the more perfect a watch it will be.[64] Likewise, if we know that a person is a firefighter, we regularly conclude that he ought to fight fires. The ought conclusion flows from the function or purpose identified in the predicate of each sentence (i.e., is a fireman).[65]

At the heart of classical natural law jurisprudence's understanding of law as an ordinance of reason is this claim that rules of action ("ought" conclusions) can be known from speculative knowledge about the nature (or end or "that for the sake of which") of things. By rationally considering what human beings do we can discover what they can do, their potencies for perfection. Rules can then be formulated directing human action toward these potencies of perfections. It is in this sense that we can say that an ordinance of reason is a rule derived from nature. This claim is at the heart of the fundamental break of the so-called new natural law school of jurisprudence, which abandons this leg of the three-part classical understanding of law as historically and communally situated commands that agree with ordinances of reason derived from the natural end of human nature. For classical authors, all law must be rooted in the metaphysical realities of human nature, properly understood. Porter explains this cleavage with classical jurisprudence by means of a compelling example:

> There is more fundamental difference between the "new natural law" of Grisez and Finnis and the scholastic conception of the natural law that cannot be brought out simply by a comparison of relevant texts on the natural law and reason. That is, Grisez and Finnis share in the modern view that nature, understood in terms of whatever is pre- or non-rational, stands in contrast to reason. This is implied by their insistence that moral norms must be derived from reason alone: that is, from pure rational intuitions that are in no way dependent on empirical or metaphysical claims about the world. They insist on this point because they are persuaded by Hume's argument that moral claims cannot be derived from factual premises but, as a result, they are forced to deny the moral relevance of all those aspects of our humanity that we share with other animals. Even the traditional Catholic prohibition of the use of contraceptives is interpreted by them as a sin against life, which represents the same stance of will as is present in murder, rather than as a violation of the natural processes of sexuality. No scholastic would interpret reason in such a way as to drive a wedge between the pre-rational aspects of our nature and rationality.[66]

Law as Command: Promulgated by One
Who Has Care of a Community

As we have seen from Aquinas, law may not be made by just anyone but only "by him who has care of the community" (*ab eo qui curam communitatis habet*).[67] It is not someone merely in authority or in possession of power. The rule maker must have care of the community. Note that this formulation is not regime-type specific. It does not require the law be made by a king, or a legislative body, or the people at large. The test of legitimacy (that which binds) is that the lawgiver has care of the relevant community. There must be a relationship of entrustment and responsibility between the community and the legitimate lawgiver. The order of reason must not just exist in the mind of the lawgiver but must be externalized; it must become word; it must be publicly spoken or "promulgated" (*promulgata*). Although born of reason, law becomes an act of the will, not just a product of speculation. Reason gives rise to the act of promulgation.

Although much of this book is critical of legal positivism's claim that human law should be understood solely or primarily as a volitional act, that criticism does not mean that positivists are wrong in understanding lawmaking to involve an act of the will. The enacting of human law involves a free human choice, albeit a choice that is still constrained by ordinances of reason. That we must drive on the right as opposed to the left side of the road is not determined by human nature or an ordinance of reason. A lawmaker must make a choice between left and right. Higher law would preclude a choice requiring random changes in driving direction, as that would unduly endanger human life. Yet, within the constraints imposed by higher law, the choice of left or right is reserved to the election of the lawmaker. Law is an ordinance of reason, yet it is more than pure intellectual speculation. It involves willed human choice.

Law is a product of both reason and will. Errors occur when either one or the other is overemphasized. As Brian Tierney has demonstrated in his discussion of Villey's theory of Aquinas on natural law, Aquinas maintains a distinction between law as describing things the way they are and ought to be and law as a set of precepts.[68] Law is both a system that explains things as they are and a system of precepts directing action. Yet, after Aquinas, the volitional sense of law as precept seems to dominate later natural law thinkers' understanding of all kinds of law, to the exclusion of the first. This emphasis on the volitional aspect predates and in some senses prepares the way for Austin. Francisco Suárez, although still clearly a natural law jurist in the Thomistic tradition, tends to emphasize law as "binding precepts, promulgated to rational creatures only, who are directed to a morally good life."[69] As the centuries have gone by, this second concept of law, law as willed precepts, and not the former, law as that which is and ought to be, has come to dominate. Therefore, contemporary defenses of natural law may err either by overemphasizing the intellectual component of natural law jurisprudence or by focusing on natural law as a list of commanded precepts. The two aspects are indispensable and related for Aquinas. Law is not merely an ordinance of reason. To be law, it must be promulgated by a real person in time. Law, in the first sense of the state of affairs that exists and that ought to exist, produces precepts. Reason is necessary to produce the precepts. It is in this sense that human laws (as precepts) are derived from the natural law principles, which in turn are derived from the proper ends contained in the exemplar, idea, and type of all laws, the eternal law. In chapter 7, we shall explore in more depth the greatness of the power to make human laws. It is nothing other than a participation in the authority of God himself. This participation involves moving from the purely intellectual—knowing the nature of things and therefore what they ought to do—to an act of the will, the promulgation of a precept. Austin is correct that laws are commands of one with the authority to utter them. Yet, natural law jurisprudence qualifies this claim by limiting the scope of those commands to commands consonant with reason and human nature.

Although law is more than precepts, Suárez is correct that law is a system of binding precepts that direct human, that is, rational, action. The incorporation of the idea that natural law is a set of rules or precepts into natural law jurisprudence is one of the contributions of Stoicism to the tradition. Although it is certainly true that the classical natural law tradition is rooted in Aristotle's distinction between natural justice and conventional justice, Aristotle does not discuss natural justice as a system of laws containing precepts. The Stoics later add to the more general understanding of Aristotle a definite law-like quality to their understanding of natural law. The Stoics develop Aristotle's notions of natural justice or a natural order into laws that create duties on us.⁷⁰ By the time of Aquinas, the natural and eternal laws are not seen as analogous to law or merely law-like. His argument sets out to prove that they clearly satisfy all the criteria of a real law. To do so each of them must contain real rules or precepts that have been promulgated.⁷¹ Natural law is an ordinance of divine reason and contains precepts promulgated by God.

In so doing, Aquinas distinguishes two aspects of the concept of legal precept. Law is both a rule (*regula*) and a measure (*mensura*).⁷² These two terms indicate that to be a law a thing must both direct an action toward an end and must serve as a basis for evaluating a completed action. A rule directs or restricts action by binding or requiring actions to conform to a standard. Aquinas notes that one Latin word for law, *lex, legis*, is derived from *ligare* ("to bind").⁷³ Law binds specific acts to their proper ends. As a rule, a law has a dual function of proscribing and prescribing actions that hinder or further, respectively, the end of human nature. As a measure, law serves as a way of evaluating or measuring acts to see to what extent they conform to the rule. Did a chosen action bind the actor to a proper end, or was the act unhinged from human perfection? The measure is not simply a binary evaluation (it complies or not) but determines how far along the line formed by the directing rule an action lies. Precepts involve both prospective and retrospective evaluation. In this dual function, we can again see Aquinas's understanding of law both normatively directing action (a rule) and descriptively telling us about the state of affairs (a measure).

However, not all precepts are of the same species. All laws are precepts, but not all precepts are of the same level of generality. Consideration of laws must therefore take account of whether the particular ordinance of reason is a general or a specific rule. Both types of laws can bind to varying degrees. Both aim at the same end but with lesser or greater specificity. If one asks for directions, one may receive a general or a specific rule of action: "Head north" or "turn left on a particular street, right on another." Both types of rule are necessary due to the variety of contingent circumstances in which people find themselves. Rules that are drafted in more general language encompass more contingent circumstances and thus apply to more people. The more particular and concrete the rule, the more limited circumstances to which it will apply. The complexity emerges once we understand that every human act is a means to some end; the act is oriented either toward the end, or goods, of human nature, or it is directed away from this end. It is in this context that we can introduce the concept of intrinsically evil acts.

Chapters 2, 3, and 4 will define in more detail the concept of "good" and its relation to "end." For now, we can state in general that an action is good if it directs the actor toward a perfection or end of human nature, and evil if it directs toward its opposite. In this sense, we consider objectively the relation of the act to its end and not the subjective awareness of the actor of this relation. For example, if a person is walking north objectively, the relation between his act, walking, and its end, the north, exists irrespective of whether or not the person subjectively knows or wants to walk north. A person who is in fact walking north but erroneously believes he is walking south is objectively walking north.[74] Yet, all human acts cannot simply be categorized as good or evil. Some acts are indispensable for the attainment of the end of human existence and are therefore called "intrinsically good." Others are incapable of being oriented to the end of human existence regardless of circumstances and are designated as "intrinsically evil."[75] A third category of acts comprise those that in and of themselves are indifferent toward the end; they can be related either to the end of human nature or its opposite.[76] An act that in and of itself is incapable of having a transcendental relationship of harmony with the end of human nature is intrinsically evil. Thus, a rule of a general nature can be formulated that applies objectively to all beings who share this common nature or end. Such a rule would be a general principle of natural law that universally directs them to that end. Disregarding the subjective knowledge and hence culpability of an actor, one who engages in an intrinsically evil act is objectively not oriented to his proper end and hence objectively acting contrary to the universally binding precept of natural law. The person's culpability or responsibility for so doing is another matter. He may be inculpably ignorant of this fact.

Many human acts fall into the third category. They are by their very nature capable either of being oriented toward one's end or toward its contrary. For example, if a person must travel from Dallas to Chicago, we can say that his end is Chicago. The simple act of boarding a plane is not intrinsically oriented toward or opposed to this end. If the airplane is traveling to Chicago, then the act of boarding the plane is oriented to the end, but if it is flying to Mexico City, then the act of boarding the plane is not oriented to the end. Acts of this third category may become good or evil acts not by any intrinsic quality of the act. Once the owner of a plane decides that a particular flight is flying to Chicago, then the act of boarding the plane becomes oriented to the end of the person wanting to go to Chicago, not by the act of boarding the plane itself but by the extrinsic choice of the owner. Acts oriented to an end of human nature not by virtue of the act but by the willed choice of someone can be called extrinsically good, and acts oriented to the opposite of an end of human nature by virtue of a determination are extrinsically evil.[77] For example, stopping one's car when encountering a light that is red in color is not in and of itself good or evil. Once a legitimate authority has determined that in order to protect human life from unnecessary danger that a red light means a car should stop, then doing so becomes oriented to the end of the preservation of life and hence extrinsically good. We will return to this example in chapter 7.

Rules that state what actions are intrinsically good or evil are therefore of the general type, because they apply to all human beings in all circumstances. Rules that change the nature of an otherwise neutral act to good or evil are specific rules because they apply only to the circumstances enumerated in the rule in which the otherwise neutral act will be good or evil. The determination of the owner of the airplane to fly to Chicago applies only to the particular time a particular flight is departing, not to all flights and all passengers in general.

Rules of law can thus be distinguished as either general or specific. General rules are universal in application. They direct human nature not by the choice of any human lawgiver, but by the intrinsic nature of the act and its intrinsic compatibility, or not, with universal human nature. Specific rules are more limited in scope. They apply extrinsic criteria, chosen by the applicable legislator, to otherwise neutral acts (vis-à-vis the end of human nature), and the fact of the rule itself is what establishes a transcendental relation between the act and the end of human nature by virtue of the specific rule. The two types of rules are distinct, yet not unrelated. Specific rules are limited to those that conform to general rules. Thus, an intrinsically evil act cannot be made good by a specific rule. General rules limit and define the scope of specific rules.

Legal positivism in all of its various forms emphasizes law as a collection of individual rules. For the pure positivists, such as Austin, law is composed of whatever particular collection of rules the sovereign declares. More nuanced positivists such as Hart surround this core concept with procedures, such as Hart's own concept of the Rule of Recognition. Yet even for Hart, a legal system is composed of those rules from the internal point of view that one in the system would recognize as law. Rules are detached from reason. Although more moderate positivists such as Hart and Raz might advise that a legal system would be a better system if its rules were formulated and promulgated in a rational manner, the quality of reasonableness is not a necessary condition for the rules to be recognized as law. They might be poorly crafted rules, but they are law nonetheless. As we will examine throughout this book, classical natural law jurisprudence accepts that law is composed of rules, but those rules promulgated by the will of a lawgiver must be consonant with the precepts of natural law that are known to human reason.

Custom and Mores

Historicism understands law merely as the product of particular communities' societal evolution. Laws develop out of the lived experience of cultures. In a certain sense, historicism is a form of collective positivism. Positivism relies upon the will of a particular person or persons at a point in time. The law is whatever the sovereign decrees. Historicism sees law as an undirected and unconstrained social phenomenon arising out of the collective will of a community that reveals itself over time. Despite rejecting historicism's exclusive reliance on a historically unfolding collective will as the only source of law, natural law jurisprudence does recognize a role for historically developing societal practices. As Aquinas's definition makes clear, law is more than an abstract ordinance of reason; it is a rule promulgated by a particular lawgiver, one who has care of the community, for the purpose of the common good of a particular community. Law encompasses both general principles of reason applicable to all communities and particular laws made for historically situated communities.

Natural law reasoning involves discovering general rules of action from rational consideration of human nature. Yet, human nature is not disembodied. It is encountered in historically situated contexts. Leo Strauss explains that at the heart of the emergence of philosophy is the recognition of the distinction between natural and conventional, between natural and ancestral.[78] Likewise Aristotle recognizes that justice can be divided into general or natural justice and political or conventional justice.[79] Something natural is that which it is simply by its own being; whereas something conventional is what it is due to the convention of human society. Although this distinction seems clear at first, the complexity lies in the fact that the natural and conventional are intermingled. The natural is not simply known naturally. It is hidden within the conventional. The ancestral conventions contain principles incorporated from nature and practices established merely by the community. Philosophy is the quest to disentangle them and to find the distinction. The quest ultimately leads to questions about the first things and the nature of man as perfect or imperfect.[80] As we shall see in chapter 6, one task that natural law jurisprudence assigns to human lawmakers is to distinguish within the ancestral conventions of a community those consonant with nature and those opposed to it. To separate the natural from the conventional and the good customs from the evil ones, we require principles, rules against which to measure historically situated customs. The precepts of the natural law provide these principles against which the customs of a people must be measured. Historicism is correct in seeing that laws have evolved through historical circumstances. Yet, it attains this insight at the cost of losing sight of the natural that is intertwined within this process.

Further confusion arises in contemporary jurisprudence when jurists such as Hart confuse morality with *mores*, or the customs of a people. The contemporary notion of morality differs dramatically from our ancient and medieval ancestors' understanding of the subject. The word "morality" as used to mean a compartmentalized set of nonlegal norms (primarily negative) governing personal behavior did not even exist in the vocabulary of classical or medieval philosophers.[81] The concept of a distinct body of nonlegal rules directing individual action as a science or discipline distinct from law or politics was alien to classical and medieval writers. Ethics was an integral part of politics for Aristotle.[82] One of the most important, and least noted, achievements of Porter's work on law and morality is to remind us that our grouping of natural law and morality on one side and human laws on the other is alien to classical and medieval philosophy and jurisprudence, including that of Aristotle and Aquinas.[83] As we shall see throughout this work, morality is inseparable from law, not in the sense that law embodies moral rules but that moral rules embody law. "Morality," as used in this book, includes the determination of natural law precepts by individuals applying them to their personal actions, as distinguished from determinations of natural law made by authorities (either personal or political superiors), and applicable to multiple members of a community.[84] We shall see that morality is distinct from human law, but merely as a different species of the same genus, not as belonging to a different genus or normative system.

The root of the confusion over law and morality can be seen in Hart's introduction of the subjectivist idea of understanding law as the concept that most people in the community or legal officials have of law.[85] Finnis adopts this concept approach to law.[86] Hart sees both law and morality as the concepts a society has of these terms. He refers to "morality of a social group"[87] rather than morality as such. For Hart, morality is virtually synonymous with the tradition or customs of a society. He struggles to distinguish law and morality from the custom of a man taking his hat off indoors.[88] He argues that morality does not have to conform to reason.[89] Morality can be whatever a people consider as morality as long as it contains certain characteristics; there can be such a thing as a barbarous morality for Hart.[90]

In contrast, classical philosophy anchors both morality and human-made law in the same source, the eternal law that is known through the natural law. Grenier defines morality as "the transcendental relation of a free act to its object as in conformity or disconformity with the rules of morals, i.e., with right reason and the eternal law."[91] Morality is therefore not distinct from law but rather ultimately derived from the eternal law. Yet, morality involves a particular type of conformity. It is the conformity of a free act. A bee that produces honey conforms to the eternal law in a different, unfree way. A free act is one in which the intellect knows and the will choses the act in conformity with the eternal law. Therefore, as Grenier states, the "proximate rule of morality is right reason, and its supreme rule is the eternal law."[92] The proximate rule of both morality and law is therefore natural law (or right reason), but the remote rule is eternal law. Yet, this conformity is known and willed in three distinct ways, corresponding to the classical three-part division of morality, based upon the person establishing the conformity of acts to right reason and the eternal law—individuals (monastics, or ethics), domestic superiors (morality of the family), and legal authorities (politics, or the morality of civil society).[93] Rather than attempting to divide "law" and "morality" as Hart sought to do,[94] classical philosophy and hence jurisprudence understood that human beings are whole beings who live not only as individuals but within domestic and political communities. Their freely chosen actions are directed to their proper end ultimately by the eternal law and proximately by their own determinations (ethics), their personal superiors (domestic commands), and political authorities (civil laws). To separate morality from law is to separate morality from its origin.

The development of human law unfolds in the context of historical communities—families, social groups, and political communities—all making determinations of natural law precepts. Human lawmaking is a part of this integrated system of developing rules of ethics (or monastics), customs, and human laws.

Throughout the remainder of the book, we will see how the classical natural law tradition requires a dialectical interaction of three components. Law must be an ordinance of reason that results from reflection upon the natural ends of human nature. The conclusions of reason must be embodied in actual rules promulgated following a willed choice of one who has care of a community. Finally, the specific laws of a community must be devised and revised in light of the developing and evolving practices of that community.

THE COMMON GOOD

This chapter has continually referred to the end or object of human acts. Chapters 2, 4, and 9 will consider the end of human acts in greater detail, but for now we need to make a few clarifications. The end or object of human activity is incorporated into the definition of law in the phrase "for the common good." This part of the definition indicates the purpose of law: it answers the question, "Why does law exist?" Law exists to orient human actions to their common natural end. Law is a rule and measure that directs the human intellect and will toward the object or end that is common to all human beings. Yet, like the false dichotomy between law and morality, the term "common good" can be misunderstood as in opposition to the individual end, the object of the life of an individual human being. Like the false dichotomy between law and morality, we will see that there is no dichotomy between common and individual good: they are parts of the same whole.

As we move through the different layers of the legal edifice, we will continually add to our understanding of this purpose of law, but for now it is sufficient to establish that for something to be part of the common good it must be both *good* (i.e., objectively oriented to a good) and *common* to members of the species. The concept of "good" will be developed in greater detail in chapters 2 and 4, but now we can state that something which is good is a perfection of the intrinsic nature of a thing. The more perfectly a thing conforms to what it is, the more it partakes of the attribute of goodness. Since an individual exists as a particular instantiation of a universal, individuals transcendentally related to the same universal share a common nature and hence a common mode of perfection. That which is therefore good for all instances of a universal is a common good. To be common, a good must be a good that is not unique to one individual or group of individuals but it must be a good common to all in the relevant species. "Common" here means capable of being participated in by more than an individual. A purely personal good is one that is good only for the individual and cannot be participated in by others. A common good is more universal in that it can be the good or end not of one singular person, but of many persons. The common good is the composite of all the goods common to human nature and is equivalent to the end of human nature. The common good is more than the collection of the private good of each person. It is, however, not separable from the good of the individual members because that which is good for an individual is always consonant with that good common to all. As De Koninck explains, "The common good is not a good other than the good of the particulars, a good which is merely the good of the collectivity looked upon as a kind of singular."[95] Because of this connection, an individual can say that the common good is his good and by that claim he does not mean it is his good in opposition to the good of other members of society. The common good is his good and also the good of others. Since the common good transcends the singular good, it is each member's good simultaneously because it is the end of each member by virtue of their common metaphysical composition.

As we will see in chapter 2, good and being are deeply related. The good or end of something is to attain the perfection of its being. The common good is the attainment of the perfection of each person that is common to all people. Thus, the end or perfection of man, as we shall see in chapter 3, is fixed by his nature. The particular end of each man is therefore the same or common end of all men, to attain the perfection of their common nature.

Although the term "common good" has been abused by collectivists of various stripes, it is opposed to a collectivist agenda that obliterates the particular good of individuals. The common good is greater than the singular good in that it is a good, a final cause for the singular, but it transcends the singular: "It reaches the singular more than the singular good: it is the greater good of the singular."[96] The common good is greater in the sense that it is a genus that includes the species of the singular good. The family presents a good example. If the father of a family obtains a new job for higher pay, this is a good for the father, but it is also a good for the entire family. The new job is a good that diffuses itself throughout the whole family, while also being a singular good for the father. The highest end of the singular is to desire that which is good for itself and good for the entire species. The collectivist error conflates the common good of man with the political common good. Collapsing all into the individual and the political state, the collectivist limits the common good of man to the political aspect of man's nature. But as Aquinas notes, "Man is not ordained to the body politic, according to all that he is and has."[97] As De Koninck explains:

> It is not according to all of himself that man is a part of political society, since the common good of the latter is only a subordinate common good. Man is ordered to this society as a citizen only. Though man, the individual, the family member, the civil citizen, the celestial citizen, etc., are the same subject, they are different formally. Totalitarianism identifies the formality "man" with the formality "citizen." . . . Man cannot order himself to the good of political society alone; he must order him-

self to the good of that whole which is perfectly universal, to which
every inferior common good must be expressly ordered.[98]

This profound reflection of De Koninck points out the poverty of understanding wrought by a simplistic debate between collectivists, who understand the common good to consist solely in the political good of the
state, and the personalists, who combat collectivism by exalting the particular good of individuals. As De Koninck indicates, the common good is
composed of many common goods. There are as many common goods as
societies—family, local communities, the nation. Yet these component
common goods are themselves part of the ultimate common good of man
and are hierarchically related as moving from smaller to greater, each
higher good encompassing the lower ones.[99] Just as the simplified dichotomy of morality and law has obscured the more complex nature of
morality, so too modern discussion of the common good has become
two-dimensional, individual and common, whereas in reality the common good is composed of a variety of common goods, all related to aspects of common human nature.

The common good is also distinguishable from the aggregate good of
some forms of utilitarianism that measure good by that which is good for
the greatest number of singulars. The common good is not the aggregate
good. As De Koninck explains, "The common good is greater not because
it includes the singular good of all the singulars; in that case it would not
have the unity of the common good which comes from a certain kind of
universality in the latter, but would merely be a collection, and only materially better than the singular good."[100] Recognizing the singular good as a
component of a more comprehensive common good flows from the
statement that whatever is good for the part is also good for the whole.
Utilitarianism, on the other hand, can only understand the good of the
part to be oriented to the good of many other parts as parts, rather than
the good of the whole. Education provides a good example. To truly educate an individual is good for the one educated, but, by being good for the
one, education is also good for the entire community because the educated individual as a social animal communicates this good throughout
the society through the shared natural inclination to know the truth. By
perfecting an aspect of the individual through education, the common

good is also perfected. Collectivism sees the common good as a good in itself but ultimately an instrumental end to satisfying singular goods. The communist collective is seen as good because it is seen as superior at satisfying the material needs of individuals. The proper understanding of common and personal good recognizes that neither is a merely instrumental good for the attainment of the other. The common good is an end in and of itself, which includes within it the singular good of the members of the community. De Koninck explains:

> It is the singular itself, which, by nature, desires more the good of the species than its particular good. This desire for the common good is in the singular itself. Hence the common good does not have the character of an alien good—*bonum alienum*—as in the case of the good of another considered as such. Is it not this which, in the social order, distinguishes our position profoundly from collectivism, which latter errs by abstraction, by demanding an alienation from the proper good as such and consequently from the common good since the latter is the greatest of proper goods?[101]

The collectivists create a good of the whole that is distinct from the good of the individual. The true notion of the common good is not in contrast to the singular good because, as we shall see in examining the natural law, the desire for the good of the society in which one lives is a part of the natural end or perfection of each individual as a social being. Jeremiah Newman explains that it is important to note that when men are considered parts of the common good, they are not parts only. The common good is the unity of order proper to the group. But the parts of the whole are also wholes themselves possessing their own end.[102] They are part-wholes of a larger whole. This is why the common good of the part-wholes also implies concern for the part-wholes as wholes. Likewise, the common good does not mean the good of a majority, but the good common to each and every member.[103] It is more than the sum of the individual goods.

We moderns have a difficult time comprehending this conclusion because when we hear the phrase "the good of the individual" we tend to understand that to mean "the good chosen by the individual." We ask: What if the individual chooses a good other than that of other individuals? We often see conflict between individual good and common good because we conceive of good as something arbitrary, chosen, or selected. In reality, as we will see in chapter 2, individual good is distinct from individual desire. Modern individualism with its basis in individual and competitive passions cannot conceive of this commonality of good. We harbor a notion that it is possible in theory, at least, for an individual to cheat the system, acting on his own outside the given qualities of human nature to achieve "his" uniquely chosen good, which differs from other humans' good. But the meaning of man being a social and political animal is that this is impossible. Man needs society to attain his end common with other men. As Aristotle noted, a man living outside society is either a beast or a god—he is either below or above human nature. The common good corrects this erroneous understanding by reminding us that the good of the individual is not chosen, but given. It is the good common to all individual humans.

To work explicitly for the common good is proper to the perfection of each person, and it is a good denied to lower creatures. This inclination to work for the common good is a distinguishing trait of human existence. De Koninck continues:

> Beings are more perfect to the degree that their desire extends to a good more distant from their mere singular good. The knowledge of irrational animals is bound to the sensible singular, and hence their desire cannot extend beyond the singular and private good; explicit action for a common good presupposes a knowledge which is universal. Intellectual substance being "*comprehensiva totius entis*," being in other words a part of the universe in which the perfection of the entire universe can exist according to knowledge, the most proper good of it taken as intellectual substance is the good of the universe, an essentially common good.[104]

In sum, "imperfect beings tend towards the mere good of the individual as properly understood; perfect beings tend towards the good of the species; and the most perfect beings towards the good of the genus."[105] The common good is not desirable by individuals merely because it benefits them, but it is desired by individuals in itself as a good common to all people. As Aquinas explains, "Therefore, to love the good in which the blessed participate so that it might be had or possessed does not make man well-disposed toward beatitude, because the wicked also desire this good. But to love that good for its own sake in order that it might remain and be made wide-spread, and that nothing might act against that good, this does dispose man well toward that society of the blessed."[106]

Aquinas summarizes this interdependence of individual and common good: "The goodness of any part is considered in comparison with the whole. . . . Since then every man is a part of the state, it is impossible that a man be good, unless he be well proportionate to the common good: nor can the whole be well consistent unless its parts be proportionate to it."[107] De Koninck comments on this statement of Aquinas:

> This ordering is so integral that those who strive towards the common good strive towards their own proper good *ex consequenti*: "because, first, the proper good cannot exist without the common good of the family, of the city, or of the kingdom." . . . And because, in the second place, as man is a part of the household and of the city, it is necessary for him to judge what is good for himself in the light of prudence, whose object is the good of the multitude; for the right disposition of the part is found in its relation with the whole.[108]

The exaltation of private individual goods over a common good, which is a hallmark of modern philosophy and jurisprudence, has been understood by those rooted in classical jurisprudence to lead to tyranny. As De Koninck states, "A society constituted by persons who love their private good above the common good, or who identify the common good with the private good, is a society not of free men, but of tyrants . . . who lead each other by force, in which the ultimate head is no one other than the most clever and strong among the tyrants, the subjects being merely frustrated tyrants."[109]

Still, the foregoing has not described what the matter of the common good is. We now understand its nature in general but need to bring more specificity to its content. A complete consideration will be deferred until chapter 4. Since the common good is the perfection of human nature, we need to understand the components of human nature. It is precisely the primary precepts of natural law that define for us those aspects of human nature and hence the common good. Yet we can summarize, in general, the content of the natural or temporal common good.[110] It can be summarized as the "'unity of order' . . . [a] dynamic order, the good life of the multitude."[111] The proximate aspect of the common good of a political community is peace, prosperity, and training in virtue as necessary elements to living the good life.[112] Its more remote and more primary aspect is the actualization of the good life by the members of the community as members of the community.[113] Thus there are two different purposes for which any law made for the care for a political community can aim. The proximate end can be to prohibit and require acts necessary to bring about the potency for individuals to perfect their nature by living a good life. Those acts that are contrary to this proximate end require law, or the potency cannot exist. Those acts that prevent actualization of the remote end are also subject to law, but if they do not affect the proximate end, then they are less urgently addressed by law. The prudential balancing of which acts of virtue to prohibit is a balancing between these proximate and remote ends of law.

Since a prong of Aquinas's definition of law is that it is directed toward the common good, the effect or end of law must be the common good of those subject to the law. As this section has argued, the common good of man is his "proper virtue" or "that which makes its subject [man] good."[114] In order to make men good, law fixes punishment with respect to three kinds of human acts: (1) those intrinsically good (*ex genere*, having connotations of birth or generation), (2) intrinsically evil (*ex genere*), or (3) intrinsically indifferent (again *ex genere*). As to the first type of acts, the law may order or command (*praecipere vel imperare*) that these acts be done, as political prudence requires. With respect to the second, the law prohibits (*prohibere*) them as political prudence requires. As to those acts neither good nor evil in themselves, the law leaves them alone (*permittere*), neither requiring nor forbidding them by the fear of punishment. Although discretion is left to those who have care of the community as to the details of which acts to require, prohibit, or permit, the bounds of the exercise of political prudence are fixed by the nature of the acts. A lawgiver may for political prudence refrain from prohibiting a particular intrinsically evil act, but he may not require it. Something may be against natural law and therefore contrary to the end of human existence but not be a violation of positive law because due to political prudence it has not been enacted in civil law. But whenever individual action affects the common good, it becomes proper matter for positive law to address.

OVERVIEW OF THE EDIFICE: DO WE NEED TO KNOW ITS ORIGIN?

Combining the elements of Aquinas's definition and effects of law produces an understanding of law as a rule and measure of human acts ordained by reason toward the common good, which is promulgated by one who has care of the community and which makes use of punishment to make men good by commanding good, forbidding evil, and permitting neutral acts. This definition identifies the genus of law, but when we penetrate deeper we see that law is composed of different species. To help understand these distinctions we can draw upon the image of an architectural structure. Just as a building is composed of many levels, so too the genus of law is composed of several levels of law. Before looking at individual levels, however, it is necessary to survey the design of the overall structure. How do the pieces fit together?

Gratian begins his treatise on laws with the following division of the types of law making up the legal structure: "The human race is ruled by two things: natural law and long-standing human customs."[115] Gratian immediately sheds more light on this two-part division of law in the first *causa* of this first distinction when he quotes Isidore of Seville:

All the laws that exist are either of divine or human origin. Divine laws are constituted [*constant*] by nature, but human laws are constituted by human customs, and therefore human laws differ from community to community because certain things are pleasing to different communities. The immutable divine will [*fas*] is the content of divinely made law, and political or conventional justice [*ius*] is the content of human law. That is why it is in accordance with divine law [*fas*] to cross through the field of another person, but it is contrary to human-made law [*ius*].[116]

The passage begins with a differently worded two-part division. Whereas the first division was between *natural law* and *custom*, the second is between *divine law* and *human law*. The terms "divine" or "human" can be reconciled to the earlier division, natural law and custom. The second division refers to their respective origins, whereas the first refers to a representative type of each genus produced by divine or human agency. Huguccio in his commentary on Gratian confirms the divine origin of natural law and verbally links Gratian's opening division to the passage of Isidore quoted by Gratian.[117] He also explains that custom (*mos*) is human law (*jus humanum*), which is invented by man.[118] Isidore says that divine laws stand in or are based on (*constant*) nature, whereas human law is based on long-standing practices. Hence, natural law has its origin in God, and custom is the creation of human law. The Ordinary Gloss on this opening passage explains natural law is "divine," and "custom" is "customary law or written or unwritten human law."[119] Isidore further notes that since human laws are rooted in the customs of nations, they can vary from nation to nation and are not universal. The implication is that divine law, rooted in nature, does not so vary. The divine law is immutable because it has its source in nature, which is universal.

Gratian's text then introduces yet another pair of words to identify each of these two categories. First it calls laws of divine origin (that which stands in the nature of things) "*fas.*" This Latin word means that which is "right or fitting or proper according to the will or command of God."[120] Its universality and unchangeable nature is conveyed even by its grammatical status as an indeclinable noun—a noun that, uncharacteristically for Latin, does not change its ending according to its function in a sentence. Huguccio describes *fas* as whatever is "permitted," "said to be appropriate and good," and "ought to be said to be pleasing."[121] As opposed to customs that may please one people but not another, *fas* ought to be pleasing to all. The text then calls all human laws "*jus.*" This is a general Latin term often translated as "law," but as Kenneth Pennington has argued, it conveys a rich penumbrae of meanings beyond mere legal enactments.[122] It encompasses the sense of that which is right or just in light of human judgment.[123] Justinian's *Digest* contains a general definition of *jus* as that which is "always equitable and good" (*semper aequum ac bonum*).[124] Cicero in a letter to Atticus uses the same construction of *fas* and *jus* to refer to everything that is right according both to divine and human reckoning.[125] Natural law (*jus naturale*) and long-standing custom (*mos*) thus stand in the opening lines of the *Decretum* as representatives of these two overarching groupings of everything that is right and good, from both the perspective of God (*fas*, rooted in the nature of things or natural law) and man (*jus*, rooted in human determinations of what is right or of long-standing customs). Both sides of this coin of what is right and good must be examined to determine a rule and measure for conduct. Man is ruled by both natural law and custom, *fas* and *jus*. Gratian gives a specific example to illustrate the need to consult both types of law for a complete answer: human law (*lex humana*) might prohibit something that could be permissible by divine law (*lex divina*). Passing through another's field may be permitted by divine law (*fas*), but prohibited by human ordinance (*ius*).

Thus, for a complete understanding of the rule and measure of human action, both groupings of law must be consulted. In this vein, Justinian's *Digest* defines jurisprudence (the wisdom of law) as "the knowledge of divine and human things, and the knowledge of justice and injustice."[126] Natural law is a component of a dual system. To understand natural law, one must know it in this context.

As Gratian comments, this two-part division of law is itself subdivided into many species.[127] This first category of law identified by Gratian, divine, contains the three types of law, which Aquinas calls eternal law (*lex aeterna*), natural law (*lex naturalis*), and divine law (*lex divina*), the last sometimes referred to as the law of the scriptures (*lex scripturae*). Each of these types has been promulgated directly by God. Gratian's second category contains written statutes and long-standing customs, both promulgated by human lawgivers. Each of these species of law is epistemologically and jurisdictionally related to the others. One can understand neither one of these individual species nor the entire concept of law as a whole without understanding the essence of each species. Most contemporary jurisprudence proceeds on the assumption, stated or implied, that either (1) only the species contained under the heading "human law" exist and the others are not real, or (2) if the other species under "divine law" exist, knowledge of them is unnecessary to understanding human law. Classical jurisprudence rejects both assumptions. Simply because the trim carpenter cannot see the foundation or the wall studs does not mean they do not exist. At least some knowledge of the entire edifice is indispensable to anyone who works on or within its walls.

As we will explore in chapter 2, the eternal law is the most general and foundational element of the structure. It contains the definition of all created finite beings. Its precepts, legislated from the foundation of the world, determine the end or perfection of each substance and provide means for the attainment of that end. The eternal law does not directly tell rational creatures how to act. It rather invites rational creatures to participate in the determination of human action by electing means to the end established by eternal law. In this sense, eternal law limits action by limiting the end of human action. The natural law is deeply connected to the eternal law and provides precepts orienting rational beings to their end established by the eternal law. The precepts of natural law provide generally worded principles of action that orient freely chosen human action to the perfection of human nature. Natural law precepts thus rise up out of the eternal law as a frame of a building rises out of the foundation. A frame gives more concrete definition to the structure of a building, which is constrained by the footprint of the foundation. Yet, the frame only generally defines the final appearance of the building. Many more details will determine its final appearance. Likewise, the natural law, by identifying hierarchically related ends of various aspects of human nature, provides more direction for electing means to attain the end of human nature. Yet, these precepts of natural law by their very design require further determination or specification, which specification is left to legal authorities, personal superiors, and individual persons, depending upon the nature and effect of the particular action contemplated. Human beings thus participate in making specific laws or rules of action at varying levels depending upon the circumstances. Likewise, artisans and craftsmen add detailed work and decoration to a frame to give the structure its final appearance.

To decorate the legal structure, practitioners of the legal craft must understand the eternal and natural law to know what it is they are decorating. This knowledge is not merely interesting but essential. Even the pagan philosopher Cicero understood that knowledge of these fundamental laws was necessary to the study and practice of law. In *De Legibus*, which is written as a dialogue, Atticus and Quintus want Cicero to begin discussing the details of the civil laws of Rome. Cicero responds that he cannot start a discourse on law at that point. First the most basic truths about human nature and the purpose of human existence must be understood:

> You must understand that there is no subject for discussion in which it can be made so clear what nature has given to humans; what a quantity of wonderful things the human mind embraces; for the sake of performing and fulfilling what function we are born and brought into the world; what serves to unite people; and what natural bond there is among them. Once we have explained these things, we can find the source of laws and of justice.[128]

Atticus then objects that in this plan of discourse Cicero is departing from the common practice that the understanding of law should be drawn from the "praetor's edict . . . or from the Twelve Tables."[129] To which Cicero responds:

> In this discussion we must embrace the whole subject of universal justice and law, so that what we call "civil law" will be limited to a small and narrow area. We must explain the nature of law, and that needs to be looked for in human nature; we must consider the legislation through which states ought to be governed; and then we must deal with the laws and decrees of peoples as they are composed and written, in which the so-called civil laws of our people will not be left out.[130]

Cicero understood that the study of law must begin with the most fundamental principles of human nature, which are known through the eternal and natural laws, but contemporary legal scholarship and education in American law schools limit themselves to cataloging, interpreting, and discussing the details of the edicts and other texts of civil law. If Cicero were alive today, he likely would say all of this work needs to follow and be subordinate to a knowledge of these higher laws.

Later Christian philosophers and jurists add to Cicero's understanding a new font of knowledge. In addition to the eternal and natural law, which all rational creatures can come to know by use of their innate reason, God has promulgated a third type of law, referred to as the "divine law" or the "law of the scriptures." One of the roles of the precepts of this type of law is to reveal principles of natural law more clearly. In addition to relying on our own, fallible reason to discover these fundamental laws, Gratian and Aquinas argue that we have direct access through revelation. Gratian makes this point clear in the opening passage of the *Decretum* when he introduces the division of law into natural law and long-standing custom. He explains that the natural law is contained in the Law (by which he means the law revealed in the Old Testament) and the Gospels, which he summarizes by quoting the Golden Rule (Matt. 7:12).[131]

Cicero's insistence that we must start with cosmological and ontological truths, and later Christian jurists' insistence that we must consult the divine law, before studying the details of civil laws raises an important question that will surface throughout this book. The classical natural law tradition is rooted in a theological perspective. For the pagan philosophers and jurists this perspective was a vaguely articulated perspective, sometimes pantheist and sometimes a monotheist tendency, that transcended the popular polytheist religions of Greece and Rome. Upon the dawning of Christianity, the perspective shifted to a clearly articulated Christian theology. For Cicero, the eternal and natural laws had their origin in a vague supreme power in the universe. For Gratian and Aquinas, jurisprudence was firmly rooted in the soil of Christian theology, and the origin of all law was more than a cosmic force—it was a personal God who became incarnate to save mankind and make the contents of divinely promulgated law more clearly and widely known.

The question then arises for jurists who are committed to the natural law tradition but are living in a pluralist and largely secular and atheistic world: To what extent is belief in and knowledge of God (either vaguely as for Aristotle and Cicero, or as with the revealed God of the Trinity) a prerequisite to accepting, understanding, and using natural law in legal practice? We will return to consider this important question throughout the book, but we can sketch a preliminary answer here.

Scholars such as Michael S. Moore have argued that commitment to natural law jurisprudence is possible without any theological commitments. Unlike Moore, a professed atheist,[132] Finnis clearly professes Christianity but argues that although one who accepts Christian revelation may understand the purpose and origin of natural law better than one who does not, Christian revelation and theological commitments are not necessary to come to know natural law or, in the nomenclature of Finnis, the principles of practical reason. Theological truths may be important to Finnis in other contexts, but they are not necessary to articulate his understanding of practical reason. On the other end of the spectrum from the claims of Moore and Finnis, Kai Nielsen has argued that "if there is no God or if we have only the God of the Deist, the classical natural law theory is absurd, for there will then be no providential governing of creation, no plan for man of which the natural law is a part."[133] Although Nielsen is no fan of classical natural law, his reading of Aquinas is more faithful to the Angelic Doctor than that of Finnis. Nielsen rightly sees that Aquinas's, and hence all classical natural lawyers', understanding of and justification for natural law is dependent upon specific theological (at least those of natural theology) claims: "For such [Aquinas's] natural law theory to be justified, God, in fact, must exist; and it must be a further fact that God's nature is essentially what Aquinas says it is."[134] Although on this point, and not on many others, I agree generally with Nielsen's claim that at the end of the analysis God and particular aspects of His nature are ultimately indispensable to a complete justification for and understanding of natural law, my own answer, however, does add a nuanced distinction to Nielsen's claim. The philosophers and jurists of antiquity demonstrate that one can come to know that natural and even eternal law exist and can come to know specific precepts thereof. Thus far, Finnis and Moore are correct that some knowledge of and argument in favor of natural law can be had without specific theological commitments. Yet, I will argue, owing to failures of both the human will and reason, a theologically neutered approach is ultimately incomplete and likely to persist in erroneous conclusions. One who follows the thread of natural law reasoning, because it argues from final ends, that is, teleology, must one day reach the question: From where did these final causes arise? Since these final causes as precepts of eternal law are an ordinance of reason, they must come from somebody's reason. As Aquinas argues, to be law they must be promulgated by someone. Ultimately, a natural law jurist must confront this question. Likewise, as we will argue in chapter 5, anyone's ability to accurately know all of those principles of natural law and, more to the point, correctly apply them to particular circumstances is severely limited without recourse to divine law. The history of unjust and evil laws and legal regimes throughout history is evidence of the difficult work of knowing and correctly applying the principles of the natural law. Succeeding in this task without recourse to divine revelation is analogous to building an edifice without consulting an architect. The approach of Finnis to minimize the role of God in natural law jurisprudence may have some initial success and overcome the initial mocking of critics like Nielsen, but I will argue it will be ultimately unsatisfactory.

Moore offers a categorization of different metaphysical foundations for a natural law that can be very useful in explaining my answer to this question. Moore first formulates a two-pronged, general definition of any form of natural law theory: "(1) there are objective moral truths; and (2) the truth of any legal proposition necessarily depends, at least in part, on the truth of some corresponding moral proposition(s)."[135] This definition clearly distinguishes natural law jurisprudence from positivism because it requires that laws (legal propositions) have a relationship to truths outside of the legal system. Yet, according to Moore, different proponents of this relational view can have very different understandings of the nonlegal truths. Moore identifies four possibilities:

1. Moral realists who hold that the nonlegal propositions to which law must relate really exist independently of both (1) what people think them to be (mind-independent) and (2) human conventions (convention-independent) regardless of whether those truths both exist naturally and are known naturally (or through some suprasensible faculty).

2. Naturalist moral realists who hold that the nonlegal propositions to which law must relate really exist, are mind- and convention-independent, and exist in the natural world and can be known by a natural power or faculty.

3. A particular species of naturalist who holds that "a universal and discrete human nature" determines the content of the nonlegal moral truths to which legal propositions must relate.

4. Religious tradition-grounded naturalists who hold that the "(human) mind- and convention-independent" nonlegal truths to which legal propositions must relate "depend on the natural fact of divine command."[136]

I will argue that one can fully comprehend the essence of law (speculative knowledge) and have greater success in reaching good (meaning true) judgments about what human laws ought to contain (practical knowledge) only from a perspective that combines both the third and fourth categories. A jurist who accepts both the real, naturally existing moral truths and their ontological origin in and revelation by the mind of God will attain greater speculative and practical knowledge of law than one who approaches jurisprudence from one of the other limited perspectives. Classical antiquity demonstrates that philosophers and jurists such as Aristotle, Plato, and Cicero accepted a natural law philosophy and jurisprudence and had significant success in acquiring speculative and practical knowledge of the law. Yet, their advocacy for natural law was inchoate because they could not clearly articulate the attributes of the divine origin. Their work, despite its greatness in some areas, clearly contains conclusions about the content of natural law that are, in light of Christian revelation, strikingly false. Aristotle's claim that slavery is a natural and good state for some is only one example. Augustine, Gratian, and Aquinas surpassed the achievements of the ancients because they had recourse to the fuller source of knowledge in revelation.

A critical difference between natural law jurisprudence undertaken from one of the first three perspectives (listed above) alone and the combination of the third and fourth is the same difference that John L. Hill identifies between Greek philosophy and Christian philosophy. The former "tries to explain the world by giving us a pattern, whereas Christianity gives us a Person."[137] The revelation of the three divine persons within God makes philosophy, and hence law, personal rather than merely conceptual. Throughout this work, we shall note how classical natural law jurisprudence makes law personal in contrast not only to the jurisprudence of Hart and Raz but also to that of Moore and Finnis.

Notwithstanding this and other differences, one can certainly be persuaded to accept and practice aspects of natural law jurisprudence without necessarily accepting the theological commitments of the fourth category, and fruitful conversation and dialectic can occur among scholars coming from all four perspectives. Yet, as we shall see in more detail in chapter 5, the fourth perspective offers the most complete and successful approach to solving the epistemological problems inherent in unaided natural law jurisprudence. Although intelligent conversation is possible and fruitful among those coming from all four categories, the benefits to be gained from accepting the commitments of the fourth category should not be ignored and left out of the discussion simply for the sake of gaining wider acceptance for natural law jurisprudence. Since all of those who argue from the first three categories lack the ultimate metaphysical foundation for law (and all of reality), they can only reach a certain extent of knowledge. Those who tend to try to appeal to positivists (or other non–natural law jurists) by arguing exclusively from the first three metaphysical positions do a disservice to, and ultimately undermine the deep metaphysical grounding of, natural law jurisprudence. Ignoring or downplaying the metaphysical foundations ultimately leads to their dismissal. As Jonathan Crowe has observed, the result is that, for Finnis, law does not really have an ontology; it is merely a hermeneutic to explain and justify normative social practices.[138]

The remainder of this book will provide more complete answers to these questions and further elaborate these critiques. The metaphysical and theological claims of the natural law tradition are ultimately the most unique contribution they can bring to jurisprudence and should therefore not be left out of the discussion.

TWO

Building Law on
a Solid Foundation

The Eternal Law

God is himself law and therefore law is dear to him.[1]

It is usually best to begin at the beginning. Following a brief introduction, Aquinas begins his discussion of law with the eternal law (*lex aeterna*). This is because for Aquinas the eternal law is the beginning, or rather before the beginning, of all other species of law. It is the law from which all other laws will be derived. Aquinas was not the first to argue that a discussion of law must begin with this eternal foundation. The Roman philosopher and jurist Cicero insisted that a commonwealth, a political community of law, cannot exist without an agreement about law, a *consensu juris*.[2] Although more will have to be said later about this rich Latin word *jus, juris* in chapter 9 concerning justice, for now we can note that the word possesses a rich penumbra of meanings beyond that of the simple English word "law."[3] The range of meanings of *jus* includes "law, justice, right, rights, procedures of justice, just behavior, court, regulations, power, authority."[4]

"*Ius* also has the connotation of 'justice'—that is, the broader principles of equity or morality which a legal system is supposed to embody."[5] This rich word is distinguished from the Latin word *lex*, also rendered in English as "law," which has a more specific meaning than *jus*. It refers merely to written rules adopted by a constitutionally approved legislative authority. Thus, when Cicero requires a consensus on *jus* before discussing the best form of civil laws, he is referring to a much deeper consensus than a mere agreement on the specific laws of a polity. He insists upon a consensus on the very nature of law and justice. In his discourse on the best form of laws for a commonwealth, the reader must wait until book 2 of *De Legibus* before Cicero begins listing these laws. Cicero puts aside his own philosophical skepticism to require from his philosophically pluralist discussion partners[6] at least a tentative agreement on fundamental philosophical principles, drawn from Stoic philosophy, before describing specific civil laws.[7] Cicero agrees that in order to discuss specific civil laws, the "nature of law" must be explained, which cannot be done by drawing from the "praetor's edict" or the "Twelve Tables" but from the "deepest core of philosophy."[8] It is in this discussion of first principles that Cicero introduces the idea of an eternal law transcending all civil laws. Although his understanding of the eternal law is less precise than Aquinas's, Cicero grasps the concept that law has its origin somewhere beyond mere legislation: "Law was not thought up by human minds; that it is not some piece of legislation by popular assemblies; but it is something eternal which rules the entire universe through the wisdom of its commands and prohibitions. Therefore . . . [the] first and final law is the mind of the god who compels or forbids all things by reason."[9]

Implicit in Cicero's discussion is the same definition of law we discussed in chapter 1. The eternal law is a product of reason. It is a rule in that it is the "first law" that compels or forbids behavior. It is a measure as the last law in the sense that it is the ultimate evaluative criteria of all law. Although Cicero's understanding of God is incomplete, he does acknowledge that the origin of this eternal law is beyond the realm of mere humans. It is the product of the mind of a god.

St. Augustine likewise preserves the notion of a law that is eternal and that brings order to the universe. He defines the eternal law as "the divine reason or the will of God, which commands that the natural order be preserved and forbids that it be disturbed."[10] In a passage that will be quoted by Aquinas, Augustine defines the eternal law as the highest type (*summa ratio*) that all people must obey.[11] Like Cicero, Augustine does not provide a detailed explanation of this eternal law and its relation to the "natural order" or natural law other than to say that it is its source and origin. He does connect the eternal law to creation[12] and uses the analogy of art, critical to Aquinas, when he describes the eternal law as "the law of all arts and the law of the omnipotent artificer."[13] A more detailed analysis awaited Aquinas. This chapter explores the nature of this foundation of all law based on Aquinas's explanation. In it we will first argue that the eternal law is really law in the proper sense of the definition we gave in chapter 1. Although really a law, the eternal law is a unique species of law. In the second section of this chapter we will examine a particular attribute of eternal law, namely, a tension between fixed, unchanging determinations and the allowance for variations. This tension will dominate the remainder of this book.

THE ETERNAL LAW AS THE REAL LAW OF CREATION

The essence of Aquinas's definition of the eternal law is "the type [*ratio*] of Divine Wisdom, as directing all actions and movements" to their "due end [*debitum finem*]."[14] The elements of eternal law are neatly summarized in this succinct definition. Eternal law comprises an act of the intellect, divine wisdom, and the will, in the act of directing. It is a type or system out of which other laws will emerge. The legislation of the eternal law directs all law by fixing the due ends of all created beings. As such, eternal law maintains the entire rational plan (*rationem*) of law.

The term *ratio*, critical to the definition of eternal law, is a complex word, the meaning of which grew with use. One Latin text explains that from the original meaning of a "reckoning, a business transaction," the term came to mean "plan, mode, method of procedure, nature, kind. The word then comes to be applied to that faculty of the mind which calculates and plans, namely, the reason. From this it is applied to certain properties of the reason, such as reasonableness, order, method. From being applied to the reason itself it is used to indicate some product of the reason, such as theory, doctrine, system, or the operation itself of the reason."[15]

Yet, this one word, complex as it is, is insufficient to capture the essence of the eternal law. Since the eternal law flows from the divine reason of God it is connected with the great mystery of the mind of God. It is thus difficult for our human intellect to express with precision its reality. Aquinas uses several words and images, drawn from the discipline of art, to capture the rich nature of this *ratio divinae sapientiae*:

> Just as in every artificer there preexists a type [*ratio*] of the things that are made by his art, so too in every governor there must preexist the type of the order of those things that are to be done by those who are subject to his government. And just as the type of the things yet to be made by an art is called the art [*ars*] or exemplar [*exemplar*] of the products of that art, so too the type in him who governs the acts of his subjects bears the character of a law, provided the other conditions be present, which we have mentioned above (Question 90). Now God, by His wisdom, is the Creator of all things in relation to which He stands as the artificer to the products of His art, as stated in the First Part, Question 14, Article 8. Moreover He governs all the acts and movements that are to be found in each single creature, as was also stated in the First Part, Question 103, Article 5. Wherefore as the type of the Divine Wisdom, inasmuch as by It all things are created, has the character of art, exemplar or idea; so the type of Divine Wisdom, as moving all things to their due end, bears the character of law. Accordingly the eternal law is nothing else than the type of Divine Wisdom, as directing all actions and movements.[16]

Eternal law has the system (*rationem*) of art (*artis*) or exemplar (*exemplaris*) or eternal prototype (*ideae*, with its allusions to the Platonic concept). Significantly, all these terms contain the concept of origin, direction, and perfection. Each word contains the idea of defining and directing both the end of and manner in which a future act or movement is to be done. The analogy to art is strong in this passage: Aquinas refers to God several times as an artificer or artist. Before an artist begins to construct his product, he needs an idea (a general impression of what he is to create). The idea identifies what is to be made. The artist then applies an *exemplar*, or a "style," as Pauline Westerman interprets it,[17] to guide the nature of the specific representation of the chosen idea. Finally, the artist employs a set of skills (art) to execute the idea in the style chosen. It is in this sense that the eternal law permeates the universe and all creation. The eternal law is the idea of the universe in all its particulars flowing from the mind of God. It contains the due end to which all things are directed. It also contains the exemplar or the pattern for the universe, the style each creature is to use in pursuing that end. Finally, it contains the skill or art needed to achieve the particular idea. Each of these aspects needs further explanation.

The eternal law determines the due ends of everything in the universe. Aquinas refers to God as creator. He indicates that all things are created by this type (*ratio*) of the divine wisdom. Since the type of divine wisdom is part of Aquinas's definition of eternal law, he is placing this law in the heart of creation. John Rziha has noted that the very notion of creation contains an aspect of law, an ordered plan delimiting things, in the sense that creation is not a production of a jumbled mass of things but rather is a "planned limitation of diverse beings."[18] In fact, the language of this definition of eternal law is linguistically related to Aquinas's earlier proof of the creation of all things by God.[19]

Aquinas argues that we observe there are different types of things in the world. We do not merely encounter disconnected individual things. We identify that things can be grouped into common categories based on shared attributes. Modern science is predicated on the assumption that not every piece of matter in the universe is completely unique but there are degrees of shared characteristics. There is not simply Spot and Rover, but a group of individual things that can all be identified as dogs. Therefore, there exists a standard, a rule and measure, establishing that Spot is a dog and Fluffy is not a dog but a cat. In Aquinas's words, "Now it is manifest that things made by nature receive determinate forms."[20] These forms, the rule that directs whether something is of a particular type or not by virtue of its measuring of the thing, are contained within the eternal law. This is Aquinas's explanation of the reality:

> This determination of forms must be reduced to the divine wisdom as its first principle, for divine wisdom devised the order of the universe, which order consists in the variety of things. And therefore we

must say that in the divine wisdom are the types of all things, which types we have called ideas—that is, exemplar forms existing in the divine mind (q. 15, a. 1). And these ideas, though multiplied by their relations to things, in reality are not apart from the divine essence, according as the likeness to that essence can be shared diversely by different things. In this manner therefore God Himself is the first exemplar of all things.[21]

Creation establishes all individual types of things in their form or their nature through the eternal law, which contains the ideas or exemplars of all things.[22] The fixing of the nature of things involves the establishment of their purposes or ends.[23] Aquinas explains: "So God imprints on the whole of nature the principles of its proper actions. And so, in this way, God is said to command the whole of nature."[24] The eternal law determines the essence of things by commanding the end of each thing, or its proper actions, and also the possible means at its disposal to reach that end. In this sense Aquinas says that although men can make laws about what men do, human-made laws cannot decide and imprint what makes a man a man: "But what pertains to the nature of man is not subject to human government; for instance, that he should have a soul, hands or feet."[25] The eternal law determines the "respective inclinations to their [each creature's] respective proper actions and ends."[26] It fixes what makes a dog a dog and a man a man by determining the function and end of each thing. This order is ruled by eternal law by imprinting the exemplar or style on each class of created beings. In creating, God subjects all creatures to the eternal law that establishes these ends to which each is directed. Just as an architect forms a plan (*ratio*) that will establish the purpose or end of the various building materials within the structure, the *ratio* of divine wisdom establishes the due ends of creation or, in the words of Augustine, the natural order.

Each creature is created with purposes and designed with attributes suitable for those due ends. As a result, the eternal law is a rule because it fixes that due end that governs all action in the universe. Humans are creatures possessing their own created will—the power to knowingly choose the means to attain their due end. The eternal law establishes a particular due end for man, which takes into account this created will with which he is endowed. As Aquinas explains: "But every created will has rectitude of act so far only as it is regulated according to the divine will, to which the last end is to be referred: as every desire of a subordinate ought to be regulated by the will of his superior; for instance, the soldier's will, according to the will of his commanding officer."[27]

In chapter 3 we will explore more completely the essence of the due end of a creature possessing a free will. For now we are only establishing the fundamental principle that the content of the eternal law, or divine wisdom, comprises the fixing of the purpose or due ends of all creatures, including that of man, who possesses a will to choose. This due end is the rule and measure of the use of man's will.

As the law that establishes all things to be what they are, the eternal law establishes the reality or the truth of things. Without an eternal law there would be no such thing as truth. As Henri Grenier explains: "The true is distinguished from the fictitious or false by its transcendental truth. But this distinction between the true and the false depends on some rule, i.e., on some measure. Hence there must be some rule from which the transcendental truth of a thing is derived."[28]

Something can only be true to the extent it conforms to a law, an established rule. That law then can be used to measure the truth of a judgment about a thing. Does the judgment measure up to the rule? After considering several different possibilities, Grenier distinguishes several methods for knowing the truth from the law establishing the truth:

> Therefore we come to the conclusion that the real measure of transcendental truth is the proper and original cause from which every specific determination of reality and essence derive. This first and original cause is the divine ideas, i.e., the divine intellect.
>
> Hence the transcendental truth of things is derived from the divine intellect. Therefore transcendental truth is defined: *being as conformed to the divine intellect.*[29]

Thus, Grenier identifies the first cause of something as the source of truth. Peter Lombard argued that the eternal law in God is this first cause that establishes the natures of each creature:

> With regard to this, it is to be known that the causes of all things are in God from eternity; for it has been in God's power and disposition from eternity that man, or a horse and suchlike, should be so made.

And these are called primordial causes, because they are not preceded by other causes, but they precede the others, and are the causes of causes. But although divine power, disposition, or will is one thing, and so the principal cause of all things is one, yet, because of its different effects, Augustine says in the plural that the primordial causes of all things are in God, using the metaphor of the artificer in whose disposition lies what kind of box is to be made. So also the cause of each future thing preceded in God.[30]

These first causes are the rules of the eternal law defining what makes a horse a horse and a man a man. Like Aquinas, Lombard reminds us that Augustine used the same metaphor of one planning a work of art to describe this first of all laws.

In order for something to truly be gold, the thing must be conformed to the rule defining the essence or nature of gold, what gold is to be. A thing when measured by this essence is truly gold if it conforms, and is not gold if it does not. As Grenier explains, the only source of truth is the true cause of something. The eternal law, which, as Aquinas explains, contains the idea of the divine wisdom for each individual thing, is thus the ultimate cause of each thing and the source of truth. Without eternal law there is no rule or measure, external to the thing itself, to determine its truth or falsity. This function of the eternal law deals with the existence of truth, not with our ability to know that truth (a topic that will be dealt with in subsequent chapters). Any person may truly or falsely judge a thing to be gold. Yet, the truth, the fact that it is gold, is separate from anyone's knowledge of that truth. The eternal law establishes the existence of the truth of things. The possibility of our knowledge of that truth is connected with a different law, the natural law.

Eternal law is not just analogically like law; it is truly law. It is a rule and measure of all that is. The definition of law we considered in chapter 1 requires law to be a rule and measure ordained of reason. The eternal law is the reason or *ratio* of Reason Himself. *Ratio* implies more than simply reasonable or reasonableness. The word suggests an order, a plan, or a system that rules action since it is "moving all things to their due end."[31] Beyond this directing of things to their end, this *ratio* also serves as the "measure of things," the type that measures the truth of things.[32] It prescribes the end of each thing and thereby prescribes that not directed to such end. It contains an ordered system, an exemplar, which measures the proportions of all things with respect to their due end. The eternal law is ordained of reason, the divine wisdom.

It might be objected that this phrase, "divine wisdom," merely refers to God's knowledge of all things, His providence or foreknowledge. Law is more than knowledge; it involves an ordering, a command. As Rziha has remarked, the eternal law is "the governing wisdom of God."[33] It is an active wisdom that knows and governs. He explains that although God's providence and eternal law are essentially the same, God's wisdom, we can distinguish different aspects by the terms "providence" and "law." Providence "emphasizes the wisdom ordering something to the end, the term law emphasizes the aspect of the command that moves something to its end."[34] There is thus no dichotomy between knowledge and commanding causation: "God's command of what He has foreseen in His providential wisdom is the eternal law."[35]

Yet, the definition of law involves more than a rule or measure ordained of reason. To complete the consideration of eternal law as law it is necessary to consider its promulgation by one having care of the community. Once again, the connection to creation will be strong.

The eternal law is directed to the most common good, the due end of the created universe. It has its origin in He who has care of the community of the universe, God the Creator and Sustainer of all things. Finally, it has been promulgated through the act of creation, that moment when the idea of each thing passed from the *ratio divinae sapientiae* where it existed *in potentia* to created reality where it existed *in actualitate*. There is a time when the law is promulgated, and that time is at creation. Yet, it is still an eternal law because the type of each thing existed in potency within God's divine wisdom even before its creation.

I believe Aquinas gives a hint to resolving the apparent paradox that the eternal law is really eternal yet has been promulgated through the act of creation. Promulgation, it will be recalled, requires a public utterance of the law.[36] Aquinas explains that through eternal law "all things have been created" (*per eam cuncta sunt creata*). This phrase echoes scripture's reference to the role of the Word (*verbum*), Christ in creation. St. Paul says "*omnia per ipsum et in ipso creata sunt*."[37] St. John's Gospel says of the

Word, "*omnia per ipsum facta sunt*."[38] Thus the eternal law is really promulgated through the utterance of the Word, by which all things were made.

Having made a reference to the way creation occurs through the Word, Aquinas makes explicit that the eternal law is promulgated through the Word (*etiam ipsa lex aeterna verbo ipso exprimitur*).[39] Just as all things created by God are expressed through the Word (*Dei opera exprimuntur hoc verbo*), so too the eternal law is really promulgated through the Word.[40] Since this Word is a personal name of God (who is eternal), this Word's expression or promulgation of the rational plan of God (eternal law) is also eternal. Eternal law is really a law and is really eternal.

Such an understanding provides an answer to later natural law scholars who struggled to understand how the eternal law could be a "real" law, that is, how it fulfilled the requirement of promulgation in the definition of a law. For example, Suárez concludes that if a law is eternal, it cannot be promulgated[41] since there would be no time before its promulgation. Thus, he reasoned that eternal law could not really be a law. Suárez considers only the later in time posited divine law (which for Aquinas is a distinct category) as real law; the eternal law is not properly speaking a law.[42] If Suárez had understood the promulgation of the eternal law as part of the theological understanding of the Word, this may have resolved his difficulty with the eternal law. The promulgation of the eternal law occurs through the Word in the same way that the Word is eternally begotten. Eternal law is really a law, one inextricably linked to creation. Through creation, the types of all created beings are legislated as they move from potency to act. That law is ordained of the Eternal Reason, which has care for the community He has created. Finally, the eternal law is promulgated eternally through the Eternal Word.

We have followed the advice of Cicero in beginning our discussion of law. It is necessary to establish fundamental principles of reality. As Cicero vaguely understood, the universe is ruled by some god's law, which law is the eternal law establishing the unique essence of each type of creature. Aquinas argues that this law is a real law and thus it possesses the authority of law. This law is a product of reason, the reason of eternal wisdom. It contains the rational idea, exemplar, and type of each creature and as such legislates their due end or the good they are to seek.[43] Without this foundational rule and measure there could not even be the possibility of truth, for truth itself needs a rule and measure. Yet, the terms used to describe the content of the eternal law, in addition to their connotation of establishing and directing, contain another attribute suggesting diversity. We will next turn to this aspect of the eternal law.

THE VARIETY CONTAINED WITHIN EXEMPLARS

Aquinas used the terms "idea," "art," "type," and "exemplar" to describe the eternal law. Our first section in this chapter established that the eternal law legislates the nature, and hence the end or purpose, of all things. Yet these terms drawn from the realm of art add an important nuance to our understanding of the way in which the eternal law functions.

Visual art, as opposed to literature or music, relies solely on the artist's depiction of the images to communicate a story or represent an emotion to the viewer. Whereas authors use vocabulary and musicians use music to express their story, artists rely solely on the images and the arrangement of those images in a work of art to communicate its meaning to the viewer.[44]

Over time, artists developed exemplars in the visual arts, through which meaning and representation could be communicated by use of a standard depiction enabling the viewer to readily identify and understand the meaning behind the work of art.[45] These standard paradigms or exemplars were so prolific and became so familiar that viewers were able to easily recognize the story behind the visual depiction.[46] The Virgin Mary seated on a throne-like chair with the Christ Child is an example of this type of exemplar or ideal that is immediately recognizable simply from the standard way it is depicted time and time again throughout the centuries.

However, artists often make various alterations to exemplars such as the Virgin Mary and Christ Child in order to reflect their particular artistic style or to render it more relevant to their generation.[47] Every artist has a style all his or her own, and through the application of unique artistic styles to a standard image such as the Virgin Mary and Christ Child, the exemplar develops in detail over time.[48] The study and interpretation of these variations of details to a recognizable standard exemplar can provide even more insight to the artist's meaning, depending on what aspects he or she elects to modify and, therefore, to emphasize through the modification employed.[49] Such an alteration by a particular artist can signal a change in meaning or interpretation.[50] These changes can also build on one another, inspire other artists to adopt these changes, and slowly rework the standard image over the centuries, eventually creating a new standard or exemplar.[51] However, the scope of variation within an exemplar is limited. A radical change to an exemplar or ideal can lead to confusion as to the meaning behind the work of art, thus defeating the purpose of conveying a meaning through art. Therefore, when artists make changes to the exemplar or standard, the alterations must fit within a certain set of parameters. When an artist follows a particular exemplar or ideal, the changes to that established exemplar must not be too drastic. If the changes are too drastic, the meaning that the exemplar has developed over time will be lost on the viewer.[52]

Each style of art is defined by certain formal, artistic characteristics or artistic elements that identify which style of art the work exemplifies and, in some cases, the time period within which the artist is working.[53] Similarly, every exemplar is defined by certain formal characteristics that make it recognizable. The parameters of a style of art or of a particular exemplar, such as the Virgin Mary and Christ Child, allow for some changes and variations in the details according to the vision of the individual artist, the way that artist has chosen to represent the subject matter, and the message the artist wishes to communicate through the employment of the exemplar. Although artists can make variations to these elements that make up the exemplar to reflect his or her individual style, the artist must be careful not to combine, change, or eliminate too many different artistic elements in a work of art. If the artist combines elements of one style with elements of a different style, or eliminates the most vital elements, or changes the important elements to the point that they are no longer recognizable to the viewer, then the artist's work may no longer fit into the parameters set by the exemplar and the limits that define a particular style of art.

Styles and exemplars thus contain an important dialectical tension between (1) formal requirements contained in definitional elements of the exemplar image or the style of art and (2) scope for individual creative adaptation of the style. The exemplar or the constituent elements of a style establish the limits within which an artist can work. Their formal elements, recognizable over time, make the very act of communication possible. If the variations exceed a due limit, the style or exemplar is lost and the intended message may fail to be received. Joseph Vining eloquently explains this necessary relationship between defined authoritative parameters and creativity: "What allows not only any one of us but humanity itself to navigate the material world is creativity, individual, then joint, then individual again. Authority unleashes creativity and pursuit of a purpose that is not just an individual purpose and that takes more than an individual arm and more than any merely calculating mind to achieve."[54]

When the precepts of eternal law are understood as exemplars, an important attribute of all law is revealed. Law constitutes an extrinsic formal cause. It directs from the outside the conformity of something to a *ratio*. A model selected for a painting determines the end for which the painter acts and then the model carves out space for creative variation over time. It is not determinative of something like an intrinsic cause would be.[55] Being an extrinsic cause is an attribute of law that determines actions externally to the thing ruled. Yet, the law also enters into the thing ruled by providing the scope for application and variation. Aquinas explains how law is in both the lawgiver and the thing subject to the law: "Since law is a kind of rule and measure, it may be in something in two ways. First, as in that which measures and rules: and since this is proper to reason, it follows that, in this way, law is in the reason alone. Second, as in that which is measured and ruled. In this way, law is in all those things that are inclined to something by reason of some law."[56]

Aquinas uses the word "imprint" several times to describe this relationship between the eternal law and all of creation.[57] Thus, although an extrinsic formal cause, the eternal law also exists within creatures, for it has been imprinted into them. Thus the eternal law directs externally and internally the movement of creatures to their due end.

It is important to understand in what sense the universe is impressed by the eternal law. The eternal law, even though it is the art, exemplar, and eternal prototype of all that exists, provides for variation within the individuation of each example of a particular type. Any type or exemplar can be individuated in different matter.[58] There can be more than one horse or more than one man. Distinct beings can possess the same nature, be ruled and measured by the same exemplar of the eternal law, and still exhibit accidental differences.[59] We know there can be white, brown, and black horses, all of which are horses. The eternal law establishes fixed natures that determine each creature while permitting accidental variation within each species.

Eternal law involves variety within its uniformity. It acts differently upon different aspects of creation. Eternal law has imprinted on all of nature the principles of action,[60] but different things in nature are imprinted in different ways, depending on whether they are rational or irrational.[61] To understand this statement, one needs to grasp how eternal law is imprinted on things. Eternal law contains direction to the end of each thing in the sense of the idea of the end, as the exemplar guiding the route to that end and the skill to achieve it. Thus, eternal law determines the essence of things by determining the end of each thing and the available means to reach that end. The end of the sun is to provide light and warmth to the earth. The available means is the combustion of gases within the sun. Yet, the sun may not always attain that end. The moon may intervene, as seen during an eclipse, and block the light of the sun. Since all created beings are contingent and capable of not attaining their end, they may fail to achieve their due end, notwithstanding the availability of means.[62]

Eternal law imprints an end on all creatures and equips them with available means. The end may or may not be achieved. Yet, the imprinting of the end occurs in different ways suited to different creatures. The eternal law contains different ideas or exemplars for different species of creatures. Each type of creature will thus participate in the eternal law differently, depending on its nature.

Grenier identifies three ways in which the ends established by the eternal law can be imprinted in creatures: (1) Some creatures tend toward an end of which they have no knowledge—"A stone has no knowledge of the centre to which it tends."[63] Such things are simply moved without any awareness toward the end imprinted upon them. (2) Other creatures apprehend the end as a thing but do not know the end as an end nor do they know the relation and proportion of the end to its means.[64] The bee apprehends pollen as the object of its activity in the sense that it distinguishes the pollen from the leaf and then flies to the pollen. Yet, the bee does not understand the purpose of the end. nor can the bee consider the various means to reach the pollen; it merely flies to it. Finally, (3) rational creatures not only apprehend the end but know it as an end and can have knowledge of the proportion of the means to the end—they can under-stand how the means relate to the end.[65] Man can know he desires to be happy and understand that happiness is the end he seeks and can choose among means to reach that end. Rational creatures are subject to the eternal law in all aspects of their nature, including their rationality. Irrational creatures, by definition lacking rationality, are not imprinted with the eternal law in a rational way. Thus, irrational creatures are imprinted with the eternal law in that they are moved or propelled by it through instinct. Human beings are imprinted partly in this way, but they possess an additional attribute, reason, which the eternal law also imprints through reason, or understanding of the eternal law. "Consequently irrational creatures are subject to the eternal law through being moved by divine providence; but not as rational creatures are, through understanding the divine commandment," states Aquinas.[66] Thus, the way the eternal law works in men is that it "imprints on their minds a rule that is a principle of action."[67] This "rule" is imprinted in the nature of man, and man cannot help but be subject to it. However, the rule serves as a principle for choosing action, and since human action is a product of the will of man, actions are a matter of choice. Thus, rational creatures, unlike irrational creatures, can choose actions that either accord with the rule imprinted on the mind or those that do not. A builder's product may or may not measure up to the designs, just as man's actions may or may not measure up to the idea and exemplar set by eternal law.

Since this impression of eternal law relates to the will of man, we must pause to distinguish between two aspects of the will—the *act of simple volition* as opposed to the *act of free choice*.[68] The act of simple volition occurs when the will desires an end for itself. The act of choice is when the will desires an object in relation to something else. Health is an object of simple volition, whereas medicine is an act of choice.[69] Strictly speaking, desiring health is only analogously an act of simple volition because health is desired for another end, to live. Thus, there is only one end, strictly speaking, which is the object of simple volition. This last end is what the will desires by its very nature and in this sense it is necessary.[70] As we will explore in chapter 3, this last end desired naturally by the will we call "the good." For now, we are not exploring the content of the good, but merely establishing the principle that the good as an ultimate end is the object of the will in the aspect of simple volition. Aquinas proves that this first act of the will is not an object of free choice or election. First, he establishes the metaphysical principle that anything which has both the potential to act and actually acts must be initially moved from the state of potency to act by some mover.[71] Our will clearly moves from potency to act, because we can identify times before we will something, and therefore the human will must be moved at some point from potency to act.[72] Aquinas explains that the will moves itself only[73] "insofar as through willing the end it reduces itself to the act of willing the means."[74] The will must have been moved to will the means by having been previously moved to desire the end to which those means are proportionate: "But this process could not go on to infinity. Wherefore we must, of necessity, suppose that the will advanced to its first movement in virtue of the instigation of some exterior mover."[75] This instigation by some exterior mover is the divine legislator through His promulgation of the eternal law. The original object of the will is moved (ruled) exteriorly and therefore does not involve a self-movement, or a free election. As Jean-Michel Gleize explains: "Human will is not master of its own end; it is the Divine Will that assigns it the first and necessary object of its fundamental act, which is simple willing."[76] This end is assigned or imprinted by the eternal law. Simple volition is not a deliberate act, since the object of volition is not an object of deliberation, but rather it is an object fixed by the eternal law. By contrast, the objects of the act of choice are the means by which the will has moved itself to choose, not as the last end but as more or less intermediate ends to the last end. The act of choice is a deliberate act because it involves the election among a range of indeterminate means.[77] Since the choice of particular means to the last end is not imprinted naturally in the will (as the instinct to seek the pollen is imprinted in the bee), the election of means by the will is properly speaking the act of free will.[78] Since free will is what distinguishes a simple act as a truly human act,[79] the act of choice by the will is the locus for human acts. As to irrational creatures, the eternal law legislates both the due end and the particular means to that end, which may or may not be apprehended by them. With respect to rational creatures, the eternal law establishes the last end of man, which in this chapter will be left undefined, and leaves as an object of choice the election of the means proportionate to that end. Gleize summarizes this truth: "The exercise of human freedom rests, then, in the last analysis, on a certain measure of determinism or of dependence. More precisely, freedom merely makes explicit the virtualities already contained in germ in nature. The human manner of proceeding to the attainment of the end remains radically a natural operation, in the sense in which nature is defined as what is determined in its fundamental tendency toward a perfection inscribed within it."[80]

Human free choice is therefore not completely free. It is a bounded freedom. Free election is restrained by the predetermined—or, in legal parlance, legislated—end. As Jean Porter has observed, this restraint is not surprising. The most free being, the author of the eternal law, is in His operations outside Himself, in a certain sense, also constrained by the eternal law He has created.[81] She explains that we should not expect to exercise more freedom than God:

> Certainly, the eternal law can in no way be said to exist apart from or exterior to God. It is an order grounded in God's own wisdom, informing God's free creative act. Nonetheless, even God's own actions *ad extra* are to some degree structured and delimited by the providential ordering of the eternal law. We should not expect human reason in its practical operations to be freer, in the sense of independence from the constraints of some sapiential ordering, than God's own freedom.[82]

A classic example of this extrinsic limitation is that God cannot make a square circle. This limitation does not express a defect or lack within God but a limitation in the object, which limitation was legislated by God in the eternal promulgation of the eternal law. The eternal law having established the essence of a square and a circle as mutually exclusive, God is then, in a certain sense, bound by His eternal legislation to respect the definitional distinction. Porter's claim is that we cannot claim a greater freedom to alter the precepts of eternal law than God has reserved to Himself. Yet, within this limitation there is a nearly infinite range of variations of a circle possible without it violating the limit on being a circle. The eternal law constrains within definitional limits while allowing extensive variation.

The tendency of the will to the act of choice, or free will, allows for two different types of variation within willed human acts. First, as we observed with nature generally, the eternal law being imprinted in corruptible matter—something with the potency to nonexistence—permits variations of imperfection. Not all individuations of the species actually attain the end established by the eternal law. Although not a product of free will, analogically we can compare privations in natural generation to understand this concept. Part of the nature of man involves the capacity of sight, yet some men are born blind. Free will thus permits the possibility of failed means, freely chosen means that in fact are not proportionate to man's determined end. Man is obligated to his last end by eternal law, but he can fail to achieve it by electing means not proportionate to that end. As Patrick Brennan explains: "The key to Thomas's solution is, in a phrase, the *hypothetical necessity* that comes from the rational creature's being ordered, by virtue of his created nature, to his due end, an end he must freely choose (or flout). The key to the classical position is that the rational creature is created with an end that he truly *ought*—'*debeat*' is one of the usual Latin terms to express this notion of obligation—to achieve."[83]

The first variation is one of failure. Man flouts the end he ought to achieve by choosing inappropriate means. He chooses poison rather than medicine, even though he desires health. The second form of variation is not one of failure. The act of choice is the election of indeterminate means or means that are contained in the eternal law in germ. Indeterminacy arises from the fact that there is more than one choice of means proportionate to the due end. If there were only a determinate means, there would be no such thing as free will, in this second sense, since freedom involves the election of means. Thus, the eternal law fixes the end, an end whose attainment is not guaranteed, and guides the election of indeterminate means.

Human laws are means to ends, since the purpose of law is to make men good.[84] This means there can be a variety of human laws, all of which are still law and all of which can still be contained within the eternal law as first cause. Human actions involve willed election and thus involve human choice as an instrumental cause of action.[85] Man participates in the eternal law in causing actions. This participation involves man causing a particular determination of each individual act or operation.[86] The eternal law is the extrinsic first cause of all of men's actions, including the making of particular human laws. Yet, God has provided for the cooperation of rational creatures in the causation of willed actions. Men act as secondary efficient causes of their own actions. Such secondary participation does not mean that God does not rule the universe, because each human act as secondary cause has its primary cause in the eternal law of God.[87] Since humans act as secondary causes of each determination they make, the eternal law does not itself fully determine the course of human actions. Thus the eternal law does not determine the content of human-made laws without the cooperation of men. At the same time, since the eternal law is the ultimate cause of human determinations it is the ultimate cause of every human-made law.

Notwithstanding the variation, the unity of form still exists. As Westerman observes: "The exemplar God has in mind directs the way the world is and should be. In short, the world is created in such a way that it is best fitted to these ends. It is because of the directive power of the exemplar that it [eternal law] can properly be called 'law.' "[88] The analogy to art is illuminating in understanding the relationship between a determinate end and either corrupting variations or conforming variations. Two artists might have the same idea for a painting (of a Madonna and Child). They each have a fixed end to paint a picture portraying this subject. They each might elect to follow the same exemplar image (that of the school of Raphael) and both may have attained the same level of artistic skill. Yet, the individual paintings of each artist flowing from the determined end and following the same exemplar will exhibit differences. The products, the paintings, are both caused by the same idea, exemplar, or type that governs the products and by the individual cooperation of the artist adopting them. Thus, the individual elements of the created world will exhibit variety and difference but are united by the *ratio* of the eternal law that directs their due end. This end, in turn, provides the exemplar to be followed. There may be a third artist who pursues the same end, Madonna and Child, and even chooses the same exemplar, yet he may produce a bad painting. He may lack artistic skill or choose poor material components, such as inappropriate paint. The painting will be ruled by the end and the exemplar, but fail to express either in reality.

In this light, human law, the laws we encounter on a daily basis, are also contained within the eternal law. We will explore the nature, purpose, and limitations of human laws in greater depth in chapter 6, but at this point we can consider the relationship between human laws and the eternal law in light of what we have established about eternal law. Aquinas notes that eternal law, as the complete ordering of the universe, contains within it "each single truth," including "the particular determinations of individual cases."[89] This phrase can be easily misunderstood to mean only that all particular human laws have been formulated in the eternal law, and human law must merely discover them. This conclusion would be similar to Ronald Dworkin's argument that there are "right answers" to all legal questions.[90] Such a conclusion is an oversimplification of the concept of the eternal law and human participation in it. To draw the distinction it is important to examine this statement in context with Aquinas:

> The human reason cannot have a full participation of the dictate of the Divine Reason, but according to its own mode, and imperfectly. Consequently, as on the part of the speculative reason, by a natural participation of Divine Wisdom, there is in us the knowledge of certain general principles, but not proper knowledge of each single truth, such as that contained in the Divine Wisdom; so too, on the part of the practical reason, man has a natural participation of the eternal law, according to certain general principles, but not as regards the particular determinations of individual cases, which are, however, contained in the eternal law. Hence the need for human reason to proceed further to sanction them by law.[91]

The phrases Divine Reason and Divine Wisdom preceding the reference to eternal law recall the connection—critical for Aquinas—between the knowledge of God and the eternal law. The eternal law contains general principles of action (the nature of things and the ends to which those things are directed). But these general principles also contain within them the particular actions determined by them, just as a conclusion is said to be contained in the premises.[92] In the case of humans, God has permitted the participation, as a secondary efficient cause, of human reason in the formation of those particular determinations. The particular shape these determinations will take is dependent upon the type or *exemplar* of eternal law and instrumentally on the practical reason of human beings participating in making particular determinations of the general principles. To the extent these particular determinations are reasonable determinations in harmony with the general principles—or, in Westerman's language, follow the divine style—they are contained within eternal law in two different ways. First, they are contained in the general principles, just as a particular work of art following a style is contained in the *exemplar* of that style. Likewise, more than one conclusion can be contained in a major premise depending upon the contingent minor premise selected. Taking the major premise "A human being is a rational animal," we can reach both of the conclusions "John Smith is a rational animal" and "Mary Jones is a rational animal," because both minor premises "John Smith is a human being" and "Mary Jones is a human being" can be paired with this major premise. Although both conclusions are contained in the major premise, the particular conclusion to a given syllogism is contingent upon the selection of the minor premise.[93]

Second, divine wisdom both knows all things and is the first cause of all things. Divine wisdom thus contains all particular laws, both in the sense of having knowledge and as an ultimate cause of them. Divine wisdom knows the particular determinations that will in fact be made instrumentally by the human laws, even though this foreknowledge is denied to man so that he may participate in the lawmaking process by using his reason, rather than divine revelation, to make the determinations. Likewise, although divine wisdom is the first cause of all particular laws, God provides for the participation of human agency as efficient causes of such laws. It is this element of intellectual and volitional (knowledge and instrumental causality) participation in lawmaking that distinguishes the process of lawmaking from a mechanical discovery of particular human laws that already exist and need merely be made known by the promulgation of human laws. If this were all that occurred, human laws would only participate in one aspect of lawmaking, promulgation. By contrast, the rules governing the operation of nonrational creatures already exist in particular determinations. For example, dropping something causes it to fall by virtue of gravity, and the bee seeks pollen. Man does not participate in formulating the law of gravity or the instinct of the bee in the same way he does with respect to laws governing human action. He merely discovers its operation and attempts to understand its causes. As to laws governing human actions, man is charged with the task of not only discovering but also causing, by determining the details of, the rule according to the general principles implanted in man's reason through the natural law. At the same time that God permits this active participation, the divine wisdom already knows and ultimately causes the determinations that will be made.

However, this participation in lawmaking that God has granted is not a "full participation of the dictate of the Divine Reason" but only "a natural participation in the Divine Wisdom [source of eternal law]" consisting of "a natural participation of the eternal law, according to certain general principles."[94] Thus, we can know that there exist objectively true determinations of individual cases (contained within the divine wisdom or eternal law), but our knowledge of these singular truths is not "natural." Unlike the general principles of the natural law, which are "impressed on it [our reason] by nature"[95] or "imparted to us by nature,"[96] the particular determinations are arrived at by the "effort of reason" (*industriam rationis*).[97] Making these particular determinations involves work or industry. It is not something like a proposition *per se nota*, which once explained to us is easily grasped by the mind.[98] This difficulty of making determinations in individual cases further explains the need for human laws. Since making these particular determinations is hard work for each individual and there is significant risk of error and hence confusion,[99] there is a need for human law to "sanction" particular determinations.[100] Not all of these sanctioned determinations will be perfectly contained within the eternal law (in the sense of being perfect determinations, even though they are contained in the sense of being foreknown by God). The error is not an error in God but rather in the weakness of human reason. It is an error not in God but tolerated by Him as a consequence of permitting human, fallible participation in the lawmaking process for human action.

THE NECESSITY AND PROBLEMS OF A FOUNDATION

The first two sections of this chapter have argued that the eternal law is the source and foundation of all other law. Through it, God establishes the natures of all things, including their ends or purposes. Without eternal law, truth itself would not be possible. As we will see in later chapters, this foundation becomes necessary to understand the nature and content of the natural law and human laws made in accordance with it.

Not all jurists, and not all jurists committed to natural law jurisprudence, agree on the fundamental importance of the eternal law. Theories of law that fail to fully accept the eternal law as a real law and as indispensable to the entire legal system are forced either to reject the natural law altogether or minimize it to such an extent that natural law becomes irrelevant.

We already observed in our first section in this chapter that Suárez rejects the proposition that eternal law is really a law because he cannot identify its promulgation. As a result, Suárez rejects the idea that man can rationally discover correct principles of action. Thus God had to promulgate a law, the first real law in Suárez's system, the natural law.[101] As Westerman observes: "The decline of the unified notion of eternal law results in the decline of the notion of practical reason."[102] She goes on to argue that this removal of eternal law as the "pillar"[103] of natural law reduces law to merely the rules commanded by God without reference to a created, intelligible order.[104]

Following Suárez, Hugo Grotius is famous for the impious hypothesis that natural law could exist even if God himself did not exist or did not order the universe.[105] Although Grotius personally may have accepted the existence of God, his hypothesis that natural law could exist even without God either eliminates the eternal law or minimizes its effect solely to the desire for self-preservation, and may limit it only to the realm of human beings and not all of creation.[106]

Following Grotius's hypothesis, three centuries later, advocates of the so-called new natural law theory, such as John Finnis, though professing a personal belief in God, have attempted to develop a natural law jurisprudence as if God did not exist or was not necessary to the argument. Finnis, in defense of his position, is correct in saying that it is not the same as a secularist position,[107] but the omissions from his system do unravel the argument. Finnis appears to share Grotius's position. When wearing his hat of a simple man, he holds a truly sincere belief in the existence of God, but that sincerely held belief is relegated to irrelevance when Finnis puts on his hat as legal philosopher. Finnis's legal philosophy of practical reason includes little attention to the eternal law. He dismisses God's existence and nature as unnecessary to the study of natural law early on in his *Natural Law and Natural Rights*.[108] He describes the project of his work as demonstrating that "natural law can be understood, assented to, applied, and reflectively analysed without adverting to the question of the existence of God."[109] Finnis leaves this original claim unchanged in his second edition of *Natural Law and Natural Rights*, even though he admits that natural reason can know more about the nature of God than the "austere, minimalist view" he articulated in the first edition.[110] Certainly in his *Aquinas: Moral, Political, and Legal Theory*, Finnis offers more than the minimalist conception in *Natural Law and Natural Rights*. Yet, notwithstanding the added detail, the discussion still comes as an appendage or afterthought to the discussion of morality, politics, and law. The discussion waits until the last chapter of the book. Although the word "God" appears somewhat more frequently, the impersonal "D" (which letter Finnis uses in *Natural Law and Natural Rights* to represent "a state of affairs" he implies to be God) is replaced by "X."[111] Most importantly, notwithstanding the more detailed examination of God's nature, Finnis reaffirms after the publication of *Aquinas: Moral, Political, and Legal Theory* adherence to the proposition that this knowledge is unnecessary to the presentation of his jurisprudence.[112] He remains committed to the claim that knowing the answers to questions about the existence and nature of God and the features of this world, although leaving "somehow 'subjective' and 'questionable' the whole structure of basic principles and requirements of practical reasonableness and human flourishing . . . does not unravel that structure or affect its internal order or weaken its claim to be more reasonable than any logically possible alternative structure."[113]

Even so, Finnis does not fool the atheist moral philosopher. As Michael Moore has keenly observed,

> Finnis eschews most of the theology/ethics connections . . . while yet coming back, at the end of the day, to theology in order to save ethics from a kind of relativity to the merely human. Finnis rightly rejects any use for God, either in making out the objective existence of moral qualities, in justifying our moral beliefs, or in accepting that such moral qualities give each of us sufficient objective reasons to act in accordance with them. Yet despite this autonomous ethics, "practical reasonableness," as Finnis calls it, he nonetheless brings in God to save morality from "a certain relativity." . . .
>
> Finnis then ultimately concludes that "God is the basis of obligation," despite his own clear-headed refusal to explain obligation generally in terms of conformity to superior will.[114]

Tacking God on to his theory as an appendix does not in the end convince an atheist like Moore; it merely opens Finnis up to the criticism of inconsistency, purporting to exclude God from moral philosophy as he sneaks him in the back door. Placing God at the foundation avoids this justified criticism.

Finnis does include a brief discussion of the eternal law, but it is literally an appendage to his theory. Not only is any discussion of God and eternal law placed at the very end of the book, but Finnis also concludes that if God and eternal law exist, they are superfluous to natural law and his seven incommensurable goods: "What can be established by argumentation from the existence and general features of this world, concerning the uncaused cause of the world, does not directly assist us in answering those practical questions."[115] Finnis's thesis consistently remains that consideration of first principles about God and the universe can be detached from considerations of practical reason: "The kinds of 'detachability' . . . never went much beyond the simple thought that, as it is possible to do physics without raising or pressing further questions, so to some extent it is possible to have a practical and theoretical understanding of practical reason's principles and their implications for reasonable choice, and so for individual and communal self-constitution, without raising further or pressing questions."[116]

The furthest Finnis goes is to agree that "adherence to the natural law is rationally unstable in the absence of a certain sort of theistic stance."[117] Yet, this statement suggests only an instability in the will to consistently adhere to the principles of natural law. Finnis continues to deny the necessity of these truths for the intellect to know the natural law.

Finnis's explanation is the very position rejected by Cicero in his *De Legibus*. Notwithstanding the weaknesses of Cicero's philosophy[118] as a philosophy, he at least sees this necessary connection between knowledge of nature, or what we would call "natural law," and knowledge of core facts about the supernatural: "He who is to live in accordance with nature must base his principles upon the system and government of the entire world. Nor again can anyone judge truly of things good and evil, save by a knowledge of the whole plan of nature and also of the gods, and of the answer to the question whether the nature of man is or is not in harmony with that of universe."[119] Without dispute, Cicero's understanding of eternal law was vague and incomplete. Yet, he rejects Finnis's partition of these questions from questions of practical reason and action. He acknowledges a system and governance of the universe that is necessary for one wishing to live in accordance with nature.

At the core of Finnis's position is this rejection of the unity of knowledge, a rejection of the interdependence of speculative and practical reason, which we introduced in chapter 1. Finnis asserts one can attain sufficient knowledge in one area, be that physics or jurisprudence, while remaining wholly detached from knowledge in another area. The consequences of such position for our ability to know the natural law will be explored in subsequent chapters. Knowledge of certain truths about God and the world are indispensable to practical reasoning. Finnis's refusal to admit the interdependence of speculative and practical reason is why, in the preface to *Natural Law and Natural Rights*, he can advise someone "whose concerns are limited to jurisprudence" that they can omit reading the chapter concerning "D."[120] Yet, as we suggested in chapter 1 and as we will argue further, one interested in "jurisprudence" or even practical reason more generally cannot be disinterested in what speculative reason tells us about the way the world is and its relationship to God.

Finnis also undermines the status of eternal law as a real law by eliminating a personal lawgiver (one who has care of the community). He does not discuss God as a personal being but rather as a "state of affairs," which can be conveniently labeled "D."[121] He asserts that "it is impossible to have sufficient assurance . . . without some revelation more revealing than any that Plato or Aristotle may have experienced," such as that God is a personal God whom we could "love, personal in a way that one might imitate, a guide that one might follow, or a guarantor of anyone's practical reasonableness."[122] Finnis subsequently reaffirmed that anything we might know about God being a personal God is also subject to his conclusion of irrelevancy with respect to knowing and applying the principles of practical reasonableness.[123]

There are two problems with Finnis's dismissal of God's personal nature. The first, which we will take up again in subsequent chapters, is the obvious fact that we have received "some revelation more revealing than any that Plato or Aristotle may have experienced."[124] The legitimate hesitancy of Plato and Aristotle is no longer acceptable in a world after the

revelation of a personal God made man has occurred. Once that information becomes available it cannot simply be ignored. That is why Aquinas's
legal philosophy goes beyond the teaching of Plato and Aristotle. His account of law and justice incorporates this more revealing revelation. Finnis's approach is to act as if this revelation had never happened, a position
only made possible by his tenacious belief in the severability of speculative and practical reason.

Second, without a personal lawgiver, eternal law cannot be a real law.
Finnis ends as Suárez does, dismissing eternal law as a real law relevant to
our understanding of other forms of law. Accordingly, Finnis states that
"it [eternal law] must not be treated as a theory which could guide investigation and verification of suggested norms in any of the four orders;
rather, it is a speculation about why those norms whose holding has been
appropriately verified or established do hold. . . . [And] the speculation
that the norms intelligible to us in any of the four orders are expressions
or indications of D's[125] creative plan in no way warrants the further speculation that D's creative plan is understood by us."[126] Not only is eternal law
not law, it is not even a theory. Eternal law is only a hypothesis, and not a
very useful one at that. Finnis concludes that "if there is an Eternal Law,
we do not know enough of it to be able to judge . . . in terms of it."[127] Porter
contrasts Finnis's insistence that "natural law does not depend on specific
theological or broadly natural beliefs for its foundations or content"[128]
with "a pervasive theme running through both Jewish and Christian
thought, namely, the deep connections between law and cosmic order."[129]
As the remainder of this book will argue, I agree with her conclusion that
an attempt to ground a theory of natural law solely in "pure . . . reason" is
"ultimately fruitless."[130] It bears no fruit because it is only planted in the
soil of pure reason, not the eternal law.

And so this failure to place eternal law in a foundational position
does more than call into question Finnis's system based on pure practical
reason. It destroys law's entire ontology. Vining has asked a penetrating
question for modern jurisprudence: Does law have its own ontology?[131]
Steven Smith has identified this question as the great quandary of today's
jurisprudence.[132] Smith convincingly argues that although we still speak
as if something called "the law" really exists, most jurists, practitioners,
and ordinary people no longer actually believe it exists as a distinct reality,

a problem he calls an "ontological gap."[133] Smith's judgment—that today our "law-talk" makes use of an ontology that we reject[134]—aptly applies to the jurisprudence of Finnis. For although Finnis finally reveals he does believe in an ontology of law, his entire argument is based on the premise that law can be understood and utilized without acceptance of that ontology, recourse to which is merely optional for a greater appreciation of law. Thus, even if not rejecting law's ontology per se, Finnis rejects its necessity for jurisprudence. Westerman argues that although Finnis's dismissal of eternal law may avoid the so-called naturalist fallacy (which accusation itself is a fallacy, as we discuss in chapter 1), it results in Finnis creating "the far more serious problem of a lacking foundation."[135] Understanding things involves understanding their causes, yet Finnis asserts we can understand law, including natural law, independently of its cause, eternal law. Finnis admits his "failure . . . to identify the unifying source of the nine 'methodological principles' or 'requirements' of practical reasonableness."[136] Since the unity of moral principles is found in the eternal law, in the second edition of *Natural Law and Natural Rights* Finnis can only correct this failure by a self-referential justification of their unity. All he can offer is a master principle that "all one's choices . . . should be *open to* integral human fulfillment."[137] However, this master principle has no source or ontology of its own. It is merely asserted as a master moral principle that can unify the requirements. And as we shall see in subsequent chapters, the lack of a foundation in eternal law has consequences for failures in ordering a hierarchy of goods and in identifying a satisfactory answer to the question of law's obligation. Ultimately, Finnis's hesitation to embrace the eternal law as foundation seems to derive from his refusal to accept that there is an epistemological relationship between speculative and practical reason or that we can derive principles of practical reason from speculative knowledge.[138]

Brennan, after long puzzling over an answer to the ontological question raised by Smith and Vining, and unlike Finnis, concluded that the laws we make must have their own reality and that reality requires a necessary source—a higher law.[139] According to Brennan,

> Higher law is "in" us as a distinct reality. We are not laws unto ourselves, and we do not make laws except as giving specification or determination to that higher law in which we "participate." If Vining

[and we might add Finnis] does not affirm this participation in a higher law, I am not sure what it would mean to say that law has its own ontology. On such a view, law is just one among the many artefacts we create that are explicable in the ways in which our other artefacts are (or are not) explicable.[140]

Without the ontological foundation of eternal law, our laws are merely figments of our creation lacking a metaphysical reality.

Unlike Suárez, Grotius, and Finnis, Aquinas places eternal law as a real and ontologically necessary law at the very heart of his jurisprudence.[141] It encompasses the entire ordering of the universe by determining what makes each thing what it is (by measuring all things) and by fixing each thing's end (setting its rule). It is the source of obligation, for as we have seen, the eternal law fixes the end and the style for achieving that end. As we will discuss in chapter 3, natural law involves discovering those ends and types. Yet, the source of their obligatory nature is located not in the fact of their discovery but in this foundation of eternal law. As Aquinas says: "Accordingly all that is in things created by God, whether it be contingent or necessary, is subject to the eternal law."[142] The source of the obligation to conform to the eternal law, a question that plagues those who think about law after David Hume, is contained in this nature of eternal law as designating the ends of all things. Men have no choice. Men cannot stop being rational or corporeal. They can choose actions that are disoriented—not oriented to the end incorporated in their nature—but they cannot change the imprint of the eternal law on them that defines their due end, their style, and their art. Likewise, a builder can build a house either well or poorly, but his action is necessarily directed by the personal lawgiver who lays down the idea and style of building, the architect.

This conclusion suggests the objection: not everyone shares a common understanding of the existence and nature of this architect. Is not the position of Finnis understandable in such an age? Must we not take God and the eternal law out of the argument in light of these deep discrepancies in theology? Essentially, these questions are the heart of Finnis's response to traditional Thomists' initial critique of his work. He argues that his project excising God and the eternal law from the argument was meant to "meet modern secular students as and where they are."[143]

The answer to these objections is at once simple and nuanced. As Cicero insisted, we cannot simply take the big issues off the table. We cannot discuss the details of jurisprudence without some agreed first principles relating to the nature of the world and man. If meeting people where they are requires the removal of the foundation of the argument, ultimately the argument will fail from lack of support. Core agreement on basic metaphysical principles was a requirement for Cicero, even among discussion partners of various philosophical persuasions. Removing the eternal law from the argument removes the ontology of law itself, for it removes its ultimate cause. It becomes a painting without a purpose or a style. It becomes mere disembodied skill. Thus, any jurisprudence beyond a jurisprudence of arbitrary rules imposed by the powerful on the powerless out of pure malice must come to grips with the ontology, or cause, of law. To explain, understand, make, and evaluate law presupposes some understanding of its ontology.

Now the nuanced aspect of the objection involves a distinction as to the extent of the agreement on first principles. This agreement does not require complete agreement on all points of dogmatic theology to make progress in understanding the ontology of law. The necessary agreement to engage in the discussion was shared by the pagans Aristotle and Cicero and the Christians Augustine and Aquinas. This minimal agreement requires only the acceptance of what Thomists call "the preambles of faith," which are "truths about God which can be known by men independently of revelation."[144] It would involve acceptance of the truth that everything that exists has been made by a rational being who has established ends or natures of each thing. This rational being orders the universe reasonably and according to law. He governs the universe. In essence, agreement must only reach that required by Cicero, that there is an eternal law to things. Disagreements on finer points of knowledge about this lawgiver and his revelations will affect later stages of the natural law argument, but at this point the fact of eternal law and the fact that it establishes due ends for all things is sufficient.

Although quite general, this prerequisite does make further discussion impossible with some people. Anyone who insists that no order or reason exists in the universe denies the very existence of an eternal law regardless of the contents of its precepts. A pure nihilist who holds that there is no point to life or the universe, no purpose in anything, will not accept Cicero's minimal agreement. The fatal flaw of the jurisprudence of Grotius and Finnis is a refusal to demand Cicero's minimal prerequisites. As a result, Finnis's "indemonstrable goods" lack a proper ontology. He may argue that they simply exist and we accept them as such, but he eludes the issue of their causes. Where did the indemonstrable goods come from? Why are they goods? Only the concept of an eternal law fixing the goods can provide an ontological foundation. The next several chapters will touch on the contentious issues surrounding the definition of those goods, a discussion to which Finnis has much to contribute. Yet, Finnis's discussion is free-floating without foundation unless it begins with the eternal law. It involves an attempt to build law in thin air.

THREE

Discovering the Framework

The Natural Law

There can be but one essential justice, which cements society,
and one law which establishes this justice.
This law is right reason, which is the true rule
of all commandments and prohibitions.
Whoever neglects this law, whether written or unwritten,
is necessarily unjust and wicked.[1]

In the discussion of eternal law in chapter 2 we explained that all creatures are not only governed by but also participate in the eternal law, but they do so in different ways. Rational creatures participate by being imprinted with a particular end that serves as a principle for choosing action. This chapter turns from the foundation of eternal law to the framework that rises out of it, the natural law. As a frame of a house is connected to its foundation, our consideration of natural law will begin with this relationship between eternal and natural law. As Aquinas says, natural law is nothing other than "the participation (*participatio*) of the eternal law in the rational creature[s]."[2] We will thus begin our consideration by examining the nature of such participation. Once understood, we can build on this concept to examine how rational creatures come to know the content of the natural law. With this epistemological ground laid, we can turn to the substance of that content and conclude by considering the hierarchical nature of the principles of natural law.

MAN'S PARTICIPATION IN THE ETERNAL LAW

In accord with Aquinas, Patrick Brennan has affirmed that natural law is really not a different law from eternal law but a participation in it.[3] Participation, meaning to take part in (*partem capere*), indicates a process whereby one receives something that belongs to another and makes it his own.[4] The one participating takes "part (*partem capere*) in something in a partial manner that belongs to another fully."[5] Plato developed the idea of participation to describe the relation between the one (ideas or forms) and the many (sensible matter).[6] Individual matter participates in the applicable form related to that type of matter. Aquinas uses the relationship of potency and act to describe participation. The act of being is the participation in God, who is pure being, limited only by the potency of man's nature.[7] Man's potency to anything—to being, to good action, and so on—becomes act through participation in the complete perfection of each within God. Aquinas uses metaphorical language evocative of the discussion of eternal law to describe two aspects of this participation: "Insofar as created things imitate in their own manner the idea of the divine mind, as artifacts imitate the form that is in the mind of the artificer; insofar as created things imitate somehow the divine nature itself, in the sense that from the first Being, other beings proceed, and from the Good, good things, and the like for others."[8] Such participation is more than mere copying of another. The participation involves an imitation of God's very nature, His being, and it results in active production of "artifacts," which participate in the idea of them existing in God.

This definition of participation as a relationship between God and creatures recalls the point of Aquinas, referenced in chapter 2, that a law exists both in the mind of the lawgiver and in the mind of the one governed.[9] This dual mode of existence of law is possible through participation. A rational creature is both ruled and governed by the eternal law from above but also makes that eternal law his own by using it to develop knowledge of the principles of natural law, and then uses those principles to form the basis of willed choices, and in such a way participates in eternal law.

As we established in chapter 2, eternal law establishes the ends of all creatures and provides for the means to attain that end. This law of the end exists in all creatures, directing them to their end. Nonrational animals participate less perfectly, as they simply fulfill the precepts of the *ratio* of eternal law by being moved to their end without their knowing cooperation. Man more perfectly makes eternal law his own by working out a *ratio*, a system of coherent principles, which are used knowingly to direct his actions to an end.[10] Man's end is not a matter of election but rather merely a given to be desired. Free choice exists at the level of election of the means to the willed end. Thus, man participates in the eternal law, or makes it his own, not by being involuntarily moved to the end, but by exercising free choice in the election of the means to that end. The natural law, which is the "first direction of our acts,"[11] is the rule and measure used to know and choose means suited to the given end. Rational creatures do not merely receive these ends but formulate the means through a *ratio* of their own. As the *ratio* of natural law is a participation in the *ratio* of eternal law, it involves the use of both intellect (a *ratio* is a rational plan) and will (a *ratio* gives direction).[12] Understanding the end or good[13] that we seek is at the heart of this participation of eternal law. We have seen how Aquinas describes the eternal law as being impressed upon us. In his description of the natural law, he returns to this image of impression or imprinting to describe the nature of the participation. Impressing captures the idea of something existing in two places. If one impresses a seal into wax, the seal exists in the mold and in the wax, which now participates in the image of the seal. Aquinas locates the instrument of this impression as the power of reason when he says: "The light of natural reason, whereby we discern what is good and what is evil, which is the function of the natural law, is nothing else than an imprint on us of the divine light."[14] We discern a good or an end to the extent that we understand that a given means is proportionate to that end and then choose it as such. To understand the good or the end legislated for man indicates that we know it through its causes, the means to it.[15] This ability to understand the relation of the means to the end is the impression of eternal law on us.

The nature of this participation may be understood by looking at Plato's Cave.[16] A group of prisoners are chained in a cave. They watch shadows on the cave wall in front of them cast by people raised on a platform carrying objects behind those chained. They pass their time speculating about the shadows they see on the wall. One person, the philosopher, or the one making the "philosophical turn," is unchained and turns around to see the source of the shadows—the light of a fire and the sun illuminating the artifacts being carried. Although the prisoners made use of their reason to speculate about the images they see on the cave wall, they cannot see (until one was turned around) the source of those images. Socrates explains that the light causing the shadows represents "the idea of the good" and "the cause for all things of all that is right and beautiful, giving birth in the visible world to light, and the author of light and itself in the intelligible world being the authentic source of truth and reason."[17] Even though they are initially unaware of the nature of the source of the light, the prisoners' speculation is directed and guided (ruled) by that source—imperfectly, since they see it as in a shadow. In this sense they participate in that source. It directs the form of their speculation. Yet that direction provided a limited scope for participation since the light is seen only through shadows. This metaphor also applies to the participation of man in the eternal law that guides or directs. As Joel Prentice Bishop commented, man "has a partially dormant and partially active power of reason. Feebly, and as in the twilight, he distinguishes between right and wrong."[18]

Eternal law has its source outside of the cave of man's rational thought, but it penetrates into and casts shadows on the cave. Eternal law rules and measures the use of man's reason, but it allows for the participation of that reason in the formation of conclusions. If anyone has seen children make shadow figures, one immediately realizes that there is scope for "seeing" different images in the shadow, but that scope is not unlimited. Its limits are ruled by the form of the shadow cast. The use of the power of rationality to consider the shadows cast by the eternal law is the participation of natural law. These shadows illuminate the end of man. Man is capable of understanding this end through his reason. Such an insight adds a dimension to the statement that man is the image and likeness of God.[19] As John Finnis rightly points out, man is not an image of God in the sense of a static photograph,[20] but rather in the sense that the original of the image serves as an exemplar or rule or idea of man. As Aquinas explains, a created thing "approaches that likeness of God more perfectly than if it were only good in itself, if it is not only good but also is able to act for the good of others."[21] Note that to attain perfection in this rule or measure involves individual action (the ability to do good to others). A few lines later, Aquinas comments that all creation is good singly in its individual nature, "but all creation taken together, they are exceedingly [*valde*] good, according to the order of the universe, which is the final and noblest perfection of creation."[22] The eternal law, the order of the universe, provides the exemplar of man, the image of God. This image progresses in perfection toward that likeness through willed actions (ability to do good to others). Natural law, then, is the ability of humans, as rational creatures, to understand this order of the universe reflecting on and in them, to have a share in the eternal reason that promulgated this eternal law, and to understand and thus choose actions in accordance with that order.[23]

THE EPISTEMOLOGICAL PROBLEM

Aquinas has defined the natural law as "the participation of the eternal law in man," the rational creature. The eternal law establishes and illuminates the end of man, and natural law involves man's participation in achieving this end. The nature of this participation is by contemplating the inclinations present in the form of man as a rational animal.[24] Natural law consists in the "natural inclination to its proper [in the sense of obligatory] act[s] and end[s] [*inclinationem ad debitum actum et finem*]."[25] Gratian likewise locates the origin of natural law not in some detailed enactment, but in natural inclinations present in all peoples.[26] These inclinations, imprinted in the form of man through which man can come to know the natural law, have their origin in the eternal law.[27] Yet, as the metaphor of Plato's Cave illustrates, the participation is complex and often indirect. How do we first come to know this end of man, and, second, how do we use the natural law to participate in working out principles of action oriented to that end? Put simply, how do we know the natural law? This section will explore the answer to this question in theory, and chapter 4 will then examine the content known through these processes in more detail. Henri Grenier explains that the attainment of all knowledge, which would include practical knowledge of good or right actions, involves a faculty, habits, and acts. The necessary faculty is reason, the ability of man to acquire any knowledge. The habits of reason are "three in number: (a) *synderesis*, i.e., the habit of first principles of the practical order, which is natural; (b) *moral science*, i.e., ethics, which is concerned with general conclusions, and is acquired; (c) *prudence*, which is concerned with operations which are actually operative, i.e., with individual operations in the concrete."[28]

Each one of these habits of reason involves a different type of epistemological process. There are some truths known naturally, others become known as truths closely connected with the first truths, and finally there are truths discovered through human ingenuity.[29] Thus, we will examine the way we come to know the natural law in three subsections. The first subsection will examine the way things are known naturally—the hinge between eternal law and the first principle of natural law, synderesis. The second subsection will turn to the habit of natural inclinations whereby we come to know the self-evident primary principles of natural law closely connected with the first principle. The third subsection will examine the habit whereby we demonstrate or deduce secondary precepts of natural law, or more particular conclusions drawn from the primary principles.

Synderesis: The Hinge to Eternal Law

Since the eternal law is a plan or type of all things, including man, it therefore contains determinations regarding each thing's purpose. Analogously, an architectural plan exists for the purpose of determining the end of various building materials. The way that the eternal law establishes this end is by fixing the natures or essences of creatures so that they are suited to their decreed end. The end of man established by the eternal law is the purpose of man's existence. The function of the natural law is to enable man to know this end and, once known, to obligate him to choose actions in accordance with it. Accordingly, the first principle of the natural law is the point of contact between the framework of natural law and the foundation of eternal law. The first principle of natural law is a concise restatement of the created end of man: *good is to be done*.[30] "All other precepts of the natural law are based upon this [first precept]" as elaborations of what constitutes good.[31]

How does Aquinas make the leap from the ability to know the "good" (as yet undefined) to being obligated to do it? The obligation arises from the definition of the "good" spoken of by this first principle of the natural law as an end. The "good" is none other than the end of man, fixed by eternal law. Aquinas considers "end" and "good" to be related: "Every agent acts for an end under the aspect of good."[32] Good and end are also related to a third concept, being. The end of man is the correspondence of man to what he is designed to be by the eternal law. Aquinas explains: "The good or evil of an action, as of other things, depends on its fullness of being or its lack of that fullness."[33] To make the logic explicit, the end of something is defined as the "good" of that thing; something is judged as good to the extent it achieves the fullness of being. Thus, by substitution, the end of something is to achieve the fullness of being, which is "good."[34]

But how is this end (this fullness of being, the good) known? Aquinas says: "Consequently the first principle of the practical reason is one founded on the notion of good, namely, that 'good is that which all things seek after.'"[35] All things by virtue of the imprint of the eternal law seek after their natural type, exemplar, or idea. The definition of what man is contains the definition of man's end. As Maria T. Carl states: "St. Thomas holds that good and being are really the same, although they differ in their concept or notion (*secundum rationem*) or in thought in that they are not predicated of a thing in the same way. Being signifies that something is, either absolutely (*per se*) as a substance is, or relatively (*per aliud*) as an accident is. Goodness expresses actuality and perfection, and ultimate goodness expresses the complete actuality of a being."[36]

The Aristotelian tradition considers the highest knowledge of something to consist in knowing it through its causes.[37] Among the four types of causes identified by Aristotle,[38] the final cause identifies the end or "that for the sake of which" of the thing. Thus, knowing what something is involves knowledge of what it ought to be. The end is the good of being of a thing, for each thing is its end in potency—even before it attains its end in actuality. For the Aristotelian tradition, final causes are not merely a component of knowledge but that through which the world is ultimately comprehended.[39] Final causes are that link between "is" and "ought" that has eluded thinkers for so many centuries. The epistemological error originated in the Enlightenment's failed attempt to reduce all causality, and hence all knowledge, to mechanical and efficient causes.[40]

Man is obligated to do good in the sense that man is obligated to be himself. Goodness is the perfection (fullness) of man's very existence. Porter has explained the connection between being and good thus: "The desire for the good . . . represents the creature's natural orientation towards its own existence, including the fullest possible exercise of its proper causal powers. Correlatively, the operations through which anything can be said to pursue the good are not only means towards the attainment of an end; they are also themselves intrinsic constituents of that end, that is to say, the dynamic, active development and expression of the creature's natural capacities and powers."[41]

Pope Benedict XVI echoed this connection between natural law and being when he defined natural law as "the ethical message contained in being."[42] Hence, the relationship between properly discerned natural inclinations and goodness lies in the fact that man is inclined to be what he is. Men thus desire, or are inclined toward, the good, the complete or perfect actualization of their own being (which as we shall see is not equivalent to every appetite or feeling they might experience). In this sense, man cannot help but be obligated to do good because he cannot help but be what he is. How he knows this fact about himself is another matter, but the sense of obligation has been located in existence as established by eternal law. Good is to be pursued because the good is the appropriate end established by the authority of a law, the eternal law. Thus, the eternal law is the answer to the so-called is/ought dilemma: How can an obligation be derived from existence?[43] It is derived by the major premise that the "is" of being is established by a law ruling that being: the eternal law as a rational plan for the universe. Things do not just exist, but exist according to a rational plan, a plan that is a law obligating conformity to that plan of being.

More precisely, how do we find the point of contact between eternal and natural law that makes natural law obligatory by connecting it to the eternal law? How is it that we know this first principle? The answer is the hinge that connects the framework to the foundation at this point of contact: it is what Aquinas calls *synderesis*.[44] Through synderesis, all men know the first principle that good ought to be done.[45] Let us consider Aquinas's definition of synderesis as a habit of reason:

> Man's act of reasoning, since it is a kind of movement, proceeds from the understanding of certain things—namely, those which are naturally known [*naturaliter notorum*] without any investigation on the part of reason, as from an immovable principle—and ends also at the understanding, inasmuch as by means of those principles naturally known [*naturaliter nota*], we judge of those things which we have discovered by reasoning. Now it is clear that, as the speculative reason argues about speculative things, so that practical reason argues about practical things. Therefore we must have, bestowed on us by nature [*naturaliter nobis esse indita*], not only speculative principles, but also practical principles. . . . Wherefore the first practical principles, bestowed on us by nature [*nobis naturaliter indita*], do not belong to a special power, but to a special natural habit [*specialem habitum naturalem*], which we call "synderesis." Whence "synderesis" is said to incite to good, and to murmur at evil, inasmuch as through first principles we proceed to discover, and judge of what we have discovered.[46]

Aquinas characterizes the act of reasoning as discursive, a movement from something known to something unknown through a process of investigation.[47] Yet, as with one of his proofs for the existence of God that all movement must begin from a fixed point or prime mover,[48] he argues that our ability to reason must begin from an immovable principle.[49] Since humans reason discursively, by moving from what is known already to what becomes known, there must be a point of departure, some original knowledge from which the movement of reason proceeds. The point at which all knowledge begins is "given instantly to the intellect."[50] This same fixed knowledge also serves as a point of return, a measure to evaluate the results of discursive reasoning. All reasoning occurs within these fixed points of departure and arrival. Using the example of the immobility from which we begin and to which we return when taking a step, Pauline Westerman concludes that the immovable principles known by synderesis are indispensable to the very act of reasoning: "We would be lost in our own train of reasoning if we had no fixed points that guided our reasoning . . . [for] it would be impossible *to reason at all* without fixed principles."[51]

In contrast to discursive reasoning, which moves from one thing to the next, the first principles of speculative and practical knowledge are put or introduced into (*indita*) our intellect without the movement of investigation. The word that dominates description of this bestowal is "natural." The first principle, do good, is "naturally known" because it is bestowed naturally. Understanding exactly what it means to be "naturally known" or "bestowed by nature" has been the subject of philosophical debate for centuries.[52] This debate has its genesis in a tension introduced in Justinian's *Digest* relating to the term "natural law," or *jus naturale*. The tension is between seeing "naturally" in this context as referring either to (1) the force in animals by which they are directed to action (or what in modern English we call "animal instinct"), or (2) some other force differing from animal instinct located in the rational aspect of man's nature. In the opening pages of the *Digest*, the jurist Ulpian introduces two terms referring to a universally applicable general law: *jus natural* and *jus gentium*.[53] Ulpian defines natural law, *jus naturale*, as "that which nature teaches to all animals, for this law is not peculiar to the human race, but affects all creatures."[54] Such a definition suggests a force, such as animal instinct, lying behind natural law. A few lines later he defines *jus gentium* as "that used by the human race, and it is easy to understand that it differs from natural law, for the reason that the latter is common to all animals, while the former only concerns men in their relations to one another."[55] This appears to distinguish *jus gentium* as a universal law applicable only to humans. A quotation from Gaius a few lines later defines *jus gentium* as that which "natural reason has established among all men,"[56] suggesting a natural source in reason differing from the animal instinct underlying natural law. A passage from the jurist Paulus complicates matters further by referring to *jus naturale* as "whatever is just and good."[57] Animals as nonrational creatures cannot be just, and thus natural law—contrary to Ulpian's statement—does appear to apply uniquely to man and involve rationality. Four centuries later, Isidore of Seville adapted Ulpian's definition of *jus naturale* with several significant alterations relevant to this tension. First, he apparently blurred any distinction between *jus naturale* and *jus gentium* by declaring *jus naturale* to be the "law common to all nations"[58] as opposed to a law common to all animals.[59] Second, he inserted the phrase *instinctus naturae*, or "instinct of nature," into the definition to explain how *jus naturale* is known.[60] Eventually the phrase *instinctus naturae* would become equated to the term "synderesis."[61] This tension results in a dilemma. Is this universal law applicable to all mankind known through a nonrational impulse as the bee knows to gather pollen? Or is it known through an instinct of higher rationality? Is knowledge of nature, in the sense of the observation of nonrational creatures (or in modern parlance, natural science), the source of our knowledge of the first principle of natural law?

The phrase "instinct of nature" carries with it certain ambiguities. To modern readers, instinct connotes animal impulse. The phrase seems to tip the tension toward understanding synderesis in light of nonrational animal behavior. Yet in classical Latin, *instinctus* has a range of connotations. It could refer to a nonrational, uncontrollable impulse of madness or passion,[62] or it could connote an incitement or inspiration that is unique to human behavior, such as inspiration by speeches or arguments.[63] In addition, it "is often understood to be extra-human in origin, frequently divine."[64] An anonymous medieval commentary uses the phrase "instinct of nature" in apposition to the phrase "divine disposition"[65] when describing natural law. This phrase "instinct of nature" does seem to combine aspects of animal compulsion (Aquinas uses the word "incites," *instigare*, in defining synderesis) with uniquely human rational action and with inspiration from God.

The word "nature" likewise is laden with ambiguity as to its relation to things animal, human, or divine. Johannes Teutonicus lists three meanings of nature: (1) "the force seated in things that produces like from like," (2) "a certain stimulus or instinct of nature proceeding from sense to experience to a desire for procreating or rearing," and (3) "an instinct of nature proceeding from reason," which he associates with natural equity and natural law.[66] Thus, the term "nature" has connotations touching animal impulse but also human rationality. Johannes Teutonicus specifically connects this third sense with *instinctus naturae* and natural law.

I believe this tension can be resolved by understanding the metaphysical relationship of human beings to pure spirits on one hand and lower animals on the other. Just as the eternal law originates in the oneness of God and is then divided into exemplars of individual beings, so too a scheme of relation can be observed in all that exists with more precise categorization of beings made possible by identifying the point of differentiation. Recalling that the eternal law is a rational plan of all that exists, different genera and species[67] are not disconnected groupings, but rather points on a continuous spectrum of being. They are distinct by virtue of the differentiae distinguishing them, yet related to what comes before and after in the spectrum. All that is participates to different degrees in the same Being, which is God. This notion—differing participation in the one Being—explains the continuity and difference between species. The tree of Porphyry (fig. 3.1) can visually assist in picturing this conception of related yet distinct species of being.

All substances, all that exist, can be divided based on properties constituting differentiae. The differentiae exist between genera of the same level and from superior to inferior genus and from genus to species. Thus, the property of having a body distinguishes corporeal from incorporeal substances (a horizontal differentia), and the property of being either living or nonliving distinguishes each subgenera of corporeal from its superior genus, corporeal. The definition of a species includes all of the differentiae distinguishing its superior genera and the differentia distinguishing the species from its immediately superior genus. In figure 3.1, the lightest boxes represent individual examples of the species known as "man," which can thus be defined as a rational, sentient, living, corporeal substance. Because a species contains the superior differentiae, it will contain the sum of the differentiae of other species related to it at some point in the tree. Thus, man contains the differentiae of sentience, life, and corporality—which are also differentiae contained in different species of animals.[68] There will therefore be some properties common to man and irrational animals. Yet there is another relationship of being among creatures. There is another order of perfection whereby creatures are more or less proximate to a pure substance (the superior being in the tree of Por-

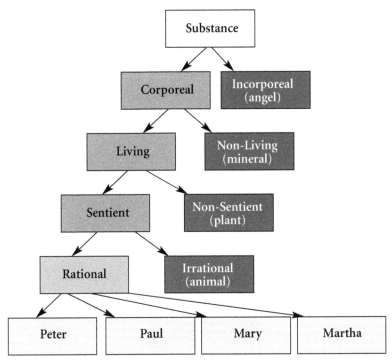

Figure 3.1. Tree of Porphyry
Source: Adapted from Grenier, *Logic,* 179.

phyry), or pure unlimited being.[69] Angels, as pure spirits, do not have their being limited by corporality and are thus more proximate to pure being. Man possessing rationality and choice is related but in a less proximate way because of the limitation of lack of pure spirituality. This type of relationship can be demonstrated by figure 3.2. Man is metaphysically between animals and angels. As Aquinas explains:

> In the human soul there is a twofold form: one through which it corresponds to the angels, in so far as it is a spirit, and this is the higher form; and another, the lower form, through which it gives life to the body, in so far as it is a soul. . . .[70]
>
> For natures that are ordained to one another are related to each other as contiguous bodies, the upper limit of the lower body being in contact with the lower limit of the higher one. Hence, at its highest

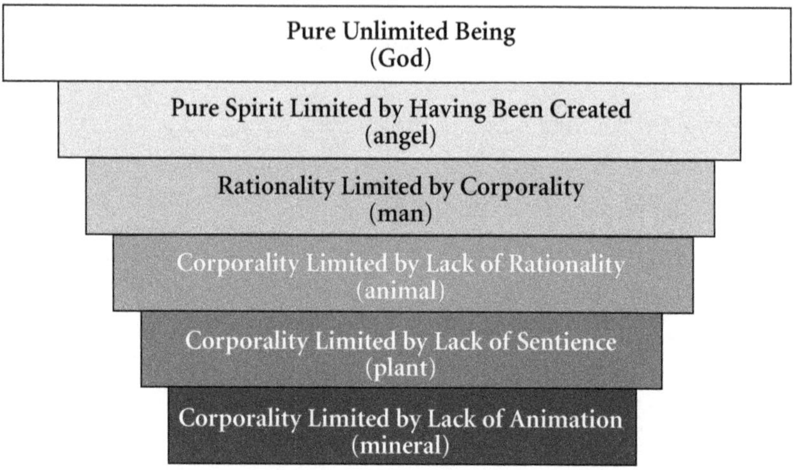

Fig. 3.2. Perfection of Being

point a lower nature attains to something that is proper to the higher nature and shares in it imperfectly.[71]

All beings are ruled and measured by the eternal law, but in different ways appropriate to their natures. All creatures are endowed with an *instinctus naturae*, an impulse placed in their essence, that impulse being the eternal law. Yet owing to the differences of species, the form of that *instinctus naturae* differs and at the same time is related to that within other species, more or less depending upon their proximity within the hierarchy of being. They each are imprinted naturally with a form of *instinctus naturae*, resembling each other yet differing because of differences of form. In this sense we can interpret *instinctus naturae* more generally as an instinct of a specific creature's nature rather than an instinct of some universalized nature. For man, the *instinctus naturae* resembles to a certain extent the lower reason in animals, which, although moving themselves through the input of sense, merely apprehend the object of sense but do not propose or understand that object as an end.[72] Forty percent of the time that Aquinas uses the phrase *instinctus naturae*, he sets it "in opposition to discursive reason and its attendant freedom of choice."[73] Nicholas of Ockham highlights this comparison between man and animal instincts: "For as we see on the part of sensitive beings that a sheep, seeing a wolf, flees at once by natural instinct and that a lamb follows its mother, so we are able to understand that there is such a natural instinct in the rational soul stimulating to the pursuit of honorable good and flight from evil."[74] Thus, in the sense that man does not freely will his last end but is merely in the initial stage moved to it by synderesis, he is ruled by an instinct of nature, as are sentient animals.

In the other direction, however, man also resembles, imperfectly, the higher reason of angels, who, unlike animals, truly know and understand this *instinctus naturae*. But angels do not come to their knowledge through discursive reasoning. According to Aquinas, "The natural and proper manner of knowing for an angelic nature is to know truth without investigation or movement of reason."[75] Westerman describes this process as the "angel's eye," by which she means the ability to "grasp things at a glance. The total picture is immediately seen and understood. There is no 'running from one point to another,' there is no movement involved, as in reasoning. It is essentially immobile, indeed just like the contemplation of a picture."[76]

Sometimes the process of knowing this first principle is compared to this higher reason rather than animal instinct. St. Bonaventure uses the term *apex mentis* ("height of the mind") to refer to "the spark of synderesis."[77] Aquinas describes synderesis as a "habitual light."[78] Through this metaphor he explains that this light is known without reason, because this light is imprinted on, or on part of, the soul and is therefore known as part of its own self: "For this light belongs to the nature of the soul, since by reason of 'this the soul is intellectual.'"[79] Without synderesis, discursive moral reasoning is not possible.[80] Without this light, intellection is not possible. Aquinas also explicitly equates human knowledge of the first principle of the natural law with angelic knowledge, while noting the difference: "Hence, the human soul, according to that which is highest in it, attains to that which is proper to angelic nature, so that it knows some things [i.e., the first principle of natural law] at once and without investigation, although it is lower than angels in this, [namely] that it can know the truth in these things only by receiving something from sense."[81]

Likewise, Robert Greene explains that this *instinctus naturae* "operates in mankind as a stimulus, source, or ground of the natural law. It is contrasted with discursive reason represented here by learning."[82] The first principle is known not in the way that man learns other things, but in the way that angels see and understand.[83]

The point of connection between eternal and natural law is anterior to free will or choice, and in this sense is similar to animal instinct. The eternal law fixes the end of man, with respect to which there is no free will. Synderesis is the point of contact where this fixed end—to do good—is made known to the intellect and the will not as an act of free election: "We have free will with respect to what we will not of necessity, nor by natural instinct. For our will to be happy does not appertain to free will, but to natural instinct. Hence other animals, that are moved to act by natural instinct, are not said to be moved by free will."[84] This is why Aquinas explains that "the first act of the will is not due to the direction of the reason but to the instigation of nature, or of a higher cause."[85] That higher cause is the eternal law made known through synderesis. Aquinas explains that this movement of the will directs the agent to the perfection of its own being: "Natural inclination of the will is present in every volitional agent to will and to love its own perfection so that it cannot will the contrary of this."[86]

Unlike animals, man is not simply moved to all his individual acts in a mechanical way as from an extrinsic cause; he understands and chooses his actions, even if he does not choose his final end. Aquinas explains this difference between rational (and hence free) and irrational creatures: "It is left, then, to the agent's choice, to order his own proper perfection to a higher end. In fact, this is the difference between those agents who have a will and those things which are devoid of will: the possessors of will order themselves and their actions to the end, and so they are said to be free in their choice."[87] This ability to understand the relation of acts to the final end, based upon the first principle of the natural law, makes the instinct of nature in man similar to that of angels, who know and understand the relationship between their end and their actions. As will be developed more in the next subsection, what man does with this imprinted knowledge becomes the subject of discursive reason. It is this discursive reasoning that is the distinguishing aspect of man's hinge to the eternal law, as distinct from angels and animals. Unlike animals, man will reason about the implications of the first principle (discussed in the next subsection). Unlike the angels, even though he knows and understands this first principle without movement, man must determine what actions he should choose to conform to it through his use of discursive reasoning. This understanding of an eternal law applicable to all animals, including man, in analogous yet different ways, helps to explain the tension in Roman jurisprudence. The instinct of nature exists in all animals, yet there is an aspect of this instinct that results in a law unique to the nations of men. The similarity to animal instinct explains the texts that note this universal application. Roman jurists had an imperfect grasp of the difference between the participation of men and animals, and therefore some of them developed a vague and confusing distinction between *jus naturalis* and *jus gentium*.[88]

Although Cicero likewise acknowledged a vague notion of an eternal law, neither he nor the jurists defined its operation and relation to *jus naturalis* or *jus gentium* with clarity or precision. Such work required a clearer understanding of the nature of the eternal law. Consequently, the precise similarity and distinction between *instinctus naturae animalium* and *instinctus naturae hominum* was not possible until the Scholastics. In retrospect, we can translate the Roman jurists' vague understanding in this way: The law that they recognized as being common to and teaching all animals, including man, is not (as they mislabeled it) the natural law, but rather the eternal law. The eternal law is common to all creatures. The law common to all men is the law of man's rational participation in the eternal law, which the *Digest* refers to as *jus gentium*.

Synderesis brings both man's will and intellect into contact with the eternal law. It fixes his will to the last end, just as animals are moved without choice, and it enlightens his intellect to begin the process of discursive reasoning to further define the good that is to be sought after. Through a similar insight, Robert Greene argues that the Scholastic debate over whether synderesis is a habit of the intellect or of the will[89] resulted in a widespread use of the term "synderesis" "to cover both intellectual recognition of practical principles and the spontaneous movement of the will and affections towards the good."[90] Synderesis makes known to the intellect the end fixed by eternal law and orients the will to choose it; it can therefore be defined as a "spontaneous movement of the will towards the good . . . simultaneous with the recognition of the 'first illumination' of the practical intellect, the first and basic precept of the natural law."[91]

Greene, in describing the intellectual consensus regarding synderesis by the time of Bonaventure, presents a useful summary of what we have established so far and indicates a few final points to be considered about this hinge to the eternal law: "The consensus that Bonaventure inherited was that synderesis was an intellectual habit of primary practical principles that operated in an intuitive, indefectible, inextinguishable and nondiscursive manner."[92]

So far we have established that synderesis makes known the primary principle of natural law—the obligation to do good—in a nondiscursive manner, or intuitively. The two other modifiers that need to be considered are *indefectible* (unable to fail) and *inextinguishable* (unable to be removed from the human soul).

Likewise, Aquinas asserts that what is known by synderesis is "unchangeable," and that "no one errs" with respect to such knowledge.[93] St. Paul refers to a "law written in their hearts."[94] The two concepts of indefectibility and inerrancy are related. The principle cannot fail to be true, and no person lacks knowledge of the principle. An immediate objection arises—which has often been raised against natural law in general—namely, his knowledge does fail, and can be lost, as evidenced by the history of mankind, which is littered with examples of people doing evil. This objection can be answered by avoiding the attribution to synderesis, and the principle it makes known, of a greater scope than exists in reality. All that the first principle of natural law states is that "good" must be done. Synderesis does not provide for man a definition of the good (but, as we shall see, it directs him to a starting point for discovering that definition, his own being). Synderesis is a "limited" concept that merely "enables us to see that it is the general tendency of creatures, including ourselves, to move upwards on the scales of being and goodness and that there are several ends, which are hierarchically ordered."[95] Synderesis does not infuse knowledge that defines what those ends are. Such definition will be the product of discursive reasoning based on inclinations (discussed in the next subsection). As Westerman explains: "We may deliberate about how to pursue good, we may deliberate about our personal conceptions of the good, but *that* we are bound to pursue good . . . is not open to criticism."[96] Even Aristotle began his ethical philosophy with this basic principle known by synderesis: everything that acts does so on account of a good (or end).[97] The principle that there is an end to be pursued cannot be called into question because without it moral discussion is impossible.[98] If we do not start with the principle that whatever is good is to be done, what are we even talking about? We may have a heated debate about what is good in a given circumstance, but a starting premise of such a debate must be that we ought to do whatever in fact is good. Aquinas gives an example from speculative knowledge that demonstrates that differences regarding application of a principle (what is actually good) do not call into question the principle itself: "A thing is also said to be unchangeable because of the necessity of a truth, although the truth may concern things which according to their nature can change. Thus the truth: every whole is greater than its part, is unchangeably true even in changeable things. Synderesis is said to refer to unchangeable things in this way."[99]

The principle grasped by synderesis acts like fixed points within which reasoning occurs. It is the beginning of reasoning since it fixes the purpose for reasoning—to know what constitutes the good that we seek. It is the end of reasoning since it serves as a measure against which we can evaluate to what extent our reasoning has attained its purpose.[100] It functions as both a regulative principle and a principle of judgment.[101]

That synderesis can never err means that it "never falls down in a general principle" even though "error can happen in some application of a general principle to some particular case because of a false deduction, or because of a false assumption."[102] What fails is not synderesis but another process that "applies the general judgment of synderesis to particular matters."[103] Aquinas gives an example to help distinguish the failure of a principle and the failure of an application. That worship should be given to God was the principle used by those who killed the apostles (John 16:2). Killing them was a wrong judgment. Yet, it was not the principle that erred—worship should be given—but the application: the assumption that killing the apostles is giving worship to God.[104] Presenting evidence of someone making a choice to do something that is in fact evil does not disprove the first principle of natural law that we are obligated to do good. These actors—by the very act of choosing—thought, erroneously, that they would be choosing good.

But is synderesis really indelible? Is this precept of the natural law really written indelibly on the heart so that all people know it? The answer to this question is related to the previous answer that the principle cannot fail. Aquinas uses the metaphor of a light,[105] which he says "belongs to the nature of the soul, since by reason of this the soul is intellectual."[106] The soul is only capable of willed action if illuminated by the light of synderesis; thus to say that synderesis is extinguished is to say the very soul of man is extinguished, since it is of the nature of the soul. Anyone who acts, acts for an end: so long as one is capable of human action, synderesis cannot be destroyed.

The difficulty is that synderesis appears not to function in some people, or to be extinguished in that they do not do the good. Yet this objection is based on a misunderstanding of the limited role of synderesis. It is not synderesis that fails, but rather something impedes the proper effect of synderesis. Aquinas explains that such obstacles arise in two ways:

> In one, the act of synderesis is said to be extinguished inasmuch as it is completely interfered with. This happens in those who do not have the use of free choice or of reason because of an impediment due to an injury to the bodily organs from which our reason needs help. In the other way, the act of synderesis is deflected toward the contrary of synderesis. It is impossible for the universal judgment of synderesis to be destroyed in this way, but in a particular activity it is destroyed whenever one sins in choice. For the force of concupiscence, or of another passion, so absorbs reason that in choice the universal judgment of synderesis is not applied to the particular act. But this does not destroy synderesis altogether, but only in some respect. Hence, absolutely speaking, we concede that synderesis is never destroyed.[107]

In the first case, synderesis is itself not destroyed, but the person in which it is a habit of the mind is not capable of making use of synderesis due to a physical impediment. This would be the case, for example, with respect to an unconscious person. Likewise, a person in a coma still might have eyes and therefore the ability to see even though an injury prevents his making use of sight. The second case involves one who acts contrary to the rule of synderesis by choosing evil. But this is not a failure of synderesis, but rather a failure to properly apply its principle to the act. The failure is in a later stage of natural law reasoning, which we will turn to shortly, but not with synderesis itself. Aquinas uses an example that aids our understanding of this distinction. As we shall see, notwithstanding the self-evidence of the next-level principles (those immediately following from the first principle), men can err in knowledge of them. In the same article where he affirms that the general principle of the natural law is "equally known to all" he gives the example of the Germans, who believed theft to be good in some cases.[108] Their error is possible because it is not a failure or extinguishment of synderesis but an error in "conclusion" drawn from the principle, which conclusions are "not equally known to all."[109] This is an error of a most basic kind (since, as we shall see, it involves a proximate conclusion), but the error does not involve a loss of synderesis since the Germans wrongly concluded theft was good. In fact, another term refers to the habit by which the principle known from synderesis is applied. It is "conscience," and that habit *is* capable of error.[110] The error in the objection to the inerrancy of synderesis is a confusion between the habit of conscience and synderesis. This confusion is not new. It is related to the ambiguous and at times equivocal meaning of the phrase "instinct of nature," which in its proper sense (as used thus far) is synonymous with synderesis. Yet, the phrase has also been used to refer to other influences upon human reason, many not always for the better. As Jean Gerson observes, instinct of nature is sometimes used to refer not to synderesis, but to "appetite of nature," which has been "corrupted in its sensual aspect" and "through not heeding the rule of reason (i.e., synderesis) is a strong tendency of the sensual aspect towards its own objects" rather than the real object of action, the good.[111] He explains that the origin of this dysfunctional appetite does not flow through the hinge of synderesis to the eternal law, but rather "it comes to us from the sin of our first parents."[112]

Self-Evident Principles and Inclinations

In the previous subsection we established that the habit of synderesis makes known to all men the intuitive, indefectible, and inerrant principle that good ought to be done and evil avoided. Aquinas asserts that like the principle of noncontradiction, this first principle (that good ought to be done and evil avoided) is the foundation of all other precepts of natural law.[113] As Ross Armstrong has observed, this foundation does not mean that all the subsequent principles can simply be deduced from this foundational principle alone.[114] A framework does not rise up out of the foundation using the materials of the foundation alone. What then is the function of this first principle? As Armstrong observes, it is not, strictly speaking, a moral principle but rather a "logical principle."[115] Yet, neither Armstrong nor the scholars he cites clearly articulate the function of this logical principle in deducing the primary moral precepts of natural law. It is true that one cannot logically reason simply from "good ought to be done and evil ought to be avoided" to "one should not commit adultery."[116] The role of the first principle is to fill the logical gap sought after by David Hume and those who repeat his challenge that one cannot make the logical leap from "is" to "ought." The first principle of natural law is the premise that answers Hume. Thus, all syllogisms ending in a conclusion containing a precept of natural law (a rule and measure directing action) will take either of the following two forms:

Form 1
Major: Good ought to be done and evil ought to be avoided.
Minor: X is good.
Conclusion: Therefore X ought to be done.

Form 2
Major: Good ought to be done and evil ought to be avoided.
Minor: Y is evil.
Conclusion: Y ought not to be done.

In this way the first principle of natural law is the foundation of all future discursive reasoning by which we come to know the precepts of natural law, because it is the major premise necessary to reach the conclusion that some act (or general category of acts) ought to be done or not to be done.

Identifying this role in formal logic for the first principle immediately begs the next question. How do we arrive at the minor premises: X is good or Y is evil? This epistemological question brings us to the next level of natural law, the general primary precepts defining in general what is good. Because we are dealing with the method of knowledge at this stage, as opposed to the content of these precepts, we need to address—as with the first principle—how people come to know these primary precepts.

There is a vacillation in Aquinas between claiming that synderesis grasps a principle or grasps several principles.[117] This vacillation might lead us to conclude that we come to know these primary principles of natural law through synderesis in the same way we know the first principle of natural law. This is not the case, nor is it the teaching of Aquinas, notwithstanding some ambiguity in the text. The reason is that Aquinas is clear, as demonstrated in the previous subsection: all men infallibly know what synderesis imprints in the mind. It cannot be extinguished. Yet, Aquinas acknowledges a continuum of fallibility exists with respect to the content of natural law: "The more we descend to matters of detail, the more frequently we encounter defects."[118] What distinguishes a principle that is infallibly known to all by synderesis from principles that might not be known by at least some people? The principle at issue is a conclusion. "As to the proper *conclusions* of the practical reason," says Aquinas, the truth is not "equally known by all."[119] The breaking point is a conclusion, a term that implies the presence of discursive reasoning, or movement from premises to conclusions. The knowledge of synderesis is immobile; it involves no conclusion drawn from premises but rather involves simple apprehension imprinted in the mind. Once we move from this first principle to any principle, such as "X ought to be done" whenever X is something less than the most general term the good, a conclusion has to be deduced: X is good. Thus with respect to any general principle of natural law,[120] other than the foundational principle, error is possible and thus knowledge of it cannot solely be apprehended through synderesis. But Aquinas clearly uses the plural "principles" at times when discussing knowledge grasped by synderesis.[121]

The answer to this dilemma lies in the teaching of Aristotle. This first principle of natural law is a restatement of the first principle announced in Aristotle's *Nicomachean Ethics*: good (or end) is what all seek.[122] In the next sentence, however, Aristotle notes that there is a diversity of ends. Is there one end or a diversity of ends? Aquinas explains that the good or end is sought through a diversity of subends, or incomplete goods, proportionate to the ultimate end. These are the matter of free choice.[123] These subends are not really ends at all but rather means to the one end. For convenience we often speak of these means as ends since they function like principles directing particular action. Aquinas gives the example of health.[124] For a doctor, health of the patient is the end his actions seek. But from the broader perspective of the well-being of the overall person, health is merely a means or a component of the end, and not the ultimate end. In chapter 2 we noted that human free choice involves knowingly choosing these subends as proportionate means to the invariable ultimate end. Thus our knowledge of these subordinate goods or ends, although related to it, is distinct from our knowledge of the first principle, known by synderesis. Assuming X is a component of good, we know we should do X, a specific subordinate good, because we know by virtue of synderesis we should do good. Although we can thus speak of knowing the goods by synderesis, we do not mean the same thing as apprehending the first principle by synderesis. In the latter case, the apprehension of synderesis is the beginning and ending of the knowledge of the first principle. In the former, the imprinted knowledge of synderesis is only a part of the process. This is why Aquinas can say that "we judge [which involves drawing conclusions] naturally *both* by our reason and by 'synderesis.'"[125] Likewise, he describes a two-part process of choosing human actions. The end is known by one method, and the means (or subends) by another: "For every act of reasoning is based on principles that are known naturally [*synderesis*], and every act of appetite in respect of the means is derived from the natural appetite in respect of the last end."[126] Aquinas can thus be understood to say that we know the first principle exclusively by synderesis, and we know the general principles of natural law by synderesis combined with knowledge of the minor premises defining the good. Because these general principles will be themselves conclusions, their relation to synderesis differs from the way in which synderesis imprints the first principle—which is not a conclusion.[127]

Things that follow in a hierarchical continuum to an imperfect extent resemble that which exists above them. Thus, the process of knowing the general principles of natural law that come immediately below the first principle will to some extent resemble the process of synderesis. In addition to the principle known by synderesis, there are some "truths closely connected" to the first principle.[128] There will be some movement in the process, but the movement will be fairly small.

Aquinas places a linguistic signal in his text to indicate that a shift has occurred from synderesis to another habit of knowing principles. We have seen that the phrase *instinctus naturae* had become, by the time of Aquinas, a term used synonymously with synderesis. Isidore of Seville had incorporated the phrase *instinctus naturae* into Ulpian's original definition of natural law.[129] When Aquinas includes an unattributed reference to this definition of Ulpian, he substitutes natural inclination (*inclinatio naturalis*) for Isidore's insertion of *instinctus naturae*.[130] Although we will turn shortly to explore the implications of this new phrase, for now it can be read as demarcating a shift from synderesis, or *instinctus naturae*, to another concept, *inclinatio naturalis*, which Aquinas employs when talking about our knowledge of the general principles (as opposed to the first principle) of natural law.

The phrase that Aquinas uses to describe the epistemology of these first-tier general principles (those coming immediately after the first principle) is *per se nota*, which is usually translated as "self-evident" but literally means "known through themselves." Since this process is closest to synderesis it resembles it in some ways, but it will also resemble discursive reasoning in others. Propositions known through themselves are principles that contain within their own terms the proofs of their own truth, because the predicate of the subject is contained in the subject. As long as we know the meaning of the subject and predicate, we instantly can apprehend the truth of their relationship.[131] Thus there is movement from ignorance to knowledge as the terms are understood first and then the proposition apprehended, but it is not the syllogistic movement of discursive reasoning. Aquinas gives two examples. A whole is greater than any one of its parts. As long as we know that a whole is composed of parts, it necessarily follows that the whole (which contains any one part in addition to additional parts) must be greater than any one part. Likewise we can say that man is a rational animal, and once we know that man is defined as an animal that possesses rationality, we can instantly see that the equation of "man" to "rational animal" is true because the predicate is included within the subject. The process resembles discursive reasoning in that we move from our knowledge of the subject and predicate to our knowledge of their relationship. It resembles synderesis in that the conclusion is apprehended instantly upon knowing the terms.

Unlike knowledge of the first principle, knowledge of these self-evident propositions is not universally and indefectibly known, because, unlike knowledge from synderesis, it depends upon knowledge of the terms in the proposition. Thus, Aquinas makes clear that although some propositions are self-evident in themselves, they are not always self-evidently known to everyone. The degree to which people actually apprehend the truth of self-evident propositions is a function of the universality of knowledge of the terms. Thus the proposition "a whole is greater than any of its individual parts" is nearly universally known since most people know the meanings of "whole" and "part." Yet the self-evident proposition "man is a rational animal" is not universally known because some people have never come to know that man is defined as being in the genus of animal and differentiated by the differentia of rationality. There are even some propositions that, although capable of being known through themselves, are only known to the wise, since the terms used are only known to the learned.[132] Thus, unlike the principle that good ought to be done and evil avoided, the self-evident primary principles of the natural law will be known in varying degrees depending on how well known the terms of the principles tend to be known. Self-evident precepts of natural law, which employ terms widely known, will be widely grasped. Others less widely known will be less widely gasped. As a corollary to this statement, the knowledge of self-evident principles of natural law can vary over time to the extent that knowledge of the relevant terms becomes more or less universally known. This corollary provides one explanation why progress and regression can occur in knowledge of the natural law over time (other reasons will relate to knowledge of secondary principles that are not self-evident). Knowledge of particular terms may become more sparsely attained and thus knowledge of the precepts employing them will be reduced.

Aquinas's teacher, St. Albert the Great, uses the metaphysical concepts of *potency* and *act* to explain self-evident propositions. Such propositions naturally contain within themselves the potency for their apprehension by all. Rather than movement from premises to conclusion, Albert describes it as a movement from potency to act caused by knowledge of the terms. Albert explains:

> There is a knowledge of the law which is a first potency with respect to the general matters of the law, concerning which it is only necessary to know the terms of the commandment, that is to say, what is stealing and what is adultery, and then through knowledge of these terms, it is evident that one should not steal or commit adultery. Hence, the knowledge of these principles is not acquired except in an accidental sense, namely, through the knowledge of the terms, and not through anything that is prior [to these principles] themselves, as

the knowledge of conclusions is acquired. Thus, the knowledge of such principles is placed in us by nature, simply speaking, and is acquired in an accidental sense through knowledge of the terms.[133]

Propositions are *per se nota*, or self-evident, in the sense that the propositions contain within themselves all that is necessary for a rational creature to come to the knowledge of them. They are potentially known by all rational creatures. They will only become actually known by all rational creatures when the potency becomes actual by discovery of the terms.

Now that we understand in general the process of knowing self-evident propositions through knowledge of the terms, we can turn to how the primary self-evident principles of natural law become known. The primary principles begin to specify the means or subends or subgoods that ought to be done as proportionate to the good that we ought do, and those that ought to be avoided as not proportionate to the good. Aquinas holds with Aristotle that "good is convertible with being."[134] The good or end is interchangeable with being in the sense that the good or end sought after by all things is that which is commensurate with what they are. The good is perfect conformity to the nature of being. As Shakespeare has Polonius say: "To thy own self be true."[135] Given this convertibility of good and being, we can begin to see that the role of natural inclinations is to know what something is by knowing the inclinations that follow from its being.

Because of the contemporary confusion over, and equivocal uses of, the term "natural," arguments proceeding from natural inclinations to precepts are often misunderstood. "Natural" often brings to mind the concept of "uncultivated," the state of being as we find it. "Natural" often implies lacking rational ordering. Yet for Aristotle, "nature"—with respect to man—has a very different connotation. Aristotle understood nature as related to the aspect of being that relates to the final cause or end of being. Aristotle understands the term "natural" in three senses: (1) something "immanent in the primordial constitution of man, as a potentiality of development"; (2) "a growth in which his 'art,' or creative mind . . . has cooperated with . . . his instinct"; (3) "part of his final cause or purpose."[136] All three senses include within them the notion of becoming or tending to a goal. "Natural" is associated not with the merely existing but with becoming. The nature of something is in one sense fixed and unchanging since the natural is part of its constitution. Yet it is dynamic; the natural is the

principle of growth and development in that constitution. It is the cooperation of that which exists as a means of striving toward the final cause of the
constitution of being. To refer to a natural inclination is to refer to that aspect of man's constitution that inclines toward his final end or purpose.

If the primary principles of the natural law are in the form "X ought
to be done" and "Y ought not to be done," they will be self-evident to the
extent that we know that X is and Y is not contained within the term
"good"—as a component of the constituted end of man—toward which
we are obliged to tend by the first principle. If X is a component part of
the good, then it will be obligatory, and, in fact, the constitution of our
being is inclined toward it. If Y is in opposition to the good, then it is prohibited. Since good is convertible with being, then the subgoods or the
component goods must be components of being. The primary precepts of
natural law thus specify the primary aspects of man's nature, his being,
which compose the good for him. Once these aspects are known to be elements of his being—elements of the good—it is self-evident that they
are to be done. How do we come to a knowledge of the components of
human nature? The answer is the linguistic signal Aquinas gives to distinguish synderesis by substituting "natural inclination" for "natural instinct" in the definition of natural law. We can come to know the essence
of man, his being, by following the trail of the natural inclinations that
lead to the aspects of his being.

The eternal law legislates an end or purpose for all beings by establishing a type, or form, or nature of each being. In order to attain the purpose or end of its being, each form possesses natural inclinations, which
can be defined as "aptitude towards its natural form."[137] To better understand what an aptitude toward a form is, we need to look at the different
aptitudes that exist. Although natural inclination is a general tendency
found in all beings, it exists in beings differently according to the different
types of forms. Aquinas identifies three classes of beings that permit differentiation among natural inclinations:[138]

> All things in their own way are inclined by appetite towards good, but
> in different ways. Some are inclined to good by their natural inclina-
> tion, without knowledge, as plants and inanimate bodies. Such incli-
> nation towards good is called "a natural appetite." Others, again, are

inclined towards good, but with some knowledge; not that they know the aspect of goodness, but that they apprehend some particular good; as in the sense, which knows the sweet, the white, and so on. The inclination which follows this apprehension is called "a sensitive appetite." Other things, again, have an inclination towards good, but with a knowledge whereby they perceive the aspect of goodness; this belongs to the intellect. This is most perfectly inclined towards what is good; not, indeed, as if it were merely guided by another towards some particular good only, like things devoid of knowledge, nor towards some particular good only, as things which have only sensitive knowledge, but as inclined towards good in general. Such inclination is termed "will."[139]

The common thread is that each of the three types of being is drawn toward that which makes it what it is, or its form; in other words, all things incline to "something suitable to itself."[140] The concept is easiest to understand in the lowest form of being—nonsentient beings. Fire inclines to rise and spread because to do so is suitable to the nature of fire.[141] The fire does not sense that it is spreading or make any choice to spread. Likewise, when a rock is dropped it falls because it is inclined by its weight to do so. Having an inclination does not mean that the being will attain its end. The fire may encounter a nonflammable substance and stop. The stone may be caught before it falls. Yet the inclination is the aptitude to rise or fall, respectively.

The eternal law acts upon creatures differently according to their form. Some beings have the power of sense. Their natural inclination involves an apprehension, an awareness of the object of their natural inclination. A cat senses a mouse and a warm blanket and can apprehend that the former is suitable for it to eat and the latter is suitable for it to sleep upon. Yet the cat merely apprehends the mouse and the blanket as such but does not understand why a mouse is good for it to eat or why a blanket will be suited to its rest. The cat is merely guided to the mouse and blanket by "another" who legislated through the eternal law the objects of the cat's sensitive appetite.[142]

Finally, rational creatures not only apprehend the things they are inclined toward, but they also possess "a knowledge whereby they perceive the aspect of goodness."[143] R. A. Armstrong summarizes Aquinas's explanation of the unique aspect of the natural inclination in rational creatures that inclines them "towards the good in general . . . rather than to any particular good. . . . Insofar as the will has as its proper object the good in general it possesses a certain power of choice over and above that possessed on the sensitive level. By virtue of the reason it possesses, it can discriminate among the various particulars which appeal to the sensitive faculty."[144]

Although we noted the restraint on human freedom by virtue of the eternal law's legislation of man's last end, the freedom of human choice comes into play at the level of natural inclinations. For a rational creature, there is an inclination to the end in general, with freedom of choice among the various subends. A rational creature not only apprehends a suitable object of desire, but it can also know that it is suitable. Thus all things possess inclinations tending toward what is suitable, but they function in different manners, or as Aquinas summarizes: "Since all things flow from the divine will [i.e., eternal law], all things in their own way are inclined by appetite towards good, but in different ways."[145] In many ways this sentence could be seen as a correction to Ulpian's definition of natural law as "that which nature teaches all animals." Understood in light of the diversity of natural inclinations that direct all things, Ulpian was correct. Yet it is not natural law but the eternal law that fixes the ends and therefore the natural inclinations that "teach" all creatures how to obey the eternal law.

So far we have considered the first two types of natural inclinations operating in nonsentient and sentient but nonrational beings, but I have not given an example of the third type of natural inclination. One might assume that this would be man. However, the quoted language describing the three types of natural inclinations comes from an article discussing angels (beings of pure rationality without bodies), not man. The third type is characterized by these beings of pure rationality. Recognizing this fact will help us appreciate the more complex functioning of the natural inclinations within man.

Man is a creature who touches pure rational beings above and sentient but nonrational animals below him in the order of being. Thus, man is not a simple corporeal being, or a sentient corporeal being, or simply a rational being; he is a *rational animal,* a rational being in a corporeal and sentient state of being. As an animal he will possess a variety of sentient and natural inclinations (he will recognize food as food, and he will fall if pushed off a ledge).[146] Yet as a rational creature he has the potential to understand, order, and choose those things to which his inclinations tend. Notwithstanding the presence of different types of inclinations, man is a unified being. He thus has the capacity to know and choose or not choose objects toward which various inclinations tend and to order his choices.

The way in which man has an inclination to proper acts and ends is similar to but also different from the sentient appetite of irrational animals. Animals tend to their proper actions by a force of innate compulsion, which they do not understand and which can be signified in modern English by the term "instinct." "Inclination" has a connotation of bending toward something but not necessarily doing so by automatic reflex. As a result, Aquinas tends to use, but not exclusively, "inclination" rather than "instinct" when talking about human action. Greene explains the distinction: "Although Thomas does not explain why he substitutes *inclinatio naturae* for Isidore's *instinctus naturae* here and generally in his discussions of the natural law, it seems likely that he chose *inclinatio* because it did not preclude, as *instinctus* did, the exercise of the discursive reason and free choice required by any moral law. An *inclinatio* is not an *instinctus*, despite Thomas's occasional use of the first term where the second seems called for, and never the reverse."[147]

Etymologically, inclination, although incorporating the idea of a force propelling action, incorporates a particularly human context. For example, Cicero uses the term "inclination" to describe the changing attitude of the republic when he says "a certain inclination toward a better hope has been seen to come about."[148] Earlier in the *Summa Theologica*, Aquinas distinguished man as rational from irrational animals, which are moved only by their sentient appetite.[149] Man can knowingly choose his actions, even those objects of a sentient appetite, which appetite "in man, has a certain share of liberty, in so far as it obeys reason."[150] Man can reasonably overrule the inclination of sentient appetite. Man's natural inclinations are like instincts in animals in that they are not chosen or willed in themselves: they simply exist in his nature. In this respect, man's natural inclinations resemble those of animals. Yet man possesses an intellect that can consider and evaluate—or is naturally inclined to contemplate and consider—the objects of these sentient appetites. Man also has the free will to pursue or ignore the objects proposed by the lower inclinations. Aquinas explains: "We have free will with respect to what we will not of necessity, nor by natural instinct. For our will to be happy does not appertain to free will, but to natural instinct. Hence other animals, that are moved to act by natural instinct, are not said to be moved by free will."[151]

This ability of man to evaluate and choose the objects of natural inclinations makes him more like the higher form of the angels. In this way, he participates more than animals in the eternal law. He is capable of being moved to action by more than simple natural instincts. Unlike irrational animals, he can be moved by law. Since man's nature includes more than irrational animals, he needs more than senses to move him: "Therefore, over and above this, something must be given to men whereby they may be directed in their own personal acts. And this we call law."[152] As a result, man has a natural inclination toward participation in law. He thus not only is moved by the eternal law as it directs all things to their end, but he actually participates in freely choosing for himself subends, or means, proportionate to the end established by the eternal law. It is through the selection of means through known law that man participates in a manner commensurate with his nature in the eternal law. As Aquinas explains: "Now, the form is found to have a more perfect existence in those things which participate in knowledge than in those which lack knowledge."[153] Aquinas uses this very word "participation" in his definition of the natural law, known through these natural inclinations.

Man in his nature possesses an innate inclination to the good, but his acceptance of this end as an object of action and the choice of means to it are not preordained, as the ends of animals are. Man possesses two additional faculties, the power to know and the power to choose. These faculties interact with this natural inclination, or, we might say, these faculties demonstrate the presence of an additional inclination, the inclination to reasonably evaluate the other natural inclinations. Man is naturally inclined to consider and sometimes overrule other innate forces of compulsion. In explaining the distinction between the operation of natural inclinations in animals and in man, Aquinas says: "Hence such animals as move themselves in respect to an end they themselves propose.[154] [Men] are superior to these [animals]. This can only be done by reason and intellect; whose province it is to know the proportion between the end and the means to that end, and duly coordinate them."[155]

The various inclinations thus direct to certain categories of action that are appropriate or suited to an aspect of man's being. This relationship between the inclinations and the ends to which they tend helps elucidate how we come to know the natural inclinations and distinguish them from other forces. Contrary to what we might suppose, the order of knowledge advocated by the classical natural law theory moved from knowledge of the ends to knowledge of the inclinations, and not vice versa. We come to know the inclinations only from the vantage point of the ends to which they are directed. Leo Strauss explains this epistemological perspective in terms of potency and act when examining the relationship between virtues and the facts of human nature. He argues that we do not move from a knowledge of human nature to a knowledge of virtues. Rather, from what we know about the virtues we can come to know human nature. He says: "One could say that the relation of virtue to human nature is comparable to that of act and potency, and the act cannot be determined by starting from the potency, but on the contrary, the potency becomes known by looking back to it from the act."[156] Likewise, the natural inclinations are related to the ends of those inclinations as potency is related to act. The natural inclinations are potencies for certain ends. Epistemologically we come to distinguish the natural inclinations not from experience of them per se but rather by our knowledge of their ends. By coming to know the ends of the aspects of human nature we can then identify them in potency as natural inclinations. We will come to examine in detail the particular objects of the natural inclinations when we begin to explore the content of the first precepts of natural law. To assist in our present discussion, we can simply summarily list them: (1) preservation of life, (2) begetting and rearing of children, (3) living sociably in society, and (4) knowledge of truth. In light of these component ends of man, we can identify natural inclinations to preserve one's own life, to produce and rear children, to live in society, and to seek the knowledge of truth.[157] Each of these objects toward which men have a natural inclination are subends or component goods composing the good for man, just as they each relate to an aspect of man's being. He knows these ends because they are part of his very nature. They are legislated into his knowledge by the natural law. But man also participates in this law through the use of reason. Man does not simply involuntarily perform actions prescribed by natural law and indicated by these inclinations. He is inclined to understand the relation of these inclinations to their natural ends, and to the ultimate end, and to choose them as willed ends. Aquinas continues to insist upon the distinction between the ends of natural inclinations and the ultimate end in relation to which they are means. He does not say man determines or chooses these natural inclinations. Since they are components of the end about which man has no choice, he does not choose them as such. They exist in him by virtue of being human. What distinguishes man from animals is the ability to truly apprehend the ends of the natural inclinations (what they tend toward) as components of the good and to choose them as appropriate means to it.

The fact that man has the ability to discern and understand the natural inclinations implies that he can fail to know them. Since he has the mere potentiality to know them, he can also fail in actualizing it. In addition to the freedom of his will, man also differs from the angels in that he possesses a body that brings with it certain aspects of natural inclinations akin to those felt by animals. The higher natural inclinations of man as *rational* animal can be confused with the lower tendencies or desires of man as rational *animal*, some innate and some acquired. This is because, in addition to his rational natural inclination, man also has impulses (impelled desires similar to the instincts operative in other animals), and he also can develop other tendencies acquired by habit.[158] The good to which the natural inclinations point is not necessarily the object of any felt desires.[159] Irrational animals cannot be confused about the instincts they have; rational man can confuse impulses and feelings originating in lower inclinations with his proper natural inclinations as a rational animal. If man were like irrational animals in this respect, there would be no work in the participation in the eternal law. Man would just know the proper ends and automatically do what appears to be a means to that end. Beyond impulses based in lower-level natural inclinations, man can also develop habits of vice (i.e., ways of acting that are contrary to the natural inclinations of man), but that through force of habit can appear to be present naturally. These conatural inclinations can become entrenched and become confused with natural inclinations.[160] The rational participation in the eternal law involves the discernment (knowledge) of the uncorrupted higher-level natural inclinations as opposed to the impulses and corrupted inclinations. The work of natural law, and a trap for the poor practitioners of it, is to properly separate other feelings or impulses (which the reason and will can redirect and control) from the proper natural inclinations of man. Likewise, Jean Porter argues that natural inclinations in and of themselves are not enough to determine the precepts of the natural law, since "the moral significance of the [natural] inclinations cannot be established apart from some reflection on the virtues."[161] Here, she echoes Aquinas when he explains: "The virtues perfect us to follow natural inclinations in an appropriate way, which inclinations pertain to the law of nature. And therefore to the determination of each natural inclination there is ordered a particular virtue."[162]

What is the basis of distinguishing among these forces? The natural inclinations can be distinguished as those compelling not merely toward something desired but toward something suitable to the nature of man as a whole. By "nature of man" is meant not simply man as we might find him but man as he is constituted, including the end or purpose of his being. It involves not merely following feelings but following the inclinations proper to man as coordinated by his natural inclination to be rational. The statement "natural law involves doing what is natural to man" is laden with potentially dangerous ambiguity due to the modern dissociation of the concept of "natural" from the final end of being so important to Aristotle's thought. Natural law is not about merely following innate instinctive feelings but rather orienting them in light of the ordered natural inclination that directs to the purpose of being for man. J. Budziszewski coherently distinguishes these two different senses of what is "natural" with the terminology of "higher" and "lower" nature. He explains:

According to what might be called the lower meaning, the natural is the spontaneous, the haphazard, the unimproved: Think of our first parents in the jungle, or for that matter, think of the jungle itself. From this point of view a human being is at his most natural when he is driven by raw desires, "doing what comes naturally," as we say. But according to what might be called the higher meaning, the natural is what perfects us, what unfolds the inbuilt purposes of our design, what unlocks our directed potentialities. This time think of our first parents not in the jungle but in the Garden, or for that matter, think of the Garden itself. From this point of view, a human being is most genuinely "doing what comes naturally" when he is at his best and bravest and truest—when he fulfills his creational design, when he "comes into his own."[163]

We might even add to the end of his last sentence "even when doing so does not 'feel' natural." Failing to recognize these different senses of "natural" and to recognize that the work of participation in the eternal law is to distinguish and redirect the lower sense of natural has been a great failing of certain natural law critics and supporters alike. Budziszewski goes so far as to describe this tension between the lower inclinations and the natural inclination of man as the great "scandal" of natural law—a scandal that often frightens people away from the fact of natural law. He says: "The natural law scandalizes us because our actual inclinations are at war with our natural inclinations, because our hearts are riddled with desires that oppose their deepest longings, because we demand to have happiness on terms that make happiness impossible."[164]

St. Paul seems to be alluding to this very tension when he says: "For the flesh lusteth against the spirit: and the spirit against the flesh; for these are contrary one to another: so that you do not the things that you would."[165] This war, this scandal within the process of participating in the eternal law (this conflict between the natural inclinations and the actual desires or impulses we may feel), is itself not "natural" but a consequence of the Fall.[166] As Aquinas explains: "As a result of original justice, the reason had perfect hold over the lower parts of the soul, while reason itself was perfected by God, and was subject to Him. Now this same original justice was forfeited through the sin of our first parent, as already stated (Question 81, Article 2); so that all the powers of the soul are left, as it were, destitute of their proper order, whereby they are naturally directed to virtue; which destitution is called a wounding of nature."[167]

The original sin of the first human beings results in a wounding of the human nature passed on to each subsequent generation. Thus, the natural powers of the soul are less disposed to know the natural inclinations to the proper end of human nature. In addition to this wounding of nature by the Fall, "the inclination to the good of virtue [the natural inclination] is diminished in each individual on account of actual sin."[168] Each person participates in the eternal law with the disadvantage of inheriting the

wounds of original sin and then exacerbates those wounds by actual trans-
gressions committed. Thus, men cannot always trust their felt inclinations:
Are they the true natural inclinations, disordered lower inclinations, or
conatural corrupted inclinations? Men need to use their reason to work to
distinguish the natural inclinations placed in them according to the plan of
God, the eternal law, from other impulses lacking proper orientation. The
call of the natural inclination within man is weaker than it ought to be (it
is diminished) as a consequence of both original and actual sin. The more
one sins the greater the diminishment, which accounts for the differing
struggles of people in making this critical distinction. This insight answers
a challenge to natural law jurisprudence. If a natural law exists, why does
following it not seem to come naturally, or why do so many people get it
wrong? Why have men tolerated evils such as slavery, abortion, and genocide if the natural law directs otherwise? The answer: men have been participating in the eternal law with a great handicap caused by the effect of
sin. There is a shadow obscuring the light cast from the eternal law on the
mind of man.

This shadow, conflicting with the natural inclinations, constitutes the
first and most basic conflict of laws. Aquinas actually calls this false guide
competing with the natural inclinations a law, the law of the *fomes peccati*.
This tendency to act contrary to the good obligated by the first principle
of the natural law, although not strictly speaking a law, has "the nature
of a law."[169] This law of the *fomes peccati* (often neglected in analyses of
Aquinas's natural law doctrine) will be examined in more detail in chapter 5. For present purposes, this law of the *fomes* functions like a law that
acts in opposition to, or we might say in competition with, the eternal law
and by doing so interferes with the discernment of the objects of the natural inclinations.

The process of discerning the natural inclinations (and their relationship to law) is described metaphorically in Plato's image of the puppet.[170]
Plato uses the metaphor of a puppet to illustrate how man "has within
himself a pair of unwise and conflicting counselors . . . besides, anticipa-
tions of the future. . . . And on the top of all, there is *judgment* . . . and when
judgment takes the form of a public decision of a city, it has the name of
law."[171] He then analogizes this fact to a puppet controlled by a series of
strings representing these internal forces within each person. These strings

"are opposed to one another, and pull us with opposite tensions in the direction of opposite actions."[172] In addition to these "hard and ironlike" strings, the puppet has a soft golden thread representing judgment. To find fulfillment (the good each seeks after, "fulfillment" being a name for the most complete good) the puppet must yield to this golden string. Since judgment "needs supporters," this judgment should be embodied in law, which the city does by embodying in law this true judgment of the correct golden string, which it receives either from a god or from a human discoverer of it.[173] Thus, the human puppet is filled with conflicting strings, one of which is the natural inclinations, which is difficult to discern. The correct discernment and choice of the golden string needs to be supported by law. Human lawmakers can find the golden string either by being told it by a being above nature (God, the subject of chapter 5) or by a human discoverer of the string. The process of discovering the golden thread is the process of discovering the natural law, which human reason is capable of doing (but not infallibly, also discussed in chapter 5). Thus, we observe a dialectical process. Human beings each need to find and follow the golden thread of natural inclinations among the mess of other strings pulling them. Because of this difficulty, they need to look to law to assist in this endeavor. Yet, putting aside revelation by God, human lawmakers also need to discover natural inclinations. Thus, there is a dialectical process of human rational reflection upon the strings within all men interacting with the established law, which is meant to embody discoveries thus far.

How does a discoverer distinguish the golden string from the mess of other strings? It is clear that merely examining the felt tendencies is insufficient. Aquinas argues that it involves two faculties. First, there is the act of the intellect: we "discern what is good and what is evil" by "the light of natural reason . . . which is the function of the natural law."[174] When Aquinas announces the first precept of the natural law, he explains the relation between this knowledge of what is to be done and the second faculty, action: "Whatever the practical reason naturally apprehends as man's good (or evil) belongs to the precepts of the natural law as something to be done or avoided."[175] We now see the connection between the eternal and natural law—the eternal law, or order of the universe, fixes man's end and illuminates that end through the natural inclinations. This connection is at the heart of Porter's observation that the difference between Christian tradition and Nietzsche is the different inclinations that are considered natural or good.[176] Nietzsche emphasizes the unnatural inclinations—those felt inclinations that do not have their source in the legislated ordered natural inclinations of eternal law. Failing to find the golden thread spun out of the eternal law and to identify the ordered natural inclinations has serious consequences; it can end in the worldview of Nietzsche.

Aquinas's understanding of this first principle of the natural law (good ought to be done, evil avoided) can be restated as "what is suitable to man ought to be done." This understanding is consistent with the way both Gratian and earlier Roman law scholars understood the basic precept of natural law. In the opening of the *Decretum*, Gratian sums up natural law as the Golden Rule: Do to others what you want done to yourself, and do not do to others what you do not want done to yourself.[177] Since what everyone seeks (in the sense of what we are naturally inclined to) is the good—the perfection of one's nature—the Golden Rule commands that we "do" what the natural law says ought to be done and avoid the opposite. What man wants done to him is associated with what man is. This connotation is stressed by the common gloss on the text, which says "interpret 'wants' as 'ought to want.'"[178] This gloss emphasizes the objective nature of inclinations and hence the Golden Rule. It is "not do unto others what one subjectively may feel he wants done to himself," but "what he ought to want done to himself," which is *jus suum* ("one's own right" or "one's own law"). The *Digest* contains a text from Ulpian stating this same first principle of the natural law when he defines the basic principles of *jus* as "to live honestly, to not injure other people, and to render everyone their due [*jus*]."[179] Again, the ideas all tie back to doing good, consistent with the exemplar of human nature as established by eternal law. The *Digest* includes in the notion of *jus* that which is always "good and equitable," which is thus *jus naturale*.[180] Aquinas, Gratian, and the *Digest* are in agreement about the essence of natural law.

But how do we know what we ought to want? How do we find what is suitable toward our nature and thus the object of uncorrupted natural inclinations? The answer is we have to use the power by which we uniquely participate in the eternal law, the power of reason to examine the aspects of our nature and thereby determine what natural inclinations follow each aspect of it. The erroneous path is to search feelings, find felt inclinations, and then discern our nature, even though this might at first seem the logi-cal course. Because of the confusion of tendencies, to say nothing of the law of the *fomes*, we need to begin with our nature and rationally identify its component powers and from there determine which felt forces are natu-ral inclinations following our form.

Demonstrations: Reason and the Secondary Precepts of Natural Law

In the prior subsection we concluded that the natural law contains gen-eral principles that specify the component goods that compose the good for man, which is the end of man established by the eternal law. Although we will turn to consider the content of these general principles in chap-ter 4, for now we can posit that these general principles specify aspects of man's nature that are to be perfected or sought after as subgoods toward the ultimate end of man. Yet, it is one thing to know that something is good; it is another to know how to attain it. Thus, it is not enough to es-tablish that men ought to live together in society. To choose actions con-forming to this principle will require the application of this principle to particular concrete actions. To determine if a particular action is obliga-tory, prohibited, or permitted under natural law, we need to apply more particular principles specifying in greater detail which types of actions are necessary, prohibited, and permitted by the primary principles known through the natural inclinations. We can refer to these more specified pre-cepts as secondary principles of natural law. There are some natural law scholars who have limited the content of the natural law to either the first principle of natural law (some form of "do good") or the most general pri-mary principles, those discussed in the prior subsection as being known through natural inclination.[181] Generally, such writers recognize that we require more specified precepts to rule our choices of action. Yet, many au-thors consider the activity of formulating more particular precepts of ac-tion beyond the most general to be the province not of natural law, but rather of human positive law.[182] Yet, such a limited understanding of natu-ral law is hardly different from that of legal positivism. In its most basic form, the argument says that natural law only requires us to be good or act rationally. Defining what constitutes good or rational is left to the choice of human law. I would doubt even the most hardened legal positivist would argue that lawmakers are supposed to make bad or irrational laws. Given the indestructibility of synderesis, all know they are supposed to seek the good. The heart of the matter is to know what actions conform to the good. To leave this determination to human law essentially renders eternal and natural law a pious irrelevance. We are obligated to do the good, but the good is whatever human law tells us. To be a real framework for human law, a real rule and measure, natural law must contain some more specific precepts to rule and measure human action.

Throughout his writing on natural law, Aquinas refers not only to general primary principles, known either through synderesis or through their own terms as self-evident principles, but also to more particular precepts connected to these more general precepts.[183]

In chapter 4 we will turn to the content of these secondary precepts. As this chapter has focused on the essence of the natural law and the epistemological problem in knowing its contents, we will limit our consideration to the process of coming to know the secondary precepts, a process that differs in significant respects from both synderesis and self-evident principles.

Aquinas argues that human knowledge moves from the more general and abstract to the more distinct and specified.[184] He gives the example of seeing a person from a far distance. First, we know what we see to be a body of some sort; then as it moves closer we see it move and know it to be an animal. As it comes closer we can discern that it is a specific type of animal—a man. Finally, as it comes even closer we can discern the particular man, for example, Socrates. The catalyst bringing our knowledge of Socrates from potency to actuality is the movement toward seeing more marks of distinction, more details. Likewise, we first know the primary principles of natural law that abstractly[185] and generally help us to recognize, from far off, the aspects of our good. In addition to these general primary precepts, natural law also contains more specific precepts, which are conclusions drawn from the general primary precepts.[186] We come to see these greater details by looking at, or reflecting upon, the good we first know indistinctly and generally. Thus, unlike the self-evident propositions that are immediately known once the terms are understood, the secondary precepts are known following reflection upon the goods indicated by the natural inclinations.

By considering and coming to know in more specific detail of what these goods are composed, we can deduce or demonstrate certain principles that identify which classes of actions are necessary for, conflict with, or are consistent with the good. The secondary precepts are not particularizations of the good but specifications. They do not involve the recognition of Socrates but of a species, man. The decision to do a particular act involves the application of a law; the specification of classes of actions bearing a certain relationship to the good is the function of the secondary precepts.

To understand the nature of the epistemological process of coming to know secondary precepts—and to distinguish natural law from human positive law—we need to consider the distinction Aquinas makes between deducing conclusions and making determinations:[187] "But it must be noted that something may be derived from the natural law in two ways: first, as a conclusion from premises, second, by way of determination of certain generalities."[188] The first process involves the drawing of a more specific conclusion based upon a general premise. For example, from the general principle "it is evil to intentionally and deliberately will harm to another man," and the minor premise "murder is the intentional and deliberate ending of a man's life," we can conclude that murder is evil. More specifically, "demonstrated conclusions [murder is evil] are drawn from the principles,"[189] but a judgment concerning a particular human act in all its attendant circumstances—the killing of Socrates—is not reached. The conclusion follows necessarily from the premises. If the premises are correct, the conclusion is correct. By contrast, the second process of determination does not involve such rational necessity. It involves the particularization of a principle in a specific instantiation. Returning to the familiar analogy of art, Aquinas explains that making a determination is "likened to that whereby, in the arts, general forms are particularized as to details: thus the craftsman needs to determine the general form of a house to some particular shape."[190] The general definition of a house does limit the work of the architect. There are specific properties that must be present in the design to constitute a house. Yet, the particular design and shape of a house are not determined by the general principle defining a house. There is an element of freedom of choice on the part of the architect. Within and bounded by the general form of the house, he chooses among the vast array of possible particularizations and determines the details of this house.

This movement from logical or rational necessity to a bounded free determination of particulars distinguishes making determinations from demonstrating conclusions, and it also marks the boundary between natural law and human positive law. Porter summarizes the point of distinction between natural law and human law, and their relationship:

> The general imperatives of the natural law must be translated into social practices through the conventions of a particular society in order to be practically effective. These conventions are not themselves part of the natural law in a primary sense, and they stand in a complex relationship to it. At the same time, they can be described as the natural law in a derivative sense, since they are expressions of the natural law properly so called, and are in some cases very nearly as universal as the natural law itself. . . . Moreover even those precepts of the natural law that are revealed by God cannot be translated directly into social practices without a considerable degree of interpretation.[191]

Once this point of interpretation or particular determination through the conventions of a people is reached, we have crossed into human law. Yet even at this point, human law can be considered at least derivatively as part of natural law since it is a particular interpretation, or to use Aquinas's term, a "determination," of the natural law.

The legal example given by Aquinas to illustrate the difference between deduction of secondary precepts and determination of human laws is the punishment of wrongdoers.[192] He argues that the principle wrongdoers should be punished is a secondary precept of natural law. But, that a wrongdoer be punished in a particular way is not a necessary rational conclusion that can be drawn from the principle. Human law is entrusted with the choice of determining a particular punishment. The choice is bounded. The granting of a reward or privilege would not constitute punishment. Likewise, disproportionate harm rising to the level of torture would not constitute punishment. Between these two extremes there is a vast possible collection of punishments among which human law can choose for a particular wrongdoing.

Thus, we have identified the process whereby secondary precepts of natural law are grasped. Unlike primary precepts, they are not understood merely through knowledge of their terms. Simply knowing what a wrong-doer is and what punishment is will not be sufficient to reach the conclusion that wrongdoers should be punished. Understanding secondary precepts will involve reflection upon the primary precepts. Aquinas explains this process:

> As every judgment of speculative reason proceeds from the natural knowledge of first principles, so every judgment of practical reason proceeds from principles known naturally, as stated above (Question 4, Articles 2, 4): from which principles one may proceed in various ways to judge of various matters. For some matters connected with human actions are so evident, that after very little consideration (*cum modica consideratione*) one is able at once to approve or disapprove of them by means of these general first principles: while some matters cannot be the subject of judgment without much consideration (*multa consideratio*) of the various circumstances, which all are not competent to do carefully, but only those who are wise: just as it is not possible for all to consider the particular conclusions of sciences, but only for those who are versed in philosophy: and lastly there are some matters of which man cannot judge unless he be helped by Divine instruction; such as the articles of faith.[193]

The key term Aquinas uses is *consideratio*, which can be translated as "consideration" or "contemplation."[194] Unlike with self-evident propositions, more than the terms of the principle need to be considered to arrive at conclusions. To reach the conclusions constituting secondary precepts, the "various circumstances" must be considered together with the general principles. These circumstances constitute the details, providing greater clarity to the more specific description of human action. To return to the earlier analogy: as the figure approaches, we need to consider the newly seen details to consider what the object might be. As we discern specific features, we can consider them in light of the definitions of different bodies to judge what the figure is. So too, as more circumstances of the human act are specified, we need to consider them in light of the general principles to reach conclusions. Aquinas continues to use this analogy of movement to distinguish among the secondary precepts. Some conclusions follow "closely [*propinquus*] from first principles," which we can refer to as proximate conclusions.[195] But in the same passage he also refers to "other" secondary precepts, which by implication do not follow "closely" the primary principles, and these we can refer to as remote conclusions.[196] The distinction between the proximate and remote conclusions is not an ontological difference, but rather a mere difference of degree.[197] We only need a little consideration to come to know the proximate conclusions but much consideration to understand the remote conclusions. Since consideration requires taking into account the relevant circumstances, the more we "descend to matters of detail," the more circumstances we must consider, and thus we will require more consideration.[198]

This distinction between proximate and remote conclusions explains the variation in the extent of knowledge of the secondary precepts. We have already seen that knowledge of the first principle of natural law is known by all through synderesis. As self-evident principles, the primary principles are capable of being known by all, but they are not always universally known due to a lack of knowledge of the natural inclinations. Since the secondary precepts require not only knowledge of the primary principles but also consideration of matters of detail, knowledge of the secondary precepts will be far from universal. As Aquinas observes, "in matters of detail, it [the truth] is not equally known to all."[199] We will return to how we cope with a more or less widespread lack of knowledge of the secondary precepts in later chapters, but for now we are merely concerned with the fact that as we move from the more abstract and general precepts of natural law to the more concrete and specific, the greater possibility of ignorance arises. To anticipate our consideration of human positive law, one function of human law is to instruct people in the more remote conclusions of natural law, and thus human law may promulgate or enact as law the secondary precepts of natural law. Yet, these precepts do not have their origin in human law but in natural law. Aquinas comments that those laws which are merely demonstrated conclusions from the natural law "are contained in human law not as emanating therefrom exclusively, but have some force from the natural law also."[200] Only human laws which are not formulated solely by demonstration from the primary principles, but which are determinations of precepts of natural law, "have no other force than that of human law."[201]

In this chapter we have discovered that the epistemological question of natural law is a complex topic. There is no single answer to the question of how we participate in the eternal law or how we come to know the principles of natural law. At points there is little intellectual effort on our part. We all know by synderesis the abstract axiomatic first principle that "good is what we ought to do and evil what we ought not to do." Due to the convertibility of good and being, we can come to know generally the aspects composing the good by coming to know our nature through the natural inclinations. Although these primary precepts of natural law are accessible to the knowledge of all men because they are self-evident, not all men will in fact know them. Knowledge of self-evident propositions requires knowledge of their terms. In this case, that requires knowledge of those aspects of our nature indicated by the natural inclinations. Because of our difficulty in properly discerning the natural inclinations, we all may fail to properly know the terms. Beyond the general principles of natural law lie more specific conclusions that can be drawn from them, either after a little or much consideration, depending upon the extent of the detailed circumstances to be considered. Knowledge of these secondary precepts or conclusions can vary even more since it depends upon consideration of details. When we reach the remote conclusions, we reach the extent of the framework, the limit of natural law. To proceed to an action beyond the secondary precepts will require not only rational consideration, but also an act of the will. A bounded choice among permissible actions all conforming to the secondary precepts must be determined. This determination will be added to the frame through the craft of human lawmaking. But before the frame can be decorated with determinations, we must explore the details of the framework more closely and consider the content of the primary and secondary precepts of natural law. Following which, we must return to the problem of epistemological failure. Since men, and entire societies, can fail to know both the primary and secondary precepts of natural law, can we locate a source of assistance to overcome this failure?

Examining the Framework

The Content of the Natural Law

Wherefore according to the order of natural inclinations,
is the order of the precepts of the natural law.[1]

In chapter 3, we looked at the framework of natural law as a whole. We considered how we come to know its component parts. We discussed three distinct processes corresponding to three levels of the framework. The first principle of the natural law—good ought to be done and evil avoided—is universally known through synderesis. The primary principles elaborating the good could come to be known through an examination of the natural inclinations, but such knowledge is not universally achieved. Finally, the secondary precepts are conclusions drawn either proximately or remotely from the primary precepts through a process of reflection on more specific circumstances of human actions. We met at this point the limit of natural law, where the framework meets the interior of the structure. Once a precept can no longer be demonstrated through rational consideration, but a choice of the will must be made to determine the precise rule, we have reached the details of human law.

As Ross Armstrong observes, many writers on natural law have been content to end their discussion at this epistemological level and merely conclude that there are self-evident precepts of natural law known through the natural inclinations without ever discussing what these precepts state.[2] To stop here is "of no value to us at all."[3] If human law is to be the active participation of man in lawmaking by determining the particular enactment of natural law's precepts in human law, then we must consider the principles to be determined in more specificity than their abstract existence. Therefore, in this chapter we will peer inside the framework of natural law and discuss the content of its primary and secondary principles. In the first section we will consider the primary precepts of natural law and their hierarchical relationship. In the second section we will turn to the secondary precepts and consider their content, their relationship among themselves and to the primary precepts, and their variability. Having reached the end of the two-chapter consideration of natural law, in the third section we will evaluate and assess the role of natural law in the overall architecture of law.

ELABORATING THE PRIMARY PRINCIPLES

Content of the Primary Principles

We have already seen that the first principle of natural law—good is to be done and evil avoided—is ontological, that is, a principle of being.[4] The good is obligatory because it is a function of being. Yet, as Ana Marta González has said, "the reference to good, at the principle level, involves a reference to a not yet specified content."[5] The next logical step must be to further specify the primary precept by defining the nature of "good" based on the ontological nature of man. The self-evidence of the primary principles of natural law is "intimately bound up with the ontological tendencies or propensities inherent in the very nature of man, the *naturales inclinationes.*"[6] As Aquinas argues, "There must be definite kinds of operations which are appropriate to a definite nature, whenever things have such a definite nature. In fact, the operation appropriate to a given being is a consequent of that nature. Now, it is obvious that there is a determinate kind of nature for man. Therefore, there must be some operations that are in themselves appropriate for man."[7] Man's certain nature is legislated by the eternal law, which establishes the type, idea, or exemplar of all things. Since the "good" is a function of the nature of things, it is what all things seek after or are inclined toward by their nature, fixed by the eternal law. The content can be specified by considering what all things seek after. Put another way, the content summarized by "good" can be found by considering the essence or being of man as man, in all his hierarchy of activities (or to use Aquinas's term, "operations") proper to his nature. The good must be broken down into more specific statements relating to the various aspects of man's essence, which are known from the activities proper to man's nature.

In chapter 3 we discussed the hierarchy of being within the natural world. Man's nature can be broken down by considering the elements of his nature he shares with other creatures and the *differentiae* that distinguish him from them. We also noted in chapter 3 that this approach to the problem was imperfectly present in Ulpian's ancient definition of natural law contained in the *Digest*. Ulpian had defined *jus naturale* as "that which nature teaches to all animals, for this law is not peculiar to the human race, but affects all creatures."[8] This definition seemed to be in tension with the understanding of natural law as the *rational* participation of man in the eternal law. Put another way, since irrational animals could not be subject to the natural law, as man is, since they cannot rationally participate, how then could it be that which nature teaches all animals? The answer lies in this hierarchical understanding of human nature. Since this nature includes the lower orders of being, such as irrational animals, the natural inclinations that man shares with them are relevant to an understanding of man's good through his nature, but merely examining these lower inclinations is insufficient since man's nature includes other natural inclinations and since these goods are not indifferent but hierarchically ordered, as we shall see in the next section. This more refined understanding of the Roman jurists' conception of natural law is also reflected in Isidore of Seville's revision of the definition of law (*jus*) contained in the *Digest*. Part of Paulus's definition of *jus* includes this statement: "Whatever is just[9] [*aequum*] and good [*bonum*] is called law [*jus*], as is the case with natural law [*jus naturale*]."[10] Isidore incorporates this phrase at the end of his list of some precepts of natural law, which he concludes are part of natural law because they are held to be "natural and equitable" (*natu-rale equumque*).[11] His substitution of natural (*naturale*) for good (*bonum*) underscores the ontological understanding of the good as that which is incorporated into the nature of things through the eternal law. That which exists by, and is in harmony with, nature (*cum natura*) is that which is good (*bonum*).

In formulating a list of the primary precepts of natural law, Aquinas follows this approach of the order of nature and the natural inclinations related thereto:

> Wherefore according to the order of natural inclinations, is the order of the precepts of the natural law. Because in man there is first of all an inclination to good in accordance with the nature which he has in common with all substances: inasmuch as every substance seeks the preservation of its own being, according to its nature: and by reason of this inclination, whatever is a means of preserving human life, and of warding off its obstacles, belongs to the natural law. Secondly, there is in man an inclination to things that pertain to him more specially, according to that nature which he has in common with other animals: and in virtue of this inclination, those things are said to belong to the natural law, "which nature has taught to all animals" [Pandect. Just. I; tit. i], such as sexual intercourse, education of offspring, and so forth. Thirdly, there is in man an inclination to good, according to the nature of his reason, which nature is proper to him: thus man has a natural inclination to know the truth about God, and to live in society: and in this respect, whatever pertains to this inclination belongs to the natural law.[12]

Aquinas explains that man is actually a composite of different natural aspects. The good can be defined as a composite construction of the various principles derived from these individual aspects. The inclinations to which each aspect of human nature gives rise can be identified by returning to the definition of man constructed from the genera within which man is a species and the specific differentiae that distinguish the species of man from its immediately preceding genus.[13] Man's good will include both the goods to which lower-order beings are inclined in addition to the aspect of the good to which man is uniquely inclined. Thus, to know man's good we can also look to the good of other beings who share common inclinations with man. John Finnis insists that animal nature tells us nothing about natural law.[14] As a result of rejecting the inclinations held in common with other beings, Finnis is forced to look exclusively to our internal experiences to identify the basic human goods.[15] Armstrong, on the other hand, explains that for Aquinas, "Man possesses inclinations characteristic not only of his own rational nature but also of other levels of created nature. He shares inclinations with beings at . . . the natural and physical level as well as those at the sensible or animal level."[16]

As a result, Aquinas begins his construction of the precepts by identifying the characteristic man shares with all other substances; they exist and are therefore inclined to remain in existence. Existence is the first aspect of man's good, and the corresponding precept of natural law can be formulated as "Do what is a means of preserving human existence" and avoid "its obstacles." Yet more can be said about this principle. Since man is a corporeal substance, he exists in a body; part of preserving his existence is preserving his corporeal existence. The phrase "human existence" thus includes the preservation of corporality. In addition to being a living corporeal substance, man is an animal. All animals are inclined to undertake acts that lead to the procreation of more like themselves and, to the extent consistent with their particular form, care for their young. As man is a rational animal, capable of being educated, this inclination includes for man both the inclination to produce other beings like himself and the "education" of children. These inclinations indicate that the procreation and education of children is a component of the good for man. Thus, the next precept of natural law can be formulated as "What assists both the procreation and education of children ought to be done, and what is opposed to it should be avoided." Next, man is distinguished from animals by the *differentia* of a rational soul, one that can know and choose. This dual aspect of man's soul leads to two more objects of good: knowledge of truth and coordinated willed action consistent with man's social nature. The attribute of an intellect makes man capable of, and therefore suited or inclined to, knowledge of the truth. For Aristotle, it is an "activity in which the mind contemplates the unchanging and eternal aspects of things, an activity in which the mind, in virtue of that within it which is divine, contemplates in a way that reproduces the activity of God."[17] It also makes communication among men possible. Second, man's ability to think about and then choose actions makes man, in the words of Aristotle, "a social and political animal."[18] Irrational animals can live in groups, but there interaction is governed by instinct and irrational desire. Man is capable of, and therefore inclined toward, comprehending the implications of his interactions and capable of choosing among a range of possible interactions. This aspect of man's nature, unique among animals, makes man both social (coming from *societas*, "a chosen association or community of people") and political (from the Greek *polis*, an association that is willed). Contrary to the modern political philosophy, rooted in Enlightenment skepticism, that says political societies are necessary evils, for natural law jurists, since man possesses a natural inclination to live together in society, organized communities, including authorities within them, are natural for man.[19] These two final goods indicated by the twofold nature of man's rational soul are therefore the related goods of the acquisition of truth and the coordinated life in a willed society. The corresponding precepts are (1) one ought to do what causes increased knowledge of the truth and avoid ignorance, and (2) one ought to do what facilitates coordinated life in society and avoid what destroys society. Aristotle understood these two aspects of human nature to be interdependent. One needs to be a member of societies, such as the family and the *polis*, to be able to achieve one's own good.[20] By proclaiming that man was a social and political animal, Aristotle was making more than an observation; he was making a normative statement. Not only was society natural in the sense of it being unsurprising to find man actually living in societies, but it was a necessary component of achieving virtue and the good alike. Man needed to be in society to achieve his ultimate end. Alasdair MacIntyre explains: "Aristotle ... represents a tradition of thought, in which he is preceded by Homer and Sophocles, according to which the human being who is separated from his social group is also deprived of the capacity for justice."[21] In fact, a human being deprived of a *polis* is deprived of central attributes of a human being.[22] One deprived of a *polis* is deprived of the ability to develop and perfect the virtue of justice and even the ability to make use of practical reasoning itself.[23] In a certain sense, a person severed from soci-

Table 4.1. Aspects of Being, Associated Goods, and Precepts of Natural Law

Level of Being	Good Identified	Corresponding Primary Precept
Corporeal Substance	Corporeal Existence (being alive)	Human corporeal existence ought to be preserved, and obstacles to it ought to be avoided.
Sentient Animal	Bearing and Education of Children	The conception and education of children ought to be done, and obstacles to these goods ought to be avoided.
Rational Soul Comprising an Intellect and a Will	Truth and Living in a Political Society	Truth ought to be sought after and life in political society ought to be fostered, and obstacles to these ought to be avoided.

ety is lacking in a critical aspect of human nature, and in this sense we can understand that "living in society" is more than an observation. It is an obligatory precept of natural law. Men need society to be fully human, to fulfill the other unique ends of being a rational creature.[24]

The results of this examination of natural inclinations following the order of being can be summarized in table 4.1.

Before leaving our consideration of the primary precepts of natural law, we must pause on an aspect of the final component of good listed by Aquinas, for it serves as the bridge between the natural and supernatural ends of man and the natural and divine law.[25] Aquinas not only lists "knowledge of truth" but specifically "knowledge of the truth about God." Much has been discussed over the centuries about Aquinas's conception of the relationship between and separation of the natural and supernatural spheres. I do not intend to engage in that question directly but only wish to note that, at least with respect to natural law, Aquinas clearly sees a relation between man's natural end and his supernatural end (*beatitudo*), that is, knowledge of God. Thus, although Aquinas understands that complete knowledge of God requires supernatural virtues and grace (which are beyond the reach of natural law), some knowledge of God is suitable to human nature. At least the inclination to know the truth about God is present. Man's nature, the soul, is suited to know about God even if he lacks the natural powers to attain that knowledge without assistance. Since man is inclined to know the truth about God, Aquinas presents five proofs for the existence of God in the *Summa Theologica*, which are based completely on the use of natural reason (not on any supernatural revelation). Although many aspects of the nature of God are unknowable by unaided human reason (i.e., the Trinitarian nature of God), God's existence, his role as uncaused cause of the material world, and so on are accessible by the use of natural reason and obligatory under the precepts of natural law. In fact, man has an inclination to know about these ultimate questions of origin. The connection between natural knowledge of God and supernatural knowledge is analogous to the relationship between eternal and natural law. Man does not know the eternal law directly in its entirety. As we have seen, the eternal law is the divine reason itself, thus beyond man's natural reason. But natural law has been defined as the "participation" of man in the eternal law. Thus, natural law, as its very name suggests, functions on the level of the natural world (in man's natural rational capabilities), but it touches the supernatural in that it is a participation in the eternal law.

The Demonstration and Hierarchy of the Primary Precepts

Aquinas's presentation of the primary precepts of natural law differs significantly from the presentation of the indemonstrable goods by Finnis in his "new natural law." Notwithstanding some overlap in Aquinas's and Finnis's lists of aspects of the good,[26] their understanding of these goods is radically different. The two points of departure are the issue of demonstrability and commensurability. Finnis maintains that the goods are both indemonstrable and incommensurable; whereas Aquinas understands the goods to be demonstrable from the natural inclinations, and he understands them to exist in a hierarchical relationship.

Finnis understands self-evident principles differently from Aquinas. He says a self-evident principle is "obvious" and "it cannot be demonstrated, but equally it needs not demonstration."[27] Finnis's definition of self-evident as "obvious" leads him to the conclusion that self-evident principles are indemonstrable.[28] As we observed in chapter 3, this definition differs significantly from Aquinas's understanding of self-evident, or *per se nota.* For Aquinas, these propositions are not known through syllogistic reasoning but through the terms themselves. This does not mean the proposition is utterly indemonstrable. It is demonstrable, not through syllogistic reasoning, but rather through the knowledge of the very terms contained within the proposition. The primary precepts, according to Aquinas, are self-evident, but the terms necessary to know the precepts are not themselves self-evident or obvious. Aquinas makes this clear when discussing the differing degrees of difficulty in actually coming to know the self-evident precepts. He notes that the meaning of the term "man" is not known to everyone.[29]

Within this last observation of Aquinas lies the root cause of Finnis's departure from Aquinas's epistemology. For Aquinas, the primary principles of natural law are *per se nota* once one knows the definition of the terms involved in the principles. But these terms, as we have seen, are the definition of man's being, or the various aspects of man's nature. As Louis Cortez has keenly observed, Finnis is committed to the primacy of human practical reason over nature.[30] Actions are wrong because they are contrary to practical reason, which makes them contrary to nature.[31] Since Aquinas starts with nature and then uses reason to recognize and deduce principles, nature precedes the application of human reason both in the order of being and the order of knowledge. Granted, reasoning from natural facts is only possible because God's rational plan underlies nature, but this places the eternal reason, not practical reason, before nature. For Finnis, this order is reversed, and he thus begins his considerations from reason and ends with nature. Thus, there are no facts, such as the composite nature of man, to serve as points of departure from which reason proceeds. As a result, Finnis has to merely postulate indemonstrable goods and defend them as obvious since nature is not there as a factual departure point. For Aquinas—unlike Finnis—discovering the goods is not merely a process of recognizing obvious goods. Rather than a systemic, rational exploration of the reality of man's nature, Finnis merely claims that "it is obvious that those who are well informed, etc., simply *are* better off. . . . Am I not compelled to admit it, willy-nilly?"[32] For Finnis, self-evident principles are not "formulated reflectively."[33] Aquinas thinks we can offer more than obviousness. Knowledge of the self-evident primary principles of natural law is attained by reflecting on the nature of man.

Reflection on man's nature leads one to identify the activities suitable to such a nature. Understanding rationality as an activity proper to the soul or to which the soul is inclined demonstrates that knowledge is a good suited to a being composed, at least in part, of a rational soul. Only once these components of man's nature are known and reflected upon do the self-evident precepts become known through the terms. Placing reason before nature ironically makes Finnis's approach less rational than Aquinas's since Finnis can only assert without rational reflection that the goods simply are obvious. As Porter observes, the Scholastics did not derive natural law precepts simply from observing nature, because nature needs to be interpreted: "They are aware that the facts of human nature and experience must be interpreted in light of our best theological and philosophical understandings in order to become morally significant."[34] The natural law precepts do not simply emerge as obvious from looking around at "nature." They become known through a philosophical exploration of man's nature. Only in light of these "theological and philosophical understandings" of man's nature do the precepts become self-evident and carry moral significance. For Aquinas and other Scholastics, some speculative knowledge is essential to knowledge of the first principles of practical reason. By contrast, and notwithstanding his protestations of not deriving "ought" statements from "is" statements,[35] Finnis simply asserts that the basic goods are goods because it is obviously so. His fallacious derivation is that the goods are goods because they are obviously goods.

Finnis's rejection of the primacy of nature also leads to a rejection of the natural inclinations as the basis of discovering the aspects of the good. He exhibits a very different and less precise understanding of inclinations than the one we developed in chapter 3. Finnis speaks of "felt inclinations,"[36] using the term synonymously with subjective "desires" and "felt want."[37] We were careful in chapter 3 to distinguish the term "natural inclination" from subjectively felt wants or desires; there I expressed agreement with Finnis's claim that subjectively felt desires are not the means to knowing the primary precepts of the natural law;[38] they do not represent the natural inclinations, properly understood. If we feel a desire for the good, among other confused and confusing desires, the felt desire does not usefully serve as the basis of our knowledge of the good, since we need to distinguish this one felt desire from the other (often contradictory ones). We at times feel the desire toward the good because it is good and thus an object suited to our nature, but our experience of feeling it cannot alone serve as our means of knowing the good. Contrary to Finnis's claim that Aquinas does not base his understanding of natural law on metaphysical knowledge,[39] Aquinas does found his understanding of natural law on primary philosophical truths concerning the essence of man. The primary precepts of natural law are only *per se nota* once the term "man" is known and reflected upon. Thus, when Finnis dismisses inclinations as a component of demonstrating through themselves the primary precepts, he is really, rightly, rejecting subjectively felt desires, not the natural inclinations. The natural inclinations are fundamental philosophical concepts that identify those actions suitable for a particular nature. These fitting actions are the terms through which the precepts of natural law can be known—not as obvious, but as necessarily true by virtue of their own definition. Yet since Finnis rejects such essential speculative knowledge as the basis of knowledge of the primary goods, he ultimately returns full circle to felt desires and urges as the source of knowledge of the goods. The need to experience feelings subjectively creeps into Finnis's argument as a necessary component: "The value of truth becomes obvious only to one who has experienced the urge to question . . . who likewise could enjoy the advantage of attaining correct answers."[40]

The second difference between the natural law espoused by Aquinas and the "new" natural law of Finnis involves the relationship among the aspects of the good. Aquinas's list of the primary precepts includes the Aristotelian notion[41] that they exist in an ordered hierarchy. The Aristotelian tradition, which in this respect accords with the Platonic, precludes any conflict of goods. Rooted in a metaphysics of cosmic order and harmony, Plato, Aristotle, and Aquinas all agree that "there exists a cosmic order which dictates the place of each virtue in a total harmonious scheme of human life."[42] The cosmic hierarchy involves a dependence of each good upon the others: "The presence of each requires the presence of all."[43] The components or parts of the good are inextricably connected to their ordering with the whole, which corresponds to the cosmic order. This cosmic unity precludes the goods composing it from coming into conflict. Any apparent conflict among goods results from our misunderstanding of the cosmic order or our pursuit of goods in a manner and to an extent out of place in this order. The Platonic/Aristotelian tradition finds a principle of unity that orders but leaves in place a plurality of goods. A hierarchical relationship is the key holding this unity in plurality together: "For Aristotle, as for Plato, the good life for man is itself single and unitary, compounded of a hierarchy of goods."[44] The perverted natural law doctrine of Thomas Hobbes attempts to resolve the apparent conflict of goods in a different way. He finds unity by eliminating plurality. He collapses the components of the good into a one-dimensional good. He reduced all natural law to one passion (as distinguished from natural inclination) and one good— self-preservation from violent death.[45] In contrast, the Platonic/Aristotelian/ Thomistic tradition, which Hobbes was leveling with his one right of self-preservation, was three-dimensional in an ascending hierarchy. Although in general Finnis has more in common with Aquinas than Hobbes (since he acknowledges multiple goods and not merely one), his philosophy makes a distinct break with this tradition and results, like Hobbes's, in a one-dimensional account of the good, albeit for a different reason. Although Finnis accepts the multiplicity of goods, they all reside on a one-dimensional plane of incommensurability. For Aquinas, the list of goods is not an incommensurable list of elements of the aspects constituting the good. The list ascends in an ordered hierarchical structure of definitions based on the hierarchical composite nature of man.[46] The goods that serve as the ends of the primary precepts of natural law are not independent autonomous incommensurable ends. They are deeply interconnected. As MacIntyre explains: "It is important that these *inclinationes* are ordered. We educate our children for the sake of their being able to participate in the pursuit of knowledge; we subordinate our need for self-preservation if the lives of our children or the security of our community are gravely endangered."[47] The good of education of youth is oriented toward the good of the pursuit of knowledge. The good of preserving one's life must be understood in the context of the higher ordered goods, the education of children and the life in a community. An example of the relevance of this hierarchy to practical reason is present in Aquinas's consideration of whether every lie is a sin. Aquinas concludes that one cannot lie to preserve the property, bodily integrity, or even the life of a person.[48] Although the good intention of saving a life may mitigate the gravity of the lie, because a lie is inordinate by excess or defect with respect to the good of truth, a lie is always wrong. This conclusion is understandable if the good of truth is a higher-ranked good than life. It becomes incomprehensible, or at least difficult to understand, if truth and life are incommensurable.

As MacIntyre's work—on the relationship among the virtues, the narrative unity of a human life, and the ultimate good—suggests, the unifying good is more complex than the one-dimensional good of Hobbes. MacIntyre's position at first may appear contradictory. He asserts the reality of a unifying good that gives order and meaning to the goods that are ends relative to the virtues, yet he acknowledges the variety of the forms that good takes in different lives unfolding their own narrative.[49] Thus, his approach to identification of the unifying good follows this method. First we must ask: "What is the good for me?"[50] Subsequently, when I ask the question, "What is the good for man?," the answer to that question involves determining what answers to the former question, with respect to different lives, have in common.[51] The answer to the particular question will vary from person to person, depending upon their own personal narrative, which will include its own particular setting and character roles intersecting the narratives of different characters. Thus, his answer appears to be both a single unified good and a variety of different goods. This apparent contradiction can be resolved by what we have already said about the eternal law and its relationship to the natural law.

MacIntyre is certainly not advocating the pluralist liberalism of limitless variation in conceptions of human good. Although not explicitly stated by MacIntyre, the unstated premise that saves his explanation from sliding into pluralistic liberalism is the eternal law. As we have seen, the eternal law fixes the ultimate, supernatural, and natural end of man and legislates it into human nature. Yet this legislation is not in the mode of detailed precept specifying means, but rather the form of a type or an exemplar. Through the freedom to elect particular means to weave a life narrative that arrives at a product still governed by the type, the eternal law permits a variation in the precise narrative nature of the good life while restraining that variation within the type or exemplar. That which is good for a monk, a teacher, a parent, an architect, and so on will vary in details; those details will be constrained within the pattern formed by what within each of these types of narratives is common to all the narratives. The medieval concept of "station in life" is a concept that captures this diversity in unity. All stations in life vary in the details of what is good for them. The particular good for a contemplative monk is not the same as what is good for a crusading knight.[52] Yet each of these stations in life is an alternative route to that which is good for man as such—on the natural level, the happiness of conformity of all aspects of life to the common unity of purpose, which brings knowledge of the truth, and on the supernatural level, eternal union with the source of that truth, God. MacIntyre's analysis is significantly strengthened by reference to the eternal law so as to avoid the misconception of the ultimate good being seen as pluralistic liberalism, which simply seeks to facilitate each writing his life however he wills. What was established about the nature of an exemplar in chapter 2 is the bulwark preventing this distortion. The eternal law legislates the ultimate end by way of exemplar, which permits the election of means that do in fact lead to this ultimate end. Thus, not every narrative and not every election of a plot turn in every narrative is possible under the ultimate exemplar, just as not every painting of every woman and a child is consistent with an exemplar of the Madonna and Child. A narrative that effectively lives a story that elects the vices and not the virtues, or in other words elects choices contrary to natural law, is not a narrative written according to the exemplar of eternal law. Transferring the exemplar to the artistic realm emphasized by MacIntyre—the telling of stories—helps illustrate this point. A story containing characters named King Arthur and Sir Gowen and Sir Perceval in which the characters engage in guerrilla war with the Anglo-Saxons, slaughter the innocent, and seek demonic preternatural powers rather than the Holy Grail is a story, but it is not one following the exemplar called Arthurian legend. Yet the genre of Arthurian legends contains a vast variety of different stories that are consistent with this type of narrative. Although every correct answer to the question "What is good for me?" is consistent with the correct answer to the question "What is good for man?," since the former will follow the exemplar of the latter, not every willed narrative life is consistent with the correct answer to the latter question, or for that matter the former.

MacIntyre leaves this understanding of the eternal law as an unstated premise in his argument for a plurality of goods, ordered by and to an ultimate unitary good, but Finnis explicitly refuses MacIntyre's conclusion and this unstated premise. He feels compelled to depart from Aquinas's understanding of the goods as corresponding to the hierarchical aspect of man's essence. Finnis aligns himself with the modern dogma, "which holds that the variety and heterogeneity of human goods is such that their pursuit cannot be reconciled in any single moral order."[53] Although many societies, particularly modern totalitarian societies, have attempted to impose a false hegemony of order over the variety of goods with disastrous consequences, the failure lies in these societies' violation of the cosmic order by imposing an artificial order of their own making, not in their belief in a hierarchical harmony of the goods. To reject the Platonic/Aristotelian/Thomistic tradition on this point by identifying totalitarian failures is equivalent to arguing that because one chef failed to combine the ingredients of a chocolate cake in a satisfactory manner to produce an edible dessert, those ingredients are incapable of being ordered in any satisfying combination. For Finnis, the definition of the good (which he calls the "basic goods") accepts this modern dogma, and he maintains that the good is composed of disparate elements, because they are incommensurable.[54] Although Finnis cannot deny that Aquinas lists the elements of the good in a threefold hierarchy, as with eternal law, he dismisses the ordering as irrelevant, a "questionable example" that "plays no part in his [Aquinas's] practical (ethical) elaboration of the significance and consequences of the primary precept of natural law."[55] Just as modern liberal individualism rejects the social nature of man and apprehends each person as a disconnected and incommensurable end disconnected from society, in like manner Finnis rejects the component nature of the various goods and denies that these goods are ordered parts of a whole, the supreme good. Pauline Westerman understands this difference to be a radical departure from Aquinas's philosophy. Synderesis, which infallibly imparts the knowledge that good ought to be done, "enables us to see that it is the general tendency of creatures, including ourselves, to move upwards on the scale of being and goodness and that there are several ends, which are hierarchically ordered."[56] Finnis, by departing from this hierarchy, not only aligns himself with modernity rather than Aristotle,[57] but also opens his approach to an important error in rationality. According to Aristotle, one of the sources of error in practical rationality is to mistake a means for an end and an intermediate end for the supreme end. Without an ordered conception of the components of the supreme good, Finnis's conception of practical rationality is open to failure when the components need to be ordered so as to actually compose the supreme good, which is the end of all of the component goods. MacIntyre summarizes this failure of some forms of practical reasoning:

> One mark of educational failure will be a tendency on the part of individual citizens to identify as *the* good and *the* best some good which is merely an external by-product of those activities in which excellence is achieved. . . . Such errors are evidence of an individual having failed to understand the way in which goods are rank-ordered, a failure which involves a defective conception of the overall character of the best life for human beings as structured in the best kind of *polis*.[58]

One who sees the goods of life as incommensurable and not capable of an ordered ranking only reaches such conclusion by misunderstanding or misconceiving of the goods composing the supreme good. According to MacIntyre, apparently unresolvable conflict among goods "arises from the inadequacies of reason, not from the character of moral reality."[59] The goods are not really incommensurable; if they seem to be, it is only because we err in understanding them.

Possibly, Finnis's hostility to the hierarchical definition of the elements defining the "good" results from a particular visualization of hierarchy. The image of hierarchy Finnis may have in mind might be a product of the positivist notion of legal hierarchy, such as the supremacy clause of the U.S. Constitution. Hierarchy, from this perspective, is a method for determining whose will wins. The top of the hierarchy gets to obliterate or supersede the will of the lower level. In the U.S. system, a federal statute is supreme over that of a state or municipality. Hierarchy in this sense implies power and victory of the higher level over the lower.

An alternative understanding of hierarchy, which Aquinas likely had in mind, is necessary to understand the way Aquinas speaks of the hierarchy of the precepts of the natural law. Hierarchy can involve not the victory of one thing over another but the enlargement of the lower levels within the higher. Each higher level does not take priority over the lower but rather contains the lower levels within itself, plus something additional. Ralph McInerny uses the image of a "telescoping effect" to describe

Hierarchy as Narrowing

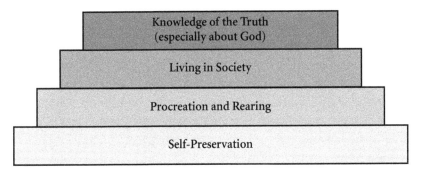

Hierarchy as Incorporating Lower Levels

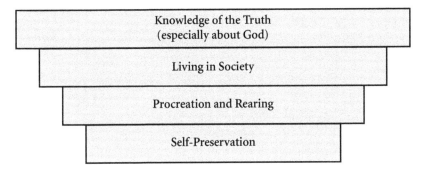

Fig. 4.1. Concepts of Hierarchy of the Good

the relationship of this hierarchy.[60] Architecturally, one may picture a hierarchy as a pyramid, which implies a narrowing as the hierarchy is ascended. Alternatively, the image of an inverted pyramid more accurately portrays this second type of hierarchy. Thus, the narrowing and enlarging notions of hierarchy can be constructed as shown in figure 4.1.

An understanding of the nature of man, as Aquinas sees it, clarifies the relationship among the elements of the hierarchy of the good required to be done by the natural law. For Aquinas, man is on a higher level of being than other animals (occupies a higher position in the hierarchy). He more perfectly reflects the completeness of being. Yet man is not in opposition to animal, but rather animal is contained within the definition of man.[61] Man is a *rational animal.* The higher order, man, in addition to his unique rationality, contains the lower attributes of irrational animals, which include inclinations to procreation and care of offspring. For Finnis, admitting a hierarchy of elements of the good may necessitate choices among them.[62] It would entail a moral system where one resolves conflicts by choosing between conflicting goods, choosing knowledge in opposition to preserving life. Although Finnis concedes that people can and should subjectively order their commitment to one or more of the basic goods,[63] he maintains that "there is no objective hierarchy amongst them."[64] They are incommensurable.[65] He may be concerned that a hierarchy necessitates moral rules, which choose one element in opposition to the other, or where one element can become merely instrumental to the higher ranked element.[66] Such a moral system would result in choosing to pursue knowledge and destroy life since knowledge is higher than life in the hierarchy. This may be what Finnis means when he suggests that a hierarchical commensuration of the elements of the good results in fanaticism.[67]

Yet hierarchy understood as the inverted pyramid, where each higher level contains the lower, can never involve an imperative to do something furthering an aspect of the good that necessitates the destruction of another lower element of the hierarchy, because the higher good contains within its very own definition the lower. Remembering that for Aquinas "end" and "good" are self-referential, he explains this relation among the hierarchical ends of man in his commentary on Aristotle's *Ethics:*

> There are also, it seems, many degrees of ends. Some of these we choose purely for the sake of something else, riches, for instance, which are sought for their utility in human living. . . . All such instruments are ends sought merely because of their usefulness. It is obvious that such ends are imperfect [incomplete]. The best end, namely, the ultimate end, must be perfect [complete]. Therefore, if there is only one such end, it must be the ultimate end we are looking for. If, however, there are many perfect ends, the most perfect [complete] of these should be the best and the ultimate.[68]

Thus a command to do the highest-ranked good must be a complete end, which contains within it the incomplete ends. If the highest good were in opposition to a lower good, the higher good would not be more perfect as it would lack the good of the lower. Aristotle expresses the concept: "Human good turns out to be activity of soul in accordance with virtue, and if there are more than one virtue, in accordance with the best and most complete."[69] The best end necessarily contains within itself all of the other elements of the hierarchy of the definition of that end, since to be the best it must be the most complete. In this way one could never say that the injunction to do the good identified as procreation could require one to choose to kill (violate the good of the lower good of preservation of life), because contained within procreation is the element of life preservation, which is a lower order (less complete good). For example, complying with the highest element of the hierarchy to know the truth about God can never involve a requirement to violate the precept to preserve life. Thus, if one concluded that one will know the truth about God only after this life, and then concluded he should commit suicide so as to further this inclination, this conclusion would be checked by the fact that the element of the good called "knowledge of the truth about God" contains within it the preservation of human life, and thus it would be a violation of the very element of knowing the truth about God to take one's life (since not taking life is part of the element of knowing the truth about God).

This proper understanding of the hierarchy of the primary ends or goods and their corresponding natural law primary precepts not only conveys the idea that each higher level contains the lower orders, but also indicates a directional movement, or rule. Recall that Aquinas has defined the "good" commanded by the first principle of the natural law both as the "end" of man (his fullness of being) and as "that which all things seek after."[70] The cognitive and volitional elements of human action are interrelated. The good involves knowing the end and seeking after it or moving toward it. Aquinas combines these two elements in a passage in *De Veritate*:

Since the essence of good consists in this, that something perfects another as an end, whatever is found to have the character of an end also has that of good. [The first element of good is that we know it by that which equates to its perfection or its end.] Now two things are essential to an end: it must be sought or desired by things which have not attained the end, and it must be loved by things which share the end, and be, as it were, enjoyable to them. [The inclination shared by men or that which all things seek after.][71]

As Aquinas argued in the *Commentary on the Nichomachean Ethics*,[72] when faced with a hierarchy of ends we should be ruled by the most complete of those ends, the end that contains all the lower order of ends. Thus, the inclination of man directs him ultimately upward in the fullness of being toward a higher end (and ultimately nudges him to consider the possibility of a supernatural end). A higher good is to be chosen over a lower good, not in the sense of being in opposition to it, but rather in the sense that the choice of the lower good must be informed by, or subsumed by, consideration of the highest good. Thus, in choosing the highest good we also choose the lower. We can understand this relationship by considering Aquinas's criterion of *inconvenientem* in the relationship between lower-ranked and higher-ranked goods. In his *Commentary on the Sentences*,[73] Aquinas explains: "Whatever renders an action improportionate [*inconvenientem*[74]] to the end which nature intends to obtain by a certain work is said to be contrary to the natural law."[75] Thus, the lower-order goods must be pursued in a way that is not *inconvenientem* to the attainment of the more complete, higher good. Armstrong gives the following examples of what it would mean to be *inconvenientem*: expecting a piano to perform a task suited to a mangle or expecting a toadstool to be a tree. Assisting and washing clothes is a good, but a good suitable not to a piano but to a mangle.[76] There is nothing wrong with being a tree, but being such does not come together with being a toadstool.

The first principle of the natural law also contains a rule of direction in decision-making oriented toward the higher (most complete) and eventually the ultimate and complete good.[77]

Some conclusions about the content of the primary principles of the natural law can be drawn from this hierarchy of goods or ends. The first precept of the natural law is the most complete: "Do good." Good is defined as "an end directing action." Based on these premises, Aquinas concludes that the natural law commands all virtuous acts, acts that are directed toward the hierarchically supreme end of man:

> Thus all virtuous acts belong to the natural law. For it has been stated (Article 2) that to the natural law belongs everything to which man is inclined according to his nature. Now each thing is inclined naturally to an operation that is suitable to it according to its form: thus fire is inclined to give heat. Wherefore, since the rational soul is the proper

form of man, there is in every man a natural inclination to act according to reason: and this is to act according to virtue. Consequently, considered thus, all acts of virtue are prescribed by the natural law: since each one's reason naturally dictates to him to act virtuously.[78]

Since reason is the hierarchical peak of man's nature, it is the good that completes all the lower goods. A life that fosters and educates new life in a human society is most complete when it accords with reason. Thus, reason completes the lower goods by indicating that they are to be pursued, but pursued in accordance with reason. This highest natural good in man thus interacts dialectically with the inclinations common to other beings. Thus, the particular way in which man is to live, procreate, rear children, and live together differs from other animals in that these inclinations are all directed toward the good of reason. Huguccio considers an example of this interaction of the lower good of procreation and rearing of children with the higher good of reason:

Marriage is the natural law, that is, its effect, that is, it derives from it.... But of what kind of union is it to be understood? Of souls, or of bodies? I respond: Of souls, because that is marriage. Hence, the jurist [Ulpian] says, "The union of husband and wife, which we call marriage, derives from this." But marriage is nothing else than a union of souls. But from which natural law does this union arise? From reason, which directs a man that he should be joined with a woman through marriage, either for the sake of offspring, or on account of incontinence. For by such a law, that is, led by reason, did Adam consent to take Eve in marriage, when he said, "this now is bone of my bones," and so on; and so does anyone consent, who now contracts marriage. ... And this latter union is derived both from that natural law which is said to be an instinct of nature, and from that which is said to be reason. For man is moved by a certain appetite of the natural sensuality, that he should be joined in the flesh to a woman, and immediately reason follows, directing him that he should not be joined with anyone except a wife, and in a legitimate way, that is, for the sake of children, or to pay his debt; for any other union, whatever with the wife or with another woman is not derived from any natural law, but is contrary to it.[79]

Although this passage verges into secondary precepts of the natural law, which will be treated more extensively in the next section, it demonstrates how the natural inclinations of nonrational beings are only a starting point for the consideration of the inclinations of man. These common inclinations (toward physical union) are affected by the higher good of reason, which imprints a particular character on the same inclination. As Porter points out, for the Scholastics, the human inclination to procreate involves more than the inclination in other animals. For humans, in addition to the joining of male and female to produce an offspring, it is also about procreating a being that is fully human, which involves—because of the human rational nature—educating and socializing offspring.[80] Coming to know the primary principles through the natural inclinations involves more than simply "observing nature." As Porter commented, it involves examining these observations in light of "our best theological and philosophical understandings."[81]

Gratian emphasizes this connection between the aspects of the good and their perfection in reason, but he also acknowledges a connection to the supernatural end of man, when he explains that law "will be all that reason has already confirmed—all, at least, that is congruent with religion, consistent with discipline, and helpful to salvation."[82] Again, the interconnection of being (form), inclination to an end, and reason are evident. Since natural law obligates man to act always in accordance with his end, or that which is good in light of his nature, all acts of virtue are prescribed by the obligation to do good.

Law, in prescribing one act, prohibits its opposite.[83] The other half of the first precept is the mirror image of the first half—"avoid evil." Thus, the command "to do always what is good" contains the opposite command to avoid that which is contrary to the hierarchy of the ends of man. This would include pursuing a lower end in opposition to its completion or preserving life unreasonably. Thus, Aquinas's primary definition of the natural law contains a command and prohibition: "Do good and avoid evil."[84] Gratian opens his general examination of law with this same double-edged precept, expressed through the words of scripture in the Golden Rule: Do to others what you ought to want done to you, and do not do to others what you ought not to want done to you.[85] Gratian's use of the Golden Rule as an expression of this precept emphasizes its connection to nature and natural inclination. Man is inclined, as Aquinas would say, to what is good for man, in accordance with his form and proper ends. Thus, what man is properly inclined toward is what he ought to want done unto himself and what he ought to do to others.

THE CONTENT OF SECONDARY PRECEPTS

The primary precepts of the natural law elaborate in more detail the first precept of the natural law: good is to be done and evil avoided. They begin to elaborate the most general concept, the good. The primary precepts, like the first precept, are ontological. They oblige us to live in harmony with the hierarchically ordered components of our nature. The primary precepts oblige us to preserve our existence, advance the propagation and education of the species, live in a society and pursue truth, and to avoid their opposites: extinction, termination of the species, anarchy, and ignorance. Yet these component aspects of the good, although more specific, still require further specification in light of particular choices. There is still a great gap between the precept "live in society" and the choice of a particular action, for example, should I take my neighbor's food while he sleeps? The primary precepts must be instantiated in more particular rules of action. Thus, in addition to the primary precepts, the natural law contains secondary precepts, which, as we discussed in chapter 3, are rational conclusions that can be drawn from the primary precepts.[86] The secondary precepts related to any primary precept involve whatever "pertains to this inclination . . . for instance, to shun ignorance, to avoid offending those among whom one has to live, and other such things regarding the above inclination."[87] The number of the primary precepts was limited by the component aspects of man's nature; the secondary precepts will be more numerous because they involve precepts adapted to factual circumstances in which choices relating to these aspects of the good are made. Since the nature of man is fixed by the eternal law, the primary precepts will be fixed according to that nature. Yet that nature can interact with a vast number of circumstances, and therefore the conclusions about what actions are consistent with natural law will be much more numerous due to the multiplicity of circumstances. We cannot produce a simple chart listing the secondary precepts. Likewise, an axiom in geometry can be stated succinctly, but from that one axiom, many different conclusions can be drawn.

A law can involve any one of three attitudes toward a particular act. We can therefore divide the secondary precepts into three types: prescriptions, prohibitions, and indications. The natural law, through the secondary precepts, "commands what is beneficial, as to love God; it prohibits what is harmful, as forbidding us to kill; and it indicates what is appropriate, as that all persons should be free."[88] Since the secondary precepts are conclusions drawn from the primary precepts, we can understand them in light of the three possible types of conclusions we can draw about the relationship about a possible means to an end. The proposed means might be indispensable to attaining a particular end. The proposed means might make the attainment of the end impossible, and the proposed means might not be necessary to attaining the end, but might be helpful and consistent in attaining the end. The secondary precepts embody these different types of conclusions. Thus, knowledge of truth is indicated by the rational nature of man. If God is by definition the perfection of truth, we are obligated by nature to love (desire) God as the perfection of truth. The following syllogism demonstrates how this prescription is a conclusion drawn from the first precept and the primary precept of natural law:

- Man ought to do good and avoid evil.
- A rational being is inclined (or suited) to acquire knowledge, the possession in the intellect of truth.
- Knowledge of truth is good for a rational creature.
- God is the complete perfection of truth.[89]
- Therefore, man is obligated to desire (love) God.

Since preservation of human life is a good, the intentional (willed) killing of a human being utterly destroys this good and is therefore prohibited. Again, we can demonstrate this with a syllogism:

- Man ought to do good and avoid evil.
- As a living substance, it is good for man to be alive.
- To intend as the object of an action to end the life of another living human being is contrary to the good of preserving life, or evil.
- Therefore, man ought not intentionally kill another human being.

Yet the prohibitions are more complex than this simple example suggests. The complexity lies in the relationship between actions and ends, or goods. We have already seen that the guiding principle of human choice is to elect actions proportionate to the end fixed by the eternal law.[90] Two different complexities in this proportionality of means, or actions, to ends are identified by Aquinas in a rather dense passage.[91] To assist in understanding them, I have disentangled the two discussions so we can consider them separately. Let us begin by considering the first argument extracted from the passage:

> Now, whatever renders an action improportionate [*inconvenientem*] to the end that nature intends to obtain by a certain work is said to be contrary to the natural law.... This happens in two ways. First, on account of something which wholly hinders the end.... Second, on account of something that renders the attainment of the principal end or secondary end difficult, or less satisfactory.... Accordingly, if an action be improportionate [*inconveniens*] to the end, through altogether hindering the principal end directly, it is forbidden by the first precepts of the natural law, which hold the same place in practical matters, as the general concepts of the mind in speculative matters. If, however, it be in any way improportionate to the ... end, ... as rendering its attainment difficult or less satisfactory, it is forbidden, not indeed by the first precepts of the natural law, but by the second, which are derived from the first even as conclusions in speculative matters receive our assent by virtue of self-known principles: and thus the act in question is said to be against the law of nature.[92]

A particular action may be completely contrary to one of the primary principles of natural law by being diametrically opposed to one of the primary goods of human nature. The action directly renders impossible the attainment of one of the goods. Committing suicide will intentionally terminate the good of the preservation of one's life. Thus, the act of suicide violates the first general precept of natural law, namely, that human life ought to be preserved and its early extinguishment avoided. That suicide must be avoided is thus a secondary precept of the natural law, as it is a conclusion that can be drawn from the primary principle that human life ought to be preserved. Thus, the first type of secondary principle is one that forbids in further detail (the taking of one's own life) an action that is directly contrary to a primary principle.

Yet other actions may tend to make attainment of the good more difficult, or they may render the good less satisfactory without completely preventing the attainment of the relevant good. Thus, eating poorly either by eating to excess or by starvation will wear down the health of the body, potentially leading to its premature death. Thus, that one ought not to eat to excess or deficiency is a secondary precept of the natural law, as such acts hinder the realization of the good of life, but in a more remote manner than suicide. Thus, some secondary precepts forbid actions that remotely hinder attainment of one of the primary goods.

Understanding this difference between completely violating the end and merely rendering it more difficult makes more understandable an otherwise difficult comment of Aquinas on the nature of the secondary precepts of the natural law:

> It is therefore evident that, as regards the general principles whether of speculative or of practical reason, truth or rectitude is the same for all. . . . As to the proper conclusions of the speculative reason, the truth is the same for all . . . thus it is true for all that the three angles of a triangle are together equal to two right angles. . . . But as to the proper conclusions of the practical reason [i.e., the secondary precepts of the natural law], neither is the truth or rectitude the same for all, nor, where it is the same, is it equally known by all. Thus it is right and true for all to act according to reason: and from this principle it follows as a proper conclusion [secondary precept], that goods entrusted to another should be restored to their owner. Now this is true for the majority of cases: but it may happen in a particular case that it would be injurious, and therefore unreasonable, to restore goods held in trust; for instance, if they are claimed for the purpose of fighting against one's country. And this principle will be found to fail the more, according as we descend further into detail . . . so that it be not right to restore or not to restore.[93]

First, Aquinas explains that the general precepts, which identify and obligate us to seek the component goods of our nature, are universally true. This universality is a consequence of the universality of human nature. As all men share the same nature, so they are all obligated to the same goods. Their application is absolutely binding in all circumstances. No human action may obey the first principle, "do good," and directly contravene a general principle by electing the opposite of a good of human nature. Turning to the secondary precepts, Aquinas notes that the conclusions drawn from the general precepts of the natural law differ from conclusions drawn in speculative matters. These secondary precepts sometimes are found to fail in the sense that they are inapplicable to what otherwise appears to be relevant circumstances. The secondary precepts that forbid actions that obliterate a primary good are universally obligatory. Yet some secondary precepts involve conclusions that certain acts frustrate but do not completely obliterate a known good. These precepts are not absolutely universally obligatory because they do not absolutely frustrate the primary goods but more remotely make them more difficult. The complexity giving rise to this element of variability in their application is a consequence of the complexity of human actions. One action may involve a conflict among the primary goods. One act might appear obligatory to preserve one good while at the same time making attainment of another more difficult. Secondary precepts prohibiting actions that only hinder a good are therefore subject to an exception to their application in circumstances where following the secondary precept would hinder another good. The exception must be navigated in a manner that does not result in the obliteration of a primary good.

The example Aquinas cites is useful to understand this complexity of variable application of some secondary precepts. We have seen that a primary principle of the natural law is that men should live peacefully in society and should avoid actions destructive of peaceful social living. One of the many conclusions that can be drawn from this primary precept is that when one borrows the goods of another he should return them. Otherwise, social life would experience strife and discord because the owner will seek to recover his property and produce discord, strife, and perhaps violence. Yet Aquinas says this precept, "return borrowed property," can fail to obligate in certain rare circumstances. If someone seeks the return of his sword from his countryman so as to attack his own country, the sword should not be returned. What we have established, concerning prevention and interference with the end, can help explain this variability in the application of the secondary precept that borrowed goods should be returned. Returning the sword to someone bent on attacking his country would interfere with the good of the preservation of human life and the good of peaceful social life. As a result, returning the sword would hinder realization of these primary goods. Thus, the secondary precept, "return the sword," is suspended from application to the circumstances, because following it would interfere with other primary goods. In the unusual case, the holder of the property may not absolutely disregard the secondary precept to return borrowed property by arrogating the sword to his absolute ownership. He may retain possession for so long as the rightful owner intends to cause the abovementioned harms. In reaching this conclusion, the secondary precept to "return borrowed goods" is not violated but merely delayed due to the complexity of the harm that will be caused by returning it now. Since the way in which this secondary precept applies does not completely frustrate the good sought, peaceful society, a variation in application is possible—delay of return until the impeding circumstance is removed. In a certain sense, we can understand the result not as the violation of the secondary precept, "return borrowed property," but rather as the drawing of a more remote and detailed secondary precept related to it but containing greater specificity. Thus, the more remote secondary precept, which is consistent with the more proximate secondary precept from which it is derived, can be phrased thus: "Return borrowed property unless its return will cause the violation of another precept of natural law, in which case delay return until such an impediment is removed." This precept is not contradictory to the more general secondary precept but merely a more particular specification of it.[94] It is in this sense that Aquinas says the secondary precepts sometimes "fail." By "fail" he means certain secondary precepts fail to apply to certain circumstances, because the result of following the precept would be "unreasonable," meaning that one of the primary goods identified by the primary principles of the natural law would be hindered or destroyed. The failure must be rectified by deducing a more reasonable specific secondary precept, which takes account of the complex interaction of the act with the primary goods. The more specific secondary precept must not obligate a complete obliteration of the secondary precept from which it is derived, but must rather more particularly specify a more complex manner in which it is to be followed.

Aquinas also explains another way in which the secondary precepts relate to the basic goods of human nature. Once again, this second argument has been extracted from the intertwined arguments of Aquinas:

> Now whatever renders an action improportionate [*inconvenientem*] to the end which nature intends to obtain by a certain work is said to be contrary to the natural law. But an action may be improportionate either to the principal or to the secondary end. . . . [For] instance a very great excess or a very great deficiency in eating hinders both the health of the body, which is the principal end of food, and aptitude for conducting business, which is its secondary end. If, however, it be in any way improportionate to the secondary end . . . it is forbidden, not indeed by the first precepts of the natural law, but by the second which are derived from the first even as conclusions in speculative matters receive our assent by virtue of self-known principles: and thus the act in question is said to be against the law of nature.[95]

The argument can be confusing because the same term "end" is employed but in a different sense than in the previous discussion. Previously, we were considering the relationship of acts to the primary goods identified by the principal precepts. Those acts could be necessary to, directly opposed to, or a hindrance to attaining the primary ends. In this passage, when Aquinas speaks of ends he is not referring to these basic goods but rather to the ends of actions. Like beings, acts (or operations) have natural ends to which they are inclined. As we have discussed several times, an end is interchangeable with a good. Thus, when the first principle of the natural law obligates man to do good and avoid evil, this also requires man, in the selection of acts as means to his own end, to use those acts in conformity to their own ends. Like man, acts can be oriented to a diversity of ends.[96] An act can be related to both a primary, or principal, end and to one or more secondary ends. The secondary ends are secondary in that they are merely instrumental means that are useful for the attainment of some other good. Aquinas gives the example of the act of eating food to illustrate the difference. The principal good or end of eating food is to sustain the health of the body, an end directly related to a primary good of man, the preservation of man's life. Yet eating food can also serve as an instrumental end to other goods. Eating food nourishes the body so that it is capable of conducting business. If one is starving or lethargic due to disproportionate eating, not only is his health impeded but secondarily his ability to conduct business in society is also hindered. The ability to conduct business with other people is not a principal good of man's nature, but rather a secondary good, a means to facilitate the principal good of the sustaining of a peaceful societal existence among men. Thus, the eating of food has as its primary end the sustaining of the life of the body and as a secondary end providing useful conditions for the conduct of business. Excess or defect in eating to the point of harming one's health is thus a violation of the primary end of health, and thus the secondary precept to eat in moderation is a proximate conclusion drawn from a principal precept of the natural law. As a more remote consequence, excess or defect of eating can also hinder the conduct of business, which can hinder the goal of a peaceful society. This conclusion yields the more remote secondary precept: "Eat to such an extent that you are fit to conduct your affairs in society." The more proximate secondary precept is a conclusion drawn from the fact that poor eating will hinder the primary good of life. The more remote secondary precept is drawn from the conclusion that poor eating will harm one's ability to function, which will hinder the obligation to live and work together in society. Again, the more remote the conclusion, the more it may be capable of exception.

Aquinas uses this discussion of the variability of secondary precepts to explain why it was not a violation of natural law, or reason, for God to grant an exception to the natural and divine precept forbidding the taking of multiple wives.[97] He explains the prohibition derives both from a primary and a secondary end of the act of marriage, the primary end of which is the principal good of procreation and education of offspring. Marriage also has a secondary end, the faithful mutual support of the married. Aquinas explains:

> Plurality of wives neither wholly destroys nor in any way hinders the first end of marriage, since one man is sufficient to get children of several wives, and to rear the children born of them. But though it

does not wholly destroy the second end, it hinders it considerably, for there cannot easily be peace in a family where several wives are joined to one husband, since one husband cannot suffice to satisfy the requisitions of several wives, and again because the sharing of several in one occupation is a cause of strife. . . . It is therefore evident from what has been said that plurality of wives is in a way against the law of nature, and in a way not against it.[98]

Since plurality of wives is said to be against the natural law, Aquinas then considers if God violated the natural law by permitting polygamy to the Old Testament Jews. He explains that polygamy is not a violation of the natural law as regards the first precepts, "but as regards the secondary precepts, which like conclusions are drawn from its first precepts. Since, however, human acts must needs vary according to the various conditions of persons, times, and other circumstances, the aforesaid conclusions do not proceed from the first precepts of the natural law, so as to be binding in all cases, but only in the majority. . . . Hence, when they cease to be binding, it is lawful to disregard them."[99]

Polygamy hinders the secondary instrumental good of marriage by hindering the peaceful mutual support of the spouses, but it does not completely destroy the primary end, the procreation and education of children. The prohibition is thus a secondary precept of the natural law, which, as we have seen, may fail to apply in unusual circumstances where following the secondary precept would violate a primary precept. In the time of the Old Testament, Aquinas explains, the propagation of the human race dedicated to the worship of God was limited to the nation of the Jews.[100] In order to increase the size of this small nation, it was convenient to permit the taking of multiple wives to increase the number of offspring. Thus, to further the primary end of marriage it was necessary for a dispensation from the secondary precept forbidding multiple wives: "For the principal end is ever to be borne in mind before the secondary end."[101] Note: the secondary end is not disregarded but is borne in mind after the primary end. This dispensation is still consistent with natural law because by it the two ends of marriage are not completely obliterated, but the secondary end of peaceful mutual support is only made more difficult. To attain the primary end, a means less suited, but not wholly opposed to, the secondary end can be chosen.

This example highlights another important distinction regarding certain circumstances when secondary precepts fail to apply. In the case of the borrowed sword, we did not speak of a dispensation from a secondary precept, but rather the application of a more detailed, refined secondary precept that took account of the new factual complexity—the owner planning to use it to attack his country. In this question of polygamy, Aquinas does not claim that men can deduce a more refined secondary precept permitting polygamy in certain cases as with the sword. Rather he states:

> It belongs exclusively to him from whose authority he derives its binding force to permit the nonobservance of the law in those cases to which the force of the law ought not to extend, and this permission is called a dispensation. Now the law prescribing the one wife was framed not by man but by God. . . . Consequently a dispensation in this matter could be granted by God alone . . . in order to ensure the multiplication of the offspring to be brought up in the worship of God.[102]

Thus, the permission to take multiple wives is not contained in a further, more specific secondary precept but in a dispensation that could only be granted by God. The reasons for this restriction to God alone appear to be twofold. Aquinas claims that one reason is that, in some cases, the variations in the circumstances are so difficult to understand that man cannot see them on his own. This criterion is not a very clear mark of distinction between cases requiring a new secondary precept deduced by man and a dispensation granted only by God. The reason does introduce the need for a law beyond the natural law to assist in the formulation of secondary precepts. We will return to this theme in chapter 5 when we consider the divine law. The second reason a dispensation is necessary is only implicit in the argument of Aquinas. The prohibition of polygamy involves not only the natural law but also a precept of the divine positive law. Beyond the natural law, Aquinas indicates that the obligation to marry one wife was also given directly by God. Thus, the new situation involves not only a conflict with the natural law but also with the divine positive law. Further, it is not a precept of the natural law that only the offspring of a specific nation would preserve the worship of God, but rather this matter was provided by divine positive law. Since precepts of both the natural and divine laws are implicated in the situation, a dispensation from God was necessary in this case.

So far we have considered secondary precepts, which either prohibit action that destroys or hinders attainment of a good, or which prescribe necessary action for the attainment of a good. Beyond these two categories of secondary precepts, there are others whose force is not as absolute as these. Certain secondary precepts are classified as "indications."[103] They involve the recommendation of actions that are not indispensable to a good but which do not make the attainment of a good impossible. The relevant action may be done consistently with the good, and the secondary precept thus permits it, but does not prescribe it absolutely. The precepts constituting indications are not as absolute in their terms and permit a wider variation in their application. In the words of one medieval legal commentary: "The law of nature . . . cannot be modified with respect to its prohibitions and prescriptions, but it is modified in part with respect to the indications."[104] To understand how the indications of natural law may be modified, and the limits on such modification, which may only occur "in part," we can examine the issue of private property.

The private ownership of things, or private property, is an activity that relates to two primary goods: the preservation of life and the peaceful organization of society. Aquinas states the obvious observation that man "may use lower things for the needs of his life."[105] Since all men require the use of material things to sustain life, the principle that the things of the earth should be available for all to use to sustain life—or as commonly expressed by Scholastics and canon lawyers, "the common possession of all things"[106]—can be deduced as a secondary precept of natural law. Notwithstanding this common possession of all things by the human race, it would be against reason for the disproportionate use by an individual of material things since "there is a definite measure according to which the use of the aforesaid things is proper to human life."[107] The natural law thus indicates that some common possession of things is suited to preserving human life.

Yet since all material goods are to be used by all of human society, the use of material things also implicates the good of peaceful existence in society. From this good, many secondary precepts can be deduced concerning actions that affect society. As Aquinas says: "The things without which human society cannot be maintained are naturally appropriate to man."[108] At least since the time Aristotle disputed Plato's claim that all property should be owned and used in common,[109] natural law philosophers and jurists have argued that some division of material things into private ownership is necessary for the good of society. Christian thinkers made their own Aristotle's arguments in favor of private property, which were essentially that private property (1) better keeps peace among men by avoiding many quarrels, (2) provides an efficient allocation of work and avoids labor-shirking and complaining, (3) is needed to practice the virtue of liberality (generosity), and (4) provides pleasure of ownership.[110] Aquinas summarizes three benefits to social life of private property:

> First because every man is more careful to procure what is for himself alone than that which is common to many or to all: since each one would shirk the labor and leave to another that which concerns the community, as happens where there is a great number of servants. Secondly, because human affairs are conducted in more orderly fashion if each man is charged with taking care of some particular thing himself, whereas there would be confusion if everyone had to look after any one thing indeterminately. Thirdly, because a more peaceful state is ensured to man if each one is contented with his own. Hence it is to be observed that quarrels arise more frequently where there is no division of the things possessed.[111]

Thus, private ownership is also indicated by the natural law as a means to achieve the social good. Aquinas acknowledges that private ownership is not a primary precept of the natural law but a secondary precept deduced from the consideration of these benefits to social life.[112] Yet he acknowledges that private property seems to be in conflict with the conclusion drawn from the good of human life that property should be possessed in common. He explains that the maintenance of private property is an addition to the natural law by way of a partial modification of each of these two precepts: common possession and private ownership. The modification involves the distinction between ownership and use. Things should be owned privately so as to obtain the aforementioned benefits, but the use made of them must take account of the common need of all men with respect to goods. Aquinas explains that "man ought to possess external things, not as his own, but as common, so that, to wit, he is ready to communicate them to others in their need."[113] The secondary precept of the natural law thus refines the more general precept on common possession so that property is to be divided among private owners but used consistently with the common need of all. Thus, private property is not an absolute end or good, but rather is simply useful for attaining the benefits put forward in the Aristotelian argument. Thus, private ownership is not an absolute end, but must be subject to the good of preserving life, which requires an element of common use. It is thus possible to acquire things "as your own," but not to use them exclusively "as your own" but "in common." The right to use may not be exercised solely with an eye to the individual benefit of the owner. Individual use must be considered in light of the common good. The notion of hierarchy explained in the first section of this chapter explains how these two concepts, private ownership and common use, can be harmonized. Social life is a higher good, as its inclination arises from the rational nature of man. Yet the higher goods do not supersede but include the lower goods. Thus, the good of preserving life is included within the higher good. The benefit to the good of society that private property provides must be achieved in a manner that respects the lower-order good of preservation of life. A practical example of the harmonization of these goods is the secondary precept of natural law entitling one in desperate need to make use of property owned by someone else. As Aquinas explains: "It is lawful for a man to succor his own need by means of another's property, by taking it either openly or secretly: nor is this properly speaking theft or robbery."[114]

When a person faces extreme need to maintain life, private ownership of property, which supports a peaceful social order, must take account of the obligation to preserve life, and goods must be shared with the one in need.[115] By noting that the one in need who takes the things needed commits no theft or robbery, Aquinas emphasizes that private property is not violated in this case. The necessities actually belong to the one in need.[116] The institution of private property as a secondary precept contains within its very terms this qualification of private ownership derived from the more general secondary precept of common use.

Yet it would appear that this analysis has wrought a change within natural law. Aquinas explains that the secondary precept permitting private property does not repudiate the secondary precept regarding common ownership, but merely partially modifies it. The precept regarding common possession was of the nature of an indication, which is subject to such partial modification that still respects the good at the root of the precept being modified. Huguccio confirms that the interaction of these two precepts, private ownership and common possession, is possible because both are indications of natural law, not prohibitions or prescriptions:

> The law consists in three, that is, in prescriptions, prohibition, and indications: it prescribes that which is profitable, as, "you shall love the Lord your God"; it prohibits that which is harmful, as, "you shall not steal"; it indicates what is appropriate and advantageous, namely, that all things should be held in common . . . and one should claim what is his own, or not claim it; the natural law did not prescribe or prohibit these and other singular things, but indicated that they are permissible. Hence, those laws by which the property of one is appropriated by another can be established contrary to this indication of the natural law; for there can be no modification of the natural law . . . with respect to its precepts and prohibitions, but with respect to its indications, there can be a partial modification.[117]

Beyond illustrating the variable nature of the secondary precepts, private property can also serve as an instrument for examining the line between the framework (natural law) and the decoration (human law). We observed in chapter 3 that precepts formulated by deduction of more specific precepts belong to the secondary precepts of natural law, but matters of determination of the manner in which those precepts are to be fulfilled lie within the purview of human law. The institution of private property can illuminate this difference.

The *Digest* explains that questions of private property involve both natural law and positive human law: "We obtain the ownership of certain property by the Law of Nations, which is everywhere observed among men, according to the dictates of natural reason; and we obtain the ownership of other things by the Civil Law, that is to say, by the law of our own country."[118] Thus, we have seen that a secondary precept of natural law indicates that the allocation of private property is beneficial for society, subject to the need for some common use. The natural law also gives some indication of how property should be acquired. Gratian refers to "the acquisition of things that are taken from the heavens, earth, or sea."[119] Many other methods are indicated by the natural law: inheritance, sale and exchange, and so on. Yet many particular details must be determined with respect to these general indications of natural law. What form of words or actions constitutes a sale? How long must one possess something to become its owner? What precisely must one do to abandon property so that it becomes eligible to be taken from the air or the sea? What must be done to indicate who is to inherit property? Once we reach these detailed questions we can see that we have reached the need to make determinations and thus reached precepts of human law. These precepts of human law are framed by the prohibitions, prescriptions, and indications of the natural law and must be elected in light of them. Yet the details, such as the formalities to complete a sale, the formalities of a will, the length of time for adverse possession to affect transfer, and so on, are left by natural law to be determined by human law. The process of this determination will be taken up in chapter 6. Human law, however, exists in tension. It is a rule and measure, to the extent it determines the permissibility of certain human actions. Yet it is also "a rule or measure ruled or measured by a higher measure."[120]

ASSESSING THE FRAMEWORK

Having reached the conclusion of a two-chapter examination of the frame of natural law built upon the foundation of eternal law, it is opportune to pause and survey the edifice. Stepping back from the specifications of the parts of this edifice of laws, what can be said about the relationship between the foundation (eternal law) and the frame built on it (natural law)? First, eternal law and natural law really are law. They are not, as Finnis claims, "only analogically law."[121] It is not in the form of "title 3, chapter 12, subparagraph 4" and such, but the form of verbosely written laws with which moderns have become all too familiar is not essential to the definition of law. Positivism has limited the nature of law to sets of arbitrary, detailed precepts promulgated by one with power to do so. The "new" natural law defenders such as Finnis have not gone quite so far. They admit the existence of eternal law, but have relegated it to an "extended nonfocal sense" of law. For classical natural law thinkers like Aquinas, law is a much richer, broader concept. Before precepts, the eternal law contains the idea or the exemplar of that which is always good, right, and equitable. The idea of law is the exemplar of the just thing itself. It is in this way that law is understood as a rule and measure, and the eternal law is not simply an analogous concept but is, in fact, the focal—ontologically first—meaning of law. The eternal law, in which rational creatures participate through the natural law, is a real law. It is "the act of God's practical reason commanding all creation to act for its divinely appointed end."[122]

With this understanding of law in mind, *jus naturale* is really a rule and measure of willed action, conformed to the nature of man, fixed by the idea or exemplar of the eternal law. It is a rule, because its principles guide action to the exemplar of the proper ends of man's nature. It acts as a directing rule because its principles identify and elucidate the hierarchy of goods of man's nature, fixed by the eternal law. In light of these ends, men can measure to what extent proposed courses of action are oriented toward or in opposition to one or more of those ends. As a rule, a principle such as "preserve human life" exists to guide decision-making by providing a goal or end. It serves to measure the advisability of a proposed course of action in light of the good embodied in it. Thus, if it is proposed that elderly people should be euthanized to save money for the health-care system, this does not measure up to the end of preservation of life as a rule.

Eternal and natural law have also been promulgated by one having care for the common good of the community. As a universal law, the community affected is all of mankind. He who promulgated the eternal and the natural law is the One with ultimate care for this community, its Creator. Natural law is concerned with the common good of that community as its principles address the common ends (or goods) of all members of that community, men. The natural law has really been promulgated by God through the eternal law, which itself has been promulgated through the mystery of the Word. Yet God has not merely promulgated the eternal law, but provided for the participation of man in the eternal law. This participation involves the speculative intellect in that man is endowed with the capability to know the goods composing his own ends and to deduce principles of action consistent with those ends: "The practical intellect participates in the eternal law by supernaturally determining the actions that are most in accord with the ultimate end of humans."[123]

This participation involves a three-part epistemological process. The process is not simply one of the syllogisms of deductive reasoning. It involves habitual knowledge, dialectical consideration, and inductive and deductive reasoning. Aquinas emphasizes this broad multidimensional epistemological process when he explains that the practice of the virtues is a source of our knowledge of the natural inclinations and the principles of natural law.[124]

In the first epistemological stage, man knows that he is to obey the precepts of the natural law through the habit of synderesis, which infallibly informs all men that they act for an end, the good. Once something is known to be good, the habit of synderesis informs man that he ought to do it and avoid its opposite. Although man cannot help but know he is to do the good, knowing what constitutes the good involves a second, more difficult process: identifying the goods through dialectical consideration of the natural inclinations connected with the various aspects of human nature. Although these primary principles of natural law are *per se nota*, or self-evident, knowledge of them is, contrary to Finnis's claims, not obvious. The primary principles are proved through their own terms; the good for man is composed of the goods or ends of the various aspects making up the definition of man. If one knows the definition of man and the corresponding inclinations of each aspect of that definition, one knows through the definition itself the primary precepts. Yet not everyone knows this definition of man. Thus, although knowing the primary precepts of natural law does not involve deductive reasoning, it does involve considerable thought and discernment. The natural inclinations of man's nature can be confused with other feelings and impulses. Further, some of them resemble the natural inclinations of lower species but differ when combined with man's rational nature. Some men may be confused about the natural inclinations and thus fail to know the primary precepts. But since they derive from human nature itself, which is the same for all people, the primary precepts universally apply to all without exception.

Only the third epistemological phase is dominated by deductive reasoning, through which further precepts are deduced (from the primary principles formulated through dialectical consideration of human nature), either (1) specifying types of acts necessary for, or a complete obstruction of, the primary goods, or (2) indicating actions that, although not indispensable, can be useful for attainment of the good. Yet, as will be examined more deeply in chapter 6, even this deductive phase relies on inductive reasoning. The secondary precepts are formulated by the intellect considering the variety of contexts in which the primary goods are sought. Since the possible actions to be chosen and the circumstances in which they arise vary greatly among people, there are a greater number of secondary precepts than primary precepts. Further, since the secondary precepts are deduced from premises involving not only the primary precepts but also facts about the circumstances in which actions occur, the secondary precepts are not as universally applicable, since variations in circumstances may call for adaptations of secondary precepts to take account of the relevant factual differences. This process of demonstration of secondary precepts is further complicated by the involvement of more than one primary good in a given action, and also variability in the proximity and remoteness of the action to the goods at issue. Thus, more refined secondary precepts are often required to resolve conflicts that arise when an action might be useful for the attainment of one good but detrimental for the attainment of another. The primary and secondary precepts differ in their quality. For "the natural law is altogether unchangeable in its first principles: but in its secondary principles, which, as we have said, are certain detailed proximate conclusions drawn from the first principles, the natural law is not changed so that what it prescribes be not right in most cases. But it may be changed in some particular cases of rare occurrence, through some special causes hindering the observance of such precepts."[125]

The realm of the secondary precepts is quite vast. Within the secondary precepts there are some conclusions following more closely the primary precepts, and others that involve more detailed deduction and considerably more thought to discern.[126] It requires more reflection to understand that overeating is contrary to man's nature than it does to reach such a conclusion with respect to drunkenness.[127] As Porter has observed, traditional natural law jurists, theologians, and philosophers have always been quite comfortable with this developing participation involving a rational refinement of the secondary precepts: "Some of them [the Scholastics] brought considerable sophistication to this interpretive task; recall, for example, Bonaventure's interpretation of the prohibition against killing in the light of the different aspects of human life, or Philip the Chancellor's analysis of the way considerations introduced at different levels of human nature lead us to reformulate and refine our understanding of the precepts of the natural law."[128]

This tension between invariability as to the ultimate end and the primary precepts and the bounded variability of the secondary precepts is a necessary element of the participation through time of a rational creature whose intellect moves discursively from more general to more particular knowledge. This nuanced understanding of the intransigence as to general principles, but openness to refinement, is a necessary component of the full participation in the eternal law so that we remain ruled and measured, and participants in the rule and measure.

Once the most appropriate secondary precept has been demonstrated for a particular circumstance, its application may still require a further choice among actions, all of which would be permitted by the secondary precept. At this point, the intellect cannot complete the choice. An election of will among the possibilities must be determined. At this point, the process has crossed out of the jurisdiction of natural law and entered the realm of human law. To use an example of Aquinas, "the law of nature has it that the evildoer should be punished, but that he be punished in this or that way is a determination of the law of nature [by human law]."[129] The discernment of the natural inclinations and the deduction of secondary principles of action reside in the intellect, for it is here that the eternal law has made its imprint. This intellectual act of discerning the natural inclinations and their corresponding hierarchy of ends gives rise to an act of the will, the choice among possible actions.

Understanding the relation between intellect and will in this theory of natural law returns an important balance to the process of thinking about the making of human laws. After centuries of legal positivism, lawmaking is generally associated with an act of the will. A law is a law because it has been willed by the applicable legislator. The alternative vision places a striking emphasis on the intellectual capacity of the soul. The participation of natural law requires the intellectual act of discerning amidst the shadows of inclinations the natural inclinations, identifying the ends to which they tend, and drawing correct conclusions from them.

Clearly, natural law involves volition; its first precept is that "good must be done." Yet complying with "do good" presupposes an intellectual activity of discerning what is good or what is an end. Natural inclinations do not point to just any end, but toward a "proper act and end" (*ad debitum actum et finem*).[130] The process is analogous to the act of building a house, which presupposes knowledge about what properly constitutes a house. Loss of attention to the intellectual prerequisite to the process of lawmaking has resulted in a philosophy and a legal system rooted in power manipulation and coalition forming. Modern law is all about exercising power. A law can be shown to be rational because it is internally consistent; it is actually directed to whatever end the will of the legislator, or the will of those he represents, has chosen. Natural law involves demonstrating not only internal consistency but also that the end of the law is inclined to a due end contained in the idea and exemplar of the blueprints of the eternal law. Human lawmaking is itself thus subject to the foundational eternal law and the framework rising out of it. Human law is itself subject to a higher legal tribunal located in the rational nature of man. As Aquinas explains: "Divine providence has endowed men with a natural tribunal of reason [*naturale judicatorium rationis*]. . . . There are certain activities naturally suited to man, and these activities are in themselves right, and not merely by positive law."[131] Patrick Brennan has summarized this dependence of the volitional act of the determination of human law upon this rational participation in higher law: "The natural law is the discovered basis on which humans can frame laws for themselves. The process of making human law is always and without exception about implementing the requirements of—or, as St. Thomas says, giving determinate or specific content to—the natural law, that is, about leading men and women to what is *good* (for them)."[132] In this sense, we are all both subject to and participants in natural law. Our volitional election of human law is necessarily dependent upon our rational participation in the eternal law. Human law "is a rule or measure ruled or measured by a higher measure."[133]

Yet constructing natural law on this foundation of the eternal law raises a fundamental question. Traditional natural law theory is an entire metaphysical system of law. It is a grand design of law. Natural law rests on the foundation of the eternal law. The natural inclinations toward the good (or ends of men) bind men to rule and measure decisions in light of them, because those natural inclinations have been fixed and promulgated through the eternal law. The obligatory nature of natural law is connected to the process of the rational participation in the eternal law, the attempt to conform the order of man's mind to the order of its reality. Men cannot help but participate in the eternal law because it is imprinted in their very being. Men can participate well or poorly, but their rational nature makes men inextricably bounded by the natural law, which itself is ruled by the style of the eternal law. This question therefore can be phrased thus: "Is the natural law of any practical relevance to one who does not acknowledge God's existence?" Put more parochially, can an atheist talk about and accept natural law? Are arguments of natural law lawyers of no use in an atheistic age? More pointedly, does Finnis's new natural law, which dispenses with the necessity of God and eternal law, establish a kind of natural law free of this foundation?

The answer to this question is qualified. In one sense, the answer is no. The natural law is utterly dependent upon the entire grand design of an edifice of law of which it is a part.[134] One cannot ultimately explain the obligatory nature of the first principle of natural law—good ought to be done—without eventually some reference to the foundation on which it rests: "If they [laws] be just, they have the power of binding in conscience, from the eternal law whence they are derived."[135] Otherwise, one is merely deriving the ultimate "ought" not even from an "is" statement. One is merely positing its existence without explanation. Only the eternal law provides an adequate explanation for the existence (the "is") of this "ought." Thus, the obligatory nature of all law is rooted in the foundation of the eternal law. To the extent a law is derived correctly through the process of participation in the eternal law, it is obligatory. If the eternal law is struck out from the system, natural law is a loose frame, floating in space. The foundation of its obligation has been severed. When thinkers like Finnis dismiss God's will (expressed through the eternal law) as the ultimate source of obligation,[136] all that remains is a justification of obligation, which bears an air of utilitarianism. Law, and for that matter all moral reasoning, is obligatory because we need it to be. The ultimate source of obligation for Finnis lies in the following principles: "That the common good is to be advanced, that authoritative determination of co-ordination problems is for the common good, and that legal regulation is (presumptively) a good method of authoritative determination."[137] Law is obligatory because it is a good (useful) method for solving coordination problems.[138] Even Finnis acknowledges that this need-based justification for law's obligatory force leaves questions unanswered.[139] When natural law theory is rooted in the eternal law, principles of natural law are recognized by the use of reason but are obligatory because they are contained within the eternal law.

Yet the understanding of legal obligation rooted in the foundation of eternal law does not lead to legal obligation becoming mere "mechanics,"[140] as it may in extreme voluntarist theories of legal obligations. As this and the prior two chapters have shown, the will of God expressed in the eternal law is "the type of divine wisdom."[141] Thus, a theory of natural law rooted in the eternal law is inextricably connected to both reason (eternal law is the plan of the divine wisdom) and an act of the will (in the promulgation of the eternal law).[142] Natural law is obligatory because it is the participation in a higher law, a law of reason promulgated by the command of an ultimate lawgiver. Severed from eternal law, explanations of the obligatory aspect of natural law ultimately end at an unsatisfactory and incomplete utilitarian argument of some sort. Thus, it would seem that it is impossible to discuss natural law without reference to at least some understanding of the rational divine lawgiver.

Yet the rational nature of man means that he cannot, in a certain sense, help but participate in the eternal law (by being rational). Whether he is aware of it or not, the "natural guide of reason impels toward that which is contained in the law of God."[143] Thus, even one not acknowledging God (and hence the eternal law), if following the natural guide of reason,[144] is participating, albeit unconsciously, in the eternal law. The denial of God's existence may affect one's ability to observe and consider the natural inclinations, but it does not obliterate them. Even if he does not turn around and see the source of the shadows cast by the eternal law in the cave of rationality, a man is still able to consider what the shadows, as shadows, mean. He may not know the source of light causing them, but he sees them nonetheless. As Aquinas says: "Since all things . . . are ruled and measured by the eternal law . . . it is evident that all things partake somewhat of the eternal law, insofar as, namely, from its being imprinted on them, they derive their respective inclinations to their proper acts and ends."[145]

By making use of reason to discern the ends illuminated by the natural inclinations, one is participating in the eternal law. As the example of Aristotle shows, even without revelation or a clear articulated understanding of eternal law, human rationality can arrive at certain primary principles and even secondary conclusions of the natural law. As scripture affirms, the natural law is available to all—even those who have not heard the specific revelation of the Artificer of the eternal law: "For when the Gentiles, who have not the law, do by nature those things that are of the law; these having not the law are a law to themselves: Who shew the work of the law written in their hearts, their conscience bearing witness to them."[146] The law written on the heart, the natural inclinations, is the starting point of all reasoning. This is because all rationality begins with what is known naturally. As Aquinas explains early in *Summa Theologica*: "Every act of reason and will in us is based on that which is according to nature . . . for every act of reasoning is based on principles that are known naturally. . . . Accordingly the first direction of our acts to their end must needs be in virtue of the natural law."[147]

Men begin reasoning by examining what is known naturally. They hence begin to participate in the eternal law without realizing they are doing so.[148] When they do so, they are making use of the eternal and natural law even if not calling it such. In a sense, one can engage all men in discussion of the natural law; particularly at the level of its most basic principles that are directly derived from the natural inclinations. Yet as Aquinas emphasizes, this step is only the "first direction" on which the use of reason is "based." Ultimately, contemplating the framework of what is known naturally will lead to questions of origin. Some knowledge of God is accessible to the mind even without the supernatural aid of grace (as demonstrated by Aquinas's proofs for God's existence). Participating in a reasonable inquiry based on what is known naturally will, naturally, lead to the eternal law since it is none other than a participation in it. Thus, discussions of natural law may commence without explicit incorporation of truths about God and the eternal law, but it is unnatural to think the entire exercise can proceed without reaching, eventually, that in which one is participating. The time for integration of the framework with the foundation may vary, but the eternal law is not, as Finnis suggests, irrelevant for natural law, just as the foundation of a house is not irrelevant to the frame, even though one may not initially see the foundation covered over by the frame.

Not seeing the foundation at first is one thing; removing the frame from it is quite another. Such an exercise is doomed to ultimate failure. Doing so leaves the natural law drifting without a mooring where it cannot stand. Natural law itself will eventually crumble, leaving only human positive law subject to no other rule or measure than that which it makes for itself. Natural law without God, although capable of stumbling upon individual successes along the way, ultimately is building a house on bare ground. As J. Budziszewski remarks: "That was the Enlightenment's project. Little by little, natural law thinkers scrubbed from their little cups of theory whatever grime of influence might have remained from the centuries of faith, whatever benefit they might have gained from the teacher's help. . . . In the end they found that they had scoured away the ground that they were standing on."[149]

To avoid such a collapse, natural law theory needs to be firmly rooted within the context of the entire edifice of which it is a part. This does not mean that every argument regarding a particular contingent matter needs to explicitly reference the eternal law. Yet to avoid ultimate collapse at the theoretical level, defense and exposition of natural law must rest explicitly on an understanding of the foundational role of eternal law. Since the very concept of justice itself is caught up in the idea of eternal law, even justice itself cannot stand without the foundation.

In 1993, John Paul II clearly rejected building natural law on pure rationality not rooted in recognition of the eternal law:

> Some people, . . . disregarding the dependence of human reason on Divine Wisdom and the need, given the present state of fallen nature, for Divine Revelation as an effective means for knowing moral truths, even those of the natural order, have actually posited a *complete sovereignty of reason* in the domain of moral norms regarding the right orderings of life in this world. . . . In no way could God be considered the Author of this law. . . . These trends of thought have led to a denial, in opposition to Sacred Scripture (Matt. 15:3–6) and the Church's constant teaching, of the fact that the natural moral law has God as its author, and that man, by the use of reason, participates in the eternal law, which it is not for him to establish.[150]

Since we have seen that the goods constituting man's end are not incommensurable, but are bound in a hierarchical ascent to a more complete good that incorporates the lower levels, choosing the good requires movement toward the highest good. Although this highest good is fixed by the eternal law, we are free to break this law written on the heart by choosing a lower-ordered good and treating it as if it were the ultimate good. Even Aristotle recognized such choice as a moral failure.[151] The ultimate end is that end sought for itself (Aristotle), and others may be ends and therefore good, but only to the extent chosen in relation to the ultimate end and not as ends in themselves. Choosing a subend as an ultimate end is not choosing good in the widest sense. Aquinas defined the object of this natural inclination of man as the "will to be happy."[152] Maria Carl explains:

> St. Thomas distinguishes two senses of happiness, perfect or supernatural and imperfect or natural. His notion of imperfect happiness, the happiness which can be attained in this life, is a complex concept which explicitly accords with Thomas' understanding of Aristotle's definition of happiness.... Final and perfect happiness consists in the direct and immediate contemplation of God, which is attainable only through grace in the afterlife.... St. Thomas is clear that the natural law is ordered to man's natural end and is thus inadequate to direct man to his supernatural end.[153]

Although Carl is correct that the natural law is directly operative in relation to the imperfect or natural end of man, her conclusion may fail to recognize a connection between these two ends. The hierarchy directs movement upward toward the most complete end. Although the natural law is inadequate to attain the supernatural end of man, it is still necessary to attain that end. One might say the natural law is directly oriented to the imperfect happiness but proximately oriented to the perfect. Although the relationship between the natural and divine law requires further elaboration, for now it is sufficient to note that there is a relationship between the natural and the supernatural. The two ends of man are not disjointed ends of separate roads; the supernatural end subsumes the natural end, and thus the natural end is related, as a part to the whole, to the supernatural end. Similarly, Gratian, when defining human law, explains that it consists in laws established by men "for divine or human reasons."[154]

Likewise, Gratian explains that human-made laws "will be all that reason [which term we have seen is an aspect of the natural law] has already confirmed—all, at least, that is congruent with religion, consistent with discipline, and helpful to salvation."[155] Thus, the natural end of man, recognized even by Aristotle, is not disconnected from the supernatural end but is a necessary component of it. Although natural law is directly related to the natural aspect of the end of man, one cannot spend significant time rationally participating in the eternal law without being forced at some point to face its ultimate source and hence the supernatural.

Consulting the Architect
When Problems Arise

The Divine Law

The law of the Lord is unspotted, converting souls:
the testimony of the Lord is faithful, giving wisdom to little ones.[1]

In chapter 2, we began laying the foundation for a particular form of legal architecture. Taking inspiration from St. Thomas Aquinas's description of God as the artificer or architect, I argued that the law is a multistoried edifice composed of different types of law. Chapter 2 explored the nature of the foundational law—the eternal law. In chapter 3, we considered how the frame of natural law rises up out of, or participates in, the foundation of eternal law. This participation is a threefold epistemological process involving the first principle known through synderesis, the primary principles known through the natural inclinations, and the secondary principles, which were conclusions deduced from the primary principles. In chapter 4 we surveyed some of the precepts of the natural law and argued that they are accessible to all men who simply consider the nature of man as a rational animal and derive principles of action based upon the ends associated with the various aspects of man's nature.

Yet as any experienced builder knows, even with a solid foundation and a sturdy frame, things can go wrong during construction. Problems arise. In the work of rationally participating in the eternal law, men make mistakes. We have already established that although the first principle of the natural law is infallibly known by all, the primary and secondary precepts are not known by all to the same level of detail. We touched upon some of the causes of failures to properly discern the precepts. The natural inclinations can be confused with other impulses. The details involved in formulating secondary precepts can be complex, involving intricate interaction of primary and secondary ends and affecting the hierarchy of goods at various levels. That all human societies, even the best, have made unjust laws should be a statement that evokes no controversy. Just like the best plans for building a house, experience demonstrates that we get law and justice wrong, at least sometimes.

So what can be done to correct man's serious errors in legal reasoning despite the perfect foundation of the eternal and natural law? This chapter presents several aids to natural law reasoning, but we conclude that recourse to the Architect is indispensable. God, the artificer and author of natural law, has provided additional specifications for the implementation of the natural law in the form of the divine law. We explore the role of divine law in natural law jurisprudence. Pope Leo XIII observed that the fates of natural and divine law are intertwined when he lamented the "spreading wish to supplant natural and divine law by human law."[2] To sustain an effective frame for human law, the natural law needs to be accessed in conjunction with the divine law.

The first section, "The Problems in Applying Natural Law," analyzes some of the problems faced by man in deducing natural law precepts. After diagnosing the pitfalls, the second section, "Nonlegal Solutions to the Problems," presents some nonlegal remedies to assist human reasoning about the natural law: taking good counsel, equity, habit, and advice of the wise. Yet even these remedies are insufficient for proper use of the natural law. "The Legal Solution," our third section, argues that since the natural law within us has been destroyed, we need a new law to assist reason. This additional law is the divine law. The final section of the chapter,

"The Role of Recourse to the Architect," concludes the examination of the divine law by summarizing the reasons for its necessity and arguing that a natural law project that ignores the necessity of divine law is doomed to failure. Just as it would be folly to work through a building crisis without recourse to the original architect, the natural law cannot be used properly without some recourse to the divine law.

THE PROBLEMS IN APPLYING NATURAL LAW: THE NEED FOR OTHER FORMS OF LAW

It should be unnecessary to prove that, over the thousands of years of history, human beings have not always deduced correct principles of natural law, or always determined good actions pursuant to correct principles. The sources of all the errors and misapplications are essentially twofold: (1) errors in arriving at proper conclusions about the precepts of the natural law, and (2) errors in judgment in applying correct principles to reach good determinations.[3] An example of the first problem would be a conclusion that the natural law requires all persons of a certain type to be enslaved to others. An example of the second would be recognition of enforced slavery as contrary to the natural law, but at the same time a failure to prohibit, as contrary to the natural law, the slave trade from Africa in the seventeenth century.

Failure to Know the Natural Law

Since the principles of the natural law are derived from the being or essence of man, knowledge of them is within the capabilities of all. The degree of difficulty or ease in actually arriving at knowledge of the precepts of the natural law depends on the level of the principles at issue. The more general and basic the proposition, the more accessible it is to human knowledge. The more remote and particular, the more opportunity exists for errors. Thus, Aquinas explains:

> It is therefore evident that, as regards the general principles, whether of speculative or of practical reason, truth or rectitude is the same for

all, and is equally known by all. As to the proper conclusions of the speculative reason, the truth is the same for all, but is not equally known to all: thus it is true for all that the three angles of a triangle are together equal to two right angles, although it is not known to all. But as to the proper conclusions of the practical reason, neither is the truth or rectitude the same for all, nor, where it is the same, is it equally known by all.[4]

Natural law reasoning involves both speculative and practical reason.[5] Speculative reason is necessary to understand the basic truths on which the existence and obligatory nature of natural law rest: the end and nature of man. Practical reason is necessary to reach conclusions oriented toward actions based on these truths.[6] Thus, the first principle of the natural law—which rests on speculative knowledge about the being, end, and good of man—is not only universally true, but it is also universally accessible by the reason of all men. Aquinas refers to this basic knowledge of natural law as things that are *per se nota*, or "known through the thing itself." By knowing the aspects of man's nature and by knowing that actions commensurate with that nature are good, it is possible to formulate general principles of action specifying the general good to be done and evil avoided. These general principles are not known through the operation of a syllogism, a conclusion drawn by inference from premises. It is instead known by itself, or through the definitions contained therein.

Aquinas describes the process of knowing something known through itself. Once seen, it is simply known without syllogistic demonstration. Yet in man this process can only occur when a particular man is exposed to the elements of the thing that is known through itself. Two examples used by Aquinas make the point clearly. It is *per se nota* that a whole is greater than its parts, yet one only apprehends this truth after he knows what is a "whole" and what are "parts."[7] Likewise, the proposition that man is an animal is *per se nota* once one knows that the nature of man contains within it the nature of an animal.[8] To know that social life is a good that ought to be fostered, one must know that man is a social animal. Although the knowledge of all things that are *per se nota* is equally accessible to all, in that once observed they are immediately knowable by any man, not all men actually know them. Since human knowledge of even *per se nota* propositions is contingent on sense experience, some people may not be acquainted with the sense impressions necessary to know the *per se nota* proposition. Thus, Aquinas explains: "Certain axioms or proposition are universally [*per se nota*] to all; and such are those propositions whose terms are known to all. . . . But some propositions are [*per se nota*] only to the wise, who understand the meaning of the terms of such propositions; thus to one who understands that an angel is not a body it is [*per se nota*] that an angel is not circumscriptively in a place: but this is not evident to the unlearned for they cannot grasp it."[9]

Although all men have the rational ability to know all things that are *per se nota*, the degree of universal actual knowledge of these principles varies with the universality of sense experience necessary to know the principles. The more common the knowledge of the definitions, the more common is the knowledge of the principle known through the components of the definition. Thus, the most general principles of the natural law, although not known by all people, are more universally comprehended than the more detailed principles. Once one knows the definition of "good"—that which is suitable to the form of man or that which is consistent with the hierarchy of ends of man[10]—the conclusion to do this "good" is known without further inference. As Aquinas explains, once being is apprehended by speculative reason, practical reason is busied with orienting that knowledge toward action. Thus, speculative reason apprehends being, and practical reason knows how to do what is consistent with being. In this sense, we cannot help but be what we are. We are ordered to be what our nature makes us. Yet not all are aware of even the most general principles known through the natural inclinations, which identify the terms of the general precepts of natural law.

Even though we cannot help but have the basic natural inclinations toward the hierarchy of goods (preservation of life, procreation and rearing of children, acquisition of knowledge, and living in society), proper knowledge of these ends of the natural inclinations is less commonly known. Thus, the conclusions drawn from them are not always known to the same extent. As Aquinas says, "the more we descend into detail" the more uncertainty exists as to conclusions.[11] Thus, the general principles of natural law are universally valid for all men, but, depending on the level of detail, not universally known by all men.[12]

Failures in Applying Principles of Natural Law to Actual Cases

In addition to formulating principles of decision-making (i.e., preserve human life), the practical reason—oriented by its nature to operations—needs to apply those principles to particular and varied factual situations that Aquinas calls "contingent matters."[13] Certainty in reaching correct conclusions of the practical reason is not assured owing to two problems: (1) the infinite nature of varying circumstances, and (2) a wounding of human nature affecting reason.

The Problem of Too Many Contingencies

First, the principles may not actually resolve a particular case at hand. As Aquinas notes, general principles are true for the majority of cases.[14] They sometimes fail to apply to a particular situation out of the presence of an unusual circumstance. For example, a general precept of the natural law is that property held in trust should be returned, but such property should not be returned if it is a weapon to be used to fight against one's country.[15] That a principle of the natural law does not always apply to similar cases is understandable given the hierarchy of goods and ends that give rise to the precepts of natural law. The secondary principle of returning property is a precept of natural law deduced from man's social nature, but the principle should not be followed when it would lead to a result that comes into conflict with another good subsumed in the hierarchy (as when a madman seeks the return of a deposited weapon to harm others).[16] Here, the result of applying the precept to return entrusted property would conflict with the precept to protect human life. Thus, even if a man were able to know all of the principles of the natural law with complete precision, an unrealistic assumption, as we concluded in chapter 4, he might still err in applying the correct combination of precepts to the particular action in a contingent situation.[17] Because of the complexity of human affairs, the application of the principles may lead to misapplication of precepts.

The virtue of prudence enables one to judge which principle should be used to resolve a particular conflict. Aquinas says that prudence is a virtue used "to apply right reason to action."[18] As in the case of the madman wanting his sword back, prudence enables one to know that return of the sword should be delayed so as to fulfill the end of preserving life. To apply natural law principles correctly, one must take account of all the individual circumstances of an action. Yet the human mind is incapable of contemplating the infinite number of singular facts and must reduce them to a finite number of factors to be considered.[19] Because the finite mind of man is incapable of considering the infinite number of singular facts, Aquinas quotes the book of Wisdom as concluding that "our counsels are uncertain,"[20] by which he seems to mean that our decisions in light of natural law are not certain to be correct in all circumstances. Thus, even though the principles of the natural law are capable of being known by all men, knowledge of the principles will not always lead to correct applications to particular contingent matters, because man's reason is finite.

Problems Caused by a Fallen Human Nature

Beyond the difficulty of applying general principles to many contingent situations, another explanation for the failure of reason to lead to correct action in all cases is that man is not a creature of perfect reason. As we noted in chapter 3, our passions and sensible appetites can obscure our discernment of the natural inclinations that lead us to the primary precepts of natural law. We may desire a particular course of action out of our concupiscence, and this desire can cloud our judgment in discerning the natural inclinations, formulating principles resulting from them, and in applying principles to particular circumstances.

Aristotle had observed that the use of practical reason becomes impossible for one subject to the forces of unrestrained passions: "For he who lives as passion directs will not hear argument that dissuades him, nor understand it if he does." Aquinas expands upon the role of passion as an impediment to rational thought by explaining that the habit of uncontrolled passion can build into evil dispositions, which then become conatural, like a second acquired nature. These obstacles impede an individual's ability to make use of practical reason, or participate in the eternal law, both at the level of demonstrating principles and determining action. Thus:

> In some few cases it may fail, both as to rectitude [i.e., the principle does not apply to what appears to be a similar case], by reason of

certain obstacles [*impedimenta*] (just as natures subject to generation and corruption fail in some few cases on account of some obstacle) and as to knowledge [*ad notitiam*] [i.e., the principle leads to a correct conclusion but this conclusion is unknown], since in some the reason is perverted by passion, or evil habit, or an evil disposition of nature; thus formerly, theft, although it is expressly contrary to the natural law, was not considered wrong among the Germans as Julius Caesar relates.[21]

Thus, we see that our reason may fail in identifying the correct precept of the natural law to resolve a particular contingent matter, because the principle that seems to be applicable is, in fact, inapplicable due to other complicating factors. This is a failure of prudence to take counsel of all relevant singular facts. Aquinas says the unaccounted-for fact creates an impediment to the correct decision, just like impediments can thwart natural generation. As a rule, the mating of a male and female produce a normal offspring. Yet because of an intervening contingency—an infection, for example—the offspring may fail to be as expected.

Beyond failures of prudence, Aquinas identifies a second reason men reach false conclusions from the precepts of natural law: our passions may pose impediments to our reason in knowing and applying the principles properly. Aquinas explains that this failure of practical reasoning is a result of the Fall: "As a result of original justice, the reason had perfect hold over the lower parts of the soul, while reason itself was perfected by God, and was subject to Him. Now this same original justice was forfeited through the sin of our first parent . . . so that all the powers of the soul are left, as it were, destitute of their proper order, whereby they are naturally directed to virtue; which destitution is called a wounding of nature."[22]

As a result of this wounding of nature, "the inclination to the good of virtue [the natural inclination] is diminished in each individual on account of actual sin."[23] Beyond the limitations of a finite mind to exercise prudence fully, man engages in practical reasoning after the Fall with a birth defect: the passions are not properly ordered to the conclusions of reason. Aquinas explains: "The body was made subject in all things to the soul or to reason. But later the devil led man through suggestion from the observation of the divine precept. Then the body was made disobedient to reason. Although it was right for man to desire the good according to reason, nonetheless he became inclined to the contrary due to concupiscence."[24]

Man exacerbates this original wound by engaging in vicious actions. Evil habits are developed, enlarging this original wound.[25] Thus, even though the precepts of the natural law necessarily flow from premises originating in the first precept of the natural law, sometimes our reason cannot see the clarity of the syllogism through the fog created by the wounding of our nature. Aquinas gives the example of the Germans, who were mistaken in thinking that theft was good, even though properly functioning reason necessarily concludes theft to be contrary to the good of living socially.[26] The problem compounds itself since errors in living according to the natural law lead to a deepening of this wound. Thus, the more vice one engages in, the greater the diminishment of the original state of the intellect. John Rziha summarizes the causes of the inevitable weaknesses in properly understanding and applying natural law: "Natural reason is subject to error and ignorance both on account of its fallenness (vice and susceptibility to be blinded by the passions) and on account of its natural weakness."[27] Aquinas argues that it is impossible for people to attain perfect natural goodness, embodied in the natural end of the natural law, as a result of this wounding of nature after the Fall.[28]

In one of his last works, *De Duobus Praeceptis Caritatis*, Aquinas is even more pessimistic about man's ability to correctly reason using principles of natural law. He explains that originally man was given the natural law as a light to guide him in his actions. He then describes the wounding of nature as another form of law operating in contradiction to the natural law. He explains, "The devil nevertheless has planted in man another law, namely, of concupiscence."[29] This other law has actually destroyed the natural law in us.[30] Yet this destruction of the natural law by the law of concupiscence does not relieve man of responsibility. His ignorance of natural law caused by this wound of nature does not excuse man from obeying the natural law.[31] Man would appear to have an intractable problem: he is obligated to the natural law and ignorance of it is not an excuse, yet he seems hopelessly incapable of overcoming ignorance of general and detailed principles of the natural law.

NONLEGAL SOLUTIONS TO THE PROBLEMS

Given these great potentials for error, how can man proceed in the use of his practical reason to make correct decisions (*secundum rectitudinem*)? Is it hopelessly futile? How can he avoid the pitfalls in determining courses of action due to the influence of his passions? Aquinas's answer is that man requires four aids: (1) counsel, (2) equity, (3) the nurturing of good habits, and (4) the advice and example of a good man. These things can aid in overcoming the complexity of details and the wound of the law of concupiscence.

Counsel and Equity

Despite the ability to reason, men err in making proper determinations of action—that is, fail to identify the "good" obligated by the natural law—owing to the complexity of the factual scenarios in which the principles must be applied. Man's reason appears incapable of taking proper account of so many details. Yet two other attributes, when combined with the use of reason, can correct for this difficulty: prudence aided by taking complete counsel, and moderating decisions by applying the principle of equity.

We have seen that the virtue of prudence enables man to judge which principle should be used to resolve the recurring conflicts among principles of the natural law.[32] Which particular decision is necessitated by the ends of man is a matter of prudence. Yet for prudence to resolve these conflicts, it must take account of all the relevant circumstances and all applicable principles. This process involves taking counsel, which Aquinas describes as an *inquisitio*, or "investigation."[33] Commenting on Aristotle, Aquinas describes taking counsel as a "deliberative inquiry" to determine the means to a given end.[34] Part of the virtue of prudence is taking counsel.[35] The virtue of counsel enables the intellect to organize the detailed facts so that prudence can choose the appropriate resolution of principles. Yet the varying circumstances, with respect to which the counsels of man must be taken, are infinite. The integration of infinite details requires an infinite intellect, and thus the perfect source of assistance in this matter is God. Only through the divine gift of counsel[36] can man truly "deliberate well."[37] As Aquinas explains: "Hence, in the research of counsel, man requires to be directed by God, who comprehends all things: and this is done through the gift of counsel, whereby man is directed as though counseled by God, just as, in human affairs, those who are unable to take counsel for themselves, seek counsel from those who are wiser."[38]

The analogy to the human level is proof of our need for God's involvement if we wish to succeed in reasoning according to natural law principles. Just as we recognize that we often need to take counsel with a wise person in making a decision, we realize that our finite intellect is incapable of taking account of all the singular factors that make up complex moral decisions. We thus recognize a need for God in the process of exercising prudence. He fills this need through the gift of counsel, which perfects the process of exercising the virtue of prudence.

Beyond the gift of counsel, another aid exists to remedy the difficulty of applying natural law principles to an infinite array of contingent matters. This aid is equity. Equity is shown by Aquinas to be a part of justice, which is the purpose or end of natural law.[39] Equity is that virtue that reviews and, in some cases, modifies the direct conclusions of the principles of natural law. Aquinas is clear that there is no defect in natural law itself, but rather in our ability to formulate the principles of the natural law. Since our ability to completely and accurately give form to the hierarchy of principles is imperfect, equity is the virtue that provides, when necessary, a corrective. Aquinas explains:

> Since particulars are infinite, our mind cannot embrace them to make a law that applies to every individual case. Therefore a law must be framed in a universal way, for example, whoever commits murder will be put to death. It is evident that our intellect can predicate something universally true about some things, in the case of what is necessary [i.e., in matters of speculative reason only] where no defect can occur. But about other things it is not possible that something true be predicated universally, in the case of what is contingent [i.e., the realm of practical reason]. Here, even though something is true in most instances, nevertheless it errs as we know in a few instances. And of such a nature are human acts about which laws are framed. . . .
>
> The previously mentioned defect does not destroy the rectitude of law or of legal justice. . . . Although a fault may be committed in some cases by the observance of the law, nevertheless the law is good because that fault is not on the part of the law (since it was made

according to reason) nor on the part of the legislator (who legislated according to the condition of the material), but the fault arises from the nature of the thing. Such is the nature of human actions that they are not done always in the same way but are done otherwise in certain infrequent instances.[40]

We might be tempted to respond to this problem by claiming we merely need to formulate the principles of natural law in more detail by listing within them all exceptions. This is not a satisfactory solution. Since human actions and circumstances are potentially infinite, our finite reason cannot form principles for infinite possibilities. Moreover, the more we delve into detail, the greater the likelihood that an error occurs. If we were to formulate the principles of natural law in more detail (i.e., return a deposit unless the person is a madman, etc.), there would be more opportunities for the principle to fail.[41]

The virtue of equity is the corrective to this failing of human reason to formulate a principle applicable in all eventualities. But what is equity? Aquinas says it is "a just thing."[42] Elsewhere, he defines it as "the equality of justice" and "the dictates of justice and the common good."[43] Yet these are the same as the definition of *jus*, the just thing itself.[44] The end of *jus*, and hence the end of law (including natural law), is that which is just, equitable, and for that good common to man (the hierarchy of ends). In this sense, equity is "the directive of the law [including natural law] where the law is deficient for some particular case."[45] The role of equity seems absent or minimized in a natural law system according to thinkers like Suárez, who focus exclusively—or nearly so—on formulating exact precepts. For Aquinas, such work is part of the use of practical reason. Yet this process must be directed or ruled by another method: the review of those principles in particular cases in light of the ends of the entire exercise. The end of *jus* and justice itself must be present in the operation of natural law so that it can direct the outcome in particularly difficult cases in light of the good or end of justice.

The Role of Habit

Even when the principle of equity moderates prudential decisions and proper counsel is taken, the virtue of justice involves constantly choosing the right (*jus*) over time. Aquinas defines justice as the "perpetual and constant will to render to each one his right [*jus*]."[46] It is not surprising that developing this perpetual and constant will involves the cultivation of good habits. Developing good habits of action thus becomes a means of overcoming the difficulties in using the natural law as a guide of action. Aquinas describes habit: "The mode or determination of the subject, in regard to the nature of the thing, belongs to the first species of quality, which is habit and disposition: for the Philosopher says . . . , when speaking of habits of the soul and of the body, that they are 'dispositions of the perfect to the best; and by perfect I mean that which is disposed in accordance with its nature.'"[47]

A good habit is a disposition toward that which is perfect, and the end of one's nature. Good habits are, in this sense, the practice of recognizing and following the natural inclinations. Accordingly, Aquinas claims that "human virtues are habits."[48] Recall that the definition of justice is the constant and perpetual will to do what is just.[49] In the reply to objection 1 in the article containing this definition, Aquinas shows the relationship between will and habit. An act of will is an act produced by the power of habit.[50] With a causal relationship established between habit and will, Aquinas can reconcile the definition of justice given by Aristotle as "that habit by which men are disposed to just works, and by which they actually perform and will just deeds."[51] Thus, one way to aid our use of natural law is to develop a habit of acting in particular cases according to its principles. This habituates the intellect and the will to the *jus*, and thus makes it easier for us to apprehend and comprehend it. Commenting on Aristotle's discussion of the necessity of knowledge of particulars (or we might say experience), Aquinas says, "Hence it is that certain people not possessing the knowledge of universals are more effective about some particulars than those who have universal knowledge from the fact that they are expert in [i.e., experienced in] other particulars."[52]

Adapting the example of Aristotle and Aquinas slightly, we can conclude that a man might know that uncooked chicken can result in sickness and death by one of two ways. He may know about the existence and nature of salmonella, and how cooking kills the bacteria, or he may simply observe that those who cook their chicken do not contract the disease. Thus, one way to proceed in making practical decisions in accordance with natural law is by being familiar with particular cases or instances and the right results. One may be able to reason by analogy and reach good results, rather than making deductions from the general principles of natural law. By doing so, one would build a habit of familiarity with natural law through particulars rather than through the general principles. In a sense, this process has characterized the common law method of legal reasoning by analogizing from past precedents. As with the common law, Aquinas does not present reasoning by analogy as an exclusive alternative to deductive reasoning.

This process of analogizing is not necessarily a sufficient method, as it may fail from insufficient breadth of particulars, a risk of all inductive reasoning, or from using erroneous results to form the habit, resulting in "corrupt habits."[53] Thus, habit cannot be completely controlling; there must be a possibility of overturning *stare decisis* when the results clearly contradict the general principles derived through deduction.

Gratian includes authorities that maintain this principle with respect to custom, which can be considered a sort of collective habit. Customs are a community's cultivated patterns of living, whereas habits are an individual's cultivated patterns of living. Gratian demonstrates great respect for custom, beginning his *Treatise on Laws* by elevating custom to the level of natural law by claiming that humans are ruled by two things: natural law and long-standing custom.[54] Notwithstanding his respect for custom, Gratian includes the admonition of Pope Nicholas that evil custom must be "torn up by its roots."[55]

The cure for bad custom is to submit it to the test of reason. Customs must be set aside if they conflict with truth or reason.[56] Since the natural law is the rational participation in the eternal law, the reference to reason can be read as a reference to natural law. Such a reading adds a new connotation to the opening line of the *Decretum*. The two pillars of law ruling the human race, natural law and custom, are not independent laws. They are symbiotically related. Natural law reasoning must respect custom, but custom must also yield to the dictates of reason. Notwithstanding its benefits, custom, if not harmonized with reason, can perpetrate errors: "An evil custom is no more to be tolerated than a dangerous infection because, unless the custom is quickly torn up by its roots, it will be adopted by wicked men as entitling them to a privilege. And then, unchecked deviations and various infractions will soon be revered as lawful and honored as immemorial privileges."[57]

What is said of custom applies to habit on the level of the individual. Habit is necessary to complement natural law reasoning, but reason is necessary to keep a check on habit. Both methods, deduction and habitual reasoning from analogy, are necessary, as each one supplements or corrects the other.

The Advice of a Good Man

Habit can aid in making decisions that accord with the principles of natural law, but it is still insufficient to ensure universal success. If unchecked by reason, a bad habit, like a bad custom, can spread error like a disease. Therefore, an additional aid must be brought to bear. The source of reason must not be limited to the interior mind of the individual. The reason of a good man has a role to play. As Vernon Bourke explains, this concept is drawn from Aristotle's ethical system: "At times [Aristotle] suggests that we have to depend on observing what the 'good man,' the pillar of society [*spoudaios*] approves and tends to, in order to discover what is morally good. . . . Certainly [Aristotle's theory] is not a [purely] deductive system, which starts from a certain definition of man and reasons to definite rules governing human activity."[58]

Although Aquinas believes that perfect knowledge comes from understanding and knowing the causes of conclusions, he admits that some people can learn a principle by "accept[ing] it as a probable opinion because wise men or most men teach it."[59] In discussing the principles of the natural law contained in the Ten Commandments, Aquinas acknowledges that one way people learn the principles is by "being taught by wise men."[60] As we have seen already, even truths that are *per se nota* are not always known to all, but only to the learned. Aquinas explains: "There are some precepts [of natural law] the reason of which is not so evident to everyone, but only the wise."[61] The instruction of a wise man may be necessary if one is dealing with a more particular principle of natural law:

There are certain things which the natural reason of every man, of its own accord and at once, judges to be done or not to be done: e.g., "Honor thy father and thy mother," and "Thou shalt not kill, Thou shalt not steal": and these belong to the law of nature absolutely. And there are certain things which, after a more careful consideration, wise men deem obligatory. *Such belong to the law of nature, yet so that they need to be inculcated, the wiser teaching the less wise.*[62]

Thus, although it is a more complete knowledge to know for one's self the general and particular principles of natural law (and how one is derived from the other), Aquinas nonetheless recognizes that this goal is not attainable by all. Some must be aided by the wise, who will teach the unwise. As with habit, this is not an infallible solution. Even the wise can err because they labor under the same difficulties identified in our first section above. Yet combined together, the wise provide methods that can buttress the use of individual reason in arriving at conclusions and determinations. Such recognition of the corrective of wise opinion may explain the importance of jurists' opinions and "custom" (*mos*) in the legal systems of Rome and the philosophies of Aquinas and Gratian.[63] The custom of collecting and referring to the opinions of those jurists whose comments have stood the test of time is a method of accessing the advice of the wise.

THE LEGAL SOLUTION:
THE ADVICE OF THE ARCHITECT—DIVINE LAW

The effects of original sin, exacerbated by individual sin, handicap our ability to reason using the natural law. Because reason is impaired and passions are disordered, we can buttress the use of deductive reason by forming good habits in light of the advice and opinion of the wise.

Yet even the wise labor under the same impediments to reason. Thus, the advice of the wise is only as good as the extent to which they have overcome these impediments. Aquinas actually casts this problem as a conflict of law. The conflict between the natural law known through natural inclinations and the law of sin (*fomes peccati*) is a conflict of law. A contemporary of Aquinas defined the law of sin as "the tinder of sin, that is, concupiscence, or a tendency to concupiscence, which is at times called the law of the limbs of the body, at times the weakness of nature, at times the tyrant who is in our limbs, at times the law of the flesh."[64]

These internal conflicts result from what Aquinas calls "the law of sin." He explains the legal implications:

The law, as to its essence, resides in him that rules and measures; but, by way of participation, in that which is ruled and measured; so that every inclination or ordination which may be found in things subject to the law is called a law by participation. . . . Now, those who are subject to a law may receive a twofold inclination from the lawgiver. First, insofar as he directly inclines his subjects to something; sometimes indeed different subjects to different acts; in this way we may say that there is a military law and a mercantile law. Secondly, indirectly; thus by the very fact that a lawgiver deprives a subject of some dignity, the latter passes into another order, so as to be under another law, as it were: thus if a soldier be turned out of the army, he becomes a subject of rural or of mercantile legislation. Accordingly, under the Divine Lawgiver various creatures have various natural inclinations, so that what is, as it were, a law for one, is against the law for another: thus I might say that fierceness is, in a way, the law of a dog, but against the law of a sheep or another meek animal. And so the law of man, which, by the Divine ordinance, is allotted to him, according to his proper natural condition, is that he should act in accordance with reason: and this law was so effective in the primitive state, that nothing either beside or against reason could take man unawares. But when man turned his back on God, he fell under the influence of his sensual impulses: in fact this happens to each one individually, the more he deviates from the path of reason, so that, after a fashion, he is likened to the beasts that are led by the impulse of sensuality. . . .

So, then, this very inclination of sensuality, which is called the "fomes," in other animals has simply the nature of a law (yet only in so far as a law may be said to be in such things), by reason of a direct inclination. But in man, it has not the nature of law in this way, rather is it a deviation from the law of reason. But since, by the just sentence of God, man is destitute of original justice, and his reason bereft of its vigor, this impulse of sensuality, whereby he is led, insofar as it is a penalty following from the Divine law depriving man of his proper dignity, has the nature of a law.[65]

Originally, man was only subject to his proper natural inclinations, which were all oriented to reason. As a result of violating the divine law, the first man was subject to various punishments, one of which changed human nature so that the passions can move men toward pleasures that are contrary to reason.[66] Posterity can thus inherit only this altered nature, and thus all who live after the first man are born with both natural inclinations, ordered to the rational nature of man, and with disordered inclinations.[67] The other felt impulses or desires, which in animals constitute their own natural inclinations, were ordered to reason. The punishment for the original transgression of the divine law was the presence in man of sensual impulses not of themselves subordinate to reason, which produces the conflicting inclinations felt in man, which in turn obscure the ordered natural inclinations. Aquinas explains concerning Plato's puppet analogy[68] why the puppet is subject to so many strings and not merely the one golden string. The other strings are a legal punishment man is left to "wrestle with"[69] when searching for the golden string of the proper natural inclinations. The law of sin, which is nothing other than the inclination to act contrary to reason, is not a specific species of law, as are the eternal, natural, and divine law. Rather, this law of sin has "the nature of law" to the extent that it participates in law by constituting a new (deprived) status for man as a result of violating the divine law. This law of sin is a legal punishment; it subjects man not only to his own natural inclinations but also to the natural inclination proper to a lower animal, irrational sensual appetite. The result of this law of sin is a legal conflict within man producing a "state of spiritual disorderliness."[70] He is aware of the natural inclination of his composite nature, which is ordered to reason. But he is also subject to an irrational appetite, which needs to be ordered to reason. This legal conflict of laws requires a legal solution to resolve the disorderliness.

Recognizing this legal plight after the destruction of the natural law in us, Aquinas argues that God saw the need for a legal solution, a different law to intervene in the natural law to counterbalance the law of sin. Immediately after making his startling statement that the law of nature has been destroyed in us, Aquinas continues: "It was necessary for man to be redirected to the works of virtue and turned away from vice, for which reasons the law of the scriptures was necessary."[71] To understand the nature of the legal solution, the law of the scriptures, we must pause to examine more precisely what Aquinas meant when he claimed the natural law is destroyed in us.

By the destruction of the natural law, Aquinas clearly does not mean the natural law itself ceased to exist since, and in the very next phrase, he indicates the purpose of the law of the scriptures was to redirect man to it. Recalling that law exists both in the lawgiver and in the one subject to the law,[72] Aquinas must mean that the natural law is destroyed within man but not within the lawgiver, God. It is destroyed in us in the sense that human nature was so altered as to create the conflict of laws between natural law and the law of the *fomes peccati.* Instead of natural law and the natural inclinations existing as the law within man, now he can be misled by the conflict of laws. Yet Aquinas does not say that human nature itself was destroyed, only the undisputed dominance of the natural law within man. In another passage in the *Summa Theologica,* Aquinas makes clear that the constitutive elements of human nature, a rational animal, are not destroyed or even diminished.[73] If we place the phrase *destructa erat* in the context of all of Aquinas's writings, we can see that Aquinas clearly does not mean that the natural law is completely obliterated for us,[74] but rather its unchallenged supremacy over our faculties is destroyed. All is not lost, even if the proper order within our nature has been destroyed. It is still possible to know some of the natural law and even to perform some acts according to its precepts.[75] All is not lost. The law of sin destroys the ordered control of reason through the natural law, resulting in a weakening, not the destruction, of the inclination to virtue, or the inclination to order appetites rationally.[76] Thus, man is still constitutively capable of following the natural law; he has merely lost his way and needs redirection. He needs a third law to resolve the conflict between natural law and the law of sin. This law is the *lex scripturae.*

The law of the scriptures is the first part of a two-part division of the divine law. Aquinas emphasizes that the divine law is obligatory and necessary for knowing what is good, what the natural law obligates us to do. He uses the word *oportebat* to indicate that it was necessary for the law of the scriptures to be promulgated for men to attain virtue. Divine law is not optional or gratuitous; it is not merely a helpful light as one of many ways leading back to the natural law. It is necessary for the rational participation in the eternal law, or the natural law: "Because we recognize the weakness of the human intellect, it is necessary to judge the precepts of our reason by the divine law."[77] Aquinas drives this point home when he argues, "It is obvious that all people are not able to persevere in knowledge, and therefore a brief summary of the law was given by Christ so that it might be able to be known by all, and nobody would be able to be excused of the observation of it [the law] through ignorance."[78]

Aquinas's emphasis of the necessity of the divine law, briefly given by Christ for all people, is striking. He is emphasizing that we cannot persevere[79] in knowing what is right without this additional law. Later, he repeats that "human action cannot be good unless it is harmonized with delight in the divine rules."[80] He repeats that the divine "law ought to be a rule of all human actions."[81] Both of these passages invoke the very definition of law itself as a rule of human action.[82] This reference to the definition of law indicates that he is speaking of divine law as a real law, not just metaphorically.

Alasdair MacIntyre has drawn particular attention to a scene in Greek tragedy, which demonstrates the role of divine intervention in the process of rational exploration of the requirements of the natural law.[83] In Sophocles's *Philoctetes*, Odysseus and Neptolemus have been sent to obtain the magical bow of Philoctetes, which has been prophesized as necessary to end the Trojan War. Philoctetes has been wronged by the Greeks and abandoned on an island. Odysseus and Neptolemus argue over what course of action is right. Should they use cunning and deceive Philoctetes, so as to secure the bow and achieve victory for the Greeks? Or should they act in a way that will give the wronged Philoctetes his due, even if that results in failure to obtain the bow? The characters are locked in what appears to be an intractable moral conflict over the nature of justice—as either effectiveness or fairness—from which they cannot extract themselves, and they remain suspended in inaction. The only way to resolve this deadlock is by a revelation from the gods on the right standard by which to choose their action.[84] Thus, although Sophocles lacked knowledge of the actual divine revelation, his play pointed to its necessity in resolving failures to know the correct choice of human actions. It is interesting to note that the intervention of the gods does not reveal a third standard, something external to the moral reasoning of the human agents. It rather intervenes to clarify—within their moral discourse—the solution to the difficulty.

Likewise, Aquinas maintains that the precepts of divine law are not something alien to the natural law, but rather encompass all that the natural law obligates us to do, the whole law: "He who observes the divine command and law, fulfils the whole law."[85] The phrase "the whole law" (*totam legem*) appears to be a reference to the eternal law. Since the eternal law is the entire rule and measure of the universe, it represents the whole of the law, including natural law, which is nothing but a participation in it. Yet the "Divine Law participates in the eternal law more perfectly" than the natural law since the divine law is not mediated through weakened human reason.[86] To persevere in this participation in the whole law it is necessary to consult the instructions of the architect of the whole law, the divine wisdom. This verbal allusion to the discussion of eternal law in the *Summa Theologica* is emphasized by an invocation of an image that runs throughout the discussion of eternal law: art.[87] Aquinas explains that "as we see in the arts, an object is said to be good and right if it is equalized by rules; so too any human work is good and virtuous when it is harmonized with love of Divine rules."[88] A love of the original artificer of the eternal law's rules is necessary for the work of participating in that law to be good and right, or *jus*.

What then is this other type of law, made necessary by the law of sin? The divine law is the revelation of God contained in the Old Testament — the law of the scriptures (*lex scipturae*), also called the law of Moses (*lex Moisi*), or the law out of fear (*lex ex timore*)[89] — and the Gospels (*lex evangelica*), also called the law of Christ (*lex Christi*), or the law of love (*lex amoris*).[90] All of these various appellations for a divine law refer to a rule and measure different from eternal law. Unlike eternal law, the divine law consists of particular principles, conclusions, and determinations originating in the eternal law of creation, but given or revealed at particular points in history. Whereas the eternal law is eternally promulgated,[91] the divine law is promulgated at particular moments in history. Many of these principles were originally promulgated through the natural law but have become illuminated directly by the promulgation of the revealed word of God.

Divine law serves several discrete purposes. Aquinas lists four reasons for a divine law, the second of which is directly relevant to the problems identified in the first section of this chapter. First, he explains that because natural law is the participation of man's nature in the eternal law, it deals primarily with the natural ends of man: preservation, procreation and rearing of children, social existence, and knowledge. Yet, as we observed in chapter 4, even the natural law points to an end beyond these — a supernatural end, which is not attainable by mere natural means alone. As Aquinas explains: "Man's perfect Happiness . . . consists in the vision of the Divine Essence. Now the vision of God's Essence surpasses the nature not only of man, but also of every creature.... Consequently neither man, nor any creature, can attain final Happiness by his natural powers."[92]

Because natural law operates on the level of man's natural abilities (reason), it is insufficient to attain the highest and most complete end— the beatific vision—because this end is above nature. Although man can come to the knowledge that God exists by use of natural reason, he cannot know all that he needs to know about God to attain this end from reason alone.[93] Divine law fills this gap in natural ability, or rather it elevates natural ability to a higher plane. Thus, the first purpose of divine law is to make known principles necessary to transcend nature and attain supernatural beatitude.

The second reason given by Aquinas directly addresses the problem considered in the second section of this chapter. Because of the legal conflict between the natural law and the law of the *fomes peccati*, men have reached and continue to reach differing conclusions on the content of the natural law and its applications in particular contexts. For the natural law to be a useful element of human decision-making, man needs a level of certainty as to both the conclusions reached about the general precepts of the natural law based on the ends of man and their application to particular contingent circumstances. Divine law provides this assistance. "Because," Aquinas explains, "on account of the uncertainty of human judgment, especially on contingent and particular matters, different people form different judgments on human acts; whence also different and contrary laws result. In order, therefore, that man may know without any doubt what he ought to do and what he ought to avoid, it was necessary for man to be directed in his proper acts by a law given by God, for it is certain that such a law cannot err."[94]

Divine law is of particular assistance to man in working out his participation in the eternal law. Conclusions, and particularly determinations about contingent matters, can be uncertain. Specifically, we have seen that the law of the *fomes peccati* brought disorder within the internal life of man so that it became difficult to discern the inclinations proper to man's nature from the lower impulses, which, due to the law of sin, have lost their subjection to reason. As Jean Porter explains, to the Scholastic philosophers, the law of the scriptures provides the means to identify those aspects of our experience of human nature "that are normative."[95] The scriptures identify those experiences that illustrate the norm of our composite human nature. Aristotle turned to the good man for such advice, but Aquinas expanded this solution to include the ultimate good and wise man—God himself, the artificer of the eternal law. The divine law serves as the detailed specifications of the architect, to assist man in constructing rules and measures in accordance with the exemplar of eternal law. Thus, although man is capable of knowing the natural law, natural law jurists must admit they will not have a perfect knowledge of the natural law on their own. Yet by accepting the divine law, man has a supernatural tool available to aid in the natural use of his reason.

The third and fourth functions of divine law relate to filling insufficiencies in human law's ability to work complete justice.[96] Essentially, human law is limited in its ability to achieve perfect justice. The first reason for this is that some acts of virtue and vice are dependent upon the intention of the one performing them. Men can only know the intentions of other men indirectly, through circumstantial evidence, but not perfectly and directly. Thus, some acts of injustice cannot be corrected by human law because of this imperfect knowledge. Further, in other cases human law might be able to correct injustice, yet for other reasons it must choose to leave the injustice unpunished, when to do so is for the greater good. In these cases, justice would not be done. The divine law fills this gap by applying the precepts of natural law to every human action, even those left unpunished by human law, so "that no evil might remain unforbidden and unpunished."[97]

Returning to the second function of the divine law, we can see how it completes the work of natural law. As we saw in the discussion of justice, its definition incorporated the concept of a habit. The virtue of justice therefore is a habit that requires time to develop. Aquinas uses the term "instruction" or "training" (*disciplina*), which appears to be related to the idea of building a habit as used in the definition of justice. He says,

> Man has a natural aptitude for virtue; but the perfection of virtue must be acquired by man by means of some kind of training [*disciplinam*]. . . . Now it is difficult to see how man could suffice for himself in the matter of this training: since the perfection of virtue

consists chiefly in withdrawing man from undue pleasures, to which above all man is inclined [i.e., by the law of the *fomes peccati*], and especially the young, who are more capable of being trained. Consequently a man needs to receive this training from another, whereby to arrive at the perfection of virtue.[98]

Thus, although man has the ability to know the natural law through the use of reason, he cannot do so perfectly alone. He needs to acquire the habit through instruction. Divine law provides the instruction. Understanding this critical function of divine law is essential to answering one of the fallacious criticisms leveled against natural law advocates. A critic could point to periods of human cruelty and vice (such as genocide or slavery) and say, "If natural law exists and is naturally accessible to man, how does it lead to such results?" The answer is that these vices can arise when man rejects the necessary aid to natural law provided by God, the divine law. When divine law is rejected per se (as in contemporary American public discourse) or accepted in theory but ignored in practice (as in certain Christian societies that advocated enforced slavery), then the human determinations of natural law will not be aided by the divine law and will be more likely to err.

Beyond its division by function, Aquinas also divides the divine law by type of precept: moral, ceremonial, and judicial. The ceremonial precepts relate solely to the supernatural end of man by determining the particular way in which God should be worshiped,[99] and are thus not directly relevant to a consideration of natural law. Thus, we will ignore their place in this discussion.

The moral precepts are those that most directly relate to consideration of natural law and the second function of divine law. As Aquinas says, "The Old Law is distinct from the natural law, not as being altogether different from it, but as something added thereto. For just as grace presupposes nature, so must the Divine law presuppose the natural law."[100]

The most obvious examples are the precepts of the Decalogue. The Decalogue contains principles that can be known by human reason alone, namely, natural law. God's revelation of the Decalogue in divine law is not gratuitous, however. Aquinas explains the purpose such moral precepts serve:

It was fitting that the Divine law should come to man's assistance not only in those things for which reason is insufficient [i.e., the super- natural end], but also in those things in which human reason may happen to be impeded. Now human reason could not go astray in the abstract, as to the universal principles of the natural law; but through being habituated to sin, it became obscured in the point of things to be done in detail. But with regard to the other moral precepts, which are like conclusions drawn from the universal principles of the natu- ral law, the reason of many men went astray, to the extent of judging to be lawful, things that are evil in themselves. Hence there was need for the authority of the Divine law to rescue man from both these de- fects. Thus among the articles of faith not only are those things set forth to which reason cannot reach, such as the Trinity of the God- head; but also those to which right reason can attain, such as the Unity of the Godhead; in order to remove the manifold errors to which rea- son is liable.[101]

Man needs assistance in three areas. First, he may err in formulating the most general principles of the natural law. These principles are based directly upon the ends of man, such as men should be sociable in doing to others as they would have done to them. Errors in this area are less fre- quent. Second, he may err in formulating conclusions based on these principles, such as one should not steal. Third, man may err in particular determinations. This includes specific contexts, such as a situation where a deposit should not be returned for another intervening reason. These problems feed on each other. The more corrupted man becomes (the more "habituated to sin"), the more his reason becomes impaired and the more errors he can make. Thus, unaided man can fall into a downward spiral of error, as when he calls evil good, acts accordingly, and thus becomes more habituated. Habituation (or discipline) is related to the attainment of vir- tue. The moral precepts of the divine law assist man with the first two areas of difficulty. They call man back from this downward spiral by formulat- ing, in words, the general principles of the natural law, such as "Do unto others," and more particular conclusions like "Thou shalt not steal."

All that is contained within the term "natural law" is accessible to reason in theory, because by its very definition natural law is the rational participation of man in the eternal law. As Aquinas says, "Every judgment of practical reason [the work of natural law] proceeds from principles known naturally."[102] Although in theory anyone having the use of reason can know the general and more detailed principles of the natural law by only the use of reason, in practice most people can recognize only the basic principles, which are *per se nota*. Only the wise (those not habituated to sin) will actually reach the proper conclusion of practical reason.[103] Whereas Aristotle believes our only means of knowing the natural law for certain is through the intervention of wise men, Aquinas understands that the moral precepts of the divine law fulfill this role more effectively and authoritatively, as the divine law is more certain than relying on the presence of wise men in every society. It is equivalent to enlisting the assistance of an outside consultant or the original architect when interpreting an architectural drawing. These precepts of divine law promulgate no new law but resolve the legal conflict within man by lighting the way to the precepts of natural law. Aquinas explains: "The moral precepts derive their efficacy from the very dictate of natural reason, even if they were never included in the Law."[104] Unlike precepts of divine law dealing with the supernatural end of man, the moral precepts merely adopt the preexisting natural law precepts into the divine law so as to make them better known.

Aquinas breaks down the contents of the moral precepts of the divine law into three categories depending on their relation to the general precepts of natural law, the proximate conclusions of the secondary precepts, and the more remote conclusions of the secondary precepts:

> Now of these there are three grades: for some are most certain, and so evident as to need no promulgation; such as the commandments of the love of God and our neighbour, and others like these . . . which are, as it were, the ends of the commandments; wherefore no man can have an erroneous judgment about them. Some precepts are more detailed, the reason of which even an uneducated man can easily grasp; and yet they need to be promulgated, because human judgment, in a few instances, happens to be led astray concerning them: these are the precepts of the decalogue. Again, there are some precepts the reason of which is not so evident to everyone, but only the wise; these are moral precepts added to the decalogue, and given to the people by God through Moses and Aaron.[105]

Such a relationship between divine and natural law appears to undergird Gratian's opening of the *Decretum*, where he initially defines natural law simply as what is contained in the Law and the Gospels, collectively the divine law.[106] The divine law, or more precisely the moral precepts of it, is in a sense unnecessary. All of the moral precepts, from the most general to the most particular,[107] are accessible to man. Yet as a conclusion becomes more particular, it becomes less accessible to the minds of men. Hence, as a corrective aid, the general principles and detailed proximate and remote conclusions of the natural law have been promulgated through, or are contained in, the moral precepts of the divine law.

This understanding of the second role of divine law explains why Aquinas considered a love of the divine commands and rules as absolutely necessary for knowing the goodness of human actions. No matter how proficient or wise one might be in knowing the natural law, perfection is impossible because of the law of sin. Although habituation and consultation with the opinions of the wise can improve knowledge of the natural law, complete certainty of knowledge is not possible. The only source of certainty in interpreting and knowing the precepts of the natural law exists in the mind that promulgated the eternal law. God, as the artificer of the eternal law, makes it known to rational creatures through the natural law. Yet the obstructions to this light shining in the cave of man's reason must be illuminated by another source. As the nature of the shadows in Plato's Cave were only made known by turning to their source, the light,[108] complete knowledge of natural law can only be attained by turning to its source as manifest in the moral precepts of the divine law. Man's rationality needs these rules. Without them, knowledge of good actions and human works cannot be good and right. Our natural law reasoning, like art, needs to be harmonized with the divine law.

The function of the divine law within Aquinas's system of law reconciles the volitional and intellectual aspects of the divine law, both of which must be maintained for divine law to be a real species of law. First, it is rational and knowable by the rational mind. Since the moral precepts of the divine law are contained within the natural law, which is itself a participation in the divine rationality, they are a product of reason. In one sense, all men could know the contents of the moral precepts of the divine law without the divine law, just as in a certain sense all men can know all *per se nota* truths. Yet experience demonstrates that all men do not actually know all *per se nota* truths. Some truths must be "inculcated, the wiser teaching the less wise."[109] Inculcation involves an act of the will that translates knowledge into action. The divine law is more than a useful memory aid; it is a real law promulgated by one who has care of the community for the common good of illuminating the principles of natural law.[110] The divine law is obligatory, both because it conforms to the rational nature of man, in that through the divine law man can rationally participate in the eternal law, and because these precepts of reason have become law by being promulgated as such within the divine law. Although it is unlikely that Joseph Vining had in mind Aquinas's understanding of the divine law, his comparison of the presuppositions of law and religion provides an apt expression of the intertwined relationship between intellect and will within the divine law. The divine law is binding as a dictate of reason and a promulgated expression of that dictate from the mind of a person. Vining writes: "That which evokes no sense of obligation is not law. It is only an appearance of law, the legalistic, the authoritarian, not sovereign but an enemy. Principal among the presuppositions of legal work are that a person speaks through the texts; that there is mind; that mind is caring mind. These are the links between the experience of law and religious experience."[111]

An understanding of the moral principles of the divine law sheds an interesting light on the controversy surrounding the placement of the Ten Commandments at our courthouses.[112] Placing the Decalogue in a courtroom can be seen as a real act of humility for a judge. It reminds him to be conscious of the limits of his wisdom. He may err in applying natural principles of justice. The presence of the Decalogue is there to help remind him of what he should, but does not always, know. Its presence alludes to all the pitfalls in using only our reason to formulate and apply the law; it reminds us that, as Aquinas said, another law is necessary and obligatory. Despite the Supreme Court's purported reconciliation of the 2005 companion cases on the grounds that one instance involved the religious message of the Ten Commandments, the historic role of the Ten Commandments in lawmaking is inseparable from their theological message. They are the auxiliary instructions of the artificer, the God of law.

The most difficult problem involved in natural law reasoning is the determination of particular actions based upon the principles of the natural law. Due to the variety of so many contingent situations, these answers are not easily universalized. God has provided assistance in making these determinations, but in different ways under the Old and the New Law. Both have the same end—the proper ordering of man's relationship to God—but they achieve this end by different methods.[113]

Prior to the coming of Christ, man was in greater need of assistance because of the lack of the fullness of grace.[114] As Aquinas says, "the Old Law is like a pedagogue of children."[115] Because men were in need of more habituation to correct determinations, the Old Law contained judicial precepts. The judicial precepts made particular determinations as a matter of divine promulgation. The particular conclusions were not binding by force of reason (as are the general principles of natural law), but were binding as particular determinations implementing principles of reason by the ultimate lawgiver, God himself.

The judicial precepts contained in the Old Law were "determinations of general principles" that are "derived from reason."[116] To lead to actual decisions about what to do, the universal principles of the natural law, as confirmed in the moral precepts of the divine law, need to be "determined by Divine or human law."[117]

Because of the absence of the fullness of grace prior to the coming of Christ, man needed more assistance in these determinations. Again, Aquinas's prior discussion of the relationship between habituation or training and the ability to reach correct conclusions or determinations is necessary to understand this distinction. In the time of the Old Law, men were not yet "possessed of a virtuous habit," and thus needed direct divine determination of judicial precepts.[118]

After the advent of grace, which Aquinas calls "an interior habit bestowed on us and inclining us to act aright,"[119] men could be "endowed with virtuous habits," and thus were no longer in such need of divine determinations, such as the judicial precepts.[120] Previously, God chose to give certain judicial precepts, which were particular determinations of the natural law. These included, for example, particular rules about forgiveness of debts, treatment of laborers, and care for the poor. Later, when the human mind was aided by the availability of grace, the new divine law, or law of love, became a "law of liberty,"[121] and the particular determinations of natural law contained in the judicial precepts ceased to bind directly, leaving such matters to human determination.[122] With the availability of grace to help discipline men in virtue, the moral precepts of the divine law remained in force, as "they are essential to virtue," being synonymous with the general principles of the natural law.[123] However, the particular determinations of the judicial precepts were "left to the decision of men."[124] We meet here again the point of demarcation between, on one hand, the natural law and the divine law and, on the other hand, human law, the species of law we will consider in chapter 6. Despite leaving particular determinations to human law, the moral precepts of the divine law were not removed but briefly given again by Christ. Thus, the withdrawal of direct divine determinations presupposed the continuation of the moral precepts of the divine law.

The abolition of the binding force of the judicial precepts did not occur because the precepts are inherently contrary to the moral precepts of natural law and reason, but rather because of the changed circumstances of human existence.[125] Unlike the ceremonial precepts, which are completely abolished by the New Law, the judicial precepts have merely been revoked as binding in and of themselves. But a human sovereign would not err by adopting any of them as particular determinations of natural law.[126] Unlike the ceremonial precepts, the judicial precepts were repealed because man was more capable of making determinations for himself, but they remain as valid possible determinations of the natural law. Aquinas does note that a sovereign would err if he prescribed the judicial precepts, because they were binding in and of themselves as part of the binding natural law. Yet he distinguishes this error from simply adopting a particular determination that happens to coincide with the older judicial precepts, which would not be an error.[127]

Before even reaching this topic of human law, we see how the divine law will be relevant to its jurisdiction. The divine law is a multijurisdictional law touching both the natural and supernatural ends of man. The natural jurisdiction of the divine law makes known those precepts of the natural law left for human law to determine. Thus, the information illuminated by this part of the divine law is epistemologically important for those attempting to determine human law. Human lawmakers who dismiss as irrelevant a source of necessary knowledge greatly increase the likelihood of making incorrect determinations based on inaccurate deductions of principle. Although the ends of man and laws relating to each end remain distinct, we see a significant public role for the Church in making laws concerning only the natural end of man. Like the divine law, the Church has a multifaceted existence. The Church's primary mission is to make known the supernatural end of man and the means to attaining that end. Yet beyond and connected to this end, the Church is also the guardian of the divine law, which is necessary to correct our failures in making false deductions of natural law principles. Refusal to seek such recourse leads to dire legal consequences. Leo XIII explained the consequences of such willful blindness:

> To exclude the Church, founded by God Himself, from life, from laws, from the education of youth, from domestic society is a grave and fatal error. A State from which religion is banished can never be well regulated; and already perhaps more than is desirable is known of the nature and tendency of the so-called civil philosophy of life and morals. The Church of Christ is the true and sole teacher of virtue and guardian of morals. She it is who preserves in their purity the principles from which duties flow, and, by setting forth most urgent reasons for virtuous life, bids us not only to turn away from wicked deeds, but even to curb all movements of the mind that are opposed to reason, even though they be not carried out in action.[128]

Put another way, the jurisdictions of civil government and the Church are distinct, just as the natural and supernatural ends of man are distinct, and as the divine and natural law are distinct. Yet they are not independent; they overlap. Both the government of the Church and of civil society take place under the natural and divine laws, and both are participations in the eternal law within their sphere. The Church and the civil authorities are meant to work together: the Church providing the certainty of knowledge with respect to the principles of natural and divine law, and the civil government applying them through particular human law.

The eminent English jurist John of Salisbury developed the image of the body politic to describe this relationship between the civil and ecclesiastical societies. The Church is the soul of the body politic, and civil society is the body. Just as the soul directs the specific actions of the body, so too the Church is meant to guide the direction of the body under its head, the governors.[129] Leo XIII invokes this image of John of Salisbury when he describes the harmonious relation of the Church and state:

The Almighty, therefore, has given the charge of the human race to two powers, the ecclesiastical and the civil, the one being set over divine, and the other over human, things. Each in its kind is supreme, each has fixed limits within which it is contained. . . . But, inasmuch as each of these two powers has authority over the same subjects . . . therefore God, who foresees all things, and who is the author of these two powers, has marked out the course of each in right correlation to the other. . . . There must, accordingly, exist between these two powers a certain orderly connection, which may be compared to the union of the soul and body in man.[130]

Thus, the civil and religious authorities are to be distinct in their operations, yet distinct does not mean wholly independent and unrelated. This nuanced distinction without separation is the opposite of the philosophy preached by Martin Luther: "Assuredly a prince can be a Christian, but it is not as a Christian that he should govern. As a ruler he is not called a Christian, but a prince. The man is Christian but his function does not concern his religion."[131] Rather than having the knowledge obtained through revelation informing the determinations of lawmakers, Luther advocates willful blindness by hiding this knowledge behind a wall of separation. The first "Catholic" president of the United States, John F. Kennedy, echoed this philosophy of separation when he merely paraphrased these words in his famous speech in Houston in 1960. He boldly proclaimed the utter separation of knowledge, declaring a belief "in an America where the separation of church and state is absolute," where no leader should be informed by the knowledge revealed in the divine law "on birth control, divorce, censorship, gambling or any other subject."[132] It is one thing to lack knowledge of the divine law, or even to refuse belief in its existence; it is quite another to profess belief in it and then dismiss its epistemological relevance.

In contrast to Martin Luther's and President Kennedy's vision of a human ruler of nations hiding behind his wall of epistemological sequestration, Aquinas describes a truly Christian—and therefore truly human—ruler: "It pertains to the king's office to promote the good life of the multitude . . . that is to say, he should command those things which lead to the happiness of Heaven and, as far as possible, forbid the contrary.

What conduces to true beatitude and what hinders it are learned from the law of God, the teaching of which belongs to the office of the priest."[133]

Divine law fulfills many functions for man: natural and supernatural. With respect to natural law, it serves as a clear measure to check errors of natural reason. The moral precepts of the divine law are like life rafts that can pull our rationality back from a drowning sea of errors. As we reach conclusions about principles of the natural law and particular determinations, we can compare them to the moral precepts of the divine law as a litmus test of their propriety. At a prior time in history, the divine law also provided direct aid in formulating particular determinations. More freedom in this regard is now granted to temporal and spiritual authority. Yet this freedom expects those authorities to access the instructions of the artificer in the moral precepts of the divine law.

THE ROLE OF RECOURSE TO THE ARCHITECT

This chapter has returned to consider natural law from a perspective that might be called optimistically pessimistic or idealistically realistic. The process of knowing and acting according to the details of the natural law is fraught with perils, congenital and self-inflicted. Over time, some remedies—taking wider counsel, equity, habit, and advice of the wise—have been partially successful. Man can become an artisan of the natural law, building more or less sound edifices of natural law principles. Yet, just as even the most proficient artisan can err by straying unguided from the overall architectural plan, so too these perfecting skills can only take our work so far. An artisan might build a soundly constructed barn only to find it resting on top of a septic field unable to support its weight. Even the artisan needs the guidance of the designing mind of the architect to guide his artistry. Aquinas evokes this very image of the dependence of the artisan on the architect in his discussion of law in the *Summa Contra Gentiles*:

> Since law is nothing but a rational plan of operation, and since the rational plan of any kind of work is derived from the end, anyone capable of receiving the law receives it from he who shows the way to the end. Thus does the lower artisan depend on the architect, and the soldier

on the leader of the army. But the rational creature attains his ultimate end in God, and from God, as we have seen in the foregoing. Therefore, it is appropriate for law to be given men by God.[134]

In this light, the divine law is not merely an exercise of divine will, but rather an assistance offered to man to illuminate the way to the end. Divine law is not opposed to natural law. Their contents, though not completely coextensive, are completely consistent. Yet the divine law is not redundant, but rather a necessary corrective. It does not correct the natural law, which needs no correction, but rather it corrects man's understanding of the natural law. Although speaking about the relationship between reason and faith generally, Pope Pius IX's comments apply equally to the relationship between divine and natural law, and to the relation of both of them to eternal law:

> Although faith is above reason, no real disagreement or opposition can ever be found between them; this is because both of them come from the same greatest source of unchanging and eternal truth, God. They give such reciprocal help to each other that true reason shows, maintains and protects the truth of faith, while faith frees reason from all errors and wondrously enlightens, strengthens and perfects reason with the knowledge of divine matters.[135]

Only in understanding the dead end of pure natural law reasoning, without the enlightenment, strength, and perfection brought by divine law, can one understand the obligatory nature of the divine law. It obligates not as an act of the will but as a necessary legal guide to human reason through the error-prone task of discovering and applying the natural law. Divine law thus perfects the participation in the eternal law. To ignore it is akin to an artisan, a plumber, performing his work without consulting the overall architectural plan. The kitchen sink might end up in the living room. From this perspective, some of the dissatisfaction with natural law theorizing over the past few centuries is an inevitable consequence of removing access to the mind of the architect by the lower artisans of the law.

In chapter 4, we noted that the "new" natural law of Finnis rejected nature as a source of natural law. His explanation likewise eliminates any need for the divine law, resulting in a jurisprudence dependent solely on reason. Germain Grisez, his partner in the "new" natural law project, agrees that our knowledge of the natural law depends on reason alone.[136] Even Michael Moore, who denies the existence of God, recognizes that if God were to exist and "if morality is God's will or thoughts, we need God to know morality, that is, what is on his mind."[137] Yet Finnis, who professes belief that God exists, dispenses with any real necessity for knowing what is in His mind. For the "old" natural lawyers, that is, the entire Christian tradition prior to the "new" natural law,[138] the *loci* of knowledge were three: nature, reason, and scripture.[139] Nature, reason, and scripture are "mutually interpreting sources of moral norms."[140] The three sources can mutually participate in this dialectical interpretation of norms because each derives from its own law: nature (eternal law), reason (natural law), and scripture (divine law). In the words of Aquinas, it was necessary that God promulgate the *lex scripturae* for us to find our way back to the natural law. For Finnis and Grisez, the scriptures may be useful but are not necessary. Thus, Finnis must pour forth hundreds of pages proving his indemonstrable goods; whereas Aquinas can allude to the core principles of natural law in a few lines. For Scholastics like Aquinas, "scripture provides . . . their account of the core normative content of the natural law."[141] The second section of this chapter argued that experience demonstrates the impossibility of attaining complete knowledge of the natural law through unaided reason. Porter has likewise concluded that any attempt to ground natural law in reason alone would be "fruitless."[142]

This conclusion adds a further dimension to one of the arguments I advanced in chapter 1, where I concluded that removing God and the eternal law from natural law "leaves the natural law drifting without a mooring where it cannot stand."[143] An examination of the necessity of divine law has demonstrated another reason for the futility of pursuing a natural law jurisprudence that excludes God and the divine law. Such an approach holds out the hope of establishing a legal regime rooted in practical reason, but where "ethical positions and their political applications are matter for open public debate, to be proposed and defended as defensible and acceptable without appeal to the authority of revelation or its author."[144] This approach not only removes the foundation, wherein lies the obligatory nature of all law, but also the necessary corrective instructions of the divine law. As we argued in the first section, above, natural law reasoning on its own is doomed to incomplete success in attaining justice. Legislating natural law without the "authority of revelation [divine law] or its author" is a recipe for an ultimate rejection of natural law. It is akin to hiring an artisan to build a structure without engaging an architect. Some level of success will eventually lead to collapse, calling into question the skill of the artisan.

Ever since Grotius speculated more than three centuries ago on natural law without God,[145] the cleavage between natural law jurisprudence and God has widened. Although insistence on the need for the supernatural in natural law jurisprudence is likely to alienate some from the concept altogether, the retention of parts of the audience by omitting, or reducing to an obscure minimum as does Finnis,[146] the role of eternal and divine law may prove short-lived. When the inevitable shortcomings of the artistry of natural law reasoning are manifest, the whole project may be abandoned as intractably flawed. Only by restoring the buttress of the instructions of the original architect may natural law jurisprudence remain standing.

SIX

Decorating the Structure

The Art of Making Human Law

All ordinances are either divine or human.
Divine ordinances are determined by nature, human ordinances by usages;
and thus the latter vary since different things please different people.[1]

In chapter 2, I described the eternal law as a foundation on which human law is built. The eternal law, which is God's providential ordering of the universe, establishes the natures of things and thereby determines their ends. Aquinas uses the two concepts of *exemplar* and *type* to describe the eternal law. These concepts are helpful in understanding how the eternal law moves particular creatures—humans—to their end. Since man is distinguished by a faculty for reason, it is this very rationality that is decreed as the method of achieving his end. Thus, the eternal law does not specify the means of attaining this end with particularity, but rather, like an *exemplar* in the field of art, it guides toward that end while leaving scope for detailed variations. On the basis of this *exemplar*, human reason deduces a framework of general principles of action, or precepts of the natural law, and thereby participates in the eternal law. Yet, as I examined in chapter 5, man's capacity to deduce and specify these precepts correctly has been seriously distorted, so much so that Aquinas claimed the natural law had been destroyed in us. To assist in overcoming this infirmity, God promulgated a new law, the *lex scripturae*, or the revealed divine law. The divine law contains general principles of action that are part of the natural law in order to present a more reliable guide than unaided human reason in deducing and specifying the principles of the natural law.

Having explored the foundation and framework for making particular law, it is now possible to turn to that law first in our order of knowledge—but last in the order of being—human positive law. The first section of this chapter, "Adorning the Structure with Human Laws," describes the nature and purpose of, and process for formulating, human law. Notwithstanding having argued strongly in prior chapters that natural law is an indispensable form of law that must undergird all human laws for them to be truly law, one might expect this chapter to argue for the simple proposition that law is merely whatever the natural law establishes. Yet, as the first section demonstrates, the relationship between natural law and human law is more complex. The general precepts of natural law are in need of specific determination through a complex dialectical process involving the general principles of natural law, historically developing communal customs, and statutory enactments. The second section, "Application to Particular Issues in Human Lawmaking," applies the analysis from the first section to two specific questions confronting the process of human lawmaking: (1) What are the benefits and shortcomings of a common law (or "case law") tradition versus the civil law (or "code") tradition?; and (2) What is the problem of the significant proliferation and complexity of modern legislation?

ADORNING THE STRUCTURE WITH HUMAN LAWS

How Human Lawmaking Fits into the Structure

Having examined the foundation (eternal law), the framing structure (natural law), and the on-site instructions of the architect (divine law), a survey of law can finally turn to the detailed completion of the edifice accomplished by what Jean Porter, relying on Scholastic precedent, calls the "ministers of the law."[2] In the architectural analogy, these "ministers" can be viewed as the skilled "craftsmen" of the law. They particularize the details of natural law's general precepts, reinforced by divine law, which arise out of the foundation of eternal law.[3] To reach this level of specificity, a long road of analysis has been necessary. This is natural, since unlike for the legal positivist, human law is not the alpha and omega of the field of law. As the prior chapters have demonstrated, human law has a limited, albeit significant, role in the grand edifice of law—but is only one part of a vast system of law—eternal, natural, and divine—that is interrelated and interdependent.[4] I have already argued that the purpose of human lawmaking is the specification of natural law's principles, which is accomplished by formulating specific determinations of those principles when they affect the common good. As I will argue in this section, this understanding already places a significant qualification on the process of human lawmaking. Human laws are dependent upon the natural law because the very reason for the existence of human law is to make particular determinations of the principles of this higher law.[5] Human law cannot exist as such without the natural law. Returning to the architectural analogy, one cannot paint a fresco until a wall has been erected on a foundation; crown molding cannot be installed until the walls have been erected. Likewise, human law cannot be properly made outside the foundation and framework of eternal and natural law.

Yet, in a certain sense, natural law cannot exist without human law because natural law needs to be made particular, to be specified. As Porter has observed, natural law is not a self-executing legal code that merely needs enforcement.[6] Rather, its general principles require further specification.[7] An architectural plan might call for a fresco of the Last Supper, but the fresco does not exist until an actual fresco is painted by an artist. The natural law contains general principles to guide human action: do good, preserve life, and so forth. As Aquinas explains, the content of natural law "has to be determined by Divine or human law, because naturally known principles are universal, both in speculative and in practical matters. Accordingly, just as the determination of the universal principle about Divine worship is effected by the ceremonial precepts, so the determination of the general precepts of that justice which is to be observed among men is effected by the judicial precepts."[8]

Aquinas's example is helpful to understand this need for additional law beyond natural law. We can know from the use of our reason that if the world has been created by a being, then that being deserves in justice to be adored as the source of our existence. Yet, such knowledge, although making known the obligation, does not explain to us specifically how we should perform this act of justice toward our Creator. God therefore revealed particular determinations of this general and universal principle.[9] Likewise, natural law obligates men to act justly. As with the ceremonial precepts, judicial precepts are needed to specify how to live justly.

Prior to the coming of Christ, because of the absence of the fullness of grace, man needed more assistance in these determinations. Again, Aquinas's discussion of the relationship between habituation or training, and the ability to reach correct conclusions or determinations, is necessary to understand this distinction.[10] In the time of the Old Law, men were not yet "possessed of a virtuous habit" and thus needed direct divine determination of more particular laws.[11] Thus, in addition to promulgating certain principles of the natural law as moral precepts of divine law, God also revealed specific determinations of those general precepts in the judicial precepts of the divine law.[12] Although human lawmakers existed, much lawmaking was done directly by God by revealing particular determinations of the natural law, such as rules regarding the forgiveness of debts,[13] the time of payment of wages to laborers,[14] the particular punishments for crimes, and measures of damages for deliberate or negligent harms caused to others.[15] After the advent of grace—which Aquinas calls "an interior *habit* bestowed on us and inclining us to act aright"[16]—men could be "endowed with virtuous habits," and thus were no longer in such need of divine determinations as in the judicial precepts.[17] Once the human mind was capable of receiving the aid of an additional habit or training through the availability of the fullness of grace, the new divine law became a "law of liberty,"[18] and the particular determinations of natural law contained in the judicial precepts ceased to bind directly.[19] With the availability of this grace to help discipline men in virtue, the moral precepts of the divine law remained in force because "they are of themselves essential to virtue," being synonymous with the general principles of the natural law.[20] However, the particular determinations of the judicial precepts were "left to the decision of [men]."[21] Put another way, once the habit of grace was made available, God could readjust the responsibilities for particular law-making, leaving more to the discretion of human agents.

These particular determinations are made within what Russell Hittinger calls three orders of prudence: the individual, the familial, and the regnative.[22] Some of these necessary determinations are left to individuals to decide for themselves.[23] Others are determined for individuals by their personal superiors,[24] such as parents for children, and those determinations that affect the common good[25] are left "to the discretion of those who were to have spiritual or temporal charge of others."[26] This same threefold division traditionally divided the study of moral philosophy into (1) "monastics," or ethics—the study of the relation of individual acts of man to his end; (2) morality of the family, or economics—the study of the operations of domestic society; and (3) political philosophy, or morality of civil society—the study of the operations of civil society.[27] With the coming of the fullness of grace, which made the perfection of reason possible, God allowed more freedom in the determination of particular acts and withdrew the specific judicial precepts of the Old Law that ruled this third order, civil society, thereby entrusting the formulation of particular determinations related to civil society to laws made by humans rather than to divine law.[28] It is in making these particular determinations of natural law that human beings participate in the eternal law or, put another way, participate in God's providential lawmaking for the universe.

Just as Aquinas's consideration of the eternal law highlighted both God's rationality and volition,[29] human lawmaking employs both aspects of human nature. As we have seen, human law is dependent upon natural law, or the rational participation of man in the eternal law. Human laws are the "particular determinations, devised by human reason" from the precepts of the natural law.[30] Thus, the process of making human law must employ the use of right reason. The matter used by human reason in the process is the "singular and contingent,"[31] "individual cases" presented by actual circumstances of human existence.[32] Gratian's *Decretum* also recognizes the connection between reason and human law.[33] He includes a text explaining that "reason . . . supports [human laws]" (*legem ratio commendat*) and ordinances "[will be] determined by reason," and therefore ordinances are "all that reason has already confirmed" (*lex erit omne iam quod ratione constiterit*).[34]

Yet, the relationship of human law to reason also involves a relation to eternal law. Aquinas notes that eternal law, as the complete ordering of the universe, contains within it "each single truth," including "the particular determinations of individual cases."[35] This phrase easily can be misunderstood to mean that all particular human laws have already been formulated in the eternal law, and human law must merely discover and conform to them. This conclusion would be similar to Ronald Dworkin's argument that there are "right answers" to all legal questions.[36] Such a conclusion is an oversimplification of the concept of the eternal law and human participation in it. To draw the distinction, it is important to examine this statement in context:

> The human reason cannot have a full participation of the dictate of the Divine Reason, but according to its own mode, and imperfectly. Consequently, as on the part of the speculative reason, by a natural participation of Divine Wisdom, there is in us the knowledge of certain general principles, but not proper knowledge of each single truth, such as that contained in the Divine Wisdom; so too, on the part of the practical reason, man has a natural participation of the eternal law, according to certain general principles, but not as regards the particular determinations of individual cases, which are, however, contained in the eternal law. Hence the need for human reason to proceed further to sanction them by law.[37]

The phrases "divine reason" and "divine wisdom" preceding the reference to eternal law recall the connection between the knowledge of God and the eternal law that is critical for Aquinas.[38] The eternal law establishes the nature of things and the ends to which those things are directed. Yet, these general principles also contain within them the particular actions determined by those ends, just as a conclusion is said to be contained in the premises.[39] Yet, God has in the case of humans permitted the participation of human reason in the formation of those particular determinations. The particular shape these determinations will take is dependent both upon the type, or *exemplar*, of eternal law, and instrumentally on the practical reason of human beings participating in making particular determinations of the general principles. Human lawmaking is a participation in the eternal law in the sense that human laws are meant to be derived from the general principles of eternal law made known through natural law and the natural inclinations.[40]

To the extent these particular determinations are reasonable determinations in harmony with the established ends, they are contained within eternal law in two different ways. First, they are contained in the general principles, just as a particular work of art following a style is contained in the *exemplar* of that style.[41] Likewise, more than one conclusion can be contained in a major premise depending upon the contingent minor premise selected.[42] Taking the major premise that "A human being is a rational animal," we can show that both of the conclusions—"John Smith is a rational animal" and "Mary Jones is a rational animal"—are contained in the major premise. This is because both minor premises—"John Smith is a human being" and "Mary Jones is a human being"—can be paired with this major premise. Although both conclusions are contained in the major premise, the particular conclusion to a given syllogism is contingent upon the selection of the minor premise.[43]

Second, divine wisdom, knowing all things, knows the particular determinations that will in fact be made instrumentally by the human laws.[44] This foreknowledge, however, is denied to man so that he may participate in the lawmaking process by using his reason and not divine revelation to make those determinations.[45] It is this element of participation in lawmaking that distinguishes the process of lawmaking from a mechanical discovery of particular human laws that already exist, which need merely be made known by the promulgation of human laws. If this were all that occurred, human laws would only participate in one aspect of lawmaking—promulgation. By contrast, the rules governing the operation of nonrational creatures already exist in particular determinations. For example, dropping something causes it to fall by virtue of gravity. Man does not participate in formulating this law in the same way he does with respect to laws of human action.[46] He merely discovers its operation and attempts to understand its causes. As to laws governing human actions, man is charged with the task of not only discovering but also determining the rule's details according to the general principles implanted in man's reason through the natural law.[47] At the same time that God permits this active participation, the divine wisdom already knows the determination that will be made.

Yet, this participation in lawmaking God has granted is not a "full participation of the dictate of the divine reason," but only "a natural participation of divine wisdom [source of eternal law]" consisting of "a natural participation of the eternal law, according to certain general principles."[48] Thus, we can know that there exist objectively true determinations of individual cases, contained within the divine wisdom or eternal law, but our knowledge of these singular truths is not "natural." Unlike the general principles of the natural law that are "impressed on it [our reason] by nature"[49] or "imparted to us by nature,"[50] the particular determinations are arrived at by the "efforts of reason" (*industriam rationis*).[51] Making these particular determinations involves work or industry. It is not something that we know like a proposition *per se nota*, which once explained is easily grasped by the mind.[52] This difficulty of making determinations in individual cases further explains the need for human laws. Because making these particular determinations is hard work for each individual accompanied by a significant risk of error, and hence confusion,[53] there is a need for human law to "sanction" particular determinations.[54] Not all of these sanctioned determinations will be perfectly contained within the eternal law, in the sense of being perfect determinations, even though they are contained in the sense of being foreknown by God. The error is not an error in God but rather in the weakness of human reason. It is not an error in God but rather tolerated by Him as a consequence of permitting human, fallible participation in the lawmaking process for human action.[55]

Understanding the imperfect nature of man's participation helps to explain why Aquinas argued for the limited jurisdiction of lawmaking by constituted authorities.[56] Not all rules of human action are to be determined by legal authorities. Some are left to individuals and others to personal superiors. What marks the jurisdictional boundary of the determinations to be made by communal, as opposed to personal, superiors? The answer is contained in our discussion in chapter 1: the answer is those determinations touching upon the "common good." The definition of law according to Aquinas includes a dictate of reason oriented to the common good.[57] A text from Isidore contained in the *Decretum* exemplifies this limitation on human law. He says: "Furthermore, if ordinance is determined by reason, then ordinance will be all that reason has already confirmed— all, at least, that is congruent with religion, consistent with discipline, and helpful for salvation."[58] Notice, human law (ordinance) is not all that reason has confirmed but that which is related to a phrase that summarizes the supernatural and natural common good of man: religion, discipline, and salvation. Aquinas uses another phrase to encapsulate the common good sought by human law: peace within the community and attainment of individual habits of virtue of its members.[59] Thus, human laws should not determine all actions, but only those related to the common good.

Why is the sanction of human law better than each deciding for himself between all the individual choices of action presented in life? The answer to this question depends on the volitional aspect of lawmaking. In addition to being consistent with reason, status as a law requires that a volitional choice of the will be made and promulgated.[60] An act of the will is necessary because the common good requires it. Decisions affecting the common good should not be left to individual choice because, as they involve contingent matters, there may be more than one reasonable way of determining them.[61] Reason may not be enough to determine the precise choice, because reason may provide for a number of reasonable alternatives. Hence each individual would be a law unto himself, with the result that the order of civil society would be harmed or destroyed. Civil society is a heterogeneous organism that attains only a unity of order. This fact means that members of society have individual ends that they pursue that require coordination to the heterogeneous society's common end.[62] Such coordination requires that choices be made by an authority and followed by the members, so as to preserve the unity of order that is necessary to attain the common good.[63]

An example will aid in understanding this argument. Natural law contains the precept to preserve human life.[64] In the course of pursuing their individual end, people operate vehicles capable of killing innocent human beings. Easily we can conclude the principle that cars should be driven in a safe and orderly manner so as to avoid killing innocent people. A more particular conclusion flowing from this general conclusion is that cars traveling in the same direction should travel on the same side of the road so as not to collide with those traveling in the opposite direction. All of these deductions can be reached by merely applying rules of practical reason. Yet, the final conclusion still does not tell the driver on which side to drive when going north on a particular road. Should it be the right side or the left side? The principle permits either; there is no inherently more reasonable side to choose. We thus reach a point where humans must make a volitional choice between two reasonable determinations. A choice must be made to preserve that aspect of the common good called orderly safety; it must not be determined by individual drivers, because each would be capable of rationally determining different sides from one another. Hence, a volitional act of an authority must bring a unity of order to the individual ends pursued by drivers by definitively choosing right or left for the community. This example demonstrates a case for necessitating the formation of a law, in the proper sense of the term, in contrast to individual determination. The common good requires a legal determination of the natural law principle by the authority with interests in the care of the community. Once selected, driving on the side not selected by the legal authority now would violate the natural law precept to preserve life.

One of Porter's greatest contributions to contemporary natural law theory has been to reemphasize the underdetermination of natural law, the principles of which allow for a variety of specific contingent determinations.[65] Given the contingency of practical matters to which precepts of natural law are applied, the precepts do not automatically determine a particular choice, such as the left or right side of the road. There is a realm of choice reserved for an authority with care of the community. Even though natural law precepts foreclose some choices, such as a law requiring people to drive into oncoming traffic, they leave choices, often broader than the binary one in the traffic law example, to be made by authorities as a participation in the eternal law.[66]

This underdetermination by natural law does not mean that natural law and human law's determinations of it lack the quality of truth. As Aquinas explains, the correspondence constituting truth differs for speculative and practical matters.[67] For speculative matters this correspondence is "conformity between the intellect and the thing."[68] For practical matters it is the "conformity with right appetite."[69] The difference is that speculative knowledge is oriented to necessary things, whereas practical matters are oriented to contingent things, choices of action that could be other than they are.[70] The end of actions, or the goods to be obtained, are determined by nature and thus cannot be chosen to be good but only willed or desired as such.[71] The means to attain these goods or ends, however, can be the ob-

ject of a real human choice because they are contingent.[72] The choice of
the right side could have been the left side (and in fact is in other countries than the United States). But it is still a true choice. The choice corresponds to a right appetite, the willing of a contingency that truly conforms
to a good—safe travel on the roads. Since necessary things cannot be but
what they are, there can only be one true speculative judgment—for example, this particular shape is a circle. Yet, because human actions as means
are contingent—different choices can all correspond to a right appetite for
the good—there can be more than one true practical judgment.[73] Either
the right or the left side could be a true judgment because either can correspond to willing the good of orderly and safe driving. These practical
judgments are choices of intermediate—as opposed to ultimate—ends, or
a choice of means, so this conclusion is consistent with the reality that there
may be more than one means to the same end.[74] If the judgment to be
made were whether travel should be safe or unnecessarily dangerous, this
would be a speculative judgment with only one possible answer, safe.

　　This traffic law example also demonstrates why some particular determinations or choices of means must be made by human law rather
than left to individual determination. Those individual acts whose nature
require coordination to the common good need to be determined by individuals having "spiritual or temporal charge of others."[75] Everyone
choosing for themselves would create dangerous chaos. Yet, the requirement for a communal determination in some circumstances does not
mandate that all choices should be determined by one in a superior position in our community.

　　On the other side of the coin are the actions proximately tied to the
personal good but remote to the common good.[76] As a result of the remoteness to the common good, these choices are left to private individuals. Human law may justly regulate the manner in which these individual
choices are lived out in the community and affect the common good, but
the choice itself is left to the individual.[77] For example, an individual's
choice of profession or career is one primarily oriented to his personal
good. Natural law principles will provide the boundaries for this choice
by, for example, foreclosing the choice of being a professional mass murderer. Yet, the particular determination within the range permitted by
natural law is rightly left to individual determination. Prior to making this

determination and to prepare for it, some education must be provided. This decision about education affects more directly the individual good of the person and should be made by his personal superior, such as his parent, who is charged with making determinations affecting his personal good on his behalf. Yet, once the choice of career is made, the legal authority in a community may have promulgated laws regarding the way this choice is lived out in the community. For example, a civil authority may determine the level of knowledge and skill that must be demonstrated before someone choosing to be a doctor can begin treating other members of the community. The choice of individual profession is an individual determination; the determination of licensing for publicly carrying out that profession is rightly reserved to the authority caring for the community.

Marriage presents another example. The law would wrongly exercise authority to determine that an individual must marry or must marry a particular person. Yet, the requirements of form to enter into a legal marriage, once chosen, and the public consequences of that choice in terms of property, for example, are determinations properly to be made in conformity to the precepts of natural law by those having "spiritual or temporal charge of others."[78]

As a natural law thinker, Aquinas is admittedly idealistic (he argues for the existence of an objective truth in practical matters), but he balances this idealism with a healthy practicality.[79] Truth is the correspondence of a chosen means to a truly desirable good. Multiple choices of means may all correspond truly with a given objective, which allows for a variety of legal systems making different, but all true, choices. A worldwide harmonized legal system is not necessary for law to be true. Further, even the wise can err, and we need not be scandalized by this fact. In reality, no legal system will always be perfect. In other words, each particular determination of a given legal system may not be a correct correspondence to the proper ends under every circumstance. It is sufficient for human societal well-being that the wise get particular determinations as correct as is possible given their abilities. Some error in the system is inevitable and does not undermine the legitimacy of the entire system. Ultimately, although God has withdrawn from direct legislation for man after the promulgation of the New Law, He nevertheless wills the temporal and spiritual leaders, who may not in fact even be wise, to do their best in reaching particular determinations.

Human lawmaking thus involves an act of both the intellect and the will.[80] Human laws must conform to the divine wisdom of eternal law as known through the principles of natural and divine law. The natural law does put constraints on the content of human law. As Porter observes: "The canonists and theologians do consider the natural law to have direct moral and social implications, even in human society as it now exists. It is true that for them, as well as for the civilians, the natural law must be expressed through human conventions in order to have practical force in the present historical order. Nonetheless, they also believe that the natural law places definite moral constraints on the legitimate forms of institutional life."[81] Even within these constraints and under certain circumstances, the principles of natural law permit real human choices, some of which must be made for a community. The following subsection will address these determinations more closely and consider their source and the process that produces the choice of the will in light of principles of reason.

The Processes and Sources of Human Lawmaking

The prior subsection explored the nature and purpose of human law as the process of rationally making particular determinations of natural law's general precepts, which are necessary to promote the common good. For Gratian and Aquinas, the natural law must serve as the framework onto which particular human laws are added. Gratian expresses this dependence by explaining that human laws are constituted by, confirmed by, or stand with reason.[82] Aquinas explains the relation: "Every human law has just so much of the nature of law, as it is derived from the law of nature."[83] In other words, human law's character as law is a product of its derivation from natural law. This subsection will examine the dialectical process of working out this derivation. The process involves two stages of intellectual activity. First, there are human laws that belong to the "law of nations" (*jus gentium*) and, second, those that belong to the "civil law" of a particular people (*jus civile*).[84]

The first set of human laws contains "those things that are derived from the law of nature, as conclusions from premises."[85] These are general principles of law deduced directly from the speculative knowledge of the end of man. They have become general principles underlying various legal systems, operating in the absence of the legal system's particular

determination. Aquinas provides as an example the conclusion that buying and selling should be on just terms, because just commercial activity,
"without which men [could not] live together," is necessary as man must
live together as "a social animal."[86] Thus the general law of nations contains a principle that exchange transactions should be just. The civil law of
a particular community, on the other hand, contains more particular laws
"that are derived from the law of nature by way of particular determination."[87] These laws are particular determinations of what constitutes just
exchange, such as the particular scope of factual misrepresentation that
will render an exchange transaction unjust and unenforceable by a particular community's court system.[88]

Aquinas also proffers an example of the relationship between *jus gentium* and *jus civile.* The *jus gentium* contains a conclusion that "evildoer[s]
should be punished."[89] In contrast, the *jus civile* contains a law requiring
that an evildoer "be punished in this or that way."[90] Roman law provides
an example illustrating the use of the *jus gentium.* The particular law of
Rome (the *jus civile*) was not applicable to non-Romans.[91] Yet as Rome's
power spread beyond its original territory, disputes arose involving non-
Roman citizens. In 247 B.C., the position of a second praetor, "praetor
peregrinus," was created to decide cases involving non-Romans by applying not the *jus civile* but the principles of the *jus gentium* to reach judgment.[92] Since the *jus civile* was inapplicable, this praetor used the universal
principles of the *jus gentium* to render particular judgments.[93] With this
distinction between *jus gentium* and *jus civile* in mind, we can now turn
our attention to the process by which human law moves from the general
precepts of the natural law, to the universal principles of the *jus gentium,*
and then to the particular determinations of various legal systems.

Cicero is one of the earliest authors to describe this process of trans-
lating principles of natural law into laws of particular peoples.[94] He summarizes the process thus:

> Justice is a habit [*habitus*] of the mind that attributes its proper dig-
> nity to everything, preserving a due regard to the general welfare.
> Its first principles proceed from nature [*ab natura*]. Afterwards cer-
> tain things come into common usage [*in consuetudinem*] due to the
> reasonableness of their utility; afterwards, the fear of both the laws

[*legum*] and religion sanctioned these things [e.g., the things that have been adopted as part of common usages], both having been established by nature [*ab natura*] and having been approved by common usage [*ab consuetudine*]. . . .

Law by common usages [*consuetudine jus*[95]] is that which (1) having been drawn out of nature quietly, use [*usus*] has nourished and made great, like religion; (2) if we see preserved any of those things that we have already spoken of as having been produced by nature and made stronger by common usage [*consuetudine*], or (3) that which antiquity has carried through into custom [*morem*] by the approval of the common people: such as a covenant that has been made, fairness, and cases that have already been decided. A covenant is that which is agreed upon between some people; fairness is that which is equitable in all cases; a case previously decided concerns that which is already decreed by the opinions of some person or persons. Law by statute [*lege ius*[96]] is contained in that which is in writing, which is made known to the people in order that it might be observed.[97]

There are several key concepts contained in this passage: justice (*justitia*), nature (*natura*), usages (*consuetudine* or *usus*), custom (*mos*), and law (*jus*), which can be caused by common usages (*consuetudine*) or by written ordinances (*lege*). The beginning of human law (*jus*) is justice.[98] Justice has its origin in nature. Eventually this natural justice is formulated into law, either in the form of law by customs (law by usages) or written statutes (law by written laws).[99] Yet, Cicero's explanation of the process helps to disabuse us of a notion that has dominated natural law jurisprudence since the Enlightenment. When it is said that these principles are deduced from nature, this phrase conjures images of a thinker—such as René Descartes—interacting directly with abstract principles and closed within the confines of his mind, where he abstractly deduces more abstract principles. Yet, Cicero describes a more concrete process. Certain common practices develop naturally because they appear useful.[100] These constitute the *jus gentium*—general principles of justice in common usage. Over the course of time, some particularities of these principles enter into the customs of a people, and eventually these practices become sanctioned or confirmed by long-standing and constant use.[101] Some of these long-standing practices receive formal sanction by religion or the law—recall Aquinas's reference to spiritual or temporal authorities in his discussion of the greater freedom left for determinations by them under divine law following the redemption.

Not all practices or usages become part of the law, but only those that are carried through time by long-standing antiquity or are confirmed by written statutes. Significantly, Cicero mentions no particular person engaging in abstract deductions. These practices are drawn out of nature quietly or softly (*leviter*). Thus, more particular principles of natural law and their particular determinations within a commonwealth are deduced, not scientifically by an abstract thinker, but collectively over the course of time by the practices of a people and the evaluation of those practices by religious and legal authorities, periodically lending sanction to them.[102] In many ways, this reading of Cicero corresponds to Porter's understanding of how we interact with the natural law. She explains that natural law principles are always mediated through a particular culture.[103] The general propositions are not encountered in the abstract but through their particular instantiation in a legal culture.[104] For medieval lawgivers, she explains, "Adjudication and even legislation presupposed a basis of generally accepted norms and practices . . . to provide starting points and substance for new law."[105] This does not mean that philosophers and jurists did not formulate and articulate abstract principles of the natural law and deductively reason from them. Yet, those abstract principles are first encountered not in the abstract, but through some particular legal culture or cultures.[106] As Porter explains, "A natural law analysis is directed towards identifying the natural purposes served by a conventional practice or institution, with the aim . . . of rendering this practice intelligible as one aspect of the 'unified set of goal-ordered capacities' that jointly inform human existence."[107]

Cicero would certainly agree with her characterization. He contrasts the discussion of the best legal regime in his *De Republica* to the more abstract discussion in Plato's *Republic*.[108] For this Roman philosopher, the best method of discussing the philosophy of the commonwealth is by examining its actual instantiation in the history of the Roman Republic rather than a theoretical construct of pure rationality, as in Plato's *Republic*.[109] As Laelius observes during the discussion of Roman history:

We see that you have introduced a new kind of analysis, something to be found nowhere in the writings of the Greeks. . . . All the others wrote about the types and principles of states without any specific model or form of commonwealth. You seem to me to be doing both: from the outset, you have preferred to attribute your own discoveries to others [e.g., Romulus and the other critical figures in the history of Rome] rather than inventing it all yourself in the manner of Plato's Socrates.[110]

This contrast in methodology is useful in understanding the relationship between the general, rational principles of natural law and actual human laws. Rather than conceiving the transition from natural law to human law as a purely descending deductive process—starting with the first principle of natural law from which general principles are deduced, from which more specific principles are deduced and following which particular legal determinations are made—the process is more fluid.[111] Over the course of time, practices and usages come into being to usefully address natural inclinations, some of which, being reasonable, stand the test of time and become common. From these practices, the inclinations[112] underlying them can be discerned, and principles from them can be articulated. Once formulated, these principles can be used to normatively evaluate the same practices and customs to determine if they should be strengthened and carried through time by acquiring legal sanction. Such an inductive or deductive process of reasoning involving both speculative and practical knowledge is similar to the methodology for moral reasoning employed by Aquinas, as described by Maria Carl.[113] The result is a dialectical process running from the particular instantiation of a practice up to general principles induced from it, and running back down to the particular practices to evaluate them. This model of lawmaking also resembles Moore's functionalist jurisprudence. Moore argues that since law is a functional kind, we come to know law by starting with a hypothesis about law's goal, which must then be tested by examining its structural components so as finally to come to know law's goal.[114]

Such a process also correlates to MacIntyre's important contribution to modern Thomistic Aristotelianism, which emphasizes the same need for particular contexts in which to understand universal principles.[115]

Thaddeus Kozinski succinctly explains MacIntyre's concept of tradition-constituted rationality: "MacIntyre insists that it is only through active participation in particular authentic traditions that men are rendered capable of discovering and achieving their ultimate good; for, it is only through a *particular* tradition that we can properly apprehend *universal* truth."[116] MacIntyre explains that for the Aristotelian or Thomistic tradition, ethics or moral reasoning involves a dialectic process involving three points of reference: (1) man-as-he-happens-to-be, which can be reflected in customs; (2) the precepts of the natural law; and (3) man-as-he-could-be-if-he-realized-his-essential-nature.[117]

We can translate MacIntyre's epistemological claim into the language of our current discussion. The universal principles of the natural law can only be discovered and explored through a particular community's determinations of human law, its tradition. The universal and particular are both part of the process.

We can use the practice of enforcing a contract (*pactum*), mentioned by Cicero, as an example of this process.[118] Over time a community requires the fulfillment of certain promises, called "contracts" in the U.S. legal tradition.[119] By examining this practice we can conclude that the peace and efficiency of human society depend to some extent upon the practice of enforcing certain promises. This requirement can be seen as an inclination related to man's social nature. To live in society and work on projects jointly, people need to depend upon—be justified in relying on—the commitments of others. It is therefore unjust to break a pact. Yet, we can observe that the practice does not universally enforce all promises. For example, in the U.S. legal tradition, promises made under duress,[120] promises made for no legal consideration,[121] promises made pursuant to a mistake,[122] or promises whose enforcement would be unconscionable[123] may not be enforced. We can determine if a particular promise should be enforced according to the common practice by comparing the particular promise that someone seeks to enforce to contracts that long-standing practice has enforced, all in light of the general principles related to man's social nature as discerned by examining this practice.

Lawyers, philosophers, and theologians in the natural law tradition took the institution of private property as another example of this dialectical relationship between societal conventions and natural law principles.[124] The legal forms for the creation, transfer, and inheritance of property are developed through communal customs. Yet, these forms are constrained by natural law principles, such as the Decalogue precept prohibiting theft.[125]

Roman law provides another example of this important relationship between natural law and the customs of particular communities. By declining to apply the law of the city of Rome, the *jus civile*, to non-Roman citizens,[126] the praetor peregrinus acknowledged that the Roman particular customary instantiation of natural law was not applicable to other peoples not part of that tradition. In the absence of the applicable particular *jus civile*, the praetor peregrinus had to abstract from common usages the principles of *jus gentium* to decide cases.[127] This law of nations appears to function as a type of law that resides between natural law and the human laws of a particular people. It resembles natural law precepts in that its rules are general; it resembles the particular law of a nation in that its principles are derived from the study of common practices of all nations.[128] Justinian's *Institutes* define it thus: "The law that natural reason has established among all mankind and that is equally observed among all peoples is called the Law of Nations, as being that which all nations make use of."[129]

The *jus gentium* appears similar to natural law because it is established by natural reason. Yet, it includes more than general abstract principles; these principles have been in fact observed by different nations in their formulation and administration of their law. In a certain sense, the *jus gentium* looks to a broader definition of customs than the application of a particular people's law. It looks to the entire human race to discern common principles across legal systems, which in varying contexts have been derived by the use of reason from the principles of the natural law.[130] And so, as the praetor peregrinus decided cases under the *jus gentium*, common usages and practices started to develop. The *jus gentium* is thus gradually determined into a new communal set of practices: the *jus gentium* as applied to non-Roman citizens. Unlike natural law, which remains at the level of more or less general principles, within the system of Roman law the *jus gentium* becomes a new communal tradition, a body of more particular rules developed over time through particular case decisions. For present purposes, the creation of the praetor peregrinus and the development of a distinct category of Roman positive law applicable to non-Romans based on the *jus gentium* demonstrate that the particularity of communal customary practices was critical to the development of law by Roman jurists. Abstract principles were insufficient; concrete customary practices needed to be examined. It would be inappropriate to apply Roman customary law to non-Romans, and thus a broader examination of human custom was necessary, leading to the development of a more particular legal tradition based on the natural law principles reflected in the *jus gentium.*

Within both the *jus civile* and the *jus gentium* not all practices become part of the law, as Cicero himself observed.[131] The process involves both historical repetition and particular rational evaluation. Cicero's definition of justice (near the beginning of this subsection) contains another concept that can help us understand better how certain long-standing practices become part of the law. Justice is defined as a habit.[132] A habit consists of a repetition of certain actions that become part of our nature.[133] Aristotle explains that virtue is instilled by good habits—the repetition of virtuous acts.[134] As the virtue of justice is instilled in an individual by the habitual performance of virtuous acts, so too communities acquire the virtue of justice—the object of law (*jus*)—by long-standing customs, which become virtuous customs.[135]

Aquinas explains that in Greek and Latin the words "ethics" and "morality" (the study of human actions) are related to the word for customs.[136] Just as an individual develops virtues by repeated human actions or habits, likewise the community develops its law by repeated human actions or customs.[137] If the customs are good, law of the community will attain its end, which is justice. Similarly, a person possessing good habits will attain his end, which is virtue.[138] But habits can be good or bad, and bad habits produce vices, not virtues.[139] Not all habits are good, and individuals must rationally review their habitual actions to root out bad habits and instill good ones. Aristotle and Aquinas analogize to the arts and explain that this is why builders need a teacher to guide them to build well or else they will become bad builders through the habit of building poorly.[140] Just as those learning the art of building need a teacher to guide the development of their habit, the community needs an authority to guide the development of usages. This analogy will assist in understanding the relationship between the two means of making law discussed by Cicero—law by usages and law by statute (*consuetudine jus* and *lege jus*).

To understand this relationship between communal usages and written statutes, we turn to Gratian. He begins his treatise on canon law by emphasizing that human actions are governed both by laws made by God and laws made by humans.[141] The laws made by God include the natural law.[142] Gratian defines the laws made by humans as the long-standing customs (*mores*) "drawn up in writing and passed on as law."[143] He offers a somewhat confusing definition of custom (*mos*): *Mos est longa consuetudo, de moribus tantummodo tracta.*[144] This definition can be rendered: "Long-standing custom (*mos*) is long usage (*consuetudo*) simply handed on from customs (*moribus*)."[145] The gloss identifies the confusing nature of this definition in that the word *mos* appears in the definition of itself.[146] The gloss resolves this ambiguity by suggesting three distinct meanings for the related words used in the text of D.1, C.4: *mos* (which I translated as the concept of custom and the term being defined here), *consuetudo* (which I translated as usage), and *moribus* (which I translated as individual customs). Custom (*mos*) is the term used for unwritten law (*iure non scripta*).[147] Usage (*consuetudo*) is used for human-made "law [*iure*] whether written or unwritten."[148] Customs (*moribus*) means "frequently performed human actions."[149] Thus according to the Ordinary Gloss, the concept of custom (*mos*) as unwritten human law (as opposed to written laws, or *leges*) is the body of long-standing usage (*consuetudo)* that has been assembled out of some customs—in the sense of frequently repeated actions. Thus, not all *moribus*, or frequently performed human actions, become usage (*consuetudo*). Those that do are either incorporated into written laws (*leges*) or unwritten custom (*mos*). Once a certain common practice moves from mere repeated actions to law, it can either take the form of a written statutory law or an unwritten customary law.[150] Before examining the relationship between written and unwritten law, we will first consider how the multitude of customs are sifted so as to become, or remain, part of human customary law (*consuetudo*).

Pope Nicholas declared that evil usage (*consuetudo*) must be "torn up by its roots."[151] Those vested with care of the common good, those possessing legal authority, are to tear up evil customs that have become part of the law by enacting written laws prohibiting bad customs, just as bad habits are to be driven out of a person by the guidance of a teacher. Legislators must set aside customs if they conflict with truth or reason.[152] The example of chattel slavery in the United States presents a case where a deeply rooted customary practice needed to be rooted out.[153] As quoted by Gratian, Pope Nicholas states: "An evil custom is no more to be tolerated than a dangerous infection because, unless the custom is quickly torn up by its roots, it will be adopted by wicked men as entitling them to a privilege. And then unchecked deviations and various infractions will soon be revered as lawful and honored as immemorial privileges."[154] This rooting up must be done by legislation enacted by the legal authorities.[155] "Let practice yield to authority; let ordinance and reason vanquish bad practice."[156] It is ordinance and legal authority that accomplish this pruning action. Since it must be "rooted up," it is not to be left to development by repeated practices, but rather definitively declared to be outside the law.

Even with respect to a law that overturns a practice, the law is still connected to common practices. The development of the bad practice has given rise to the definitive declaration by statute. The pruning is guided by the natural law, which provides a standard for determining which customs are evil. Wicked customs are those that conflict with truth or reason, terms which clearly refer to the natural law as the rational participation in the eternal law, the source of truth.[157] Although the normal disposition of legal authority should be to respect long-standing practices and not to interfere with them,[158] such respect does not extend to practices that are contrary to natural law, which practices should be "held null and void."[159] Aquinas agrees that although human law, including custom, is a rule and measure, it must itself be ruled and measured by a higher law—divine and natural law.[160]

The analogy to building is useful yet again. When a painter paints an inside section of the house, he engages in a similar process. He begins applying the paint, and then steps back periodically to evaluate the result to determine if it correlates well or poorly with the general intention. Does the color as actually applied reflect the original intention? Does the thickness present the desired effect or is another coat of paint required? The painter does not make such evaluations with every paint stroke, but rather periodically evaluates his repeated actions.

Before leaving this aspect of the relationship, it must be emphasized that the ability of a statute to reverse long-standing customs should not be misunderstood as a plenary authority to overturn customs at will. The normal position is that custom must be respected.[161] The amount of respect due to a custom, and hence the extent of the limitation on the legal authorities' ability to tamper with it, is a function of its relationship to natural law. If "truth supports custom, nothing should be embraced more firmly."[162] The pruning is limited to bad customs only.

The roles of custom and legislation are more complex than statutes merely overturning bad customs. Sometimes statutes restate in written form that which is already law by custom.[163] Recall that Cicero's historical explanation noted that practices can become sanctioned by the written laws. Another purpose of statutes can be to confirm or make more known the laws made by custom. The earliest written collection of Roman law, the Twelve Tables, was such a collection of customary Roman law written down so that all subject to it could know its contents.[164] Written law can perform two different functions—sanctioning/confirming customs or abolishing bad customs.[165]

Even those customs not confirmed by statute still carry the force of law. Law made by developing customs includes both customs that have been written down and those that although unwritten are still part of a community's legal system.[166] Unwritten customs having the force of law provide legal answers to some questions not specifically addressed by statutes. So Gratian: "Usage [*consuetudo*] is a type of law [*jus*] established by customs and which is treated like a written statute [*pro lege*] when a written statute [*lex*] on the subject is lacking."[167] Custom can thus supplement the written law by expanding its application to broader contexts. In a gloss to this section, the jurist Johannes Teutonicus cites several cases where custom "has force against written law."[168] One of these examples is provided in a later *causa* in the *Decretum*, wherein an answer is provided to the question of which clerics are bound to observe clerical celibacy.[169] The *causa* references a written statute requiring only bishops, priests, and deacons to observe clerical celibacy, but concludes that clerics of other ranks are also obligated to observe the Church's custom (*consuetudenem*) of clerical celibacy, even though not specifically subject to the statute.[170] In this case, the customary law supplements the specific ordinance applicable only to the three highest classes of clerics.

Aquinas also explains that law can and is made by both speech (statute) and action (customs).[171] To support this conclusion, he uses an analogy to common experience. People express practical judgments made in their mind both by speech and by deeds.[172] Analogously, a community can express its rationally chosen law by written statutes and repeated deeds, or through habitual customs.

The analysis thus far could suggest only a gap-filling function for custom; it is law only when no statute addresses a topic. If custom were limited to this role, it would be subordinate to and at the mercy of enacted statutes. Individual passages within the *Decretum* can be read to support this conclusion; however, others seem to contradict it. The thirteenth-century jurist Johannes Teutonicus observes that some authorities can be cited to support the proposition that custom cannot judge statutes, and other authorities can be cited to support the proposition that it can.[173] This apparent contradiction of authorities can be seen as a necessary tension between custom and written law within a legal system. Denying absolute controlling authority to one or the other allows for a continued dialectical relationship between the two sources of law, by statute and by custom. Since one function of statutes is to uproot bad customs, statutes require a certain priority over custom. Yet, written laws are, like customary laws, subject to evaluation by a higher standard.[174] Like custom, they are also subordinate to natural law and must give way to it when they stand in contradiction. According to Gratian, "Both ecclesiastical and secular enactments are to be rejected entirely if they are contrary to natural law."[175] One method for overturning bad enactments is the development of a practice abrogating them. Gratian comments: "Some ordinances have now been abrogated by the usage of those acting contrary to them because ordinances are confirmed by the usages of those who observe them."[176] Aquinas agrees that an established contrary custom that demonstrates why a previously enacted statute "is no longer useful" can abrogate that statute "just as it might be declared by the verbal promulgation of a law to the contrary."[177]

In a gloss on a later section of the *Decretum*, Johannes Teutonicus returns to this question of customary practice abrogating statutes. He compiles a list of criteria drawn from various authorities that appear to circumscribe the precedence of custom over enactment. The enumerated criteria include the following:

1. The contrary custom must "gain force through the passage of time";
2. the custom must be "maintained by a contrary popular judgment";
3. those maintaining the practice must do so "in the belief that they are acting rightfully"
4. and "with the intention of acting the same way in the future";
5. the object of the custom must be a matter with respect to which "rights may change with the passage of time";[178]
6. the custom must be "ancient and approved";
7. the practice must "contain natural equity";
8. its introduction must be "with the knowledge of the prince and not merely tolerated" by him;
9. the custom must not be introduced "through error"; and
10. a "greater part of the people must be accustomed to the use of this custom."[179]

Several important elements can be observed in this list. First, the practice contrary to the statute must be in accord with natural law: it must contain natural equity, and it must concern a contingent matter left to determination by human law. Second, the nature of time runs forward and backward from the adoption of the statute. The statute must be one that is overturning an ancient custom, and the contrary practice must continue for some time after enactment. The people must act against the statute *deliberately*—the act is described as one of exercising a judgment—which suggests they must have a real knowledge of the statute and deliberately disregard it. The list is a bit ambiguous about which "people" must be engaging in this practice. It must be more than a mere majority of the people, but it also appears that the government must be involved in some way.[180] The "prince" must to some extent approve of the abrogation in that he must not merely tolerate the contrary practice. The use of the word "prince" is somewhat ambiguous. It may imply that the one who enacted the statute must consent to its change by custom. On the other hand, not all legislation is by the prince but sometimes by a legislative body, so it could suggest the prince in exercising his executive or judicial capacity disapproves of the enactment.

The key elements of the conditions can be distilled down to two. The contrary practice must be (1) a deliberately chosen act consistent with natural law, which (2) sustains an ancient practice of the community.

Such is the summary conclusion appended to this list by another jurist, Bartholomew of Brescia: "Briefly . . . it suffices . . . that custom be reasonable and have gained force through passage of time."[181] The same jurist warns the reader of the *Decretum* not to focus too literally on this list but rather to focus on the principles of natural law and antiquity when he states that "rational and long-standing custom detracts from written law . . . even if the other elements mentioned by Ioan [Johannes Teutonicus] at D.8, C.7 are not present."[182] A later canonical source maintains the conclusion that customary practices can take precedence over statutes, but only if they are rational and legitimate.[183] The more detailed criteria of Johannes Teutonicus can thus be seen as a way of expressing cases in which these principles would be fulfilled in a way maintaining a tension among the following: law and customary practice, the people and their governors, natural reason and particular determinations, and ancient and contemporary usages.[184]

Beyond supporting the theoretical justification for customs abrogating statutes, the *Decretum* also can be read to place customary use within the legislative process itself. Gratian introduces an example showing how a particular statute is not part of the law, because of a contrary use. He quotes a lengthy papal ordinance mandating all clerics to fast from Quinquagesima Sunday. Immediately following the quotation, Gratian asserts that clerics cannot be held guilty for transgressing these statutes "because they were not approved by common use."[185] The process of written statutes entering into law involves more than adoption by the legislator. Gratian describes a two-part process following deliberation over a new written ordinance: "Ordinances are *instituted* when they are promulgated; they are *confirmed* when they have been approved by the usage of those who observe them."[186] Institution of a statute is complete when the written rule is made public and then a second phase begins: the rule's confirmation by reception into common use. Refusal of a community to confirm a statute is curtailed by the conditions described by Johannes Teutonicus, summarized by saying that the contrary practice must be rational and consistent with ancient custom.[187] The ability of common customs to abrogate a statute can be understood to be embedded in the lawmaking process itself. In the language of H. L. A. Hart, part of any "Rule of Recognition"[188] is confirmation by reception into practice. To form part of the binding written law, a statute must be promulgated and then confirmed by the practice of observing it.[189] The particular ordinance concerning fasting from Quinquagesima Sunday is not part of the law because it was never received into practice and hence never confirmed.

Thus, rather than custom and written law being in a static one-way relationship wherein statute either confirms or abolishes custom, they appear in a more fluid dialectical relationship.[190] Statutes and customs can supplement each other by addressing cases different than or distinguishable from those addressed by the other. Statutes can overturn bad customs, and custom can abrogate statutes, in each case based on the higher authority of the natural and divine law. As Porter has explained, "His [Gratian's] point . . . is that custom and ordinance represent two distinct *but interrelated* ways of expressing the demands of natural law in a particular time and place."[191] Harold Berman has similarly described the medieval lawmaking process as involving law coming up from the customs of the people and coming down from the will of the legislator, by which process "law helps to integrate the two."[192]

Yet, the question still remains: Can a judge before whom a case arises abolish a statute that conflicts with natural law, or must it be enforced until changed by the legislator?[193] It would seem that if a statute can be abrogated by custom, a judge can refuse to enforce a statute that has been abrogated by contrary practice. In this case, the judge is not abrogating a written ordinance, but rather enforcing the law (*jus*) in its totality, taking into account that a contrary custom has either abrogated a statute or failed to confirm it. This leaves another case (which as we shall see is composed of two subcases) where a statute contradicting natural law has not been abrogated by custom. It would seem that, according to the *Decretum*, the judge is not permitted to abrogate written laws: "In the case of temporal ordinances, although men pass judgment on them when they are being instituted, a judge may not pass judgment on them after they are instituted and confirmed, but only according to them."[194] A careful read of this passage leaves open the possibility of abrogating a written statute after enactment but before confirmation. It states that a judge may not pass judgment on written statutes after they have been "enacted" *and* "confirmed."[195] This would indicate that a judge may judge a statute during its period of entry into the legal system, after enactment but before confirmation.[196] This would be a logical conclusion because one way a statute is confirmed is by its reception into the customs of the people. One way of entering the customs of a people would be the customary enforcement of the statute by courts. Thus, judicial evaluation of newly enacted statutes that reverse long-standing customs, subject to the qualifications and limitations on this process we discussed above, appears to be part of the necessary process of confirming statutes, failure of which results in their abrogation.

Yet, this leaves a case where a statute has been instituted and confirmed, including by enforcement of the statute by courts. In essence, a bad statute has been instituted and confirmed and enforced for a significant time by courts. A judge realizes that the statute violates natural or divine law. An example might be the fugitive slave laws at issue in the infamous *Dred Scott* decision.[197] The Fugitive Slave Act was a restatement of the common practice of forcefully returning slaves to their owners, a practice dating back to the fugitive slave clause in the U.S. Constitution.[198] Forcibly enforcing slavery of the type in existence in the nineteenth-century United States[199] was contrary to the principle of the "identical liberty of all" contained in natural law.[200] Assuming the judge cannot avoid concluding the ordinance has been confirmed by use, what may such a judge do? This subcase goes beyond the first, in which the statute was not yet confirmed. The analysis thus far would suggest that he cannot simply abrogate the Fugitive Slave Act, again assuming its confirmation by accepted use. But many authorities assert that, absent the exceptions discussed earlier, the judge must judge according to the statute.[201] In one provision of Roman law, magistrates who failed to enforce a law regarding burial of the dead outside of towns were ordered to pay the same fine for failing to enforce the statute as the offenders themselves.[202] Absent the exceptions discussed in the prior two cases, it would seem the judge would have no other choice but to enforce the bad law.

Another exception may be available to our troubled judge. A long tradition dating from St. Augustine holds that "a law which is not just does not seem to me to be a law."[203] The tradition following Augustine is important to understand the extent of the binding obligation of the law generally. For now we can observe, however, that at least in extreme cases, human laws, of whatever origin, that compel a violation of the revealed divine law are not laws at all and must be refused.[204] This topic is broader than current purposes, but it is enough to note that the principle does not mean all unjust laws (those that transgress the natural law) are abrogated. As we have already observed, human law will never be a perfect participation in eternal law, and some error must be tolerated for the common good. A more nuanced evaluation is necessary, and even some unjust laws ought to be obeyed for the common good.[205] Yet, we can still conclude that if a judge is confronted by a statute whose enforcement would compel the judge to transgress the divine law, the judge must refuse the statute as no law at all.[206] Thus, a statute could be abrogated by a judge. Outside of this narrow exception, it would seem that the judge would be required to enforce the offensive law. Once again the relationship between practice and statute is complex, without one having complete precedence over the other. Their respective authority varies depending upon the context and the conformity, or transgression, of each to natural law.

Having examined the relationship between ordinance and custom within the general category of human law, we can conclude this subsection by turning from resolving conflicts among sources of law to examining the criteria for the process of human legislating. We can begin with written ordinances. Gratian includes a useful summary of the characteristics of well-written laws by Isidore: "A[n] ordinance, then, shall be proper, just, possible, in accord with nature, in accord with the custom of the country, suitable to the place and time, necessary, useful, clear enough so that it contain no hidden deception, and not accommodated to some private individual, but composed for the common utility of the citizens."[207]

This passage succinctly integrates many of the themes we have been examining. Human law must be woven out of a dialectical interaction between natural law and the customs of the community for whom they are made. To the extent they accord with natural law they will be proper and just, as suited to human nature. To the extent they accord with the customs of the people, the laws will be suitable for the time and place in which they appear. A third element woven through this dialectical tension between nature and custom is the common good. Laws must be written so as to address the common good of the community and not just the individual good of some members. The skill of a lawmaker is to draft clear ordinances that express general natural law principles in a particular manner suited to the particular instantiation of the common good in an actual community. Human laws cannot be made in the abstract but only in the particular context of the customs of a community.[208]

The requirement that good laws are written according to the customs of a particular community points to another relationship between written law and custom. Since written law should be framed in accordance with the customs of the community, those laws should be interpreted likewise. If one criteria of written law is that it be suited to a time and place, it should be read and understood in the same context. Part of the gloss on the phrase "customs of the country" in this passage from the *Decretum* says that "ordinances are interpreted according to custom."[209] Aquinas likewise lists three legal effects of custom: "Custom has the force of a law, abolishes law, and is the interpreter of law."[210] The dialectical relationship of statute and custom thus continues, even when custom does not abrogate law, in that laws should be interpreted in accordance with custom and not merely according to a presumed original intent of the statute if that intent is seen as an abstraction devoid of connection to the customs of the people.

Yet, as we have noted, not all customs are good. Although morality calls individuals to strive to maintain only good habits, in reality the habits of individuals at any point in time are usually both good and bad ones. It is hoped that the individual is working to nurture the good and extirpate the bad. Communities also have a mixture of good and bad customs. Although bad customs need to be rooted up, the practical idealism of Aquinas's Aristotelianism recognizes that the rooting up is an act of prudence that may take time to achieve:[211] "The purpose of human law is to lead men to virtue, not suddenly, but gradually."[212] Aquinas clearly teaches that the end or goal of human law is perfect conformity to natural law.[213] Still, he recognizes that at any given moment in time, systems of human laws will fall short of that goal in different respects.

Human laws need to be made in the context of particular communities, taking into account the particular state of the virtue of the customs maintained. Interpreting Isidore's description of well-written law, Aquinas explains that for a law to be proper, it must be proportional to the nature of the people for whom it is made.[214] Thus, different rules are framed for adults and children in light of their differing capacities.[215] Likewise, because "human law is framed for a number of human beings, the majority of whom are not perfect in virtue,"[216] human laws do not, and Aquinas argues should not, prescribe every virtue or punish every vice.[217] Human law cannot approve of or compel violations of natural and divine law, or otherwise it would be no law at all, but it may, by certain omissions, necessitated by the state of a community's customs, neglect to forbid or punish all infractions.[218] Doing so does not leave the vice unregulated. As human law is merely the lowest level in a hierarchy of law, the action remains subject to divine and natural law.

Returning to the architectural analogy, even if a builder neglects to have a wall painted, that does not mean the wall does not exist. Likewise, simply because a community's law has not yet enacted a particular determination of a natural law precept does not mean that precept ceases to stand to rule the choices of individuals. Even before the first particular traffic rule was framed, the natural law obligated people to drive safely.

Aquinas explains the omissions in human law: "Human law is given to the people among whom there are many lacking virtue, and it is not given to the virtuous alone. Hence human law was unable to forbid all that is contrary to virtue, and it suffices for it to prohibit whatever is destructive of human intercourse, while it treats other matters as though they were lawful, not by approving of them, but by not punishing them. . . . On the other hand the divine law leaves nothing unpunished that is contrary to virtue."[219]

Human law cannot actually approve of vice; it may merely omit to punish a particular instance. Since human law has concurrent jurisdiction with the other forms of law, man is still accountable for vice under other law.[220] The process of rooting up bad customs and leading men to virtue is a slow and gradual process. Lines must be drawn. Once again, the principle of the common good is what guides the fixing of the line between enacting a particular law and abstaining in light of the particular situation of a community. Those violations of natural law that are "destructive of human intercourse," or destructive of living in society for the common good, are those human law must root up.[221]

In recognizing this important limitation on human law's ability to prescribe virtue and proscribe vice, we can again observe the important tension between universal and particular, and between the desired perfect good and the accepted practical reality. This dialectical tension is resolved by the necessity of orienting the law to the common good of a real community with a particular customary history. Thus, no two legal systems will be identical, but, to be real legal systems, they will exhibit a commonality of purpose and orientation. Likewise, no two houses will be identical in detail but will have to exhibit a commonality of form to be recognizable as houses.

In summary, the process of human lawmaking is multidimensional. It is a deductive or inductive process making use of general principles of natural reason known through common practices (*jus gentium*) and particular practices of the particular community. Law emerges out of tensions between written ordinance and customary usages. Each cause of law possesses certain precedence over the other, and vice versa. Custom can confirm—or refuse to confirm—law, make law, abrogate law, and interpret it. Classical natural law jurisprudence conceives of the role of the human legislator, the lawgiver, in fairly modest terms. Human legislators are a part of a complex dialectical process, not the alpha and the omega of the legal system. Statutes they promulgate can root up bad custom and give sanction to good custom. Dante's portrayal of Justinian, "the Empire's greatest law-giver,"[222] in his *Divine Comedy* aptly expresses this limited conception of legislators. Justinian introduces himself and describes his great work of codifying centuries of Roman law: "I was Caesar and am Justinian, who, by will of the Primal Love which moves me, removed from the laws what was superfluous and vain."[223] Rather than describing his work as commanding newly devised precepts, he characterizes it as pruning, removing from the existing civil laws what had become superfluous or vain. Dante's Justinian, rather than seeing the lawgiver as supreme commander of new precepts born of his will, places the lawgiver within the midst of a historically developing dialectical process of refining the decoration of the preexisting legal framework of the natural law.

APPLICATION TO PARTICULAR ISSUES IN HUMAN LAWMAKING

The first section elucidated the purpose of human law as a process of making more explicit and particular the principles of the natural law, as reinforced by divine law. Essentially, making human law involves selecting appropriate means to a predetermined end. From ancient times, this process has been seen as a long and gradual process of discovering with more precision the principles of natural law and developing expressions of those principles within a people's particular customary tradition.[224]

The history of Roman jurisprudence exemplifies this understanding of human law in many respects. Cicero explained the development of law as an evolution of customs from natural law over time. Roman law developed through case law decisions of the praetors applying either the *jus civile* to Roman citizens or the *jus gentium* to aliens. Yet, Roman law was more than pure casuistry. Throughout its development, legislation would interact with developing jurisprudence. Finally, various jurists would survey the legal history and attempt to elucidate the principles underlying the particular decisions.[225] The *Corpus Juris Civilis* of Justinian represents the final product of the Roman system. It contains a compilation of specific legislative determinations,[226] summaries of specific resolutions of various particular cases,[227] and a systematic summary of the principles underlying these particular laws.[228] Gratian, writing at the time of the great revival of Roman law, applied this approach to the organization of the law of the Church. His *Decretum* contains an introductory summary of the principles of law,[229] followed by a collection of case law decisions and legislative enactments drawn from the past thousand-year history of the Church organized by subject matter. Structurally, the work presents cases, or *causae*, which are resolved by comparison with the collection of prior decisions and enactments. Both the *Corpus Juris Civilis* and the *Decretum* are compilations of temporal and ecclesiastical law drawn from the varied customary and statutory sources that developed over time.

In this section we turn from this theoretical and historical overview of human lawmaking from a natural law perspective to consider several contemporary issues facing jurisprudence.

Common versus Civil Law

Modern law rooted in the history of the Western legal tradition[230] can be divided into two main types or systems, generally referred to as *common law* and *civil law*.[231] Although most legal systems are not pure examples, and in fact contain elements of both types,[232] individual systems tend to be dominated by more of the characteristics of common law or of civil law. In recent decades, debate has ensued over the superiority of one ap-proach over the other.[233] This subsection will examine what contribution the foregoing natural law analysis of human lawmaking brings to this de-bate between the two types of legal systems.

Although simple definitions are underinclusive, we must begin at some point. The differences between legal systems characterized as com-mon law and civil law touch many areas, such as court procedure and criminal presumption.[234] The particular aspect we shall examine in rela-tion to each system is the method for making and developing law exem-plified by each. In light of this specific purpose, the following definitions can serve to present the contrast between the two systems. A common law system is characterized by appellate judge-made law formulated in re-sponse to specific controversies.[235] Legal rules emerge as particular re-sponses to resolving individual disputes. As new disputes arise, prior rules are refined and developed in light of previously formulated rules and the new factual scenarios. The term *case law* can function as a synonym for our intended definition of common law. Common law identifies a legal system in which (1) a significant portion of laws (2) are formulated over periods of time (3) in response to specific disputes (4) by judges who see themselves as refining or further specifying an ordered system of law not of their own creation and preexisting their tenure, (5) periodically refined and even overturned either by legislative enactments or in grave cases ju-dicial reversals of prior decisions.

Civil law systems are dominated not by judge-made law, but rather by comprehensive codes, which can be defined as "a statute which covers the whole law, or the whole of some branch or province of the law."[236] The term "code" is ambiguous, referring to two very different objects. The Code of Justinian and the United States Code represent one type, which, for the purpose of distinction, we can call a "code of compilation." The Code Napoleon or the Uniform Commercial Code are another type of code, which we can refer to as a "comprehensive code." A code of compila-tion merely collects and organizes by subject matter prior laws enacted over the course of time.[237] A comprehensive code is a newly written law enacted to supersede all prior legislation covering the field of law of the code.[238] A code of compilation enacts no new law but merely brings a sys-tematized order to legislation adopted over the course of time. As new statutes are enacted, they are integrated or appended to the code.[239] Although produced after a study of prior legislation, comprehensive codes go beyond merely organizing existing law. They rewrite and supersede all prior law. The Code Napoleon adopted points of law that were completely new and in some cases reversed prior law. The concept of legality that emerged from the French Revolution and was spread throughout continental Europe by Napoleon rejects the "lawmaking role of the courts" and "resulted in the articulation of the primacy of the legislature."[240] Therefore, for purposes of this subsection, civil law jurisdiction refers to a collection of the following characteristics: (1) a comprehensive code or codes, (2) which is or are intended to be complete and final in the applicable area, (3) enacted on the premise that statutes are preeminent over customs and history, (4) by a legislator who is the actual normative source of law and not just the determiner of law within a positive legal system.

The process of making law in common law systems is embedded in the facts, and in the analogizing and distinguishing of new scenarios.[241] Even when reading a new statute, common law courts employ analogical reasoning and appeal to precedent.[242] This characterization makes common law sound purely inductive: "The common law exalts the particulars, which, as the court encodes them in its narrative, become a set of givens, enabling the formation of the legal standard or proposition for which the pending case will stand in the future, for others to claim as legal precedent."[243]

Yet the process is also permeated with deductive reasoning in addition to the inductive formulation of rules from case-specific facts. Once legal rules have been formulated out of particular disputes, those rules become general principles from which new rules and applications can be deduced:

> Within the common-law legal system, for example, by virtue of the courts' crafting of legal principles, each precedent stands for a legal norm from which applications to future pending cases can be deduced. Common-law reasoning thus clearly contains a deductive component that is as intrinsic to its nature as the analogical reasoning by similarity and dissimilarity which dominates the comparative process of evaluating the legal significance of a pending case by weighing it against prior case law.[244]

Harold Berman describes this type of legal method as having been developed by the medieval jurists working with the texts of Roman law:

> The jurists thus gave the West its characteristic methods of analysis and synthesis of texts. They taught the West to synthesize cases into rules, rules into principles, principles into a system. Their method, which is still that of legal science in the United States today, was to determine what various particulars have in common, to see the whole as the interaction of the parts. . . . It took the customs and rules as data and adduced from the data the regularities—the "laws"—that explained them.[245]

This description highlights the connection between inductive reasoning from particular cases and deductive creation of a system of principles, which characterizes the common law system. This dialectical process of making law by judicial case decision resembles the description of the role of custom contained in our first section.[246] Human law contained in case decisions is developed over time in response to the particular developing practices of a legal community. Justice Cardozo similarly connected the case law method to customs when he said, "The judge in shaping the rules of law must heed the *mores* of his day."[247] James Whitman likewise connects the development of the historicism of English common law to its deep respect for custom.[248] Case law, like general customs, develops gradually and in light of an adherence to precedent. Its default starting point is the transmission of existing practices. The late nineteenth-century defender of the common law Joel Prentiss Bishop described the common law in language reminiscent of Cicero and the natural law tradition we described in the first section:

> They [laws] are the visible product of invisible laws,—imperfect and incomplete in their first formations, because man is imperfect, but capable of being gradually improved and perfected by reason. . . .
>
>   Following instinct, or conscience, or whatever else we call it,— in other words, moved by impulses from the nature given by God to man,—he, while living as all must in society, establishes various customs and usages. After they become universal the court takes judicial cognizance of them as law. When statutes are enacted it takes the like cognizance of them also.[249]

This common law attachment to precedent as custom resembles the attitude toward custom we described in the first section. The developing case law contains the usages and customs of the legal community.

Although custom is to be a general guide for human law, bad customs need to be rooted out. Likewise, the common law limits the adherence to custom. The principle of *stare decisis*—particularly as applied by the U.S. judiciary—is a principle subject to exception.[250] Whereas some jurists have struggled to articulate a consistent standard for when *stare decisis* is to be followed[251] and when it is to be overruled, the analysis in the first section provides an answer. When a precedent represents a bad custom, it should be rooted up.[252] Bad precedents can and should be overturned when they are contrary to reason, or to natural law principles.[253] Bishop described the relationship between natural law principles and changes in law:

> Now, for a court to decide a question differing from what has gone before, it must take cognizance of the law engraved, not by man, but by God, on the nature of man. In other words, it must take cognizance of what our predecessors have named the unwritten law, or common law. This law has already been discovered by judicial wisdom to consist of a beautiful and harmonious something not palpable to the visible sight, yet to the understanding obvious and plain, called principles.[254]

As Bishop explains, the deductive or inductive nature of the common law process allows for the discovery of general principles of reason, or the natural law, which then can be used to correct prior mistakes by overruling bad precedents. He argues, "What is termed the law's progress or growth consists, more than in anything else, in discoveries of its just and true reasons, and in correcting old mistakes as to them."[255]

Still, courts are not the entire legal system, even in common law countries; statutes also have a role in traditional common law systems, particularly in correcting such old mistakes.[256] Yet their function is often understood as more akin to the role of enactment of a tailored pruning of the gradually developing case law as opposed to a way to supplant it. Legislation is episodic and often focused on reversing a particular line of case law that is considered unsatisfactory.[257] This narrower role of legislation is reinforced by the principle of construing strictly derogations of existing common law.[258] This principle reinforces the idea that law develops gradually through decisions, with legislation weaving in and out of the process to guide its development. Roscoe Pound observed that notwithstanding claims of legislative supremacy, the interpretive power of courts means that judges possess a de facto supremacy in their ability to narrowly interpret and apply statutes:[259]

> The proposition that statutes in derogation of the common law are to be construed strictly . . . assumes that legislation is something to be deprecated. As no statute of any consequence dealing with any relation of private law can be anything but in derogation of the common law, . . . [one] must always face the situation that the legislative act . . . will find no sympathy in those who apply it, will be construed strictly, and will be made to interfere with the *status quo* as little as possible.[260]

The approach described by Pound resembles the dialectical interaction between ordinance and custom, especially the role of confirmation of statutes, discussed in the first section. The final part of the legislative process involves confirmation by the community, which in common law countries occurs through the acceptance and application of the statute by courts. To the extent that it is narrowly interpreted and applied, it is confirmed.[261]

The philosophical vision of human lawmaking described in the first section appears to justify a common law tradition allowing for a dialectical development of law over time. As Jeremiah Newman explains, for the natural law tradition, the primary image of a political ruler is the judge, rather than the legislator, who declares and enforces the law.[262] For Aristotle, a ruler discovers and declares law rather than enacts it,[263] since in his vision, law "is no code: it is the custom, written and unwritten, which has developed with the development of a state."[264] Law is made through courts and legislatures transmitting and pruning custom. A qualified respect for custom is shown in the process through a doctrine of *stare decisis*, which still permits either legislatures or courts to overrule laws made in opposition to reason.

The civil law system, by contrast, places the emphasis on comprehensive legal codes. A comprehensive code is written on a clean slate and is meant to supersede all prior law as a final and comprehensive statement of the whole law or of the law of a particular subtopic. As Curran explains: "By contrast, the civil law focuses on codes, written texts designed to govern throughout time, designed to embody the immutably true, to embody principles so reliable that they supersede and can withstand the vicissitudes of the particular, of the temporal, of the myriad contextual elements that connect human beings to the legal issues they ask courts to adjudicate."[265]

Civil law codes use legislation to formulate axiomatic principles of Kantian reasoning and are held out to be "a coherent and complete representation of law, all of its parts mutually reconcilable."[266] Although prior laws may be studied in preparing the code, the project aims at a complete articulation of law, or a part of law, at a particular moment in history. Tunc likewise summarizes the philosophy of the prototype of modern civil law codes, which is the French Napoleonic Code: "Portalis' excellent *Discours préliminaire*, which so admirably explains the thought of the drafters of the *Code civil*, suggests that the French concept of the law rests on three fundamental principles: A code ought to be complete in its field; it ought to be drafted in relatively general principles rather than in detailed rules; and it ought at the same time to fit them together logically as a coherent whole and to be based on experience."[267]

Codes aspire to be complete, axiomatic, and logically comprehensive as a whole.[268] They are written rather than developed over time. By its abstract axioms, the code remains detached from particulars or the contingent matter of life. The English utilitarian Jeremy Bentham[269] was a great admirer and advocate of modern codes. He also believed that codes could be formulated so completely as to answer all legal questions once and for all, in a sense outside of history. He boasted: "Were any such all-comprehensive Code in existence, and executed as it ought to be and might be, seldom would there be any such question as a question of law: never any other question of law than a question concerning the import of this or that portion of the existing text of the really existing law."[270]

One might conclude that this process seems commensurate with natural law legal jurisprudence, which argues that the natural law contains comprehensive general principles of action derived from a unified systemic whole, the eternal law. Yet, despite the similarities, the civil law process errs by conflating the two levels of law. These characteristics—general axioms, completeness, wholeness, a transcendence of particular times and places—typify the natural law. Human law, as we described in the first section, is more detailed, particular, and incomplete. The very claim of the code to be complete, to make law for all cases, directly contradicts Aquinas's conclusion, described in the first section, that human law not only cannot, but should not, address all vices. In an attempt to be complete, the code fails to take account of the particular situation of the people for whom it is made. Human law should involve particular determinations of the general principles in relevant evolving historical contexts. Becauase of weaknesses in the reasoning process, lawmakers are prone to err in the elucidation and refinement of natural law principles.[271] A common law system of historical development limited to particular cases contains the effect of any one person's mistakes. Chancellor Kent in his famous commentary on U.S. law quotes Sir Matthew Hale: "The common law of England is, 'not the product of the wisdom of some one man, or society of men, in any one age; but of the wisdom, counsel, experience, and observation of many ages of wise and observing men.'"[272]

Another nineteenth-century advocate of retaining the common law in the United States, J. Bleecker Miller, looked to the Roman law as a historical example of a legal system developed not by one man but across generations. For Miller, Roman law was not the prototype of civil law codes but rather an example of a historically rooted common law tradition.[273] He explained, "The great merit of the Roman Law being, that it is a natural product of one people, with which no legislator interfered before its perfection."[274] Once it reached a maturity of historical development, its components—case decisions, ordinances, and general principles—could then be gathered into the systemic whole by Justinian.

Civil law codes, contrary to Miller's understanding of the evolution of Roman law, attempt to usurp the place of natural law and also the customary evolution of its determination. The legislator is charged with the task of composing the general axioms that natural law considers merely as given.[275] The axioms serve as means for reaching particular determinations through the guidance of evolving customs. By contrast, the premise of the Napoleonic Civil Code and its progeny is that the legislator posits the axioms, which places them at the wrong level of the legal edifice. According to the civil law system, legislation deals in absolutes,[276] whereas for natural law jurisprudence, human legislation deals in contingent matters—decisions that could be made in more than one way.[277] The levels of absolute truth are the eternal, natural, and divine law; human law is contingent and contextualized. This difference between the common law and civil law understanding of the contingent nature of human law is epitomized by the terminology used to refer to court action. Common law courts tend to refer to their products as opinions, whereas the civil law system typically refers to decisions: *décision* in French and *Entscheidung* in German.[278]

Within the civil law system, the legislator is supreme.[279] Hobbes expressed this supremacy by holding the following three principles, among five others, to be fundamental to the legal order: "First, that the sovereign is the *sole* legislator; second, that the sovereign is effectively *immune to civil laws*, since they may change those laws at will; and third, that any norms or conventions only become law because the sovereign *indicates a tolerance* for them by his inaction."[280]

Rather than making particular periodic determinations bounded by general principles of natural law, the Hobbsian sovereign enacts the whole law in the code. The code may be changed at will by the sovereign, and changes are limited by neither principles of natural law nor custom.[281] Custom is only law to the extent the legislative sovereign permits it to continue. The general principles of the code are stated in the abstract and derive from the enactment of the code, not from the evolution of customary practices. This exaltation of the legislator, the author of the code, has consequences for the civil law's understanding of the judiciary. French opinions, taken to exemplify the civil law approach, tend to be short, anonymous, and abstract, and lack reasoning, dissent, or concurrence.[282] Additionally, civil law court opinions tend to avoid detailed recitation or analysis of the particular facts of the case decided.[283] This tendency is a consequence of understanding the code as containing all the law through unfailing abstract principles. As a result, the judge is viewed as merely logically applying the absolute abstract principle.

Common law opinions by contrast typically contain lengthy discussions of the particular facts of the case.[284] As a result, common law reasoning arrives at general principles, not through legislative *fiat*, but through the inductive process of case resolution. Such a process keeps ever present the reminder that general principles are capable of exceptions. As Aquinas explained, because natural law precepts are applied to contingent human actions, "although there is necessity in the general principles, the more we descend to matters of detail, the more frequently we encounter defects."[285] By defect, he does not mean that the principle is defective, but rather its application in the particular facts would fail "because the greater the number of conditions added, the greater the number of ways in which the principle may fail."[286] Aquinas gives the example of the principle of the natural law that if one accepts possession of goods for safekeeping, he should return them.[287] Yet, in some cases this principle fails, as when for example the one to whom they will be returned is planning to use them to fight one's country.[288] The common law's determination of law's general principles based on application to discrete facts, and the process of distinguishing precedents on the facts, reminds the judge of this tendency of principles to fail to apply in some contingent cases.[289]

Oliver Wendell Holmes contrasted the abstract logical formalism of civil law courts to the more fluid experiential common law process: "The life of the law has not been logic: it has been experience."[290] By which, he does not mean that the common law is illogical, but rather, it is a logic worked out through experience rather than axiom. Common law judges discover the logic by applying principles over time and thereby gaining experience.[291] Civil law achieves a logical code by having a legislature impose the logical whole upon the law independent of the particular facts of a case.[292] By contrast, the common law assumes the logical whole exists in the law, and judges are merely attempting to knit together and shine a light upon the various intersecting threads in the tapestry that preexists. The civil law system thus appears to lack the appropriate dialectical tension between legislature and judiciary that was part of the development of law rooted in custom we described in the first section.

The philosophy of common law jurisprudence thus appears more commensurate with the understanding of the relationship of human law to natural law described in the first section. Legislation is understood as a more limited and constrained process, which interacts dialectically with evolving customs to prune and guide the development of a community's particular determinations.[293] Judicial conflicts are resolved through a deductive or inductive process of inducting general principles from particular facts and deductively developing those principles. The entire process is factually and historically rooted in particular contingent details, the matter of human lawmaking. By contrast, the civil law approach usurps the level of natural law by transforming human law into a legislature of general abstract principles, which are seen to be the entire law mechanically applied by courts.[294] The law is disconnected both from preexisting natural law norms and evolving customs. The result is the supremacy of the legislature in civil law jurisprudence, in contrast to a more fluid relationship in common law jurisprudence. J. N. Figgis extolled the common law tradition for this very reason. It trusts no single legislator to know and articulate all principles of natural reason perfectly, but rather allows their discovery across time. As he explains: "Common Law is the perfect ideal of law; for it is natural reason developed and expounded by the collective wisdom of many generations."[295] Aquinas would agree: "No man is so wise as to be able to take account of every single case; wherefore he is not able sufficiently to express in words all those things that are suitable for the end he has in view."[296]

Ironically, one of the drafters of Napoleon's Civil Code, Portalis, expressed an understanding of the limitations and necessary historical contextualization of law that stands in sharp contrast to the way his code has come to be seen in civil law jurisdictions: "Laws are not pure acts of will; they are acts of wisdom, of justice, and of reason. The legislator does not so much exercise a power as he fulfills a sacred trust. One ought never to forget that laws are made for men, not men for laws; that they must be adapted to the character, to the habits, to the situation of the people for whom they are drafted; that one ought to be wary of innovations in matters of legislation."[297]

A common law system that fosters dialectical interaction among existing precedent, natural law principles, case decisions, and targeted legislation seems to fulfill Portalis's criteria more than his abstract, transhistorical code.

The Problem of Legislation

Both common law and civil law systems rely to varying degrees on legislation. This subsection will argue that legislation, both in civil law jurisdictions with their comprehensive codes and in common law jurisdictions that have yielded much of the field of law to statutes, "is a problem in law."[298] One problem of modern legislation is its volume. As Brennan has remarked: "The statutory codes swell, the case reporters go into new series, and the Government Printing Office can barely keep up with our zeal to regulate from soup to intrauterine devices. . . . We are awash in the badges and incidents of law."[299] As a result, we are "surrounded . . . by law on all sides."[300] The United States Code comprises approximately 269 volumes.[301] The typical code of laws of a state in the United States comprises anywhere from twenty to hundreds of volumes.[302] In the 111th Congress alone (2009–11), the federal government passed more than 300 new laws, including the 906-page Affordable Care Act.[303] Not only are we surrounded by laws, but the laws we are surrounded by are longer than the Bible, which took thousands of years to complete. Grant Gilmore once quipped that after the 1930s, our government engaged in an "orgy of statute making."[304] Although founded as a common law jurisdiction, the United States no longer represents a pure form of this system. Although never conquered by the Code Napoleon, the United States allowed its law to be conquered over the course of the twentieth century by a creeping or, more accurately, a flooding, invasion of legislation.[305] This subsection will first consider the causes of this massive expansion of legislation and then outline some of the deleterious effects of it.

The primary reason for the expansion of legislation is a belief, fostered by supporters of codes, now permeating even common law jurisdictions,[306] that legislation can be complete. One attribute of modern codification is the claim that the new legislation includes all law, or all law with respect to a particular subject area. Notwithstanding this claim to completeness, the enactment by Napoleon of the Code did not bring an end to lawmaking. In the twentieth century changes in daily life led many to call for wholesale change of the Code and a new type of statute emerged, with detailed and regulatory minute rules.[307] France has seen the growth of executive decrees making detailed rules to enforce the allegedly complete Code.[308] Further, in many areas French courts have developed new areas of law, such as unjust enrichment and products liability.[309] John Henry Merryman has argued that Napoleon's attempt to draft and promulgate a code that was complete, coherent, and clear failed quickly, and then sardonically he has added that France forgot to communicate this failure to the countries that adopted the code system, so the other countries clung tenaciously to belief in this theory and restricted judicial scope to develop the law.[310]

Why has the goal of completeness inevitably failed? Aquinas rendered the answer centuries ago. Law by definition includes rules.[311] Yet, rules can be understood in two very different senses, one detailed and precise, specifically addressing all variables, and the other more general and less complete in its formulation.[312] Brennan, in commenting on the work of Joseph Vining, uses the rules of a game to exemplify the first class.[313] Rules in games produce binary results. In Monopoly, when one rolls doubles three times, one must go directly to jail without passing Go.[314] Yet, in life and hence in law, rules are part of a "methodical process that is not itself governed by any 'rule' (or standard) of law that we have made."[315] Put another way, life is more complicated than a game, which by definition is played in an artificially simplified universe, no matter how complicated the particular game may be.

Life, and hence law, is radically more contingent than a game. Law is applied to contingent matters,[316] which vary greatly across time and space. Legislation can attempt to address such multiplicity of contingent matters in two ways. First, it can merely contain a rule written as a general standard of conduct written at a level of generality (a "Standards Rule").[317] Alternatively, law can attempt to write a series of rules, each meant to address a different particular contingent matter to which the law might need to be applied (a "Game Rule").[318]

To explain, we can adapt an example used by Brennan[319] of two forms of a statute meant to cover the same conduct. Example 1 (Game Rule): "It shall be a crime to cry 'fire' in a crowded theatre."[320] Example 2 (Standards Rule): "It shall be a crime to cry 'fire' in a crowded theatre if all things considered this was a dangerous thing to do."[321] The Game Rule is clear and precise, yet incomplete. It does not, on its face, prohibit shouting "earthquake" in a crowded stadium. The Standards Rule is very general and does not specifically address many situations. All things considered, what constitutes "dangerous"? If one makes law from a premise that the only law that legitimately exists is the complete statutory law made by a legislator to the exclusion of (1) the natural law, (2) custom, and (3) law made by the judiciary as it tries cases, one would find the Game Rule woefully underinclusive. The only solution is to write more Game Rules that address other possible scenarios—other shouts and other locations—until all possible contingent matters have been covered. Yet, unlike a board game with a limited number of spaces on which to land, life is not as finite in its possibilities. The result is that one would continue writing more and more Game Rules addressing every conceivable scenario and then, after completing this task, someone will shout something not yet conceived in a new location, and the legislator must go back to expand the legislation to add one more Game Rule to cover the new space added to the "game board." The result is an endless cycle of amending and expanding the written law to cover every possible scenario. This has been the pattern and problem of U.S. legislation involved in the orgy described by Gilmore. Since the United States never adopted a code with more abstract standard rules, its legal system has tended to adopt Game Rules. Yet, as legislation comes to be seen as all-inclusive, the failure of the Game Rules and the proliferation of their number follows.

If the Game Rule in such a system leads to a legislative orgy, then what of the Standards Rule typically found in a code system? It would appear to be the only alternative to an ever-expanding set of rules trying to overturn the last unjust result, when the Game Rule failed to cover a new scenario. In fact, the Standards Rule has been the form of many civil law codes, which contain abstract general standards.[322] Yet, once the Standards Rule is selected, it eventually becomes necessary to further determine the meaning of the standard in varying contingent circumstances. New law is made every time judgment is given that determines the specific meaning of the standard in the particular facts. Yet, the court in a code system is, at least in theory, handicapped in this role by three limitations. First, it must labor under the pretext that it is not making law and thus limit its justification for the new rule to a fictional mechanical application of the existing legislation.[323] This trait is observed in the perfunctory decisions of civil law countries already noted. Second, custom has been obliterated as a source of law.[324] Thus, in theory the judge is precluded from using custom as a source of law, unless it has been incorporated into the code, to define the general terms. Third, the purpose the law was meant to fulfill cannot be uncovered by asking what principles of natural law this rule is meant to determine and then using the background natural law precepts to understand the meaning of the general rule.[325] In addition to these problems, the court faces the problem of a case in which the general rule fails. The case of the person who, all things considered, *should* shout "fire" in the crowded theater — as when, for example, the fire-detection system is broken and nobody is listening to his quiet warnings. As Aquinas explains, the more contingent conditions that are added to a case, the more likely a general precept will not work a just result in some cases or, in other words, the precept will fail.[326] It may be that shouting "fire" is, all things considered, dangerous but nonetheless should be done in the circumstances. Thus, even the general rule deserves to go unobserved in this particular case. The judiciary in such a system is precluded from legislating an exception or dispensing from the law, since it cannot make law.[327]

Turning to a legal system built on the understanding of human law I advocate in this book, we can see that the Game Rule is useful and nonproblematic as a statute. It appears to be a particular determination of the natural law precepts of preservation and protection of human life and also the obligations of living in a society of social animals.[328] It makes the determination that in this particular case — a crowded theater — these natural law precepts would be transgressed by shouting "fire." Since statutes only make particular determinations that are not meant to be complete, the enactment of the rule contains no danger of authorizing other equally dangerous behavior that may be prohibited by custom and judicial analogizing to a similar scenario, such as shouting "earthquake" in the crowded stadium. The Game Rule in such a system poses no danger of triggering a flood of further necessary specifications. It is supplemented by custom and judicial lawmaking by analogy.

Why then should this Game Rule be adopted in the first place? The answer might be that it need not be, absent a particular cause relating to shouting "fire" in theaters. Custom may already specify that shouting "fire" in a theater is a violation of the relevant natural law precepts, and courts will hold one violating it accountable under tort law, for example. In such a situation, the Game Rule is redundant and should not be enacted. On the other hand, a legislator may find it necessary to enact the Game Rule because a court either has attempted to overturn the old custom, such as by exonerating a "fire" shouter in circumstances that in the past would have incurred liability, or has attempted the initiation of a new bad custom encouraging the "fire" shouting, or because the community has itself developed a bad custom of shouting "fire" in crowded theaters, notwithstanding existing judicially enforced liability. In these scenarios, the court, or perhaps even the community as a whole, needs to be reminded of the forgotten general principle of natural law.[329] In the job of pruning the development of law, the legislator enacts this specific Game Rule in response to one of these particular failings but without attempting to address all similar cases. In some cases, a Standards Rule may be appropriate to remind the communal conscience of the general principle of natural law.[330] In such a case, the human law does not really make law, but rather repeats an existing precept of natural law in need of reinforcement. Thus, a Game Rule and a Standards Rule are possible legislative responses to an apparent need for a statutory correction of some flaw in the legal system. Yet, because both a Game Rule and a Standards Rule will function within the integrated hierarchy of law, natural and customary included, the problems identified in each type within a legislatively closed legal system can be avoided.

Turning from the hypothetical example of the "fire" shouting, we can see the implications of the foregoing analysis in the regulation of the financial markets, which markets in the United States have become dominated by legislative law in the form of statutes and administrative rules. In 2000, credit default swaps were completely exempted from state-made common law, including state common law affecting gambling contracts by legislative *fiat*.[331] Yet, these products that resembled financial gambling[332] fell outside the complex of Game Rules contained in federal securities and commodities regulation.[333] Due to the federal preemption, common law courts were precluded from addressing the problems these instruments posed and were unable to use evolving common law standards holding gambling contracts unenforceable as against public policy.[334] The unregulated credit default swaps contributed at least in part to the financial collapse epitomized by the failure of Bear Stearns and Lehman Brothers.[335] Following the financial collapse, the Dodd–Frank Act's 848 pages were an attempt to add more Game Rules to address the new contingent matters added to the game board, such as the role of risk-multiplying credit default swaps in the financial collapse.[336] Yet, just as its 2000 predecessor statute, it exempted the area from all common law.[337] Thus, the federal government remains committed to churning out more Game Rules fighting the last crisis as the financial markets continue to evolve. The one legal institution containing the flexibility to adapt and analogize to the changes, the common law courts, remains excluded from lawmaking under this federal tyranny of legislative preemption.[338] Thus, even in a historically common law system, areas of U.S. law have been subjected to voluminous Game Rules to the exclusion of the common law.

The approach that allows law to be made from a variety of sources thus eliminates many of the problems of legislation in common or civil law contexts.[339] The Game Rule is no longer underinclusive because it is nonexclusive. Detailed case-by-case judgments can be made and explained so as to guide development. Because the Game Rule forces a court doing anything other than simply applying the rule to the precise case to analogize to similar situations or to explain a dispensation from the law, it encourages the articulation of reasons.[340] As Brennan explains: "Judges, unlike legislators and legislatures, are required to give reasons. It is true that legislators often give explanations for what they are up to in proposing or supporting legislation, but there is little by way of culture that demands that their reasons be argued rather than asserted. Legislators can often get by with progandistic, half-hearted explanations for their decisions."[341]

Statutes, although enacted for reasons, lack a forum for making the reasons part of the law. Civil law judges hesitate to articulate reasons underpinning their decisions, because they are not supposed to be making law.[342] As a result, a system that embraces law generated through case law will not only address more particular and contingent situations with equitable rules, but it will also embody reasoned decisions.[343] Reason then becomes a source of law. As R. Floyd Clarke observed:

> It follows that in cases whose subject-matter involves considerations of equity, a system of decisions of special cases will produce more justice than a system of general rules expressed so as to govern all cases. The Case Law decides one case, the Statute Law attempts to solve many. In short, it is easier to decide one case correctly and give a true reason therefor, than it is to decide all cases that may possibly arise correctly, and by one form of words express the general rule, and its exceptions.[344]

This is not to say that case law always gets the rule correct. Still, it implants the rule within a larger system, providing opportunities to correct the error through distinguishing other cases or, in appropriate cases, exposing the faulty reasoning and overturning the rule.[345] The "imperfection of human reasoning powers" results in the imperfection of the common law system, but this problem is compounded when imperfection in reasoning produces a rigid fixed statutory rule applicable to all cases in theory.[346] Rather than the tripartite sources of law formerly recognized in the Western tradition—reason, custom, and commands[347]—all Western legal systems, including both those historically identified as common law and those as civil law, are being overwhelmed by tyrannical legislation that collapses the three sources into one—legislative command. The result in both common and civil law systems has been a great increase in the quantity of laws.[348]

The consequences of the growing exclusivity and quantity of legislation are many, but I will focus on two here. First, it detaches lawmaking from reasoning and customary history. I have already noted the emphasis in common law on the reasoned opinion that is generally absent from massive legislation, which may be explained in general terms but rarely contains rational explanations of adopted rules. Law no longer appears to be a reasoned evolution of rules based upon a rational analysis of the dialectical interaction of natural law principles and customary practices.

In turn, this detachment of law from rationality contributes to a growing disrespect for law, the violation of which is no longer connected either to the transgression of transcendental moral principles, since human law is no longer seen as determinations of them, or to the traditions of the community. Experts debate the causes, but our current U.S. prison population is greater than any country's in recorded history, and it continues to grow.[349] In particular, instances of white-collar crime are increasing,[350] which indicates a socioeconomically broader disrespect for law. The typical white-collar criminal is not an innercity economically deprived criminal but rather affluent and possibly a community leader.[351] The increase in white-collar crime demonstrates a weakening concern for respecting the congressionally generated statutes designed to regulate the industries in which they work. These crimes often impact our societies to a much greater extent than violent crimes, at least in purely economic terms.[352] This disregard of law by wealthy individuals is exemplified through the individual cases of Martha Stewart,[353] James Paul Lewis, Jr.,[354] and Bernard Madoff,[355] and also by the corporate cases of WorldCom, Enron, Tyco, and Adelphia.[356] Some academics even argue that corporations should violate the law whenever it is economically efficient to do so, and then pay the financial price.[357] As Harold Berman has remarked:

> Almost all the nations of the West are threatened today by a cynicism about law, leading to a contempt for law, on the part of all classes of the population. The cities have become increasingly unsafe. The welfare system has almost broken down under unenforceable regulations. There is wholesale violation of the tax laws by the rich and the poor and those in between. There is hardly a profession that is not caught up in evasion of one or another form of governmental regulation. And the government itself, from bottom to top, is caught up in illegalities.[358]

Thus, the more commands not based in reason and custom come to dominate the source of law, the less respect law seems to hold among the governed.

The second major impact upon human law is the eroding of the legal principle that ignorance of the law is no excuse, which "is deep in our law."[359] How can U.S. citizens still be presumed to know the law when the law is composed of libraries of statute books of Game Rules? In the area of tax law, ignorance of the law "is a defense, not just in the constitutional sense of vagueness, but as the flat, unadorned lack of knowledge of the law."[360] Sharon Davies has even argued that ignorance of law is slowly becoming a defense to all crimes.[361] The legal maxim made sense when laws were either restatements of natural law, which is able to be known by all, such as "do not murder the innocent,"[362] or were the product of long-standing customs, which because of their age were clearly known by the community in general. Specific enactments must be promulgated and accepted so that variations from long-standing customs become well known. The maxim is reasonable in such a context. Yet, it becomes a legal fiction, and arguably an absurd one, when the law has become a mountain of detailed Game Rules or vague Standards Rules lacking connections to both natural law and long-standing custom. Obviously, the policy implications of allowing such a defense are significant. Yet, is justice really worked when the law through its sheer quantity and disconnection to natural law or custom becomes unknowable?

In the first section we described the role of human lawmaking within the grand architecture of law as the progressive decoration of the structure with specific determinations of the general principles. The process weaves deductive reasoning from principles of practical reason together with inductive discovery of principles through developing customs. Statutory and customary law interact dialectically to prune customary development of human determinations of the natural law. Unlike Hart, who saw natural law—and morality generally—and human positive law as opposed to each other, or at least existing on separate planes,[363] the natural law tradition deems them coterminous: "The immutable idea of right [natural law or *jus*] dwells in the changing positive law."[364]

This second section has applied this jurisprudential framework to a more detailed consideration of the nature of a legal system. Among the two idealized types, the common law tradition, with its developing judge-made law with a flexible rule of *stare decisis* interacting with periodic necessary statutes, appeared to embody the philosophy of the first section more than civil law codes. We have also lamented the takeover of law by legislative statutes, not only in the realm of civil law codes but also in formerly common law systems, which are increasingly dominated by voluminous Game Rules. The explosion of legislation either in the form of codes of abstract standards or U.S.-style exponentially growing Game Rules appears to contribute to a lack of respect for law. The elimination, or at least the overwhelming by sheer volume, of reason (natural law principles) and developing custom has eliminated both knowledge of and respect for law, leading some to challenge the viability of the maxim that ignorance of the law is no excuse.[365] To return to the architecture analogy, the vision of human lawmaking we described in the first section may result in the decoration of a structure slowly and eclectically transcending various architectural styles. Like Chartres Cathedral, the law may be a structure decorated with Romanesque, Gothic, and Baroque ornamentation woven together. Yet, the triumph of legislation has papered over the structure with a dizzying array of disjointed pieces of paper, piled so high that they obscure the foundation and the architectural structure. Whereas code countries have whitewashed the interconnected architectural styles with a uniform abstract code, common law countries continue to churn out paper to obscure the structure. The aesthetically displeasing result was poetically predicted by Bishop in his polemical arguments against the adoption of the legislation-dominated code system:

> And she [England] threatens to substitute acts of Parliament for all her common law of reason; and make it possible for sluggards and fools to practise at her bar and preside in her courts. If she does it, it requires no gift of prophecy to foresee that her encompassing seas will weep upon the dripping rocks around that little island a more mournful re-quiem to her entombed empire than was ever before sung over fallen greatness and glory.[366]

SEVEN

Appointing a Foreman

The Basis of Authority and Obligation

Law, if it is law, is authoritative,
and the authoritative is voice, voice heard.[1]

In chapter 6, we considered in detail the process for making particular determinations of natural law through human law. Underlying this examination we find an assumption: that there are individuals who possess the authority to make these determinations. This premise needs further examination, because it has been a source of consternation in modern legal philosophy. Throughout history some men have questioned whether authority of some over others is consistent with human nature.[2] Is it possible for a law made by one man to bind the conscience of another, or is such a claim merely tyranny?[3] If such a power to bind to laws made by humans is justified, what is its scope? The answers to these related questions explored in this chapter will be both descriptive and normative. I will offer an explanation of the nature of authority and the extent of the obligation to obey the law and also explain how the architecture of natural law jurisprudence exposited in this book explains and justifies both the authority and the obligation. To introduce the subject, I will offer a preliminary definition of authority and obligation. The first section will then survey some of the competing theories of authority and obligation and demonstrate their lack of an ontology and a satisfying justification. The second section will present the natural law–based justification for legal authority and obligation that can be derived from the jurisprudence of the prior chapters and will examine the scope, and particularly the limits, of legal authority and obligation to obey the laws.

Before commencing the discussion, the parameters of the questions can be narrowed somewhat by defining the terms "authority" and "obligation." *Auctoritas*, from which the English word "authority" is derived, is a "liberty, ability, [or] power" to express one's will as a "command, precept, [or] decree."[4] Yet, such a general definition would encompass the power or ability of a thug to order a person to hand over his wallet. Distinguishing authority from threats backed by force was one of the primary concerns of H. L. A. Hart in defining the concept of law.[5] As Joseph Raz observed, justifying authority involves distinguishing *authority* to direct action from the mere *power* to direct action.[6] At the very basic level of definition we can see how the descriptive answer to the question of legal authority is inextricably linked to the normative claim. That which distinguishes authority from threats backed by force, or authoritarianism, is legitimacy. The power or ability to command is a legitimate or justified power, an attribute lacking in the case of the gunman. Authority involves both an ability to impose one's choice of a law upon others and a normative justification for doing so.[7] Yet, to constitute legitimate authority one must not only have the power to command but that power must also include a duty on the part of the one commanded to obey.[8] Obedience to the law involves conforming one's actions to the requirements of the law.[9] Legitimate authority entails an obligation to conform one's action to the command in a way that the threat of the gunman does not. The effect may be the same, the completion of an action complying with the instructions of another, but the nature of that conformity is different. In the case of the gunman, conformity may be necessary to avoid harm but it is not normatively obligatory. It is not an act of obedience to conform to the gunman even if it becomes prudentially expedient. In contrast, the claim of authority involves more than a threat of harm making conformity expedi-

ent, but a threat may be added to the instruction of law to encourage obedience.[10] It is not the threat that makes the law obligatory. The threat is legitimate if and only if the one giving the instruction is possessed of authority in contrast to mere force. As Randy Barnett explains: "A lawmaking
system is legitimate . . . if it creates commands that citizens have a moral
duty to obey."[11] In the pithy words of Joseph Vining, legal authority produces "willing obedience."[12] Willing obedience is not the same as being
happy or pleased about one's obedience. It means being willing to obey
even when we do not want to obey. Although Raz would dispute a general
duty to obey the law,[13] he does understand the concept of authority as a
power to give another an exclusionary reason for acting when one does
not understand the reasons or when one would choose otherwise.[14] If not
morally obligatory, for Raz, authoritative law can at least give one a preemptive reason to act.[15] As Philip Soper has noted, recognizing an authority
preempts in some way individual choice, in the sense that a command or
precept given by one with authority takes some degree of freedom away
from deliberating personally about the regulated action.[16] Soper describes
this autonomy-limiting role of authority as a "content-independent" reason for action, meaning that the reason for action is rooted in the authority
of the one commanding or enacting the law and not in the content of the
command or law being correct.[17] In other words the power referred to in
the definition of authority is a power to require others to act on the authority's determination of the correctness of the content of the authoritative claim. Abner Greene argues that this preemption of individual determination requires justification.[18] Hart and Kelsen, in contrast, proceed in
their jurisprudence without providing a complete justification for legal
authority but merely assume its presence in the system. Kelsen merely assumes the existence of a "basic norm," which he calls a "juristic hypothesis."[19] Hart acknowledges that without some "minimal content" no person
would have a reason to obey the law and no legal system would exist.[20] Yet,
he merely assumes the existence of this minimum content as a rational
necessity without normatively justifying or rigorously defining it. This
lack of metaphysical justification is most obvious in his treatment of the
"Rule of Recognition,"[21] which he asserts exists simply because it must
exist and thereby sidesteps any rigorous ontological treatment of this
foundational rule and its causes. Both Kelsen's "basic norm" and Hart's

Rule of Recognition are used to ground their concept of the legal system. Yet, the most that either thinker can do is simply posit the existence of such a lynchpin of authority as a logical necessity. Hart simply introduces the Rule of Recognition as that rule which tells you what rules count as rules.[22] Hart offers no explanation for the origin of such a Rule of Recognition other than it just exists in every legal system. Ultimately Hart's analysis ends at an ultimate Rule of Recognition that has no rule to evaluate its own validity. It is "'assumed or postulated' or it is a hypothesis."[23] A Rule of Recognition can "neither be valid nor invalid but is simply accepted as appropriate for use."[24] For Hart and his disciples the Rule of Recognition is asserted as an uncaused cause of legal systems. It is merely a fact devoid of any metaphysical explanation or proof that a certain Rule of Recognition exists in a particular legal system.[25] The basic norm and the Rule of Recognition are assumed as givens, and authority is therefore assumed to exist. Even Ronald Dworkin, who is claimed by some as a proponent of moral reasoning in jurisprudence,[26] asserts the justification of coercive authority. For Dworkin, current adjudications are based on past political decisions, which are assumed into the system without justification.[27]

The examination of authority in this chapter makes the stronger claim that legal authority can be justified and not simply assumed. Yet, even Raz's minimalist notion of authority as a mere reason for acting requires some justification. Why should the adoption of a rule by a political ruler present a particular reason for choice? Thus, even Raz needs to identify the ontological and normative grounding of his minimalist legal authority to give exclusionary reasons. The contention of this chapter is that the architecture onto which human law is layered justifies legal authority. The authority of human laws can be justified and explained only in light of the eternal and natural law.

Contra Raz, the concept of authority articulated in this chapter necessarily entails an obligation located beyond the mere command of the one claiming authority to compel obedience to the command. The power of authority in its essence is the power not merely to persuade one to choose an action one might otherwise not choose, but, as Perry has defined it, the power "to change persons' normative situations."[28] By which he means, to change their normative situation by creating a specific obligation to act that did not exist prior to the authoritative act. Authority in the strongest sense of the word is not merely a claimed ability to superior knowledge of what should be done.[29] To hold authority involves more than merely repeating the content of a preexisting obligation for the purpose of clarifying and publicizing its content (although those possessing authority may do this). The strongest form of the concept of authority involves a power to legitimately bring obligations into existence by choosing to enact particular laws. This strong form of authority will be defined, delineated, and defended in this chapter. Stephen Perry offers a useful definition of this strong form of authority that is the subject of this chapter: "If a directive was issued by an organ of a government which not only claims but also possesses legitimate authority, then those persons who fall within the scope of the directive have an obligation to obey it. Because legitimate authority is moral authority, this obligation is a moral obligation."[30] The definition contains a criterion for distinguishing between what Patrick Brennan calls "authoritarian" and "authority."[31] The definition of legitimate authority will enable us to distinguish between a subtle gunman, the one who clothes himself in the robes of a political ruler claiming authority but who, though possessing the power to compel compliance, lacks the power to create obligations to comply. Whereas most people can recognize the gunman when they see him, it is more difficult to recognize the gunman when he is clothed with the vestments of legitimate authority, when he commands from the Kremlin or the White House, but whose claim to authority is false. By defining the precise scope of the claim to authority we can distinguish the authoritarian from the authority. By claiming the obligation to be moral, Perry points to a criterion of evaluation outside the command itself. It obligates by virtue of something beyond itself, whereas the gunman or the authoritarian merely obliges by the force of his threats.

One final definitional clarification is warranted. This chapter will consider only a species of political authority, the power specifically to create or alter laws. The definition of *auctoritas* included the power to create both commands and precepts. Political authority in the broadest sense includes both these powers. Political authority includes the power to order individuals to act in particular ways. The U.S. president may order the army to move to a specific location. The governor may order the offices of a state to close on a certain day because of inclement weather. Neither of these acts involves the creation of a law. Law involves the formulation of a rule and measure of human acts that, although capable of formulation at various levels of generality or specificity, is directed to a community or a group within a community to serve as a general guide to action—not an order to act a particular way at a particular time. A law as opposed to a command transcends any particular individuals.[32] Laws, though capable of repeal, are written to apply beyond any particular individual at any point in time. A formulated law is not directed merely to the living members of the community for which it is made but to future members (unless the law is later revoked). A command by contrast is directed to compel action by one or more particular individuals at points in time and is intended to lapse when the commanded acts are completed. The consideration of authority within this chapter is restricted to the power to change normative positions by enacting laws. This limitation is not meant to deny the existence of the power of authorities to command but merely to distinguish the power likely subject to differing justifications and limitations. Austin and Hart, two jurists who have thought deeply about authority and law, seem to neglect this distinction within political authority.[33] The following discussion is concerned solely with the authority to make obligatory law. The first section will examine the two general categories of arguments used to justify legal authority and demonstrate how they fail. The section will conclude with a brief examination of two theories of authority that do not fall into either group and that come the closest to a real justification of legal authority, those of Raz and Perry. Yet, we will see where even these attempts fail to provide a completely satisfactory answer.

ATTEMPTS TO JUSTIFY AUTHORITY
AND OBLIGATION

Innumerable attempts have been made in the history of jurisprudence to justify the power of some people to make laws that others are obligated to obey and thereby change the others' normative position. Although there are many fine distinctions among the theories, they can be grouped into two major categories: consent theories and utilitarian arguments. This section will summarize the key features of each type of justification and demonstrate their inadequacy, both in the sense of the failure of the argument on its own terms and its failure to explain the ontological goodness of authority. If the strong form of the definition of authority requires that those subject to the law should obey the law even when they believe their own calculation of the best action is superior, a complete justification of authority must prove the ontology of authority by explaining its origin and causes. It must demonstrate the good of authority in itself, and not merely instrumentally. To assist in this evaluation this section will have recourse to the criteria developed by Leslie Green to evaluate whether a particular purported legal system entails an obligation to obey its laws. Although these criteria are not formulated to prove the reality and goodness of authority in the universal context, they are helpful when applied to particular communities. Perry has provided a succinct recitation of Green's criteria:

> To justify the conclusion that there is, within a given legal system, a general obligation to obey the law, the supporting argument or arguments must, according to Green, show that this obligation is (i) a moral reason for action; (ii) a content-independent reason for action, meaning a reason to do as the state directs because the state directs it and not because its directives have a certain content; (iii) a binding or mandatory reason for action, as opposed to a reason which simply happens to outweigh other relevant reasons; (iv) a particular reason for action, meaning a reason that arises only for the directives of a citizen's (or subject's) own state, and not for the directives of other states; and, finally, (v) a universal reason for action, in the double sense that it binds all of a state's citizens to all of that state's laws.[34]

Throughout the analysis of authority we will use these five criteria as a hermeneutic for judging the success or failure of theories of authority.

Consent Theories

When the natural law–based justification of authority, described in the next section, was rejected in the early modern era, philosophers and jurists not willing to abandon themselves to anarchism searched for a substitute. They turned to a familiar area of the law, contracts. Contract law is the law of voluntarily created obligations. If successful, consent theory would satisfy the five conditions for authority since it provides a binding content-independent moral reason for obeying the law made by others universally applicable only to the members of the relevant community. The reason for obeying the law would be the antecedent contractual promise to do so, not because of its content, but because one promised to obey the law. The moral obligation to obey the law would be entailed by the moral obligation to honor voluntary contracted obligations (which if such a moral obligation can be proven, it would support public contracts consenting to obey the law). If the consent were valid, such an obligation would be binding. If the consent as given applied universally to all laws made at any time, the obligation would be universal and at the same time limited only to those members of the community made such by consent and not individuals consenting to different states. Although the five conditions would be met, the problem is that consent theory has not been able to establish the existence of the requisite voluntary consent to a universal obligation to obey the laws of a particular legal system by each member of the relevant legal community. Contracts come into existence upon the freely given consent of the contracting parties. From Rousseau to Locke, many who rejected traditional natural law saw a potential substitute theory in this basic act of voluntary consent. Legal authority and the entailed obligation could be the product of voluntary consent of the governed entering into a compact imposing an obligation to obey the law.[35] But contracts only impose binding obligations on the parties actually consenting thereto, and consent of the governed is at best a myth. The consent myth has played a significant role in attempting to justify legal authority in the United States. Americans must obey the law because the consent of "We the People" legitimized our government.[36] Our first president invoked this argument to urge obedience to the laws during his Farewell Address: "The basis of our political systems is the right of the people to make and to alter their own constitutions of government.... The very idea of the power and the right of the people to establish government presupposes the duty of every individual to obey the established government."[37] Christopher Ferrara has exploded such rhetoric by demonstrating that "We the People" was no more than a tiny minority of the people living in the former American colonies, now thirteen states, at the time of ratification of the U.S. Constitution.[38] According to Ferrara, "no more than about five percent of the total American population at the time, or about 160,000 white male voters, actually cast votes for delegates to the ratifying conventions. Of these 160,000 voters probably about 60,000 were opposed to ratification. Thus . . . it was . . . only a few hundred *ad hoc* delegates at ratifying conventions whose votes represented the will of about 100,000 propertied electors in a nation of some 3.5 million people, not including the slave population."[39] Beyond this problem, how does this consent of a majority of 5 percent of the population hundreds of years ago express the voluntary consent of those living today? As Randy Barnett quipped, "In what sense can a small minority of inhabitants presuming to call themselves 'We the People' bind anyone but themselves? And assuming they could somehow bind everyone then alive, how could they bind, by their consent, their posterity?"[40] Yet, these few hundred men's votes are treated by the myth of "We the People" to be sufficient to express a voluntary consent to be morally obligated universally to obey the laws of the government ratified hundreds of years ago when none of us were even alive to be excluded from the elite electorate.

Even Jean-Jacques Rousseau recognized that the only way to justify legal authority—and an obligation on the part of each member of a society to obey the law—is through unanimous consent to this social contract.[41] Yet, even this early pioneer of consent theory recognized his social contract was only a myth and not a real contract. Unlike real contracts, which require a real objective manifestation to be bound by the contract, Rousseau admitted that requiring real universal consent was impossible and some form of tacit consent would be necessary to hold his theory together.[42] The weakest form of tacit consent attempts to imply consent from other acts or passive states, including voting, residing in a territory, the failure to engage in rebellion,[43] or the receipt by a resident of a territory of some benefit.[44] The voting or political participation version of implied consent relies on the ambiguity of an act like voting, which may not imply consent to the system but merely be an act of self-defense to avoid a worse evil.[45] As to passive acts, such as living in a territory or benefiting from living in a society,[46] these arguments run afoul of the principle that mere silence cannot bind an offeree to a contract.[47] A car company cannot drop off a car in your driveway and say you owe us if we do not hear from you. As Barnett observes, "It is still not clear, however, that one is obligated to pay for all unsolicited benefits one receives from others."[48] If taken to its logical extension, the receipt of benefits legitimizes slavery at least in the case of a beneficent master who provides enough benefits.[49] At a minimum, the resting of a claim to tacit consent on the threat of removal of basic benefits flowing from communal life of any society would seem to constitute undue influence or even duress. Any attempt at implying consent by the receipt of benefits must prove that an easy and realistic option exists for exiting the purportedly beneficial system. We are born into a territory, into a family, and have very little real choice to leave or rebel. The absence of a realistic, inexpensive exit option from the territory means that remaining in a territory is a poor argument for the presence of freely given consent.[50] Thus, tacit consent is really a method for imposing the desired consent on those who do not affirmatively do so. As Barnett wryly notes: "It is a queer sort of 'consent' where there is no way to refuse. 'Heads I win, tails you lose,' is the way to describe a rigged contest. 'Heads' you consent, 'tails' you consent, 'didn't flip the coin,' guess what? You consent as well. This is simply not consent."[51] The logical fallacy in all consent arguments consists in a faulty leap from the legitimate principle of consent in personal relationships and contracts to implied consent in impersonal groups.[52] Rawls's approach represents a desperate last-ditch effort to invent consent. If real and tacit consent fail to exist, we can imply a "hypothetical consent." People have consented to that to which they ought to consent. Rawls argues: "The choice which rational men would make in this hypothetical situation of equal liberty . . . determines the principles of justice."[53] Thus, "We the People" must obey the laws because we have hypothetically consented to what Rawls says we would have consented to if he asked us, which in fact he never did. Consent has turned into hypothetical or imagined consent. Paul W. Kahn makes explicit the imaginary nature of consent:

> To see through the constitution to the popular sovereign whose act it records is what makes it literally *our* constitution, despite the fact that we, as finite individuals, neither wrote it nor approved it. This is not a matter of "implicit consent" but of a social imaginary that grounds faith. The constitution claims us not because it is just—although we want it to be just . . . but because it is a remnant of a politics of authenticity that we still imagine as our own.[54]

Beyond the failure to actually prove the existence of any real, meaning-ful consent to legal authority, the consent argument fails for another rea-son of ontology. Even if we could all somehow engage in an evergreen free and voluntary consent, what proof is there that we possess the ability to confer such a power in the first place? It is an ancient legal maxim that no-body can transfer more authority than one possesses.[55] The proponents of consent merely argue about the legitimacy of the process of passing along legitimate authority from "We the People" to lawmakers. Yet, as Kelsen ar-gues, legitimate authority must rest on a chain of authorization back to a source.[56] Consent theory if successful merely proves that a power was passed legitimately. It has no answer for the origin of the power to change others' normative situation. It has no answer to the question how one or more human beings can change the normative position of another crea-ture sharing an equal nature. As Abner Greene observes, consent theory only works if you start with the premise that individuals possess authority to be given up in the consenting.[57] Whence does the power to choose our own actions originate? By focusing on the process of transmission, consent theories ignore the larger ontological problem of the justification of the power supposedly transmitted. Perry glimpses this problem with acts of consent justifying the categorical power to obligate everyone to obey the law.[58] Michael Moore explains that the failure of consent theories (or other theories based upon the will of individuals) lies in the unjustified move from the fact that sometimes individuals engage in obligation-creating acts (by making a promise, for example) to the claim that individuals pos-sess a limitless sovereignty to create obligations. This limitless sovereignty that consent theorists assume to reside in the individual can then be trans-mitted by some real or fictitious consent. Yet, as Moore argues: "We should see these obligation-creating acts as part of our limited moral sovereignty, that is, the capacity which each person possesses to alter the moral land-scape through his exercise of will. . . . That we have some such sovereignty at all is only because other obligation-creating norms permit us to have and to exercise such powers."[59] Even if actual consent were possible, which it is not, it would not transmit a plenary obligation-creating authority since individuals lack such limitless authority. Thus, consent theories of vary-ing stripes fail to fulfill, at the very minimum, Leslie Green's first and third criteria. Absent real unanimous consent, the theory does not establish a moral reason to obey the law, because the authority supposedly conferred by consent has no ontological or moral basis, and consent theories lack a plausible reason why those who do not consent to the system in general or particular laws with which they disagree are obligated, notwithstanding their lack of consent, universally to obey the law.

This lack of reasonable plausibility evacuates human law of the quality of rationality. For consent theorists such as Thomas Hobbes, the starting point is not a universally valid rational law but rather each person's right to self-preservation.[60] Since the foundation of modern authority is not a rational law, the rule of the wise in which rulers deserve to make law because they are skilled in the love of truth advocated by the ancient philosophers is no longer considered the best regime.[61] One does not rule by virtue of wisdom but by virtue of having received some volitional consent in the mythical state of nature. Law no longer needs to be reasonable but simply be a willed act of the hypothetically consented to authority.[62]

Utilitarian Justifications

Beyond consent theories, another group of jurists attempt to justify authority on utilitarian grounds. By this term I do not mean that all of these theorists are utilitarian in the strict sense of the term. They all approach the topic from different philosophical premises. What they all have in common is that they justify authority only instrumentally. Authority is good because it is instrumentally useful or effective for achieving some other good. Certainly there is nothing wrong with authority being efficient or useful in achieving other goods. The problem is that usefulness does not justify authority as a real good. If it is only instrumentally good, then authority cannot bind universally in conscience. Doing so begs the question if in a particular situation obedience to authority is not useful or effective, why should one obey the law? Even if one takes such terms in their most long-term perspective, where obedience may not be useful in a particular case but disobedience may diminish respect for law, including for the actor, and thus it is useful to obey in the one case, why should one obey the law? One should obey a legal authority in such a case only if doing so is in and of itself good. To say anything less about authority may justify authority as useful but does not justify a universal obligation to obey the law because doing so is good.

For the utilitarian justification, the presence of an authority to make laws that people are obligated to obey is useful for communities. We are better off with authority than without. Although the prior sentence may sound like a truism to all but the most committed anarchist, it does not really justify authority in and of itself. It only justifies it as a less offensive alternative to anarchy. Ultimately, although some of the utilitarians use moral language (and would likely object to being labeled utilitarian), all among the wide variety of utilitarian theories fail to support an authority that gives a content-independent moral reason to obey the law universally.

The negative utilitarian argument—authority is a lesser evil than anarchy—is rooted in the state of nature myth used by the consent theorists, even though the argument avoids the need for consent. The state of nature is so dangerous and horrid that we are all better off with an authority that can keep us from slipping back into the state of nature.[63] The two main problems with this argument are that it is unverifiable. First, since it compares life with authority to a never-existent myth, it can never prove its claim of life being better now. It sets up a false dichotomy between life with authority and a nonexistent situation, and thus it simply asserts the conclusion that authority is useful. Second, the theory fails criterion (ii) (content-independence), criterion (iii) (a binding obligation and not merely the best among other reasons), and criterion (v) (universality). Since the end of authority, for the utilitarian approach, is merely avoiding a worse fate, its goodness is dependent upon the extent to which it is in fact the best means to that end in all cases. The problem of legal cheating confronts the theory. To use a classic example, if I can know for certain that driving through a red light at a deserted intersection entails no risk of slipping into the dreaded state of nature, and if in fact I can argue that my arriving at my destination on time will contribute to a stable and orderly society (perhaps I am on my way to my shift as a police officer), then I can conclude that running the light is more utilitarian. I do sweep some complexity under the carpet. There is the argument that not obeying the law wears down respect for the law and thus it should be universally obeyed even when a particular instance suggests it is unnecessary in that context. Yet, if it could be proven that I am a perfect utilitarian in that I will not lose my sense of respect for laws that are really justified on a case-by-case basis to avoid the slip into the state of nature, then I have no duty to obey a law that does not instrumentally serve the given end. The negative utilitarian argument thus fails to bind universally, but only when a particular law is in fact an effective means to avoid the slip into the state of nature. It also fails to offer a content-independent reason for obeying the law. Each law is only worthy of obedience to the extent its content actually fulfills the utilitarian criterion of effectiveness.

The more successful utilitarian arguments approach the problem positively. The good that authority is useful for achieving is not simply avoiding a worse mythical state but making possible some positive good. For John Finnis, authority is essentially utilitarian in that it makes possible the good of coordination. First, Finnis argues that authority is needed because people are selfish and foolish in pursuing the common good.[64] This argument is merely a reformulated version of the state of nature argument. Without authority we will be at the mercy of selfish and foolish people. Authority is needed to avoid this worse fate. But Finnis progresses to a more interesting question: "In a community free from these vices, would authority be needed, or justified?"[65] Finnis asserts that "more authority" may be necessary in such an idyllic community to solve coordination problems.[66] Practical reasonableness will often support several reasonable and appropriate solutions to a problem. Authority is needed to choose among them since unanimity of choice is practically impossible and consent theory is merely a form of unattainable unanimity. Having an authority is the only other possibility.[67] Authority is thus only an instrumental good "because required for the realization of the common good."[68] Although less morbid than the negative utilitarians (since Finnis talks about achieving a positive common good, not merely avoiding a worse evil), in the end Finnis can only argue that authority is good by default. Nothing else works to coordinate effort toward the common good, so authority must be good. Authority is thus not good in the broadest sense in which Finnis uses the term (and for which he introduces the word "value").[69] To be such it must be "desirable for its own sake and not merely as something sought after under some such description as . . . 'what will contribute to my survival.'"[70] Consistently Finnis does not include authority in his list of basic goods.[71] It is only good if it is the only means to achieve coordination, which itself is only an instrumental and not a basic good. If it could be proven that either in a society of devils or of angels, coordination and the common good could be achieved without authority, then authority would lose its purpose and cease to be an instrumental good. Finnis offers no real ontology for authority as a good in itself. His theory of authority thus fails criteria (ii), (iii), and (v). The only reason to obey authority is because it appears to be the only useful means of coordinating action. Thus, to the extent authority fails to do so it is sapped of its moral authority and is thus not content-independent. As understood by Finnis, authority lacks universality in that it would cease to exist in the presence of other, more effective methods of coordination.

Although Finnis ultimately concludes that "God is the basis of obligation,"[72] he denies that knowledge of God helps answer questions about obligation.[73] Finnis clearly states that he does not ground his understanding of obligation in terms of conformity to God's supreme will,[74] but he does admit that God is the ultimate origin of obligation. As with the eternal law, Finnis's ultimate conclusion is that God is practically irrelevant for understanding and justifying authority. Such a conclusion runs counter to the entire Aristotelian tradition, which holds that we must know things through their causes. The ultimate causality of God for authority is dismissed by Finnis from necessary consideration.

Stripped of a necessary ontology of its own, Finnis's theory contains, for all practical purposes, no origin of authority, no transmission, delegation, or consent. Tellingly, when Finnis quotes Fortescue's famous discussion of authority, he can't abide his statement that authority comes from "natural law" and changes it to "practical reasonableness."[75] If authority comes from natural law, that suggests it has an ontology. We shall see in the next section that Fortescue's claim that the law of nature establishes authority, which Finnis dismisses as "lawyers' jargon,"[76] is central to the ontological justification of authority. For Finnis, there is only a fact: that people acquiesce to someone as an authority explains that there is authority.[77] Lawyers try to legalize the devolution of undevolved authority:[78] "The sheer fact that virtually everybody *will* acquiesce in somebody's say-so is the presumptively necessary and defeasibly sufficient condition for the normative judgment that that person has (i.e., is justified in exercising) authority in that community."[79] Ironically, although Finnis goes to great lengths to claim he is avoiding the "is" entails "ought" so-called fallacy (rather than rejecting its universal application as a fallacy), this argument simply asserts that authority ought to exist because people nearly universally do acquiesce to someone. To this "scandalously stark principle" he adds two riders. First, the person exercising authority has to comply with the constitutional provisions applicable to gaining the position at the time and place, if any. Finnis's rule is merely a reincarnation of Hart's Rule of Recognition, which simply exists without an ontological foundation or explained and justified origin.[80] As long as one complies with the fact of the Rule of Recognition, authority is justified. Further, Finnis recognizes that not all people to whom enough people acquiesce are deserving of authority, so he has to borrow from consent theorists and create his own myth, as Rousseau and Rawls do. His is this: "When practically reasonable subjects, with the common good in view, would think they *ought* to consent to it," then they should.[81] Thus, a real community has an obligation to accept an authority when a mythic community of mythic people would have to do so. When ought they accept an authority? The full force of Finnis's utilitarianism is on display in the answer to this question: "Authority (and thus the *responsibility* of governing) in a community is to be exercised by those who can in fact effectively settle co-ordination problems for that community."[82] This is another form of fictitious consent: people are deemed to have consented when they ought to consent. They ought to obey simply because there is a fact of authority and there is no other way to get things done.

Some scholars attempt to avoid the utilitarian justification by claiming that authority is valuable in itself, yet upon closer examination their theory is at heart utilitarian. Raz, although rejecting a universal obligation to obey the law, does recognize that respect for authority is at least permissible. Raz concedes that it is permissible to respect the law (at least in a good legal system), and if you do in fact respect the law, then you may be obligated to obey the law.[83] Thus, there is only a contingent duty to obey an authority; if you respect a particular legal system's law, then that respect is the source of your obligation. Raz's duty can never become completely content-independent. The contingent duty only arises if one judges the content of a legal system to be good. A flaw in Raz's argument can be observed by considering an analogy he uses: friendship. He argues there is no duty to have friendships, but if one in fact has a friendship, then he has a duty to act as a friend toward the friend.[84] For Raz, there is no good in being a legal system or a good in law itself (regardless of content). Likewise there is no good in friendship itself. He fails to see that although we may have no duty to be a friend to a particular person (or to be subject to a particular legal system), we do have an obligation to pursue the good of friendship (due to the social component of our nature) and law in general. Friendship and, as we will discuss more in the next section, law are both good because they are a component of man's nature, specifically his social and political nature, for which man has a natural inclination.[85] Although there may be no obligation to establish a friendship with a particular person, one is obligated—naturally inclined by nature—to friendships, and the attainment of friendship is a good (though there certainly can be degrees of goodness of any particular friendship). As discussed more in the next section, man is inclined to law, and therefore having law is good (but there are degrees of goodness). For Raz, on the other hand, the attribute of authority of law is not good in and of itself, but only good if one chooses to respect a given legal system. Raz's conception thus clearly fails criterion (v), because the obligation is not universal, but only effective for those who have chosen to respect the law.

It is also not content-independent. Unlike the consent theorists, Raz does argue that legal authorities are to act based on reasons: "All authoritative directives should be based, in the main, on reasons which already independently apply to the subjects of the directives and are relevant to their action in the circumstances covered by the directive."[86] It is notable, however, that Raz does not consider these reasons to be themselves legal. The authority in issuing a directive is not necessarily relying on law, but in general it should be relying on some undefined type of reasons. The work done by authority for Raz is simply to add preemptive force to the pre-existing undefined reasons on which the authority's determination depends. Raz develops this argument into what he calls a "service conception of authority." Justifying authority "involves showing that the alleged subject is likely better to comply with reasons which apply to him . . . if he accepts the directives of the alleged authority as authoritatively binding and tries to follow them, rather than trying to follow the reasons which apply to him directly."[87] Hugo Cyr demonstrates the utilitarian nature of Raz's theory by characterizing the service performed by authority as merely a "resource-saving" service.[88] Rather than having to spend the time analyzing all our reasons for action, we can simply obey the decision made by the authority. Yet, as Cyr has pointed out, if Raz's theory is taken literally, there is really no resource saving because in order to know if we should obey an authority we have to conclude that they do in fact perform this service—they do primarily base decisions on the reasons that individuals would otherwise weight for themselves. Cyr explains: "Moreover, to actually determine whether or not an authority is worth accepting, according to the Service Conception, the subject will ultimately have to engage in the very deliberations that the 'resource-saving' feature of the Service Conception was meant to help the subject avoid."[89]

In making this evaluation, the subject is analyzing the content of the authoritative decisions to see if they meet the standard of being primarily based on the reasons that would have been considered. Thus, announced rules are not content-independent; they rely for legitimacy on their content meeting this standard. In undertaking this exercise to determine the legitimacy of an entity as an authority, the subjects end up "destroy[ing] the authority function of that entity"[90] because the subject has to engage in the same deliberations from which the authority was supposed to save him. The only way to avoid destroying the utilitarian benefit of the authority-saving decision-making resources of subjects is to abstain from conducting the necessary evaluation of whether the authority meets the standard and accept the conclusion "that an entity has a legitimate authority over us would be ultimately a matter of faith."[91]

Perry summarizes Raz's argument: "Roughly speaking, the general idea is that, if one will better comply with right reason in a specified set of circumstances by allowing oneself to be guided by the judgment of another rather than by trying to act according to one's own judgment about what ought to be done, then one is justified in subjecting one's will to that of the other."[92] Perry argues that although Raz's theory might explain the subjection to the directives of another on some occasions (i.e., when subjection serves conformity with practical reason), it does not ever provide justification for the power of an authority to change people's normative positions in and of itself.[93] Essentially, Raz's position collapses into a form of greater-knowledge defense: one who possesses greater expertise becomes an authority based on that expertise. Their authority is justified because it is based, though not exclusively, on what he calls "dependent reasons,"[94] reasons that are merely assumed by Raz to exist and that are not given an ontological, and specifically legal ontological, explanation. Ultimately any obligation to obey the law of an authority is rooted in the claim that in the ideal (i.e., if acting as the experts they are meant to be) they are supposed to be accessing undefined dependent reasons that apply to their subjects. Yet, as Perry points out, the fact that I am morally obligated to conform to an expert's advice due to the wisdom of that advice does not itself prove the expert has moral power to command me to follow him.[95] The good advice of the expert contains its own reason for conformity, its inherent goodness. The reason for conformity does not reside in the expert but in the advice. As Perry observes according to Raz's view: "So long as I have reason to know that I will in general do better in complying with the reasons that apply to me in a given type of case by following the views of another person rather than by acting on my own judgment, it does not matter whether those views are offered in the form of advice or in the form of directives."[96] Raz himself seems to concede that his theory is no more than the expert explanation of following authority when he admits that the conditions for the service conception are unlikely to obtain.[97] In the end, the advice of authority may be useful to acting reasonably, but it is only authoritative subjectively for those who respect a particular legal system and see its laws as expert advice worthy of respect. In the end, authority may be useful, but it is not justified. Raz's theory fails the universality condition—criterion (v)—because, in Raz's view, a legal directive binds except when it does not due to other reasons, such as arbitrariness or violation of fundamental human rights.[98] Ultimately, Raz's service conception of authority is merely that—at the service of other undefined, preexisting reasons that already apply to people. The authority is justified if its decisions are most of the time dependent on those reasons, except if a particular decision violates other vague nonlegal concepts, such as "human rights." For Raz, authority may most of the time make me more likely to act rationally, but the rationality is the good and the authority is only most of the time useful. There is no particular good to authority itself.

The two thinkers who come closest to avoiding the utilitarian trap and locating the justification for legal authority are Perry and Barnett. Perry's value theory of authority appears to transcend utilitarianism and to be sound in substantive moral argument. He argues that authority is a moral power conceived as a value-based power. His value-based conception argues that "legitimate moral authority can only exist if there is something sufficiently good or valuable about one person being able intentionally to change the normative situation of another person."[99] "The moral and conceptual core of the concept of legitimate political authority" is that "one person has practical authority over another if there is sufficient value in the former person's being able intentionally to change the normative situation of the latter."[100] Unlike Raz, Perry recognizes that to justify authority as such, and not just the authority of a good system or a moral or legal expert, the exercise of authority must be shown to be a good or valuable. As Perry argues: "One person *A* has a power to effect a certain kind of change in the normative situation of another person *B* if there is reason for regarding actions which *A* takes with the intention of effecting a change of the relevant kind as in fact effecting such a change, where the justification for so regarding *A*'s actions is the sufficiency of the value or desirability of enabling *A* to make this kind of normative change by means of this kind of act."[101] Perry sees what utilitarian arguments miss, that the act of changing people's normative positions must be explained as a good act regardless of its instrumental usefulness for some independent good. The problem that ultimately turns Perry's argument into a utilitarian one is that he leaves indeterminate this value that is authority. He claims that his value theory of authority "is not intended to be a substantive theory addressed to the justification problem, nor can it operate as such. It is not self-applying; further moral argument is required to determine what kinds of value (if any) will justify *A*'s possession of such a power, as well as to determine the sufficiency of that value. This information will be provided by particular substantive theories of justification."[102] Thus, in the end, the value of authority is utilitarian for Perry because authority is only valuable if it can be found to support attainment of some other undefined value. In other words, authority is merely the best way to reach some other moral goal by imposing obligations necessary to achieve it.[103] At most, Perry's theory provides a hypothetical method for attempting to justify legal authority. If we can prove that there is a value served by legal authority, then legal authority can be justified. To the extent that this conclusion frames the issue for consideration it is useful, but only in such a modest capacity. Although it uses the language of moral justification, the value theory still reduces legal authority to a utilitarian role; authority is still instrumental to another undefined value. I believe Perry would accept my evaluation, because by his own admission he is only offering a conception of authority and not a justification of it, which he says must come from political moral theory. The closest Perry's theory comes to a real justification is in its functional or teleological argument. The goal of the state is to "accomplish particularly important moral goals that states are uniquely suited, or at least particularly well suited, to achieve on behalf of their subjects."[104] A power that fulfills this function of states is good in that it is suited to the function. Authority fits this function by "means of the normative instrument of a capacity to impose obligations."[105] Ultimately, Perry's argument becomes circular. Authority is justified because authority serves the function of the state achieving important moral goals. That is exactly what a theory of authority is supposed to justify, namely, that another person or institution should direct individuals to or away from certain actions. Perry thus only transfers the discussion to the realm of "moral political philosophy." If the function of the state as Perry defines it can be justified in this other epistemological field, then authority is justified because authority fulfills that function. Authority is left unjustified other than by this utilitarian conclusion. As with the other utilitarian theories, this leaves criteria (ii) and (v) unmet, since authority is only good to the extent its use or content actually fulfills the state's purpose. Also, authority would not bind in a hypothetical situation in which it could be shown that some other instrument could better fulfill this function.[106]

Barnett skillfully exposes the inadequacy of consent theories of legal authority. He keenly notes that even if universal consent were possible, which it is not, consent would only be meaningful if there were a real right not to consent.[107] Thus, even on the consent theorists' own terms, something must preexist consent—the right to consent or not. Barnett uses this realization to ground legal authority not in consent but in rights: "The assumption that 'first come rights, then comes government' helps explain how lawmaking can be legitimate in the absence of consent. For a law would be *just*, and therefore binding in conscience, if its restrictions on a citizen's freedom were (1) *necessary* to protect the rights of others, and (2) *proper* insofar as they did not violate the preexisting rights of the persons on whom they were imposed. The second of these requirements dispenses with the need to obtain the consent of the person on whom a law is imposed."[108] He explains: "Therefore, when we move outside a community constituted by unanimous consent, laws must be scrutinized to ensure both that they are necessary and that they do not improperly infringe upon the rights retained by the people."[109] As perceptive as Barnett's argument is in exposing the failure of consent theories, it fails to ground his "rights come first" theory in a solid ontology and ultimately succumbs to the utilitarian trap. First, he substitutes rights for consent in his legal ontology. In the order of being, first come rights and then comes law, which is legitimized through its respect for the preexisting rights. Yet, Barnett fails to find an origin for the preexisting rights. He merely assumes their existence and dispenses with the need for any particular content informing the rights on which legal legitimacy rests: "One need not accept any particular formulation of background rights, however, to accept the conception of constitutional legitimacy advanced here."[110] If he is correct that respect for rights removes the need for consent, the conclusion begs the question of the nature and origin of these rights. Barnett fails to answer this question. If rights are going to legitimize the power to coerce action independently of the content of the command, how can one evaluate the claim to legitimacy without knowing the content of those rights that are determinative in the justification? Thus, ultimately his theory of legal authority is based in a presupposed abstract rule, such as Hart's Rule of Recognition and Kelsen's basic norm. Barnett's rights simply exist without cause, explanation, or necessary definition. They, like the Rule of Recognition and the basic norm, are an unjustified black box.[111] Once the ontologically empty concept of rights is assumed, then Barnett falls into the utilitarian trap. Laws are justified to the extent that they are useful to safeguard the preexisting rights. Laws remain utilitarian for Barnett, but he has simply substituted rights for happiness, or pleasure, or whatever term the particular utilitarian chooses to employ. There is no good in law itself. It is merely useful to protect the merely assumed but undefined background rights.

Ultimately, all the utilitarian claims to justification of authority as instrumentally good amount to the unproven and unprovable claim that some group processes some unique skill set that will allow them to manage society better than others for some purpose, value, or undefined set of rights. As Alasdair MacIntyre has argued, this claim is merely a fiction created to justify the fact of the power of managerial bureaucrats over society.[112] Essentially the utilitarian claim to legal authority is open to use by those in power or those seeking to overthrow those in power by simply asserting that "we are the best experts in lawmaking and you are better off under our control." Such assertion lacks any justified reason for believing the claim to be true.

Consent and utilitarian theories fail to justify the power to change people's normative positions. All the theories considered fail because they lack any ontological grounding. They fail to identify anything other than a myth to explain the origin of authority, and they fail to articulate any goodness in authority other than its usefulness.

THE NATURAL LAW JUSTIFICATION OF AUTHORITY

Having failed to find a satisfactory justification for authority in consent or utilitarian theories, in this section we will argue that traditional natural law theory as articulated in prior chapters provides a satisfactory grounding for legal authority. In the first subsection, we will show that the natural law justification provides an ontology for human legal authority. It provides a home for legal authority within the architecture of law by resting on a solid ontological foundation. In doing so we will begin as Perry suggests, by addressing the "'existence conditions' for a power to change through legal authority people's normative position rather than on conditions that will justify the supposedly mediating conclusion that there exists a (general) moral obligation to obey the law."[113] After exploring the proof of such power's existence, we will explain in the second and third subsections how authority and obedience to it are not only necessary but also a good in themselves. In the fourth subsection we will reconsider the role of consent and argue that although consent is inadequate to ground legal authority, there can be a role for consent in designating the persons holding legal authority. In the fifth subsection we will draw out of the prior analysis several characteristics of legal authority and emphasize those that suggest limitations on the obligation to obey the law. We will conclude the chapter by demonstrating that the natural law argument satisfies Leslie Green's criteria for a successful argument for an obligation to obey the law.

The Creation of Legal Ontology

The natural law justification of authority can be summed up in the old saying: "All authority comes from God."[114] Leo XIII noted that the notion of legal authority deriving from the people was a departure from classical Catholic jurisprudence, which held "the right to rule is from God, as from a natural and necessary principle."[115] Raz admits that all authority must be conferred by another.[116] Raz explains that Kelsen's legal theory recognizes the need for an external single norm to move from "is" to "ought" and validate all laws. According to Raz, Kelsen admits some natural law is needed to have any law.[117] Kelsen admits that without his basic norm as presupposed there is no law: "An anarchist . . . who denied the validity of the hypothetical basic norm of positive law . . . will view its positive regulation of human relationship . . . as mere power relations."[118] It is the basic norm that saves Kelsen's system from being Hart's gunman. But for Kelsen there is no ontology for this basic norm; it is just an uncaused cause for the entire legal system, which he has assumed to exist because it must exist.[119] In Raz's words, for Kelsen, "It does not make sense with regard to any basic norm to ask when it was created, by whom or how. These categories simply do not apply to it."[120] Without admitting so, Kelsen and Raz have simply come to the same conclusion philosophers reached thousands of years ago. If the principle of origin of law is an uncaused cause, then that principle must be the uncaused cause of everything. As C. G. Bateman observes: "From Hammurabi to Hadrian, and even on past to the Hapsburgs, the only affective benefactor of sovereignty was, at least in theory, the deity. In societies where religion was the fundamental framework of daily life for all classes, rulers, for the sake of legitimacy, had to acknowledge that it was the God or 'the gods' who had bequeathed their sovereignty. In this context sovereignty was never aggregately or individually understood as solely attached to either the will or skill of personages, it came from the deity."[121] St. Paul expresses the same argument succinctly: "Authority comes from God only, and all authorities that hold sway are of his ordinance."[122] J. D. Goldsworthy concludes that only with God can morality successfully claim that "its precepts are authoritatively binding in a sense which transcends even enlightened self-interest."[123] His claim holds equally true for law. Even if Moore's argument is correct, which I do not believe to be the case, and we could have "good without God,"[124] he fails to even raise the related question: Can we have authority without God? Even if Moore proves that there is good and that people should do good because of the reality of morality, such proof fails to explain why any person should have the power to change the normative position of another by determining what is good for him in a particular circumstance when good can be done in two or more morally ambivalent ways. Socrates, unlike Moore, saw the good, God, and authority as intimately linked: "For Socrates, it is not enough that kings or oligarchs, or even citizens, wield the largest share of political power in their states, it is whether that sovereign power is the product of the 'good.' As to the fountainhead of this notion of 'good,' like many of the theorists who ended up weighing in on sovereignty after Socrates, he appealed to God."[125] Even Emperor Frederick II, not the most pious of Christian rulers, felt the need to acknowledge in promulgating legislation for the Kingdom of Sicily the ultimate origin of law in God: "After Divine Providence had formed the universe. . . . [God] put [His rational creatures] under a certain law."[126] The modern crisis of justifying authority emerged when the notion of legal authority became detached completely from God so that political theory could imagine the state as being sovereign in its own right, whereas since the time of Constantine, sovereign authority was "only thought to be under the jurisdiction and control of God."[127]

In Kelsen's language (and this may be the bit of natural law Raz admits Kelsen needs), the basic norm is therefore the eternal law, an omnipresent foundation or starting point. Whereas Kelsen merely asserts the necessity of a basic norm, which has no ontology other than to fulfill a need to make Kelsen's jurisprudence complete, the eternal law has a complete ontology, which we discussed in detail in chapter 2. The eternal law is the only law that is an uncaused cause since the eternal law is nothing other than the divine wisdom ordering the universe. The eternal law legislates the ends of things, including legal authority and human law. If we can find authority legislated into the eternal law, we will have found a source from which all subsequent authority can be derived. Yet, as we showed in chapter 4, we come to know the content of the eternal law not directly but through our participation in the eternal law, or through the natural law. Likewise, we encounter the natural law not solely in the abstract but through the developing customary history of real political communities. Thus, by dialectically examining the authority exercised in actual historically developing communities, we can find the origin of authority in the eternal law. In this sense Leo XIII argued that the principle that all authority comes from God is a "natural and necessary principle."[128] It is necessary since, as even Kelsen acknowledged, authority must ultimately derive from a necessary being or an uncaused cause. It is natural because we come to know of its existence through the natural law.

Aquinas begins his consideration of sovereign authority by considering man's ends.[129] In doing so he begins with the eternal and natural law. As we discussed in chapter 2, the eternal law establishes the ends of man's nature. Those ends become known through the natural inclinations, which direct man. Therefore, as Jean Porter argues, even though the principles of natural law "are accessible to reflective judgement," their relative indeterminacy means they are not sufficient in themselves "to govern conduct or to provide adequate structures for social activities."[130] The principles permit a realm of choice among particular ways of conforming to natural law. Some of those elections must be made by individuals but others cannot be left to each individual. A component of man's end is living in society. The existence of communities is therefore commensurate with human nature.[131] Man is meant to live in a society. Since a community is a heterogeneous organism, it needs a principle of order to unify it.[132] Authority is therefore both "appropriate and sometimes necessary" because in order to be effective in a social context, the determinations of natural law that affect the common good will have to be "public and relatively stable."[133] However, since the indeterminacy of natural law allows for more than one (although not an unlimited) rational choice, there will be an element of contingency to any particular choice made (the right as opposed to the left side of the road, for example).[134] As a result, Porter concludes that "it must be imposed in some way if it is to yield a cogent claim, having binding force within a context of human relations."[135] The nature of making particular determinations for a society requires that the choice be both an act of reason—it must conform to the rational principles of natural law—and an act of the will—be an authoritative, binding choice among permissible possibilities: "Authority serves to bring a relatively final, public, and generally acceptable specificity to indeterminate rational and natural principles in such a way as to create a framework for shared activities of diverse kinds."[136]

From Necessary to Good

This justification appears on the surface to be utilitarian. Authority is justified because it is necessary to make social life possible. But this appearance is only superficial. Authority is not only necessary but, as Porter says, appropriate, and is in fact good. Authority fulfills a particular need for public and definitive determinations to be made for individuals in a social context. Both that social context and the necessity that authority satisfies have been willed by divine providence. The indeterminacy of natural law and hence the need for authority is not accidental but has been intentionally written into the legal fabric of the universe. Put another way, human authority was not strictly necessary. The eternal law could have specified all principles of action in the natural and divine law, leaving no room for determination. God chose to leave this task, in a sense, unfinished and thus intended the need that authority satisfies. Unlike the Scholastic jurists of the classical natural law tradition, early modern natural law theorists like Blackstone envisioned human law as being made by copying necessary specific precepts of natural law into human law.[137] In contrast, the medieval Scholastics understood the relationship to be more complex—natural law, and even to some extent, divine positive law,[138] was indeterminate and in fact required human lawmakers to actively provide that determination. As Porter explains:

> Rather than regarding social conventions as more or less direct and unchangeable expressions of human nature, they emphasize the need for processes of rational, communally shared deliberations, in order to move from natural principles to their conventional formulations. . . . These general principles [of natural law] are accessible to reflective judgment, and yet they remain relatively indeterminate, in such a way that they are not sufficient to govern conduct or to provide adequate structures for social activities. Seen in this context, relations of authority appear as appropriate and sometimes necessary elements in the social life of rational animals. The rational principles of natural law must be specified in order to be put into practice, and yet these specifications cannot be left to individual judgments; they must be generally accepted in order to provide a framework for social activities, and that means at least that they must be public and relatively stable.[139]

The indeterminacy of natural law is not a fault or failing of natural law that needs to be fixed by inventing the concept of legal authority. It is an intentional indeterminacy legislated into the legal system by the ultimate legislator through the eternal law. God wanted rational creatures to participate more actively than in Blackstone's idea of copying out preformulated precepts. If natural and divine law explicitly contained all particular determinations of right action, there would be no room for the election of means—the realm of human liberty. Human authority is necessary and useful (as the instrumental arguments of the utilitarians suggest), yet it is more than that. It is good because God, the author of law, wishes humans to participate in the making of laws that govern their communal activity. He provides for the further specification and determination of general public precepts by one having care of a community, by particular human beings exercising lawmaking authority. This authority ultimately resides in God, but is delegated and shared with human agents through the intentional indeterminacy contained in the revelation of eternal law through natural and divine positive law. To fully understand human legal authority in these terms we must return to what has been established about eternal law and its relation to natural law and human positive law in prior chapters.

As we saw in chapter 2, the eternal law, although fixing the ends of creatures, does not fix for man the means to those ends. The eternal law legislates the course of these means only in general by implanting the natural inclinations. The eternal law requires the cooperation of human agents in determining the particular election of proportionate means through working out determinations of the principles of natural law in contingent circumstances.[140]

These particular determinations are made within a threefold order of authorities: the individual, the familial, and the regnative.[141] The eternal and natural laws leave some of these necessary determinations to each individual to determine.[142] Others are determined for individuals by the authority of their personal, not strictly speaking legal, superiors[143] (those possessing authority in an imperfect or nonpolitical community, e.g., parents for children in a family). Finally, those determinations that affect the "common good"[144] are left "to the discretion of those who were to have spiritual or temporal charge of others."[145] The first two orders are only analogous to law, which properly exists only in the third. Why is the sanction of law better than each determining for himself (or each superior of a nonpolitical community determining for it) all the individual cases? The first answer is that the common good requires it. By definition the individual cases that should be addressed by human law rather than individual decision are those affecting the common good. Just as those decisions not affecting the common but only a personal good should be left out of human law, those cases that do affect the common good should be determined not by private individuals but by those having "spiritual or temporal charge of others."[146]

Francisco Suárez demonstrates that such an authority is needed to govern any society.[147] He explains: "No body can be preserved unless there exists some principle whose function it is to provide for and seek after the common good thereof, such a principle as clearly exists in the natural body, and likewise (so experience teaches) in the political."[148] A homogeneous body such as an animal has instincts that serve the unifying purpose of directing the whole animal to its end, survival. In man, the rational soul serves this purpose. Thus in the heterogeneous body of politics a principle of order must govern the heterogeneous parts because each individual in a society looks after his own cares, and these sometimes are contrary to the common good. Also, sometimes there are things that are necessary for the common good but are not directly pertinent all the time to individuals, so not all will work toward them without direction.[149] Governed society thus provides for peace and order among people and families and for the avoidance and correction of injustices.[150] Beyond the organic unity of the individual, the heterogeneous organisms of the family and a perfect community thus require a principle of order to govern determinations necessary under natural law to reach man's end. Although the form and nature of the authority to determine rules of action varies from the individual to civil society, the source and principle is the same: the provision for human determination of principles of natural law provided by the divine wisdom in the eternal law. God could have provided this principle of order directly, but he chose to provide for the participation of human agents—the individual's reason and will, the personal superior, and legal authorities. These authorities are good not by virtue of any internal cause but because they participate in the ultimate legal authority ruling the universe, God. The third form of authority, to make laws for a community, is the subject of this chapter, and so we will turn to consider its origin and nature.

Aquinas explains that when one is directed to an end exterior to oneself, one needs a guide to direct to that end.[151] The word *gubernator* (meaning one in authority of a *polis*) developed from the original meaning of a pilot of a ship,[152] one who directs a ship to an exterior end, the port. Since the end of the common good is external to man, there is need for such a guide, an authority. As a social being, man's individual end, the fulfillment of his nature, is inextricably caught up in the end of the society of which he forms a part, the common good. Thus, a need for a directive authority in the sphere of determinations beyond those within the determination of the individual is part of the legal architecture itself and would be present even in a theoretical community of saints not affected by the "wounding of nature."[153]

Classical natural law jurisprudence understands legal authority to be existential rather than functional. The good or end of a thing is the fullness of its being. Cyr distinguishes the former type of authority as one in which those subject to it see their existence and identity as existentially connected to the authority. He contrasts this type of authority to mere functional authority, which exists solely for instrumental efficiency.[154] Clearly, utilitarian theories can only justify the thin functional form of authority. Although consent theories may come closer to justifying existential authorities since they see authority as the expression of popular consent, ultimately they fail to do so. The consent is only fictional, at best. Beyond its expositive failure, being rooted in consent it only justifies authority because it is useful or beneficial to the consenting parties. The natural law tradition understands legal authority to be existential and an inherent part of a person's identity as part of a common political community, through which the perfection of human nature must be pursued by obeying the determinations of natural law made by those entrusted with care of that community. It is not simply that authority makes life more efficient. Authority is existentially connected to a social being, and we are existentially connected to society by the natural inclination to live in society. Without authority we could not be fully what our nature is designed to be. As Porter has observed, "It [authority] addresses one of the pervasive needs of human life, since without a whole range of shared activities, we as rational, social animals could not live—fully, or perhaps at all—in the way characteristic to us as a specific kind of living creature."[155]

Authority is thus more than a necessary evil instituted after the loss of original justice; ordered determination by an authority predates destruction of the natural law in us.[156] The eternal law, by fixing a social element in man's nature and by entrusting particular determinations to human agents, makes the presence of an authority, one charged with care of the social community in its quest for the common good,[157] a good. The making of determinations of law that guide toward the common good is the end or purpose of authority fixed by the eternal law. A proper understanding of the necessity and goodness for human determination of natural law refutes Kelsen's claim that knowledge of natural law would make human positive law superfluous.[158] Far from being a "foolish effort at artificial illumination in bright sunshine,"[159] the making of human law involves the rational selection among several determinations in the bright light of natural law. Perhaps Kelsen's dismissal of natural law resulted from his misunderstanding the classical doctrine's explanation of the divinely desired indispensable role for human law in making determinations of the general principles of natural law. The making of human law is a good: it is the attainment of a natural end.[160] Human society, or the social aspect of human nature, is naturally inclined to be directed by law. Thus, the fulfillment of that natural inclination—the formulation of determinate laws—is good. In the words of Porter, "Authority thus shares in the goodness, the attractive power, and the rational cogency proper to human life as such."[161]

From the Good of Authority to the Virtue of Obedience

Not only do consent and utilitarian theories fail to adequately explain the origin of legal authority, but they also consider authority, or the power to affect the normative position of others, at best neutral and at worst an evil, albeit a necessary evil. Obedience may be necessary, but it is not good according to this dim view of authority. Utilitarian theories find no good in this power to change normative duties and the obligation to obey, but they accept the fact as justified only to the extent that it can produce other goods. Consent theorists start from the premise that authority restricts individual freedom and is therefore problematic. This problematic interference with freedom that a duty to obey another person creates can then only be justified if freely given consent accepts it. Obedience is justified only as an act of freedom through consent. The understanding of authority rooted in the natural law tradition offers a much stronger ontology—one that accepts authority as not merely necessary but as good. Obeying the law is therefore not only necessary but an authentic good commensurate with human nature. Leo Strauss argues that since man is naturally social, and therefore the restraint of freedom is natural to, and therefore good for, man, one cannot associate without restraint on freedom. He explains: "Man is so built that he cannot achieve the perfection of his humanity except by keeping down his lower impulses. He cannot rule his body by persuasion. . . . What is true of self-restraint, self-coercion, and power over one's self applies in principle to the restraint and coercion of others and to power over others. . . . To say that power as such is evil or corrupting would therefore amount to saying that virtue is evil or corrupting."[162]

The dim view of restraint as unnatural and evil is evident in Enlightenment authors such as Rousseau[163] and constitutes an often unstated premise of consent and utilitarian justifications of authority. For this contrary view, restraint (and therefore every virtue) is corrupting of freedom. Law involves restraint and this restrain is unnatural, at best conventional. For the classical tradition, however, restraint of action is, on the contrary, good and natural, in fact virtuous. Strauss explains: "If restraint is as natural to man as is freedom, and restraint must in many cases be forcible restraint in order to be effective, one cannot say that the city is conventional or against nature because it is coercive society."[164]

Postclassical jurisprudence is therefore uncomfortable with and thus continually in search of a justification for a coercive authority. The distinction with the armed gunman haunts Hart's analysis. The best jurists committed to positivism can produce is an assumed basic norm or rule that must exist to justify the existence of a legal system. Hart and Austin were wrong in concluding that various societies each need their own absolute, in the absence of which there would be no legal system.[165] This assumption arises from the premise that law and authority are not natural and therefore only conventional. In the absence of convention there would therefore be no legal system. Yet, a legal order, although making use of conventional elements, is ontologically natural. There is always a cosmic legal system by virtue of the existence of the ultimate sovereign, the promulgator of eternal law. There may be no specifically *human* legal system in a particular time and space (in a civil grouping in a state of anarchy, for example). This lack of a human legal system in a particular area would stem not from the lack of an unlimited human sovereign but rather the lack of someone with care of a community to make the necessary legal determinations of natural law for that civil society. There is no need for a sovereign in Austin's terms, but there is a need for someone filling the office of determination-maker under natural law, or in the phrase of Porter, a "minister of the law."[166] If such an office is vacant, there is no functioning particular human legal system in such area, but a legal system still exists, albeit one requiring further determination. There is always a legal system because no one is outside the eternal, natural, and divine law. The need for a human authority arises from the intentional indeterminacy of natural law. Unlike Hart, who lamented the indeterminacy "handicap" in law,[167] this view of authority rejoices in the indeterminacy within the natural law. This indeterminacy is a gift of God providing the opportunity for us to participate in the divine action of making law by determining the natural law. The conforming of our individual actions to the determinations of those charged by the eternal law with this responsibility of making determinations is thus a fulfillment of an aspect of human nature. Obedience to the law is thus a natural inclination in the sense we discussed in chapters 3 and 4. Because of the social aspect of our nature, we have a natural inclination to obey the law. As we will discuss more in chapter 9, this inclination to obey the law is the particular virtue of legal justice. According to the Thomist Jeremiah Newman, justice is good under the aspect of due, and legal justice involves a case in which due arises under the divine or human law.[168] Thus doing what is due under the determinations of human law constitutes a good act because it is a legally just act. Aristotle argues that good government consists in two essential elements: good laws and the obedience of citizens to the laws.[169] Aquinas treats the virtue of obedience as a species of the virtue of justice.[170] Obedience is the virtue whereby individuals allow their free determination of actions to be directed by the command of another.[171] Aquinas explains the naturalness of obedience to authority: "Wherefore just as in virtue of the divinely established natural order the lower natural things need to be subject to the movement of the higher, so too in human affairs, in virtue of the order of natural and divine law, inferiors are bound to obey their superiors."[172] Not only is the power to make determinations affecting the common good derived from the eternal law, but the obligation to obey is also found in the eternal law through the natural law, which contains a secondary precept that superiors ought to be obeyed within the scope of their authority. Obedience to the law is thus a good in and of itself because one who obeys participates in the end of good government of society. All laws that are just and ordained to the common good are binding in conscience. The law binds by virtue of legal justice. Its breach may, in a particular case, constitute merely a minor infringement of legal justice, but it still impugns it. Obedience to these laws is thus a moral act. There is no such thing as purely penal laws (laws that do not bind in conscience but for which one must pay the price if caught), as some modern theorists have suggested.[173]

This conclusion requires a different analysis of Raz's traffic light example.[174] He posits as a legitimate law the requirement to stop at a red traffic light. He then assumes a case in which disregarding the red light will not result in any danger to anyone, including the driver, and will not diminish anyone's respect for law or those who make it, including the driver's. Since in this case disobedience would not affect any of the purposes of the law (specific and general) as Raz conceives of them, Raz concludes "that in this case or a similar case the utterances of authority can be held to be legitimate without holding them to constitute reasons for action."[175] Raz does not see that obeying the law even in such a circumstance is good because doing so constitutes a good act—a virtuous act of legal justice and participation in good government by obeying the particular determinations of the constituted authority. The only difference between a normal case and this special case of a deserted intersection is that fewer social consequences result from an act of disobedience in the deserted intersection. For the motorist, however, he has forfeited the opportunity to practice the virtue of legal justice. Thus, there is only a difference in the scope of the consequences flowing from running the red light, not a change in the binding obligation to stop as stated by human legal determination.

Beyond the goodness of authoritative determinations in and of themselves, another good of obedience to legal authorities can be discov-

ered in light of the obstacles to virtue created by the wounding of nature.[176] Aristotle in his discussion of virtue noted this good of obedience.
His argument in favor of authority is based on the observation that virtue
requires not simply understanding but action.[177] It is not enough to know
what is virtuous to be virtuous, one has to do it. Some people, either
through a gift of nature or good training, will act according to virtue once
they hear an argument as to what is virtuous. But not all are this way.
Some are ruled more by their passions and will not be persuaded by argument. They require an act of the will to be moved to virtue because passions respond more to force than argument. Therefore laws are needed
both to urge people to virtue by directing to the good they can will themselves and to compel others, "for most people obey necessity rather than
argument."[178] The *Digest* agrees that it is of the very essence of law to command.[179] Aquinas defines a command as the act of moving "by reason and
will."[180] Law must be a dictate of natural reason whereby it guides the reason of those under the law to know the good. Since the wounding of nature affects both the reason and the will, human law cannot remain
merely a dictate of reason (which would merely support the expert notion
of authority). Since passions, which can direct the will away from the true
good, respond to commands not rational arguments, human law must
also be an act of coercion.

To understand this further value of authority we must discuss the interdependent relationship between personal moral virtue and the common
good, which is the end of law. Although law is directed to the common
good, in contrast to individual or purely personal goods, the common good
is related to individuals. In the preface to Charles De Koninck's work dedicated to the relationship of the common good to individuals, J. M. Cardinal
Villeneuve summarizes the interconnectedness of them thus:

> [The common good is] the greatest good of the singular, not by being
> a collection of singular goods, but best for each of the particular indi-
> viduals who participate in it precisely on account of its being com-
> mon. Those who defend the primacy of the singular good of the sin-
> gular person suppose a false notion of the common good as if it were
> alien to the good of the singular; whereas it is natural and proper that
> the singular seek more the good of the species than his singular good.

Since the person, an intellectual substance, is a part of the universe in whom the perfection of the whole universe can exist according to knowledge, his most proper good as intellectual substance will be the good of the universe, which is an essentially common good. Rational creatures, persons, are distinguished from irrational, by being more ordered to the common good and by being able to act expressly for its sake. It is true also that a person can perversely prefer his own singular good to the common good, attaching himself to the singularity of his person, or as we say today to his personality, set up as a common measure of all good. Furthermore, if the reasonable creature cannot entirely limit himself to a subordinate common good, such as the family or political society, this is not because his particular good as such is greater; it is because of his proper ordination to a superior common good to which he is principally ordered. In this case, the common good is not sacrificed to the good of the individual as individual, but to the good of the individual insofar as the latter is ordered to a more universal common good, indeed to God. A society consisting of persons who love their private good above the common good, or who identify the common good with a private good, is not a society of free men, but of tyrants, who menace each other by force, and in which the final head is merely the most astute and the strongest among the tyrants, the subjects being nothing but frustrated tyrants.[181]

The common good is that external good or end common to all members of the society. Attainment of the common good cannot be achieved separately from individuals pursuing their individual end or good because the common good of the society is constituted by the same end as individuals, the perfection of the aspects of human nature. Since human nature involves a social aspect, the perfection of virtue of each individual is a component of attainment of the common good. Thus in pursuing the common good, the law has an interest in the individual moral determinations of the individuals of society. As a social animal, man works toward his individual good as part of a society, as part of a whole working to the common good of all. Thus, part of the purpose of law in pursuing the common good is to assist individuals in making personal determinations conforming to the natural law. We need to consider the nature of this relationship between law and personal determinations.

In chapter 5 we discovered that any human participation in the eternal law will be imperfect. The act of determining individual cases in conformance to virtue is difficult (involving an effort of reason). In the words of Aquinas, "It is difficult to see how man could suffice for himself in this matter [training himself to be virtuous]."[182] Consequently, Aristotle and Aquinas suggest recourse to a proven good, or a wise man. Those possessing the habit of justice, the wise, are more likely to be correct in particular determinations. Their conclusions are more likely to correspond to the specific truths contained in the eternal wisdom. Thus, contrary to modern liberal individualistic philosophy, the determination of acts solely by autonomous individuals is not an ideal that would be preferable except for the practical need to coordinate choices. Individual choice aided by recourse to the wisdom of human law is preferable. The difficulty in making good determinations indicates that individuals need to look outside themselves for assistance when determining their own particular acts. For this reason, Aquinas explains that a system of formulated human laws should include general principles of action in addition to the particular determinations affecting the common good. Human laws include not only specific determinations but also deductions of principles from natural law.[183] Particular individual decisions are aided by having recourse to general principles deduced from natural law by a legal authority. Although he is speaking about the relationship between judges and lawmakers, his analysis applies more generally:

> As the Philosopher says (Rhet. i, 1), "it is better that all things be regulated by law, than left to be decided by judges": and this for three reasons. First, because it is easier to find a few wise men competent to frame right laws than to find the many who would be necessary to judge aright of each single case. Secondly, because those who make laws consider long beforehand what laws to make; whereas judgment on each single case has to be pronounced as soon as it arises: and it is easier for man to see what is right, by taking many instances into consideration, than by considering one solitary fact. Thirdly, because lawgivers judge in the abstract and of future events; whereas those who sit in judgment of things present, towards which they are affected by love, hatred, or some kind of cupidity; wherefore their judgment is perverted. Since then the animated justice of the judge is not found in

every man, and since it can be deflected, therefore it was necessary, whenever possible, for the law to determine how to judge, and for very few matters to be left to the decision of men.[184]

Note, this is a tempered assessment of the question. Aquinas does leave room for some "few" case-by-case determinations but argues that "whenever possible" there should be laws formulated in general by a few wise men, who would, being distanced from human emotions that can distort the consideration of specific cases, be more likely to reach the just conclusion.[185] In a sense, Aquinas is stating an old legal maxim familiar to most lawyers—"bad facts make bad law." If law is solely a product of unrelated case-by-case rulings of particulars by individuals, it is likely that the unique and potentially emotionally compelling aspects of the individual case will lead to a bad law, a bad decision. Thus, *ex ante* formulation of a general rule can be more likely to be correct. He does not advocate the formulation of an all-encompassing omnibus code, for "certain individual facts that cannot be covered by the law" need to be left to individual judgment.[186] MacIntyre uses the analogy of a craft to describe the development of virtue.[187] One learning a craft must advance under the direction of a master who guides by virtue of his authority the transformation within the apprentice into one who has internally mastered the craft. Just as those learning the art of building need a teacher to guide the development of their habit, the community needs an authority to guide the development of individual choices. Laws that contain deductions of general principles from natural law guide without completely determining individual actions, leaving the final choices of action to individuals within the bounds of the general principles. Such laws are ones that generally prescribe virtue rather than laws that prohibit vice. Thus human law directs individual acts and coordinates those acts to the common good. In guiding individual determinations, law does not exceed the bounds of its direction to the common good. Since assisting individuals in making good individual determinations is inextricably connected to the common good, the law orients to the common good even when it guides individuals in making particular determinations for themselves.

For Aristotle and Aquinas, the two major qualifications for one to assume legal authority in a regime are that he be virtuous (the wise) and act for the common good.[188] Thus, it is prudent to leave the determination of particular rules affecting the common good to those who are supposed to be wise and virtuous, to the ruling authorities temporal and spiritual.[189] The reference to both temporal and spiritual authorities as instruments of human determinations is an important point to note for our time. Both religious and civil authorities have the obligation and freedom to make particular determinations of the natural law within the appropriate spheres of their jurisdiction, temporal and spiritual. Thus, not all laws enacted to aid individual moral determinations need be made by temporal authorities. Aquinas is speaking of authority in general, and he envisions a plurality of authority in distinct but overlapping spheres, overlapping in that they all relate to the same subject—individuals making determinations of actions under the eternal law. Harold Berman argues that this plurality of overlapping jurisdictions was a central feature of the traditional understanding of legal authority.[190] This conception differs greatly from contemporary visions of authority as monolithic and as monopolistically controlled by a single human legal sovereign, as Austin envisions.

Thus, authority serves two distinct but related roles that can be summarized in the statement that "authorities make laws that directly or indirectly affect the common good." Some laws directly affect the common good by making particular determinations for actions so as to orient those actions to, and coordinate them with respect to, the common good. Some laws also aid individuals in attaining their personal end, their personal good, by providing guidance in the form of deduced principles of natural law. In such a way the law indirectly aims at the common good by guiding individuals whose individual choices inextricably affect the common good.

This insight provides part of the answer to Hart's question of what distinguishes the coerced compliance with the demand of a gunman from the obedience to the law.[191] First, the lawmaker is entrusted with the power to require obedience to a command that is a determination of natural law; the gunman is a self-appointed commander. The legal authority is empowered to command for the purposes of guiding individuals to actions oriented to the common good, a good that by its very nature includes the good of the individual commanded. The gunman commands action oriented solely to his individual advantage and not to the common good. Second, the power to command is entrusted to the legal authority from a superior authority, God and His eternal law. God provides for the exercise of authority by those entrusted with care of the common good. The gunman usurps authority for himself for the purposes of advancing his own personal good. Even though both a legitimate authority and the gunman coupled their command with a threat of consequences for disobedience, the difference between the two is that a legal authority is given this power to command and threaten from a superior authority. The gunman usurps the power for himself. As Hart rightly argued, the presence of a threat of punishment is insignificant to legitimize authority.[192] Yet, since Hart rejects the delegation of authority from outside a particular legal system, he is forced to ground the obligation to obey legal authority on the negative consequences of disobedience, albeit defined more broadly than those of a gunman. Hart explains: "Rules are conceived and spoken of as imposing obligations when the general demand for conformity is insistent and the social pressure brought to bear upon those who deviate or threaten to deviate is great."[193] Hart thus ends up basing the obligation to obey internally on social pressures to conform, resulting in no qualitative difference between law and the gunman. The difference is only one of quantity. The gunman's threat is backed only by himself and his gun; the law's threat is backed by broader social pressure. It is still a threat that makes a law obligatory for Hart. The classical natural law explanation avoids reliance on threats of consequences that constitute the main obligation to obey the law. The threats merely remain as potential consequences of violating the otherwise justified duty to obey legitimate laws. Obligation derives from the provision of eternal law for rational determinations of natural law by human authorities. Rather than deriving an obligation to obey from the existence of a legitimate threat of punishment, the classical theory derives the legitimacy of a threat of punishment from the presence of a legitimate obligation to obey. Legal authorities can threaten consequences because they possess legitimate authority, delegated to them to create the obligation that will later be coupled with a threat. Punishment derives from obligation, not vice versa.

To distinguish this power to obligate from the demand of a gunman, it is necessary to recognize that, unlike the gunman's, the legal authority's power is delegated from above. The legal authority's power originates in the power to guide toward the development of virtue and to make determinations of natural law provided by God. Since all humans share an equal human nature (though differing in accidentals to that nature), no person can confer authority to command on another person, as both are equal in nature. Authority must come from a superior. Hart recognizes this need when he argues that a legal system must have a supreme lawmaker from whom subordinated lawmakers receive their authority.[194] The indeterminacy of natural law as provided for in the plan of the eternal law provides for the delegation of authority from a superior. Beyond this important distinction, the lawmaker's command must not only be a product of a delegated authority but it must also be a product of reason—a deduction or determination of natural law—whereas the gunman's demand is the product solely of his will and need not be rational. The exercise of legal authority involves the making of rational deductions or determinations of the rational principles of natural law and is thus an act not only of the will but of the intellect. Yet, since after the Fall law has served the purpose of guiding the subjection of the disordered passions to the intellect, it also must involve a coercive act of the will. As we will see in chapter 8, the absence of both intellectual and volitional elements renders a purported act of a lawmaker nothing other than an act of violence. When the necessary rational connection to natural law is removed, the lawmaker becomes merely Hart's gunman, notwithstanding his possession of titles suggesting legitimate authority.

The Proper Role of Consent in the Delegation and Exercise of Legal Authority

Although we have seen that the ontological reality of legal authority does not rest upon a real, presumed, tacit, or fictitious consent but rather upon the design of the original lawgiver in the eternal law, this does not mean that the consent of the governed plays no role in the transmission and exercise of legal authority. Even though, as demonstrated thus far, consent of the governed is an insufficient foundation for the existence of legal authority, the concept of consent is an integral component of classical natural law jurisprudence. Consent does not create legal authority but it has an important role to play in the transmission and exercise thereof. The claim that all authority comes from God involves a more nuanced claim than may at first appear evident from the consideration so far. To appreciate the full impact of the claim, we must explore both how that authority is transmitted and how the power to bind the consciences of other rational agents is transmitted and exercised in relation to its source.

First, the claim means that all authority ultimately finds its origin in the ultimate efficient cause of all things,[195] the eternal law, the structure of law as established by divine providence. In this sense the exalted good of legal authority is found in its source. Leo XIII explained the relationship between the truth that all authority comes from God and the inherent goodness of authority itself: "The power to rule comes from God, and is, as it were, a participation in His, the highest of all sovereignties."[196] The eternal law provides for this participation of man in the highest sovereignty through its requirement that deductions and determination of natural law precepts be made by human agents. The power to change normative positions by determining natural law is built into the fabric of the legal architecture. Whereas God is the ultimate efficient cause of legal obligation, the determinations by human authorities are proximate instrumental causes.

Yet, this conclusion does not explain how this authority is transmitted from God to individual governors of particular communities. Other than a few particular extraordinary interventions (the appointment of rulers for the Israelite nation in the Bible, for example), He does not normally confer this authority directly.[197] Rather, He makes use of secondary causes.[198] He confers authority as "a characteristic property resulting from nature."[199] The existence of an authority to determine natural law for the common good is a conclusion flowing from the natural inclinations of man. Natural law provides that there should be an authority as an inherent characteristic of a community. The nature of that authority will be a function of the type of community—perfect or imperfect—involved. The selection of the recipient of that authority, as with the making of human law, will involve a particular determination for a specific political community of this natural inclination toward legal authority. As we examine this process of the formation of a political community (possessing the property of authority) and the process for designating those who will exercise the property, the true role of consent will become evident. Consent serves not as an ontological foundation of the property, but a component of its use.

Communities can be either perfect[200] or imperfect.[201] A perfect community possesses both the perfect or most complete end and the complete means of attaining such an end.[202] In a word, the perfect community is completely self-sufficient.[203] A community that aims at a complete common good rather than a limited particular good and thus incorporates the goods of all lesser communities is this perfect community.[204] The nation[205] is a perfect community because it pursues the ultimate end, human happiness, and is self-sufficient in the means to attain that end.[206] The perfect community is composed of a variety of different imperfect communities, such as families, households, villages, and so on.[207] Each of these associations shares a particular common end, but each is only to some extent self-sufficient.[208] The family's purpose is to provide the basic nourishments of life for one household and the begetting and rearing of children.[209] The village[210] aims at the necessities for a particular trade or profession. Families and other imperfect communities are not sufficient either to provide all that is needed for human life or to attain all necessary knowledge.[211] The perfect community—city or province—has the aim of achieving all the necessities of human life and defense against external danger.[212] Each imperfect community aims to an aspect of the complete good but does not encompass all of that complete good, the good life or human happiness; they are parts of a whole.[213] The end of a perfect community is called the common good because it corresponds to the good or end of the common nature of the component parts of the heterogeneous whole rather than to the aggregate of individual ends or goods.[214] As Aristotle argues, the end or good of the individual is identified with the same end or good of the political community, not as an aggregation of preferences, but as the common natural end of all individuals composing the community.[215]

When a family is formed, this imperfect community necessarily contains the property of familial authority to govern the community toward the imperfect ends of the family. Authority is transmitted to the parents of the family as the efficient cause of the family.[216] Parents receive their authority as a necessary property attached to becoming a parent. They do not receive the authority from their children nor from themselves. The consent of the parents is necessary to form the familial society, yet it is not their consent that creates their authority. Their consent is instrumental in the formation of the familial society, which once brought into existence, possesses the property of familial authority.

The formation and establishment of the imperfect community of a family is analogous to the formation of a perfect community containing the necessary property of political or legal authority. Yet, parents do not possess legal authority strictly speaking but only analogically.[217] Law is not the directing of individuals but the directing of a community to the common good. Authority in a family is analogous but not identical to the political authority of a perfect community.[218] And the transmission of parental authority to parents in the formation of a family is analogous to the transmission of legal authority in a political community. Once a community whose end encompasses the common good and not merely a particular good comes into existence,[219] the power to govern exists as an essential property of the perfect community[220] by nature as designed by God. The principle of transmission in this case is the superiority of the whole over the parts.[221] Suárez analogizes this process to the conferral of powers inherent in the soul of man with the infusion of the form of the organism. He explains that the bestowal of the form involves the "bestowal of that which is consequent upon the form."[222] Once God creates the nature of man, if the form of man is bestowed upon certain matter, those capacities or powers essential to the form, that is, rationality and volition, are necessarily bestowed with the form. Once a community comes into being (a process analogous to the development of law by custom we described in chapter 6), the power to govern is transmitted to the community by virtue of it being a perfect community, but it is not bestowed by the members of the community. Just as the essential powers of the soul are not conferred by the material members of the body with respect to which the soul is the form, the members that materially compose the community do not confer these powers. The people act as instrumental efficient causes of the conferral— they produce the material cause, the community, which is capable of receiving the conferral of authority. The people are neither the formal cause nor the ultimate efficient cause of the authority. The people are merely the instrumental causes bringing about the formation of a group that becomes a political community.[223] The transmission of this authority to the community is analogous to human procreation. The parents' involvement is necessary to bring into existence a new person, but they do not confer the form, they only dispose the matter to receive the form. They do not have to consent to the granting of the constituents of human nature (that the child will be sentient or rational) but merely consent to the actions that dispose the matter to receive the form. Likewise the people forming a perfect community may participate in (and thereby consent to) the formation of the matter into a community, but once it emerges as a community the authority is conferred by God as author of the form. This understanding solves the problem of popular sovereignty as manifested in the consent theories. The consent or agreement of the members who at a time in history formed the disparate mass of people into a community is sufficient to bring the perfect community, with the related power of authority, into being.[224] There is no need for a renewed consent once the body politic is formed, just as there is no need for continual consent after the physical act that disposed the matter to receive the form and conceive the child. The perfect community once brought into existence possesses the governing authority and does not require the consent of each successive generation. Since the consent given is merely the consent to dispose a group of people to receive authority from God and not consent to the transmission of a power to govern residing in each individual that is somehow conferred on the ruling authority, the continual reconsenting by new members is unnecessary. The original members who bring a particular polity into existence do not create or transmit from themselves the legal authority of the whole but merely participate in the disposition of the mass of people to receive the form of a perfect community from God. The authority comes not from the founding individuals of the community but from God through the nature of things upon the emergence of a community formed through the actions of its members. A type of consent is present in the founding members of a perfect community, but this consent is not the ontological foundation of legal authority but merely an instrumental cause in its transmission from above.

Consent may also play a role in the future life of the political community. Members beyond the founders of a community may be able to transfer the possession and manifestation of that God-given authority from one person or persons to another person or persons by consenting to the transfer.[225] The transfer of this preexistent authority to a new holder does not involve any consent to the power of legal authority itself. In a system in which the transfer of legal authority is from one holder to another, the people do not continually consent to being governed by authority but merely to the identity of the particular holder of the power. Thus, if done in a just manner consistent with the particular law of the community, the citizens of a political community can act by consent to transfer the holding of authority from one member of the community to another. As Leo XIII pointed out, there is an important distinction between the designation of a particular person to exercise the given authority for the common good of the community and the conferral of the authority: "And by this choice, in truth, the ruler is designated, but the rights of ruling are not thereby conferred. Nor is the authority delegated to him, but the person by whom it is to be exercised is determined upon."[226] The consent theories fail to make this critical distinction between the source of authority itself and the designation of the individuals who will exercise it.[227] This understanding of authority is analogous to the overall understanding of law as a participation of man in the lawmaking by God. Authority "in its essence, is undoubtedly derived from God . . . yet the fact that it resides in a particular individual . . . pertains to human law."[228] Thus a notion of consent of the community may be relevant to determine the legitimacy of an individual's claim to possess the power of authority in a community, but consent is not relevant to the establishment of the power itself.

Beyond the formation of a particular perfect community out of the mass of people and the transfer of the property of authority within the community, consent has also played an important role in the exercise of that authority. Some form of consent or acceptance of the actual exercise of the God-given authority has long figured in classical natural law jurisprudence. Yet, as we shall now show, this use of consent is very different from its use by the consent theorists examined in the first section of this chapter.

The process of making human law is multidimensional. It is a dialectical interaction among natural law precepts, posited legislation, and the developing customs of the people. Thus, a component of this dialectical development of law is the developing usages of the members of the political community. The people of a community through usages can not only make law in the absence of statute but also approve enacted statutes and can act to abrogate ordinances. Gratian's description of the legislative process involves a form of consent through the confirmation of statutes by their accepted usage by the people: "Ordinances are instituted when they are promulgated; they are confirmed when they have been approved by the usage of those who observe them."[229] Consent through usages is also an element of the process of custom becoming law on an equal footing with statutes: "Long-standing usages approved by the consent of those following them are like ordinances."[230] Medieval jurists discerned a general principle transcending the particular roles of consent in various aspects of the legislative process: "What touches all ought to be approved by all" (*Quod omnes tangit, ab omnibus approbari debet*).[231] Consent in this context again did not mean that the people conferred authority on their governors. Jurists utilizing and interpreting this maxim maintain a clear distinction between those who exercise legal authority and those who participate in that exercise through forms of consent. The maxim does not dictate any particular form of government, such as popular democracy. Rather, regardless of the form of political authority in any society, the consent of those subject to the law is an integral part of the operation of the system, but not a source of authority. As Kenneth Pennington notes, the extended uses of the maxim *Quod omnes tangit, ab omnibus approbari debet* to require consultations with and the consent of those affected by the laws "were not just alternatives to monarchical rule. The jurists argued that these norms of corporate governance should be integrated into princely government."[232] Aquinas refers in a general way to this legal tradition when he argues that human laws cannot be made simply in the abstract, but in light of the particular circumstances and conditions of the people for which they are made. Although Aquinas explains that all human law must be derived from the general precepts of natural law, his jurisprudence is firmly rooted in the reality of actual living communities. Deduction and determination of human law must always be done in light of the particularities of the community to which it will apply. According to Aquinas, "Human laws should be proportionate to the common good. Now, the common good comprises many things. Wherefore law should take account of many things, as to persons, as to matters, and as to times. Because the community of the state is composed of many persons; and its good is procured by many actions; nor is it established to endure for only a short time, but to last for all time."[233] As human law serves as a measure of human action, a "measure should be homogeneous with that which it measures . . . since different things are measured by different measures. Wherefore laws imposed on men should also be in keeping with their condition, for . . . law should be 'possible both according to nature, and according to the customs of the country.'"[234] Although Aquinas's discussion does not dwell on the specific topics of consent discussed by the jurists, he insists that a lawmaker must be sensitively attuned to the particularities of the members of the political community. He thereby provides a theoretical justification for the jurists who were insisting on practical procedures that ensure the consultation with and consent of the people to the laws that regulate their behavior.[235] Yet, within classical natural law jurisprudence and practice, the consent of the governed is not an ontological basis of the legal authority of the ruler but rather a prudentially good means for the holder of that authority to make use of it wisely and efficaciously. The consent of those affected by the laws of a community does not create legal authority but rather assists one exercising that authority to ensure that determinations are in fact oriented to the particular instantiation of the community as it exists in history. A lawgiver can better attain the end of human law, to orient human action to the common good, if the lawmaking process requires the actual particularities of the people subject to the law be taken into account. Ensuring such participation is the purpose of the legal maxim *Quod omnes tangit, ab omnibus approbari debet.* Consent thus serves a more limited instrumental function in the operation of a legal system rather than the ontologically necessary role unsuccessfully advocated by consent scholars. Pope Honorius III's explanation of his ruling overturning the exclusion of representatives of cathedral chapters from a local legislative council clearly identifies the issue of consent as one necessary to the proper exercise of legal authority. Pope Honorius explains that involving the participation and consent of the members of the community is essential to the harmonious function of the whole: "When the head gives the members their due, the body shall not experience the ravages of schism but will remain whole in the unity of love."[236]

The examination of the legitimate role of consent in the exercise of legal authority has highlighted an important feature of classical natural law jurisprudence. The system avoids the extremes of pure idealism and excessive particularism. Consent has been a concept that made jurisprudence more than abstract general precepts of universal law. The universally applicable general precepts of natural law must be particularized by real communities in a variety of circumstances. The transmission and exercise of legal authority from above must be mediated through practical involvement from below. Understanding legal authority as the power necessary for particular lawmakers to fulfill their duty under the eternal law to determine natural law precepts for their communities locates a dual basis for the obligation to obey the law in the universal and the particular. The obligation to obey a particular law derives from both (1) the natural law precept that has been determined and (2) the particular determination made by the legitimate authority taking into account the circumstances of those touched by the law. As Suaréz observed, all obligations either proximately or remotely come from the natural law. An obligation may arise upon the will of the human lawgiver choosing among possible determinations, but that will is only a part of the process of establishing an obligation.[237] He uses three examples to demonstrate the dual source of obligations. First, an obligation to fulfill a vow comes in part from the will of the one making the vow but also from the general natural law precept requiring that vows once made should be fulfilled. Both parts of the process, the general natural law precept and the particular determination of a specific vow by the maker, are necessary for the obligation to act according to the vow to arise. Likewise, second, one is obligated not to take away property transferred by prescription. The source of this obligation includes both a particular human law transferring property from one owner to another following a specified period of prescription and the natural law precept prohibiting theft of another's property.[238] Whereas a particular obligation comes proximately from a human law, the obligation to obey that particular law comes from the natural law, because the conclusion that a human law ought to be obeyed is "deduced from natural principles."[239]

Finally, third, to come full circle to the universal foundation of all legal authority, human law, although proximately dependent upon natural law, is ultimately dependent upon the eternal law. This entire second section of this chapter can be summarized by considering more precisely the relationship between human law and eternal law. Aquinas notes that eternal law, as the complete ordering of the universe, contains within it "each single truth," including "the particular determinations of individual cases."[240] Yet, God has not granted us a "full participation of the dictate of the divine reason" but only "a natural participation in the divine wisdom [source of eternal law]" consisting of "a natural participation of the eternal law, according to certain general principles."[241] Thus, we can know that there exist objectively true determinations of individual cases (contained within the divine wisdom or eternal law), but our knowledge of these single truths is not "natural." Unlike the general principles of the natural law, which are "impressed on it [our reason] by nature"[242] or "imparted to us by nature,"[243] the particular determinations are arrived at by the "efforts of reason" (*industriam rationis*).[244] Making these particular determinations involves work or industry. It is not something that we know, like a proposition *per se nota* that once explained to us is easily grasped by the reason. This difficulty of making determinations in individual cases is the precise reason for the very existence of human laws. Since making these particular determinations is hard work for each individual and there is significant risk of error, there is a need for human law to "sanction" particular determinations.[245] This is another reason why man is a social and political animal. He is aided by being in society where these determinations are made to assist him.

Which determinations of reason should human law sanction? The answer is contained in our prior discussion—those touching upon the "common good." Recall that the definition of law involves a dictate of reason oriented to the common good. A text from Isidore contained in the *Decretum* exemplifies this limitation on human law as the dictate of reason. He says: "Furthermore, if ordinance is determined by reason, then ordinance will be all that reason has already confirmed—all, at least, that is congruent with religion, consistent with discipline, and helpful for salvation."[246] Notice, human law (ordinance) is not all that reason has confirmed but that which is related to a phrase that can be seen as a summary of the natural and supernatural common good of man: religion, discipline, and salvation. Aquinas uses another phrase to summarize the common good sought by human law: peace within the community and attainment of individual habits of virtue of its members.[247] Thus, human laws need not determine all actions but only those directly and indirectly related to these concepts of the common good.

In discussing the judicial precepts in chapter 5 we noted that discretion in making determinations was left to the individual, private superiors, and governing authorities, respectively. The last group has been entrusted with determinations affecting the common good. Thus, human law is distinguished from purely personal choices when the determination affects the common good of the respective community. The next subsection develops a more detailed understanding of this process.

The Nature of Authoritative Determinations

The prior subsections developed an ontology of legal authority located in the delegated power to determine the general principles of natural law into particular rules of action. Pius XI summarized this bounded freedom of the will of authorities to rationally determine the requirements of the natural law under the guidance of divine law: "To define these duties in detail when necessity requires and the natural law has not done so, is the function of those in charge of the State. Therefore, public authority, under the guiding light always of the natural and divine law, can determine more accurately upon consideration of the true requirements of the common good."[248] This power to determine human law involves both the rational and volitional powers. Since human law is a further specification of the natural law, which can be known by the use of reason, the process must be reasonable. The definition of human law is dependent upon that of natural law (the rational participation of man in the eternal law). Human laws are the "particular determinations devised by human reason . . . from the precepts of the natural law."[249] Thus, the process of making human law involves the use of reason. The matter used by human reason is the precepts of the natural law and the "singular and contingent"[250] "individual cases" that require a definitive determination.[251] Gratian's *Decretum* also recognizes the connection between reason and human law. He includes a text explaining that "reason supports human laws" (*legem ratio commendat*) and ordinances "will be determined by reason" and therefore ordinances are "all that reason has already confirmed" (*lex erit omne iam quod ratione constiterit*).[252] Yet, the process is not *solely* a product of reason. Since the making of determinations may involve the election of one determination among several possible determinations, an act of the will is involved in choosing among them. The essence of authority is the power to require subjects to conform to one particular rational determination chosen by the authority rather than either an irrational determination or all other possible rational determinations. As Philip Soper has observed, this power involves the ability to command conformity "even though others may disagree and even though the state's judgment may be wrong."[253] There are limits on how wrong that determination can be and still count as law,[254] and we will discuss this in chapter 8, but for now we will concentrate on the exercise of this power within those limits. As long as a human law is not an unjust law, as we will define in chapter 8, it retains its status as a human law notwithstanding imperfections. Even if the lawmakers of a society are in fact the wisest of the society, there is no guarantee that every decision of the wise will be correct.[255] Aquinas quoted Aristotle as saying that the formulation of laws by a few wise men was "better" than determinations by the many; he did not say it was perfect. As Aquinas admits: "Wherefore human laws cannot have that inerrancy that belongs to the demonstrated conclusions of sciences. Nor is it necessary for every measure to be altogether unerring and certain, but according as it is possible in its own particular genus."[256]

Within the bounds we will discuss in chapter 8, human laws are better than individual determinations of all matters, but they do not have to be prudentially perfect to qualify as laws. Laws and those who make them derive their authority not from the perfection of every act of lawmaking but from the authority conferred by God through the natural law.

Returning to the red light example, a law requiring a motorist to stop at a red light involves several determinations of the natural law precept that innocent human life should not be unduly placed in danger. In the case of a particular intersection, an authority has determined that to fulfill this obligation the traffic flowing in one direction should stop for a period of time before proceeding. In addition, the authority has determined that the indication to stop will be conveyed by a red light. This determination removes any discretion from the motorist in determining the safety of crossing the particular intersection. By contrast, at other intersections, the absence of a stoplight leaves discretion to the individual regarding the need to stop or slow down. A particular motorist might believe that the authority is wrong in this particular choice; the particular intersection is traveled so infrequently that it is unnecessary to stop for a period of time at a red light. The motorist may also believe that the authority should have determined that one must wait at the red light unless he is certain no other cars are present. Finally, he might rightly believe a bright yellow light would be more effective as a signal to stop. The power of legal authority means that he must stop and wait at the red light regardless of these considerations. Therein lies the power of authority. Since God has entrusted this determination to the authorities of a community and not to the individual, the individual is obligated to obey the authority and not his own judgment about the particular instance. The very fact that other determinations were possible is a necessary condition for the determination of law to be a voluntary election. If the natural law specified the content of every law, the act of human lawmaking would involve no free discretion and lawmakers would merely be scribes. Lawmaking would merely involve transcribing the content of natural law. The determination chosen may be wrong in the sense that it is not the most optimal possibility. Although still supporting conformity to the underlying natural law precept, a different determination may have been made more efficiently or directly. The fact that the eternal and natural law entrust such determinations to the applicable legal authority gives that authority the power to "claim that it has a right to create and enforce norms that reflect its judgment about correct action."[257] Contrary to the conclusion of Raz, the citizen is obligated to stop and wait because the authority has so determined, even when doing so in a particular instance is in fact unnecessary.

There is another sense in which human laws can err, by omission. Human laws do not, and in fact cannot, state every possible conclusion that could be deduced from natural law or determine every choice. Human law will always, and in certain cases must, be incomplete. Aquinas explains:

> Human law is given to the people among whom there are many lacking virtue, and it is not given to the virtuous alone. Hence human law was unable to forbid all that is contrary to virtue; and it suffices for it to prohibit whatever is destructive of human intercourse, while it treats other matters as though they were lawful, not by approving of them, but by not punishing them. . . . On the other hand the divine law leaves nothing unpunished that is contrary to virtue.[258]

Human law may omit to regulate a particular area of virtue or vice. Sometimes this omission may be a failure of lawmakers. They should prohibit a certain act but fail to see its discordance with natural law. Sometimes their omission is actually preferable as a means to the common good. Aquinas notes that one of the requirements of law is that it be possible to take into account the condition of the particular people.[259] Laws must be suited to the state of the community. Aquinas notes that sometimes a

community may be so perverse that if human law were explicitly to punish a particular vice, it could do more harm to the community than good.
He explains that "these imperfect ones, being unable to bear such precepts, would break out into yet greater evils: thus it is written (Ps. 30:33):
'He that violently bloweth his nose, bringeth out blood'; and (Matt. 9:17)
that if 'new wine,' i.e., precepts of a perfect life, 'is put into old bottles,' i.e.,
into imperfect men, 'the bottles break, and the wine runneth out,' i.e., the
precepts are despised, and those men, from contempt, break into evils
worse still."[260] In addition to declining to adopt a particular human law
prohibiting a digression from the natural law, human authorities may decline to apply particular legal sanctions to certain violations of human law
when doing so is deemed beneficial for other reasons. Examples of commonly recognized doctrines in human law justifying an omission of application of a particular law include agreements not to prosecute, diplo-
matic immunity, immunities for charities, and presidential immunity.[261]
Although human law may omit to prohibit or decline to enforce some
laws prohibiting action that is against the natural law, human law may not
positively prescribe or approve of vice.[262] Failing to forbid or punish a certain act does not contradict the applicable natural law precept, and no
conflict of laws exists. Requiring or facilitating violation of a natural law
precept does contradict natural law and thereby creates a conflict of
laws.[263] Human law may, mistakenly or intentionally, omit to forbid or
punish a particular act. There is no absolute duty to adopt and universally
enforce every conceivable deduction and determination of natural law.
Choices can be made. Yet, since human law has concurrent jurisdiction
with the other forms of law, man is still accountable for acts violating the
natural law in another forum. The particular act of vice is not outside the
law but is left solely to higher law, which "leaves nothing unpunished that
is contrary to virtue."[264] Aquinas discusses the example of selling something for more than it is worth, by which he shows that our actions are
subject to more law than human laws. He concludes that it is "unlawful"
to sell something for more than it is worth, notwithstanding the fact that
positive human law does not punish all instances of doing so, and he cites
the Code of Justinian as an example.[265] Although human law may omit
punishing every instance of selling something for more than it is worth, it
may not affirmatively approve of such injustice.[266]

This understanding of the basis of human legal authority residing in the determination of natural law by real human agents applicable to societies of real people, who are at different stages in the journey of perfection, has the important benefit of humanizing authority. Patrick Brennan has, with his usual passion and wit, argued that modern law has become inhuman and depersonalized.[267] In reaction to Hobbes, Rousseau, and Austin, who posited a superhuman absolute sovereign above all law, Thomas Paine and the late Justice Antonin Scalia attempt to make the law itself the absolute sovereign. They thereby strive to make an abstract concept take the role of a person—sovereign law in lieu of unconstrained personal sovereign.[268] To Brennan's comparison we could add Kelsen. His substitution of a hypothetical abstract basic norm for God depersonalizes the nature of sovereignty. Brennan explains that textualists like Scalia are on a "systemic campaign to eliminate the problem of authority in law by eliminating the source of authority."[269] By "source of authority" Brennan means the intention of the lawgiver. But his comment has a deeper meaning. Not only do textualists attempt to excise the intention of the human lawgiver of a particular statute, they also excise the source of the human lawgiver's authority, which is itself a personal lawgiver, God, who has expressed His intention through eternal, natural, and divine law. Human laws are produced by the prudential decisions of real people, not by abstract rules or principles. The principles that guide those real people in making determinations are themselves promulgated laws of a real person. Human laws certainly must be the determinations or deductions from general principles of natural or divine law, but they are the determinations made by real fallible human authorities not claiming that authority of their own right but of that of the ultimate lawgiver, the author of eternal law. For the legal positivist, be he Hart, Raz, or Kelsen, human laws ultimately derive from a depersonalized text—whether it is called a Rule of Recognition or a basic norm. For utilitarians of various stripes, human laws ultimately derive from an abstract rule, a utilitarian principle of maximization of something. For the consent theorists, although they purport to locate authority in people, it is still impersonal. Authority is located in a text of consent by a fictitious abstract metaphor of real people. "We the People" is an abstraction that never actually existed. It is not surprising that once the ultimate source of law is no longer understood to be a real person, but a text or an abstract principle or a metaphor, the proximate source of particular human law would also cease to be understood as a person but would be seen only as an abstract disembodied text. Joseph Vining keenly observes that basing legal authority on dehumanized concepts such as these produces not authority but authoritarianism: "There is always a temptation in law to approach a statute as if its words had meanings in themselves and by themselves—the authoritarianism sometimes shown by those devoted to maintaining the supremacy of democratic politics and legislative authority."[270] In another place, Vining poetically emphasizes the location of legal authority in human activity. Law is not in the things produced, the rules, but in the rationality of the lawmaker, or, to use a phrase out of the classical natural law tradition, law is in the mind of the lawgiver. Vining writes:

> Decision making consists of weighing purposes, values, factors, channels of thought. Rules are not self-executing, in law. There is always, in law, a decision maker, and what are called rules in law are expressions of considerations to be taken into account by a decision maker. They focus not on themselves as a self-contained system but upon decision-making activity pointing forward. Talk of rights and rules of a static kind, projecting an image of law standing off by itself, obscures the focus that legal rules have in fact, always a decision that must be made, at the edge of lives that have not been lived before, in a world that has not been seen before.[271]

This dehumanization noted by Vining is a consequence of grounding legal authority in abstract texts and propositions rather than real persons. Brennan concludes that the way to humanize law and thereby be ruled by authority and not by authoritarianism is to once again put persons back into law.[272] Ultimately the only way to make particular human lawmaking personal again is to see lawmaking as an act of a person from start to finish, to put a person at the top of the legal system and not simply a piece of paper, such as a constitution or an abstract rationalist natural law like that of Finnis. This is exactly where the classical natural law located authority—in real people making rational judgments. First, legal authority is located in God, the person who created the legal system. Second, He locates human legal authority in real fallible human beings participating in

His authority by making rational and prudential choices among possible determinations of law. Consequently, the classical natural law theory understood the authority of law to be in people—all the way up and all the way down the entire legal system—and not in the rule itself or the paper containing the rule.[273] As Brennan concludes elsewhere: "The crux of the matter is that law is an ordinance of reason, not a piece of paper; the law is only 'in' the paper metaphorically. To know law, is to receive something from the mind of the lawgiver."[274] This legal ontology can be a bulwark against the authoritarianism of textualism that rightly concerns Vining.

Unlike Finnis's utilitarian rationale for the existence of human law that ought to be obeyed, the traditional natural law jurisprudence understands the making of particular human laws to be a good in and of itself because the authority is fulfilling a purpose established by the eternal law. Human lawmaking is not merely instrumentally good as a useful means to coordinating group actions. *Contra* Finnis, the justification of authority defended in this chapter holds that authority, the choice or election among possible legal determinations of natural law precepts, is a good in and of itself because it is legislated into the system by the eternal law, which provides that such determinations ought to be made by those with care of the community. Making human laws is thus a participation in God's governance of the universe, which God has entrusted to men. As an aspect of God's nature, authority thus is a good in its own right and not merely an instrumental good to solve a coordination problem. Finnis bases the need for authoritative rulers on a requirement for "speed and certainty" that is not provided by a coordination solution by custom.[275] At his most utilitarian he says: "Authority (and thus the *responsibility* of governing) in a community is to be exercised by those who can in fact effectively settle co-ordination problems for that community."[276] Particular authorities may vary widely in their effectiveness in performing their task, but the activity has value regardless because it is a participation in God's lawmaking. For this reason, Aquinas held that one could not be removed from an office of legal authority simply for making bad laws.[277] A tyrannical prince may be participating poorly in God's authority, but that does not detract from the goodness of that authority itself.

Grounding human authority in the eternal law provides the only answer to what Steven Smith has called "law's quandary": Does the law exist or is it only a conceptual construct?[278] Utilitarian and consent, or popular sovereignty, theories might say something about law or something about why some people obey it, but none of them provides answers to the big question. If law and legal authority really exist, from where did they come? As Vining has commented about Smith's work, the classical view of law running from the ancient world through Christian jurisprudence maintained that the key to the big question lay in the divine. Vining observes: "Smith begins with an overarching sense of law, 'classical' or 'traditional,' preceding the developments of the twentieth century. One view, which he outlines, is that this overarching sense depended upon and linked human law to divine law with divine judgment and sanction."[279] The modern break with this ontology created a metaphysical problem that the modern theories of authority fail to solve satisfactorily. Finnis resists relying on this classical understanding of law and its grounding of authority and obligation in God. He seems to believe that unless he removes God from the explanation of authority and obligation, his argument can be defeated by this question: "Why should we obey God?"[280] Yet, that question can be answered in the same way that one would answer the question of a worker on a building site: "Why should we obey the architect?" The answer is because he has in his mind the entire plan and can see better than the individual contractor the purpose of his particular action and how it fits into the overall structure. Ultimately, we should obey God not simply because, in the words of Moore, he is some "Big Person."[281] As Brennan has observed, the Thomistic definition of law does not contain an element of coercion.[282] Obedience to the law is not a result of law being coercive. Some forms of coercion may be justified once an obligation to obey the law has been established. But this use of coercion is a consequence of legitimate authority, not a constituent of it. Ultimately, we should obey God's law because the world is objectively rational and He is the source of that rationality. He can see the entire architecture, and thus we should obey Him. This rational obligation to obey God's law is the source of the rational obligation to obey the authorities He has permitted to participate in His lawmaking, by entrusting them with perfecting His architectural design by making particular determination.

Recognizing the necessity of God in the foundation of legal authority returns us to the issue we raised at the end of chapter 2: Should natural law theory be articulated so that it depends upon belief in God? Some may fear

losing an audience for the argument over this issue. There are two possibilities of avoiding God's fundamental role in legal authority. Either deny his
necessity or reduce that necessity to virtually nothing. The first solution
leads to the dead-end justifications of utilitarianism and consent theory.
The attempts to justify legal authority without God have all failed to present a cogent, complete, and satisfactory explanation for the ontology and
origin of legal authority. Eliminating God also leads to the destruction of
real limitations on legal authority and the consequent obligation to obey
the law. Those who wish to diminish the central role of God in the origin
of law and legal authority likewise end up in an unsatisfactory conclusion.
For minimalists, as with Finnis, God exists, and perhaps He created the
world, but He is not a part of the legal system. He created man and man
created law. We saw in chapter 3 that for Finnis, natural law is only law
by analogy to the law made by men. Brennan vividly describes the bleak
world of legal theory built on a Deist's notions of a minimalist God:

> The world to which the Deist would consign us looks like this. On
> the one hand, irrational, unfree creatures—such as puppies and
> petunias—would be infallibly moved by God through their created
> inclinations to their respective ends. Rational human creatures, on the
> other hand, would suffer their inclinations to their end(s), alright [sic],
> but would enjoy no authoritative measure for freely achieving them.
> What this would mean, in other words, is that the creator created with
> the certainty that his rational creatures would not, absent divine inter-
> vention (as in Scripture), be commanded to the end(s) for which God
> created them. Created by God but not commanded by God, to vary
> Hittinger's phrase. Or, to vary the phrase yet again, no measures, or
> rules, or law imposed by another by which to choose and act. Kant cele-
> brated the putative result as "autonomy." But is this true?[283]

For this reason Brennan argues that the very notion of law and legal
authority must be based on presuppositions about God:

> And here the connection with religion, the work to make law heard
> proceeds only on presuppositions. If it does not proceed on those
> presuppositions, it does not produce anything to which there is any
> sense of obligation. That which evokes no sense of obligation is not

law. It is only an appearance of law, the legalistic, the authoritarian, not sovereign but an enemy. Principal among the presuppositions of legal work are that a person speaks through the texts; that there is mind; that mind is caring mind. These are the links between the experience of law and religious experience.[284]

One need not accept everything that theology teaches about God to find the origin of authority in Him.[285] Yet, at least one must recognize God as a God of law, a person who orders the universe with authority and entrusts a portion of that authority to rational creatures to do likewise. Only here can we find not only a satisfactory explanation of authority— an answer to the question of why the fallible determinations of other fallible rational creatures should be obeyed as law by us—but we can also regain a humanized authority. If law is only words and text, then, as Brennan observes, it easily becomes authoritarian. If law is in a rational mind it can resist authoritarianism. As we shall see in chapter 8, locating human legal authority within the person of God secures limits to the exercise of that authority by human minds and produces the duty to obey the laws they enact.

Finally, the natural law explanation satisfies Leslie Green's requirements for an authority that can obligate obedience to laws. The natural law provides a moral reason (in the sense of a reason independent of the human law itself) for action, criterion (i), because the natural law entrusts to human authorities the responsibility to determine particular action to be done or avoided pursuant to its own general precepts. Thus, the precept of natural law that we are to live well in society obligates us to conform to the determinations of applicable authorities independently of those determinations themselves. The foregoing justification of legal authority provides a content-independent reason for action, criterion (ii), because the general precepts of natural law permit a variety of possible conforming determinations, and the particular one to be obeyed is to be obeyed because the applicable authority in fact so determined. Subjects do not obey human laws because, all things considered, they would have selected this particular determination of natural law. They must obey because natural law has delegated election of this type of determination to human authorities. Stephen Perry argues that to satisfy criterion (ii) we must not refer to an independent moral obligation to do X but rather only to the legal directive to do X.[286] If we parse more precisely what we mean by X, we can see how a human law requiring citizens to do X is content-independent under the natural law understanding of law. For example, the human law requiring one to drive on the right side of the road is rooted in the obligation under natural law to drive safely, but the specific obligation to do such by driving on the right side as opposed to the left is dependent solely on the determination by a human lawmaker, even if that determination derives its obligatory force from a more general precept of natural law. Before the drive on the right law was enacted, each person was free to conform to the general precept of driving safely by making individual determinations about which side appeared to be the safest in the particular context. Yet, once the determination is made by human law, all drivers must drive on the right because the lawmaker has now made the determination for the community. Punishment for murder provides another example. The natural law obligates one not to murder, but the obligation to be confined to prison for life if one murders is obligatory once a human authority has determined a life sentence to be the punishment due to those who commit murder. Although both rooted in the natural law precepts prohibiting murder and requiring evildoers to be punished, the specific nature of the punishment is content-independent because it arises from the legitimate determination of the authority in selecting this particular punishment. Human law provides a binding or mandatory reason for action, criterion (iii), because God through natural law delegates the power to determine natural law to human authorities. The mandatory nature of legitimate human determinations thus derives from the mandatory nature of the ends of human existence established in the eternal law. Although the election of means in relation to that end is left to human choice, it is not always left to each individual for all choices. Some determinations are left to the superiors of families, imperfect communities, and perfect communities. Yet, the power to determine is derived from the eternal law. Human law is a particular reason for action only for the directives of a citizen's (or subject's) own state, criterion (iv), because natural law entrusts determination not to one superior but to a variety of temporal and spiritual superiors dispersed throughout the variety of perfect communities around the globe. The various imperfect and perfect communities are constituted by nature, with their own particular superiors entrusted with a specific jurisdictional limit for making determinations for their particular community. Those determinations can legitimately differ from community to community and still be derived from the same natural law precept (see chapter 6). The developing customs of each community will result in different but still legitimate determinations of the same natural law precept. Finally, a particular determination is a universal reason for action, criterion (v), because it binds all of those subject to the applicable authority to all determinations of that authority. Unlike Raz's theory, the classical theory requires universal conformity even when individuals might deem the determination unnecessary in a particular case. Many theorists have argued that this universality condition can never be met, because in every society there will at some point be a law that should not be obeyed.[287] At some point another normative principle demands disobedience to a law. Such a conclusion is necessitated by restricting the idea of legal system to human-made laws. Thus, when a human-made law must be disobeyed, it appears to lack legal universality. Yet, if we see the legal system as larger than the determinations by human authorities to include the natural law, when those determinations that cannot be obeyed are encountered, we are still conforming our actions to the law in its fullest sense. Subjects are only bound in conscience to obey determinations of the natural law. If a human authority commands something other than a valid determination of natural law, it is not a law at all. Thus, if human law is defined to include only those acts of lawgivers that are in fact laws, the universality condition is satisfied. Those acts of lawgivers that may be disregarded are not laws because they are invalidated by higher law. Yet, to fully prove this last point we must examine more carefully the limits on human lawmaking authority conferred by the natural law. Chapter 8 will turn to this limitation. As we shall observe, once this limitation is understood, we will see how the legitimate disregarding of a human-made law is not a moral objection to a legal obligation resulting in disobedience to law; it is a legal objection based on the resolution of a conflict of laws, and the purported disobedience is rather an act of obedience to higher law.

EIGHT

Falling Off the Frame

The Limits of Legal Authority

Laws may be unjust in two ways. . . .
The like are acts of violence rather than laws; because . . . ,
"a law that is not just, seems to be no law at all."
Wherefore such laws do not bind in conscience,
except perhaps in order to avoid scandal or disturbance,
for which cause a man should even yield his right.[1]

THE LIMITS OF LEGAL AUTHORITY: UNJUST LAWS ARE NO LAWS AT ALL

H. L. A. Hart, although developing a more nuanced version of legal positivism than John Austin, ultimately reaches a similar conclusion. There is no *legal* limit on the authority of a lawmaker other than one imposed by human-made positive law itself. Hart might believe that people should disobey an immoral law, but Hart is clear this choice of the individual is not due to any legal limit on legal authority. Such a choice is not legally permitted, even if morally permitted: "It is important to understand that the legally unlimited power of the sovereign is his by definition: the theory simply asserts that there could only be legal limits on legislative power if the legislator were under the orders of another legislator whom he habitually obeyed; and in that case he would no longer be sovereign. If he is sovereign he does not obey any other legislator and hence there can be no legal limits on his legislative power."[2] Likewise, Joseph Raz, although admitting that the decisions of legal authorities can be questioned, maintains that such questions are nonlegal. As a result, the criteria for evaluating human laws are merely referenced by Raz and are never defined. For Raz, a legal decision acts as a protected reason for action, but this protection does not exclude all reasons to the contrary. Yet, these nonexcluded reasons become extralegal and, for Raz, not subject to legal definition. For example, Raz explains at one point: "Even where an authoritative decision is meant to settle finally what is to be done, it may be open to challenge on certain grounds, for example, if an emergency occurs, or if the directive violates fundamental human rights, or if the authority acted arbitrarily. The nonexcluded reasons and the grounds of challenging an authority's directives vary from case to case."[3] For Raz, these legal decisions that are subject to further questions remain law, but law that should be questioned and perhaps ignored. Within legal reasoning, Raz describes the point of reference from which we can discern legitimacy of authority as an "ideal."[4] Yet, this ideal is simply assumed and asserted "like the fundamental human rights," the violation of which can justify refusing to conform to authority.[5] Like Kelsen's basic norm, Raz merely posits this ideal authority where undefined reasons are relied upon for framing directives. They are extralegal free-floating concepts that influence our evaluation of law's merit and our decision to conform to it or not; they are in the end, however, distinctly not *legal* reasons. Raz notes that, generally, directives of authority ought to be followed even when mistaken, except when some mistakes justify not following them,[6] but ultimately he has no legal explanation for why some mistakes justify disobedience but others do not.

Because legal positivism (even of the Hartian or Razian flavor) is wedded to this legal supremacy of human legal authority, this absolute *legal* sovereignty of human law, it is intellectually incapable of formulating a defined limit, specifically a legal limit, to the use of legal authority, and correlatively the theory requires a legally unqualified obedience to the law.

Hart argues that there are no *legal limits* on the sovereign. Nonlegal prudential and other practical restraints may in fact exist, but they do not legally limit the sovereign:[7] "The law courts, in considering whether they have before them a law of the sovereign, would not listen to the argument that its divergence from the requirements of popular opinion or morality prevented it from ranking as law, unless there was an order of the sovereign that they should."[8] The only possible limit is circular. The sovereign's authority is limited only to the extent the sovereign limits himself. Hart, relying on Austin, adopts a popular sovereignty foundation for the power of the sovereign.[9] Although grounding the authority of the unlimited sovereign in the populace may appear to limit the authority of the sovereign, in reality the people turn out to be an empty limitation. Popular sovereignty provides no stable limitation on legal authority. If the people delegate they can later revoke their consent and the terms of the authority. Any restraints in delegated authority are only as good as the last constitutional amendment. Hart cites provisions of the U.S. Constitution forbidding amendments to the slave clause and depriving states of equal representation in the Senate.[10] Yet, since the Constitution is merely a product of popular delegation, the people can amend the clauses that restrict any changes and then make those changes. Ultimately, the sovereign people can do anything they wish. If they elect someone who wants to torture and if they pass a constitutional amendment authorizing torture, torture is legal. The notion of popular sovereignty can only limit authority if the people themselves are a subordinate sovereign possessing only a limited delegated authority. The justification of legal authority we described in chapter 7 requires a diametrically opposed conclusion to legal positivism and the theory of popular sovereignty. Human lawmaking authority is most certainly circumscribed within legal limits. This chapter explores the nature and implications of those limits, or, returning to the architectural analogy, the points at which lawmakers fall off the architectural structure.

Francisco Suárez observes that to fulfill the function of providing a unity of order to a heterogeneous community, such as a political community, lawmakers need to bind members and compel action.[11] This lawmaking power is thus a form of "dominion," but it is not a dominion of "servitude to a despot"[12] because the power to bind is limited. Two key features of authority produce this limitation: (1) the end or purpose of lawmaking authority and (2) the hierarchical source of human authority that delegates only a limited scope of authority.[13] The limitations of human legal authority are intimately connected to the justification of legal authority we developed in chapter 7. Since human lawmakers derive their authority to make determinations from the natural law—and ultimately the eternal law—that authority is legally circumscribed by this higher law. The natural law allows significant freedom of choice to design the particulars of a legal system, but not all conceivable possibilities are permissible.[14] This section explores the ancient argument of natural law lawyers that an unjust law is no law at all, which adage summarizes a nuanced understanding of the limitations on human legal authorities to obligate subjects to obey their pronouncements.

Jonathan Crowe has summarized this fundamental claim of traditional natural law jurisprudence: "A rational defect (R) in a norm or system of norms (N) necessarily renders it invalid or defective as Law (L)."[15] Crowe then identifies four critical questions about the natural law thesis:

1. Is the thesis about the concept of law, the nature of law, or the linguistic meaning of the term?
2. What counts as a rational defect?
3. What does it mean to say a norm is invalid or defective as law?
4. Does it apply to individual norms of a system or to normative systems as a whole?[16]

We will see how the grounding of legal authority in the eternal and natural law provides answers to these questions.

First we must understand that the virtue of obedience—which is the practical end of legal authority—is itself subject to limitations. These limitations will assist in understanding the limitation on legal authority. Aquinas identifies two categories of exceptions to the obligation to obey one in authority. In the first category, Aquinas acknowledges a hierarchy of superiors. One may disobey the order of a direct superior if required to do so by a higher authority.[17] He quotes St. Augustine to illustrate the operation of this type of exception: "If a commissioner issue an order, are you to comply, if it is contrary to the bidding of the proconsul? Again if the proconsul command one thing, and the emperor another, will you hesitate, to disregard the former and serve the latter? Therefore if the emperor commands one thing and God another, you must disregard the former and obey God."[18] Thus, if human legal authority is not a source of its own authority but received from another (e.g., God), there is a hierarchy in obedience. The lower authority must be disobeyed if and to the extent that a different act is required to obey the command of the higher authority. Since chapter 7 argued that all human authorities receive their power to make law from God, the obligation to obey those authorities is always subject to the greater obligation to obey the higher authority.

The second category involves cases in which the one possessing authority orders something outside the scope of his authority.[19] Only the ultimate source of authority possesses limitless authority. Thus, only God himself can command with unbounded authority. Since all other authority is transferred from God, its scope is necessarily finite and limited in scope to the extent of the particular authority granted. Thus, one subject to obedience is obligated to obey only to the extent of the delegated authority: "In matters concerning the disposal of actions and human affairs, a subject is bound to obey his superior within the sphere of his authority; for instance, a soldier must obey his general in matters relating to war, a servant his master in matters touching the execution of the duties of his service, a son his father in matters relating to the conduct of his life and the care of the household, and so forth."[20] Thus, a citizen is not obligated to obey the human-made law of his society when either that law contradicts a higher law or when the human law exceeds the scope of human lawmaking authority. Since, for Austin and Hart, the sovereign or the people are the source of their own authority, they cannot locate any higher legal authority or any matter outside the scope of legal authority. The remainder of this section will flush out the particular nature of these limitations on the obligation to obey the law that elude legal positivism.

The legal authority delegated to human lawmakers is the power to determine the choice on behalf of their political community among particular permissible courses of action pursuant to the primary and secondary precepts of the natural law consistently with the developing customs of the people. We have established that the goodness of legal authority consists in the fact that it involves a participation in the sovereign legislative power of God. Ultimately, however, it is only a participation in sovereignty, not sovereignty itself. Although this grandeur of human legal authority is provided for by the indeterminacy of natural law precepts, Jean Porter reminds us that this indeterminacy is not open-ended but is bounded. She explains, "Certainly, the universally applicable scriptural norms, considered as a revealed formulation of natural law, place stringent restrictions on human activity."[21] Human lawmakers are thus bound by the very source of their authority to respect the limits imposed at the source. Yet, granting human beings the ability to make determinations within these stringent restrictions does not ensure that those authorities will always respect those restrictions. Human authorities are capable of misusing the great good given to them.

Determinations, even those made by the wise—a requirement for those assuming the role of spiritual or temporal authorities—are not infallible. Recall that we observed (chapter 7) that Aquinas quoted Aristotle as saying that the formulation of laws by a few wise men was "better" than determinations by the many; he did not say it was perfect. Aquinas admits: "Wherefore human laws cannot have that inerrancy that belongs to the demonstrated conclusions of sciences. Nor is it necessary for every measure to be altogether unerring and certain, but according as it is possible in its own particular genus."[22] As a natural law jurist, Aquinas is idealistic (he argues for the existence of an objective truth in practical matters), but this idealism is balanced by a healthy practicality. Even the wise can err, and we need not be scandalized by this deficiency. It is sufficient for human societal well-being that the wise get particular determinations as correctly worked out as is possible given their abilities. On this point, natural law advocates can agree with positivists: some error in the legal system is inevitable and does not undermine the legitimacy of the entire legal system. Ultimately, because God has withdrawn from direct legislation for man (after the promulgation of the New Law), he wills the temporal and spiritual leaders to do the best they can in making particular determinations. Yet, Aquinas maintains that lawmakers can err in qualitatively different ways. Such differences should affect the way in which those subject to law act in light of such errors. The line is not drawn simply between perfect and imperfect laws. The conclusion is not as simple as that one must obey only perfect laws and must disobey all that fail to attain perfection. More refined distinctions are necessary, particularly within the genus of imperfect determinations.

The natural law must serve as the foundation for each human law. If it does, such human law exhibits three attributes: (1) it is just, (2) it binds in conscience, and (3) it is a "legal law."[23] Aquinas uses this striking phrase, "legal laws" (*leges legales*), to describe the goal of evaluating the status of human laws. I think the phrase helps us distinguish the issue we are considering from the method of a legal positivist. A human law considered solely from the standpoint of procedure may appear to be a law (it was enacted according to the prescribed method of a particular community or, in Hart's words, according to the Rule of Recognition), yet from a natural law perspective, it may not be a legal law—and thus not binding in conscience. The positivist ends the analysis at the point of recognizing that a particular statement fulfills the procedural requirements of lawmaking in a given system. Yet, a natural law jurist proceeds to test the purported law's status further in light of natural law precepts, primary and secondary and also divine law precepts. Testing it involves evaluating particular errors made by the legislator in framing human positive law. Not all errors remove the status of legality from laws. Legal laws are just laws that bind in conscience. Thus, it is necessary to determine if an imperfect law is also an unjust law that cannot bind in conscience.

There are two types of errors in making human laws, errors in relation to which different conclusions follow. The two types of errors relate to the two ways in which human laws can be derived from natural law, as deductions of principles or determinations of actions. This division is analogous in certain respects to the divisions contained in Roman jurisprudence of human law into the *jus gentium* (law of nations) and the *jus civile* (law for the city).[24] The first types of human laws are "those things that are derived from the law of nature, as conclusions from premises."[25] These are general principles of action deduced directly from the speculative knowledge of the end of man that are true for all types of human society and thus form the law of every nation. Aquinas lists here as an example the conclusion that buying and selling should be on just terms because "without which man cannot live together," which is necessary since man must live together as "a social animal."[26] Thus, laws that state general principles of action not particularly determined for a particular legal community are applicable to any legal system. On the other hand, laws constituting specific determinations in light of the contingent facts of a particular legal system (or *jus civile*) include those laws "derived from the law of nature, by way of particular determination."[27] These laws are particular enactments with prescribed consequences, which can vary from legal system to legal system without violating any principles of the *jus gentium*. Aquinas gives an example of this type of law, which particularly determines a general precept of the *jus gentium*. The *jus gentium* contains a conclusion that "evildoers should be punished," but the *jus civile* of a particular city may contain a law stating that an evildoer "be punished in this or that way."[28] In chapter 6, we noted how Roman law would look to the general principles of the *jus gentium* when deciding cases involving people not subject to the specific determinations of the *jus civile* of Rome. The *jus gentium* contains general precepts that are more directly related to natural law because they are deductively formulated as conclusions drawn from precepts of natural law used as premises. Thus, laws of the *jus gentium* lack not only the specificity but also the element of volition found in determinations, as they are merely rational deductions. For this reason, Roman law only relied directly on *jus gentium* in the absence of applicable *jus civile*. Having drawn this distinction, we can now consider how human laws can be illegal as a result of departing from justice.

The first of the three necessary characteristics of a law is that it comports with justice. From the first chapter of his consideration of justice, Aristotle had claimed a necessary relationship between law and justice. Arguing that the just man is law-abiding, Aristotle argues that what is lawful is just.[29] This statement is not meant in the positivist sense that the law can make something that is naturally unjust into something just by merely making it law. Aristotle explains that only those laws which direct acts to the ultimate human good are just.[30] Since he has already equated lawful with just, therefore a law must be just to be a law. Therefore, for Aristotle, in order for something to qualify as a law, it necessarily must be directed to the ultimate human good and hence be just. In the *Politics*, Aristotle states the negative implication of this positive relationship between law and justice. Aristotle observes that a government, an authority in a political community, can make either just or unjust laws, and concludes that true forms of authority could only make just laws, whereas perverted authority makes unjust laws.[31] As a result of this potential for true and perverted authority, "laws must be passed, but these laws will have no authority when they miss the mark, though in all other cases retaining their authority."[32] A law that misses the mark is, like a poorly shot arrow, a law not properly oriented to its end, justice. In a passage cited by Aquinas,[33] Augustine states the same negative conclusion with more precision: since the purpose of law is to do justice, an unjust law is therefore not a law. Suárez confirms the conclusion that an unjust law is not law.[34] In Aristotle's original observation that a law that misses its mark lacks authority, we see the essence of the limitation on the authority to make laws. Laws must be just to partake of the quality of authority requiring obedience. Although we will consider in more depth the essence of justice in chapter 9, it is necessary to note that the notion of the common good has long been embedded in the concept of justice. As Kenneth Pennington has explained, medieval jurists fused together two conceptions of justice.[35] The first came from Ulpian's definition and considered justice the virtue of giving people what was lawfully due to them.[36] The second came through the Stoic tradition, which emphasized that justice is oriented to the common good. Cicero exemplifies this second emphasis when he defines justice: "Justice is a habit of the mind which attributes its proper dignity to everything, preserving a due regard to the general welfare."[37] Pennington quotes Peter Abelard as an early source who not only brings these two aspects together but explains how the notion of the common good can be read to be implied in Ulpian's definition:

> The philosophers define justice as the "habitus" of the mind to render to every person what is his as long as the common good is preserved. Justinian [by which he means Ulpian's definition included in Justinian's compilation] defined this concept in his definition when he would say, "Justice is the constant and perpetual will," etc. "His" can refer to the receiver as well as to the giver. If it refers to the receiver then [this right] ought to be regulated by the preservation of the common good. Justice refers to the common good in all matters.[38]

We have already seen how Aquinas embeds the same concept of the common good into the definition of law as a dictate of reason ordained to the common good.[39] The common good is a necessary element of both justice and law. Put another way, to be just laws must be oriented to the common good. The necessary connection among law, justice, and the common good can be found, at least implicitly, in Aristotle. Only those governments, according to Aristotle, "which have a regard to the common interest are constituted in accordance with strict principles of justice" and are true forms of government.[40] Aristotle distinguishes among true and corrupt governments because he holds that authority aims at a good.[41] We can thus discriminate between those laws that attain that good and those that miss the mark. As Aquinas observes, "Whatever is for an end should be proportionate to that end."[42] The end of human laws is the common good of the community.[43] Laws are thus a means to the end of the common good of society. Another way of understanding how justice encompasses the common good can be attained by applying Ulpian's definition of justice (the virtue of rendering to one what is due) to the community as a whole. What is due the community from its authority is the enactment of laws, which are means to their proper end, the common good. A just law is one ordained to its end, the common good.[44] An authority that attempts to impose a law not ordained to the common good does not give what is due, and thus the law is unjust and, as Aquinas echoing Augustine concludes, is thus "no law at all."[45] The reason, according to Aquinas, that an unjust law is no law is owed to the lack of conformity of the means, the law, to its end, the common good: "Consequently, since the law is chiefly ordained to the common good, any other precept in regard to some individual work, must needs be devoid of the nature of a law, save in so far as it regards the common good."[46] The power to change men's normative position by making laws is thus limited by the end of such power. As C. G. Bateman observes: "The 'right to rule' . . . necessitated a 'right' rule," and "the further back one goes in the history of authority/sovereignty as an idea, the more this moral component seems to show up."[47] The scope of lawmaking authority extends only to suitable means, just laws, that is laws that are oriented to their end.

Yet, there is another aspect to the limitation of authority by its end. The authority of lawmakers extends only to the determination of those preexisting principles of natural law that relate to the common good. For the legal authority, the sphere of operation is the temporal common good of the political community. Thus determinations that are primarily related to the sphere of the individual or the family or other imperfect communities that compose the political community should be left to the appropriate authority within such sphere (i.e., the individual, or the parents, or the leaders of a vocational organization).[48] Legal authority is thus limited to determinations primarily involving the sphere of the common good, or in other words peace, order, and justice.[49] Suárez explains this delineation of spheres: "The civil authority, or the State as it is called, has no right to refuse recognition to the proper ends determined by nature for the individual person and for the family, nor has it any right to limit them."[50] In fact, it is obligated to aid these lower spheres since the attainment of their ends is inextricably caught up in the common good of political society: "The virtue whereby the good of the individual person and of the family are directed to the end of civil society is legal justice."[51]

In addition to the limitation imposed by the end, the authority to make law is also limited by the source of that authority. The supreme lawmaker in any jurisdiction "has the power to make laws proper to its sphere; that is to say, civil or human laws which, by the force of natural law, it may validly and justly establish."[52] As I have argued in chapters 6 and 7, the source of human authority is the natural law, which leaves the determinations of its principles to appropriate authorities. Human authorities are not vested with the power to make general principles of law, which are already contained in the natural law. The authority vested in human lawmakers is restricted solely to the articulation of general precepts of natural law and their determination for the particular community.

This limitation can be examined by looking at the process of lawmaking. For Aristotle, law is made both by an act of reason and an act of the will (compulsive power).[53] The first act, of reason, functions as a constraint or limitation on the compulsive power. To be an act of reason, law must comport with reason, the principles of which are contained in natural law. Aristotle maintains that merely legitimately being the lawmaker is not sufficient for one's commands to become law. The content of the law is a relevant consideration to its legality: "Unlawful it certainly is to rule without regard to justice, for there may be might where there is no right."[54] Laws are thus volitional choices bounded by acts of reason.

It is important to recognize the complexity of the relationship between natural law and human authorities. The authorities do not simply transmit natural law like a reporter. Human authorities are not mechanical robots but rational creatures who, within the prescribed bounds of natural law precepts, actually do change people's normative positions when they enact laws. Aristotle understood the relationship between law and people in authority to be complex. All good rules must be based on well-constituted law, but people are needed to make determinations. Laws must be just or unjust, but the just ones are in accord with a good constitution.[55] As Brian Tierney has observed, natural law is not simply "a kind of detailed pattern of legislation laid up in heaven."[56] At the same time, according to Pennington, "laws were not simply reflections of different usages in various communities. All law had to be evaluated according to standards that transcended human institutions."[57] Thirteenth-century jurists began to articulate a theory of the source of legal authority, which sprung from two heads: the natural law and the will of the prince. Natural law was a source of legal authority in that "law must be moral, ethical, equitable, and, most importantly, reasonable."[58] To natural law, these jurists added "the will (*voluntas*) of the prince as [an additional necessary] source of law."[59] One of the most grandiose descriptions of the will of the prince as a source of law is found in Laurentius's commentary on a papal decretal of Innocent III: "O, how great is the power of the prince; he changes the nature of things by applying the essences of one thing to another. . . . He can make iniquity from justice by correcting any canon or law, for in these things his will is held to be reason [*pro ratione voluntas*]. . . . And there is no one in this world who would say to him, 'Why do you do this?' "[60] Laurentius recognized the ability of a legal authority to transform something that was previously iniquitous into something just by an act of the will. This power lies in the ability to determine the general principles of natural law. To understand the power, we can consider an example. A precept of natural law forbids theft,[61] the taking of the property of another. Yet, to apply the precept, one must know what constitutes private property. This determination is left to human authorities, who, for example, determine after what length of time unclaimed property works a loss of ownership. Imagine a depositor deposits money with a bank for safekeeping, and in the applicable legal system one ceases to be an owner of unclaimed property after twenty years. After eighteen years, the bank takes the entrusted money and uses it for its own purposes. The bank has committed the iniquity of theft. If, however, the legal authority has promulgated a law fixing the period to be fifteen years, then this same act (appropriation after eighteen years) is not iniquitous but just. Likewise, it is wrong to drive on the wrong side of the road, as this would violate the natural law precept not to unnecessarily endanger other people. At present it would be iniquitous to drive on the right side of the road in Great Britain. If, however, Great Britain promulgated a new law to drive on the right, doing such would be changed from iniquitous to just. It is this power to alter the justice of actions by an act of determination that Laurentius is extoling as a source of law.

But, unlike a legal positivist, who would limit the source of law to this will of the sovereign, the medieval Scholastics articulated the aphorism "the will of the prince has the force of law" in the context of a wider jurisprudence that restrained the will of the prince, requiring any act of his will to be rational. There is a serious danger in accepting the will of the legislator as the sole source of law without the accompanying other source of natural law. The acceptance of the will of the legislator without the restraint of natural law creates the possibility for unconstrained arbitrary law. A strand of jurisprudence in the later Middle Ages began to separate the will of the legislator from the natural law, making the will of the prince the *only* rather than a codependent source of law.[62] The result is a legislator who can promulgate laws contrary to reason, morality, and justice.[63] Although opposed by other strands of jurists, this exaltation of the will ultimately leads to modern legal positivism, which accepts Laurentius's identification of the will of the prince as a cause of law but rejects the other source that provides the authority for that will to operate. Prior to the separation of legislative will from natural law, "No jurist had ever made the claim that the prince could make laws that were unreasonable and unjust."[64] Notwithstanding Laurentius's extolling of the power of the will of the prince, he immediately adds to his praise that "he is held, nevertheless, to shape this power to the public good."[65]

Prior to this separation, jurists accepted this great power to change the nature of particular cases of justice and injustice by promulgating particular law only within the constraints that the determination must comport with natural law: "Natural law provided a moral basis for deciding whether a given enactment was a good and just law."[66] If under such a standard the law did not satisfy this moral basis, it was not a law since it no longer rested upon both sources of authority—natural law (rooted in the eternal law) and the will of the legislator. Cicero, who only vaguely understood the concept of eternal law, nonetheless clearly understood that "those who wrote decrees that were destructive and unjust to their peoples . . . produced something utterly different from laws . . . [so that] even if the people approve of it . . . [such an enactment will not] be a law of any kind."[67] Cicero analogizes an unjust enactment to a doctor who through ignorance or inexperience prescribes poison. An injustice prescribed by a lawmaker is no more a law than a poison prescribed by a doctor through ignorance or inexperience would be medicine.[68]

Aquinas worked out the nuanced implications of deviations from these two sources of law by interpreting Augustine's famous aphorism, which accords with Cicero's conclusion, that "a law that is not just, seems to be no law at all."[69] Aquinas first notes that laws are either just or unjust. His first conclusion is that if they are just, "they have the power of binding in conscience, from the eternal law whence they are derived."[70] Aquinas associates three concepts with the establishment of an obligation: human law, eternal law, and justice. To obligate the conscience a human law must derive from natural law and must be just. We have already established that the manner of derivation from eternal law is through the natural law. Thus, just laws are derived from eternal law by being determinations of precepts of natural law. In addition to the process of being made as determinations of natural law, Aquinas lays down three conditions for laws to be just: their end, their author, and their form each must comport with justice.[71]

Law is not an end in itself. Law serves the end of guiding human action (both of individuals and society as a whole). A just law must therefore conform to this end. All law must be an ordinance of reason directed to the common good, and every level of the legal architecture is ultimately ordered to the highest common good, the end of the eternal law, God himself. Leo XIII summarizes this requirement: "Laws only bind when they are in accordance with right reason, and, hence, with the eternal law of God."[72] Yet, each level of law has its own particular aspect of the common good, which is a component of this ultimate common good. The common good of natural law is the conformity of human acts to the common nature of man. The common good of the divine law is the supernatural relation of man to God. The common good of a particular system of human law is the political common good of the community to which the law applies. Yet, although the specific end of human law is the political common good of the society to which the law applies, this political common good is itself a component of the higher common good of the natural and divine laws and ultimately the eternal law. Thus a just law must have as its proximate end the common good of the society and as its ultimate end the ultimate common good of all men as fixed by the eternal law. Thus, all laws "should be framed, not for any private benefit, but for the common good of all the citizens."[73] The common good does not exclude the good of individual members of the community. However, individual goods are compatible with the common good only when they are not inconsistent with the common good. Suárez explains: "The good of private individuals . . . forms a part of the common good, when the former is not of a nature to exclude the latter good; being rather such that it is a necessary requisite in individuals . . . in order that the common good may result from this good enjoyed by private persons."[74]

Whereas a law requiring a governor of a society to be paid a just salary in compensation for service to the society would be directed to the common good notwithstanding that it also constitutes a private good for the governor, a law that requires all citizens to transfer half their property to the governor of the state would not have as its end the common good but only the private "cupidity or vainglory"[75] of the governor. The end or purpose of the first law is to fulfill the society's obligation in justice to compensate the governor for his service and to encourage good government of the society, notwithstanding that as a consequence of pursuing this common good the governor received an individual benefit. Good government is a common good shared by all, including the governor. On the other hand, the second law aims merely a private benefit to the governor by working a disproportionate wealth transfer. This essential element of a just law is a key safeguard against degeneration of legal authority into authoritarian power. A sovereign or the sovereign's delegate who uses legal authority to further his private benefit does not exercise legal authority but authoritarian power. The distinction is found in the end of what otherwise might appear to be the same act, the making of a legal command. When the law is oriented to private benefit rather than to the common good, the act becomes authoritarian rather than authoritative. The unsuitability of the law serving private benefit over the end of law, common good, deprives the act of legal authority because the purported law is not ordered to law's end.

The second criterion is that the law must not "exceed the power of the lawgiver."[76] This is a criterion that I suspect most legal positivists would accept, but in a more limited sense. For positivists such as Hart, the lawgiver only exceeds his authority if his lawmaking act is not in conformance with the Rule of Recognition or the primary rules about how rules are made.[77] The test of authority is internal to the particular society's legal system. The understanding of authority advanced in this chapter, however, while also accepting this internal definition of authority, also holds that the lawgiver's authority is constrained by law external to the particular legal system, that is, the higher laws. The crux of legal authority is the power to determine with more particularity the precepts of natural law as illuminated by revealed divine law. Any attempt to enact a law that is not such a determination exceeds the authority of the human lawmaker. Thus, a law that does not determine with more particularity how evildoers should be punished but rather decrees that evildoers should be rewarded would exceed such authority. The most a Hartian positivist could say is that *if* a particular legal system happened to include natural law in its Rule of Recognition, then such a constraint could exist. A natural law advocate recognizes both internal restraints of the particular legal system enshrined in its constitutional laws and this external constraint to the exercise of human legal authority.

The final requirement is in a sense a further elaboration of the first. The form of human laws must provide that the burdens created by the law "are laid on the subjects, according to an equality of proportion and with a view to the common good."[78] Pursuing the common good does not exclude pursuing something advantageous to an individual member as long as the contemplated action benefits the common good and also the private good of that individual (as in the case of a just salary being paid to a political ruler). As Mary M. Keys explains: "But to be fully just, these ordinances must be made with a view to the overarching welfare of the entire political community and reflect a reasonably equitable allocation of benefits and burdens. Likewise, any exception made to the law must conduce in some respect to the public welfare, lest it constitute an act of arbitrary privileging of one part of civil society over another."[79]

Aquinas's third requirement for a just law reminds us that the common good does not dispense with individual goods in favor of an independent good for the community as a whole, as a form of utilitarianism seeking to maximize the good of the most individuals would. It is not consistent with the common good to disproportionately burden any individual whose own good is a constituent part of the common good. As a Roman law maxim states: "By the law of nature it is fair that no one become richer by the loss and injury of another."[80] Aquinas restated this principle: "Now, whatever is established for the common advantage should not be more of a burden to one party than to another."[81] The good of the individual is not a mere means to an end to be sacrificed to the common good. The individual good is still an end, even if it is to be coordinated with the common good. Both the individual and common goods are ends to be pursued in tandem. As the twelfth-century philosopher John of Salisbury stated: "The public welfare is therefore that which fosters a secure life both universally and in each particular person."[82] Pursuing the common good may mean that the ultimate individual good is not maximized to the extent it could be if the common good were disregarded, but the individual good cannot be disproportionately affected even for the sake of a law "with a view to the common good."[83] Thus, even laws that aim at the common good can only do so in a way that does not disproportionately burden the individuals and communities who are part of the political community.

After establishing the criteria for just laws, Aquinas then answers this question: What effect does the injustice of a law have on its status as law, and in particular its ability to bind in conscience? Aquinas identifies two different consequences of just laws. First they are "binding in conscience," and second they are "legal laws [*leges legales*]."[84] This final phrase, which at first may appear redundant, underscores the legal relationship between natural law and human law. *Legales* means "of or belonging to the law, legal."[85] A legal law is a law that is a part of the legal system. It is a law in harmony with other law. In the metaphor of this book, it is part of the architecture of law. By being just, a human law moves from being a mere speech utterance to acquiring the quality of being a law that takes its place within the cosmological legal system. Justice is a necessary (but not sufficient) condition for a norm to be law. This strong view of the relationship between justice and law is summarized by Michael Moore: "A natural lawyer should say that the essence of law is such that it includes justice, among other things. *Necessarily*, that is, if some system, norm, or decision is unjust, it is not *legal*. Not as a matter of conventional usage of the word 'law' (analytical necessity); not as a matter of universal social practices (contingent necessity); but as a matter of the nature of one of the things that exists in the world, namely, law."[86]

Unjust laws, on the contrary, are "acts of violence rather than laws," which means, in the words of the famous English jurist William Blackstone, "no human laws are of any validity, if contrary to this [natural law]."[87] This conclusion directly answers one of Hart's three primary questions: What distinguishes law from coercive violence?[88] The answer is that the law is a just law; a violent command is not. At this point Aquinas carefully distinguishes the question of legal authority (is a particular act a law?) from the question of an obligation to obey (is there no obligation to obey an illegal law?). These are two distinct questions. Although subjects are obligated to obey legal laws (they are "binding in conscience"), an obligation to conform to illegal laws may[89] exist even if the illegal law has no authority by virtue of being unjust and an act of violence.[90] Some illegal laws not only fail to bind in conscience, but we are actually bound not to follow them. Others, although vested with no legal authority, should be followed nonetheless. How is one to distinguish between the two cases? As to the first, laws that induce "anything else contrary to the divine law," such as idolatry, it is not legally permitted in any manner to obey them (*nullo modo licet observare*).[91] Aquinas specifically uses the juridical word *licet*, meaning it is not legally permitted or licit to obey the purported law. The choice of words emphasizes that the conclusion is a legal conclusion based upon the application of a higher law, not simply a personal moral choice. If obeying the human law would lead (induce) one to violate a precept of the divine or natural law, it must be refused. Essentially, Aquinas sees the issue not as a conflict between morality and law (as Hart would see it) but as a conflict of laws. The divine or natural law forbids an act, but the human law requires it. The higher law wins the conflict, thereby invalidating the human law and making it an illegal law, and thus the subject must refuse obedience to it. Although Aquinas uses the phrase "divine law," he must mean to include both natural law and divine law. Because natural law is a higher law, one could not be obliged by a lower law to violate a higher law. He might be using the phrase "divine law" to refer to both natural and divine law by referring to their common source, God.[92] Alternatively,

Aquinas can be understood to be referring to natural law in the sense he has explained, that the divine law contains "a brief summary of the law . . . so that it might be able to be known by all."[93] In either case, he is establishing that if the unjust law induces a violation of higher law, the higher law binds and must be obeyed. Sophocles's *Antigone* presents a classic example of how the principle was understood even in pre-Christian Greece. In the play, Creon decrees that the body of Antigone's brother is to be refused burial and dishonored. Yet, Creon's command contravenes the religious duty of ancient Greek women to ensure the burial of their relations. Antigone refuses this unjust command as of no legal force and sternly rebukes Creon for his overreaching: "Nor did I think your edict had such force / that you, a mere mortal, could override the gods, / the great unwritten, unshakable traditions."[94]

And so we are now left with the question of what to do with illegal laws, commands that fail to enter the legal system because they are unjust. Must citizens disobey these illegal laws or may they nonetheless conform their actions to the content of the command? Some jurists, supporting a form of natural law theory, present a rather imprecise answer to this question. Philip Soper and Moore, for example, both conclude that if a law or legal system is too unjust then it ceases to be law.[95] But how unjust is too unjust? With only an issue of degree at stake, fixing a line of demarcation becomes difficult. The answer that classical natural law thinkers such as Aquinas offered to this question was more precise and nuanced. First, an absolute line is drawn: an unjust law is no law at all. There is no question of degree of injustice. An unjust law is not a law. Yet, the absence of a particular human law does not remove all law from the world, only the level of particular human determinations. An individual who must choose to act or not to act must be guided by some law. In the absence of a lower form of law, he reverts to higher laws, natural and divine. It is possible that in directly applying human law, the individual determines that, all things considered, the same action as enjoined by the illegal law, not because of the illegal law but in spite of it, should be chosen. In such a case, the chosen action under these higher laws coincides only accidentally with the unjust human law. Yet, even when the chosen action coincides with the illegal law, it is not an action chosen in obedience to the human law, which remains no law at all. In a certain sense, the action merely conforms to law accidentally, not as an effect from its cause. To understand how a citizen might at least accidentally obey the content of an unjust law, we must examine in more detail the different ways in which a law can be unjust.

An unjust law may command actions or omissions that constitute violations of natural or divine law, and as such violate the more universal common good (even if the law appears to conform to the political common good of the society), and therefore must never be obeyed. If a human law commands the murder of the innocent, one must not murder the innocent, an act directly contrary to the natural and divinely revealed law—even if the authorities claim that the murder of these innocents advances the political common good by, for example, providing greater security against terrorist attacks. The act prescribed, even if advancing the political common good, is contrary to higher law and thus contravenes the higher common good. Since the act required by this law involves a direct transgression of higher law, it "must nowise be observed, because, as stated in Acts 5:29, 'we ought to obey God rather than man.'"[96] Commanding by precept an act directly contradicting the very source of the authority to command exceeds the authority of one possessing purely delegated authority. Although the virtue of obedience, discussed earlier, normally requires one to remain within the order of a superior authority, in a circumstance in which that superior removes himself from the very order that is the source of his authority, the subject must remove himself from the order of the wayward superior so as to remain within the overriding architectural order. As Charles De Koninck explains:

> Hence the inferior may be obliged to withdraw from the order of a superior if the superior himself deviates from the order he ought to follow. But as long as the superior remains in the order prescribed, he is a superior good to which the inferior must submit. [According to Aquinas:] "For example, the soldier who is subject to the king and to the general of the army can subordinate his will to the good of the general and not to that of the king, and inversely; but if the general transgresses the order given by the king, the will of the soldier will be good if he detaches himself from the will of the general and directs his will according to the will of the king; he will do wrong, however, if he follows the will of the general against the will of the king; for the order of an inferior principle depends on the order of the superior principle."[97]

Thus, the action of the subject cannot even accidentally conform to this type of illegal law. Unlike positivists, natural law jurists can conclude that in such circumstances citizens are not only permitted but even legally required to refuse to obey such an unjust law and could be subject to punishment for so doing (as the Nazi war criminals were punished for complying with Nazi laws that required direct violation of higher law). Raz, on the other hand, holds that if any justification to disobey a human law exists, it does not exist within a liberal state, which he defines as a state that allows political participation.[98] In such a state he asserts that there is no right to civil disobedience because citizens have a right to participation to change the law. Since, consistent with positivism, he focuses exclusively on the process of lawmaking and excludes evaluation of the substance of the legal product to determine legal validity, if the process is acceptable, there is no legal criteria to evaluate the validity of a law, only private morality. A person might conclude privately that a law is unjust and should be disobeyed, but this is not a legal decision based on law but merely on personal judgment. Hence there is no legal right to refuse an unjust law as long as the legal process is acceptable. Since the substantive evaluation involves purely private morality and not law, Raz cannot even definitively justify a right of conscientious objection to unjust laws. All he can do is list arguments for and against such a right to refuse obedience.[99] A natural law advocate, however, grounds the right, and in some cases the duty, to refuse such unjust laws on higher laws, thereby ensuring that the right to disobey purported human laws is a legal right, not merely a private objection of conscience, which may or may not be recognized by human legal authorities.

Yet beyond the case of an unjust law, which requires violation of higher law, another type of unjust law may exist. A command of an authority may be unjust, but the illegal law might not require the subject to violate the higher law when performing or omitting the action subject to the unjust law. We can illustrate how this can be the case by returning to the example of the ruler who decrees the transfer of 50 percent of all subjects' property to him personally. Such a law is unjust. It violates the end of law by being ordained to the cupidity of the ruler and not the common good. Yet, obeying the law does not require the subject to violate the natural law. The natural law forbids the theft of property but does not forbid the donation of property. Thus, although it is unjust for the ruler to demand the excessive wealth transfer, it is not a violation of natural law to give the ruler more than he is entitled to in justice. This hypothetical law is illegal and not binding in conscience as a law; nonetheless performing the act specified in the illegal law is not *per se* contrary to higher law. Thus, Aquinas does not forbid conformity of action with the illegal law. The question remains: What should the subject do? The answer is more complex than the answer to the first type of illegal law. As Aquinas notes, sometimes "a man should even yield his right."[100] When might one be obliged to yield one's right? When required by a higher law. Lacking the quality of justice, the purported law is no law at all, but it is not true that there is no law at all governing the situation. Legal justice, a concept to be considered at greater length in chapter 9, would still exist in a society devoid of all law. Legal justice directs actions to the common good by conformity to law. In the absence of particular human law, legal justice directs actions in such cases through direct application of higher law.[101] No lawless society can exist. Even a society whose entire legal system is composed of "illegal laws" would still be under law, the natural and divine laws. In the absence of a command of a superior who stands between God and a person, the "subject is immediately under God, by whom he is taught either by the natural or by the written law."[102]

When there is an absence of law, as when a purported law is no law at all, we revert to being directly ruled by natural and divine law. Our obligation to advance the common good derives ultimately from our social nature, and ultimately the natural law, and not from the human law per se, which only makes particular proximate determinations of how to fulfill this duty. Thus, we might conform behavior to the content of an unjust law when doing so is required not by the unjust law but by the application by the individual of a principle of a higher law. In doing so, the subject is not obeying the unjust law but only coincidentally conforming to the unjust law. He is obeying a higher law. Aquinas explains that one might conform to an unjust law to avoid "scandal or disturbance."[103] Refusing the command of the authority in a society, even when it acts outside the scope of that authority, might lead to scandal in that some people might not know the law to be illegal and might thus be scandalized by what appears to be unjustified disobedience. Likewise, refusal to obey might lead to civil unrest and disorder that could do grave harm to the common good, harm greater than the loss of the excessively demanded property in the hypothetical. Citizens might determine in particular circumstances, by prudently applying the precepts of natural law, that for the good of all of them and the community as a whole, it is better to yield their right and yield their property that has been unjustly demanded by the ruler. They do so not by obeying the unjust human command but by applying precepts of natural law. Thus, sometimes in order to fulfill our obligations under the natural law, not unnecessarily to give scandal or disturb the public peace, we might be obligated to conform our behavior to the illegal law; we are not obligated to do such by virtue of the illegal human law, but only by application of the higher natural law. This distinction may at first appear identical to some utilitarian justifications of the legal obligation to obey the law. We are obligated to obey the law so that others will obey the law.[104] Aquinas's argument differs in that although an obligation to obey does not flow from human law, it does flow from law, natural law. The obligation arises from an application of the general principles of natural law in the absence of a particular human law determining the case (given the only applicable human law as unjust is illegal).

Notwithstanding the citizen's action of conforming to what the illegal human law required, the act is not done due to an obligation to obey the illegal human law but rather to obey the natural law. Those opposed to natural law often ignore these important nuanced distinctions regarding the effects of unjust laws. For example, Raz summarizes the natural law position as "statutes, court decisions, etc., which are contrary to natural law are not valid and hence not laws at all."[105] Such an oversimplification obscures the variation in consequences flowing from the conclusion that a law is invalid.[106]

The circumstance of an unjust law that does not necessitate violation of a higher law when conforming to the unjust command is certainly a more complicated situation. It involves a prudential judgment as to the proper course of action because justified disobedience is permitted but not required. The touchstone of the judgment is the obligation under natural law to orient actions to the common good. J. Budziszewski has argued that Aquinas calls for a dynamic analysis of such situations. Rather than a binary decision—obey or disobey this type of unjust law—he argues that choices in the manner of disobedience may tip the balance one way or the other. He explains:

Most first-time readers apply the scandal condition in a static way: If a given act of disobedience would cause grave scandal, then I should not disobey. But nothing prohibits us from applying the condition in a dynamic way instead: If I can find a *way* to disobey that does *not* cause grave scandal, then I *should* disobey. This is how Martin Luther King interpreted the condition in his famous "Letter from a Birmingham Jail," for he believed that bad moral example could be avoided if certain conditions were met. First, protestors are to disobey the unjust law only after attempts to change it through discussion with the authorities have been exhausted. Second, when protestors disobey, they must do so for the sake of justice rather than revenge, they must do so publicly rather than in secret, they must give a public explanation of their reasons for disobedience, and they must publicly accept the legal penalties for disobedience. Protestors should offer no resistance whatsoever, even if spat upon, beaten with nightsticks, sprayed with high-pressure fire hoses, bitten by police dogs, and carried off to prison.[107]

To summarize, three categories of purported human law can be distinguished: (1) just human laws; (2) unjust human laws, the conformity to which would require violation by the subject of natural or divine law; and (3) unjust human laws, the conformity to which would not require violation by the subject of natural or divine law. People are obligated to obey type (1) laws since as determinations of natural law they derive their authority to bind the conscience from their ultimate source, eternal law. The obligation exists notwithstanding that the subject might have made a different determination of the higher principle than the one chosen by the legal authority. Since the power to determine involves free human volition, the nature of authority is to require conformity to the particular determination chosen *because* the choice was made by the authority. One is not legally obligated to obey type (2) or (3) since they are not valid human laws and thus ontologically they are not laws. This conclusion represents what has been called the "strong view" of the "no unjust law is law" principle.[108] Yet, the denial of the ontological status of law does not completely answer the question whether the action the nonlaw attempted to require or prescribe should be done or omitted. A source other than human law for an obligation to act or refrain from acting in such a way might exist. Following the ontological determination, the analysis of (2) and (3) must continue under the natural law. One is always required to refuse to perform any act required by a type (2) law in obedience to the precepts of higher law. A soldier ordered to murder an innocent noncombatant has no obligation to obey and must refuse the authority, as doing such would violate the natural law. Type (3) laws can be further subdivided: (3a) those illegal laws to which people are obligated under natural law to conform their action, all things considered (because for example there is no way to disobey without giving scandal); and (3b) those illegal laws to which people are not obligated to conform their action, all things considered under natural law (by for example disobeying in a manner that does not give scandal). Cases involving (3a) are analogous to circumstances in which no human law exists. People must in the absences of law directly apply natural law to determine the correct course of action. In the absence of controlling authority by temporal rulers, the matter is left to individual determination through the virtues of prudence and legal justice exercised in light of the particular circumstances (including the practical implications for society of the illegal law having been commanded). A more particular rule cannot be formulated to distinguish between (3a) and (3b) in the abstract, since the determination will depend on the specific circumstances and likely consequences of the action. The operative rule is the obligation to advance the common good, which may be disproportionately harmed by scandal or disturbance in comparison to conforming one's action to a command of authority one otherwise need not obey. The obligation to conform behavior to illegal laws does not derive from the purported human law but only from the natural law as applied to the concrete situation. Likewise, in the case of (3a), since the act subject to the illegal law is not itself contrary to natural or divine law, the injustice of (3a) is committed by the authority in attempting to promulgate an illegal law, not in the subject conforming his action to it. Only in the case in which one obeys a type (1) law commanding violation of higher law does the subject commit an injustice by violating natural or divine law.

We can conclude by considering a final example of (3a). Suppose that a particular society enacts a tax law that disproportionately places the tax burden on some citizens by requiring more than what would otherwise be their fair share of taxes ($X) to be paid. This would be an illegal law because it fails Aquinas's requirement that burdens required by the common good not be distributed disproportionately. Suppose further that the amount of variation from the fair tax ($X) is only slight ($X + 0.5%). One could conclude that refusing to pay the additional tax could lead to scandal or disorder in the society (or in one's family), especially if one would be convicted of a crime, unjustly of course, and imprisoned for refusal to pay.[109] One could determine that for the good of one's family and for the common good of society, all things considered, it is prudent to pay ($X + .05%). Since, the act of giving more than one is obligated in justice to give is not contrary to natural law but permitted by it, the act is permissible. In another case, the injustice of the purported law might be so great ($X + 1,000%) that the common good would require, or at least permit, an act of resistance to the unjust command (which act itself must comport with natural law) so as to persuade the authority to cease its act of violence (trying to enforce an unjust law). As Dr. King stated in his famous letter from the Birmingham jail: "There comes a time when the cup of endurance runs over."[110] Thus, human law remains limited in its power to impose unjust laws without throwing every imperfect human enactment out the window of the human legal artifice. In contrast to Finnis's characterization of the maxim that an unjust law is no law at all is "pure nonsense" and "self-contradictory,"[111] the traditional distinction among the consequences attendant upon an unjust law being illegal shows the principle carefully to balance between avoiding vesting unjust laws with legal authority and unleashing unnecessary and imprudent civil disobedience contrary to the common good. Finnis, on the other hand, defends only a weak view[112] of the principle and essentially concedes victory to the positivists, who admit that some laws can be considered unjust for moral reasons, but they are still laws since moral reasons are not legal reasons to invalidate a law.[113] Finnis agrees with the positivists that the unjust laws remain law, and he merely tacks on a qualification that a legal defect, not capable of invalidating the law as law, exists.[114] It is unclear what the effect of a noninvalidating defect would be.

Before concluding this section, we can return to the questions raised by Jonathan Crowe and explain how the grounding of legal authority in the eternal law more precisely defines the natural law thesis in the ways for which he seeks clarification. First, this section has shown that the "no unjust law is law" thesis addresses the ontology of law. It therefore elucidates the limits of the scope of human law and thus describes the very nature of law itself. As the linguistic tension of the phrase itself demonstrates, the thesis does not necessarily address the linguistic use of the word "law," in both the subject and the negative predicate nominative in the expression "an unjust law is no law at all." It may be common linguistic usage to refer to an unjust law as a "law," but such an entity is not a member of the category "law" but only wrongly purports to belong to such category.

Second, we have clarified that what counts as an invalidating rational defect is the fact that a human law does not determine a precept of natural law. It is a defect of legal contradiction between the human law and a precept, primary or secondary, of natural law. Optimal rationality in the sense of the most efficient or prudent of all possible determinations does not count as an invalidating rational defect. The rational defect must involve a human law that either commands acts contrary to natural law or forbids acts obligatory under natural law. To say that a law is invalid under the thesis is to say that notwithstanding its linguistic dressing and even the intent of the lawgiver, the purported norm does not create an obligation in the conscience of subjects to conform to the rule as a human law (although their consciences may be similarly bound by virtue of a higher law). The thesis applies to individual norms on a case-by-case basis and not to a human legal system as a whole. In so clarifying these questions, this section has shown the strength of the thesis regarding unjust laws and also its limitations. It is a strong thesis that invalidates what otherwise appears to be obligatory laws. What the positivists who cling tenaciously to the legality of patently unjust laws fail to see is that the "critical issue is to distinguish between those authorities who possess authority and those who cloak the authoritarian in legal garb."[115] The tenacious positivist wants to judge legal authority solely by looking at the garb and not what it cloaks. Classical natural law jurisprudence refuses to judge the essence of a purported law by its garb but rather by the correspondence of that which the garb clothes with higher law.

Yet, the natural law thesis's function is not limited merely to refuting purported obligation under human laws. Since the grounding of legal authority in eternal law is inextricably linked to the thesis that human law is merely one form of law, a legal obligation to perform or omit the commanded act may exist under law other than human law.

In addition to providing a more coherent ground of legal authority than utilitarianism or popular consent theory, basing human authority on the eternal law also limits that authority.[116] It cannot be used to enact unjust laws. Notwithstanding the nuanced distinctions just discussed, political authorities can never create a legal obligation to obey an unjust law. As Randy Barnett has observed, grounding legal authority in the divine was used to limit that power. The divine source of authority "could be used to deny any intentions to the king that were unworthy of a perfect being."[117] Harold Berman has described the necessary connection between rooting legal authority in the eternal law and limiting the scope of the authority of rulers. He explains that the belief that the king was subject to some form of law himself and that citizens might in certain cases disobey him "was rooted ... in the theological conviction that the universe itself was subject to law."[118] Edmund Morgan has aptly summarized the effects of shifting the basis of authority from God and the eternal law to a fictitious consent based in popular sovereignty: "With the fictional people suddenly supreme, actual people, as embodied in local communities, found their traditional rights and liberties in jeopardy from a representative body that recognized only a fictional superior."[119] Freed of the foundation of eternal law, "the sovereignty of the people would pose graver threats not only to the wishes but also to the rights and liberties of actual people, than the divine right of kings had ever done."[120] Only when there is a nonhuman exogenous source of authority can authority be limited. If it is from the people, there is always the danger of the majoritarian problem, a Napoleonic plebiscite authorizing new authoritarianism. The limits on authority can always be revoked by the fictitiously consenting people and are only as firm as the last constitutional convention or plebiscite. For this reason the great English jurist Henry Bracton, after noting that the king was the highest legal authority within a realm, observed: "The king must not be under man but under God and under the law, because law makes the king, for there is no *rex* where will rules rather than *lex*."[121] That law that makes the king is the eternal law. Leo XIII reiterates this legal limitation on the authority of lawmakers, analogizing it to the limitations on personal liberty for the common good. He explains:

Therefore, the true liberty of human society does not consist in every man doing what he pleases, for this would simply end in turmoil and confusion, and bring on the overthrow of the State; but rather in this, that through the injunctions of the civil law all may more easily conform to the prescriptions of the eternal law. Likewise, the liberty of those who are in authority does not consist in the power to lay unreasonable and capricious commands upon their subjects, which would equally be criminal and would lead to the ruin of the commonwealth; but the binding force of human laws is in this, that they are to be regarded as applications of the eternal law, and incapable of sanctioning anything which is not contained in the eternal law, as in the principle of all law.[122]

IMPLICATIONS OF THE LIMITATION ON LEGAL AUTHORITY

Implications for the Relationship of Law and Morality

In the first section, we considered a nuanced explanation of the principle that an unjust law is no law at all, which distinguished the ontological effect of an unjust law (it ceasing to bind as human law) and the significance of such an illegal law for individual decisions (whether one should conform to an unjust law). This understanding can be used to respond to a classic assertion of legal positivists, such as Hart and Raz, for the separation of law from other normative systems, especially morality.

Hart's characterization of the difference between natural law jurisprudence and positivism is rooted in an assumption regarding a dichotomy between law and morality. Hart claims this difference stems from the fact that natural law advocates assert that an immoral law is invalid, whereas his form of positivism holds that an immoral law is still law but it might not have to be obeyed or enforced.[123] He views the end result to be the same: some laws should not be obeyed. He sees no benefit in the narrower definition of law. For Hart, leaving the determination of which purported laws count as laws to another normative system, such as morality, can only create confusion.[124] Rather, it is Hart's conflation of two metaphysically distinct categories, a command that is law and a command that is not law due to its iniquity, which creates confusion. Hart misrepresents the classical natural law argument when he objects to a separate nonlegal normative system impeding the legal obligation. As we argued in the first section of this chapter, it is not a nonlegal normative system but a higher law that can invalidate unjust laws. The result of this misunderstanding of Hart's is that he considers an unjust command can really be law, but sometimes such a law can or should be ignored. Such a contradictory conclusion eviscerates the very essence of law as a rule and measure of human action. This error of Hart's results from his failure to properly distinguish three distinct concepts: natural law, morality, and a particular society's mores. At the heart of Hart's confusion is his misstatement of the classical natural law aphorism "an unjust law is no law at all." Hart substitutes for "unjust laws" this phrase: [laws that] "offend against a society's own morality or against what we might hold to be an enlightened or true morality."[125] For Hart, natural law is simply synonymous with societal mores or some person's individual opinion of enlightened morality. The natural law claim about the invalidity of unjust laws never invoked the concepts of societal mores or personal morality, but rested upon the ontological conclusion that natural law is a real law.

Based on our prior analysis of the classical natural law arguments, we can disentangle these concepts and clarify the relationship between natural law and morality, properly defined. Natural law as we have defined it thus far is a universal set of general legal precepts concerning human action that can be known by all men (and hence all societies) by reflecting on the inclinations of human nature. At one point, Hart comes close to this concept when he alludes to a transsocietal general morality, but in the end he fails to see it as law.[126] These general principles of action enumerated by Hart are similar to what the Roman jurists recognized as *jus gentium*, the general principles of law common to all nations.[127] Yet, in his discussion of what Hart calls "social morality," he also uses the example of other social rules, such as those relating to modes of dress and ceremonies.[128] Hart seems to include such common social practices within this concept of social morality. Thus, Hart's societal morality is not identical to either natural law or *jus gentium*. In the terminology of our analysis in chapter 6, common social practices are the common historical practices of a society. Some of these practices may become part of the law of the community when through common usage they become customary law (*mos*) or when those customs are sanctioned by written law. Hart seems to acknowledge this concept of social customs, but he severs the fluid connection they have to law, described in chapter 6, since law, for Hart, is only those customs sanctioned by procedures consistent with the Rule of Recognition. Social mores or customs for Hart are never law (although they may serve as an ingredient to make law), and they have no direct relation to law for Hart; however, for the classical natural law explanation, social customs are one of the three poles of the dialectical process that makes and refines law: natural law, social customs, and written law. Common social practices can be a real source of law in the art of making human law that we described in chapter 6. Thus, any given practice, such as removing one's hat indoors, may not be law but may in a certain society become law as a particular determination of the natural law precept to cultivate respect for sacred places or people in authority, either through the development of the custom or its sanction by written law. Thus, Hart's separation of social mores from law impoverishes his understanding of both law and shared social customs.

Finally, we come to morality in the sense of personal obligations or duties with respect to the actions of individuals. Hart gives the example of the obligations of fathers to care for their families as an instance of a moral precept.[129] Hart again fails to see both the distinction and the connection between morality and law. First, in the classical natural law system, the term "morality" properly defined refers to the choice of good actions by individuals that do not directly impact the common good (but all human action at least indirectly affects the common good in some way).[130] Morality is distinguished from human-made laws but not from law itself. Morality is the determination of individual chosen actions made by individuals consistently with eternal and natural law; human law is the determination of actions according to these higher laws by human authorities. Morality applies to the individual choice of means, not primarily concerned with the common good, but with individual goods. In chapter 6, we used the example of the choice of whether to marry or not. Such a choice is in the realm of personal determination. As defined, morality cannot be societal but only personal. Morality is the realm of practical determinations left to individuals under the natural law.[131] Moral and legal determinations are thus distinguished by the primary end of the decision, for personal or common good, and by the identity of the one making the determinations, the individual or legal authority. The two (morality and human law) are distinct by nature of their end but are related to the same common cause, the general precepts of natural law that require determination. Hart fails to retain this restriction of morality to determinations oriented to personal good and conflates morality with community mores. In fact, he treats personal morality as only analogous to morality,[132] when indeed personal morality is the only sphere where morality operates. Determinations of natural law for political communities are made by human law, but determinations for individuals are made by direct personal determinations of natural law precepts. Rather than elucidating a clear distinction between law and morality, by ignoring their common origin, natural law, he actually fails to distinguish the two concepts clearly.

Hart's failure to make the proper distinctions between the field of activity of morality and human lawmaking also leads to his failure to see their connection. Natural law teaches us that human beings are not autonomous individuals, but are social and political.[133] Thus, purely personal determinations of natural law for individuals have implications for and relationships with legal determinations. Thus, personal determinations, or the manner in which personal determinations are lived, are made in the context of the individual being a part of a societal whole; personal moral choices must be made in the context of legal human determinations designed to orient those choices not only to the individual but also the common good. Thus, the choice to become a lawyer is a determination to be made by the individual, but the way in which any individual completes such a chosen action will be affected by legal determinations relating to the practice of law. Thus, law can legitimately constrain or limit the mode of living personal moral decisions so as to fulfill law's purpose of orienting them to the common good. Requiring a certain level of minimal competence to practice law may be determined appropriate by a legal system. If a human law makes such a determination, this law will thus bound the personal decision within the requirements of the human law. Returning to Raz's traffic light case can provide another example of the relationship between moral decisions and human law. The choice of where to travel on a Sunday afternoon is a choice of means within the order of prudence of the individual. It would be beyond the scope of human law to determine what every person should do with their leisure time. Consistent with her natural inclination to live in society, a person may choose to travel to visit friends in the next town. Yet, the way in which she will travel will be determined by law. If she encounters a red light during the execution of this personal choice, she is obligated to stop in a jurisdiction whose law requires motorists to stop at a red light. Thus, personal moral decisions are always affected by legal determinations, which can require the choice to be executed within the bounds of laws oriented to the common good. Yet, such a relationship does not place law over morality. It is merely a function of the fact that human beings live and make decisions in a society. Human nature has both an individual and a societal aspect, but it is also a unified nature. Put another way, natural law leaves aspects of the choice of means to both individuals and those having care of the community. The subjects of action are unified persons, and thus these spheres of choice are inseparable. The relationship is not one of subordination of one sphere to the other (either individual to societal, as in totalitarianism, or societal to individual, as in libertarianism or anarchism) but of mutual cooperation. Legitimate legal determinations are those that must be made by an authority to foster the common good. The common good serves as a limiting principle on the power to make legal determinations. Decisions capable of being oriented to the common good should be left in the sphere of individual determination. Although human laws legitimately may guide the execution of those determinations to the common good, the personal choices themselves must be left to the order of the individual or personal superior. Human legal authority is not entrusted with the power to preempt personal choices made consistently with natural law. Human legal authority is thus limited to two types of action: (1) the restraint of personal choices contrary to precepts of natural law, and thus incapable of orientation to the common good; and (2) the direction of the mode of execution of individual choices that are valid determinations of natural law precepts so that the mode of execution furthers the common good. A law prohibiting the individual from choosing to be a contract murderer as a profession is a legitimate exercise of legal authority, as this personal choice violates the precept of natural law to preserve life. Further, specifying the minimal requirements for one to practice law in a society is a determination of the manner in which one individually choosing the legal profession must execute that choice so as to protect the common good. A law determining for each individual which profession or vocation he must pursue would be illegitimate because it would be an invasion of the individual order of prudence by the regnative order of prudence. Thus, in one way Hart is correct that legal determinations are distinct from personal moral choices. Yet, in another way, he fails to see the inextricable relationship between morality and law. Since both have as their subject the same individual human actor, morality and law will always be related because they share a common subject. The distinction of the spheres of activity of each limits the determinations made by the other. Iniquitous laws are laws that exceed the jurisdictional limitations of human lawmakers granted under the natural law, thereby unduly invading the sphere of determinations left to individuals, either by compelling illegal actions or by illegitimately usurping the jurisdiction of the individual.

This delicate relationship between the individual order and the regnative order was summarized by Pope Leo XIII in his landmark encyclical, *Rerum Novarum*, in which he carefully avoids the extreme position of subordinating one to the other:

> We have said that the State must not absorb the individual or the family; both should be allowed free and untrammelled action so far as is consistent with the common good and the interest of others. Rulers should, nevertheless, anxiously safeguard the community and all its members; the community, because the conservation thereof is so emphatically the business of the supreme power, that the safety of the commonwealth is not only the first law, but it is a government's whole reason of existence.[134]

In the entire chapter in which Hart explains the separation of law and morality that he seeks to defend, he seems stuck on the point that iniquitous laws in fact exist, so they must be laws.[135] But this begs his entire definitional question of law itself. Under Hart's logic, since false gold certainly exists, we should consider it to be gold (but perhaps price it differently than real gold). But this conclusion is logically untenable. The fact that false gold exists does not prove that it exists as gold. It is of a separate species to gold, being false gold. More confusion seems to be created by conflating commands that are law and those that are not and then by appealing to a vague societal morality to direct our reaction to each.

Raz concurs with Hart's dichotomy between law and morality. He argues a legal system must have a body that is bound to make determinations based on laws it must observe regardless of the citizens' own evaluation of those laws.[136] Even if such a body, such as a court, is permitted to overrule those rules on occasions, such power to overrule is limited to less than complete discretion. A judge cannot simply overrule on the grounds that he believes a different rule would be better.[137] In finding this limit, Raz argues that normative systems that are different from law exist because judges must decide at least sometimes on the basis of a rule that they think (according to a normative system other than law) not to be the best.[138] The fact that other possible, and even better, laws, exist does not prove the separation of law and morality, as Raz seeks. Human law and morality are differentiated, yet not part of different normative systems. Both are systems of determination of the same natural law. Whereas Hart and Raz see a dichotomy between *natural law and morality* and *positive law*, the description of natural and human law developed thus far in this book conceives of the distinction as between *natural law* and *morality and human law*.[139] Both morality and human law are particular determinations of natural law made within different orders of determination. Moral reasoning involves the making by individuals of particular determinations of action, whereas human lawmaking involves determinations by legal authorities of actions affecting the common good. Morality and human law are differentiated by the scope of their activity (actions that affect predominantly either individual goods or the common good) and the scope of delegated authority to make such determinations. Legal authorities are only delegated with the power to make determinations affecting the common good, with other determinations left to individuals or superiors of nonlegal societies, such as families. Thus, morality and human lawmaking are alike in that they are both subject to natural law. Thus, when a judge, or anyone else for that matter, evaluates a human law, he does not do so according to "another" normative system. Rather he evaluates it within the same system but merely in light of the higher natural law. When a judge concludes that a particular human law is law—because when evaluated in light of higher law it is a permissible determination not exceeding the limits of human authority—he is evaluating law within the same system. When a judge recognizes that, although it is law, another determination could have been chosen rather than the existing law, and he believes such other determination to be superior, he is merely recognizing the freedom of choice of means entrusted to human lawmakers by the eternal law. Not possessing the authority to change this particular permissible determination, the judge must accept the determination as made. The judge following such jurisprudence can articulate a rule distinguishing which human laws he may overrule and which he must accept, notwithstanding his believing another rule to be better. Is this human law an unjust law such that it is no law at all or is it a permissible, if not optimal, determination? Hart and Raz fail to articulate a principle for identifying which iniquitous laws should be enforced and obeyed and which not according to the undefined other normative system. Their failure is due to their fixation on contraposing law to morality. Hart and Raz can thus merely acknowledge that some laws should not be obeyed, but they can go no further because an undefined morality of an alien normative system must be used to distinguish the two types of laws. Yet, the grounding of legal authority in the natural and eternal law—source of precepts guiding individual moral decisions and human legal determinations— points to higher law within the same normative system to differentiate the two cases. There will certainly always be hard factual cases in which the judgment of justice or injustice will be difficult, but the natural law approach at least provides a principled legal method for approaching the question, rather than abdicating the work to another normative system. For Hart and Raz, the only legal principle of distinction is merely a procedural Rule of Recognition as to what constitutes law of a particular legal system, and thus the substantive principle is up for grabs.

Hart even went so far as to suggest that considering all iniquitous laws to be laws nonetheless was more likely to foster the refusal of obedience to those iniquitous laws.[140] Yet, it seems more logical to believe that one who acknowledges that a purported law may be found legally invalid on the basis of a higher law would seem more likely to evaluate critically the duty to obey than one who accepts iniquitous laws as valid, even if they may be disobeyed. Shifting the locus of decision on the duty to obey from law to morality confuses the issue. Because morality refers to determinations affecting the individual and familial realm, there is a greater danger of confusion since the end or reference point has been shifted from the common good to the private or individual good. Laws need to be evaluated in light of their end, the common good, which is retained when the evaluative mechanism is another law rather than morality. In the end, Hart and Raz can only maintain the position that an unjust law remains a law, because they do not see a positive good in authority and law. A law can be a law while remaining unjust because legal authority and obedience to law are empty vessels devoid of ontological meaning for them.

For Hart, law is merely a human phenomenon.[141] Hart and Raz exclaim: What does it matter if there be iniquitous laws, for people can simply disobey these purely human constructs? There is no harm to the good of legal authority by simply disobeying a law that happens to be iniquitous. Yet, as we argued in chapter 7, law and legal authority are good in and of themselves. They are not human constructs, but divine. A human law is both human and eternal. It is made by humans, but it has its authority and power to bind in obedience from the eternal law. Law is not solely a human creation. There is harm to the transcendental property of goodness[142] to hold that a law can remain law while being unjust. To allow a law to remain a law and be iniquitous is metaphysically a contradiction because it denies the property of goodness to a being.[143] Obedience to law is a good, and therefore disobedience to a law is not good. Disobeying law is a violation of the first principle of the natural law—good is to be done. Thus, a command should only be disobeyed if the command is not good, in the sense of a command that satisfies the metaphysical definition of law. To preserve the ontological goodness of legal authority, one may disobey the command of an authority only if that command is not in fact law.

If, as we have argued throughout this book, law and authority are built into the fabric of the universe and our nature, then law cannot so simply be dismissed. History is rife with examples suggesting that it is not as easy as Hart and Raz presume for people to simply disobey what they hold to be real laws (Nazi Germany is a prime example). Beginning with the controversial experiments of Stanley Milgram, social scientists have demonstrated that cloaking unjust commands with the appearance of legal authority will influence individuals to act unjustly.[144] This research indicates that it is much harder for human beings to disobey the unjust command of an authority figure. Hart and Raz seem too optimistic in their assumption that human beings can simply ignore unjust laws still cloaked with the attribute of legal validity. Would it not be easier for a citizen to disregard an order of a superior if that order were decloaked of the status of law than to require the citizen to break the law when is it unjust? One facing the command of an iniquitous law (such as the killing of the innocent) would seem to be on firmer ground if the natural law legally obligated or permitted disobedience to an authoritarian command that fails to be law. Classical natural law jurisprudence holds authority in law in higher regard than Hart or Raz, and thus denies the status of authority to iniquitous law, paving the way for a legally justified disobedience of the command that fails to be law.

Implications for the Role of Judges

The general discussion of the limitations on human legal authority can raise a more specific question in a legal system that includes a separation of the aspects of legal authority into different institutions. For a judge in a system like the one in the United States, which separates legal authority among different institutions, the question inevitably will arise as to "whether courts may ever refuse to render judgment according to an enactment of the legislature, when, by the standards of the natural law, the enactment does not rise to the level of true law."[145] In the context of the U.S. legal system, with a separation of judicial and legislative power, can U.S. courts refuse to enforce legislative acts of Congress on the ground that such utterances are contrary to natural or divine law? This section will develop an answer to this question. As Budziszewski has pointed out, this question has been posed since the earliest days of the U.S. legal system.[146] As with the general question of the reaction of a citizen to an illegal law, the answer for the judge will be more nuanced than simply "always" or "never."

In a legal system in which the legislative and judicial functions are unified, this precise issue does not arise, because the adjudicator possesses the authority to alter the human-made laws and also to adjudicate. In a system that separates these aspects of legal authority, the judiciary is limited to judging cases according to the law (or perhaps to making law only when the legislator has not determined a law necessary to decide a case). Yet, in a legal system in which the judiciary is constrained to apply the human laws as written, what should a judge do if asked to apply a law that under the analysis developed in this chapter is no law at all?

Aquinas initially answers this question by simply stating that "it is necessary to judge according to the written law."[147] Thus, a judge should follow the written law. Yet, Aquinas immediately qualifies what seems to be an absolute requirement by reminding us of the dual nature of human lawmaking. In some cases a human law makes acts just or unjust, and in other cases it does not. The difference lies in human laws made by determinations and those by demonstrations. Aquinas summarizes the two types of human law:

> Now a thing becomes just in two ways: first by the very nature of the case, and this is called "natural right," secondly by some agreement between men, and this is called "positive right," as stated above (Question 57, Article 2). Now laws are written for the purpose of manifesting both these rights, but in different ways. For the written law does indeed contain natural right, but it does not establish it, for the latter derives its force, not from the law but from nature: whereas the written law both contains positive right, and establishes it by giving it force of authority.[148]

Thus, when human law declares murder to be a crime, it does not make murder unjust but simply contains the natural law precept to that effect, based upon the good of the preservation of human life. On the other hand, when human law establishes that one must drive on the left side of the road, the law not only manifests what is unjust but makes driving on the right unjust. The difference between the two cases is that in the first, human law is merely demonstrating a principle of natural law, whereas in the second it is determining a matter left to human choice. The choice between left or right involves nothing that is naturally just or unjust.[149] If a matter has been left to human determination, the judge must render judgment according to the written law made by one who has authority to make such a determination. Even if the judge would have chosen the right side of the road if writing the law himself, he must rule according the determination written of the left. Although not naturally unjust to drive on the left, it becomes unjust to do so once a legal determination has been made. This written law, drive on the right, binds the judge.

Aquinas, relying on this distinction, immediately clarifies that a judge is bound to apply the written law only to the extent the written laws are really laws. He states that "if the written law contains anything contrary to the natural right, it is unjust and has no binding force."[150] As a result, such "documents are to be called, not laws, but rather corruptions of law . . . and consequently judgment should not be delivered according to them."[151] Although it might seem Aquinas is saying both to judge according to the written law and not to do so, the apparent contradiction is removed when he reminds us that human law is not a measure of its own existence. A document purporting to be a law but one that violates the natural law is no law at all, and so a judge cannot judge according to this document. In short, a judge is bound to follow the written law in rendering judgment unless that written law cannot be afforded the status of law because of its iniquity.

Two objections can be leveled against Aquinas's injunction that human law must be followed only so long as it is not an unjust law. First, an objection might be drawn from Aquinas's distinction between an inferior and a superior judge. By superior judge, he means one who holds plenary power and can therefore change the law. At one point in his examination of justice, Aquinas argues that inferior judges must follow the letter of the law given to them and may not exempt a party from it: "Nevertheless in this respect there is a difference between judges of lower degree and the supreme judge, i.e. the sovereign, to whom the entire public authority is entrusted. For the inferior judge has no power to exempt a guilty man from punishment against the laws imposed on him by his superior."[152] Budziszewski dispenses with this objection by pointing out that in this statement Aquinas "is speaking of *just* laws."[153] If the law to be applied by the inferior judge be just, he must apply it, even if he would prefer to show mercy and exempt the one guilty of violating the law. Yet, if the law be unjust, it is no law at all, and thus must not be utilized by the judge in rendering judgment.

Another critic might argue that this conclusion permits judges to invalidate laws on the basis of their own personal moral beliefs. As Soper has explained, such a criticism is not justified: "The assumption that natural law looses a judge to do whatever she wants, ignoring even clear texts, is wrong. Natural law does not tell a judge to do whatever she wants."[154] There are two sources of the limitation on judicial authority to declare purported laws not laws at all on the basis of personal belief. First, contrary to the false dichotomy between law and morality, a judge does not declare a purported human law invalid on the basis of personal moral norms, as Ronald Dworkin suggests should happen.[155] Contrary to Dworkin, a judge in such a position could refuse to enforce a purported human law because in fact the utterance is not a legal law. Likewise, a judge refusing to enforce a state statute on the grounds that it has been preempted by a federal statute is not using personal morality to invalidate a law. The judge is resolving a conflict between two purported statements of law by recourse to the higher law. Thus, the judge confronted with a human-made law that impinges upon the natural law must engage in the legal reasoning described in the first section of this chapter. To apply and enforce the law, the judge must first identify the law. If a purported human law is not actually law, the judge does not invalidate the law, but rather merely acknowledges the preexisting reality that the document alleged to be law is not law at all. Analogously, if a litigant claimed a particular statute existed and thus should be applied, but the judge discovered that the purported law was in fact merely a bill introduced in the legislature, which had never been passed by the requisite majority, his ruling would not invalidate a law but rather declare that the text alleged by the litigant to be law is in fact not law.

To understand the distinction between judges declaring a purported law no law at all and invalidating a law based on private morality, we must recall the important distinctions among natural law, morality, and human law that we introduced in chapter 6 and developed further in the preceding subsection in this chapter. Morality involves the particular determinations left by natural law to individuals and personal superiors, as distinguished from those determinations primarily affecting the common good that are left to those possessing legal authority. Personal morality and human laws are thus metaphorically siblings of their common natural law parent. Thus, when a judge concludes that a law which violates natural law is no law at all, such a judge does not do so according to a system of personal moral norms for making determinations as an individual but applies a real law, the higher law of the natural law. The content of the natural law is independent of opinions of individuals because that content is rooted in human nature and ultimately the eternal law. Obviously, individuals may make mistakes in acquiring knowledge of that content, in all the ways we discussed in chapter 5. Yet, this is a distinct issue from a judge using a subjective norm to invalidate a human law. A case in which a judge who mistakenly rules that a human law is contrary to natural law because he has misunderstood the applicable precept of natural law is comparable to a case in which a judge invalidates a state statute based upon an erroneous understanding of a provision of that state's constitution. In both cases, the judge has simply made an erroneous legal judgment; he has not necessarily ruled on the basis of personal morality. Given the fallibility of human reasoning for all the reasons we discussed in chapter 5, some incorrect legal decisions will inevitably be rendered. That is a fact of the human condition. Yet, discrediting the principle that judges should not apply an invalid law on the basis that some judges will make mistakes in so doing is analogous to rejecting the principle of federal supremacy simply because some judges apply the principle of federal supremacy erroneously.

In refusing to judge according to an illegal law, the judge is not comparing the purported human law to what personal norm the judge might determine for herself in the absence of any applicable human law. There may be more than one possible determination of the natural law principle. The judge must compare the purported human law to the natural and divine law, on the basis of the criteria we described in the first section of this chapter. If the judge is making a new human law—in legal systems entrusting lawmaking authority to the judiciary—then the judge is free to choose among possible licit determinations. Yet, in the situation in which another human authority, such as a legislator, has purportedly made a binding determination and the judge's role in such a situation is limited to applying that determination, an aspect of such application of the prior determination involves the evaluation of whether the determination is in fact a law capable of application. Here, the judge cannot simply substitute the determination that she would have made had she made the determination. In fact Gratian concludes (based on a passage in Augustine discussed by Aquinas) that, generally, once a law is enacted judges need to render decisions according to that law rather than judging the merits of the law itself.[156] A law should be carefully considered when being written, because once the law is enacted, judges generally need to judge according to it rather than judging its perfection. Although the general rule is that the judge should not judge the enacted law, in cases of direct contradiction of the divine law or natural law such a purported human law is in reality not a law at all. In such a case the judge should not judge according to an illegal law. Thus, if a law meets the minimum requirement for justice, then the judge should not second guess the prudence of the determination. If the purported law has no force of law due to injustice, then in fact the judge is not judging a law but rather concluding that the purported command is not a law at all.

The pertinent question is whether the lawmaker exceeded his authority in making the determination (in one of the ways described in the first section). Such an understanding justifies and requires the "enforcement of laws even though they are not the laws the judge would have enacted herself."[157] Judges who are permitted to invalidate purported human laws must do so solely on the legal basis of a failure to determine a just law by reference to the natural or divine law.

Stating that judges can refuse to enforce a purported law that is no law at all does not, as Justice Samuel Iredell fears, make the judiciary omnipotent.[158] As with the case of an individual citizen, the judge is not omnipotent, possessing the power to invalidate all laws. The judge may in fact invalidate no law. He is merely constrained by reality. He may only enforce legal laws, a concept that does not include purported but illegal laws. The judge is not free to remake the law, as he would if he were the legislator. To understand this constraint on the role of judges we must remember that we discovered in chapter 7 that the natural law does not claim that all human laws are the best laws or even free from prudential error. Since there is an election of means, the legislator may fail to select the most appropriate or efficacious means to attain the common good. This toleration of bad laws differs from the standard for lack of validity, which is injustice.

A law may be imprudent without violating the natural or divine law. Returning to the traffic example, a legislator may wrongly choose the right side of the road to direct traffic flow. He may wrongly believe that the right side is a better choice from an aesthetic and efficiency point of view. Yet, not being the best prudential decision does not invalidate the law. Designating the right side for driving may not be the optimal law, but requiring such action does not transgress the natural or divine law. It is still oriented to the common good of safe driving, even if prudentially imperfect. Such errors are to be tolerated by judges applying existing law.

We can adapt Hart's example of the scorer in a game to illustrate the difference between imprudent laws and unjust laws.[159] One who makes a human law can be considered as an umpire in a baseball game. The umpire takes general rules, such as one who is tagged before he reaches the base should be called out. He then applies this general rule to a particular situation to determine the result. This runner is out. It is known and accepted that an umpire, even a good umpire, will make some bad determinations. He might fail to see and take into consideration a swift movement of the infielder. He may be distracted at a critical moment. The game must tolerate these errors in judgment for there to be an organized game. The league officials accept the results of the game as umpired, even if they know they might have made certain calls differently and thereby altered the result. Otherwise there would be no winner; each team would make its own determinations of particular plays resulting in interminable debate about the outcome. In contrast, if an umpire violates the scope of his authority by accepting bribes to make all determinations in favor of a particular team, then it is likely one team will simply walk off the field and refuse to play under such circumstances, perhaps appealing to the league officials to remove the umpire. In the former case, the umpire merely failed to make the most prudent choice among possibilities provided by the general rules and the particular situation. In the latter, his actions exceed the scope of his authority by disregarding the rules altogether, thus producing injustice so that the players would be justified in treating his calls as invalid. Likewise, legislators may make errors in selecting among possible determinations. A judge being asked to accept a particular determination of a legislator must, like the league officials, accept the legislator's call, even if it seems flawed from a prudential point of view. Yet, when the legislator has exceeded the scope of his authority to determine human law by making an unjust law, as defined in the first section of this chapter, then the judge could refuse to play. Alternatively, the judge might conclude that in the case of a particular unjust law, the action subject to the law can be reconciled to higher law, notwithstanding the injustice in the actual law itself. Likewise, a league official that watched a game (or studied a recording of it) in which the umpire was known to have been bribed to make calls favoring one team, notwithstanding the injustice of the bribe, might conclude that coincidentally the umpire made acceptable calls. In which case, a league might allow the result of the calls to stand regardless of the injustice of the bribe.

What then is a judge to do when faced with an illegal law that should be treated as invalid? The judge must then render judgment in the absence of an applicable human law, because the purported law is no law at all. How the judge proceeds will be determined by the nature of the particular legal system in which the judge functions. As we discussed in chapter 7, although the natural law requires and justifies the presence of a lawmaking authority in a political community, it does not determine the particular form of any society's legal system. Natural law is ambivalent as to forms of government and division of the legal authority among institutions within that legal system.[160] As we described in more detail in chapter 7, all legal authority comes from God, but it also comes through the particular history of each community. The mode of designating the persons holding the God-given authority is a matter of determination left to each political community. Thus, it is possible, and in fact has been the case, that a particular legal system divides the legal authority between a legislature and a judiciary to the extent that the legislature solely or primarily makes law and the judiciary solely or primarily applies and interprets the laws so made. The U.S. legal system in fact provides for a shared authority to make laws, with some areas left to the development of the common law and others left to statute, and still others subject to a dialectical interaction of both (see chapter 6). Yet, a possible division of legal authority can involve a designation by which persons are invested with the authority to make universally applicable laws, as opposed to merely deciding individual cases. If the judiciary, as in a common law system, is charged with formulating rules of law in the absence of a valid written law, then the judge may proceed to develop a rule of law to decide the case in which an illegal law has been found invalid. As with the individual deciding how to act in light of an unjust law, in such a process the judge should consider if there are any aspects of the unjust law not inconsistent with natural and divine law and base his legal analysis on those permissible aspects or policy choices underlying the unjust law. Yet, if the judiciary is prohibited from promulgating universally applicable legal rules, the judge must decide the case in the manner he would in a case where no written law applies to the case before him. Fundamentally, the question is not a question of natural law but rather a function of the chosen division of legal authority within a legal system. What is clear is that a judge cannot render a judgment that is contrary to the natural law by ordering action contrary to higher law. Yet, the judge may or may not possess the authority to make a universally applicable law in lieu of the illegal determination attempted by the law-maker. As with the Roman praetor peregrinus deciding cases involving noncitizens, the judge does not act in the absence of all law. He should apply any particular laws that do not contravene higher law, and he can then deduce a rule of decision from the *jus gentium*. In systems in which a judge cannot make new law, his determination of the particular result under natural law will not be a universally binding determination for future cases. In a different legal system, it could be.

One further question arises. In refusing to apply an unjust law, may a judge declare the law void for all citizens and thereby formally relieve them of any purported obligation of obedience? The question is one whose answer again depends on the particular divisions within a legal system. One option is that the judiciary is entrusted with the authority to declare and determine publicly that an unjust law is no law at all. On the other hand, the legal system may reserve this public power to a particular court or another organ of government. The distinction is between individuals navigating personal decisions about how to react to an unjust law in the nuanced manner we described in the first section, and a legal authority making a legal determination for all individuals. Even in the absence of such a public determination, we have seen that individuals, including an individual judge deciding a case, must refuse certain unjust laws and may refuse others, or they must exteriorly conform (due to the basis of an alternate obligation to do the same act). In this context, we are considering the competence to make a public determination that would relieve individuals of the nuanced considerations (discussed in the first section of this chapter) by removing the purported law from all consideration whatsoever. Whether this power is vested in the legislature or judiciary is, as Budziszewski points out, a matter of free determination by various legal systems.[161] Thus, a particular legal system might determine that only a legislature and not a court is vested with the authority to universally and definitively declare a purported law no law at all. As Budziszewski points out, there are a variety of reasons in favor of this power being vested in courts and also other reasons favoring legislatures.[162] In the case of the U.S. legal system, there is no clear text that resolves the determination. The U.S. Constitution certainly does not directly answer this question. As is evident from the debate between Justices Chase and Iredell, a case can be made either way that the U.S. system implicitly locates that authority one place or the other.[163] However, assuming for the moment that the U.S. system, or any other system for that matter, definitively locates the power in an institution other than courts, that does not relieve a particular judge of his obligation to refuse to enforce an unjust illegal law in a particular case.

Even if a judge is precluded by the separation of powers from making a universally binding declaration that such and such an utterance is not law, the judge must render judgment in a case before the court on the basis of law. In this context, the judge must act and must find the rule and measure of action. The judge's situation is analogous to that of a citizen deciding how to act in the face of an illegal law. Judges in rendering judgment must act. All human acts are subject to the natural and divine law. Political communities are free to distribute God-given legal authority among various individuals or institutions. There is nothing inherently necessary in the U.S. choice of allocation of legal authority among institutions. An unjust law is no law at all. The command utterance of one possessing legal authority may have an accidental appearance of law, but it is not law and it does not bind in conscience as a legal command. Yet, answering this ontological question regarding an illegal law does not answer the practical question of how people should respond to the fact of a purported but illegal law. The fact of a purported law's attempted but failed legally binding enactment leaves unanswered the prudential question of how a citizen should act in a particular case. In a case purportedly governed by an illegal law, a judge must decide the case, but if he does this according to the illegal law, he is required to violate the natural or divine law, which he cannot do. The judge, like the ordinary citizen, must in such a case "obey God rather than man."[164]

Thus, if rendering judgment according to the human law would cause the judge to violate the higher law, the judge must refuse to do so. For example, if a particular human law required that a person found guilty of terrorism should be executed along with his (innocent) children, a judge applying this human law would have to order the death of innocent people. This act would directly violate the natural and divine law against the direct killing of the innocent. The judge could not make such an order regardless of whether or not the applicable legal system permitted such a judge to declare the underlying sentencing statute no law at all.

If, on the other hand, rendering judgment would be unjust in a certain way but not directly violate the higher law, the judge would have to engage in the same prudential analysis as a citizen does when deciding how to act. These obligations are independent of a judge's authority to render a public determination of the invalidity of an illegal law.

Pope Pius XII, who reigned during one of the darkest periods (World War II) for the recognition of limitations on legal authority, noted the problem of his day lay precisely in the rejection of any law higher than the human law of the state: "State absolutism . . . consists in fact in the false principle that the authority of the state is unlimited and that in face of it—even when it gives free reign to its despotic aims, going beyond the confines between good and evil—to appeal to a higher law obliging in conscience is not admitted."[165] The obligation to obey positive law can result in great pain and suffering if there is no limit on that obligation. If the only limit on the ability to command obedience to law resides in positive law itself, it is in effect no real limit because it is self-referential. Only a higher law truly independent of human lawmakers can limit the great power to bind in conscience to obey the law. This right and, in some cases, the duty to disobey "illegal laws" is central to the architecture of law. It is the keystone that holds the entire structure together. The nuanced distinctions among the types of unjust laws and the varying consequences of them ensure that this limitation on authority does not simply degenerate into private judgments about what laws to obey. One cannot simply disobey a law because one would have framed it differently. The limitations on the obligation to obey the law are constrained to objective criteria. Is the law a legitimate deduction from or determination of natural law? This refined analysis of purported laws is on the one hand a bulwark against the blind execution of unjust commands and on the other hand a restraint on anarchy. The truth that an unjust law is no law constitutes the essence of the distinction that troubled Hart between the command of a gunman and law.

The Point of the Structure

Justice and the Causes of Law

The justices of the Lord are right, rejoicing hearts:
the commandment of the Lord is lightsome, enlightening the eyes.
The fear of the Lord is holy, enduring for ever and ever:
the judgments of the Lord are true, justified in themselves.[1]

KNOWING THINGS THROUGH THEIR CAUSES

So far in our investigation of the legal edifice we have examined the component parts, the species of law, eternal, natural, divine, and human, which compose the overall building. In chapters 7 and 8 we considered the ontology of human legal authority, the power to change people's normative positions by making authoritative utterances. We justified the authority, and in so doing explored the limits of that justification, of the legal artisans who decorate the frame of the legal edifice. Yet our ontological investigation must go further to understand the ontology not only of laws but of law itself. In the Aristotelian tradition, one knows something by knowing its causes. Aristotle identifies four causes: material, formal, efficient, and final.[2] To truly know the law we must examine all four. The law is a different sort of thing from a building and thus the nature of these causes will not be identical in each, but only analogous. The analogy with tangible beings will enlighten our understanding of that being we call the law.

The material cause is "the cause out of which a thing is made, and which exists in it."[3] A building is made out of bricks, stone, beams, and other material. The law is made out of individual laws (decrees or ordinances), particular precepts of reason. The formal cause is "the intrinsic principle by which a thing is determined to a certain mode of being, and is constituted in its species."[4] The form is what makes the bricks and stone and wood and other materials a cathedral rather than a pile of bricks. The form and not the matter is the essence or nature of a thing since it makes the thing what it is rather than something else composed of the same materials.[5] The form is what makes a brick wall a wall and not a house. With respect to law, this form is what Latin refers to as *jus*, which in this context we might translate into English as "the law." The law is what turns the collection of words or commands in a text (the matter) into law. The law, *jus*, is the object of the virtue of justice. Thus the formal cause of law is the law (or *jus*), which is the object of the virtue of justice. Aquinas expresses this relationship among the virtue of justice, the law (*jus*), and laws (*leges*) by returning to his architectural analogy used to elucidate the concept of eternal law:

> Just as there preexists in the mind of the craftsman an expression of the things to be made externally by his craft, which expression is called the rule of his craft, so too there preexists in the mind an expression of the particular just work, which the reason determines and which is a kind of rule of prudence. If this rule be expressed in writing it is called a "law" [*lex*], which according to Isidore (*Etym.* 5.1) is "a written decree": and so law [*lex*] is not the same as right [*jus*] but an expression of right [*jus*].[6]

Individual laws (*leges*) are not the law (*jus*) but rather particular expressions of the universal, the law. This understanding correlates with the argument in chapters 7 and 8 that not all utterances of authority are law. The law (*jus*) is the universal form that transforms the matter (the utterance) into part of the law. When this formal cause is lacking (as in an unjust utterance), then the matter is merely a failed law, but not part of the law.

An efficient cause is "the first positive extrinsic principle of motion."[7] Things can have a single total efficient cause or a combination of partial causes.[8] A sculptor is an efficient cause of a statue,[9] and the architect and various artisans and workers are each partial efficient causes of a building. The efficient causes of the law are the lawmakers, those with jurisdiction, the ability to speak the law.[10] We have examined how these efficient causes produce laws in chapter 6.

The final cause is "the good for whose sake an action is performed."[11] Thus a cathedral is built for the good of worshipping God. A house is built for the good of living in it. The formal and final causes of something are "inextricably linked,"[12] since what something is indicates what it can or should be. In the words of James Lennox, "The form of a living thing is . . . a unified set of goal-oriented capacities."[13] Jean Porter explains that Aristotelian metaphysics presuppose that "the purposes for which a living creature acts are inseparable from the intelligible principles giving structure and coherence to its development and activities."[14] We will argue in this chapter that the law is built to make people act justly and, ultimately, to be just. Justice is thus the reason for the law, the end of all laws. Thus, I will argue in this chapter that there is a complex, nonlinear, relationship between justice and law. Justice is the beginning and end of the law. The law (*jus*), which is the object of the virtue of justice, is the formal cause of all laws, and the attainment of justice or a just state of affairs is the final cause of the law. One cannot therefore understand the concept of law without understanding the nature of justice.

When considering not any type of law but the law itself, we can see that we have explored two of these causes. The material cause of law, the matter out of which the law is built, is the particular precepts of the various types of law—eternal, natural, divine, and human. These are the bricks, stones, and other building blocks of law. Just as a building is efficiently caused by both the architect and the artisans working under his direction, the efficient causes of law are the architect of law and those participating in His building plan. The ultimate efficient cause of the law is God, the one who caused the first type of law (eternal law) to be. With respect to human law, those human authorities who participate in God's lawmaking power act as proximate causes of human law by virtue of their participation. The jurist Bulgarus expressed this cooperation of man and God as efficient causes when he observed that "God is the author of justice whereas man is the author of human expressions of justice in law [*jus*]."[15] Even though man is the author of *jus* through promulgating laws, since *jus* is the object of justice (whose author is God), God is the ultimate author of *jus*. The *jus* may have its direct authority from man, but it "has its beginning and continued existence through God."[16] That which is good, right, and equitable is patterned on or rests upon the eternal law of God. As the eternal law determines the natures of all things, God determines through the eternal law the nature of justice. As we will see in this chapter, justice determines the nature of the law (*jus*). Laws (*leges*) made by man have their beginning and existence through God mediated by their particular exemplar or type, *jus*, the object of justice. *Jus* is the exemplar of laws (*leges*) as eternal law is the exemplar of all things. Thus, both God and human lawmakers are the efficient causes of the law.

We have not yet considered the formal and final causes of law itself. To do so we must step back from the edifice itself and search for that which informs the building and the end for which law is constructed. Much jurisprudence today, and legal education in general, restricts its attention to the material and efficient causes of law. Books and articles analyze, compare, and contrast the details of individual laws. Many writers on jurisprudence focus on the efficient cause and discuss who are the lawmakers and in what way they act. Yet a legacy of legal positivism, whether of a pure Austinian or Kelsian analytical jurisprudence or even of the softer Hartian type, focuses on material and efficient causes. Hart's Rule of Recognition is merely an efficient cause that sets the lawmakers in action. It identifies what counts as the matter of the law but does not give it form or purpose. Hart's very expression of the "internal point of view,"[17] which is the key to finding the Rule of Recognition, indicates that he is trapped within the material object and not considering it from its universal formal cause. Kelsen in a sense acknowledges the need for causes beyond the commands and the commander of law by positing his basic norm, but it is merely a logical starting point rather than a real formal or final cause. Aristotle argued that one who studies something must know both the formal and material cause. He argues that one who studies physical being, physics, must study more than matter:

But if on the other hand art imitates nature, and it is the part of the same discipline to know the form and the matter up to a point (e.g., the doctor has a knowledge of health and also of bile and phlegm, in which health is realized, and the builder both of the form of the house and of the matter, namely, that it is bricks and beams, and so forth): if this is so, it would be the part of physics also to know nature in both its senses.[18]

Put another way, would one hire an architect or a builder who professed no knowledge of what makes a house a house or a church a church or who did not know for what purpose a building was being constructed? Yet, modern legal education and jurisprudence often act as if one can know the law without knowing its form or end. Echoing the thought of Aristotle, Alasdair MacIntyre once noted on the practical level the necessary relationship between law and justice when he observed that to administer the law one must possess the virtue of justice.[19] He might have added that this is so because justice, in different senses, gives law its form and its end.

The next section examines in more detail these causal relationships between law and justice. The third section then considers in more detail this concept of justice, which informs and directs laws. Finally, in the fourth section, we must consider the role of equity as a corrective to the failure of the matter to embody the form. When laws fail to reach their end of justice, equity intervenes to redirect the laws to their end.

THE RELATIONSHIP BETWEEN LAW AND JUSTICE

Francisco Suárez notes the etymological connection between the Latin term *jus* and justice.[20] This etymological connection for Suárez symbolizes the ontological connection between the concepts the terms reference. Two distinct words in Latin are often translated into English by the same English word "law"—*jus* and *lex*. *Jus* is connected to the more universal concept, the formal and final cause of law, but *lex* refers to particular instances of law. As Pennington has noted: "Every jurist, even the pagan Roman jurists, had understood for centuries: *ius* embodies justice; and *ius naturale* in its purest form contains equity, justice, and reason in its DNA."[21] The distinction in meaning between *jus* and *lex* is evident in a

quotation we considered in chapter 6: "Custom is a sort of law [*jus*] established by usages and recognized as ordinance [*lege*] when ordinance [*lex*] is
lacking."[22] Immediately prior to this text in the *Decretum*, Gratian quotes
another statement of Isidore that makes explicit this distinction between
jus and *lex*: "Law [*ius*] is a general term; ordinance [*lex*] is a species of law
[*jus*]. Law [*jus*] is so called because it is just [*justum*]. Law [*jus*] consists of
ordinances [*lex*] and usages."[23] Hence, Gratian, through Isidore, is using
jus to signify a general universal concept and *lex* a particular type of *jus*, a
written ordinance. Gratian and Isidore also make an explicit connection
between law and justice. Law is something that is just.[24]

Huguccio also maintains this connection between laws (*lex*) and
justice when he says: "*Lex* commands what is just and prohibits the contrary."[25] As Pennington observes, "*Ius* reminded the jurists constantly
of the transcendental significance of a legal system. It existed not just to
establish right and wrong and to punish the wicked. It was the source of
justice, equity, and rights."[26]

In the course of the debate over the connection between law (*jus*)
and rights, Tierney has reminded us that for classical jurists such as
Aquinas, the universal type of law was not merely an abstract being of
reason but "*ius* was primarily a 'thing' (*rem*), something existing in external nature."[27] *Jus* as the object of justice[28] is thus not theoretical but real
and essential to the making, understanding, and interpreting of laws. In
considering the many meanings of the term *jus*, Aquinas includes the notion that it is not merely a concept but something real. It is "the just thing
itself" (*ipsam rem iustam*),[29] or as Isidore says in a passage quoted by
Aquinas, "'jus' [right] is so called because it is just [*justum*]."[30] What is
meant by the "just thing itself" or that which is by its very nature just? It
is that which is right or correct, *rectitudinem*.[31] Beyond rightness or correctness, "justice implies equality."[32] Thus, *jus* is that thing which is just,
right, and equitable.

Yet, justice is not the same thing as the just thing itself or the law (*jus*),
but is related to it. To understand this relationship it is important to understand that justice, unlike the law, is a virtue. A virtue is a habit, *habitus*. A
habit, according to Aristotle and Aquinas, is a disposition in relation to the
nature of a thing.[33] Man is a being who possesses various powers to act and
is thus a being oriented toward action. A power is a "capacity for acting,"
and in the case of a rational creature, the power is called a faculty to repre-

sent it is a conscious capacity for acting.[34] Habit thus is a disposition within the powers of man in relation to actions.[35] This relation can be either toward actions consistent with human nature (good actions) or contrary to human nature (evil).[36] Aquinas succinctly defines habit as "a disposition in relation to a thing's nature, and to its operation or end, by reason of which disposition a thing is well or ill disposed thereto."[37] Habit generally refers to an ambivalent disposition, which can be disposed either well or poorly. A virtue is a particular type of "disposition whereby the subject is well disposed according to the mode of its nature."[38] A vice is the opposite; it represents that which is "not being disposed in a way befitting its nature."[39]

Justice is a virtue—which means by definition a habit (Cicero's definition makes that explicit[40])—which disposes a man to render to each person his due.[41] The specific words used to specify what justice disposes one to render are *suum jus*, a phrase that highlights the ontological connection between the law (*jus*) and justice. Justice is the virtue that disposes men to render to each other what the law (*jus*) requires be rendered to him in particular. The phrase makes an inextricable connection between the universal and the particular. *Jus* refers to the universal formal cause of all particular laws, that which is always "good and equitable."[42] *Suum* ("his own") refers to a particular instantiation of the universal: that which for this one particular person is equitable and good for him. This relationship between the universal and the particular has been developed throughout the architecture of law in all of our preceding chapters. Law is composed of universal precepts of natural and divine law, which are particularly determined by human law. Justice can be thought of as a virtue that is the bridge between the universal and the particular. Justice is always in relation to another person.[43] Justice seeks an objective state of affairs (the just thing itself) that is right and good in relation to another particular person. *Jus*, as the object of justice, is that which is correct, due, and equitable, or as John Finnis summarizes, "acts, objects, and states of affairs, considered as subject-matters of relationships of justice."[44] Justice is the virtue that disposes men to act in relation to another particular person in a particular way suited to that person that conforms to what is always good and equitable. Knowing what constitutes a just action requires knowing the law, in all its universal and particular aspects. In this sense, law can be understood both as an objective reality (it exists) and a subjective reaction to that reality (how, in particular circumstances, that reality is determined).

For Aquinas, the law (*jus*) is not a virtue but a thing that is the object of the virtue of justice. Specific precepts or laws (*leges*) are the object of a different virtue, prudence. He says, "Justice has its own special proper object over and above the other virtues, and this object is called the just [*justum*], which is the same as 'right' [*jus*]. Hence it is evident that right [*jus*] is the object of justice. . . . Law [*lex*] is the object not of justice but of prudence."[45] Although obviously related as cause is to effect, the law (*jus*) and particular laws (*leges*) are distinct and objects of different virtues. Justice disposes one to render to everyone what is due to them according to the law (*jus*)— meaning in this instance what is always "good and equitable."[46] Yet, the term *jus* signifies more than a thing. Aquinas explains that the term has also come to mean the "art whereby it is known what is just."[47] The term *jus* bridges, in a sense, the intellectual and volitional elements necessary to the virtue of justice, the habit of acting justly. To have the constant and perpetual will to render to one his *jus*, a person must possess the art of knowing what is good and equitable. The art of making human laws (*leges*) must involve both the intellect and the will. Aquinas therefore connects two virtues, one intellectual and one volitional, in this discussion. Prudence is the intellectual virtue whereby men express in particular precepts what is "always good and equitable." As an intellectual virtue, prudence aids the mind in knowing the universal and expressing it in the particular. The volitional virtue of justice gives one the will to render the just thing (*justum*) to other people. The law (*jus*) gives form to laws so one can know what is due. The art of making law requires the art of knowing what is just. The law (*jus*) is also the end or purpose of the virtue of justice, because this virtue disposes one to render *suum jus* to others. Such thoughts led Aquinas to ask whether natural law is a habit. Although he concludes that natural law is not in itself a habit, he notes that we can hold the precepts of natural law in our mind habitually. In this sense we exercise the habit of holding natural law precepts in our mind so as to practice the virtue of justice. This argument reinforces the connection between intellectual and volitional virtues, which is indispensable for law and justice.

Aquinas uses another meaning of *jus* taken from the *Digest* to emphasize that this union of these virtues occurs within a person, one who makes law. *Jus* "refers to the place where justice is administered" and "a man, who has the office of exercising justice, administers the *jus*."[48] Law becomes justice in a particular place when a person exercising the art of knowing what is good and equitable renders to one his due, and this place is referred to by the same term for the law, *jus*. This most particular meaning of *jus* highlights the connection between *jus* and *lex*. Particular laws (*leges*), which are related to the knowledge of justice through prudence, are "an expression of right [*jus*]."[49] *Jus* is the good and right that the virtue of justice disposes one to will toward others. The term *jus* signifies both the just thing that is to be known through particular *leges* and the just thing that the will should continually and perpetually desire to render to others.

In a very subtle way, Aquinas has worked out the relationship among eternal law, justice, and particular law, and also the connection between knowing and willing good, equitable, and right actions. The just thing itself is the idea, exemplar, and art of justice, just as the eternal law acts in such a way for the other forms of law. The eternal law fixes the ends (or good) of all created things. *Jus*, as that which is right and equitable in the actions or states of affairs among people, is the idea, exemplar, or formal cause of all laws. The virtue of justice is the habit of choosing that which is *jus*, as a consequence of the *jus* having become known through the expression of the *jus* in *lex*. Justice is the imprint of the style or exemplar of the *jus* in *lex*. This virtue is expressed in particular acts of justice, or we could say, particular acts of law. Justice can also be said to contain the style for achieving the object of justice, the just thing itself. The habit of acting in accordance with that which is just requires one to practice the art of knowing what to do in relationships with other people. This art when put into practice forms the habit of doing what is good and equitable for others. All laws that follow the exemplar of *jus* are particular expressions of the idea of *jus*, and thus when rendered in a particular place are said to be given *in jure*.[50] This entire discussion is filled with expressions resonating with the language of our discussion in chapter 2 of eternal law. As the object of the virtue of justice, the law (*jus*) both transmits the form of law to command utterances and is the end for which the virtue of justice is exercised. Particular acts of the law must be performed by one practicing the virtue of justice in particular places so that the just thing may be done. Justice thus provides the form of the law and the final cause of the law— that justice may be done.

The tiny word *jus* thus summarizes and contains an elaborate system of relationships among existence, authority, and objects, and among God, the eternal law, justice, and human law. *Jus* establishes a connection between knowing that which is just and doing the just thing in a particular case (*suum jus*). By including consideration of eternal law within the architecture of law we can add an additional explanation to the already rich penumbra of meanings surrounding the legal term *jus*.[51] The purpose and meaning of a legal system of precepts are connected to the concepts of justice, equity, goodness, rightness, and the divine plan of order/wisdom (*ratio divinae sapientiae*) in the universe known as eternal law.

This elusive concept of the *jus* is made clearer by the earlier explanation of eternal law serving as idea and exemplar. *Jus* is the particular idea and exemplar for laws, which is itself contained within the eternal law's idea and exemplar of justice. Having laid this foundation for law and justice, we can understand how that which might be called the divine *jus* is expressed in particular precepts or rules. This process of particularization of *jus* is the natural law (*jus naturale*).

Justice through *jus* provides the formal and final cause of all laws. An anonymous jurist explains this essential relationship between justice and *jus*, the absence of which leaves the matter of *jus*, the *leges*, bereft of their essential form and thus they can be ignored. He says, "Justice and *ius* are in effect the same or ought to be the same. Whatever justice wants, *ius* strives to follow. It happens that sometimes . . . *ius* is not in concord with justice. When this occurs justice or equity interprets that, if *ius* openly departs from equity, we may ignore the authority of *ius* and follow equity."[52] After exploring the various kinds of justice more closely, we must return to this important virtue of equity, which readjusts the law when it departs from its formal and final causes.

Although intricately related, law (*jus*) and justice are distinct. Medieval authors drew a distinction based upon the authorship and hierarchical relationship. Stephan Kuttner quotes one such jurist, the author of the *Summa Elegantius*, as saying: "Law [*jus*] differs from justice because the author of law [*jus*] is man, but the author of justice is God. Further, justice spans more broadly than law [*ius*], containing within it many things, but law [*jus*] has been caught in many of its own traps."[53] This statement is interesting on several accounts. It distinguishes justice and law by virtue of God being the author of justice but man as the author of laws. We have seen in chapter 6 how the making of laws is a joint project of God and man. Man participates in the making of laws when deducing or determining laws for communities. God in a certain sense is the author of both justice and law since all laws have their origin in the eternal law. Yet, this attribution of the authorship of law to man is correct in that man is a necessary part of the making of particular laws by participating in God's legislative power. Yet, God is the author of justice. He establishes what is just, and what is just, as we have seen, limits the authority of man in participating in God's legislative power. Man authors the law when he authors particular laws as particular instantiations of justice. A medieval glossator expresses this concept between the preexistent justice of God (present in the precepts of natural law) and the making of law by men: "In like manner, nature encompasses more than art (science). Every art is a sum (*collectio*) of precepts while nature includes what has not yet been discovered but can be termed into precepts once it becomes known."[54] Whereas justice is the natural collection of all that is just, the principles of justice come into being in civil society when authored as legal precepts by men. Again we see this joint cooperation of men and God, but we begin to see a hierarchical relationship. Law is an incomplete set of precepts of justice, which have been authored by human lawmakers.

Yet, as the final cause of the law, justice is hierarchically superior to the law. The notion of such superiority is evident in this profound statement of the author of the *Summa Elegantius* when he notes that justice extends more widely than law. We shall explore this breadth when we consider the principle of equity, as a part of justice that gives justice a broader scope for action than the letter of the law. Justice is thus the universal of which laws are the particular. Justice is the form; laws the matter. The statement concludes by noting the limitations of law when considered only in itself. Because of its lack of breadth, it can, and has, become entangled in traps. When law is directed within itself to its strict letter, it becomes disconnected from justice and loses its ontological status as law.

Having examined the ontological relationship to the law, we need to delve into the nature of what constitutes justice in more detail so as to understand more particularly the ways in which justice causes law.

THE NATURE AND PARTS OF JUSTICE

Justice is the virtue by which we will to render to another person what is good and equitable for him (*suum jus*). Thus far we have discussed this concept of *suum jus* generally. We have noted the ontological connection between the law and justice and the general notion that *suum jus* is that which is good, right, and equitable in the circumstances for this particular person. But we still need to examine in more detail these general concepts before returning to the important corrective aspect of justice—equity. Before commencing we need to clarify terminology. Justice is a virtue and thus a habit and faculty for acting in a manner suited to human nature. The word "justice" is also used to refer to acts of the virtue, acts that in fact render *suum jus*. The virtue of justice orders acts toward due proportion. In this section we are considering the matter upon which the virtue acts: external actions and things. Justice seeks to render this matter proportionately among people.[55] Thus, Aquinas defines *suum jus* as "that which is due to him according to equality of proportion."[56] This equality of proportion can be considered from several different perspectives, hence the matter of justice can be divided into parts—commutative, distributive, and legal—for consideration.

What Is Justice?

First, we must note, as was suggested in the first section of this chapter, that justice is natural to man. By natural, we do not mean that man is automatically or necessarily just, but that the powers of human nature indicate an inclination toward acting justly. As Aristotle explains: "The power of speech is intended to set forth . . . the just and the unjust."[57] He argues that "when separated from law and justice" man is the "worst of all" animals.[58] Worst because he is acting contrary to his nature. Natural law is the law that identifies, based on the natural inclinations flowing from the qualities of human nature, what man ought to do—the good.[59] That which one ought to do in relation to another, or that which one owes to another, is a debt. Justice directs toward the good under this aspect of that which is due.[60] The great Thomistic philosopher Joseph Pieper explains that justice involves a *debitum*, a debt owed to someone. To be just is to pay a debt owed.[61] Since justice requires the rendering of that which belongs to the recipient—the reflexive pronoun *suum* ("his [very] own") in the definition of justice reinforces this notion—what is owed to him must already in a certain sense be his in order for justice to require it to be rendered.[62] To find a debt we must identify an antecedent cause establishing the claim to that which is to be rendered as belonging to the other person. Justice requires a due proportion, meaning only what is one's own (*suum*) (as opposed to another's) is due. Justice distinguishes between what is one's own (and hence due) from another's (and hence not due). Yet, in order to make this distinction, justice must know what belongs to whom. Law is that which determines that which constitutes one's own. Justice requires one to give back that which is another's, but law determines how we know what is another's. Law can only determine this distinction justly, in a cooperation between human and higher law.[63] Consistent with this cooperation between higher (divine and natural) and lower (human positive law), classical philosophy and jurisprudence has broadly distinguished two principal sources of the debt owed in justice, although referred to under different names.

Jeremiah Newman has explained that from its ancient origins in Semitic thought, justice has been associated with fitting conformity to a divine plan for an ordered cosmos. Conformity to this ordered cosmos occurs on two distinct but connected levels: the divinely established order and the order established by the individual ruler of a particular community, which is meant to reflect the cosmic order.[64] For the Greeks, rendering justice required acts of the intellect and will: knowledge of the divine order for men given by Zeus as represented by customs and the coercive enforcement of that order.[65] This dual source of the debt, both divine and human order, according to Alasdair MacIntyre, constitutes a significant difference between modern conceptions of justice and that of the ancient Greeks. He notes, "Someone in our own culture may use the word 'just' without any reference to or belief in a moral order in the universe."[66] For the Greeks, the concept of justice was inextricably linked to a cosmic order. The just man respects that cosmic order and does not violate it.[67] Although MacIntyre rightly contrasts the nature of that belief in Homeric epic and the later Athenian democracy, the debate is over the extent to which the present political order necessarily is that cosmic order and therefore can or cannot be criticized and not whether a cosmic order exists. This tension over the relation and divergence of Athenian political order to cosmic order is at the heart of a fundamental distinction within the virtue of justice that is at the heart of Aristotle's treatment and division of the virtue.

Throughout book 5 of his *Nichomachean Ethics*, Aristotle speaks of two types of justice, which can be understood to conform with this ancient division of order into "cosmological" and "local." Aristotle employs the distinction in terminology between *unqualified justice* (justice as such between men as men) and *political justice*[68] (justice between men in accordance with the law of civil society). Unqualified justice is in direct conformity to the divinely established cosmic order not mediated through political justice; political justice is justice as experienced by a particular city, a *polis*. Although he asserts that they are related, in that when Aristotle asserted that both unqualified justice (or justice as such) and political justice are both real, he differed from the Sophists, who denied any justice as such and recognized only a justice as understood by a particular political community.[69] Aquinas likewise identifies two distinct sources of a debt owed in justice, which he calls *moral* and *legal*. The moral debt is that "which is due by reason of a certain honesty [unqualified justice]" and legal debt is that which "man is compelled by law [political justice]."[70] He gives the example that by legal debt a man "owes honor and worship to those persons in positions of dignity who are placed over him," and by moral debt that "we owe worship and honor to persons in positions of dignity even though we be not their subjects."[71]

Although distinguishable, for Aristotle, unqualified and political justice are not severable. They are distinct but not different, in that unqualified justice is included within the particularization of political justice as a universal is in its particular. At least in the ideal or perfect civil society, the two will be identical.[72] The communication between unqualified justice and political justice becomes evident when we examine Aristotle's division of political justice. He divides political justice into natural and legal.[73] His division corresponds to the distinction between natural law and human law, or at least between the expression of natural law in the *jus gentium* (although Aristotle would not have used this Roman term to describe it) and particular human positive law. Political justice has two legal sources—natural law and human law, which can either express precepts of natural law directly or determine them particularly.[74] Thus unqualified justice is distinct from political justice but also included within political justice under Aristotle's term "natural justice," and so natural justice and legal justice compose political justice. Some medieval commentators understood the similarity between natural law and unqualified justice (often called natural justice by them). Kuttner has drawn attention to a late twelfth-century author who equates natural justice with natural law and political justice with customs[75] (the predominant form of human positive law at the time[76]). Natural law is the rational creature's participation in the eternal law,[77] it corresponds to the divinely ordained cosmological order, which Aristotle associates with unqualified or natural justice. Another writer also quoted by Kuttner poetically makes this connection between natural justice and the divine author of justice. The author of the *Summa Elegantius* alters an ancient definition of justice so as to include the phrase *cordibus hominum inspirata*, "inspired (literally, breathed) into the hearts of men."[78] According to Kuttner: "The new version [of this definition of justice] ... opened a wide range of associations: with the 'natural law' that God had written from time immemorial in the heart of man."[79] The divinely established natural law is breathed into human nature and is thus a source of what is due, independent of a particular human community.

Yet, this unqualified justice is not separate from political justice. It is also an inspiration for political justice. Aristotle teaches that political justice is partly natural and partly legal. Although not employing the term "natural law," his discussion correlates well with the relationship between natural law and human law we saw in chapter 6:

> Of political justice part is natural, part legal—natural, that which everywhere has the same force and does not exist by people's thinking this or that; legal, that which is originally indifferent, but when it has been laid down is not indifferent, e.g., that a prisoner's ransom shall be a mina, or that a goat and not two sheep shall be sacrificed, and again all the laws that are passed for particular cases, e.g., that sacrifice shall be made in honour of Brasidas, and the provisions of decrees.[80]

Even Aristotle had to contend in his own time with a sort of legal positivism, which in our time is merely another incarnation of the same mistaken philosophy Aristotle confronted. He admits that some believe that only political justice exists, because the specific details of what is just in one *polis* differs in another.[81] Leo Strauss confirms that these ancient critics saw the differing definitions of what is right and just among differing societies as proof that justice is merely conventional.[82] Aristotle explains that his critics have fallen prey to an overly simplified understanding of the relationship between nature and change. There is not a simple divide between that which is just by nature and that which is by convention. Justice is natural (justice qua justice), but we encounter it in particular determinations (political justice). Each society's political justice represents its chosen vision of the universal in its context. Strauss explains, "Each of those visions, taken by itself, is merely an opinion about the whole or an inadequate articulation of the fundamental awareness of the whole and thus points beyond itself to an adequate articulation."[83] Although different societies envision the details of justice differently in their context, that envisioning depends on a recognition of the whole. That which exists by nature is capable of change within what is necessary to its essence by nature. Natural or unqualified justice is the same for all, yet it allows different specifications. Aristotle gives the examples of measures.[84] If I borrow a measure of wine, I must repay the same measure in justice (rendering what is your due). Yet, among differing peoples the unit employed to determine the equality of quantity can differ. Although using differing systems of measure, they both are used to equalize the quantity so as to render what is due. A just measure of wine or corn is the same universal concept implemented by different specific quantities among different peoples. He explains: "Of things just and lawful each is related as the universal to its particulars; for the things that are done are many, but of *them* each is one, since it is universal."[85] The eradication of the Aristotelian synthesis of natural and political justice ends in the disproportionate exaltation of political justice. Legal positivism exalts the conventional justice of each legal system as the beginning and end of justice. From the internal point of view, what is legally conventional is just.

The Aristotelian synthesis of natural justice (which corresponds to the divine order) and political justice (which corresponds to the conventional order, which itself is also conformed to divine order) can be discerned in the scene from Sophocles's *Philoctetes*, which we discussed in chapter 5. When Odysseus and Neoptolemus debate the right course of action in attempting to obtain the bow of Philoctetes, Neoptolemus's obligations in political justice to the Greek community appear to conflict with his general obligations in justice to Philoctetes. To give Philoctetes his due in natural justice seems to require Neoptolemus to fail in his duty in political justice to bring about an end of the Trojan War. His dilemma in determining the just course of action is resolved by an intervention of the gods. They do not intervene by choosing one conception of what is due over the other; they resolve the apparent conflict by demonstrating that the just course of action renders what is due from both the natural and political perspective. Neoptolemus returns to Philoctetes his bow, because it had been taken by unjust cunningness, and he promises to correct the injustice done to Philoctetes by returning him to Greece. Philoctetes, in receipt of the bow destined to end the war, agrees to travel with Neoptolemus to Troy, where he helps the Greeks to defeat the Trojans and in the course of which heals his own afflictions. Thus, the apparent conflict of a duty in natural justice and a duty in political justice vanishes in a resolution that satisfies both. The cosmic order of the gods had decreed that the war must end only by Philoctetes firing the particular bow. Neoptolemus renders to Philoctetes his due under natural justice in a way that fulfills his duties to his *polis* and thereby conforms to the divinely decreed order. Likewise for Aristotle it is impossible for political justice and justice as such, albeit differing in detail, actually to conflict.

Strauss uses the concept of the common good, which figures in the definition of law itself, to explain why the ancient and modern positivists err in considering justice merely conventional:

> The law claims . . . to secure the common good. But the common good is exactly what we mean by "the just." Laws are just to the extent that they are conducive to the common good. But if the just is identical with the common good, the just or right cannot be conventional: the conventions of a city cannot make good for the city what is, in fact, fatal for it and vice versa. The nature of things and not convention then determines in each case what is just. This implies that what is just may very well differ from city to city and from period to period: the variety of just things is not only compatible with, but a consequence of, the principle of justice, namely, that the just is identical with the common good. Knowledge of what is just here and now,

which is knowledge of what is by nature, or intrinsically, good for this city now, cannot be scientific knowledge. . . . To establish what is just in each case is the function of the political art or skill. That art or skill is comparable to the art of the physician, who establishes what is in each case healthy or good for the human body."[86]

This relationship between natural and political justice both empowers and restrains the role of the human will in the determination of justice. The human will, in certain circumstances, has the power to make a particular act due in justice, but in different circumstances it lacks the power to make a particular act due in justice. The difference results from whether or not the act conforms to natural justices. Aquinas explains:

> The human will can, by common agreement, make a thing to be just provided it be not, of itself, contrary to natural justice, and it is in such matters that positive right (*jus*) has its place. Hence the Philosopher says (Ethic. v, 7) that "in the case of the legal just, it does not matter in the first instance whether it takes one form or another, it only matters when once it is laid down." If, however, a thing is, of itself, contrary to natural right (*jus*), the human will cannot make it just, for instance by decreeing that it is lawful to steal or to commit adultery. Hence it is written (Isaiah 10:1): "Woe to them that make wicked laws."[87]

Natural justice both provides for the variations of political justice and limits that variation. Natural law specifies what is generally just, and this natural justice distinguishes which purported laws are just and therefore binding in conscience. As to matters left undetermined by natural law and natural justice, particular conventional human law, customary or statutory, determines what is just (political justice) and therefore what particular behavior is obligatory pursuant to legal justice. Thus in one sense law determines what counts as just, and in another justice determines what counts as law. When one seeks to know the just thing to do so as to have the constant and perpetual will to render to others what is their due, he needs to consider both unqualified (or natural) justice and political justice. This dual relation between law and justice can be understood only once the distinction among the types of law and justice and the complex causal relation among them are understood. Natural justice is the formal cause of all law. It gives the form of law to an utterance or command by orienting it to the common good. All laws are made to determine what is just. The specific end of every particular law is the common good, and by attaining that end the law is just. Justice is thus the ultimate end or purpose of laws. As Newman notes, "The idea of justice is inseparable from the idea of law and where the latter reigns so does the former."[88] In other words, that which is just is also lawful (in the broadest sense of the word, i.e., not restricted to human law) and that which is lawful is just.[89] The law, *jus*, is the just thing itself and that which is lawful.

Beyond the distinction between general and political justice, and their relationship to law, there is another distinction within the term "justice," not related to its source, but to the nature of the relationship involved. To understand justice more fully, we must consider this distinction next.

Particular Relationships and Particular Justice

Beyond distinguishing between unqualified justice and political justice, Aristotle distinguishes between *general justice* (the complete virtue in dealings with others) and *particular justice* (which is based on particular types of equality in dealings with men).[90] General justice is merely a reference to justice in the abstract. The habit of willing to render others their due without considering the ways in which things are due. Particular justice distinguishes among the different relationships men may share with each other, which in turn require different ways of rendering *suum jus*.

According to Aquinas, the nature of the debt owed in justice "must needs vary according to various causes giving rise to the debt."[91] Pieper uses three types of relationships that cause a type of debt to arise to identify three types of particular justice: (1) individuals may directly owe something to each other through direct interaction or exchanges between them; (2) a community owes duties to the parts composing it; (3) an individual owes duties to a community of which he is a part. These three types of debts correspond to three forms of justice: *commutative, distributive,* and *legal*.[92] Pieper uses the scheme shown in figure 9.1 to summarize his explanation. Understanding the nature of these relationships helps us to understand the nature of these types of justice.

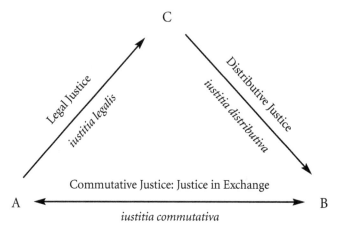

Figure 9.1. A Schematic Representation of the Basic Forms of Justice

Commutative justice considers the justice of commutations, or ex-change transactions between individuals. Aquinas defines commutative justice thus:

> In the first place there is the order of one part to another, to which corresponds the order of one private individual to another. This order is directed by commutative justice, which is concerned about the mutual dealings between two persons. . . . In commutations something is paid to an individual on account of something of his that has been received, as may be seen chiefly in selling and buying, where the notion of commutation is found primarily. Hence it is necessary to equalize thing with thing, so that the one person should pay back to the other just so much as he has become richer out of that which belonged to the other. [93]

These commutations can be voluntary, as when a person sells his car, or involuntary, as when someone steals another person's car. Commutative justice requires that a debt becomes due in equal amount when something is transferred from one to another. Aristotle held that commutative justice requires equality in all exchange transactions between individuals in society.[94] Aristotle was not unconcerned with the distribution of wealth among people,[95] but the principle of equality in exchange held that particular transactions between individuals (voluntary or involuntary) were not the way to achieve redistribution. James Gordley has explained that equality in exchange is not meant to achieve a just distribution of wealth, the achievement of which involves principles of distributive rather than commutative justice, but is meant to "avoid random redistributions" of wealth through "the system of exchange."[96] A legal system provides for commutative justice when it requires damages for involuntary commutations, such as torts like battery and conversion (liability in a civil action) and when it enforces voluntary exchanges, such as contracts. The root of commutative justice is the debt created by a transfer of something (tangible or intangible) from one to another.

Distributive justice is the aspect of justice that regulates the distribution of goods or benefits produced by a common undertaking. A community that communally produces goods owes a debt to the parts of that community. This type of debt is regulated by distributive justice. Aquinas describes distributive justice: "There is the order of the whole towards the parts, to which corresponds the order of that which belongs to the community in relation to each single person. This order is directed by distributive justice, which distributes common goods proportionately."[97]

Distributive justice does not involve the distribution of individual goods among individuals but only the distribution of common goods, goods made by the combined effort of the community. Henri Grenier explains: "In distributive justice, something is given to a private person, in as much as what belongs to the whole is due to the part, and in a quantity that is proportionate to the importance of the position of the part in relation to the whole."[98] Pieper explains that communal goods are the "total product of community life."[99] The term "product" may be misleading for our materialist generation. By this term, Pieper means more than the mere production of material goods. It is the sum total good resulting from the communal enterprise and includes things like honor and praise. Each individual is entitled to share proportionately in commonly produced benefits, "taking into account not only the thing but the person whose share is distributed, his *dignitas*, capacity and ability that is distinctively his."[100] A just distribution involves a delicate balance between considering the relevant distinctive qualities of the individual and respecting the equality of justice. For there is some measure of *dignitas* in equal proportion in each person, but there are other unique qualities relevant for a distribution that are not equal in all.[101] The fact that all people share a certain equality of dignity by virtue of a common human nature does not mean that all merit equal distribution of common goods in all communal contexts. Distributive justice does not require equality of result but rather proportionality according to merit. Aquinas explains:

> Equality of justice has its place in retribution [an aspect of commutative justice because retribution must be equal to the harm done], since equal rewards or punishments are due to equal merit or demerit. But this does not apply to things as at first instituted. For just as an architect, without injustice, places stones of the same kind in different parts of a building, not on account of any antecedent difference in the stones, but with a view to securing that perfection of the entire building, which could not be obtained except by the different positions of the stones; even so, God from the beginning, to secure perfection in the universe, has set therein creatures of various and unequal natures, according to His wisdom, and without injustice, since no diversity of merit is presupposed.[102]

There are two levels involved in applying distributive justice: (1) choosing an appropriate principle of distribution (or the principle by which we identify the relative importance of a part to the whole), and (2) applying the principle consistently. Aquinas recognizes that in different contexts, the relative importance of individuals to the whole may differ based on different distinguishing characteristics.[103] Distributive justice requires common goods be distributed proportionately, but not necessarily equally, according to merit.[104] Yet, as Aquinas observes, "all do not judge merit in distribution in agreement with the same norm."[105] Once the norm for judging distribution has been selected, distributive justice evaluates whether that norm has been applied consistently. A misapplication of a principle of equality or merit may be made in two ways: two persons who are unequal may receive equal distributions, or two people who are equal may receive unequal distributions. Aquinas gives the examples of people receiving unequal wages for equal work, and people receiving equal wages for unequal work. Thus, actions that distribute (or redistribute) goods such as wealth can be criticized on either level of distributive justice. The principle of distribution (the definition of what constitutes equality or merit) may be criticized as random or unprincipled. Alternatively, the actual distribution achieved may be criticized as contrary to the applicable definition of merit.

Finally, an individual owes a debt to the whole of which he is a part. Legal justice directs all the actions of individual men under law to conform to the common good of the political community of which he is a part.[106] Legal justice directs men to render others their due not as individuals but as parts of a whole.[107] Yet, this debt owed to the community is not to be understood in the collectivist sense that considers the collective community an entity distinct from the individual members. Aquinas explains that justice always regulates duties to other individuals but legal justice considers debts owed to other individuals in their capacity as members of a common political community. He explains:

> Justice, as stated above (Article 2) directs man in his relations with other men. Now this may happen in two ways: first as regards his relation with individuals, secondly as regards his relations with others in general, in so far as a man who serves a community, serves all those who are included in that community. Accordingly justice in its proper acceptation can be directed to another in both these senses. Now it is evident that all who are included in a community, stand in relation to that community as parts to a whole; while a part, as such, belongs to a whole, so that whatever is the good of a part can be directed to the good of the whole. It follows therefore that the good of any virtue, whether such virtue direct man in relation to himself, or in relation to certain other individual persons, is referable to the common good, to which justice directs: so that all acts of virtue can pertain to justice, in so far as it directs man to the common good.[108]

Since all acts of other virtues can be oriented to the common good — since what is good for the part is good for the whole — legal justice has often been referred to as a general virtue because it can direct all other virtues to the universal common good. Good individual acts that are the objects of individual virtues—such as temperance, fortitude, liberality, and so on—have their own end with respect to the individual, but legal justice adds another aspect of due to the particular just act. Newman has noted that writers after Aquinas began to confine the concept of legal justice solely to the common good of the state as such. This narrowing of the field of legal justice is a corruption of Aquinas because it does not fully account for the individual good of the people composing the community, nor does it include man's complete (including supernatural) end.[109] Legal justice can function in the mode of both general justice and political justice. Legal justice with reference to the particular laws of a political community (Aristotle's *polis*) directs the citizen to fulfill duties in political justice. Legal justice requires the members of a *polis* to obey the particular determinations of the political community because they determine politically just actions, that is, particular actions that are oriented to the common good of this particular *polis*. Yet, human lawmakers cannot legislate for every possible circumstance; they cannot determine what legal justice requires in all circumstances. In the absence of conventional determinations of political justice applicable to certain contingent circumstances, legal justice continues to direct that the choice of actions be oriented to the universal, not *polis* specific, common good. In this latter context, legal justice can be understood to be functioning as general rather than political justice. Aristotle understood that general justice required more than political justice. A citizen is obligated in justice to more than complying with the particular laws of the *polis*. As a result, that which is required of a good citizen is not everything required of a good man.[110] Justice and virtue are the same (for that which is just is virtuous) yet distinct. Virtue is the inclination to all good actions in general; justice is virtue in relation to others.[111] In one sense, the natural law therefore obligates with respect to all virtues, and we can say we are legally just when we act according to natural law.[112] Thus, legal justice considered as general justice obligates us to do all that natural law requires; legal justice as political justice requires us to obey the particular laws of our *polis*. In many circumstances, the obligations under both senses of legal justice will coincide because the law of the *polis* will determine what legal justice as general justice requires. Yet, human law does not forbid or require all that is forbidden or required under the natural law.[113] The scope of the obligations of legal justice as general justice is more extensive than that of legal justice as political justice. Thus, the failure of human law to prohibit a particular vicious act does not remove the legal obligation in legal justice to avoid that act under the natural law. It is in this sense of legal justice as general justice that Aquinas explains that legal justice directs all the other virtues: "Every virtue strictly speaking directs its act to that virtue's proper end: that it should happen to be directed to a further end, either always or sometimes, does not belong to that virtue considered strictly, for it needs some higher virtue to direct it to that end. Consequently there must be one supreme virtue essentially distinct from every other virtue, which directs all the virtues to the common good; and this virtue is legal justice."[114]

We can take for an example the virtue of temperance. This virtue directs to an aspect of the end or good of the individual in that self-preservation is a component of what is good for man. Temperance is oriented toward health, which has as its end self-preservation, a primary principle of natural law. Yet, temperate individuals, those who moderate their appetites, are good for their community because a component of the common good of a community is to have healthy citizens. An individual who practices the virtue of temperance is therefore pursuing his own individual good and the common good simultaneously. By furthering the common good, he thus acts justly toward others by orienting his action toward the common good. Legal justice is the virtue the practice of which inclines the individual to conform behavior to the natural law and thereby to his personal good and by the practice of the same virtue orient his acts to the common good.

Grenier explains that this type of justice is called legal because "it is the function of law to direct to the common good," and by legal justice "man conforms with the law which directs the acts of all the virtues to the common good."[115] Justice requires men to conform actions to the common good. Laws are made for the purpose of determining what is best for the common good in particular circumstances. Therefore, men owe a debt in justice to obey the laws, since those laws direct to the common good. Justice obligates citizens to obey the laws of their country not simply because they are laws, but because the end of all valid laws must be the common good. Laws that fail to conform to this final cause or end of law are no laws at all. Legal justice is a broader concept than the law, but it includes it. The duty to work for the common good is the reason for the making of all laws. Legal justice thus gives form to the laws of a society and directs them to the end of lawmaking. By paying one's debt in legal justice, "man is in harmony with the law, which directs the acts of all the virtues to the common good."[116] Since the virtue of legal justice disposes men to render what is due to other men in their capacity as members of a community by directing all actions to the common good, and since law is what determines that which constitutes the common good, law and justice are existentially connected. To orient actions to what is good one must know what is good. We know what is good through the natural law, which must be made particular and determined through human law. Legal justice is law in its fullest sense—natural, divine, human, all of which have their origin and foundation in eternal law. Aquinas emphasizes this indispensable connection between natural law (as the font of all human law) and justice by returning to the first principle of natural law in his discussion of justice. He claims that the first precept of the natural law—good ought to be done and evil avoided—is integral to justice.[117] This precept encompasses all aspects of the debt that justice disposes us to render. The rest of law—all the other precepts of natural, divine, and human—makes more specific and concrete the dimensions of that debt.

We see from this perspective of legal justice the depth of the relation between law and justice. Legal "justice means the doing of what is lawful,"[118] but here "lawful" is used in the broadest sense, what is lawful according both to positive human law and to higher natural and divine law.[119] Legal justice can direct the constancy of the will to conform to law in a narrow and particular realm, that which is politically just, but also in the wider sense of natural justice. As Newman observed: "Every virtuous act, since it is within the law, is a rendering of a *debitum* in this wide sense [of legal justice]."[120] Citizens have a "double vocation, one which is proper to him as a man and one which he, as citizen, has in common with all other citizens."[121] As social and political animals, a man's life of virtue is not only a private affair.

Having considered the breadth of the purview of legal justice (in these two senses), we can see the inherent futility in the attempt to separate law and morality by legal positivists, such as Hart and Raz. For Raz, law is merely a social institution.[122] A legal system is contrasted with other normative systems.[123] Given the existential connection between general and particular justice, we have seen how legal justice obligates one to act for both the individual and common good. If we use the term "morality" to indicate a system whereby rules for individual action in particular circumstances are determined by individuals (or personal nonlegal authorities), morality is not a different normative system from human law. As Jean Porter has insightfully commented, rather than placing a divide between natural law and morality on one side and human law on the other, it is more appropriate to place the divide between natural law on one side and morality and human laws on the other.[124] Natural law can be distinguished from both morality and human law by the level of specificity of precepts. Both morality and human laws are systems of particular determinations that apply to actual circumstances in which a choice among actions must be made. Natural law contains universal general principles that require further determination. Morality and human law can be distinguished on the basis of the actor making the determination: the individual or personal superiors in the case of morality, and political authorities in the case of law.[125] Human laws are determinations of the same natural law made by political or legal authorities. Morality and human law are both part of the same normative system rooted in natural law and ultimately the eternal law. The two can be distinguished only by the type of person making the determination. The distinction is a distinction of jurisdiction, not of normative systems. Since legal justice (in its broad sense) orients all virtues to the common good, morality is part of the architecture of the legal system established by the eternal law. Hart cannot see this connection because he ignores legal justice. In his discussion of justice in *The Concept of Law*, Hart only discusses commutative and distributive and eliminates this third type of justice.[126] Human legal systems are not merely social institutions, as Raz would have it, but part of a cosmological institution. They are the particular incarnations of the cosmological system in particular political communities.

Hart attempts to save the dichotomy between morality and justice by attempting to separate the good from the just.[127] He narrowly defines justice to exclude legal justice,[128] and since he can only admit commutative and distributive, he restricts justice to equality of treatment: like cases should be treated alike and different cases differently.[129] Although equality of treatment is just, justice encompasses more than equality of treatment. Legal justice (and general justice for that matter) requires conformity to higher law, including natural and divine law. As a general virtue, justice orders all our actions to the common good. Hart's example of distinguishing a bad action from an unjust one reveals the limitations of his definition. He argues that a father who acts cruelly to his child would be bad, but not unjust, to the child; if the father treated each of his children differently, that would be unjust.[130] Although Hart would likely consider it bad behavior, a father who beat all his children equally would not, under Hart's limited conception, be unjust. In reality, the father's actions are both bad (not good) and unjust. The father owes a debt to his child to care for and not harm the child, and acting with cruelty fails to render to the child what is due. The father has disobeyed the natural law and the divine law, which obligate parents to love and care for their children. The end of this law is the common good of the family, and the virtue of justice is the habit of willing to render what is due to one's children in justice for the common good of the family. By fulfilling this duty in legal justice to his children, the father also pursues his own personal good (a virtuous life). The cruel father, on the other hand, has violated commutative justice toward the child by not rendering to the child what is his due under natural and divine law. The cruel father has also violated legal justice by not acting for the common good of the family.

John Rawls at certain points comes close to acknowledging the obligations of legal justice thus understood. He claims we have a natural duty to support a system that is reasonably just (or establish one): "If the basic structure of society is just, or as just as it is reasonable to expect in the circumstances, everyone has a natural duty to do his part in the existing scheme."[131] This obligation is a general summary of legal justice: we are obligated to establish or obey just laws. Yet, this "natural duty" has no legal ontology. Like Kelsen, who merely posits his basic norm, Rawls simply presumes the existence of this duty without explaining its causes. As with Kelsen, even those scholars who refuse classical natural law cannot escape it completely. They need some bit of natural law to make their legal jurisprudence work.

In this examination of the types of justice, we can discern from another point of view the relationship between law and justice. Commutative and distributive justice direct relations between individuals, and between the community and the individual. Laws determine what is due in these relationships by making determinations of either the equality of exchange or the proportionate mean of distribution. Individuals must obey these laws (if truly laws) because they direct their actions toward one another and the community by directing to the common good, which in legal justice must be the end of all our actions.

WHEN LAW FAILS: EQUITY

In this chapter we have considered the causes of law. To be considered a law, a command must be infused with the form of the law, *jus*. It must be directed to the final cause of law, justice. In chapter 8 we considered when purported laws lose their connection to these causes, when they are iniquitous. We considered this situation from the perspective of one subject to these purported laws and concluded that they cease to be laws that bind in conscience. Yet, in light of exploring the ontological relationship between laws, the law, and justice in this chapter, we can revisit this issue to add a refinement and a distinction. In chapter 8 we gave two answers to the question of what one can do about an unjust law: refuse to conform to the unjust law or, for prudential reasons, conform behavior to the unjust law when possible without violating the natural or divine law. We can now reconsider a more complex situation in which a particular law may not, in and of itself, be universally unjust but in particular circumstances may fail to be oriented to the final end of law, justice. Here we are not faced with an unjust law per se but an unjust result. The legal solution to such a dilemma is equity, or *epikeia*. We have seen the deep connection between law and justice. To be just requires one to render to others their due. To determine what is due to them, one needs to know the law. Yet, there is not merely a one-dimensional relationship between law on one hand and justice on the other. Justice encompasses two pillars, law and equity. In the very beginning of Aristotle's consideration of justice, he alludes to the composition of justice involving two related but distinct concepts that correlate to law and equity. The virtue of justice, he claims, involves two aspects, law-abidingness and fairness. That which is just must be that which is according to law and is fair. That which is unjust is unlawful and unfair.[132] This conjunctive alludes to the relationship among law, equity, and justice.

In chapters 5 and 8 we considered how human lawmakers can err in making human law. As Aquinas explains, although knowledge of the principles of natural law is available to all men through rational reflection on the common human nature, those principles are not universally known by all. The degree of difficulty or ease in actually arriving at a correct understanding of the precepts of the natural law depends on the generality of principles at issue. The more general and basic the proposition, the more accessible it is to the human intellect. The more remote and particular the precept, the more opportunity exists for errors.[133] Aquinas explains that "the more we descend to matters of detail," the more uncertainty exists as to conclusions.[134] Thus, the general principles of natural law are universally valid for all men and theoretically knowable by all men, but depending on the level of detail, they are not universally known by all men.[135] Divine law has been given as a remedy to this failure, but this revelation may be rejected by some human lawmakers, and even by entire societies, thus cutting them off from this source of knowledge. In such a situation, people are likely to make more and greater errors in knowing the general precepts of natural law that need to be determined. Since human law is supposed to be a particularization of the general principles of natural and divine law, if the lawmaker errs in knowing the principles, the particular law can err. In chapter 8 we examined such cases when human authorities formulate laws that order what the natural law forbids. Thus, the laws of Nazi Germany that commanded the torture and execution of the innocent were directly contrary to the precepts of the natural law and therefore no law at all.

Yet, even a legal authority who properly understands all the applicable principles of natural law and makes a just and good determination of those higher precepts is incapable of foreseeing all circumstances to which this otherwise good law might apply. Since laws are made to apply to a multiplicity of circumstances and situations, a law can only be formulated to produce the just result in the majority of cases. The problem is not in the principles of natural and divine law themselves but rather in the contingent circumstances to which they are applied. Aquinas explains: "But as to certain matters of detail, which are conclusions, as it were, of those general principles, it is the same for all in the majority of cases . . . and yet in some few cases it may fail . . . as to rectitude, by reason of certain obstacles (just as natures subject to generation and corruption fail in some few cases on account of some obstacle)."[136] By "fail," Aquinas means that a literal application of the law would fail to direct one's action toward a good end, the objects of the natural inclinations. It is not that the law is a bad law, but rather that in a particular circumstance the law if followed would fail to direct to its proper end. For example, Aquinas says that a law compelling the return of things borrowed to their owner is a good and just law. In most cases we must obey this law. Yet, in certain extraordinary circumstances, following this rule would be unjust and wrong. For example, if one lends his sword and at the time of requesting return of it the owner is known to be mad so that he is likely to use the sword to harm himself or others, the one having possession of the sword should not comply with the law. In such a case "it is bad to follow the law, and it is good to set aside the letter of the law and to follow the dictates of justice and the common good."[137] This case differs from those considered in chapter 8. The law stating "return borrowed property" is not unjust. It does not command something contrary to the natural law. The law itself is not iniquitous, but its application in particular circumstances (the man having gone mad) is what makes complying with an otherwise just law unjust, because it would result not in orienting action toward the common good but against it.

Human history and experience teach us that unusual and unexpected things regularly happen, and the "greater the number of conditions added, the greater the number of ways in which the principle may fail."[138] Human lawmakers cannot foresee all of these virtually infinite possibilities for unusual circumstances, and, even if they could, writing particular laws to account for them would make the law unwieldy and more likely to fail. As Russell Hittinger has argued: "By and large, laws that try to reach all the contingencies and singularities of action will prove deficient not only in the order of prudence, but also in the order of art."[139] Particular laws are better written in a general way, since as we descend into detail the more errors we make.[140]

Particular law must therefore be made for the typical situations, but, having done so, lawyers and legislators must not forget this limitation when administering the law. There must be a safety valve installed in the law for dealing with circumstances in which the law fails of its essential purpose under certain conditions. Aquinas summarizes the argument: "Now, it happens often that the observance of some point of law conduces to the common weal in the majority of instances, and yet, in some cases, is very hurtful. Since then the lawgiver cannot have in view every single case, he shapes the law according to what happens most frequently, by directing his attention to the common good. Wherefore if a case arises wherein the observance of that law would be hurtful to the general welfare, it should not be observed."[141]

He then provides a useful illustration:

> For instance, suppose that in a besieged city it be an established law that the gates of the city are to be kept closed, this is good for public welfare as a general rule: but, were it to happen that the enemy are in pursuit of certain citizens, who are defenders of the city, it would be a great loss to the city if the gates were not opened to them: and so in that case the gates ought to be opened, contrary to the letter of the law, in order to maintain the common weal, which the lawgiver had in view.[142]

The virtue of equity is the safety valve that tells the guards to open the gates and the one in possession of the sword to keep it. Aquinas concludes that equity is a part of the virtue of justice that relates to legal justice. Legal justice is the part of the virtue of justice that directs our actions toward rendering to others what is due under the law. In Aquinas's view, equity is either (1) a part of legal justice that modifies what is due under the letter of the law or (2) a part of general justice that modifies what legal justice requires.[143] In either case, equity is necessary when the law applied to certain circumstances would "frustrate the equality of justice and be injurious to the common good, which the law has in view."[144] Legal justice and equity are both concerned with the same matter but from different viewpoints (the letter and spirit).[145] Normally, we presume the letter of the law is ordained to the common good, but in certain cases it may not be.

We can return to the human law that decides what side of the road to drive upon to consider another example. The law designating the right side is a good law. It is a reasonable determination of the natural law precept that we should not unnecessarily endanger ourselves or others. Yet, although a good determination for most situations, it can fail to achieve its end (providing a rule for avoiding injury to ourselves or others) in an extraordinary circumstance. If a driver were on a mountain road and rocks started falling onto the right side of the road, she could cross over to the left side of the road (especially if there were no cars on that side) to avoid injury from falling rocks. She could do this even though a specific law commands her to drive on the right side of the road. The necessity of the falling rocks suspends this otherwise good law from applying to this unusual circumstance. It is not simply that this violation of law is overlooked or excused. Equity intervenes to modify the application of the law to correct for the unusual circumstance not foreseen by the one making the law. Archbishop Amleto Giovanni Cicognani explains this interaction between law and equity by arguing that equity acts to emend the letter of the law to enable the law to achieve its ultimate end, what is good and equitable. He defines equity: "The benign application of the law according to what is good and equitable, which decides that the lawgiver does not intend that, because of exceptional circumstances, some particular case be included under his general law."[146] He goes on to explain:

> A law though just in general, may, taken literally, lead in some unforeseen cases to results which agree neither with the intent of the lawgiver nor with natural justice, but rather contravene them. In such cases the law must be expounded not according to its wording but according to the intent of the lawgiver and the general principles of natural justice. Law in the strict sense (*jus strictum*) is, therefore, positive law in its literal interpretation; equity, on the contrary, consists of the principles of natural justice so far as they are used to explain or correct a positive human law if this is not in harmony with the former.[147]

Archbishop Cicognani is merely echoing what Suárez concluded five centuries before when he concluded that "*epieikeia* is an emendation of a law, or of that which is legally just."[148] According to Suárez, equity or *epikeia* occurs when there is an act forbidden by the letter of a positive law, but that positive law is emended because the lawgiver did not intend the particular case at hand to be governed by the positive law, notwithstanding the letter of the law. This understanding of the role of equity is embodied in the old legal aphorism: that "which is not otherwise permitted, necessity allows, and necessity makes a privilege which supersedes the law."[149] Yet, the dispensation from law due to necessity is not a license to do wrong. This aphorism is an oversimplified statement. The natural law is not capable of dispensation because its principles apply universally,[150] nor can one be dispensed from the divine law, which "leaves nothing unpunished."[151] Equity cannot emend the letter of human law to require one to transgress the natural law; rather, the particular law is emended so that the higher principles of natural law are not frustrated in a particular instance. The act at issue must be prohibited only by virtue of the determination of the legislator and not by virtue of the act itself. In such a case, the legally prohibited act in light of the particular circumstances "may be permissible in consequence solely of the legislator's intention, as this intention is conjecturally deduced from an extrinsic occasion, necessity or purpose."[152]

We can consider the example of the return of a deposit (the sword) discussed above to understand this distinction. Natural law requires that which is borrowed should be returned because one should render to the owner that which is his due. The human law adopts a particular law, such as the Roman law for return of goods under a contract of *depositum* or *commodatum*.[153] As we discussed in chapter 4, natural law is not a monolithic precept, but a hierarchical ordering of goods. When returning a deposit would be harmful to life or the common good of man, it must be returned in a way that respects those goods. In the case in which a sword is to be returned to a madman, the law that would normally order the return of the sword should not compel repossession by the madman. The Roman laws concerning contracts of *depositum* and *commodatum* are not natural law precepts but particular determinations in human law of the principle that borrowed goods should be returned.[154] In those cases in which the letter of Roman law would require returning a weapon to a madman, that would be against justice, but equity provides an exception. Yet, equity cannot violate natural law, thus equity, although dispensing with the need to render possession during the madness, would not allow the one in possession simply to transfer title of the sword to himself and deprive the true owner of the value of his property. He must continue to hold it in trust, or if it can never be returned, the owner must be compensated with equal value according to commutative justice.

In a legal culture that under the influence of legal positivism has become legalistic, this role of equity is difficult to understand. When the legal system is reduced to the positive pronouncements of human actors (no matter how broadly one defines those pronouncements), the idea that the law is something larger than the body of legal texts is an alien concept. In our day, law has become abstract and depersonalized. Law is in the paper not in the mind of a person. It has become disconnected from its formal and final causes. Law is simply the material cause—the particular rule or, worse, the paper on which the rule is written. For the classical natural law jurist, law transcends the paper and the rule and is in the mind of people. Law is not an independent abstraction but directed to a final end, justice. In this sense, equity is not opposed to law, but is its sibling, born of the same parent—the same formal cause, justice. When equity dispenses with the requirements of a particular law or emends the text to make the laws conform to their formal cause and serve their final cause, equity does not reject the law but rather perfects it. As Patrick Brennan has eloquently explained: "For Aquinas the answers to these jurisprudential questions— the equity of the statute, dispensation when the common good demands or suggests it, etc.—*follow from the nature of law* (and, to be sure, prudential decisions about how to realize it); they are not, as is sometimes supposed, accidents of history or legally-unguided choices of 'policy.'"[155]

As Brennan has argued, rules in law are not like rules in simple games that produce binary results. In law, rules are part of a "methodical process that is not itself governed by any 'rule' (or standard) or law we have made."[156] Legal authorities, even when following rules, do, and should, not simply follow them mechanically. They take them into account as part of the process of doing justice. This is because the rules we make are governed by the eternal law, which contains exemplars or types, which permit variations of detail, unlike the mechanical rules of games.

Aquinas explains that it would be better for the legislator who wrote the rule himself to officially grant a dispensation or promulgate an emendation, since if each person were to grant his own dispensation, there would be disorder.[157] Yet, in a case where the peril is great and recourse to the lawgiver would not be reasonably possible, "the mere necessity brings with it a dispensation, since necessity knows no law."[158] It would be better if a police officer were present on our mountain road with falling rocks directing those on the right to move to the left, but in the absence of one, the driver can still disregard the specific law to drive on the right. However, there is an intermediate position between the legislator granting the dispensation and each individual deciding for himself. The judiciary can read, interpret, and apply the letter of the statutes according to these principles of equity, dispensing and emending in light of particular circumstances. This does not present the oft-raised specter of subverting the legislative function by legislating from the bench. The judiciary may not simply change the letter of the law as generally applied by, for example, declaring that now all must drive on the left. Rather, as Brennan suggests, the legislation must be taken into account as part of the process of doing justice in the particular case. The judge does not in applying principles of equity legislate *de novo*, but he rather smooths out the rough edges of the rule laid down by dispensing or modifying its application so that it does not fail to attain its final end, justice. Legislators and judges do have different roles, but those roles are interrelated and interdependent. One French jurist expressed this dialogue between legislator and judge:

> The task of statutory law is to express in broad terms the general maxims of the law, to settle principles fertile in consequences, and not to go down in the details of questions which may arise in every matter. It is the task of judges and lawyers, engrained with the general spirit of the law, to conduct the application of those principles. . . . There is a science for legislators as there is one for the judges; and one is not similar to the other. The legislator's science consists in finding in every matter the principles most favorable to a general rule; the judge's science is to make such principles operative, to ramify them, to extend them by a wise and reasoned application to given cases.[159]

Porter has demonstrated that this complex relationship between law and justice is incomplete without equity. Yet, equity is not merely a necessary corrective. It touches the divine. A judge not only applies but judges the laws in accordance with reason and equity. "This claim is supported by the view that reason and its judicial expressions—that is, justice or equity—are divine in origin, so much so that the jurist Martin even says that equity *is* God," states Porter.[160]

Equity is the virtue that inclines one to follow the spirit of the law and the intention of the legislator and not merely the letter of the law.[161] Because law must be oriented to an end—the common good—the particular laws made by human authorities must always serve that end. Human lawmakers may err in drafting laws out of ignorance of principles or their inability to foresee and provide for an unusual circumstance. When this occurs, the law must always be obeyed in conformity with the higher natural and divine law and according to reason, justice, and equity. If a particular contingent fact would cause obedience to a human law to fail to be oriented to the common good, one is dispensed from the particular law. Ideally, this dispensation should be granted by the proper legal authorities, but in the case of risk or peril the dispensation exists by virtue of the higher law itself. Whenever considering a particular law, we must always keep the end of that law, and in fact all law, in mind. L. J. Riley summarizes the constrained role of equity thus: "Epikeia, falling within the genus of justice, is a corrective of general justice as expressed by law, but only insofar as certain elements of that law are concerned—that is, not matters which are of the natural law, nor particular precepts or decrees, but only what is 'originally indifferent but when it has been laid down [by positive enactment] is not indifferent.'"[162]

Even Hart recognized that legal rules are formulated in general (universal terms), which will always have cases of clear applicability and those of open possibilities, or hard cases.[163] Yet, Hart cuts himself off from the legal tool to resolve these open possibilities because they are outside the legal system (unless by chance incorporated in a particular legal system's Rule of Recognition). The divine and natural law provide the context for resolving the hard cases so as to achieve justice. Hart admits that his jurisprudence results in at least some hard cases coming down to a point in which a choice simply has to be made.[164] Unfortunately, his jurisprudence, in seeking to distinguish what he calls "morality" from law, cuts off the surrounding architecture that frames, informs, and guides that choice. At some point, Hartian jurisprudence ends in a brute exercise of the will, even if Hart believed or hoped that people would use that brute choice well. His jurisprudence does not ensure that choice will be constrained by general principles of justice.

MacIntyre's understanding of a "practice" and a "virtue" can help us understand how the complex relationship between law and justice can help us escape the dead-end jurisprudence of even the milder positivism of Hart. A practice, according to MacIntyre, is "any coherent and complex

form of socially established cooperative human activity through which
goods internal to that form of activity are realized in the course of trying to
achieve those standards of excellence which are appropriate to, and partially definitive of, that form of activity, with the result that human powers
to achieve excellence, and human conceptions of the ends and goods involved, are systematically extended."[165] A virtue is "an acquired human
quality the possession and exercise of which tends to enable us to achieve
those goods which are internal to practices and the lack of which effectively prevents us from achieving any such goods."[166] We can apply his definitions to the practice of law in relation to the pursuit of the virtue of justice. Through the practice of law, the common good, which is the good
internal to the legal activity, is realized in the course of trying to achieve the
standards of justice that are appropriate to, and partially definitive of, the
practice of law, with the result that human powers to achieve the excellence
of the virtue of justice, and human conceptions of justice, are systematically extended. Justice is both constitutive of the practice of law and is at
the same time itself a practice. The practice of law becomes a virtue. The
relationship between law and justice advanced by classical natural law jurisprudence results in a very different understanding of a political community. The end of law is justice, the right ordering of members to each other,
and to and with the whole. Law has a purpose and justice has a purpose,
and those purposes are not just instrumental or facilitating. Law and justice do not aim at arranging an arena for any possible outcome. Their goal
is the fulfillment of their existential purpose, namely, cosmic justice, or
harmony with the eternal law. MacIntyre offers this succinct summary of
the difference between the classical view of the purpose of virtue (and
hence the purpose of law and justice) and the purpose of modern political
communities: "On this medieval view, as on the ancient, there is no room
for the modern liberal distinction between law and morality, and there is
no room for this because of what the medieval kingdom shares with the
polis, as Aristotle conceived it. Both are conceived as communities in which
men in company pursue the human good and not merely as—what the
modern liberal state takes itself to be—providing the arena in which each
individual seeks his or her own private good."[167]

Law and the moral virtue of justice are inextricably united components
of a shared human pursuit of a common end, the ultimate human good.
They are not merely rules of the game; they are in fact the game itself.

The Reality of the Art
(Not the Science) of Law

Unless the Lord build the house, they labour in vain that build it.
Unless the Lord keep the city, he watcheth in vain that keepeth it.[1]

THE NATURAL LAW IS A REAL LAW
THAT IS THE PRODUCT OF ART

Having made our tour through the various levels of the edifice of law, what can we say about natural law? First, we can conclude that it is really law. It is not in the form of title 3, chapter 12, subparagraph 4, and such. Rather, natural law is an ordered set of general principles of action that orient to the proper ends of human nature. The form of verbosely written rules with which we have become familiar of late is not essential to the definition of law. The reign of positivism has narrowed our understanding of law to arbitrary, detailed rules. For classical natural law jurists, detailed rules are certainly part of law, but only a part. Rules are a necessary but not a sufficient condition for law, in the fullest sense of the term. Wood, stone, and other raw materials are necessary but not sufficient to the building of a house. The role of rules within the structure of the law is analogous to the role assigned by Alasdair MacIntyre to rules within practices. As MacIntyre explains, one cannot engage in a practice like baseball without rules that must be obeyed.[2] Practices require more than simply obeying the applicable rules. A practice requires a *telos*, a real end that is the good of the practice internal to itself.[3] There is no point to the rules of baseball unless there is a point to playing the game. Likewise, law needs rules, precepts of varying specificity and generality. It also needs equally, or perhaps more, architecture. Those rules need to exist within an ordered edifice that begins and ends in its foundation. That edifice needs to have a purpose, an end toward which the rules are ordered. A collection of random and disjointed rules, even one purporting to operate as a coherent legal system, is not law if it is not incorporated into an architectural framework. As we have seen throughout this book, for classical natural law thinkers like Aquinas, law (*jus*) is much richer and broader than a set of rules. It is the idea or the exemplar of that which is always good, right, and equitable. The end of law is the just thing itself (*justum*). It is only within this more comprehensive context that Aquinas can define a law as a rule and measure.

With this understanding of *jus* in mind, *jus naturale*, natural law, is a real rule and measure of all willed human action. It is a rule because its principles are the exemplar of the proper end of human actions. It acts as a directing rule because its principles identify and elucidate the hierarchy of ends of our created nature, which are the good and right toward which our being tends as its perfection. In light of these ends, we can measure to what extent proposed courses of action are oriented toward, or in opposition to, one or more of those ends. As a rule, a principle such as "preserve human life" exists to guide our decision-making by giving us a goal or end to guide our actions. It serves to measure the advisability of a proposed course of action in light of the good embodied in it. Thus, if it is proposed that elderly people should be euthanized to save money for the healthcare system, this proposed rule does not measure up to the end of preservation of life.

Natural law has been promulgated by one having care for the common good of the community. In the case of natural law, "the community" is all of mankind. He who promulgated the natural law is the One with ultimate care for this community, its Creator. Natural law is concerned with the common good of that community, because its principles address the common ends (or good) of all members of that community, the human race. The natural law has really been promulgated by God through the eternal law being expressed in the recognition of the imprinted natural inclinations by the rational faculty of man. The eternal law that fixes the ends (or good) of mankind is made temporal and concrete in the rational mind of man to the extent the mind of man participates in this order by recognizing the imprint of eternal law. The natural law likewise is meant to imprint itself in the particular laws of political communities throughout time. In the words of Jean Porter, "The natural law is a temporal expression of the eternal law, as are all just (and therefore authentic) human laws."[4] Natural law is therefore not only analogous to law; it is really a species of law.

Throughout this book, we have considered the construction of a legal system to be analogous to the art of building a grand edifice. We have considered each part of the cosmological legal system as a component of a building project. The eternal law is the foundation; the natural law is the frame that rises out of the foundation. The divine law comprises direct instructions from the architect that correct inevitable errors in construction. Human laws more precisely define and decorate the general structure outlined by the frame of natural law within the footprint of the eternal law. Justice acts as the formal cause that orders all details of the building site and also the final cause toward which the construction is directed. Finally, we have considered the role and authority of human lawmakers who serve as foreman on the job site to implement the architectural plan contained within the eternal law in their corner of the edifice. Our consideration of law as the craft of architectural construction gives a new meaning to Aristotle's claim that "every good is the product of some art."[5] We can adapt his observation to our discussion to conclude that every law is the product of the art of lawmaking. All good laws are the product of the art of following the *exemplars* of the eternal law, which is the foundation of every art.

Law then is not, as Hans Kelsen hoped to make it, a science (in the modern sense of the term) but an art. The legal art is, in MacIntyre's language, a craft.[6] The practice of a craft involves the application of universals to particulars. An artist must do more than copy an *exemplar*. The artist must apply the *exemplar* to the particular matter and subject. A well-practiced art avoids both the extreme of acting solely in the realm of the ideal or the universal and the opposite extreme of becoming so mired in the details that the practice degenerates into casuistry. A master craftsman aims at the perfect balance between the universal and the particular. As MacIntyre explains of a craft: "Every craft is informed by some conception of a finally perfected work which serves as the shared *telos* of that craft. And what are actually produced as the best judgments or actions or objects so far are judged so because they stand in some determinate relationship to that *telos*, which furnishes them with their final cause."[7] This tension between the universal and the particular means that all crafts have two points of reference, that which is "good and best unqualifiedly" and "what is good and best for me . . . in my particular circumstances."[8] The two questions, and their answers, although distinct, are deeply related. That which is good for an individual at a given point in time is teleologically related to what is good and right unequivocally for all human beings.[9] Ultimate excellence in any craft is the rule that directs what is good for the apprentice in a particular circumstance and the measure of how his work compares to the telos. The perfection of the craftsman is in working with the matter of the here and now with all its material limitations toward the *telos* of the craft. For law, the *telos* is the eternal law within which we participate by coming to a better, meaning more specific, understanding of the precepts of natural law, and then determining their application to particular societal circumstances. What is good and right for a particular legal community is related to what is good and right for all human beings. The two cannot be in contradiction, even when the particular shape of a determination of the same general principle of natural law differs among particular communities. Unlike a sterile science of natural law that simply looks for impersonal abstract axioms of practical reason, the art of natural law works its craft between both of these poles: the ultimate excellence of the *telos* and the possible *telos* of the historically situated legal community. In the words of Father Dominic Bourmaud, the entire Christian tradition is a synthesis of a "fundamental realism" with a "spirit of all-conquering optimism."[10] The *telos*, the eternal law, provides the ultimate rule and measure for artisans of law to formulate rules and measures of real excellence in the here and now, which are participations in that excellence. Law is meant to rule and measure our progress toward a knowledge that is both speculative and practical—a knowledge of "the good and the best, both for human beings in general and for this specific kind of human being in these particular circumstances here and now."[11] The inseparability of the eternal and natural law from human laws is a direct result of the inseparability of speculative knowledge about the good as such and practical knowledge about the good to be pursued now. A craftsman acquires speculative knowledge about the craft through reflection upon the practical practice of the craft in such a way that the speculative reflection improves the practical results of the craft.

Finally, law seen as science (in the modern sense) depersonalizes the discipline. Whereas the work of (modern) science implies an outside observer who does not participate in that which he observes, a craftsman participates in making that which is brought forth. Mere observation becomes active creation; impersonal observation is transformed into personal participation. The loss of personal active participation and the rejection of the interdependence of speculative and practical knowledge are some of the ways in which jurisprudence has been impoverished by the desire to make it a mere science.

THE ART OF DERIVING LAW FROM THE NATURAL AND SUPERNATURAL ORDERS

Art Must Imitate Nature

If we can agree with Aristotle's observation that "art imitates nature,"[12] we can go further and conclude that the art of law must also imitate or be derived from nature. In chapters 3 and 4 we explored in depth the ways in which classical natural law jurisprudence derives principles of action from the consideration of the natural inclinations directed toward the perfection of human nature. Classical natural law jurisprudence is distinguished from both positivism and the "new" natural law theories on precisely this point. Both positivists and "new" natural law thinkers accept the critique of Hume that we cannot derive norms from reflection on human nature. Porter explains:

The widely influential "new natural law" theory developed by Germain Grisez and John Finnis . . . is explicitly distinguished from "old" natural law theories by the fact that it does not attempt to derive moral conclusions from observations about human nature. . . . They insist that moral conclusions cannot be derived from factual or metaphysical premises; in Finnis' words, "No value can be deduced *or otherwise inferred* from a fact or set of facts." Rather, according to them, the norms of natural law are derived from rational intuitions of basic human goods, which are self-evidently human goods.[13]

Although Finnis and Grisez may disagree with more liberal authors, such as Charles Curran, in their conclusions about particular rules, they do so from radically different principles and methods than those of classical ethicists and jurists. As Porter has observed, "Grisez and Finnis defend the moral teachings of the magisterium, including its prohibition against the use of contraceptives, but they do so on the basis of arguments that are very different from those set out by the magisterial documents themselves."[14] In fact, she rightly argues:

> There is more fundamental difference between the "new natural law" of Grisez and Finnis and the scholastic concept of the natural law that cannot be brought out simply by a comparison of relevant texts on the natural law and reason. That is, Grisez and Finnis share in the modern view that nature, understood in terms of whatever is pre- or non-rational, stands in contrast to reason. This is implied by their insistence that moral norms must be derived from reason alone: that is, from pure rational intuitions that are in no way dependent on empirical or metaphysical claims about the world. They insist on this point because they are persuaded by Hume's argument that moral claims cannot be derived from factual premises but, as a result, they are forced to deny the moral relevance of all those aspects of our humanity that we share with other animals. . . . No scholastic would interpret reason in such a way as to drive a wedge between the pre-rational aspects of our nature and rationality.[15]

Whereas Finnis and Grisez, like most post-Enlightenment thinkers, consider nature as something other than rational, that is, prerational, the classical thinkers understood nature to be inherently rational because it is the creation of a rational mind, the author of nature.

Ironically, notwithstanding the fact that Porter advocates some conclusions that no classical natural law jurist would have recognized as deductions from natural law,[16] her jurisprudential premises and methodology are more in continuity with the natural law tradition than that of Finnis and Grisez, who agree with the tradition in particular conclusions but reject its mode of reasoning. Porter fails to utilize the aid of divine law to constrain or correct her conclusions in applying the precepts of natural law regarding marriage. These failures in conclusion serve as poignant contemporary examples of the frailty of mere reliance on the natural law. Finnis's and Grisez's failure, on the other hand, is deeper in that they reject the very premises upon which their, albeit correct, conclusions rest. Yet, their admirable defense of Catholic doctrine on marriage unfortunately rests on grounds more resembling positivist thinking. Their conclusions flow from the indemonstrable goods that lack metaphysical and epistemological foundations. Their argument therefore only holds force with one who chooses to accept their posited goods.

Although classical natural law jurists reject Hume's refusal to reason from is to ought, they do not simply argue that every fact we meet in the world carries moral conclusions. As Porter explains, "Nature in the sense of sheer facticity is not incorporated into the scholastic concept of the natural law."[17] For the Scholastics, an observed fact in the natural world does not mechanically translate into a norm. "In order to be incorporated into the concept of the natural law, a given idea of nature has to carry connotations of order and intelligibility" because the Scholastics understood that the concept of natural included "the ordered totality of all creatures, and . . . the intrinsic characteristics of a given kind of creature."[18] Thus, facts encountered in the world must be evaluated in terms of whether they conform to this ordered totality that is reflected in the intrinsic characteristics of individual species that are in harmony with the cosmic order. Facts that do not harmonize with this interlocking universal and particular totality of order are facts representing departures from the natural law rather than support for its precepts. As we described in chapters 3 and 4, the epistemological process for natural law jurisprudence is therefore an interrelated deductive/inductive process. Universally observable intrinsic characteristics are used to formulate universal norms, while at the same time those universal norms are used to understand and interpret facts observed on the ground. Nature has a universal, cosmic connotation and a particular, intrinsic one. Natural law is therefore an expression of the order, intelligibility, and goodness of nature.[19] Scholastic jurists reason from the principle that man is a substance with an intelligible and discoverable fixed nature. The process of discovering the detailed characteristics of that nature involves reflecting not only on that universal nature but also on the customs and conventions which are reflections of that nature, but the degree to which any given custom or convention will be an accurate reflection (as opposed to a deviant one) will vary.[20] The art of law is therefore the process of ordering human communal life toward the natural order established by the eternal law. The more law reflects nature, understood in this sense, the more it attains its perfection.

Art also Imitates the Supernatural

For classical natural law jurists, natural law is not limited to, but rather transcends, nature. It is founded upon and participates in the supernatural. Pagan philosophers and jurists acknowledged the element of the divine in the law, even if they did not clearly understand the divine. From the Latin word *fas* to Cicero's vague concept of an eternal law, ancient writers acknowledged that although present in nature, natural law transcended it and touched the eternal. Christian philosophers and theologians could define more precisely the relationship between the natural and the supernatural. As Porter explains, for the Scholastics the term "natural" not only referred to "the human capacity for rational judgment, which gives rise to moral norms" but also to "God's will as revealed in Scripture, since the divine will certainly exists prior to all human enactments and provides their ultimate norm."[21] Aquinas understood the eternal law as that law which precedes the natural law and in a certain sense includes it. As we explained in chapters 2 and 3, natural law is for Aquinas a participation of human beings as rational creatures in the eternal law. The supernatural thus serves as a foundation for the natural.

Thus, some level of commitment to supernatural realities is inherent in a comprehensible jurisprudence of natural law. Although a commitment to all revealed truths will be more beneficial to the development of natural law jurisprudence, a minimal commitment (even a vague one, such as was held by ancient pagans) is indispensable. MacIntyre argues that the Socratic tradition (upon which classical natural law jurisprudence rests) insists that there must be a predialectical commitment to certain presuppositions. One must know the virtues before studying them.[22] Leo XIII argued that ultimately our ability to understand the natural, the temporal, was unsustainable without knowledge of the supernatural: "The things of earth cannot be understood or valued aright without taking into consideration the life to come, the life that will know no death. Exclude the idea of futurity, and forthwith the very notion of what is good and right would perish; nay, the whole scheme of the universe would become a dark and unfathomable mystery."[23]

A critical attribute for a jurist that is reinforced by this theological commitment is intellectual humility. When we accept that law is ultimately not our own creation, notwithstanding our contributions to its determination, we realize that any attempt to fully comprehend and contain "the law," whether in a self-contained scientific system like Kelsen's or a perfect codification like Bentham's, is unrealistic and impossible. With the acceptance of law's origin in God necessarily comes a recognition that any attempt to fully know and understand *jus* is futile. As Porter observes: "The scholastics remind us that we live in a world that we did not make, under the sovereignty of a Creator whose goodness we can trust but whose designs will always be to some extent opaque to us."[24]

In contrast to the classical commitment to the divine origins of law, MacIntyre describes the tradition running from Descartes that embodied "a declaration of independence by reason from the particular bonds of any particular moral and religious community."[25] Just as Descartes and his progeny strove to sever reason from theological precommitments, so too Austin, Hart, and Kelsen tried to sever law from any theological or moral precommitments. This Cartesian project also describes to a certain extent Finnis's "new" natural law, which aims in part to separate the claims of "practical reason" from the necessary claims about "D" and the eternal law that places Finnis's thought as a whole (even if not in most details) in a different tradition than that of Aristotle, Cicero, and Aquinas. I do not intend to suggest that Finnis or other "new" natural law scholars do not personally hold a commitment to theological truths or to the Catholic Faith.

They may hold to these truths, but they act as if they are practically irrelevant to jurisprudence, and certainly to legal practice. The result, intended or otherwise, is, in the words of Russell Hittinger, that "divine providence is stripped of the predicates of law [and we are left with] . . . , at best, . . . a creating but not a commanding God."[26] Ultimately, rejecting the supernatural produces an anthropomorphic sense of the law. Finnis's "new" natural law virtually eliminates the supernatural from his conception of the indemonstrable goods, which results, as Johnathan Crowe has observed, in a definition of the good that is exclusively focused on what is good for man. It ignores the other goodness in the universe, albeit goodness pursued at a different level.[27]

The rejection of the supernatural makes it difficult to remain committed to the teleological. As we have seen, modern jurisprudence is inextricably rooted in a rejection of a teleological reality. For one rejecting teleology, there are no final causes or purposes that we attain through a multiplicity of elected means. Since teleology requires purpose and a purpose can only be conceived in the mind of a rational being, then teleology requires a supernatural reality, a rational being that precedes the *telos* infused throughout the material world. Rejection of a supernatural reality leads to rejection of teleology, and, as Leo Strauss has noted, teleology is essential for classical jurisprudence: "Natural right in its classic form is connected with a teleological view of the universe. All natural beings have a natural end, a natural destiny, which determines what kind of operation is good for them."[28] Classical natural law jurisprudence is intellectually unsustainable without teleology, and teleology requires a being that is above teleological reality.

Once teleology is abandoned, explanations of the world in which we find ourselves, or purported "comprehensive doctrines," to use Rawls's phrase, become either products of history as shown by the historicist project[29] or tied to a rejection of anything other than the individual (as in the case of the approach of Max Weber).[30] Rejection of teleology thus leaves either historically contingent stories or disconnected individuals who share no common nature. The result in both cases is a rejection of the reality of any universal. There is only the historically contingent individual culture or the isolated individual. Classical jurisprudence does not offer in opposition to this rejection of universals a system of pure abstract universals or Platonic forms. The architecture of law includes universals, particular political societies, and individuals. The eternal, natural, and divine laws contain universal precepts that are determined by (1) human laws made by those who are entrusted with care of political communities and (2) human actions willed by rational individuals. We and our political communities meet the universals clothed in particular human laws, both beautifully reflective ones and in tattered and torn attire, but all human laws with varying degrees of perfection and imperfection are related to the universals of higher law.

Weber famously argued for value-free social science. The work of social scientists was with facts and their causes, not about the value of those facts and their causes. Facts and values were utterly heterogeneous.[31] Yet, Weber's heterogeneous conclusion overlooked a possible fact: *that values could themselves be facts.* Final causes are values that give meaning to choices, and if those final causes are real, then those final causes are facts. Final causes are facts that say something about how we should act. If the final cause of a knife is to cut, then it should be sharp. If the final cause of a rational creature is to attain knowledge of the truth about natural and supernatural realities, then we ought to act in a manner consistent with that cause. Final causes can be both facts and directive values. Weber's sharp distinction misses this important relation. If the classical argument is correct that final causes are facts contained in reality, then the rejection of these values and their supernatural origin is rejection of factual reality.

When we reject reality, we are faced with a void. The Enlightenment attempted to fill this void by inventing myths about the origin of law and society—the state of nature, the social contract, and so on. When supernatural realities are either unknown (pagan world) or rejected (modern world), we invent myths to take their place. The ancients developed a mythology reflecting human experience (since they had no direct knowledge of the supernatural itself). Modern pagans had to invent new myths to fill the void created by their rejection of the supernatural. Yet, these modern myths fall far short of the ancient ones at capturing reality. Ancient myths born of ignorance rather than rejection accepted the supernatural in principle, even when they could only express it inaccurately. Their inaccurate myths nonetheless reflected more accurately the human condition because the ancients understood that the human condition is connected to the supernatural. The classical mythology and worldview recognized that human beings have always existed within a legal and social framework by nature. The ancients understood that law and society are natural to man since man was placed within them by the gods of their myths. There can be no prelegal or presocial, because sociability and law are part of human nature. In contrast, the modern myths of the state of nature or the original position postulate man existing in not only a presocial but a prelegal world, but classical jurisprudence maintained that no prelegal man ever existed or could exist. The eternal law, being eternal, precedes the entire universe, including man. Even in a very simple state of organized civil society[32] lacking many positive laws, man is still subject to the eternal, natural, and divine laws. Cicero argued the same point more than two thousand years ago when he noted that Horatio's command to hold and destroy the bridge was not outside the law simply because no law yet existed requiring it, and that the rape of Lucretia was illegal, even though the law of the Romans had not yet declared it to be so:

> But in fact it should be understood that both this and other commands and prohibitions of peoples have a force for summoning to proper behavior and deterring from crime, a force which is not only older than the age of peoples and states but coeval with the god who protects and steers heaven and earth. It is not possible for there to be a divine mind without reason, nor does divine reason lack this force in sanctioning right and wrong. The fact that it was not written down anywhere that one man should stand on the bridge against all the forces of the enemy and order the bridge to be cut down behind him does not mean that we should not believe that the famous Horatius Cocles performed his great deed in accordance with the law and command of bravery; nor does the absence of a written law on sexual assault during the reign of Lucius Tarquinius mean that the violence which Sextus Tarquinius brought against Lucretia the daughter of Tricipitinus was not contrary to the eternal law. Reason existed, derived from nature, directing people to good conduct and away from crime; it did not begin to be a law only at that moment when it was written down, but when it came into being; and it came into being at the same time as the divine mind.[33]

Cicero understood that no prelegal state of nature existed prior to the founding of cities and the growth of civilizations. The state of nature is a legal and organized state existing directly under the eternal and natural law.

Rejection of a fundamental law to which man is subject from the very beginning of existence has a significant consequence. When a directing law precedes man, he is subject to that law, and he is oriented to the future, to an end or goal—living in conformity with the law that precedes him. Looking back to the origin directs man to the end. Yet, if man precedes law in the order of being, man is oriented not to the end but to the beginning. Law is subject to man. All of man's actions, including making law, must be measured not by the end identified by the antecedent law but rather by man's beginning. The presocial, prerational, and prelegal mythic state of nature becomes the guiding rule and measure rather than the end provided by the antecedent eternal law. As Strauss observed, the consequence of Rousseau's state of nature is that "civil society must therefore be transcended in the direction not of man's highest end but of his beginning, of his earliest past."[34]

Unfortunately, by accepting the Enlightenment's dichotomy between prerational nature and rationality, Finnis is forced to abandon teleology and therefore a satisfactory explanation for why the indemonstrable goods exist at all and how we can come to know them rationally.

On the other hand, what can be said about jurists like Michael S. Moore who remain committed to moral realism while overtly rejecting a supernatural source of that reality (whereas Finnis does not reject but rather marginalizes it)? Although Moore in some ways admirably defends the reality that exists, he ends up standing on shaky metaphysical and epistemological ground. It is possible for someone like Moore to accept moral reality notwithstanding his rejection of its first cause because the moral reality does in fact exist. Moore can defend its existence but has no satisfactory answer to the questions of how and why it exists. Like the inhabitants of Plato's Cave, he can admit the reality of the shadows without admitting their cause. Classical natural law jurists can reach a certain level of agreement with moral realists like Moore, at least on what exists. That is not to say that agreement on all details of that objective reality would be possible. Yet, agreement on the underlying metaphysical reality is not possible.

Further, disagreements are more likely because Moore cuts himself off from the aid of the divine law. There is no external epistemological guarantor of the general precepts of natural law. Moore is forced to downplay the obvious epistemological failures that have occurred throughout history when man rejects this supernatural aid. We often fail to properly know and abide by natural law precepts when we lack recourse to the divine law. As we argued in chapter 5, without divine assistance we will continue to fail in our search for knowledge of natural law. Certainly the "wise" atheist can attain high levels of knowledge of the natural law (as did the wise pagans), yet all epistemological failures cannot be solved solely on our own. We need recourse to the precepts of the divine law. As general precepts, they may not in practice immediately correct errors of detail in secondary conclusions, but they can serve as large signposts when laws or legal systems stray from basic primary precepts. They are like out-of-bounds markers on a playing field that mark when some errors of reasoning lead us out of legal bounds. Out-of-bounds markers will not identify all penalties committed in a game, but they will point out when players leave the field. By rejecting this role of divine law, a scholar such as Moore forsakes this safeguard. As a result, rather than admitting the real challenges to moral reasoning, Moore is forced to act as if there were no serious epistemological challenges. Toward the end of his argument that God is unnecessary to moral reasoning about the good, he states: "The plain fact of the matter is that morality is not so epistemically elusive. If we sometimes face intractable moral dilemmas, we as often face easy moral decisions."[35] History is littered with examples in which civilizations (some that in many respects understood aspects of the natural law and achieved in certain areas a high level of virtue) developed gravely unjust practices and enshrined them in their laws. Slavery (both in the ancient and modern world) and racial genocide in the twentieth century are but illustrative examples. It is precisely in times of crisis when tyranny threatens that we will feel the legal ground give way beneath us, unless the legal protections against tyranny are grounded in more than natural human faculties. These are times in which the need for divine law is greatest. Josef Pieper lived through one of those times in history, Nazi tyranny. His experience led him to observe that although we can get by without plumbing the metaphysical depths of justice in times of relative peace and stability (when the willed positive law is relatively benign), we cannot afford such omission when tyranny threatens:

For how can human nature be the *ultimate* basis when it is not founded upon itself! At this point we could certainly break off any further delving into the depth. In "moderate" periods, in fact, there would be nothing against it. When the most far-reaching denials of justice take the stage, however, it is no longer enough to go back only to penultimate roots. If man is treated as though simply nothing were due to him as his right, as a *suum* . . . at such a time mere reference to the person's freedom and to human rights will obviously not carry us very far. . . . Something must be said of the deepest roots of such rights. . . . We must learn to experience as reality the knowledge that the establishment of right and justice has not received its fullest and most valid legitimation until we have gone back to the absolute foundation.[36]

Moore's atheism prevents him from reaching those roots and that will make his jurisprudence most in danger in such times of crisis.

Because of the consequences of the Fall (wounds Moore ignores), we labor under the difficulty of seeing our natural inclinations through the shadows of other instincts and affections. The merciful lawgiver has provided an additional illumination—revealed divine law. Although in theory unnecessary for the discovery of the ends of man and the precepts that are proximate conclusions from them, in reality the divine law provides an invaluable aid in avoiding the confusion of the natural inclinations with other instincts and affections. Hittinger has aptly referred to the aid of the divine law as the "tutor of divine revelation," which makes the inferences from the naturally known "rudiments of the moral measures of action . . . easier and clearer."[37] Using the analogy of the tutor, one can learn a discipline, such as a foreign language, solely by the application of one's mind to the matter of the subject. Yet, practically one has a greater likelihood of success by humbly supplementing one's own abilities with an expert tutor, especially a native speaker. Moore not only denies the existence of the divine tutor (who is the only native speaker of the language of law), but by so doing he is also forced to act as if the tutor's aid is unnecessary.

Finally, natural law without theological presuppositions cannot provide a complete justification for an obligation to obey the law, natural or human. Natural law rests on the foundation of the eternal law. The natural inclinations toward the good (or ends of men) bind us to rule our decisions in light of them because those natural inclinations have been fixed and promulgated through the eternal law. Unless there is a universal eternal command, human law cannot be obligatory. Authority to bind in conscience can only come from above; as Aquinas states, "If they [laws] be just, they have the power of binding in conscience, from the eternal law whence they are derived."[38] Attempts to ground the obligation to obey the law in consent or utility fail to prove the existence of true authority and its correlative obedience to lawful commands. Moore might sense from observation that it is good to obey the law, but he cannot prove an obligation to obey the law that precedes human beings.

Notwithstanding the metaphysical and epistemological challenges facing an atheist committed to a natural law jurisprudence, since the rational nature of man means that an atheist cannot, in a certain sense, help but participate in the eternal law (by being rational), even a staunch atheist can make some proper use of his innate rationality. The denial of God's existence may impede the ability to observe and consider our natural inclinations, but it does not obliterate them. *Synderesis* still operates in the soul of the atheist. The obligatory nature of natural law is connected to the process of the rational participation in the eternal law, the attempt to conform the order of our mind to the order of its reality. We cannot help but participate in the eternal law as it is imprinted in our very being. We can participate well or poorly, but our rational nature makes us inextricably bound to the natural law. Moore is deeply committed to an objective real moral universe even though he denies the existence of its author.[39] Moore is left to confront directly the objective reality of natural law. He cannot explain whence this objective reality came. He can merely assert its existence without metaphysical explanation of its origin. He cannot answer the age-old question summarized by Finnis: "What makes it *obligatory* to choose the right and the due and to avoid the wrong and the undue?"[40] Moore recognizes that right and wrong exist but cannot explain why we are obligated to do them other than that is the way things are in reality. He is correct in that observation, but surely there must be a more satisfactory answer than such unexplained realism. He also lacks recourse to the Architect's designs. His natural law reasoning is unaided and thus more susceptible to error. Yet, even if he refuses to turn around and see the source of the shadows in Plato's Cave, he is still able to consider what the shadows, as shadows, mean.

He may deny that there is a light causing them, yet he sees them nonetheless. Because they are only shadows, and he refuses to look to their origin for aid, he may make many mistakes in his use of reason, but he is nonetheless participating in the eternal law. As the works of Aristotle demonstrate, even without revelation or a clear articulated understanding of eternal law, human rationality can arrive at certain precepts and conclusions of the natural law. As scripture affirms, the natural law is available to all (even those who have not heard the specific promulgation of the divine law). St. Paul says, "For when the Gentiles, who have not the law, do by nature those things that are of the law; these having not the law are a law to themselves: Who shew the work of the law written in their hearts, their conscience bearing witness to them."[41] The law written on the heart (synderesis) is the starting point of all reasoning. This is because all rationality begins with what is known naturally. As Aquinas explains in the beginning of his treatment of the topic of laws in the *Summa Theologica*: "Every act of reason and will in us is based on that which is according to nature . . . for every act of reasoning is based on principles that are known naturally. . . . Accordingly the first direction of our acts to their end must needs be in virtue of the natural law."[42] Men begin reasoning by examining what is known naturally. They can begin to participate in the eternal law without realizing they are doing so. When they do so, they are making use of the natural law even if not knowing it as such. To a point, natural law advocates can engage all people in discussion of the natural law, particularly at the level of its most basic principles that are *per se nota*. Since they can be known in themselves, there is hope that once explained people will accept them. We can attempt to demonstrate their validity from that which is known naturally. Yet, as Aquinas emphasizes, this step is only the "first direction" on which the use of reason is "based." Ultimately, contemplating the order that is known naturally will lead to questions of origin. Some knowledge of God is accessible to the mind even without the supernatural aid of grace. Participating in a reasonable inquiry based on what is known naturally will, naturally, lead to the eternal law since it is none other than a participation in it. Thus, we may begin discussion of natural law with nonbelievers without explicit incorporation of truths about God, but it is unnatural to think the entire exercise can proceed without reaching eventually that in which we are participating.

Likewise, it will be impossible to descend to the level of making particular determinations while leaving the divine law as an ignored elephant in a corner. One practicing natural law without the ultimate Aristotelian "wise man" is more likely to fall into errors in deducing remote principles and determining particular contingent matters. The war between the actual impulses and the diminished natural inclinations is arduous and prone to failure. Aristotle, who knew not the divine law, recognized that making determinations of practical reason is hard work. Judgments of practical reason are imperfect, and we should turn to the wise for guidance. Having access to the divine law does not guarantee universal infallibility in exercising practical reason, but it increases our chances of success. The law of liberty leaves much discretion to human agents; the divine law is not a Rosetta Stone for deciphering all of the particular determinations necessitated by the natural law. It is, however, an aid, a tutor. We can conclude that those who have access to the tutor will likely do better (on balance but not always) in arriving at correct conclusions and determinations than those without one. As Aristotle's accomplishments prove, it is possible to reach many objectively true conclusions about the contents of the natural law without the divine law, but it is certainly more difficult, requiring the discipline and ability of a great mind like Aristotle's. The world is not populated by Aristotles! For Aquinas, "Natural reason itself creates a presumption in favor of the divine law, which completes or perfects the natural law."[43] If one wishes to succeed in the work of coming to know and act according to natural law, he must come face-to-face with the divine law. It is this realization that led Aquinas to understand that "natural law is practically inseparable not only from natural theology . . . but even from revealed theology."[44] We can conclude, at a minimum, that those ignorant of or rejecting the revealed divine law are more likely to confuse impulses for inclinations and more likely to derive false secondary principles from general principles. They labor without a significant check on their work. To lead one to the practice of natural law without divine law is to purposefully lead one to imperfection rather than perfection. It may be a tactical decision (ruled by prudence) at which point in time to introduce this tutor into a debate, but a decision to exclude Him permanently and entirely is doomed to failure.

What then are we to make of theistic natural law thinkers who want to leave God and the eternal and divine law out of the discussion? The nonbeliever is laboring to use natural law to the best of his ability given his more limited resources, but why would those aware of the eternal law and the divine law choose to ignore them? Why would one choose to construct an entire theory of natural law detached from these critical elements entirely? It is one thing to neglect building natural law on the foundation of the eternal law or failing to prune one's conclusions in light of the divine law because one is ignorant, perhaps even willfully, of their very existence. It is quite another matter to know of and believe in their existence but consciously exclude them. It is bad enough for Grotius to impiously speculate that if God didn't exist, would natural law still bind? It is quite another to affirm God does exist but then carry on theorizing about natural law as if he did not. To submit to the authority of the order of God's idea of the created universe on the one hand but treat such submission as irrelevant to rational thought on the other is like having "Cartesian minds somehow under church discipline," in the words of Hittinger.[45] Such a compromise is doomed to failure, for as Harold Berman observed, "At the highest level, surely, the just and the holy are one, and our sense of each rests partly on our sense of the other. It is necessary to say this because conventional wisdom has separated them to the point of disaster."[46] He argues that when law is "divorced" from religion, "law tends to degenerate into legalism."[47] Since the Enlightenment, we have seen that once the foundation of natural law is discarded, natural law itself will crumble, leaving only human laws. This legalism means that law is subject to no other rule or measure than that which it makes for itself. This is what the Enlightenment's separation of faith and reason produced, the legal positivism of John Austin, John Stuart Mill, and H. L. A. Hart. Natural law without God (either the Finnis or Moore version), although capable of stumbling upon individual truths along the way, ultimately is building a house on no foundation. As J. Budziszewski remarks: "That was the Enlightenment's project. Little by little, natural law thinkers scrubbed from their little cups of theory whatever grime of influence might have remained from the centuries of faith, whatever benefit they might have gained from the teacher's help. . . . In the end they found that they had scoured away the ground that they were standing on."[48]

To avoid such a collapse, natural law theory needs to be firmly rooted within the context of the entire system of which it is a part. This does not mean that every argument regarding a particular contingent matter needs to reference explicitly the divine law or the eternal law. Yet, to avoid ultimate collapse at the theoretical level, defense and exposition of natural law must rest explicitly on an understanding of the foundational role of eternal law and incorporate to some extent the tutorial and corrective role of divine law. In response to Grotius, it is utterly pointless to speculate about whether natural law might be obligatory even if God did not exist, because what we do know is that without Him using natural law to determine human action and attain even our natural end is doomed to ultimate failure. As Aquinas understood, divine assistance is not only necessary for our supernatural end, but we also cannot achieve even our natural end "without divine assistance."[49]

As recently as 1993, the Catholic Church rejected this disembodied natural law—rooted in Cartesian rationalism under some guise of Catholic authority—when John Paul II restated the traditional understanding of the foundation of natural law:

> Some people, . . . disregarding the dependence of human reason on Divine Wisdom and the need, given the present state of fallen nature, for Divine Revelation as an effective means for knowing moral truths, even those of the natural order, have actually posited a *complete sovereignty of reason* in the domain of moral norms regarding the right orderings of life in this world. . . . In no way could God be considered the Author of this law. . . . These trends of thought have led to a denial, in opposition to Sacred Scripture (cf. Matt. 15:3–6) and the Church's constant teaching, of the fact that the natural moral law has God as its author, and that man, by the use of reason, participates in the eternal law, which it is not for him to establish. . . . No one can fail to see that such an interpretation of the autonomy of human reason involves positions incompatible with Catholic teaching.[50]

It is time to rebuild the ruined fragments of the architecture of law. This rebuilding will require that we acknowledge both the natural and supernatural components of the edifice. As Jeremiah Newman argues, the classical pagans and the Christian thinkers were agreed on the indispensability of both, even if they disagreed on the ontological ordering of the two. For Aristotle, law is primarily human (but he acknowledges a divine foundation), but for Aquinas, law is primarily divine and secondarily human.[51] For Aquinas, "Human law was but a participation in the divine law."[52] When Aquinas considers legal justice as the virtue that directs all virtuous acts to the common good by obeying law, "the law in question is not confined to state law . . . but signifies primarily the divine law of the City of God."[53]

The Refutation of Hart's Separation of Law and Morality

The foregoing understanding of law as art and not science, and the inseparability of the natural and the supernatural, permits us to return to another topic raised at the beginning of this book: Hart's argument that law must be separated not only from the supernatural but also from morality. Art requires the harmony of the parts within the whole. Severing morality from law is akin to removing a wall from a cathedral.

In *The Concept of Law*, Hart presents four arguments for the separation of law from morality.[54] We can now demonstrate how classical natural law jurisprudence refutes these arguments and maintains the argument that law and personal morality are parts of the same normative system.

First, Hart argues that morality is always about important things. Legal rules can be concerned with important things, and in those cases he admits to some overlap between moral rules and laws. Yet, unlike morality, he argues law does not necessarily have to be about important things; many laws concern insignificant or minor details.[55] But this distinction is not true. Both morality and law provide norms for a range of activity that varies in gravity. Both law and morality share an equal gravity in that they both require making particular determinations of the precepts of natural law. They are parts of the same normative system distinguished not by gravity of actions but by the identity and role of the one charged with making particular determinations: individuals, personal superiors, or political authorities. The actions to be determined by individuals or personal superiors may range in gravity depending upon the degree to which the contemplated action orients or disorients the actor from the ultimate good. Raising one's voice in anger would be less grave of a moral offense than physically striking in anger. Stealing a pencil would most likely be less important in its circumstances and effects than stealing a starving person's last loaf of bread. Like law, morality deals with both grave and less serious actions.

Further, we might be able to argue, *contra* Hart, that since laws by definition affect the common good, as opposed to the personal good, laws, even about small matters, are always about more important matters than moral determinations. Legal authorities are entrusted with the power to make determinations that transcend individual goods and affect the common good and thus the scope of matters dealt with by laws is broader than morality. In any event, Hart's argument fails to separate them into different normative systems on the basis of gravity.

Second, Hart argues that morality is immutable, but laws can be changed.[56] Hart again fails to see the proper distinction between primary and secondary deductions from natural law and determinations of natural law. The principles of natural law are immutable since they are expressions of aspects of immutable human nature, which has been legislated in the eternal law. The primary precepts of natural law, being a participation in a law that is eternal, are, by definition, immutable. As we discussed in chapter 4, more remote deductions from primary principles and determinations of natural law precepts for particular circumstances are subject to change. Both moral and legal determinations are based on the same unchanging principles of natural law, but particular moral and legal rules are subject to change depending upon circumstances (but the nature of any change is always constrained within the bounds of the immutable principles). Intrinsically evil actions are always intrinsically evil, and no moral or legal determinations have the power to alter their character. Yet, many actions are not intrinsically good or evil, and therefore rules relating to those actions, and the moral or legal character of them, are subject to change depending upon the context. Hart claims that one cannot say from January 1 it becomes immoral to do so and so, but one can say from January 1 it becomes illegal to do so and so.[57] As we have seen in the example of returning a borrowed sword to a madman, it would be immoral to refuse to return it to its owner in general, but not in the case of its owner going mad and posing a danger to himself or others. Thus remote conclusions and determinations of both law and morality are subject to change, whereas the primary principles of natural law, on which both law and morality are based, are not. Moreover, since Hart does not fully understand the moral obligation to obey just laws (as we explained in chapter 7), he cannot see that if a government determines that from January 1 motorists must drive on the left side of the road instead of the right, then one can say as of January 1 it becomes both illegal and immoral to drive on the right side of the road.

Third, Hart attempts to distinguish law and morality on the basis of the voluntary character of moral norms. Hart attempts to argue that morality always takes into account mental states and other circumstances so that moral failures must always be voluntary to be failures; however, law does not always take into account subjective mental states and circumstances to determine legal consequences.[58] In short, Hart seems to be arguing that moral analysis necessarily must always take into account internal subjective factors; law typically does not, but sometimes may (as in the case of *mens rea* for most criminal offenses). Hart's analysis seems to be dictated by his commitment to the division between law and morality, and so he fails to recognize that law and morality are not distinguishable on this basis: both moral and legal analysis have objective and subjective levels of analysis. Acts must be judged objectively as good or evil, or legal or illegal, and the actor's moral or legal responsibility or culpability for acts must also be judged. Moral analysis requires that any given action be evaluated objectively: Was the act intrinsically evil? Or, if a neutral act, evil under the circumstances? The answer to the first question is not reliant upon the next subjective question. Even for intrinsically evil actions, an individual's culpability or responsibility for performing the action will vary in degree from none to complete, depending on the extent to which he performed the act with full knowledge and consent of the will. One can conclude that lying is intrinsically evil since it is directly disoriented to the natural inclination to know the truth. Yet, in a particular circumstance, one might conclude that a person bears little or no culpability for the moral failing, due either to invincible ignorance or a volitional impairment, such as grave fear. However, this determination of subjective responsibility does not change the fact that the action was contrary to the natural law. Likewise, the law in all areas, not simply criminal law, looks to the objective acts and the degree of culpability or liability. The law may conclude that a person breached a contractual promise yet excuse liability because it was impossible to perform that promise in the particular circumstances. Hart is wrong when he argues that the "ought" of morality always requires that the actor must not be able to say, "I could not help it," but "legal responsibility is not necessarily excluded by the demonstration."[59] The excuse of impossibility is a prime example in which "I could not help it" relieves the contractual promisor of liability for the failure. Morality and law are concerned with both questions: (1) Is the act contrary to either morality or law? and (2) Is the actor liable or culpable for it?

Finally, Hart argues that the pressure to conform to law lies in the threat of physical or other harm, but for morality it is the appeal to the rightness of the rule itself, in other words, an appeal to conscience.[60] Again, Hart's purported distinction is a product of his failure to see that all valid laws bind in conscience. We are obligated to obey moral and legal determinations because they both are particular determinations of natural law. When a purported law fails in its essence, it fails to bind in conscience resulting in no binding obligation. We are bound to obey the determinations made by a personal superior or political authority to the same extent we are bound to obey moral determinations we make ourselves. The same obligation to obey moral and legal determinations rests on the same natural and eternal law. The only distinction is the identity of the person making the determination. Both law and morality bind in conscience. Further, even though some of the harmful consequences of breaking the law and breaking moral determinations can vary, the most important consequence flowing from both failures is the same. Law and moral norms direct human beings toward their natural end; they orient rational creatures to perfect their natural inclinations. A failure to obey either one constitutes a rejection, to some extent, of the end or good for which we exist. One may result in punishment, another only in shame or guilt, yet both result in a disorientation away from the good or end of being.

Ultimately, Hart's attempt to divide morality and law into two normative systems fails because his concept of law fails to reflect the ontological reality of law. He studies merely the decorations on the cathedral and believes he can understand them without reference to the entire edifice. He fails to see the foundation upon which the architectural frame and the decorations it contains rest, the eternal law.

LAW AS POWER POLITICS

The rejection of classical natural law jurisprudence not only leads to epistemological and metaphysical problems for "new" natural law theories and agnostic moral realism, but it also leads to the volitional failures of legal positivism. By design, the architecture of law with its various layers of law acts as a restraint on the human will.

The architecture of law is founded upon the eternal law, which law includes a comprehensible end or purpose of man. The elimination of the foundation by modern jurisprudence (be that legal positivism, "new" natural law, or agnostic moral realism) ultimately results in the transformation of law into a mere product of pure human will unrestrained by any universal account of the "good life," and hence a potentially arbitrary product. The lack of a comprehended end reinforces this rule of will by reversing the order of precedence. The first element of Aquinas's definition of law is an ordinance of reason. Law through the requirement of promulgation involves an act of the will, yet reason must precede the act of the will. Jurisprudence is the art of applying reason to the willed law. Reason is used to explain and interpret the willed law. The premodern notion placed reason before the willing of the law. Law is a willed ordinance of reason. "To speak the laws," "jurisdiction" (*juris dicere*), required one to come to know the law first before uttering it. Strauss explained the effects of this shift exemplified in the jurisprudence of Hobbes through a transformation of classical Epicureanism: "Hobbes's transformation of Epicureanism implied the liberation of the individual not only from all social bonds which do not originate in his will but also from any natural end. Rejecting the notion of a natural end of a man, he no longer understood by the 'good life' of the individual his compliance with, or assimilation to, a universal pattern which is apprehended before it is willed."[61]

Once law becomes disconnected from an objective end known by reason, it becomes subject to transient opinions. Lawmaking merely becomes the process of using power to give free reign to the will. As Cicero argued:

If the will of the people, the decrees of the senate, the adjudications of magistrates, were sufficient to establish justice, the only question would be how . . . to win over the votes of the majority, in order that corruption and spoliation, and the falsification of wills, should become lawful. But if the opinions and suffrages of foolish men had sufficient weight to outbalance the nature of things, might they not determine among them, that what is essentially bad and pernicious should henceforth pass for good and beneficial? Or why should not a law able to enforce injustice, take the place of equity? Would not this same law be able to change evil into good, and good into evil?[62]

For Cicero, the rejection of a natural law, and therefore a rational order and purpose in nature, leads to irrationality because justice must have a foundation in nature (which for Cicero is connected to reason since nature is a rational order) or it will rest solely on the changing desires of people: "Now we must entirely take leave of our senses, ere we can suppose that law and justice have no foundation in nature, and rely merely on the transient opinions of men."[63] For pre-Christians such as Cicero, natural reason was the check on unrestrained (and therefore by definition irrational) willful action. The Christian tradition adds a greater restraint (greater because it is external)—divine revelation. Yet, law is not simply a dictation of precepts from God. He requires human rational participation in the making of law. The purely conventional is a legitimate component of law. Yet, this conventional aspect of law, according to the classical Christian jurisprudential perspective, is restrained by both natural reason and divine revelation (which is nothing other than divine reason). As Porter explains, civilians and also canonists and theologians accepted that some institutions like property are basically conventional but are constrained by the natural law.[64] The principles of the Ten Commandments are binding in all societies, constraining institutions and conventions.[65] The human choice of conventions is a constrained choice.

As a result of rejecting the constraints of natural reason and divine revelation, modern politics and lawmaking have become, in the words of MacIntyre, "civil war carried on by other means."[66] Harold Berman observed that we have come to understand law simply as the "instrument for effectuating the policies of those who are in control,"[67] those who win this civil war. In so doing, "we deprive [law] of its capacity to do justice and possibly even its capacity to survive."[68] Law, rather than being a handmaid of justice, has become, at best, a mere peacekeeping force in the midst of this civil war. As MacIntyre points out, one central role of the Supreme Court of the United States in recent times has been to treat the rival and incommensurable moral, philosophical, and juridical systems fairly in their interminable conflict through the law.[69] Rather than existing as an alternative method of settling disputes justly, the law has become an arena that breeds conflict, which can at best hope to maintain an uneasy cease-fire. Having leveled the architecture of law, the field for interminable civil war is left bare. Berman worried that the consequences of divorcing law from faith and reason, leaving pure power, would ultimately destroy law itself: "The idea that law is wholly existential, wholly relative to circumstances of time and place, that it cannot be measured by standards of truth or of rightness but only by standards of workability . . . is . . . self-defeating."[70] Such purely pragmatic theories cause law to "lack the credibility upon which observance of law ultimately depends."[71]

Having jettisoned the foundation and framework constraining the civil war of all against all in this legal arena, Hart's gunman has been unleashed. As Strauss observed, what distinguished the classical notion of a city, ruled by law, was that it restrained and contained mere battles of the will: "The city is essentially different from a gang of robbers because it is not merely an organ, or an expression, of collective selfishness."[72] Once the final and formal causes of law are removed, law becomes merely an organ of collective selfishness. When we believe law to be an ordinance of reason directing the city toward the common good, then law has an end outside itself, a purpose other than itself. What Hart failed to realize is that what distinguishes the command of the gunman from law is a higher end, the common good. To be law and not the command of a gunman, the law must be directed to that higher end, and law therefore has a necessary element outside itself, outside Hart's closed legal system terminating in its own internal Rule of Recognition.

Without an external limit, law can be whatever the strongest, the loudest, the most powerful, or the majority will it to be. Contemporary politics are the result of the leveling of the architecture. As Newman argued: "Positivism has ended in bankruptcy. Following its teaching States have been declaring whatever they wish to be law, the only limit to their arbitrary legislation being that of their actual power to give force to its will."[73]

Higher laws, natural and divine, do not merely constrain from the outside this potential for unbridled violence in making human law. They do so as part of an integrated system. Unlike Hart, who sees law and what he calls morality as different normative systems, the precepts of natural and divine law are parts of the same system. As Newman explains, "They [civil, natural, and divine law] are not three separate systems independent of one another; rather they are related as are three concentric circles. The goals are subordinate one to another, the ultimate goal being that of the City of God and the others but intermediaries. The laws too are contained in one another, civil law within the natural and the natural within the divine."[74] Classical natural law jurisprudence thus maintains a nuanced understanding of the relationship among these different types of laws. The proper understanding of hierarchy discussed throughout this book rejects the simplistic notion of higher law negating lower law. Natural, divine, and human-made law all interact with each other to produce just laws. Natural law precepts are not simply abstract axioms from which further precepts can be deduced through disembodied rationalism. Likewise, laws cannot be made simply by inductive reasoning from the facts on the ground. Laws must be made in a dialectical process that relies upon deductive and inductive reasoning. Porter succinctly explains this tension inherent in natural law jurisprudence, both of civil and canon law lawyers, when she explains how their jurisprudence lies between self-executing general precepts and detailed conventional enactments: "The canonists and theologians do consider the natural law to have direct moral and social implications, even in human society as it now exists. It is true that for them, as well as for the civilians, the natural law must be expressed through human conventions in order to have practical force in the present historical order. Nonetheless, they also believe that the natural law places definitive moral constraints on the legitimate forms of institutional life, and repeatedly they attempt to say what those restraints are."[75]

Understanding the process of natural law reasoning returns an important balance to the process of thinking about the making of human laws. After centuries of legal positivism, lawmaking is generally associated with an act of the will—a law is a law because it has been willed by the applicable legislator. The vision of natural law articulated in this book places a striking emphasis on the intellectual capacity of the soul. The participation of natural law requires the intellectual acts of (1) discerning amidst the shadows of impulses the natural inclinations, (2) identifying the ends to which they tend, and (3) drawing correct conclusions from them. Clearly, natural law involves volition; its first precept is that "good must be done." As an aspect of practical reason, natural law jurisprudence is oriented ultimately toward action, not knowledge for its own sake. Yet, complying with "do good" presupposes an intellectual activity of discerning what is good or what is an end. The actions that may be chosen are necessarily limited by that knowledge of the end. Natural inclinations do not point to any end but "to its proper act and end" (*ad debitum actum et finem*).[76] The process is analogous to the act of building a house, which presupposes knowledge about what properly constitutes a house. Loss of attention to the intellectual prerequisite to the process of lawmaking has resulted in a philosophy and a legal system rooted in power manipulation and coalition forming. In modern times, a law can be shown to be rational simply because it is internally consistent, even if it is disoriented to an improper end chosen by the will of the legislator, or the will of those he "represents." Natural law jurisprudence requires demonstrating not only internal consistency but also that the end of the law is oriented to a proper end.

This jurisprudence simultaneously exalts and restrains human-made laws. It ennobles the art of making laws while it restrains it within proper ends. The result affects the governed and the governing. When human-made laws are determined well from the principles of the natural law, they resonate with the imprint of eternal law on the rational nature of man and bind in conscience; they are seen as "legal laws" facilitating the *jus* of each individual and the common good of the community. Yet, when we are keenly aware not only of this great promise of natural law but also the many difficulties and errors that plague the proper determinations of contingent matters, we can adopt a more realistic expectation for the success of human lawmaking. Laws no longer being written by God himself in the liberty of the new dispensation, we can admit from the outset that human laws cannot attain universal perfection in their determinations. Thus imperfection does not equate with unjust and invalid. Some poorly written laws can still bind us in conscience so long as they do not compel violation of higher law. As Aquinas would say, any human law will not be able to hold true in all cases but it will, at its best, in the majority of cases.

There is thus no need for scandal when we find that a particular human law misses the mark. Since human law is only one part of the universe of law, the inevitable gaps in human law's ability to universally perfect the measure of its rule are naturally filled by the principles of natural law and supplemented by divine law, which allow equity to be done when human laws are found wanting. The gates of the city can be opened, notwithstanding the failure of the law of the city to provide for doing so when the defenders are being pursued.

Such a balance of grandness and humility serves as a check to unrestrained idealism (or ideology), pure utilitarianism, and a revolutionary spirit. An understanding of the place of human law within the framework of eternal, natural, and divine law gives men the confidence to resist unjust laws as no law at all when necessary, but also the restraint not to see all failings of human law as perversions of law and not binding in conscience. In a time when so many of our laws fail to exhibit a clear derivation from the natural law, this latter temptation becomes great.

Classical jurisprudence restrained the will of the legislator in a three-dimensional edifice. John Dickinson in his introduction to the classic Catholic treatment of political philosophy, *The Statesman's Book of John of Salisbury*, describes the former Catholic worldview:

> It has become a historical commonplace that mediaeval thought was dominated by the conception of a body of law existing independently of the authority of any government and to which all positive law must conform and to which governments no less than individuals owed obedience. Rulers were thought of as bound by a "higher law" . . . which accordingly made it possible to apply to their acts the criterion of legality or illegality. In the words of the *Policraticus*, "between a tyrant and the true prince there is this single or chief difference, that the latter obeys the law and rules the people by its dictates." "A tyrant is one who oppresses the people by rulership based upon force while he who rules in accordance with the laws is a prince." "There are certain precepts of the law which have a perpetual necessity, having the force of law among all nations. . . . And not only do I withdraw from the hands of rulers the power of dispensing with the law, but in my opinion those laws which carry a perpetual injunction are not subject at all to their pleasure."[77]

The failed project of modernity has been, in the words of Rémi Brague, to reduce "the idea of law to a purely human phenomenon."[78] Law has become one-dimensional. In this book I have argued for its restoration on a three-dimensional plane. Three dimensions create more complexity and stress on the system. Such tensions restrain men from losing focus on the ultimate point of all law, that which is good, right, equitable—the just thing itself. As Ana Marta González states: "What appears from these tensions is not simply a programme for reform or for revolution, but an attempt to do justice to the truth of man himself, with all his paradoxes and tensions."[79]

Ultimately, a complete understanding of natural law avoids the error of merely trying to beat positivists at their own game and thus in practice becoming positivists ourselves. If we merely seize the will of the prince (or Congress) and change the corrupt perversions of human laws by force of conquering the system (voting in new politicians), we will have won a battle but lost the war. What needs to change even more desperately than individual unjust human laws (of which there are many today) is the entire philosophical and jurisprudential foundation of the system. For when the system rests on the will of the prince or the will of the Supreme Court or the will of the people, it is easily changed with a change of power or judge or public opinion. Taxpayer funding of abortion for overseas U.S. government personnel is discontinued and then resumed from administration to administration, for example. Battles are won and lost. The war will only be won when the entire understanding of the system of law is changed.

Post-Enlightenment positivism has swelled the greatness of human-made laws by exalting them as the only law, casting aside the eternal, natural, and divine law. It has also cast aside the unique role of man as rational. Law has become its own justification locked within self-contained and self-justifying texts severed from the rational participation of a rational person in the eternal plan of the universe. Aristotle left unanswered the question whether "it is more advantageous to be ruled by the best man or by the best laws."[80] John Adams chose to answer Aristotle's question by claiming that we are a "government of laws, and not of men."[81] Legal positivism has convinced us that Adams's depersonalization of law is correct. We have indeed become a government of texts and not a government of persons, human and divine. Only rational beings can attain rational participation in the eternal reason of a divine person. Only human beings (and not laws) have rational faculties. A government not of human beings is therefore not one of rational participation in the exemplar or idea of the way things ought to be. By cutting away the foundation, the texts of positive law are all that remains, making them supreme. Such an empire of laws and not of men is therefore an empire with no foundation or restraints. The laws are an illusory restraint on the government because those rules can simply be changed in an attempt to legitimize tyranny. Its laws are therefore not rational. Ironically, a government merely of laws is lawless, because law, by definition, requires an ordinance of reason by a person having care of a community. The result is exactly what Cicero predicted, the greater the law, the greater the injuries. The world has seen inflicted more injuries than Cicero could have imagined under, through, and in the name of the rule of laws. It is time that natural law put human law back where it belongs within the architectural structure of law. It is time to construct a government of persons built on the foundation of the eternal law and under the framework of the natural law.

The only thing holding our legal order together now that it has been severed from its foundation and framework is a vague collective memory of the truths known to our ancestors. MacIntyre's conclusions about modern moral utterance apply equally to modern jurisprudence and legal practice:

> Modern moral utterance and practice can only be understood as a series of fragmented survivals from an older past and that the insoluble problems which they have generated for modern moral theorists will remain insoluble until this is well understood. If the deontological character of moral judgments is the ghost of conceptions of divine law which are quite alien to the metaphysics of modernity and if the teleological character is similarly the ghost of conceptions of human nature and activity which are equally not at home in the modern world, we should expect the problems of understanding and of assigning an intelligible status to moral judgments both continually to arise and as continually to prove inhospitable to philosophical solutions.[82]

Only by reincarnating these ghosts from the past will jurisprudence and legal practice be able to offer satisfactory answers to the problems of our, or any, age.

N O T E S

ONE. Introducing the Building Project

1. Marcus Tullius Cicero, *De Officiis* 1.10.33; available at http://www.the latinlibrary.com/cicero/off.shtml (my translation).

2. See Philip Soper, "In Defense of Classical Natural Law in Legal Theory: Why Unjust Law Is No Law at All," *Canadian Journal of Law and Jurisprudence* 20, no. 1 (2007): 204–6.

3. *Quod principi placuit, legis habet vigorem*; Justinian, *Digest*, in *Corpus Iuris Civilis*, ed. Joannis L. G. Beck (Leipzig: Carolum Cnoblock, 1829), 1.4.1 (hereafter *Digest*), http://www.archive.org/stream/corpusiuriscivi00beckgoog#page /n2/mode/2up. To be fair to the ancient Roman legal theorists, this phrase was qualified by many other legal concepts, not least of which was the natural law. Thus, "what pleases the prince" was not always law but only what legitimately pleased the prince. Classical positivism rejects all of these qualifications and accepts this principle as an absolute.

4. *Princeps legibus solutus est*; Justinian, *Digest* 1.3.31.

5. Abraham Lincoln, "First Inaugural Address" (March 4, 1861), in *The Speeches of Abraham Lincoln* (London: Chesterfield Society, 1908), 310.

6. Alexander Pope, "An Essay on Man," in *The Poems of Alexander Pope: A Reduced Version of the Twickenham Text*, ed. John Butt (New Haven, CT: Yale University Press, 1966), 1.10.294.

7. See John Austin, *The Province of Jurisprudence Determined and Uses of the Study of Jurisprudence* (New York: Noonday Press, 1954), 10–13.

8. Ibid., 13.

9. Ibid., 13–14. Emphasis in quoted material is in the original throughout the book, unless I indicate it as mine.

10. Ibid.

11. Jeremy Bentham, *Of Laws in General*, ed. H. L. A. Hart (London: University of London Press, 1970), 1.

12. Thomas Hobbes, *De Homine*, trans. Charles Wood, T. S. K. Scott-Craig, and Bernard Gert (Indianapolis: Hackett, 1991), 10.5, quoted in Ted H. Miller, "Thomas Hobbes and the Constraints That Enable the Imitation of God," *Inquiry* 42, no. 2 (1999): 165.

13. See, e.g., H. L. A. Hart, *The Concept of Law* (New York: Oxford University Press, 1961), and Joseph Raz, *Practical Reason and Norms* (London: Hutchinson, 1975).

14. For a discussion of how modern positivism still retains an aspect of "might makes right," see Roger Berkowitz, *The Gift of Science: Leibniz and the Modern Legal Tradition* (Cambridge, MA: Harvard University Press, 2005), 5 (associating legal positivism with the view that law is "nothing but a willful decision" and with the idea that "might makes right").

15. Benedict XVI, "Address to Members of the International Theological Commission" (October 5, 2007), https://w2.vatican.va/content/benedict-xvi/en/speeches/2007/october/documents/hf_ben-xvi_spe_20071005_cti.html.

16. Hart, *Concept of Law*, 97–107.

17. Ibid., 99.

18. Ibid., 6–13.

19. Ibid., 7.

20. Ibid., 8–10.

21. Ibid., 15.

22. Elaine Sciolino, "French Voters Soundly Reject European Union Constitution," *New York Times*, May 30, 2005, http://www.nytimes.com/2005/05/30/world/europe/french-voters-soundly-reject-european-union-constitution.html?_r=0; Marlise Simons, "Dutch Voters Solidly Reject New European Constitution," *New York Times*, June 2, 2005, http://www.nytimes.com/2005/06/02/world/europe/dutch-voters-solidly-reject-new-european-constitution.html.

23. Vaughne Miller and Claire Taylor, *The Treaty of Lisbon: Amendments to the Treaty on European Union*, House of Commons Research Paper No. 08/09, January 24, 2008, http://researchbriefings.files.parliament.uk/documents/RP08-09/RP08-09.pdf.

24. See "Q&A: The Lisbon Treaty," BBC News, January 17, 2011, http://news.bbc.co.uk/2/hi/europe/6901353.stm.

25. Benedict XVI, "Message for the Celebration of the World Day of Peace" (January 1, 2008), http://w2.vatican.va/content/benedict-xvi/en/messages/peace/documents/hf_ben-xvi_mes_20071208_xli-world-day-peace.html.

26. Harold J. Berman, *Law and Revolution: The Formation of the Western Legal Tradition* (Cambridge, MA: Harvard University Press, 1983), 556.

27. Harold J. Berman, "An Ecumenical Christian Jurisprudence," in *The Teachings of Modern Christianity on Law, Politics, and Nature*, vol. 1, ed. John Witte, Jr., and John S. Alexander (New York: Columbia University Press, 2006), 756–57.

28. Soper identifies four schools of jurisprudence: classical natural law, classical positivism, modern positivism, and modern natural law. See Philip Soper, "In Defense of Classical Natural Law in Legal Theory," 205–6.

29. Berman, *Law and Revolution*, 529.

30. Lloyd L. Weinreb, "The Moral Point of View," in *Natural Law, Liberalism, and Morality: Contemporary Essays*, ed. Robert P. George (Oxford: Oxford University Press, 2001), 202.

31. St. Thomas Aquinas, *Summa Theologica*, trans. Fathers of the English Dominican Province (New York: Benziger Brothers, 1947), I-II, q. 90, a. 4 (unless otherwise noted all translations of the *Summa Theologica* are from this edition).

32. Ibid., I-II, q. 90, a. 4 (my translation).

33. Hart, *Concept of Law*, 6–7.

34. *Summa Theologica* I-II, q. 90, a. 4.

35. Gratian, *Concordia Discordantium Canonum*, in *Corpus Iuris Canonici* (Graz: Akademische Druck-u. Verlagsanstalt, 1959); electronic reproduction, vols. 1–2 (New York: Columbia University Libraries, 2007), D.1, C.5 (hereafter cited as *Decretum*), http://www.columbia.edu/cu/lweb/digital/collections/cul/texts/ldpd _6029936_001/pages/ldpd_6029936_001_00000059.html.

36. Ibid.

37. See, Henri Grenier, *Thomistic Philosophy*, vol. 2, *Philosophy of Nature*, trans. Rev. J. P. E. O'Hanley (Charlottetown, PEI: St. Dunstan's University Press, 1950), 220–21.

38. Ibid.

39. See ibid.

40. Marcus Tullius Cicero, *De Finibus Bonorum et Malorum*, 2nd ed., trans. H. Rackham (New York: G. P. Putnam's Sons, 1921), 293.

41. Ralph McInerny, *St. Thomas Aquinas* (Notre Dame, IN: University of Notre Dame Press, 1982), 61. See also Aquinas, *Summa Theologica* I, q. 14, a. 16, and St. Thomas Aquinas, *Commentary on the Nichomachean Ethics*, trans. C. I. Litzinger (Chicago: Henry Regnery, 1964), bk. 6, lect. 2 (discussing the relationship between speculative and practical intellect).

42. See Alasdair MacIntyre, *Three Rival Versions of Moral Enquiry: Encyclopaedia, Genealogy, and Tradition: Being Gifford Lectures Delivered in the University of Edinburgh in 1988* (Notre Dame, IN: University of Notre Dame Press, 1990), 62.

43. Ibid., 128.

44. See Leo Strauss, *Natural Right and History* (Chicago: Chicago University Press, 1953), 309–12.

45. Ibid., 311.

46. See Aaron J. Rappaport, "On the Conceptual Confusions of Jurisprudence," *Washington University Jurisprudence Review* 7, no. 1 (2014): 77–106.

47. Strauss, *Natural Right and History*, 312.

48. Charles De Koninck, "On the Primacy of the Common Good: Against the Personalists and The Principle of the New Order," *The Aquinas Review* 4 (1997): II: "Negation of the Primacy of the Speculative," http://ldataworks.com /aqr/V4_BC_text.html#BC_h003.

49. Ibid.

50. See *Summa Theologica* I, q. 84, a. 6 (citing Aristotle, *Metaphysics* 1.1, and *Posterior Analytics* 2.15).

51. John Finnis, *Natural Law and Natural Rights*, 2nd ed. (Oxford: Oxford University Press, 2011), 375.

52. Alasdair MacIntyre, *After Virtue: A Study in Moral Theory*, 2nd ed. (Notre Dame, IN: University of Notre Dame Press, 1984), 52. Some quotations herein are from the second and some from the third edition. Unless otherwise noted, all references are to the second edition.

53. On the convertibility of the concepts of being and goodness, see chapter 2 herein, and John L. Hill, *After the Natural Law: How the Classical Worldview Supports Our Modern Moral and Political Values* (San Francisco: Ignatius, 2016), 59–60.

54. MacIntyre, *After Virtue*, 53.

55. Ibid.

56. Ibid.

57. Jean Porter, *Natural and Divine Law: Reclaiming the Tradition for Christian Ethics* (Grand Rapids, MI: Eerdmans, 1999), 77.

58. Aristotle, *Physics*, in *The Basic Works of Aristotle*, ed. Richard McKeon (New York: Random House, 1941), 2.1.

59. Ibid.

60. Ibid., 2.2.

61. Ibid.

62. Ibid.

63. MacIntyre, *Three Rival Versions*, 134.

64. Edward Feser provides another excellent example that demonstrates the logical connection between being and goodness: "It is of the essence or nature of a Euclidian triangle to be a closed plane figure with three straight lines, and anything with this essence must have a number of properties, such as having angles that add up to 180 degrees. These are objective facts that we discover rather than invent; certainly it is notoriously difficult to make the opposite opinion at all plausible. Nevertheless, there are obviously triangles that fail to live up to this definition. A triangle drawn hastily on the cracked plastic seat of a moving bus might fail to be completely closed, or to have perfectly straight sides, and thus its angles will add up to something other than 180 degrees. Even a triangle drawn slowly and carefully on paper with an art pen and a ruler will contain subtle flaws. Still, the latter will far more closely approximate the essence of triangularity than the former will. It will accordingly be a *better* triangle than the former. Indeed, we would naturally describe the latter as a *good* triangle and the former as a *bad* triangle"; Edward Feser, *Neo-Scholastic Essays* (South Bend, IN: St. Augustine's Press, 2015), 298–99.

65. See MacIntyre, *After Virtue*, 57–59.

66. Porter, *Natural and Divine Law*, 93.

67. *Summa Theologica* I-II, q. 90, a. 4.

68. Brian Tierney, *The Idea of Natural Rights: Studies on Natural Rights, Natural Law, and Church Law, 1150—1625* (Grand Rapids, MI: Eerdmans, 1997), 23–24.

69. Pauline C. Westerman, *The Disintegration of Natural Law Theory: Aquinas to Finnis* (Leiden: Brill, 1998), 82.

70. See Hill, *After the Natural Law*, 53.

71. See *Summa Theologica* I-II, q. 93 and 94.

72. Ibid., I-II, q. 90, a. 1.

73. Ibid.

74. For a more complete discussion of the distinction between objective and subjective morality, see Henri Grenier, *Thomistic Philosophy*, vol. 4, *Moral Philosophy*, trans. Rev. J. P. E. O'Hanley (Charlottetown, PEI: St. Dunstan's University, 1950), 76–79.

75. Ibid., 82–86.

76. Ibid., 78.

77. See ibid., 82–86.

78. Strauss, *Natural Right and History*, 81–91.

79. See chapter 7 in this book.

80. See Strauss, *Natural Right and History*, 81–91.

81. MacIntyre, *Three Rival Versions*, 28, 191.

82. Ibid., 191.

83. See Jean Porter, *Ministers of the Law: A Natural Law Theory of Legal Authority* (Grand Rapids, MI: Eerdmans, 2010), 278–79.

84. See chapters 6 and 7 herein.

85. See Jonathan Crowe, "Clarifying the Natural Law Thesis," *Australian Journal of Legal Philosophy* 37 (2012): 161.

86. See Finnis, *Natural Law and Natural Rights*, chap. 1.

87. Hart, *Concept of Law*, 169.

88. Ibid., 9, 44, 84, 121, 122.

89. Ibid., 177.

90. Ibid.

91. Grenier, *Moral Philosophy*, 77.

92. Ibid., 89.

93. See ibid., 10–11.

94. See Hart, *Concept of Law*.

95. De Koninck, "On the Primacy of the Common Good."

96. Ibid.

97. *Summa Theologica* I-II, q. 21, a. 4, reply to obj. 3.

98. De Koninck, "On the Primacy of the Common Good."

99. See Jeremiah Newman, *Foundations of Justice: A Historico-Critical Study in Thomism* (Cork: Cork University Press, 1954), 36.

100. De Koninck, "On the Primacy of the Common Good."
101. Ibid.
102. See Newman, *Foundations of Justice*, 21 (citing Aquinas's *Commentary on the Nichomachean Ethics*, lecture 1).
103. See ibid., 34: "The good of the parts is the matter of the common good."
104. De Koninck, "On the Primacy of the Common Good."
105. Ibid.
106. Thomas Aquinas, *On Charity*, trans. Lottie H. Kendzierski (Milwaukee: Marquette University Press, 1960), art. 2.
107. *Summa Theologica* I-II, q. 92, a. 1, reply to obj. 3.
108. De Koninck, "On the Primacy of the Common Good," quoting *Summa Theologica* II-II, q. 47, a. 10, reply to obj. 2.
109. De Koninck, "On the Primacy of the Common Good."
110. As I will discuss in chapter 5, beyond man's natural end, God has through grace given a supernatural end to man that transcends this natural or temporal end. As this is a work of jurisprudence and not theology, this book is not concerned directly with this supernatural end of man other than to acknowledge its existence and the subordination of the temporal end to the attainment of this greater supernatural end. For us moderns, human society and law are primarily or exclusively material and temporal. For the classical tradition, the material is only an initial part. The purpose of law and society is to establish, preserve, and promote virtuous living in the multitude; see Newman, *Foundations of Justice*, 40 (citing Aquinas, *De Regimine Principum* 1.15). But in light of the ultimate remote end of civil society, man's supernatural end, this common living well of the multitude is also a means to attain the divine end; see *De Regimine Principum* 1.14.
111. Newman, *Foundations of Justice*, 37–38 (citing Aquinas, *De Regimine Principum* 1.14, 15, and Aquinas, *Commentary on the Aristotle's Politics*, bk. 3, lecture 5).
112. Newman, *Foundations of Justice*, 38.
113. Ibid.
114. *Summa Theologica* I-II q. 92, a. 1 (citing Aristotle, *Nicomachean Ethics* 2.6).
115. Gratian, *Decretum* D.1 (my translation of *humanum genus duobus regitur, naturali uidelicet iure et moribus.*)
116. Ibid., D.1, C.1; my translation of *omnes leges aut diuinae sunt, aut humanae. Diuinae natura, humanae moribus constant, ideoque he discrepant, quoniam aliae aliis gentibus placent. §1. Fas lex diuina est: ius lex humana. Transire per agrum alienum, fas est, ius non est.*
117. Huguccio Pisanus, *Summa Decretorum*, in *Monumenta Iuris Canonici Series A: Corpus Glossatorum*, vol. 6, ed. Oldřich Přerovský (Biblioteca Apostolica Vaticana, 2006), 13 (glossing *naturali uidelicet iure* as *id est diuino*); see also Huguccio, *Derivationes*, quoted in Stephan Kuttner, *The History of Ideas and Doctrines of*

Canon Law in the Middle Ages (London: Variorum Reprints, 1980), V, 99. Drawing a similar parallel between positive justice and natural justice, which he calls *fas*, Huguccio claims that *iustitia positiva* has been made by man whereas *naturalis justitia* is extended from the effects of nature.

118. Huguccio, *Summa Decretorum*, 14: *Quo nomine comprehenditur quodlibet ius humanum, id est ab homine inuentum.*

119. Gratian, *The Treatise on Laws (Decretum DD. 1–20)*, vol. 2, trans. Augustine Thompson and James Gordley (Washington, DC: Catholic University of America Press, 1993), Ordinary Gloss to D.1.

120. See Charlton T. Lewis et al., *A Latin Dictionary: Founded on Andrews' Edition of Freund's Latin Dictionary* (Oxford: Clarendon, 1879) (defining *fas* as "belonging to the religious language, *the dictates of religion, divine law*; opposed to *jus*, or human law"). The following are examples of the use of the word in the Bible: *audiebant autem eum usque ad hoc verbum et levaverunt vocem suam dicentes tolle de terra eiusmodi non enim fas est eum vivere* (Acts 22:22, Vulg.)—"And they heard him until this word, and then lifted up their voice, saying: Away with such an one from the earth; for it is not fit that he should live" (Acts 22:22, DV); *contigit autem et septem fratres cum matre adprehensos conpelli a rege contra fas ad carnes porcinas flagris et taureis cruciatos*" (2 Macc. 7:1, Vulg.)—"It came to pass also, that seven brethren, together with their mother, were apprehended, and compelled by the king to eat swine's flesh against the law, for which end they were tormented with whips and scourges" (2 Macc. 7:1, DV); *hii vero qui intus erant confidentes in stabilitate murorum et adparatu alimoniarum remissius agebant maledictis lacessentes Iudam ac blasphemantes et loquentes quae fas non est* (2 Macc. 12:14, Vulg.)—"But they that were within it, trusting in the strength of the walls, and the provision of victuals, behaved in a more negligent manner, and provoked Judas with railing and blaspheming, and uttering such words as were not to be spoken" (2 Macc. 12:14, DV).

121. Huguccio, *Summa Decretorum*, 20–21.

122. See Kenneth Pennington, "Lex Naturalis and Ius Naturale," *The Jurist* 68 (2008): 571–73.

123. See Lewis, *A Latin Dictionary* (*jus*: "*that which is binding* or *obligatory*; that which is binding by its nature, *right, justice, duty*").

124. Justinian, *Digest* 1.1.11.

125. Cicero, *Letters to Atticus* 1.16.6, http://www.thelatinlibrary.com/cicero /att1.shtml#6. Explaining how devastating it is to Rome when corrupt men render a wrong verdict, he says: *triginta homines populi Romani levissimos ac nequissimos nummulis acceptis ius ac fas omne delere.* The phrase sums up a complete obliteration of all rightness—*ius ac fas.*

126. Justinian, *Digest* 1.1.10.2 (my translation of *iuris prudentia est divinarum atque humanarum rerum notitia, iusti atque iniusti scientia*).

127. Gratian, *Decretum* D.1, C.1.

128. Cicero, "On the Laws," in *On the Commonwealth and On the Laws*, ed. James E. G. Zetzel (Cambridge: Cambridge University Press, 1999), 110.

129. Ibid., 110–11.

130. Ibid., 111.

131. Gratian, *Decretum* D.1.

132. See Michael S. Moore, "Good without God," in *Natural Law, Liberalism, and Morality*, ed. Robert P. George (Oxford: Clarendon, 2001), 221–70.

133. Kai Nielson, "The Myth of Natural Law," in *Law and Philosophy: A Symposium*, ed. Sidney Hook (New York: New York University Press, 1964), 129.

134. Ibid., 130.

135. Michael S. Moore, "Law as a Functional Kind," in *Natural Law Theory: Contemporary Essays*, ed. Robert P. George (Oxford: Oxford University Press, 1992), 189–90.

136. Ibid., 190–91.

137. Hill, *After the Natural Law*, 55 (paraphrasing G. K. Chesterton).

138. Crowe, "Clarifying the Natural Law Thesis," 168–70.

TWO.   Building Law on a Solid Foundation: The Eternal Law

1. Author of *Sachsenspiegel* (c. 1220), quoted in Berman, *Law and Revolution*, 521.

2. Marcus Tullius Cicero, *On the Commonwealth*, in *On the Commonwealth and On the Laws*, ed. James E. G. Zetzel (Cambridge: Cambridge University Press, 1999), 18.

3. See Pennington, "Lex Naturalis and Ius Naturale," 569.

4. Cicero, *On the Commonwealth and On the Laws*, xl.

5. Ibid.

6. Including an Epicurean; see Cicero, *On the Laws*, in *On the Commonwealth and On the Laws*, 112n25.

7. See ibid., 110.

8. Ibid., 110–11.

9. Ibid., 132.

10. Augustine, *The Works of Saint Augustine: A Translation for the 21st Century*, vol. 20, Part 1, *Answer to Faustus, a Manichean*, ed. Boniface Ramsey, trans. Roland Teske, S.J. (Hyde Park, NY: New City Press, 2007), 22.27; see also ibid., 22.30, 43, 61, and 78.

11. Augustine, *De Libero Arbitrio*, in *Patrologia Latina*, ed. J. P. Migne, 1.6, http://www.augustinus.it/latino/index.htm.

12. Jean Porter, *Natural and Divine Law*, 125–26.

13. Augustine, *De Vera Religione*, 30.56, translated in Porter, *Natural and Divine Law*, 126.

14. Aquinas, *Summa Theologica* I-II, q. 93, a. 1 (my translation).

15. Cora Carroll Scanlon and Charles L. Scanlon, *Second Latin* (Charlotte, NC: TAN, 1976), 5.

16. *Summa Theologica* I-II, q. 93, a. 1.

17. See Westerman, *Disintegration of Natural Law Theory*, 26–30. Although Aquinas does not use the word "style," Westerman has convincingly argued that it is a suitable English word to capture the essence of Aquinas's comparison to art.

18. John Rziha, *Perfecting Human Actions: St. Thomas Aquinas on Human Participation in Eternal Law* (Washington, DC: Catholic University of America Press, 2009), 26.

19. See *Summa Theologica* I, q. 44, a. 3.

20. Ibid.

21. Ibid.

22. "[God] who by His own omnipotent power at once from the beginning of time created each creature from nothing, spiritual, and corporal, namely, angelic and mundane, and finally the human, constituted as it were, alike of the spirit and the body"; see Henry Denzinger, "Decree of Lateran Council IV," in *The Sources of Catholic Dogma*, trans. Roy J. Deferrari (Fitzwilliam, NH: Loreto Publications, 2007), 428.

23. "He followed no external form or model; but contemplating, and as it were imitating, the universal model contained in the divine intelligence, the supreme Architect . . . created all things. . . . He also gave to the sun its brilliancy, and to the moon and stars their beauty; and that they might be *for signs, and for seasons, and for days and years.* He so ordered the celestial bodies in a certain and uniform course, that nothing varies more than their continual revolution, while nothing is more fixed than their variety. . . . The earth also God commanded to stand in the midst of the world, rooted in its own foundation, and *made the mountains ascend, and the plains descend into the place which he had founded for them*"; see John A. McHugh, O.P., and Charles J. Callan, O.P., trans., *Catechism of the Council of Trent* (Rockford, IL: TAN Books and Publishers, 1982), 27 (emphasis added).

24. *Summa Theologica* I-II, q. 93, a. 5.

25. Ibid., I-II, q. 93, a. 4.

26. Ibid., I-II, q. 91, a. 2.

27. Ibid., I-II, q. 63, a. 1.

28. Henri Grenier, *Thomistic Philosophy*, vol. 3, *Metaphysics*, trans. J. P. E. O'Hanley (Charlottetown, PEI: St. Dunstan's University, 1948), 47.

29. Ibid.

30. Peter Lombard, *The Sentences*, Book 2, *On Creation*, trans. Giulio Silano (Toronto: Pontifical Institute of Medieval Studies, 2008), 79.

31. *Summa Theologica* I-II, q. 93, a. 1.

32. Ibid., I-II, q. 93, a. 1, reply to obj. 3.

33. Rziha, *Perfecting Human Actions*, 29.

34. Ibid., 41.

35. Ibid., 42.

36. *Summa Theologica* I-II, q. 90, a. 4.

37. Col. 1:16 (Vulg.).

38. John 1:3 (Vulg.).

39. *Summa Theologica* I-II, q. 93, a. 1, reply to obj. 2.

40. Ibid.

41. Francisco Suárez, *De Legibus, ac Deo Legislatore*, in *Selections from Three Works of Francisco Suárez*, ed. James Brown Scott, trans. G. L. Williams, Ammi Brown, John Waldron, and Henry Davis (Oxford: Clarendon, 1944), 150.

42. See ibid., 174–75.

43. See Alexander of Hales, *Summa Fratris Alexandri* (Rome: The Trinity), 3.2.1.4. Alexander of Hales attributes each of these three attributes of eternal law to a person of the Trinity: authority to the Father, wisdom to the Son, and goodness to the Holy Ghost.

44. Arnold Hauser, *The Philosophy of Art History* (New York: A. A. Knopf, 1958), 5, 21.

45. Fred S. Kleiner and Christin J. Mamiya, *Gardner's Art through the Ages: The Western Perspective*, 12th ed. (Belmont, CA: Thomson Wadsworth, 2006), 446.

46. Ibid.

47. Ibid., 523.

48. Hugh Honour and John Fleming, *The Visual Arts: A History*, 6th ed. (New York: Harry N. Abrams, 2002), 25.

49. Hauser, *Philosophy of Art History*, 27.

50. Ibid.

51. Ibid., 3, 122.

52. Ibid., 26.

53. Honour and Fleming, *The Visual Arts*, 26.

54. Joseph Vining, "Law's Own Ontology: A Comment on Law's Quandary," *Catholic University Law Review* 55 (2006): 697.

55. St. Thomas Aquinas, *Summa Contra Gentiles*, ed. Joseph Kenny, O.P. (New York: Hanover House, 1955–57), 4.11.1–7, http://www.dhspriory.org/thomas /english/ContraGentiles4.htm#11.

56. *Summa Theologica* I-II, q. 90, a. 1, reply to obj. 1.

57. See ibid., I-II, q. 93, a. 2, *sed contra* (quoting Augustine); I-II, q. 93, a. 5; I-II, q. 93, a. 5, reply to obj. 1.

58. Grenier, *Philosophy of Nature*, 121–25.

59. Henri Grenier, *Thomistic Philosophy*, vol. 1, *General Introduction, Logic and Philosophy of Nature*, trans. J. P. E. O'Hanley (Charlottetown, PEI: St. Dunstan's University, 1948), 166; and Grenier, *Metaphysics*, 187–88.

60. *Summa Theologica* I-II, q. 93, a. 5.

61. Ibid., I-II, q. 93, a. 5, reply to obj. 2.

62. Grenier, *Philosophy of Nature*, 67.

63. Ibid., 64.

64. Ibid.

65. Ibid.

66. *Summa Theologica* I-II, q. 93, a. 5.

67. Ibid.

68. See Jean-Michel Gleize, "Laicity and Liberalism," *The Angelus* 35, no. 3 (May–June 2012): 74–75 (containing an English translation of Gleize's preface to his translation of the third volume of Cardinal Billot's treatise on the Church).

69. Ibid., 75.

70. *Summa Theologica* I, q. 82, a. 1.

71. See, ibid., I-II, q. 9, a. 4; see also Grenier, *Metaphysics*, 267: "a mover . . . reduces a mobile being from potency to act."

72. Aquinas uses the following example of how choices of the will are caused by prior choices: "When a man wills to be healed, he begins to reflect how this can be attained, and through this reflection he comes to the conclusion that he can be healed by a physician: and this he wills. But since he did not always actually will to have health, he must, of necessity, have begun, through something moving him, to will to be healed" (*Summa Theologica* I-II, q. 9, a. 4).

73. Ibid., I-II, q. 9, a. 3.

74. Ibid., I-II, q. 9, a. 4.

75. Ibid. (citing Aristotle, *Eudemian Ethics* 7.14).

76. Gleize, "Laicity and Liberalism," 75 (citing *Summa Theologica* I, q. 82, a. 1).

77. See also McInerny, *St. Thomas Aquinas*, 157–59, 164 (explaining how there is only one ultimate end to human action, but there are a variety of possible means to that end).

78. "The proper act of free will is choice: for we say that we have a free will because we can take one thing while refusing another; and this is to choose. . . . The proper object of choice is the means to the end" (*Summa Theologica* I, q. 83, a. 3).

79. See Grenier, *Moral Philosophy*, 51.

80. Gleize, "Laicity and Liberalism," 75.

81. This constraint is only analogous to that applicable to creatures. In absolute terms God is completely and existentially free, or, to use a theological term, omnipotent. Yet, God's omnipotence will not be used in a way contradictory to God's nature. Because His nature is perfectly rational, His omnipotence cannot be used irrationally. This explanation is the basis for the old quip that God although completely free cannot make a square circle. This statement is not contradictory; God remains free because technically the limitation does not exist in God but rather in the form of circle and square, which are mutually exclusive. God freely chose to create circles and squares, and once having done so, the two are limited by mutual exclusivity.

82. Porter, *Ministers of the Law*, 89.

83. Patrick McKinley Brennan, "Are Legislation and Rules a Problem in Law? Thoughts on the Work of Joseph Vining," *Villanova Law Review* 55 (2010): 1217 (citing *Summa Theologica* I, q. 21, a. 1, reply to obj. 3; I, q. 82, a. 1; I-II, q. 99, a. 1; II-II, q. 44., a. 1; and Aquinas, *De Veritate* 17.3).

84. See *Summa Theologica* I-II, q. 92, a. 1.

85. Grenier, *Metaphysics*, 219–32.

86. See Rziha, "Perfecting Human Actions," 66–78 (explaining how Aquinas understands that human acts are determined by the eternal law as primary cause but human choice as instrumental cause and showing how the eternal law really does determine all things but allows for variety in human action).

87. Ibid., 26.

88. Westerman, *Disintegration of Natural Law Theory*, 29. Westerman, despite being a legal positivist who ultimately rejects the usefulness of natural law, offers one of the best explanations of Aquinas's understanding of the eternal law, which she calls the "divine style." She argues that later natural law scholars who did not fully incorporate this idea of the eternal law in their theory erected a natural law theory on an edifice without a foundation.

89. *Summa Theologica* I-II, q. 91, a. 3, reply to obj. 1.

90. See Ronald Dworkin, *Law's Empire* (Cambridge, MA: Harvard University Press, 1986), viii–ix; and Dworkin, *Taking Rights Seriously* (Cambridge, MA: Harvard University Press, 1978), chap. 4.

91. *Summa Theologica* I-II, q. 91, a. 3, reply to obj. 1.

92. Grenier, *Logic*, 78.

93. Ibid., 77–94 (describing major and minor premises and their relation to conclusions using categorical syllogism but employing slightly different terminology).

94. *Summa Theologica* I-II, q. 91, a. 3, reply to obj. 1.

95. Ibid.

96. Ibid., I-II, q. 91, a. 3.

97. Ibid.

98. See chapter 3 for a further discussion of *per se nota* principles.

99. See chapter 5 for a discussion of the problems in knowing the natural law.

100. *Summa Theologica* I-II, q. 91, a. 3, reply to obj. 1.

101. See Westerman, *Disintegration of Natural Law Theory*, 90–91.

102. Ibid., 103.

103. Ibid., 100.

104. Ibid., 102.

105. "What we have been saying [about natural law] would have a degree of validity even if we should concede ... that there is no God, or that the affairs of men are of no concern to Him"; Hugo Grotius, "Prolegomena," in *De Jure Belli ac Pacis Libri Tres*, trans. Francis W. Kelsey (Indianapolis: Bobbs-Merrill, 1925), 11.

106. Westerman, *Disintegration of Natural Law Theory*, 136–39.

107. John Finnis, "Grounds of Law and Legal Theory: A Response," *Legal Theory* 13 (2007): 315, 340.

108. John Finnis, *Natural Law and Natural Rights*, 2nd ed. (Oxford: Oxford University Press, 2011), 49. To be fair, Finnis does not dismiss all consideration of God's existence as irrelevant in itself (per se) but as irrelevant to the study and application of natural law.

109. Ibid.

110. Ibid., 424, 442.

111. See, e.g., John Finnis, *Aquinas: Moral, Political, and Legal Theory* (Oxford: Oxford University Press, 1998), 300.

112. See, e.g., Finnis, "Grounds of Law," 339–44; and Finnis, *Natural Law and Natural Rights*, 415–17, 477–79.

113. Finnis, *Natural Law and Natural Rights*, 405, 424.

114. Moore, "Good without God," 251–52.

115. Finnis, *Natural Law and Natural Rights*, 405.

116. Finnis, "Grounds of Law," 343.

117. Ibid., 341.

118. Not least of which is the flaw of advancing Stoic beliefs in a tentative manner due to his skepticism and the danger of Stoicism itself of seeing living virtuously as the only goal without accepting the good at which virtue aims. Although Finnis presents an excellent critique of this flaw of Stoicism and its necessary reliance on piety to support the command to live virtuously (see Finnis, *Natural Law and Natural Rights*, 377–78), Finnis's own position is subject to the same critique as Stoicism is. Men can live according to practical reason even without accepting its source and foundation in an ordered universe. Even if Cicero's appropriated Stoicism lacks clarity on the nature and goodness of that universal order, he puts aside his own skeptical beliefs in *De Legibus* to acknowledge its necessity to the discussion of law.

119. Cicero, *De Finibus Bonorum et Malorum*, trans. H. Rackham (London: Macmillan, 1914), 293.

120. Finnis, *Natural Law and Natural Rights*, v.

121. Ibid., 387.

122. Ibid., 398, 424.

123. Finnis, "Grounds of Law," 339.

124. Finnis, *Natural Law and Natural Rights*, 398.

125. Finnis occasionally, and I would add with hesitation, uses "D" as his general term in referring to God.

126. Finnis, *Natural Law and Natural Rights*, 390.

127. Ibid., 391.

128. Porter, *Ministers of the Law*, 4.

129. Ibid., 2.

130. Porter, *Natural and Divine Law*, 140–41.

131. Vining, "Law's Own Ontology," 695–709.

132. Steven D. Smith, *Law's Quandary* (Cambridge, MA: Harvard University Press, 2004).

133. Ibid., 15–16.

134. Ibid., 22.

135. Westerman, *Disintegration of Natural Law Theory*, 256 (arguing that the only foundation left for Finnis is to simply assert his principles as self-evident, which foundation is unsatisfactory).

136. Finnis, *Natural Law and Natural Rights*, 419.

137. Ibid., 420.

138. See ibid., 417 (declaring his opposition to Adler and Veatch who do support such a claim).

139. Brennan, "Are Legislation and Rules a Problem in Law?," 1212n102.

140. Ibid.

141. Brennan calls the key discussion of the relationship between eternal law and human laws in *Summa Theologica* I-II, q. 91, a. 2, and I-II, q. 91, a. 3, reply to obj. 2, "canonical texts" for natural law jurisprudence (Brennan, "Are Legislation and Rules a Problem in Law?," 1212).

142. *Summa Theologica* 1-II, q. 93, a. 4.

143. Finnis, *Natural Law and Natural Rights*, 415.

144. McInerny, *St. Thomas Aquinas*, 152.

THREE.   Discovering the Framework: The Natural Law

1. Marcus Tullius Cicero, "Treatise on the Laws," in *The Political Works*, vol. 2, trans. Francis Barham (London: Edmund Spettigue, 1842), bk. 1, http://oll .libertyfund.org/index.php?option=com_staticxt&staticfile=show.php%3Ftitle =545&Itemid=99999999.

2. Aquinas, *Summa Theologica* I-II, q. 91, a. 2.

3. Brennan, "Are Legislation and Rules a Problem in Law?," 1211.

4. Rziha, *Perfecting Human Actions*, 9 (discussing one of Cornelio Fabro's insights with respect to participation and using the analogy of water participating in heat when tepid water is heated).

5. Ibid., 9–10.

6. Ibid.

7. Ibid.

8. My translation of Aquinas, *De Potentia* q. 3, a. 4; Latin text taken from Rudy A. Te Velde, *Participation and Substantiality in Thomas Aquinas* (Leiden: E. J. Brill, 1995), 173n22.

9. See *Summa Theologica* I-II, q. 90, a. 1, reply to obj. 1.

10. See ibid., I-II, q. 93, a. 5.

11. Ibid., I-II, q. 91, a. 2, reply to obj. 2.

12. Ibid.

13. R. A. Armstrong, *Primary and Secondary Precepts in Thomistic Natural Law Teaching* (The Hague: Martinus Nijhoff, 1966), 46, citing Aquinas, *De Veritate*, trans. James V. McGlynn, S.J. (Chicago: Henry Regnery, 1953), 21.1 (explaining that end and good "have a reciprocal relationship; everything in seeking its end seeks the good and everything, insofar as it attains its end, is itself good"); see also E. D'Arcy, *Conscience and Its Right to Freedom* (New York: Sheed and Ward, 1961), 52–53.

14. *Summa Theologica* I-II, q. 91, a. 2.

15. In this respect, philosophy is the science, or knowledge, of things through their causes. See Grenier, *Logic*, 14.

16. Plato, *Republic*, in *The Collected Dialogues of Plato*, ed. Edith Hamilton and Huntington Cairns (Princeton, NJ: Princeton University Press, 1961), 7.514a–517b.

17. Ibid., 517b–c.

18. Joel Prentiss Bishop, *Common Law and Codification, or, The Common Law as a System of Reasoning* (Chicago: T. H. Flood and Co., 1888), 9.

19. Gen. 1:26–27; Acts 17:28; Col. 3:10; Rom. 8:29.

20. John Finnis, "Reason, Revelation, Universality and Particularity in Ethics," *American Journal of Jurisprudence* 53 (2008): 28.

21. *Perfectius igitur accedit res creata ad Dei similitudinem si non solum bona est sed etiam ad bonitatem aliorum agere potest, quam si solum in se bona esset*; my translation of Aquinas, *Summa Contra Gentiles* 2.45.4, http://www.corpusthomisticum .org/iopera.html.

22. *Quia singula quidem sunt in suis naturis bona: simul autem omnia valde bona, propter ordinem universi, quae est ultima et nobilissima perfectio in rebus* (ibid., 2.45.10; my translation).

23. Huguccio also links natural law with the divine plan for rationality, inclination, and the order of nature; see Huguccio, *Summa Decretorum*, 18: *divine: id est a Deo tradite sine ministro, ut lex naturalis que dicitur ratio et que dicitur instinctus et ordo nature.*

24. *Summa Theologica* I, q. 80, a. 1 (observing that "some inclination follows every form").

25. Ibid., I-II, q. 91, a. 2.

26. Gratian, *Treatise on Laws*, D.1 C.7.

27. See *Summa Theologica* I, q. 91, a. 2.

28. Although not relevant to the argument at this point, the three acts correspond to the three habits: (1) speculative judgment, for example, stealing is wrong; (2) practical judgment in the universal, therefore stealing must be avoided; and

(3) practical judgment in the particular, this particular act of stealing must be avoided. See Grenier, *Moral Philosophy*, 85.

29. Aquinas, *Commentary on the Nicomachean Ethics*, bk. 5, lect. 12, no. 1018.

30. *Summa Theologica* I-II, q. 94, a. 2.

31. Ibid.

32. Ibid., I-II, q. 94, a. 2.

33. Ibid., I-II, q. 18, a. 2.

34. "Thomas argues that although humans make a distinction between goodness and being in their knowledge, they are the same in reality" (Rziha, *Perfecting Human Actions*, 36). See also Louis Cortest, *The Disfigured Face: Traditional Natural Law and Its Encounter with Modernity* (New York: Fordham University Press, 2008), 15, 98–100 (arguing that the ontological connection of goodness to being is at the heart of Aquinas's natural law philosophy).

35. *Summa Theologica* I-II, q. 94, a. 2.

36. Maria T. Carl, "The First Principles of Natural Law: A Study of the Moral Theories of Aristotle and Saint Thomas Aquinas" (PhD diss., Marquette University, 1989), 149–50, http://epublications.marquette.edu/dissertations/AAI9014051/.

37. See Grenier, *Logic*, 6.

38. See Aristotle, *Physics* 2.3.194b23–35 (the four causes: material, formal, efficient, and final).

39. See Alasdair MacIntyre, *After Virtue: A Study in Moral Theory*, 3rd ed. (Notre Dame, IN: University of Notre Dame Press, 2007), 81.

40. Ibid., 81–82.

41. Porter, *Ministers of the Law*, 92.

42. Pope Benedict XVI, "Address to the International Congress on Natural Moral Law" (February 12, 2007), https://w2.vatican.va/content/benedict-xvi/en/speeches/2007/february/documents/hf_ben-xvi_spe_20070212_pul.html.

43. See, e.g., W. D. Hudson, *The Is/Ought Question: A Collection of Papers on the Central Problems in Moral Philosophy* (London: Macmillan, 1969); Charles Pigden, "Naturalism," in *A Companion to Ethics*, ed. Peter Singer (Oxford: Wiley-Blackwell, 1993), 421–31; and Charles Pigden, "Logic and the Autonomy of Ethics," *Australasian Journal of Philosophy* 67, no. 2 (1989): 127–51.

44. See Aquinas, *De Veritate* q. 16.

45. See ibid.; *Summa Theologica* I-II, q. 94, a. 2.

46. *Summa Theologica* I, q. 79, a. 12.

47. "It is proper to human nature to reach the knowledge of truth by investigating and moving from one thing to another" (Aquinas, *De Veritate* 16.1, reply).

48. *Summa Theologica* I, q. 2, a. 3.

49. See Aquinas, *Commentary on the Sentences*, ed. Mandonnet and Moos (Paris: Lethielleux, 1929), 2.24.2.3 (arguing from the observation of physical motion proceeding from immobility to motion that all knowledge must move from immovable principles).

50. Ibid.: *subito intellectui offertur.*

51. Westerman, *Disintegration of Natural Law Theory,* 52.

52. See Robert A. Greene, "Instinct of Nature: Natural Law, Synderesis, and the Moral Sense," *Journal of the History of Ideas* 58, no. 2 (1997): 173–98.

53. Justinian, *Digest,* trans. S. P. Scott (Cincinnati, OH: Central Trust Company Executor of the Estate Samuel P. Scott, 1932), 1.1.1.3, 1.1.1.4. We will return to consider the *jus gentium* in chapter 6 when we consider in more detail human positive law.

54. Ibid., 1.1.1.3.

55. Ibid., 1.1.1.4.

56. Ibid., 1.1.1.9.

57. Ibid., 1.1.1.11.

58. Isidore of Seville, *Etymologiarum sive Originum,* ed. W. M. Lindsay (Oxford: Clarendon, 1911), 5.4: *ius naturale* [*est*] *commune omnium nationum.*

59. See Greene, "Instinct of Nature," 175–76 (describing how alterations—such as substituting "men" for "male"—and additions moved the emphasis from animals to humans).

60. See Isidore, *Etymologies* 5.4.

61. See Greene, "Instinct of Nature," 180.

62. See, e.g., Cicero, *De Domo Sua* 138 (describing someone acting *furore instinctus,* "impelled by madness"), http://www.thelatinlibrary.com/cicero/domo.shtml; Cicero, *In Verrem* 2.5.188 (describing the inspiration for sacrilegious attacks on temples as being inspired *furore et audacia instinctus,* "by an impulse of madness and audacity"), http://www.thelatinlibrary.com/cicero/verres.2.5.shtml; Livy, *Ab Urbe Condita* 1.47 (describing how Tarquin was *muliebribus instinctus furiis,* or "incited by his wife's madness"), http://www.thelatinlibrary.com/livy/liv.1.shtml.

63. Greene, "Instinct of Nature," 176; see also, e.g., Suetonius, *Divus Julius* 19.2 (describing how Caesar was *maxime iniuria instinctus,* "impelled by that great injury to act"); *Divus Julius* 14.9; Livy, *Ab Urbe Condita* 4.16.9 (describing how the people were *his uocibus instinctus,* "inspired by these words"); Tacitus, *Agricola* 16.1 (describing how words inspired each other's actions, *invicem instincti*); Vitruvius, *De Architectura* 9, preface 16 (referring to *qui litterarum iucunditatibus instinctas habent mentes,* "those who have minds inspired by the delights of literature"; Livy, *Ab Urbe Condita* 9.40.7 (explaining how Cursus led the soldiers into battle, "soldiers inspired by these words," *uocibus instinctos milites*).

64. Greene, "Instinct of Nature," 176 (emphasis added); see, e.g., Livy, *Ab Urbe Condita* 5.15.10 (describing how a soothsayer would not take back what he had said *diuino spiritu instinctus,* "inspired by the divine spirit"); ibid., 5.21.2 (relaying a prayer that a military leader would go forth *numine instinctus,* "impelled by thy [Apollo's] divine will"); Lucan, *Pharsalia* 5.150 (describing an *instinctam sacro mentem,* "a mind inspired by the sacred").

65. *Summa Institutionum Vindobonensis*, translation quoted in Greene, "Instinct of Nature," 177 (emphasis added).

66. Greene, "Instinct of Nature," 180.

67. These terms are used as terms of logic, not in the sense of modern natural science; see Grenier, *Logic*, 164–65 (defining genus as "a universal which is predicated of several specifically distinct subjects and which incompletely expresses their essence"; species as "a universal which is predicated of several numerically distinct subjects and which completely expresses their essence"; and differentia as "a universal which is affirmed of several subjects as an essential and qualifying predicate").

68. Grenier, *Logic*, 173: "Whatever are predicated of the predicate of a subject are predicated of the subject itself. . . . Example: animal is predicated of man as subject. Everything that really belongs to animal belongs also to man, as to be sensitive, animated, material." See also *Summa Theologica* I-II, q. 94, a. 2 (stating that the definition of man contains within it the definition of animal).

69. "Life is in the highest degree properly in God. In proof of which it must be considered that since a thing is said to live insofar as it operates of itself and not as moved by another, the more perfectly this power is found in anything, the more perfect is the life of that thing" (*Summa Theologica* I, q. 18, a. 3).

70. Aquinas, *De Veritate* 16.1.13.

71. Ibid., 16.1.

72. See *Summa Theologica* I, q. 18, a. 3.

73. Greene, "Instinct of Nature," 182; see, e.g., *Summa Theologica* I-II, q. 50, a. 3: "The sensitive powers can be considered in two ways: first, according as they act from natural instinct: secondly, according as they act at the command of reason."

74. Quoting Nicholas of Ockham, in Greene, "Instinct of Nature," 188.

75. Aquinas, *De Veritate* 16.1.

76. Westerman, *Disintegration of Natural Law*, 51.

77. Bonaventure, *Itinerarium Mentis in Deum*, in *Works of Saint Bonaventure*, vol. 1, ed. Philotheus Boehner, OFM, and Sr. Frances Laughlin, SMIC (St. Bonaventure, NY: Saint Bonaventure Press, 1956), chap. 6, pt. 2, 41.

78. Aquinas, *De Veritate* 16.3.

79. Ibid.

80. *Summa Theologica* I-II, q. 14, a. 2 (explaining why "the principle" in practical matters—later identified at I-II, q. 94, a. 2, as "do good"—cannot be questioned without rational consideration of what action is to be done, counsel becoming impossible).

81. Aquinas, *De Veritate* 16.1.

82. Greene, "Instinct of Nature," 183.

83. The distinction between "some things," which are known like angels, and "these things," which are known differently, will be explored further in the next

subsection when we examine how the further principles of natural law are known. Although the first principle is known by synderesis, or instinct of nature, the further precepts are known through discursive reasoning (although a distinction here will also be made between the first-level principles and second-level principles).

84. *Summa Theologica* I, q. 19, a. 10.

85. Ibid., I-II, q. 17, a. 5.

86. Aquinas, *Summa Contra Gentiles*, trans. Vernon J. Bourke (New York: Hanover House, 1955–57), 3.109.7, http://dhspriory.org/thomas/ContraGentiles3b .htm#114.

87. Ibid.

88. See J. Budziszewski, *Natural Law for Lawyers* (Nashville: ACW Press, 2006), 51–54 (discussing Roman jurist's confusion over the term "natural law").

89. Greene, "Instinct of Nature," 185–87.

90. Ibid., 189.

91. Ibid., 184.

92. Ibid., 186.

93. *Summa Theologica* I, q. 79, a. 12.

94. Rom. 2:15 (DV).

95. Westerman, *Disintegration of Natural Law*, 56.

96. Ibid., 51–52.

97. Aristotle, *Nicomachean Ethics*, in *The Basic Works of Aristotle*, ed. Richard McKeon (New York: Random House, 1941), 1.1.1094a1–1094a3.

98. *Summa Theologica* I, q. 14, a. 2.

99. Aquinas, *De Veritate* 16.1.9.

100. *Summa Theologica* I, q. 79, a. 12; Westerman, *Disintegration of Natural Law*, 52.

101. Westerman, *Disintegration of Natural Law*, 53.

102. Aquinas, *De Veritate* 16.2.1.

103. Ibid.

104. Ibid., 16.2.2.

105. The source of this light is the eternal law, which Aquinas shows by quoting Psalm 4:6 (Douai Rheims): "The light of thy countenance, O Lord, is signed upon us" (Aquinas, *De Veritate* 16.3).

106. Ibid.

107. Ibid., 16.3.

108. *Summa Theologica* I-II, q. 94, a. 4.

109. Ibid.

110. Aquinas, *De Veritate* 17.1; Westerman, *Disintegration of Natural Law*, 59–60.

111. Jean Gerson, *Definitiones Terminorum Theologiae Moralis* (1400–1415), quoted in Greene, "Instinct of Nature," 189.

112. Ibid.

113. *Summa Theologica* I-II, q. 94, a. 2.

114. Armstrong, *Primary and Secondary Precepts*, 39–40.

115. Ibid., 40, citing D'Arcy, *Conscience and Its Right to Freedom*, 52–53.

116. Ibid.

117. Westerman, *Disintegration of Natural Law*, 54.

118. *Summa Theologica* I-II, q. 94, a. 4.

119. Ibid. (emphasis added).

120. See *Summa Theologica* I-II, q. 94, a. 4 (stating that the Germans did not know the general principle that theft is evil).

121. "Thus, just as there is a natural habit of the human soul through which it knows principles of the speculative sciences, which we call understanding of principles, so, too, there is in the soul a natural habit of first principles of action, which are the universal principles of the natural law. This habit pertains to synderesis" (Aquinas, *De Veritate* 16.1).

122. See Aristotle, *Nicomachean Ethics* 1.1.1094a2–3.

123. *Summa Theologica* I-II, q. 13, a. 3.

124. Ibid.

125. Ibid., I, q. 79, a. 12, reply to obj. 3.

126. Ibid., I-II, q. 91, a. 2, reply to obj. 2.

127. See, e.g., Jacques Maritain, *The Rights of Man and Natural Law*, trans. Doris Anson (New York: Scribner, 1943), 27. Maritain likewise makes a similar distinction between the first principle, do good and avoid evil, and subsequent primary principles on the basis that the first is self-evident to all but the latter are only self-evident in themselves. He does not directly attribute the difference to synderesis, however.

128. Aquinas, *Commentary on the Nichomachean Ethics*, bk. 5, lect. 12, no. 1018.

129. See text accompanying note 60, above.

130. See Green, "Instinct of Nature," 181–82.

131. *Summa Theologica* I-II, q. 94, a. 2; see also, Armstrong, *Primary and Secondary Precepts*, 35–37.

132. *Summa Theologica* I-II, q. 94, a. 2 (giving the example "that an angel is not circumscriptively in a place" cannot be grasped by the unlearned even though it is self-evident since in the definition of an angel is included the lack of corporality and hence the lack of occupation of any space).

133. Albertus Magnus, *De Bono* (Munster: Aschendorff, 1951), 5.1.1, translation quoted in Jean Porter, *Natural and Divine Law*, 91.

134. Aquinas, *Commentary on the Nichomachean Ethics*, bk. 1, lect. 1, no. 9.

135. William Shakespeare, *Hamlet* 1.3.78.

136. Ernest Barker, introduction to *Natural Law and the Theory of Society*, by Otto Gierke, trans. Ernest Barker (Cambridge: Cambridge University Press, 1934), 35.

137. *Summa Theologica* I, q. 19, a. 1; see also I, q. 59, a. 1; I, q. 78, a. 1, reply to obj. 3; I-II, q. 26, a. 1; I-II, q. 35, a. 1; Aquinas, *De Veritate* 25.1.

138. See Armstrong, *Primary and Secondary Precepts*, 44.

139. *Summa Theologica* I, q. 59, a. 1.

140. Ibid., I, q. 78, a. 1, reply to obj. 3.

141. Ibid., I, q. 80, a. 1.

142. See also ibid., I-II, q. 26, a. 1: "Because natural things seek what is suitable to them according to their nature, by reason of an apprehension which is not in them, but in the Author of their nature."

143. Ibid., I, q. 59, a. 1.

144. Armstrong, *Primary and Secondary Precepts*, 45, citing Aquinas, *De Veritate* 25.1.

145. *Summa Theologica* I, q. 59, a. 1.

146. See, Armstrong, *Primary and Secondary Precepts*, 47.

147. Green, "Instinct of Nature,"182.

148. Cicero, *Orationes: Cum Senatui gratias egit, Cum populo gratias egit, De domo sua, De haruspicum responso, Pro Sestio, In Vatinium, De provinciis consularibus, Pro Balbo*, vol. 5, ed. Albert Clark (Oxford: Clarendon, 1952), 31.67 (my translation of *fieri quaedam ad meliorem spem inclinatio visa est*).

149. *Summa Theologica* I, q. 18, a. 3.

150. Ibid., I-II, q. 26, a. 1.

151. Ibid., I, q. 19, a. 10.

152. Aquinas, *Summa Contra Gentiles* 3.114.1.

153. *Summa Theologica* I, q. 80, a. 1.

154. Here Aquinas is using the term "end" not in the strict sense of the end but rather as subend, since, as we discussed in chapter 2, he has clearly stated that man does not choose his ultimate end but only the means to that end.

155. *Summa Theologica* I, q. 18, a. 3.

156. Strauss, *Natural Right and History*, 145.

157. *Summa Theologica* I-II, q. 94, a. 2.

158. See J. Budziszewski, *The Line through the Heart* (Wilmington, DE: ISI Books, 2009), 61–77 (discussing how unnatural inclinations can be acquired and become conatural).

159. "That such and such is the good . . . is true or false independently of whether or not . . . anyone . . . happen[s] in fact to desire that good"; Alasdair MacIntyre, *Whose Justice? Which Rationality?* (Notre Dame, IN: University of Notre Dame Press, 1988), 130.

160. *Summa Theologica* I-II, q. 85, a. 2 (arguing that the natural inclinations, or the "good of nature," cannot be completely destroyed by vice but can be "diminished").

161. See Porter, *Natural and Divine Law*, 93.

162. Ibid., quoting *Summa Theologica* II-II, q. 108, a. 2.

163. Budziszewski, *Line through the Heart*, 62–63.

164. Ibid., 5.

165. Gal. 5:17.

166. The effects of the Fall provide further proof of the eternal law's status as law. To be law, punishment must follow failure to follow law. When man acted contrary to the plan of his nature in eternal law, the law of the *fomes* became a law of punishment for him (see *Summa Theologica* I-II, q. 91, a. 6).

167. Ibid., I-II, q. 85, a. 3.

168. Ibid.

169. Ibid., I-II, q. 91, a. 6.

170. Plato, *Laws*, in *The Collected Dialogues*, ed. Edith Hamilton and Huntington Cairns (Princeton, NJ: Princeton University Press, 1961), 1.644c–d.

171. Ibid.

172. Ibid.

173. Ibid., 644e–645c.

174. *Summa Theologica* I-II, q. 91, a. 2.

175. Ibid., I-II, q. 94, a. 2.

176. See Porter, *Natural and Divine Law*, 144.

177. Gratian, *Decretum* D.1.

178. Gratian, *Ordinary Gloss* to *Decretum* D.1.

179. Justinian, *Digest* 1.1.10.1 (my translation).

180. Ibid., 1.1.11.

181. See Armstrong, *Primary and Secondary Precepts*, 3–7 (summarizing the work of Viktor Cathrein, Henri Capitant, Edgar Janssens, François Gény, C. Martyniak, and Louis Le Fur).

182. See ibid., 4.

183. See, e.g., Aquinas, *De Veritate* 16.3; Aquinas, *Commentary on the Nichomachean Ethics*, bk. 5, lect. 12; *Summa Theologica* I-II, q. 94, a. 4, and I-II, q. 100, a. 3.

184. *Summa Theologica* I, q. 85, a. 3.

185. "The primary precepts . . . are concerned with abstractions from the details of real life" (Armstrong, *Primary and Secondary Precepts*, 93).

186. See Aquinas, *De Veritate* 16.3; Aquinas, *Commentary on the Nichomachean Ethics*, bk. 5, lect. 12.

187. See *Summa Theologica* I-II, q. 95, a. 2.

188. Ibid.

189. Ibid.

190. Ibid.

191. Porter, *Natural and Divine Law*, 307.

192. *Summa Theologica* I-II, q. 95, a. 2.

193. Ibid., I-II, q. 100, a. 1.

194. See Charlton T. Lewis, *An Elementary Latin Dictionary* (Oxford: Oxford University Press, 1999).

195. *Summa Theologica* I-II, q. 94, a. 6.

196. See Armstrong, *Primary and Secondary Precepts*, 101–3 (although the term "remote" does not appear directly in the *Summa Theologica*, Armstrong uses the term to distinguish those secondary precepts not described as *propinquus*, "closely connected to," the primary precepts).

197. Ibid., 102.

198. *Summa Theologica* I-II, q. 94, a. 4.

199. Ibid.

200. Ibid., I-II, q. 95, a. 2.

201. Ibid.

FOUR.   Examining the Framework: The Content of the Natural Law

1. Aquinas, *Summa Theologica* I-II, q. 94, a. 2.

2. Armstrong, *Primary and Secondary Precepts*, 51.

3. Ibid., 52.

4. Ibid., 128.

5. Ana Marta González, "Natural Law as a Limiting Concept: A Reading of Thomas Aquinas," in *Contemporary Perspectives on Natural Law: Natural Law as a Limiting Concept*, ed. Ana Marta González (Hampshire: Ashgate, 2008), 24.

6. Armstrong, *Primary and Secondary Precepts*, 129.

7. Aquinas, *Summa Contra Gentiles* (trans. Bourke) 3.129.

8. Justinian, *Digest* 1.1.1.3.

9. "Equitable" would be a better translation of *aequum* than "just," which in Latin would be *justus*.

10. Justinian, *Digest* 1.1.1.3 and 1.1.11.

11. Gratian, *Decretum* D.1, C.7.

12. *Summa Theologica* I-II, q. 94, a. 2.

13. See ibid., Supp., q. 65, a. 1: "All natural things are imbued with certain principles whereby they are enabled not only to exercise their proper actions, but also to render those actions proportionate to their end, whether such actions belong to a thing by virtue of its generic nature, or by virtue of its specific nature: thus it belongs to a magnet to be borne downwards by virtue of its generic nature, and to attract iron by virtue of its specific nature"; and see the discussion of the definition of man in chapter 3.

14. Finnis, *Natural Law and Natural Rights*, 401.

15. See, e.g., ibid., 59–75, in the course of which Finnis argues for the value of knowledge exclusively from our subjective experience with knowledge.

16. Armstrong, *Primary and Secondary Precepts*, 47.

17. MacIntyre, *Whose Justice? Which Rationality?*, 142 (referring to Aristotle, *Nicomachean Ethics*, bk. 10).

18. Aristotle, *Politics*, in *The Basic Works of Aristotle*, ed. Richard McKeon (New York: Random House, 1941), bks. 1–2.

19. *Summa Theologica* I, q. 92, a. 1, reply to obj. 2; and I, q. 96, a. 4; Thomas Aquinas, *De Regimine Principum* (*De Regno*), in *Selected Political Writings*, ed. A. P. d'Entreves, trans. J. G. Dawson (Oxford: Blackwell, 1959), 8–9; Aquinas, *Summa Contra Gentiles* 3.129.5.

20. Aristotle, *Nicomachean Ethics* 6.8.1142a9–10.

21. MacIntyre, *Whose Justice? Which Rationality?*, 96.

22. Ibid.

23. Ibid., 98. MacIntyre notes that Aristotle does believe that to a certain extent other communities less complete than the *polis*, such as the Academy of Plato, can fill this necessary role or that very exceptional individuals could excel notwithstanding their isolation. Yet these are exceptional circumstances in which extraordinary individuals may attain their end in spite of the deficiencies. The situation of isolation is still unnatural and a deprivation.

24. Ibid., 98–99.

25. Budziszewski, *The Line through the Heart*, 195–97 (employing the image of the mezzanine level of a house to describe this relationship).

26. Finnis's list includes life, knowledge, play, aesthetic experience, sociability, practical reasonableness, "religion" (see Finnis, *Natural Law and Natural Rights*, 85–90). Unlike Aquinas's list, which remains at the general level, Finnis mixes general and specific aspects of the good, such as life and play. Also, Finnis indicates that what he means by the term "religion" is not the same as the truth about God by placing the word in quotation marks. By it he means the vague notion of conformity to some sort of order. As with Finnis's discussion of God, which was reduced to the vague "D" (discussed in chapter 2), he here empties the term "religion" of most of its particular meaning. The most he can countenance by religion is the relationship of the other goods "of the whole cosmos and to the origin, if any, of that order" (Finnis, *Natural Law and Natural Rights*, 89).

27. Ibid., 65.

28. Ibid., 85.

29. *Summa Theologica* I-II, q. 94, a. 2.

30. See Cortest, *The Disfigured Face*, 96–97.

31. See, e.g., Finnis, *Aquinas: Moral, Political, and Legal Theory*, 152–53: "for both reasons [extramarital sex] is against reason, and consequently against nature."

32. Finnis, *Natural Law and Natural Rights*, 72.

33. Ibid., 68.

34. Porter, *Natural and Divine Law*, 170; see also Aquinas, *Commentary on the Nichomachean Ethics*, bk. 5, lecture 12, no. 1019 (noting that man possesses a twofold nature, that which is common to animals and that which is unique to man, rationality requiring a more complicated analysis of natural justice than simply the observation of animals).

35. See, e.g., Finnis, *Natural Law and Natural Rights*, 33–34, 66, 81.

36. Ibid., 65.

37. Ibid., 60, 66.

38. Ibid., 69: The criterion of truth of self-evident propositions is not the "feeling of certitude" about it.

39. Ibid., 33–34: "They [the forms of good] are not inferred from metaphysical propositions about human nature, or about the nature of good and evil, or about 'the function of a human being.'"

40. Ibid., 65.

41. "But that variety [of components of the supreme good], as Aristotle conceived it, is susceptible of a kind of ordering" (see MacIntyre, *Whose Justice? Which Rationality?*, 133).

42. MacIntyre, *After Virtue* (3rd ed.), 142.

43. Ibid. Although here MacIntyre is referring to virtue rather than good, the same point applies since the virtues are habits oriented to each of the goods.

44. Ibid., 157.

45. See Strauss, *Natural Right and History*, 180–81.

46. This principle of ordering based on man's nature is the subtle correction that Aquinas makes to Aristotle, who explains the rank order as originating within the structure of the *polis* (see Strauss, *Natural Right and History*). By situating the order within the nature of the *polis*, Aristotle's argument is susceptible of being understood as the hierarchy of goods being a matter of social convention. Yet since life in the *polis* is an aspect of man's nature, the hierarchy is not a matter of mere convention. Yet Aquinas's explanation more explicitly makes the hierarchy a given ontological fact.

47. MacIntyre, *Whose Justice? Which Rationality?*, 174.

48. *Summa Theologica* II-II, q. 110, a. 3, reply to obj. 4.

49. See MacIntyre, *After Virtue* (3rd ed.), 204–25.

50. Ibid., 218.

51. Ibid., 218–19.

52. MacIntyre uses different examples but makes a similar point: "What the good life is for a fifth-century Athenian general will not be the same as what it was for a medieval nun or a seventeenth-century farmer" (ibid., 220).

53. Ibid., 142.

54. See Finnis, *Natural Law and Natural Rights*, 92–95n42.

55. Ibid., 94. See also ibid., 410 (rejecting any ranking or ordering of the basic human value so that union with God or religion is considered of a higher order).

56. Westerman, *Disintegration of Natural Law Theory*, 56.

57. See MacIntyre, *Whose Justice? Which Rationality?*, 133: "From the standpoint of modernity . . . there can be no uniquely rational way of ordering goods within a scheme of life."

58. Ibid., 127, citing Aristotle, *Politics* 1.9.1257b40–1258a14, and *Nicomachean Ethics* 1.5.1095b22–31.

59. Ibid., 142.

60. See McInerny, *St. Thomas Aquinas*, 42. McInerny uses the image to describe the relationship among the powers of the soul—intellective, sensitive, and vegetative—but his image applies equally to the precepts of natural law.

61. *Summa Theologica* I-II, q. 94, a. 1.

62. See Finnis, *Natural Law and Natural Rights*, 92–95.

63. See ibid., 93.

64. See ibid., 92.

65. See ibid., 93.

66. See ibid.

67. See ibid., 110.

68. Aquinas, *Commentary on the Nichomachean Ethics*, bk. 1, lect. 9, no. 110. I have placed the word "complete" after "perfect" as a reminder that for Aquinas perfection means completeness or fullness of being.

69. Aristotle, *Nicomachean Ethics* 1.7.1098a17–18.

70. *Summa Theologica* I-II, q. 94, a. 2.

71. Aquinas, *De Veritate* 21.2.

72. See text accompanying note 68, above.

73. This text has been incorporated into the Supplement of the *Summa Theologica*.

74. The English word "improportionate" does not completely capture the meaning of the Latin *inconvenientem*. Etymologically, the word means "not to come together with." Thus, something *inconvenientem* does not come together well with something else. Thus, the lower goods to be pursued must come together with the higher goods, or they are inconvenient. We will return to this concept in considering the secondary precepts in the next section.

75. *Summa Theologica* Supp., q. 65, a. 1.

76. Armstrong, *Primary and Secondary Precepts*, 61.

77. For a good discussion of this understanding, see Westerman, *Disintegration of Natural Law*, 47.

78. *Summa Theologica* I-II, q. 94, a. 3.

79. Quoted in Porter, *Natural and Divine Law*, 200.

80. Ibid, 205, 213.

81. Ibid., 170.

82. Gratian, *Decretum* D.1, C.5.

83. Ibid., D.1, Ordinary Gloss on "prohibited": "Where one of two contraries is commanded, the other is, as a consequence, prohibited."

84. *Summa Theologica* I-II, q. 94, a. 2.

85. Gratian, *Decretum* D.1, and Ordinary Gloss on "what he wants."

86. See, e.g., Aquinas, *Commentary on the Nichomachean Ethics*, bk. 5, lect. 12, no. 1018, and *Summa Theologica* I-II, q. 94, a. 4.

87. *Summa Theologica* I-II, q. 94, a. 2.

88. *Summa Tractaturus Magister*, quoted in Porter, *Natural and Divine Law*, 254.

89. See *Summa Theologica* I, q. 16, a. 5: "As said above (article 1), truth is found in the intellect according as it apprehends a thing as it is; and in things according as they have being conformable to an intellect. This is to the greatest degree found in God. For His being is not only conformed to His intellect, but it is the very act of His intellect; and His act of understanding is the measure and cause of every other being and of every other intellect, and He Himself is His own existence and act of understanding. Whence it follows not only that truth is in Him, but that He is truth itself, and the sovereign and first truth." Someone who refuses to accept the existence of God would dispute this conclusion, but his dispute is not with the syllogism but with the truth of this premise. He would have to admit that *if this premise were true*, the prescription in the conclusion is also true.

90. See chapter 2.

91. *Summa Theologica* Supp., q. 65, a. 1.

92. Ibid.

93. Ibid., I-II, q. 94, a. 4.

94. For another similar example, see *Summa Theologica* II-II, q. 120, a. 1, where Aquinas explains that one who has received a deposit of a sword should not return the deposited sword to a madman bent on using the sword to kill someone; see also Aquinas, *Commentary on the Nichomachean Ethics*, bk. 5, lect. 12, no. 1025 (citing the same examples).

95. *Summa Theologica* Supp., q. 65, a. 1.

96. See Aristotle, *Nichomachean Ethics* 1.1.1094a1–1094a18, and Aquinas, *Commentary on the Nichomachean Ethics*, bk. 1, lect. 1, no. 12.

97. *Summa Theologica* Supp., q. 65, a. 1.

98. Ibid.

99. Ibid., Supp., q. 65, a. 2.

100. Ibid., Supp., q. 65, a. 2, reply to obj. 4.

101. Ibid., Supp., q. 65, a. 2; see also, *Summa Contra Gentiles* 3.109.5: "A secondary end depends on a principal one, just as a secondary agent depends on a principal one."

102. *Summa Theologica* Supp., q. 65, a. 2.

103. "The divine law consists of three [kinds of precepts], that is, prescriptions, prohibitions and indications. It commands what is beneficial, as to love God; it prohibits what is harmful, as forbidding us to kill; and it indicates what is appropriate, as that all persons should be free" (see *Summa Tractaturus Magister*, trans. Weigand, no. 321, quoted in Porter, *Natural and Divine Law*, 254).

104. Ibid., 254, quoting Weigand, *Summa Reginensis*, no. 382.

105. Aquinas, *Summa Contra Gentiles* 3.129.6.

106. See, e.g., Gratian, *Decretum* D.1, C.7.

107. Aquinas, *Summa Contra Gentiles* 3.129.6.

108. Ibid., 3.129.5.

109. See Aristotle, *Politics* 2.2 and 2.4; Plato, *Republic* 3.416b et seq., 5.464c, 8.543b et seq.

110. See Odd Langholm, *Economics in the Medieval Schools: Wealth, Exchange, Value, Money and Usury according to the Paris Theological Tradition, 1200–1350* (Leiden: E. J. Brill, 1992), 171–72. Christian thinkers tended to interpret the final reason given by Aristotle as a restatement of the pleasure of generosity and thus tended to merge the final two reasons into one (ibid).

111. *Summa Theologica* II-II, q. 66, a. 2.

112. See ibid., I-II, q. 94, a. 5, reply to obj. 3: "A thing is said to belong to the natural law in two ways. First, because nature inclines thereto: e.g., that one should not do harm to another. Secondly, because nature did not bring in the contrary: thus we might say that for man to be naked is of the natural law, because nature did not give him clothes, but art invented them [i.e., is indicated as possible by the eternal law]." In this sense, "the possession of all things in common . . . are said to be of the natural law, because, to wit, the distinction of possessions . . . were not brought in by nature, but devised by human reason for the benefit of human life. Accordingly the law of nature was not changed in this respect, except by addition."

113. Ibid., II-II, q. 66, a. 2.

114. Ibid., II-II, q. 66, a. 7: "It is nonetheless true that all things should be held in common in a time of extreme necessity, since natural reason directs that the well-being of the neighbor is to be cherished in preference to one's worldly goods." See also William of Auxerre, *Summa Aurea*, 3.18.1, translation quoted in Porter, *Natural and Divine Law*, 257; Henry of Ghent, *Quodlibet*, in *Opera Omnia*, vol. 10, ed. G. A. Wilson (Leiden: E. J. Brill, 1979), 204–5.

115. See also Robert of Courson, *Summa*, 16, 5, trans. quoted in Langholm, *Economics in the Medieval Schools*, 42–43; Ambrose, quoted in *Summa Theologica* II-II, q. 66, a. 7: "It is the hungry man's bread that you withhold, the naked man's cloak that you store away."

116. See Gregory the Great, *The Book of Pastoral Rule and Selected Epistles*, trans. Rev. James Barmby, in *Nicene and Post-Nicene Fathers*, vol. 12, *Leo the Great and Gregory the Great*, ed. Schaff and Wace (Grand Rapids, MI: Eerdmans, 1979), 3.21: "For, when we administer necessaries of any kind to the indigent, we do not bestow our own, but render them what is theirs."

117. Porter, *Natural and Divine Law*, 138–39 (quoting translation of Huguccio, *Lottin*, 110.

118. Justinian, *Digest* 41.1.1

119. Gratian, *Decretum* D.1, C.7; see also Justinian, *Digest* 41.1.1.1.

120. In fact, Aquinas says it is ruled by two higher measures, both the divine law and the natural law. He says: "And this higher measure is twofold, viz. the divine law and the natural law. . . . Wherefore Isidore in determining the nature of law, lays down, at first, three conditions; viz., that it 'foster religion,' inasmuch as

it is proportionate to the divine law; that it be 'helpful to discipline,' inasmuch as it is proportionate to the nature law; and that it 'further the common weal,' inasmuch as it is proportionate to the utility of mankind" (*Summa Theologica* I-II, q. 95, a. 3).

121. Finnis, *Natural Law and Natural Rights*, 280. In this quotation, Finnis is only speaking of natural law, not eternal law. Given his dismissal of eternal law at the end of the book, I doubt he would disagree with applying this phrase to it. Also, in certain contexts, Finnis might consider some principles of eternal law as real law, but I believe in the context of the discussion where he uses this phrase (the relationship between eternal law and positive law) he clearly does not consider eternal law to function as a real law in conjunction with positive law.

122. Rziha, *Perfecting Human Actions*, 42.

123. Ibid., 90; see also ibid., 191 (explaining that as the speculative intellect participates in God's wisdom the practical intellect participates in eternal law).

124. "The virtues perfect us to follow natural inclinations in an appropriate way, which inclinations pertain to the law of nature. And therefore to the determination of each natural inclination there is ordered a particular virtue" (Porter, *Natural and Divine Law*, 93; quoting *Summa Theologica* II-II, q. 108, a. 2.

125. *Summa Theologica* I-II, q. 94, a. 5.

126. See Armstrong, *Primary and Secondary Precepts*, 79.

127. See ibid.

128. Porter, *Natural and Divine Law*, 170.

129. *Summa Theologica* I-II, q. 95, a. 2.

130. Ibid., q. 91, a. 2.

131. Aquinas, *Summa Contra Gentiles* 3.129.2.

132. Brennan, "Are Legislation and Rules a Problem in Law?," 1213–14.

133. *Summa Theologica* I-II, q. 95, a. 3.

134. Ibid., I-II, q. 19, a. 4: "It is from the eternal law . . . that human reason [i.e., eternal law] is the rule of the human will."

135. Ibid., I-II, q. 96, a. 4.

136. Finnis, *Natural Law and Natural Rights*, 342–43 (dismissing the notion of obligation in God's will as "conceptually misdirected").

137. Ibid., 335.

138. Certainly, Finnis's understanding of the common good is much more nuanced and encompassing than utilitarian notions of utility and preference. Finnis's argument is not therefore strictly speaking utilitarian; yet its source of ultimate justification bears similarity to utilitarian logic. For Finnis, law is obligatory because it works; for Aquinas it is obligatory because it conforms to the way the divine artificer intended it.

139. Ibid., 343.

140. Ibid., 342.

141. *Summa Theologica* I-II, q. 90, a. 3.

142. For Aquinas, the act of commanding (promulgating a law) is an act of reason; yet this act of reason itself involves an act of the will. See *Summa Theologica* I-II, q. 17, a. 1: "Command is an act of the reason presupposing, however, an act of the will." When considering whether law is an act of the reason or the will, Aquinas concludes it is an act of the reason, yet he references this earlier discussion as a reminder that this act of the reason in commanding presupposes an act of the will (see ibid., I-II, q. 90, a. 1, reply to obj. 3).

143. Huguccio, *Summa Decretorum*, 19 (my translation): *quia ad ea que in diuino iure continentur naturalis ductus rationis . . . impellit.*

144. *Naturalis ductus rationis* is a phrase used by Huguccio to describe the natural law. See, e.g., Huguccio, *Summa Decretorum*, 19.

145. *Summa Theologica* I-II, q. 91, a. 2.

146. Rom. 2:14–15.

147. *Summa Theologica* I-II, q. 91, a. 2, reply to obj. 2.

148. See Clifford Kossel, "Natural Law and Human Law," in *The Ethics of Aquinas*, ed. Stephen J. Pope (Washington, DC: Georgetown University Press, 2002), 171–93 (explaining that although in the order of causation the eternal law precedes the natural law, yet in the order of knowledge, we come to know the natural law first and then come to know its cause, the eternal law.)

149. Budziszewski, *The Line through the Heart*, 59.

150. Pope John Paul II, *Veritatis Splendor*, sec. 36, http://w2.vatican.va/content/john-paul-ii/en/encyclicals/documents/hf_jp-ii_enc_06081993_veritatis-splendor.html.

151. See Aristotle, *Nichomachean Ethics.*

152. *Summa Theologica* I, q. 19, a. 10.

153. Carl, "The First Principles of Natural Law," 153–55.

154. Gratian, *Decretum* D.1, C.8.

155. Ibid., D.1, C.5.

FIVE.   Consulting the Architect When Problems Arise: The Divine Law

1. Ps. 18:1.

2. Pope Leo XIII, *Arcanum Divinae Sapientiae* (1880), sec. 27, http://www.vatican.va/holy_father/leo_xiii/encyclicals/documents/hf_l-xiii_enc_10021880_arcanum_en.html.

3. See Westerman, *Disintegration of Natural Law*, 67–70, for a discussion of the difference between a deduction and a determination.

4. Aquinas, *Summa Theologica* I-II, q. 95, a. 2.

5. See Patrick Brennan, "The Place of 'Higher Law' in the Quotidian Practice of Law: Herein of Practical Reason, Natural Law, Natural Rights, and Sex Toys," *Georgetown Journal of Law & Public Policy* 7 (2009): 456 (describing speculative reason as how we know what is, and practical reason as how we know what we ought to do).

6. See Rziha, *Perfecting Human Actions*, 216 (explaining how speculative knowledge can become practical knowledge by extension by using the example that the speculative premise that men are rational becomes the practical premise that men should act rationally).

7. *Summa Theologica* I-II, q. 94, a. 2.

8. Ibid., I. q. 2, a. 1.

9. Ibid., I-II, q. 94, a. 2. I have substituted the original Latin *per se nota* for the phrase in the translation of "self-evident" because I believe this English phrase carries the connotation of "universally known" and as the current discussion makes clear not all things *per se nota* are actually known by all.

10. See chapters 3 and 4 herein.

11. *Summa Theologica* I-II, q. 94, a. 4.

12. Ibid.

13. Ibid.

14. Ibid.

15. Ibid.

16. Ibid., II-II, q. 57, a. 2, reply to obj. 1.

17. See ibid., II-II, q. 52, a. 1, reply to obj. 1. "Prudence or *euboulia* ["deliberating well"], whether acquired or infused, directs man in the research of counsel according to principles that the reason can grasp. . . . Since, however, human reason is unable to grasp the singular and contingent things which may occur, the result is that 'the thoughts of mortal men are fearful, and our counsels uncertain'" (ibid., quoting Wisd. 9:14).

18. Ibid., II-II, q. 47, a. 4.

19. Ibid., II-II, q. 47, a. 3, reply to obj. 2.

20. Ibid. (quoting Wisd. 9:14).

21. Ibid., I-II, q. 94, a. 4.

22. Ibid., I-II, q. 85, a. 3.

23. Ibid.

24. Thomas Aquinas, "Prooemium [Prologue]," in *De Duobus Praeceptis Caritatis*, http://www.corpusthomisticum.org/cac.html (my translation of *caro fuit subdita in omnibus animae vel rationi. Sed postquam Diabolus per suggestionem retraxit hominem ab observantia divinorum praeceptorum, ita etiam caro fuit inobediens rationi. Et inde accidit quod licet homo velit bonum secundum rationem, tamen ex concupiscentia ad contrarium inclinatur*).

25. See Rziha, *Perfecting Human Actions*, 118 (arguing that in the wicked the natural inclinations have been weakened by vicious habits).

26. *Summa Theologica* I-II, q. 94, a. 4.

27. Rziha, *Perfecting Human Actions*, 271.

28. See *Summa Theologica*, I-II, q. 109, a. 2.: "But in the state of corrupt nature, man falls short of what he could do by his nature, so that he is unable to fulfil it by his own natural powers"; see also Rziha, *Perfecting Human Actions*, 230: "Reason is subject to ignorance and obscured especially in practical matters."

29. Aquinas, *De Duobus Praeceptis* (my translation of *diabolus tamen in homine superseminavit aliam legem, scilicet concupiscentiae*). In chapter 4 we saw that Aquinas referred to this "other law" in the *Summa Theologica* as the law of the *fomes peccati*.

30. Ibid. (my paraphrasing of *quia ergo lex naturae per legem concupiscentiae destructa erat*).

31. Ibid.: "God gave to man this light and this law [natural law] in creation. But many believe that they are to be excused if through ignorance they do not observe this law. But against this, the prophet says in Ps. 4:6, 'Many say: "Who shows us the good?," as if they are ignorant of what is to be done." This is my translation of *Hoc lumen et hanc legem dedit Deus homini in creatione. Sed multi credunt excusari per ignorantiam, si hanc legem non observant. Sed contra eos dicit propheta in Ps. 4:6 multi dicunt: quis ostendit nobis bona? quasi ignorent quid sit operandum.*

32. See subsection "The Problem of Too Many Contingencies," in this chapter.

33. *Summa Theologica* II-II, q. 52, a. 1.

34. Aquinas, *Commentary on Aristotle's Nicomachean Ethics*, bk. 3, lect. 8, no. 73.

35. Rziha, *Perfecting Human Actions*, 42.

36. By "gift of counsel," I refer (as does Aquinas) to one of the seven gifts of the Holy Ghost, not merely the virtue of counsel. As a supernatural gift, counsel is "conferred on nature . . . [and] is above all the powers (*vires*) of created nature"; see Thomas Scannell, "Supernatural Gift," in *The Catholic Encyclopedia*, vol. 6 (New York: Robert Appleton, 1909), http://www.newadvent.org/cathen/06553a.htm.

37. *Summa Theologica* II-II, q. 52, a. 1, reply to obj. 1.

38. Ibid.

39. See chapter 9 herein for a discussion of natural law and justice.

40. Aquinas, *Commentary on the Ethics*, bk. 5, lect. 26, nos. 1083–85. Note that where the word "law" is used, we should think of it in terms of a precept of the natural law, and "legislator" should be understood as the one formulating in words a principle of the natural law. See also *Summa Theologica* II-II, q. 120, a. 1.

41. See *Summa Theologica* I-II, q. 94, a. 4.

42. Aquinas, *Commentary on the Ethics*, bk. 5, lect. 16, no. 1086.

43. *Summa Theologica* II-II, q. 120, a. 1.

44. Ibid., II-II, q. 57, a. 1.

45. Aquinas, *Commentary on the Ethics*, bk. 5, lect. 16, no. 1086.

46. *Summa Theologica* II-II, q. 58, a. 1.

47. Ibid., I-II, q. 49, a. 2.

48. Ibid., I-II, q. 55, a. 1.

49. Ibid., II-II, q. 58, a. 1.

50. Ibid.

51. Aristotle, *Nicomachean Ethics*, translation in *Commentary on the Ethics* 5.1.1129a5.

52. Aquinas, *Commentary on the Ethics*, bk. 6, lect. 6, no. 1194.

53. *Summa Theologica* I-II, q. 94, a. 6.

54. Gratian, *Decretum* D.1, pt. 1.

55. Ibid., D.8, pt. 2, C.3.

56. Ibid., D.8, C.4–6.

57. Ibid., D.8, C.3.

58. Vernon Bourke, *History of Ethics* (New York: Doubleday, 1968), 38–39.

59. *Summa Theologica* I, q. 12, a. 7.

60. Ibid., I-II, q. 100, a. 3.

61. Ibid., I-II, q. 100, a. 11.

62. Ibid., I-II, q. 100, a. 1 (emphasis added).

63. See, e.g., Justinian, *Digest* (which is a collection of various opinions of jurists); Gratian, *Decretum* D.1, D.2, C.5; *Summa Theologica* I-II, q. 97, a. 3; David Johnston, "The Jurists," in *The Cambridge History of Greek and Roman Political Thought*, ed. Christopher Rowe and Malcolm Schofield (Cambridge: Cambridge University Press 2005), 616 (describing the opinion of jurists as "pivotal" in the Roman law system).

64. Raymond Martini, *Pugio fidei adversus Mauros et Judaeos*, ed. Westmead (Paris, 1687), 3.2.6.1, translation quoted in Jeremy Cohen, "Original Sin as the Evil Inclination: A Polemicist's Appreciation of Human Nature," *Harvard Theological Review* 73 (1980): 497–98.

65. *Summa Theologica* I-II, q. 91, a. 6.

66. See Aquinas, *Summa Contra Gentiles* 4.52, in which he discusses all of the punishments flowing from the first sin.

67. Ibid.

68. See chapter 3.

69. See Denzinger, "Decree of Lateran Council IV," 792, and Council of Trent, *Decree on Original Sin*, session 3, in ibid.

70. Cohen, "Original Sin as the Evil Inclination," 505.

71. Aquinas, "Prooemium [Prologue]," in *De Duobus Praeceptis Caritatis* (my translation of *oportebat quod homo reduceretur ad opera virtutis, et retraheretur a vitiis: ad quae necessaria erat lex Scripturae*).

72. *Summa Theologica* I-II, q. 91, a. 6.

73. See ibid., I-II, q. 85, a. 1.

74. See Porter, *Natural and Divine Law*, 173–75.

75. *Summa Theologica* I-II, q. 109, a. 2, and I-II, q. 109, a. 4 (explaining that even without grace one can fulfil some of the precepts of natural law and do some good), and II-II, q. 122, a. 1 (stating it is possible to observe some of the natural law through natural virtues).

76. The third effect is described as the loss of original justice, one of the effects of which is the loss of the intellect's ordering of the sensual appetites (*Summa Theologica* I-II, q. 85, a. 1; and Cohen, "Original Sin as the Evil Inclination," 509–10).

77. Rziha, *Perfecting Human Actions*, 271.

78. Aquinas, "Prooemium [Prologue]," in *De Duobus Praeceptis Caritatis* (my translation of *Sed manifestum est quod non omnes possunt scientiae insudare; et propterea a Christo data est lex brevis, ut ab omnibus posset sciri, et nullus propter ignorantiam possit ab eius observantia excusari*).

79. The use of the verb *insudare* to express this notion demonstrates the arduous nature of persevering in knowledge of what is right. The verb means "to sweat or perspire" in doing something.

80. Aquinas, "Prooemium [Prologue]," in *De Duobus Praeceptis Caritatis* (my translation of *Ad hoc autem quod actus humani boni reddantur, oportet quod regulae divinae dilectionis concordat*).

81. Ibid. (my translation of *Sed sciendum, quod haec lex debet esse regula omnium actuum humanorum*).

82. *Summa Theologica* I-II, q. 90, a. 1.

83. MacIntyre, *After Virtue* (3rd ed.), 131–32; MacIntyre, *Whose Justice? Which Rationality?*, 61–62.

84. See MacIntyre, *Whose Justice? Which Rationality?*, 61–62.

85. Aquinas, "Prooemium [Prologue]," in *De Duobus Praeceptis Caritatis* (my translation of *Sed considerandum, quod qui mandatum et legem divinae dilectionis servat, totam legem implet*).

86. Rziha, *Perfecting Human Actions*, 271 (citing *Summa Theologica* I-II, q. 99, a. 2, reply to obj. 2).

87. See ibid., 58–60.

88. Aquinas, "Prooemium [Prologue]," in *De Duobus Praeceptis Caritatis* (my translation of *Sicut enim videmus in artificialibus quod unumquodque opus tunc bonum et rectum dicitur quando regulae coaequatur; sic etiam quodlibet humanum opus rectum est et virtuosum quando regulae divinae dilectionis concordat*).

89. See ibid.

90. See ibid.; *Summa Theologica* I-II, q. 91, a. 5.

91. See chapter 2.

92. *Summa Theologica* I-II, q. 5, a. 5.

93. See ibid., I, q. 12, a. 12.

94. Ibid., I-II, q. 91, a. 4.

95. Porter, *Natural and Divine Law*, 52.

96. Ibid. To be properly understood, the role of complete justice must be discussed after a more detailed examination of human law. See chapter 9 herein.

97. Ibid.

98. *Summa Theologica* I-II, q. 95, a. 1.

99. See Porter, *Natural and Divine Law*, 138.

100. *Summa Theologica* I-II, q. 99, a. 2.

101. Ibid.

102. Ibid., I-II, q. 100, a. 1.

103. Ibid.: "For some matters connected with human actions are so evident, that after very little consideration one is able at once to approve or disapprove of them by means of these general first principles, but some matters cannot be the subject of judgment without much consideration of the various circumstances, which all are not competent to do carefully, but only those who are wise: just as it is not possible for all to consider the particular conclusions of sciences, but only for those who are versed in philosophy."

104. Ibid., q. 100, a. 11.

105. Ibid.

106. Gratian, *Decretum* D.1.

107. Aquinas lists many examples of the more detailed principles of the natural law that stand below the Decalogue in the hierarchy of generality; see *Summa Theologica* II-II, q. 100, a. 11.

108. See chapter 2's discussion of the analogy between Plato's Cave and the eternal law.

109. See *Summa Theologica* I-II, q. 100, a. 1.

110. See chapter 1 for the definition of law.

111. Joseph Vining, *From Newton's Sleep* (Princeton, NJ: Princeton University Press, 1995), 34.

112. See, e.g., Van Orden v. Perry, 545 U.S. (2005), 677, 690–92 (plurality) (holding that the establishment clause was not violated by a Ten Commandments monument, with the plurality reasoning that the display was typical of unbroken history of official acknowledgments of religion's role in American life, and even though the Ten Commandments were undoubtedly religious, they also had undeniable historical meaning); McCreary County v. ACLU of Ky., 545 U.S. (2005), 844, 869, 881 (holding a Kentucky courthouse display unconstitutional as the county's purpose was to emphasize the religious message of the Ten Commandments).

113. See *Summa Theologica* I-II, q. 107, a. 1.

114. Ibid., I-II, q. 107, a. 1, reply to obj. 2: "The Old Law . . . was given to men who were imperfect, that is, who had not yet received spiritual grace." The New Law, after the coming of Christ, is appropriate for those who have "spiritual grace instilled into our hearts."

115. Ibid., I-II, q. 107, a. 1.

116. Ibid., I-II, q. 107, a. 4, reply to obj. 2.

117. Ibid., I-II, q. 107, a. 4.

118. Ibid., I-II, q. 107, a. 4, reply to obj. 2.

119. Ibid., I-II, q. 108, a. 1, reply to obj. 2.

120. Ibid., I-II, q. 99, a. 4, reply to obj. 2.

121. Ibid., I-II, q. 108, a. 1.

122. Ibid., I-II, q. 104, a. 3; and I-II, q. 108, a. 3, reply to obj. 3.

123. Ibid., I-II, q. 108, a. 1, reply to obj. 3.

124. Ibid., I-II, q. 108, a. 2.

125. Ibid., I-II, q. 104, a. 3; and I-II, q. 104, a. 3, reply to obj. 1.

126. Ibid., I-II, q. 104, a. 3.

127. Ibid.

128. Pope Leo XIII, *Immortale Dei* (1885), http://w2.vatican.va/content/leo
-xiii/en/encyclicals/documents/hf_l-xiii_enc_01111885_immortale-dei.html.

129. Ibid.

130. Ibid.

131. Quoted in Denis Fahey, *The Mystical Body of Christ in the Modern
World*, 3rd ed. (Palmdale, CA: Christian Book Club of America, 1994), 15.

132. John F. Kennedy, "Address to the Greater Houston Ministerial Association at the Rice Hotel in Houston, TX" (September 12, 1960), http://www.american
rhetoric.com/speeches/jfkhoustonministers.html.

133. Aquinas, *De Regimine Principum* 1.16.

134. Aquinas, *Summa Contra Gentiles* 3.114.5.

135. Pope Pius IX, *Qui pluribus: On Faith and Religion*, ed. Padraig M.
O'Cleirigh (Kansas City, MO: Angelus, 1996), sec. 6.

136. Germain Grisez, *The Way of the Lord*, vol. 1 (Quincy, IL: Franciscan
Press, 1983), 599–626. Grisez does admit that the divine law can make known certain truths, but it is not actually necessary and reason is sufficient.

137. Moore, "Good without God," 249–50.

138. See Porter, *Natural and Divine Law*, 121 (noting that connections between the law of God and the natural law go all the way back to patristic authors).

139. Ibid., 51.

140. Ibid., 140.

141. Ibid., 136.

142. Ibid., 141.

143. Pope Pius IX, *Qui pluribus*, sec. 6.

144. Finnis, "Reason, Revelation, Universality and Particularity in Ethics," 38.

145. See chapter 2, third section, herein.

146. See ibid.

SIX.   Decorating the Structure: The Art of Making Human Law

1. Gratian, *Decretum* D.1, C.1.

2. See Porter, *Ministers of the Law*, 223.

3. See ibid., 60–62.

4. See Patrick McKinley Brennan, "Persons, Participating, and 'Higher
Law,'" *Pepperdine Law Review* 36, no. 5 (2009): 484–85 (describing the role of
higher law in human lawmaking).

5. Aquinas, *Summa Theologica* I-II, q. 91, a. 3.

6. See Porter, *Natural and Divine Law*, 159.

7. See ibid., 153–54.
8. *Summa Theologica* I-II, q. 99, a. 4.
9. See ibid., I-II, q. 99, a. 3.
10. See chapter 5 herein.
11. See *Summa Theologica* I-II, q. 107, a. 1.
12. See ibid., I-II, q. 99, a. 4.
13. See Lev. 25:23–25.
14. See Deut. 24:15.
15. See Exod. 21:1–22:30.
16. *Summa Theologica* I-II, q. 108, a. 1 (emphasis added).
17. Ibid., I-II, q. 107, a. 1.
18. Ibid., I-II, q. 108, a. 1.
19. Ibid., I-II, q. 104, a. 3; I-II, q. 108, a. 3.
20. Ibid., I-II, q. 108, a. 3.
21. Ibid., I-II, q. 108, a. 2.
22. Russell Hittinger, *The First Grace: Rediscovering the Natural Law in a Post-Christian World* (Wilmington, DE: ISI Books, 2003), 99; see also *Summa Theologica* I-II, q. 90, a. 3.
23. *Summa Theologica* I-II, q. 108, a. 1.
24. Ibid., I-II, q. 108, a. 1; I-II, q. 108, a. 2.
25. Ibid., I-II, q. 108, a. 2.
26. Ibid., I-II, q. 108, a. 2.
27. Grenier, *Moral Philosophy*, 11.
28. *Summa Theologica* I-II, q. 108, a. 2; I-II, q. 108, a. 3.
29. See chapter 2 (explaining that eternal law as divine wisdom emphasized its rationality, and the act of promulgation emphasized the volitional nature).
30. *Summa Theologica* I-II, q. 91, a. 3.
31. Ibid., I-II, q. 91, a. 3.
32. Ibid.
33. See Gratian, *Decretum* D.1, C.5.
34. Ibid.
35. *Summa Theologica* I-II, q. 91, a. 3.
36. Rebecca L. Brown, "How Constitutional Theory Found Its Soul: The Contributions of Ronald Dworkin," in *Exploring Law's Empire: The Jurisprudence of Ronald Dworkin*, ed. Scott Hershovitz (Oxford: Oxford University Press, 2006), 42.
37. *Summa Theologica* I-II, q. 91, a. 3.
38. See chapter 2.
39. Grenier, *Logic*, 78.
40. *Summa Theologica* I-II, q. 93, a. 1; see also Aquinas, *Summa Contra Gentiles* 3.123.7: "Now, laws that are established should stem from the prompting of nature [*oportet quod ex naturali instinctu procedant*], if they are human; just as in the demonstrative sciences, also, every human discovery takes its origin from

naturally known principles. But, if they are divine laws, they not only develop the prompting of nature but also supplement the deficiency of natural instinct, as things that are divinely revealed surpass the capacity of human reason."

41. See *Summa Theologica* I-II, q. 93, a. 1.

42. See W. D. Ross, introduction to *Aristotle's Prior and Posterior Analytics* (Oxford: Oxford University Press, 2001), 1, 4.

43. See Grenier, *Logic*, 81–83 (describing major and minor premises and their relation to conclusions using categorical syllogism, but employing slightly different terminology).

44. See *Summa Theologica* I-II, q. 91, a. 3.

45. See Mark C. Modak-Truran, "Beyond Theocracy and Secularism (Part I): Toward a New Paradigm for Law and Religion," *Mississippi College Law Review* 27, no. 1 (2007): 168.

46. See Martin Rhonheimer, "Natural Law as a 'Work of Reason': Understanding the Metaphysics of Participated Theonomy," *American Journal of Jurisprudence* 55, no. 1 (2010): 69.

47. See *Summa Theologica* I-II, q. 91, a. 3.

48. Ibid.

49. Ibid.

50. Ibid., I-II, q. 91, a. 3.

51. Ibid.

52. See ibid., I-II, q. 94, a. 2.

53. See chapter 5.

54. *Summa Theologica* I-II, q. 91, a. 3.

55. See Rziha, *Perfecting Human Actions*, 217.

56. See *Summa Theologica* I-II, q. 108, a. 2.

57. See ibid., I-II, q. 90, a. 2.

58. Gratian, *Decretum* D.1, C.5.

59. See *Summa Theologica* I-II, q. 95, a. 1.

60. See ibid., I-II, q. 90, a. 4.

61. See ibid., I-II, q. 95, a. 3.

62. See Grenier, *Moral Philosophy*, 290.

63. See ibid., 289–90, 367–68.

64. See *Summa Theologica* I-II, q. 94, a. 2.

65. See, e.g., Porter, *Ministers of the Law*, 81–82, 221–22.

66. See ibid., 80–81.

67. See Aquinas, *Commentary on the Nicomachean Ethics*, bk. 6, lecture 2, nos. 1127–32; *Summa Theologica* I-II, q. 57, a. 5.

68. *Summa Theologica* I-II, q. 57, a. 5.

69. Ibid.

70. See ibid.

71. Aquinas, *Commentary on the Nicomachean Ethics*, bk. 3, lecture 5, no. 446.

72. Ibid., bk. 3, lecture 5, cmt. 446; bk. 3, lecture 9, no. 487; bk. 3, lecture 11, no. 496.

73. Ibid., bk. 3, lecture 5, cmt. 446; bk. 3, lecture 6, no. 452.

74. See ibid., bk. 6, lecture 2, no. 1131 (explaining that ends are determined by nature but means are left to the choice of men).

75. *Summa Theologica* I-II, q. 108, a. 2.

76. See Grenier, *Moral Philosophy*, 288, 367.

77. See ibid., 289, 368.

78. *Summa Theologica* I-II, q. 108, a. 2.

79. See ibid., I-II, q. 57, a. 5.

80. See ibid., I-II, q. 57, a. 6.

81. Porter, *Natural and Divine Law*, 250.

82. Gratian, *Decretum*, D.1, C.5.

83. *Summa Theologica* I-II, q. 95, a. 2.

84. Ibid., I-II, q. 95, a. 4.

85. Ibid.

86. Ibid.

87. Ibid.

88. See ibid.

89. Ibid., I-II, q. 95, a. 2.

90. Ibid.

91. William L. Burdick, *The Principles of Roman Law and Their Relation to Modern Law* (Clark, NJ: Lawbook Exchange, 2004), 198.

92. See ibid., 105, 200.

93. Ibid., 200.

94. Cicero, *On the Commonwealth and On the Laws*, xxiv.

95. *Consuetudine* as ablative of cause expresses the cause or reason of a thing. Thus, this sentence describes law caused by common usages. See Robert J. Henle, *Latin Grammar* (Chicago: Loyola University Press, 1958), 178. "The ablative without a preposition may also be used to express the CAUSE OR REASON [ABLATIVE OF CAUSE]" (ibid., 320).

96. The same ablative of cause is used. See ibid.

97. Cicero, *De Inventione* 2.53–54, http://www.thelatinlibrary.com/cicero/inventione2.shtml (my translation).

98. *Summa Theologica* II-II, q. 57, a. 1 (describing *jus* as "the just thing itself" [*ipsam rem iustam*]); see ibid.: "*jus* [right] is so called because it is just [*justum*]."

99. Ibid.

100. Cicero, *De Inventione* 2.54.

101. Ibid.

102. See ibid.

103. See Porter, *Ministers of the Law*, 120.

104. See, e.g., ibid., 115–22.

105. Ibid., 50.

106. See, e.g., ibid., 105–13.

107. Ibid., 117.

108. Cicero, *On the Commonwealth*, 34: "I will have an easier time in completing my task if I show you *our commonwealth* as it is born, grows up, and comes of age, and as a strong and well-established state, than if I make up some state as Socrates does in Plato" (emphasis added).

109. Thelma B. Degraff, "Plato in Cicero," *Classical Philology* 35, no. 2 (1940): 149.

110. See Cicero, *On the Commonwealth*, 39. In fairness to the Greeks, Aristotle does employ a more historically rooted approach within his theoretical treatment of politics by examining the history of certain cities. See Aristotle, *Politics* 2.8–12.

111. See Cicero, *De Inventione* 2.53–54.

112. See chapter 3 (discussing the role of inclinations in the natural law).

113. Carl, "The First Principles of Natural Law," 124–30.

114. See Moore, "Law as a Functional Kind," 188, 208–9.

115. Thaddeus J. Kozinski, *The Political Problem of Religious Pluralism: And Why Philosophers Can't Solve It* (Lanham, MD: Lexington, 2013), 150–51.

116. Ibid., 151.

117. MacIntyre, *After Virtue* (2nd ed.), 53.

118. Porter uses the example of the institution of marriage for a similar illustration. See, e.g., Porter, *Ministers of the Law*, 117.

119. See *Corpus Juris Secundum* (St. Paul, MN: West, 2013), 17§1.

120. Ibid., 81A§42.

121. Ibid., §35. The doctrine of legal consideration requires that for a promise to be legally enforceable, the promise must have been bargained for. In other words the promise must have been made in exchange some action or promise in return.

122. Ibid., §40.

123. Ibid., 17§3.

124. See Porter, *Natural and Divine Law*, 251.

125. See ibid.

126. See Burdick, *The Principles of Roman Law and Their Relation to Modern Law*, 105, 200.

127. See ibid.

128. F. S. C. Northrop, "Naturalistic and Cultural Foundations for a More Effective International Law," *Yale Law Journal* 59 (1950): 1435.

129. Justinian, *Institutes* 1.2.1.

130. Northrop, "Naturalistic and Cultural Foundations for a More Effective International Law," 1430, 1435.

131. See Cicero, *De Inventione* 2.53–54.

132. *Summa Theologica* II-II, q. 58, a. 1.

133. See Cicero, *The Second Book of the Rhetoric, or of the Treatise on Rhetorical Invention, of M. T. Cicero*, in *Orations*, vol. 4, *The Fourteen Orations against Marcus Antonius; to Which Are Appended the Treatise on Rhetorical Invention; the Orator; Topics; on Rhetorical Partitions, Etc.*, trans. C. D. Yonge (London: G. Bell and Sons, 1913–21), 373–74.

134. Aquanis,*Commentary on the Nicomachean Ethics*, bk. 5, lecture 2, nos. 908–12.

135. See Porter, *Ministers of the Law*, 139: "[Culture] represents, therefore, a kind of social analogue to the Aristotelian and Thomistic idea of virtue as *habitus*."

136. Aquinas, *Commentary on the Nicomachean Ethics*, bk. 2, lecture 1, no. 247 (explaining that in Greek *ethos* when spelled with an *epsilon* means moral virtue or habit, but when spelled with an *eta* means custom, and that the Latin word *mos* contains both meanings of habit and custom).

137. See ibid., bk. 5, lecture 2, nos. 902–3.

138. Ibid., bk. 5, lecture 2, nos. 909–11.

139. See ibid., bk. 2, lecture 2, nos. 260–64.

140. See ibid., bk. 2, lecture 1, no. 250.

141. See Gratian, *Decretum* D.1.

142. Ibid.

143. Ibid., D.1, C.1.

144. Ibid., D.1, C.4.

145. Ibid., (my translation).

146. Ibid., D.1, C.4, Ordinary Gloss.

147. Ibid.

148. Ibid.

149. Ibid.

150. Ibid., D.1, C.5.

151. Ibid., D.8, C.3.

152. See ibid., D.8, C.4–C.9.

153. See Christopher A. Ferrara, *Liberty, the God That Failed: Policing the Sacred and Constructing the Myths of the Secular State, from Locke to Obama* (New York: Angelico, 2012), 257; arguing that slavery had become integrated in the customs of the South and, as Southerners themselves admitted, could only be ended by being rooted out; and quoting John C. Calhoun as saying: "We of the South cannot, will not surrender our institutions. To maintain the existing relations between the two races inhabiting that section of the Union is indispensible to the peace and happiness of both. *It cannot be subverted without drenching the country in blood.* . . . Be it good or bad, it has grown up among our society and institutions, it is so interwoven among them that *to destroy it is to destroy us as a people.*"

154. Gratian, *Decretum* D.8, C.3.

155. See ibid., D.8, C.3–C.5.

156. Ibid., D.11, C.1.

157. Ibid., D.6, C.3.

158. See *Summa Theologica* I-II, q. 97, a. 3: "*Sed Contra*, Augustine says [Ep. ad Casulan. xxxvi]: 'The customs of God's people and the institutions of our ancestors are to be considered as laws. And those who throw contempt on the customs of the Church ought to be punished as those who disobey the law of God.'"

159. Gratian, *Decretum* D.8, C.1 (citing Augustine for the proposition that custom must be abandoned if it is contradicted by the revelation of God, or the divine law); see also ibid., D.1, C.2.

160. See *Summa Theologica* I-II, q. 95, a. 3.

161. See Burdick, *The Principles of Roman Law and Their Relation to Modern Law*, 183.

162. Gratian, *Decretum* D.8, C.7.

163. Ibid., D.1, C.5: "It does not matter whether [custom] is confirmed by writing or by reason, since reason also supports ordinances [*lex*]."

164. Burdick, *The Principles of Roman Law and Their Relation to Modern Law*, 100.

165. *Corpus Juris Secundum* 15A§16.

166. See Gratian, *Decretum* D.1, C.5: "It is apparent that usage [*consuetudo*] has been reduced in part to writing and preserved partly only in the customs [*moribus*] of those continuing to make use of those customs. That which is reduced to writing is called either an ordinance [*constitutio*] or law [*jus*], while that which is not reduced to writing is called by the generic term 'usage' [*consuetudo*]" (my translation).

167. Ibid. (my translation).

168. Ibid., D.1, C.5, Ordinary Gloss.

169. Ibid., D.32, C.13.

170. See ibid.

171. *Summa Theologica* I-II, q. 97, a. 3.

172. Ibid.

173. Gratian, *Decretum* D.1, C.5, Ordinary Gloss: "And so it may be argued that one is never to judge according to custom if law prescribes the contrary. . . . But much can be found that is against this position."

174. See ibid., D.8, C.1: "Natural law similarly prevails by dignity over custom *and enactments*. So whatever has been either received in usages *or set down in writing* is to be held null and void if it is contrary to natural law" (emphasis added); see also Kenneth Pennington, "Politics in Western Jurisprudence," in *A Treatise of Philosophy and General Jurisprudence*, vol. 7, *The Jurists' Philosophy of Law from Rome to the Seventeenth Century*, ed. Andrea Padovcani and Peter G. Stein (Dordrecht: Springer, 2007), 157, 163: "Under Gratian's schema, laws were not simply reflections of different usages in various communities. All law had to be evaluated according to standards that transcended human institutions."

175. Gratian, *Decretum* D.9, C.11.

176. Ibid., D.4, C.3; see also Pennington, "Politics in Western Jurisprudence," 157, 163.

177. *Summa Theologica* I-II, q. 97, a. 3.

178. This phrase is a translation of the word *praescriptibilis*, which appears to be a rarely used word. It could mean "capable of becoming a rule or precept" or "capable of exception by prescription," which is an exception to law created by the passage of time. The latter meaning seems appropriate in the context in that the custom may be with respect to a matter that divine and natural law leave to be determined by human law.

179. Gratian, *Decretum* D.8, C. 7–C.8, Ordinary Gloss.

180. Ibid.

181. Ibid., D.8, C.7, Ordinary Gloss.

182. Ibid., D.1, C.5 ("is lacking").

183. *Corpus Juris Canonici* 2.1.4.11.

184. Ibid.

185. Gratian, *Decretum* D.4, C.6.

186. Ibid., D.4, C.3 (emphasis added).

187. Ibid.

188. See generally Hart, *Concept of Law*, 94–107.

189. See ibid., 94–95.

190. See ibid., 95–96.

191. Porter, *Ministers of the Law*, 253 (emphasis added).

192. Berman, *Law and Revolution*, 557.

193. This very question was at the center of one of the earliest Supreme Court cases. See Calder v. Bull, 3 U.S. 386 (1798). Justices Chase and Iredell clashed in their opinions over whether the judiciary has the power to void legislation on grounds of its violation of natural law; compare 388 with 399 (Iredell, concurring). Both justices agreed on the requirement that legislation must comply with the natural law but differed over who held the power to abrogate offending statutes. Chase believed the power vested in the legislature, while Iredell believed it vested in the judiciary; see also Budziszewski, *The Line through the Heart*, 151.

194. Gratian, *Decretum* D.4, C.3.

195. Ibid.

196. Ibid.

197. Dred Scott v. Sandford, 60 U.S. 393, 452 (1856).

198. U.S. Const. art. IV, § 2, cl. 3.

199. See Ferrara, *Liberty, the God That Failed*, 297.

200. Gratian, *Decretum* D.1, C.7.

201. E.g., ibid., D.1, C.5; D.11, C.4: "The authority of long-standing custom and practice is not . . . of such moment as to prevail over . . . ordinance."

202. Justinian, *Digest* 47.12.3, para. 5.

203. St. Augustine, "The Problem of Free Choice," in *Ancient Christian Writers,* ed. Johannes Quasten and Joseph C. Plumpe (Mahwah, NJ: Paulist, 1955), 35, 44.

204. See *Summa Theologica* I-II, q. 96, a. 4.

205. See ibid.

206. See ibid.

207. Gratian, *Decretum* D.4, C.2.

208. See ibid.: "Because what is against the custom of the inhabitants is abrogated through their contrary custom."

209. Ibid.

210. *Summa Theologica* I-II, q. 97, a. 3.

211. Ibid., I-II, q. 96, a. 2.

212. Ibid.

213. See ibid., I-II, q. 95, a. 2: "Consequently every human law has just so much of the nature of law, as it is derived from the law of nature."

214. Ibid., I-II, q. 96, a. 2.

215. Ibid.

216. Ibid.

217. Ibid., I-II, q. 96, a. 2–3.

218. Ibid.

219. Ibid., II-II, q. 77, a. 1.

220. Ibid., I-II, q. 96, a. 2.

221. See ibid., II-II, q. 77, a. 1; see also ibid., I-II, q. 96, a. 2 (explaining that human law should prohibit those vices "without the prohibition of which human society could not be maintained"); I-II, q. 96, a. 3 (explaining that human law only requires virtuous acts "that are ordainable to the common good—either immediately, as when certain things are done directly for the common good,—or mediately, as when a lawgiver prescribes certain things pertaining to good order, whereby the citizens are directed in the upholding of the common good of justice and peace").

222. Dante, *The Divine Comedy,* vol. 3, *Paradiso,* trans. John D. Sinclair (London: Oxford University Press, 1939), 96. I am grateful to my colleague Jason Houston, whose on-campus lecture on canto 6 of the *Paradiso,* "Reading the Signs of History in Dante's *Paradiso,*" September 10, 2014, directed my attention to this passage.

223. Ibid., 87.

224. See, e.g., *Summa Theologica* I-II, q. 95–97.

225. For an example, see generally Gaius, *Institutes.*

226. See generally Justinian, *Codex and Novelles,* vols. 12–17.

227. See generally Justinian, *Digest,* vols. 3–11.

228. See Justinian, *Institutes,* vol. 2.

229. See Gratian, *Decretum* D.1–D.20.

230. By which I mean Western Europe, the United States, and former colonies of these nations whose legal systems have been adapted from prior colo-

nial rulers and thus exclude from the discussion two other categories of legal systems, socialist law and Islamic law. See James S. E. Opolot, *World Legal Traditions and Institutions*, rev. ed. (Jonesboro, TN: Pilgrimage, 1981), 9.

231. Rafael La Porta, Florencio Lopez-de-Silanes, and Andrei Shleifer, "The Economic Consequences of Legal Origins," *Journal of Economic Literature* 46, no. 2 (2008): 288.

232. See Opolot, *World Legal Traditions and Institutions*, 9. The United States, for example, possesses a legal system built upon the common law model, yet many areas of the law have been superseded by comprehensive codes, such as the Uniform Commercial Code and the Model Penal Code (see ibid.).

233. See, e.g., Richard B. Cappalli, "At the Point of Decision: The Common Law's Advantage over the Civil Law," *Temple International and Comparative Law Journal* 12, no. 1 (1998): 87; La Porta, Lopez-de-Silanes, and Shleifer, "The Economic Consequences of Legal Origins," 286; Paul G. Mahoney, "The Common Law and Economic Growth: Hayek Might Be Right," *Journal of Legal Studies* 30, no. 2 (2001): 519.

234. See Opolot, *World Legal Traditions and Institutions*, 13–98.

235. La Porta, Lopez-de-Silanes, and Shleifer, "The Economic Consequences of Legal Origins," 285, 288.

236. R. Floyd Clarke, *The Science of Law and Lawmaking: Being an Introduction to Law, a General View of Its Forms and Substance, and a Discussion of the Question of Codification* (New York: Macmillan, 1898), 10.

237. 1 U.S.C. § 204(a) (2012).

238. U.C.C. § 1–103(a).

239. In the case of Justinian's Code, this was done through appending the *Novels* to the Code. The United States Code is updated periodically to remove repealed legislation and insert adopted legislation.

240. Leonard Besselink, Frans Pennings, and Sacha Prechal, "Introduction: Legality in Multiple Legal Orders," in *The Eclipse of the Legality Principle in the European Union*, ed. Leonard Besselink et al. (Austin, TX: Wolters Kluwer Law & Business, 2011), 6.

241. Vivian Grosswald Curran, "Romantic Common Law, Enlightened Civil Law: Legal Uniformity and the Homogenization of the European Union," *Colombia Journal of European Law* 7 (2001): 76–77.

242. Ibid., 93.

243. Ibid.

244. Ibid., 105.

245. Berman, *Law and Revolution*, 529.

246. Porter has drawn the same conclusion. See Porter, *Ministers of the Law*, 256: "The common law tradition informing the legal systems of England and its former colonies is itself a kind of customary law, extending well beyond those areas of law explicitly identified as falling within its scope."

247. Benjamin N. Cardozo, *The Nature of the Judicial Process* (New Haven, CT: Yale University Press, 2007), 104.

248. James Q. Whitman, *The Legacy of Roman Law in the German Romantic Era: Historical Vision and Legal Change* (Princeton, NJ: Princeton University Press, 1990), 71–72.

249. Bishop, *Common Law and Codification*, 3, 9–10.

250. See Payne v. Tennessee, 501 U.S. 808, 827–28 (1991): "When governing decisions are unworkable or are badly reasoned, this Court has never felt constrained to follow precedent. *Stare decisis* is not an inexorable command; rather, it is a principle of policy and not a mechanical formula of adherence to the latest decision" (citations omitted) (internal quotation marks omitted).

251. See, e.g., Planned Parenthood of Se. Pa. v. Casey, 505 U.S. 833, 854 (1992); Robert Barnhart, Note, "Principled Pragmatic Stare Decisis in Constitutional Cases," *Notre Dame Law Review* 80 (2005): 1911; Daniel M. O'Keefe, "*Stare Decisis*: What Should the Supreme Court Do When Old Laws Are Not Necessarily Good Laws? A Comment on Justice Thomas' Call for Reassessment in the Supreme Court's Voting Rights Jurisprudence," *St. Louis University Law Journal* 40 (1996): 261–62.

252. Gratian, *Decretum* D.8, C.7 (describing truth's supremacy over custom and custom's strength when it is supported by truth).

253. See, e.g., Loving v. Virginia, 388 U.S. 1, 10–11 (1967), overturning Pace v. Alabama, 106 U.S. 583, 585 (1883) (holding that states could prohibit interracial marriages because of potential harm to white marriages); Brown v. Bd. of Educ., 347 U.S. 483, 494–95 (1954), overturning Plessy v. Ferguson, 163 U.S. 537, 547–48 (1896) (holding that separate facilities for blacks and whites were constitutional so long as they were equal); W. Coast Hotel Co. v. Parrish, 300 U.S. 379, 391–92 (1937), overturning Lochner v. New York, 198 U.S. 45, 60 (1905) (holding the Constitution included a freedom to contract with which government could not interfere).

254. Bishop, *Common Law and Codification*, 11.

255. Ibid., 12.

256. See Curran, "Romantic Common Law, Enlightened Civil Law," 83.

257. See ibid., 75.

258. Ibid., 84–85.

259. See ibid., 83; Roscoe Pound, "Common Law and Legislation," *Harvard Law Review* 21 (1908): 386.

260. Pound, "Common Law and Legislation," 387.

261. Ibid., 396.

262. See Newman, *Foundations of Justice*, 40.

263. Aristotle, *The Politics of Aristotle*, trans. Ernest Barker (Oxford: Oxford University Press, 1946), 367.

264. Ibid., lv.

265. Curran, "Romantic Common Law, Enlightened Civil Law," 100–101.

266. Ibid., 95.

267. André Tunc, "Methodology of the Civil Law in France," *Tulane Law Review* 50 (1976): 459–60 (footnote omitted).

268. Ibid., 469.

269. Bentham attempted to get himself hired to replicate Napoleon's process in any jurisdiction willing to pay; see Philip Schofield and Jonathan Harris, introduction to *"Legislator of the World": Writings on Codification, Law, and Education*, by Jeremy Bentham, ed. Philip Schofield and Jonathan Harris (Oxford: Clarendon, 2009), xi: "Bentham offered to draw up such a code, but only if he were formally requested to do so. He was not prepared to embark on the arduous task of codifying unless he were given sufficient encouragement. He therefore wished to receive an invitation from a 'constituted authority' asking him to draw up a code of law."

270. Bentham, *"Legislator of the World,"* 245.

271. See chapter 5.

272. James Kent, *Commentaries on American Law*, 12th ed., ed. O.W. Holmes, Jr. (Boston: Little, Brown, and Company, 1873), 1:536.

273. In contrast to the view that continental European legal systems form one group based on Roman law, and Anglo-American another based on a rejection of Roman law, Harold Berman has argued that all Western legal systems, including continental European and Anglo-American ones, share "common historical roots" (Berman, *Law and Revolution*, 539).

274. J. Bleecker Miller, *Destruction of Our Natural Law by Codification* (New York: H. Cherouny, 1882), 7.

275. Curran, "Romantic Common Law, Enlightened Civil Law," 95.

276. Ibid., 93.

277. See *Summa Theologica* I-II, q. 91, a. 4; I-II, q. 96, a. 1.

278. Curran, "Romantic Common Law, Enlightened Civil Law," 92.

279. See Besselink, Pennings, and Prechal, "Introduction: Legality in Multiple Legal Orders," 6.

280. Benjamin Lee Samuel Nelson, "Unwritten Law: Three Selections from the History of Political Philosophy" (unpublished manuscript, May 19, 2012), http://ssrn.com/abstract=2062924, or http://dx.doi.org/10.2139/ssrn.2062924.

281. Ibid.

282. Tunc, "Methodology of the Civil Law in France," 466–67.

283. Curran, "Romantic Common Law, Enlightened Civil Law," 87–88.

284. Ibid., 87.

285. *Summa Theologica* I-II, q. 94, a. 4.

286. Ibid.

287. Ibid.

288. Ibid., I-II, q. 94, a. 4; I-II q. 96, a. 6 (discussing exceptions to a general rule about keeping the gates of the city closed); II-II, q. 62, a. 5 (regarding exceptions to

the rule that restitution of goods to their owner must be made, but a sword should not be restored to a madman).

289. Curran, "Romantic Common Law, Enlightened Civil Law," 92 (arguing that the assembly of particular examples "no matter how numerous they may be, is vulnerable to defeat by counterexample").

290. Oliver Wendell Holmes, *The Common Law* (Clark, NJ: Lawbook Exchange, 2005), 1.

291. Ibid.

292. Curran, "Romantic Common Law, Enlightened Civil Law," 93.

293. Ibid., 92.

294. Ibid., 93.

295. John Neville Figgis, *The Divine Right of Kings*, 2nd ed. (Cambridge: Cambridge University Press, 1934), 229.

296. *Summa Theologica* I-II, q. 96, a. 6.

297. Translated in Tunc, "Methodology of the Civil Law in France," 468 (internal quotation marks omitted).

298. Vining, *From Newton's Sleep*, 155.

299. Brennan, "Persons, Participating, and 'Higher Law,'" 476.

300. Brennan, "Are Legislation and Rules a Problem in Law?," 1191.

301. See *United States Code Service*, LexisNexis, last visited September 13, 2017, https://store.lexisnexis.com/products/united-states-code-service-uscs-skuSKU 7560/details (listing the number of volumes composing the United States Code).

302. See, e.g., *Deering's California Codes Annotated*, LexisNexis, last visited September 13, 2017, https://store.lexisnexis.com/products/deerings-california -codes-annotated-skuSKU7329/details (listing the number of volumes comprising California's code as 219); *Michie's West Virginia Code Annotated*, LexisNexis, last visited September 13, 2017, https://store.lexisnexis.com/products/michies -west-virginia-code-annotated-skuSKU6989/details (listing the number of volumes comprising the code of West Virginia as twenty-nine).

303. Susan Davis, "This Congress Could Be Least Productive Since 1947," *USA Today*, August 15, 2012, http://usatoday30.usatoday.com/news/washington /story/2012-08-14/unproductive-congress-not-passing-bills/57060096/1.

304. Grant Gilmore, *The Ages of American Law* (New Haven, CT: Yale University Press, 1977), 95.

305. Ibid.

306. This subsection is premised upon the claim that, although still classed as a common law jurisdiction, the United States has allowed entire sections of the law to become dominated by legislation and codes. From the various codes of types of law to the omnibus statutes covering major sections of American life, entire areas of the law are dominated by codes or omnibus statutes, such as the Securities Act of 1933, the Dodd–Frank Act, and the Affordable Care Act.

307. Tunc, "Methodology of the Civil Law in France," 461.

308. Ibid., 462.

309. Ibid., 465–66.

310. John Henry Merryman and Rogelio Pérez-Perdomo, *The Civil Law Tradition: An Introduction to the Legal Systems of Western Europe and Latin America*, 3rd ed. (Stanford, CA: Stanford University Press, 2007), 144–45; John Henry Merryman, "The French Deviation," *American Journal of Comparative Law* 44, no. 1 (1996): 112, 116.

311. See *Summa Theologica* I-II, q. 90, a. 1: "Law is a rule and measure of acts."

312. See Brennan, "Are Legislation and Rules a Problem in Law?," 1202.

313. Ibid., 1203; commenting on Joseph Vining, "The Resilience of Law," in *Law and Democracy in the Empire of Force*, ed. H. Jefferson Powell and James Boyd White (Ann Arbor: University of Michigan Press, 2009), 151, 155–56.

314. Monopoly, Hasbro, last visited February 13, 2015, http://www.hasbro.com /common/instruct/00009.pdf.

315. Brennan, "Are Legislation and Rules a Problem in Law?," 1203 (commenting on Vining; see note 313).

316. See text accompanying note 67.

317. See Brennan, "Are Legislation and Rules a Problem in Law?," 1202.

318. Ibid.

319. Ibid.

320. Ibid.

321. Ibid.

322. See text accompanying note 318.

323. See text accompanying notes 282–94.

324. Merryman and Pérez-Perdomo, *The Civil Law*, 144–45.

325. See chapter 5.

326. See *Summa Theologica* I-II, q. 94, a. 4.

327. See ibid., I-II, q. 97, a. 4 (considering when lawgivers should dispense).

328. See chapter 4.

329. For example, just as the Germans forgot the natural law precept against all forms of theft; see *Summa Theologica* I-II, q. 94, a. 4 (noting how the Gauls had developed the custom of permitting theft from foreigners, notwithstanding theft clearly being contrary to the natural law).

330. See ibid., describing a division of human law between general principles (as in the *jus gentium*) and particular determinations (as in the *jus civile*).

331. See H. R. 5660, 106th Cong., § 408(2)(C) (2000).

332. See Brendan Sapien, "Financial Weapons of Mass Destruction: From Bucket Shops to Credit Default Swaps," *Southern California Interdisciplinary Law Journal* 19 (2010): 442.

333. See ibid.

334. See, e.g., Schrenger v. Caesars Ind., 825 N. E.2d 879, 882 (Ind. Ct. App. 2005) (declaring that, except for specifically authorized and highly regulated exceptions,

gambling contracts are against public policy); Samuel Williston, *A Treatise on the Law of Contracts*, 4th ed. (Eagan, MN: Thomson/West, 2013), 7 § 17:1.

335. See Blake Hornick and Arren Goldman, "Commentary: The End of the Reagan Era of Deregulation and Worship of the Free Markets," *Andrews Securities Litigation and Regulation Reporter* 14, no. 17 (2008): 1, 3.

336. Ibid.

337. U.S.C. § 16(e)(2) (2012): "This chapter shall supersede and preempt the application of any State or local law that prohibits or regulates gaming or the operation of bucket shops . . . in the case of . . . (B) an agreement, contract, or transaction that is excluded from this chapter under section 2(c) or 2(f) of this title or sections 27 to 27f of this title, or exempted under section 6(c) of this title [regardless of whether any such agreement, contract, or transaction is otherwise subject to this chapter]."

338. See La Porta, Lopez-de-Silanes, and Shleifer, "The Economic Consequences of Legal Origins," 64–65, arguing that one cause of the superiority of common law systems is their flexibility or (adaptability), enabling courts to catch evasions.

339. Ibid., 42–43.

340. Brennan, "The Place of 'Higher Law' in the Quotidian Practice of Law," 475–76.

341. Ibid., 476.

342. Ibid., 475–76.

343. Ibid., 476.

344. Clarke, *Science of Law and Lawmaking*, 25.

345. See ibid., 40.

346. See ibid.

347. See Berman, *Law and Revolution*, 528.

348. See Clarke, *Science of Law and Lawmaking*, 334.

349. See W.W., "What's America's Real Crime Rate?" *Economist*, February 14, 2012, http://www.economist.com/blogs/democracyinamerica/2012/02/prisons-and-crime: "In 1980, there were about two hundred and twenty people incarcerated for every hundred thousand Americans; by 2010, the number had more than tripled, to seven hundred and thirty-one. No other country even approaches that," quoting Adam Gopnik, "The Caging of America: Why Do We Lock Up So Many People?," *The New Yorker*, January 30, 2012. But see Richard Fausset, "Conservatives Latch onto Prison Reform," *Los Angeles Times*, January 28, 2011, http://articles.latimes.com/2011/jan/28/nation/la-na-conservative-crime-20110129 (describing the recent successes of Texas and other states in reducing or eliminating the trend of increasing prison populations with prison reform).

350. See Robert S. Mueller, III, *Today's FBI: Facts and Figures, 2010–2011* (Darby, PA: Diane Publishing, 2011), 37: "Since 2007, there have been more than 1,700 pending corporate, securities, commodities, and investment fraud cases," an increase of 37 percent from 2001.

351. See generally ibid., 37–39 (discussing high-profile white-collar crimes).

352. See "Corporate Crime and Abuse: Tracking the Problem," *Center for Corporate Policy*, 2003–2004, http://www.corporatepolicy.org/issues/crimedata .htm: "In its 2001 report the FBI estimated that the nation's total loss from robbery, burglary, larceny-theft and motor vehicle theft in 2001 was $17.2 billion—less than a third of what Enron alone cost investors, pensioners and employees that year."

353. "Martha Stewart Convicted," *Time*, March 5, 2004, http://www.time .com/time/nation/article/0,8599,598286,00.html.

354. Gillian Flaccus, "Calif. Man Gets 30 Years for Ponzi Scheme," *Washington Post*, May 27, 2006, http://www.washingtonpost.com/wp-dyn/content/article/2006 /05/27/AR2006052700250.html.

355. Diana B. Henriques, "Madoff Is Sentenced to 150 Years for Ponzi Scheme," *New York Times*, June 29, 2009, http://www.nytimes.com/2009/06/30 /business/30madoff.html?pagewanted=all&_r=0.

356. "WorldCom Scandal One of Many," *CNN Money*, June 27, 2002, http:// money.cnn.com/2002/06/26/news/companies/accounting_scandals/. See generally Penelope Patsuris, "The Corporate Scandal Sheet," *Forbes*, August 26, 2002, http://www.forbes.com/2002/07/25/accountingtracker.html.

357. Frank H. Easterbrook and Daniel R. Fischel, "Antitrust Suits by Targets of Tender Offers," *Michigan Law Review* 80 (1982): 1155, 1177n57: "Managers not only may but should violate the rules [economic regulatory laws] when it is profitable to do so"; see also ibid., 1168n36 (arguing that managers "have no general obligation to avoid violating regulatory laws, when violations are profitable").

358. Berman, *Law and Revolution*, 40.

359. Lambert v. California, 355 U.S. 225, 243 (1957).

360. Mark D. Yochum, "Ignorance of the Law Is No Excuse Except for Tax Crimes," *Duquesne Law Review* 27, no. 2 (1989): 223.

361. Sharon L. Davies, "The Jurisprudence of Willfulness: An Evolving Theory of Excusable Ignorance," *Duke Law Journal* 48, no. 3 (1998): 342.

362. *Summa Theologica* I-II, q. 94, a. 4: "It is therefore evident that, as regards the general principles whether of speculative or of practical reason, truth or rectitude is the same for all, and is equally known by all."

363. See generally Hart, *Concept of Law*, 81–207.

364. Heinrich A. Rommen, *The Natural Law*, trans. Thomas R. Hanley (New York: Arno Press, 1947), 17–18.

365. Davies, "The Jurisprudence of Willfulness," 343.

366. Bishop, *Common Law and Codification*, 8.

SEVEN.   Appointing a Foreman: The Basis of Authority and Obligation

1. Vining, "Law's Own Ontology," 695.

2. See Francisco Suárez, *Selections from Three Works*, vol. 2, ed. James Brown Scott, trans. G. L. Williams, Ammi Brown, John Waldron, and Henry Davis

(Oxford: Clarendon, 1944), 363 (all footnotes following in this chapter refer to volume 2.)

3. Ibid.

4. Charlton T. Lewis and Charles Short, *A Latin Dictionary* (Oxford: Oxford University Press, 1879), s.v. "auctoritas."

5. See Hart, *Concept of Law*, 7, 20.

6. Joseph Raz, "Authority and Justification," *Philosophy & Public Affairs* 14, no. 1 (1985): 5.

7. C. G. Bateman, "Sovereignty's Missing Moral Imperative," *International Zeitschrift* 8, no. 2 (2012): 40: "Sovereignty denotes two main tenets which support its legitimacy. First, there must be a political body or person with the capacity to exercise power over a specific community and place such that no higher authority exists within its jurisdiction. Second, sovereignty must insist that a positive moral imperative is placed on the person or body executing such power in practice."

8. See Raz, "Authority and Justification," 5: those claiming legitimate authority are correct "only if and to the extent that their claim is justified and they are owed a duty of obedience."

9. See ibid., 7: "I do all that the law requires of me if my actions comply with it."

10. See ibid., 5.

11. Randy E. Barnett, "Constitutional Legitimacy," *Columbia Law Review* 103, no. 1 (2003): 116.

12. Vining, "Law's Own Ontology," 696.

13. See, e.g., Joseph Raz, *The Authority of Law* (Oxford: Clarendon Press, 1979), 233.

14. Joseph Raz, *Practical Reason and Norms* (Oxford: Oxford University Press, 1999), 35–48, 58–78; Raz, *Authority of Law*, 17–19.

15. See Raz, *Practical Reason and Norms* (1999), 35–48, 58–78; Raz, "Authority and Justification," 13: "The fact that an authority requires performance of an action is a reason for its performance which is not to be added to all other relevant reasons when assessing what to do, but should exclude and take the place of some of them."

16. Philip Soper, "Legal Theory and the Claim of Authority," *Philosophy & Public Affairs* 18, no. 3 (1989): 215–21.

17. Ibid.

18. Abner S. Greene, *Against Obligation: The Multiple Sources of Authority in a Liberal Democracy* (Cambridge, MA: Harvard University Press, 2012), 102.

19. See Hans Kelsen, *General Theory of Law and State* (Cambridge, MA: Harvard University Press, 1945), xv. I adopt Raz's interpretation of Kelsen's theory with respect to the origin of the basic norm; see Raz, *Authority of Law*, 126.

20. See Hart, *Concept of Law*, 189: "In the absence of [the minimum] content men, as they are, would have no reason for obeying voluntarily any rules; and with-

out a minimum of co-operation given voluntarily by those who find that it is in their interest to submit to and maintain the rules, coercion of others who would not voluntarily conform would be impossible."

21. Ibid., 84–85, 92–93.

22. Ibid., 92.

23. Ibid., 105.

24. Ibid. See also Raz, *Authority of Law*, 69 (arguing that the ultimate rule in a legal system has no rule to establish its validity).

25. See Hart, *Concept of Law*, 107.

26. See, e.g., Rebecca L. Brown, "How Constitutional Theory Found Its Soul: The Contributions of Ronald Dworkin."

27. See Ronald Dworkin, *Law's Empire* (Cambridge, MA: Harvard University Press, 1986), 93, 97, 103, 151. See also Brian M. McCall, "Exploring the Foundations of Dworkin's Empire: The Discovery of an Underground Positivist," *Journal of Law, Philosophy and Culture* 4, no. 1 (2009): 201–2.

28. Stephen Perry, "Political Authority and Political Obligation," in *Oxford Studies in Philosophy of Law*, vol. 2, ed. Leslie Green and Brian Leiter (Oxford: Oxford University Press, 2013), 1n4.

29. See Greene, *Against Obligation*, 102.

30. Perry, "Political Authority and Political Obligation," 3.

31. Patrick McKinley Brennan, "Locating Authority in Law," in *Civilizing Authority: Society, State, and Church*, ed. Patrick Brennan (Lanham, MD: Lexington, 2007), 163.

32. See Aquinas, *Summa Theologica* I-II, q. 90, a. 4.

33. See, e.g., Hart, *Concept of Law*, 18–48; Raz, *Authority of Law*, 11–19.

34. Perry, "Political Authority and Political Obligation," 11–12.

35. See, e.g., John Locke, "Of the State of Nature," in *Second Treatise of Government* (Indianapolis: Bobbs-Merrill, 1952), chap. 2, para. 14; Locke "Of Slavery," in *Second Treatise of Government*, chap. 4, para. 22.

36. See, e.g., Barnett, "Constitutional Legitimacy," 115.

37. George Washington, "Farewell Address" (September 17, 1796), in *Documents of American History*, 9th ed., ed. Henry Steele Commager (Englewood Cliffs, NJ: Prentice-Hall, 1973), 1:169, 172.

38. Ferrara, *Liberty*, 175–87.

39. Ibid., 183.

40. Barnett, "Constitutional Legitimacy," 123.

41. Jean-Jacques Rousseau, *The Social Contract*, trans. Maurice Cranston (Harmondsworth: Penguin, 1968), 152.

42. Ibid., 135, 153.

43. Barnett, "Constitutional Legitimacy," 118.

44. Locke, "Of the Beginning of Political Societies," in *Second Treatise*, chap. 8, para. 119.

45. See Greene, *Against Obligation*, 45. Greene also points out that participation in the electoral process, even if it could imply consent to the results of the election in which one voted, cannot be used for its claimed purpose of binding one to the electoral results in the past (ibid., 47). Jeffrey Reiman summarizes the failure of the so-called electoral participation theory of consent thus: "There is nothing inherently legitimating about the electoral process. If anything, the electoral process is the problem, not the solution. . . . The policies that emerge from the electoral process will be imposed on the dissenting minority against its wishes. And then, rather than answering the question of legitimacy, this will raise the question with respect to those dissenters. Why are the exercises of power approved by the majority against the wishes of (and potentially prohibiting the desired actions of) the minority obligatory with respect to the minority? Why are such exercises of power not simply a matter of the majority tyrannizing the minority?"; Jeffrey Reiman, "The Constitution, Rights, and the Conditions of Legitimacy," in *Constitutionalism: The Philosophical Dimension*, ed. Alan S. Rosenbaum (New York: Greenwood, 1988), 127, 134.

46. See, e.g., A. John Simmons, "The Principle of Fair Play," *Philosophy & Public Affairs* 8, no. 4 (1979): 307–37; Simmons, "The Principle of Fair Play," in *The Duty to Obey the Law: Selected Philosophical Readings*, ed. Williamson A. Edmunson (New York: Rowman & Littlefield, 1999), 107, 124–25.

47. Edith R. Warkentine, "Beyond Unconscionability: The Case for Using 'Knowing Assent' as the Basis for Analyzing Unbargained-for Terms in Standard Form Contracts," *Seattle University Law Review* 31, no. 3 (2008): 502.

48. Barnett, "Constitutional Legitimacy," 133.

49. Ibid., 136.

50. Greene, *Against Obligation*, 39–40.

51. Barnett, "Constitutional Legitimacy," 120.

52. See Greene, *Against Obligation*, 81 (arguing that such a consent argument "is constitutive of intimate associations and one-to-one promise relationships, respecting the state or a state official . . . is not constitutive of citizenship").

53. John Rawls, *A Theory of Justice*, rev. ed. (Oxford: Oxford University Press, 1999), 11.

54. Paul W. Kahn, *Political Theology* (New York: Columbia University Press, 2011), 142.

55. See, e.g., Justinian, *Digest* 50.17.54: *Nemo plus iuris ad alium transferre potest, quam ipse haberet.*

56. See Raz, *Authority of Law*, 126.

57. Greene, *Against Obligation*, 36.

58. Perry, "Political Authority and Political Obligation," 24: "But the basic argument, which if correct applies to all 'voluntaristic' arguments for a general obligation to obey the law, including the argument from fair play, is this. Any argument that offers to justify the state's claimed moral power to impose obligations

cannot be conditioned on such contingencies as whether or not citizens (or, more generally, subjects of the law) have engaged in a particular kind of act—for example, the acceptance of benefits, or the making of a promise. This is so because any obligations that arise from the exercise of the power will be categorical, and as such cannot be conditioned on this kind of contingency."

59. Moore, "Good without God," 236.

60. Strauss, *Natural Right and History*, 185–86.

61. Ibid.

62. Ibid.

63. See Greene, *Against Obligation*, 94–95, for a summary of this argument.

64. See Finnis, *Natural Law and Natural Rights*, 231.

65. Ibid.

66. Ibid.

67. Ibid., 231–33.

68. Ibid., 246.

69. Ibid., 61.

70. Ibid., 62.

71. Ibid., 86–90.

72. Ibid., 407.

73. Ibid., 405.

74. Ibid., 403.

75. Ibid., 251.

76. Ibid., 252.

77. On this point, Finnis's claim becomes indistinguishable from Hart's argument that the fact of obedience to authority simply must be recognized.

78. Finnis, *Natural Law and Natural Rights*, 250.

79. Ibid.

80. Hart, *Concept of Law*, 97–98 (merely stating the existence of an unstated and often unformulated Rule of Recognition that can have virtually any content as long as it is in fact used as a rule of recognition by a society).

81. Finnis, *Natural Law and Natural Rights*, 251. Finnis does describe this rule as only a "rule of thumb" as to when to refuse to obey someone who has garnered acquiescence, leaving the reader in more of a quandary of exactly when authority is justified.

82. Ibid., 246.

83. Raz, *Authority of Law*, 250, 260.

84. Ibid., 250, 256.

85. See ibid., 53–77.

86. Raz, "Authority and Justification," 14. Raz never claims that every decision must be based exclusively on dependent reasons but that they must mostly be; see ibid., 16: "All it [the service conception] requires is that it shall act primarily for dependent reasons."

87. Ibid., 18–19; see also Joseph Raz, *The Morality of Freedom* (New York: Oxford University Press, 1986), 53.

88. Hugo Cyr, "Functional and Existential Authorities," *Canadian Journal of Law and Jurisprudence* 28, no. 2 (2015): 271.

89. Ibid., 273.

90. Ibid.

91. Ibid.

92. Perry, "Political Authority and Political Obligation," 43. Philip Soper also exposes the utilitarian basis of Raz's service conception of authority thus: "Raz designates his view the 'service conception' of authority: government exists because (and has authority just in case) it does a better job of advancing the aims of the governed (what 'ought to be their aims') than they could do on their own. The alternative conception might be called the 'leader' conception of authority: government exists because (and has authority just in case) it provides necessary direction in default of agreement about what *are* the aims of the governed" (see Soper, "Legal Theory and the Claim of Authority," 231–32).

93. Perry, "Political Authority and Political Obligation," 41–42.

94. Raz, "Authority and Justification," 15.

95. Perry, "Political Authority and Political Obligation," 43–48.

96. Ibid., 52–53.

97. Raz, *Morality of Freedom*, 70, 76–78, 104.

98. Raz, "Authority and Justification," 14. See also ibid., 15: "On the contrary, there is no point in having authorities unless their determinations are binding even if mistaken (though some mistakes may disqualify them)." In other words, law should bind except when it should not for nonlegal reasons.

99. Perry, "Political Authority and Political Obligation," 26.

100. Ibid., 72.

101. Ibid., 67.

102. Ibid.

103. Ibid., 64.

104. Ibid., 7.

105. Ibid. Perry does not actually label his argument as "teleological" or "functional" but rather, following Leslie Greene, he calls it the "task efficacy" theory of authority (ibid).

106. The traditional natural law explanation of authority meets Perry's two value criteria of authority: the intentionality condition (there must be value in someone having the power intentionally to bind others) and the prospectivity requirement, which is present expectation of future acquiescence rather than mere fact of later acquiescence. The value in intentionality is that God intends that human authorities exist to make determinations of natural law. Prospectivity exists because it is expected that people should obey because there is a delegated authority that has been transmitted from the source of the legal architecture of the universe.

107. Barnett, "Constitutional Legitimacy," 141–42.

108. Ibid., 142; see also his reiteration of this two-part test (145).

109. Ibid.

110. Ibid., 141.

111. See ibid., 144. At one point, Barnett switches his language from talking about rights to justice. As touched on later in this chapter and explored more in chapter 9, justice can serve as a source of obligation for action. Yet, Barnett fails to define justice as anything other than the rights he simply assumes to exist.

112. MacIntyre, *After Virtue* (3rd ed.), 75–77.

113. Perry, "Political Authority and Political Obligation," 4.

114. Richard Flathman, *Political Obligation* (New York: Atheneum, 1972), 215.

115. Leo XIII, *Diuturnum*, sec. 5, https://w2.vatican.va/content/leo-xiii/en/encyclicals/documents/hf_l-xiii_enc_29061881_diuturnum.html: "Very many men of more recent times, walking in the footsteps of those who in a former age assumed to themselves the name of philosophers, say that all power comes from the people; so that those who exercise it in the State do so not as their own, but as delegated to them by the people, and that, by this rule, it can be revoked by the will of the very people by whom it was delegated. But from these, Catholics dissent, who affirm that the right to rule is from God, as from a natural and necessary principle."

116. Raz, *Authority of Law*, 20.

117. Ibid., 124–25, 129, 132–33.

118. Kelsen, *General Theory of Law and State*, 413.

119. Hart's Rule of Recognition is similar in this respect in that it must exist for the legal system to exist, but Hart offers no explanation of why or how it exists other than to assume it does.

120. Raz, *Authority of Law*, 126.

121. Bateman, "Sovereignty's Missing Moral Imperative," 33.

122. Rom. 13:1 (DV).

123. J. D. Goldsworthy, "God or Mackie? The Dilemma of Secular Moral Philosophy," *American Journal of Jurisprudence* 30 (1985): 77.

124. See Moore, "Good without God."

125. Bateman, "Sovereignty's Missing Moral Imperative," 36.

126. *The Liber Augustalis or Constitutions of Melfi Promulgated by the Emperor Frederick II for the Kingdom of Sicily in 1231*, trans. James Powell (Syracuse, NY: Syracuse University Press, 1971), 3.

127. Bateman, "Sovereignty's Missing Moral Imperative," 39.

128. Leo XIII, *Diuturnum*, sec. 5.

129. Aquinas, *De Regno* 1.1.

130. Porter, *Ministers of the Law*, 81.

131. Suárez, *Selections from Three Works*, 364, citing Aristotle, *Politics*.

132. See Grenier, *Moral Philosophy*, 289.

133. Porter, *Ministers of the Law*, 81.

134. Ibid.

135. Ibid., 81–82.

136. Ibid., 82.

137. Ibid., 63–64.

138. See ibid., 75. Porter cites *Summa Theologica* I-II, q. 91, a. 3; q. 99, a. 3, reply to obj. 2; q. 99, a. 4, as demonstrating that even the divine positive law leaves "much undetermined."

139. Ibid., 81.

140. See *Summa Theologica* I-II, q. 108, a. 2.

141. See Hittinger, *The First Grace*, 99; see also *Summa Theologica* I-II, q. 90, a. 3, reply to obj. 3.

142. *Summa Theologica* I-II, q. 108, a. 1.

143. Ibid., I-II, q. 108, a. 1–2.

144. Ibid., I-II, q. 108, a. 2.

145. Ibid., I-II, q. 108, a. 2, reply to obj. 4.

146. Ibid.

147. Suárez, *Selections from Three Works*, 365–66.

148. Ibid., 366–67.

149. Ibid., 367.

150. Ibid., 365; Cicero, *De Republica* 6.13.

151. Aquinas, *De Regno* 1.15.

152. Ibid.

153. Ibid., 1.5; *Summa Theologica* I-II, q. 85, a. 3.

154. See Cyr, "Functional and Existential Authorities," 287–89.

155. Porter, *Ministers of the Law*, 82.

156. Aquinas, *De Regno* 1.5, p. 25–27.

157. See *Summa Theologica* I-II, q. 90, a. 1.

158. Kelsen, *General Theory of Law and State*, 13.

159. Ibid.

160. Moore conceives of the value of law in a similar manner by considering law a functional kind; see Moore, "Law as a Functional Kind," 188 et seq. Moore, however, does not locate the origin of the function in the eternal law.

161. Porter, *Ministers of the Law*, 133.

162. Strauss, *Natural Right in History*, 132–33.

163. See, e.g., *The Social Contract* and *Émile*, both of which understand freedom as the natural state of man and restraint as a corrupting convention.

164. Strauss, *Natural Right in History*, 132.

165. Hart, *Concept of Law*, 65.

166. As explained in her work *Ministers of the Law*.

167. Hart, *Concept of Law*, 125.

168. Newman, *Foundations of Justice*, 127.

169. Aristotle, *Politics* 4.8.1294a. We will consider the necessity of the goodness of laws further in this chapter but primarily in chapter 8.

170. *Summa Theologica* II-II, q. 104, a. 2, reply to obj. 2.

171. Ibid., II-II, q. 104, a. 1.

172. Ibid.

173. Newman, *Foundations of Justice*, 57–58.

174. Raz, *Authority of Law*, 16.

175. Ibid.

176. For a further discussion of the wounding of nature, see chapter 5.

177. Aristotle, *Nicomachean Ethics* 10.9.1179a33–1181b13.

178. Ibid., 1180a–1180a5.

179. See Justinian, *Digest* 1.3.7.

180. *Summa Theologica* II-II, q. 108, a. 1.

181. J. M. Cardinal Villeneuve, O. M. I., preface to *On the Primacy of the Common Good: Against the Personalists and The Principle of the New Order*, by Charles De Koninck (Paris: Université Laval/Éditions Fides, 1943); Sean Collins translation reprinted in *The Aquinas Review* 4 (1997), http://ldataworks.com/aqr /V4_BC_text.html.

182. *Summa Theologica* I-II, q. 95, a. 1.

183. Ibid., I-II, q. 95, a. 2: "Something may be derived from the natural law in two ways: first, as a conclusion from premises, second, by way of determination of certain generalities."

184. Ibid., I-II, q. 95, a. 1, reply to obj. 2.

185. Ibid.

186. Ibid.

187. See, e.g., MacIntyre, *Three Rival Versions of Moral Inquiry*, 60–64.

188. My presentation of this claim is a summary. See Aristotle, *Politics* 1094a–3, 1103a3–10; see Aquinas, *De Regno* 1.1, p. 5; 1.2, for more details.

189. *Summa Theologica* I-II, q. 108, a. 2, reply to obj. 4.

190. See Berman, *Law and Revolution*, 536–37 (arguing that the nature of authority "was rooted in the duality of secular and spiritual authorities" and "the belief in the supremacy of law was rooted in the pluralism of secular authorities within each kingdom, and especially in the dialectical tensions among royal, feudal, and urban polities").

191. Hart, *Concept of Law*, 6–7.

192. Ibid., 81–83 (showing that obligation must consist of more than predictions about the likelihood of suffering negative consequences for disobeying).

193. Ibid., 84. To distinguish law from morality or social convention, Hart merely makes distinctions in the type of punishment or consequences that flow from disregarding a precept. Thus, law, morality, and social convention for Hart only differ in the nature of punishments related thereto.

194. Ibid., 24–25. Hart erroneously goes further to demand independence and a supreme lawmaker. Certainly he is correct to note that for one particular legal system (England) to be distinct from another (Russia) the supreme lawmaker in

England must be independent of the one of Russia. Yet, it does not follow from this conclusion that both the supreme lawmaker of England and of Russia cannot each be independently subordinate to a lawmaker above both of them who has severally delegated a limited authority (within the respective countries) to exercise internal to that system the supreme legislative power still subject in turn to the overarching supreme lawmaker. Admitting such a dependence of both countries on a higher authority does not destroy the independence of England and Russia from each other pursuant to their separate delegation.

195. Grenier, *Moral Philosophy*, 291.

196. Leo XIII, *Rerum Novarum*, sec. 35, http://w2.vatican.va/content/leo-xiii/en/encyclicals/documents/hf_l-xiii_enc_15051891_rerum-novarum.html.

197. Suárez, *Selections from Three Works*, 379, 384–85.

198. Ibid., 367; see also Leo XIII, *Immortale Dei*, sec. 4: "For, in things visible God has fashioned secondary causes, in which His divine action can in some wise be discerned, leading up to the end to which the course of the world is ever tending."

199. Suárez, *Selections from Three Works*, 379. Grenier confirms that authority is not of the metaphysical essence of a community but rather a property of being a community. See Grenier, *Moral Philosophy*, 291.

200. In this chapter, "perfect" is used in a precise sense to mean complete or fulfilled and not necessarily good or virtuous. See Wladyslaw Tatarkiewicz, "Paradoxes of Perfection," *Dialectics and Humanism* 7, no. 1 (1980): 77–78 (contrasting the Aristotelian notion of perfection as "complete," "finished," or "flawless" with a paradoxical view of perfection as "ceaseless improvement").

201. Suárez, *Selections from Three Works*, 86.

202. See ibid., 86–87; Aquinas, *De Regno* 1.2; Nicholas Aroney, "Subsidiarity, Federalism and the Best Constitution: Thomas Aquinas on City, Province and Empire," *Law and Philosophy* 26 (2007): 174–77.

203. Suárez, *Selection from Three Works*, 86.

204. Thomas Aquinas, *Commentary on Aristotle's Politics*, trans. Richard J. Regan (Indianapolis: Hackett, 2007), 4: "And the association that is supreme and includes all other associations is the absolutely supreme good."

205. The name of this perfect community varies from age to age and author to author. Aristotle referred to the *polis*, or "city-state"; see Aroney, "Subsidiarity, Federalism," 170. Aquinas varyingly refers to the perfect community as the *civitas* ("city"), *regnum* ("kingdom"), and *provincia* ("province") (ibid., n34). Suárez uses the term *civitas* when referring to Aristotle's perfect community; see Suárez, *Selection from Three Works*, 37. The translators use the word "state" for *civitas* in this passage (ibid., 86). In the modern context, I have chosen the word "nation" as most approximating the concept of the *polis* in Aristotle's time because it lacks the negative modern connotations of the word "state"; see Aroney, "Subsidiarity, Federalism," 170.

206. Aristotle, *Politics* 1.1.1252a6; Aquinas, *Commentary on Aristotle's Politics*, 5: "And the perfect association . . . is the political community, now complete, having a self-sufficient end. . . . Therefore, the political community was instituted for the sake of protecting life and exists to promote the good life"; ibid., 7, where Aristotle shows "that the good to which the political community is directed is the supreme human good"; Aquinas, *De Regno* 1.2, p. 9: "It follows that a communal society is the more perfect to the extent that it is sufficient in providing for life's necessities."

207. See Aristotle, *Politics* 1252a24–1253a6 (showing how the union of men and women combine to form households, and households combine to form villages, and villages unite to form the political community); see also Aquinas, *Commentary on Aristotle's Politics*, 2: "Since there are indeed different grades and orders of these associations, the ultimate association is the political community directed to the things self-sufficient for human life." Aristotle continues by proposing "the true relation of other associations to the political community. . . . First, he explains the association of one person to another. Second, he explains the association of the household, which includes different associations of persons. Third, he explains the association of the village, which includes many households" (Aquinas, *Commentary on Aristotle's Politics*, 9); Aquinas, *De Regno* 1.1 (containing the same list of family, household, and city).

208. See Aquinas, *De Regno* 1.1.

209. Ibid.

210. The term *vicus*, translated "village," has an economic overtone more than the modern word "neighborhood" or "village," as can be seen when Aquinas says that a village is self-sufficient with respect to "a particular trade or calling" (*De Regno* 1.1). Elsewhere, Aquinas refers to the fact that in many medieval towns, streets or sections of a town were divided on the basis of occupation, as evidenced when he says, "In one [*vicus*] smiths practice their craft, in another of which weavers practice theirs" (Aquinas, *Commentary on Aristotle's Politics*, 15).

211. Suárez, *Selections from Three Works*, 365, relying on Aristotle's argument of sufficiency in *Politics*.

212. Aquinas, *De Regno* 1.1, p. 9.

213. Aquinas, *Commentary on Aristotle's Politics*, 7: "An association is a whole, and wholes are ordered so that one that includes another is superior. . . . And the association that includes other associations is likewise superior. But the political community clearly includes all other associations, since households and villages are included in the political community."

214. Grenier, *Moral Philosophy*, 358.

215. Aristotle, *Politics* 1324a.

216. Grenier, *Moral Philosophy*, 291.

217. See *Summa Theologica* I-II, q. 90, a. 3, reply to obj. 3.

218. See Aquinas, *De Regno* 1.2, where Aquinas explains that the analogy is expressed by the practice of calling kings fathers.

219. Cicero distinguishes this entity, a community, from a mere mass of men by an agreement about the justice and a community of interest. See Brian M. McCall, "Can a Pluralistic Commonwealth Endure?," review of *The Political Problem of Religious Pluralism and Why Philosophers Can't Solve It*, by Thaddeus J. Kozinski," *Georgetown Journal of Law and Public Policy* 11 (2013): 45–46.

220. See Aristotle, *Politics* 1.1.1252a7–26 (explaining that authority is vested in a *polis*).

221. Grenier, *Moral Philosophy*, 291.

222. Suárez, *Selections from Three Works*, 379.

223. See generally ibid., 379–80.

224. See Cicero, "*De Republica*," 18: defining the commonwealth as "the concern of a people, but a people is not any group of men assembled in any way, but an assemblage of some size associated with one another through agreement on law and community of interest."

225. Suárez, *Selections from Three Works*, 380–82.

226. Leo XIII, *Diuturnum*, sec. 6.

227. For this distinction between the source of authority as opposed to its transmission, see Grenier, *Moral Philosophy*, 291.

228. Suárez, *Selection from Three Works*, 386.

229. Graitan, *Decretum* D.4, C.3.

230. Ibid., D.12, C.6.

231. Pennington, "Politics in Western Jurisprudence," 190.

232. Ibid.

233. *Summa Theologica* I-II, q. 96, a. 1.

234. Ibid., I-II, q. 96, a. 2.

235. See, e.g., Kenneth Pennington, "Representation in Medieval Canon Law," *The Jurist* 64 (2004): 370 (discussing Pope Honorius's ruling that bishops should not deny "representatives [*procuratores*] of the cathedral chapters admittance to comprovincial councils in which matters touching their interests were treated."

236. Honorius III, *Etsi Membra*, quoted in Pennington, "Politics in Western Jurisprudence," 187.

237. See Suárez, *Selections from Three Works*, 228.

238. See ibid. for both examples. Suárez also cites the example of a law requiring a certain price be paid for a certain good. Once enacted, this particular legal determination together with the natural law prohibition of theft combine to obligate one to pay the legally determined price.

239. Suárez, *Selections from Three Works*, 230.

240. *Summa Theologica* I-II, q. 91, a. 3, reply to obj. 1.

241. Ibid.

242. Ibid., I-II, q. 91, a. 3, reply to obj. 2.

243. Ibid., I-II, q. 91, a. 3.

244. Ibid.

245. Ibid., I-II, q. 91, a. 3, reply to obj. 1.

246. Gratian, *Decretum* D.1, C.5.

247. See *Summa Theologica* I-II, q. 95, a. 1.

248. Pius XI, *Quadragesimo Anno*, sec. 49, https://w2.vatican.va/content /pius-xi/en/encyclicals/documents/hf_p-xi_enc_19310515_quadragesimo-anno .html; Pius XI is here commenting specifically on the determination of the duties flowing from the general principle supporting the private ownership of property and its use for the common good, but his comment applies equally to determinations of other principles.

249. *Summa Theologica* I-II, q. 91, a. 3.

250. Ibid., I-II, q. 91, a. 3, reply to obj. 3.

251. Ibid., I-II, q. 91, a. 3, reply to obj. 1.

252. Gratian, *Decretum* D.1, C.5.

253. Soper, "In Defense of Classical Natural Law in Legal Theory," 211.

254. Soper qualifies his assertion by adding that the law cannot coerce if it is gravely wrong (ibid., 213–18).

255. See chapter 5.

256. *Summa Theologica* I-II, q. 91, a. 3, reply to obj. 3.

257. Soper, "In Defense of Classical Natural Law in Legal Theory," 211.

258. *Summa Theologica* II-II, q. 77, a. 1, reply to obj. 1.

259. Ibid., I-II, q. 96, a. 2 (quoting Isidore to explain that human laws "should be 'possible both according to nature, and according to the customs of the country'" and explaining that "possibility or faculty of action is due to an interior habit or disposition: since the same thing is not possible to one who has not a virtuous habit, as is possible to one who has").

260. Ibid., I-II, q. 96, a. 2, reply to obj. 2.

261. Ori J. Herstein, "A Legal Right to Do Legal Wrong," *Oxford Journal of Legal Studies* 34, no. 1 (2014): 36, 42–44.

262. *Summa Theologica* II-II, q. 77, a. 1, reply to obj. 1.

263. The resolution of this conflict is the subject of chapter 8.

264. *Summa Theologica* II-II, q. 77, a. 1, reply to obj. 1.

265. Ibid.

266. Usury provides another example. Although charging usury for a loan of money is unjust and contrary to the natural law, because of the difficulties in distinguishing precisely between usury and just extrinsic titles, human law may tolerate some usury but should not promote it. See Brian M. McCall, "Redeeming Our Future," in *The Church and the Usurers: Unprofitable Lending for the Modern Economy* (Ave Maria, FL: Sapientia, 2013), chap. 7.

267. Brennan, "Locating Authority in Law," 161–95.

268. Ibid., 165.

269. Ibid., 168.

270. Vining, *From Newton's Sleep*, 240.

271. Joseph Vining, *The Authoritative and the Authoritarian* (Chicago: University of Chicago Press, 1986), 217–18.

272. Brennan, "Locating Authority in Law," 169.

273. See, e.g., *Summa Theologica* I-II, q. 90, a. 1, reply to obj. 1; I-II, q. 90, a. 3, reply to obj. 1 (stating that law is in the lawgiver and the one subject to the law); I-II q. 90, a. 2 (constantly employing the phrase of natural law being in people or in rational creatures).

274. Brennan, "Are Legislation and Rules a Problem in Law?," 1214.

275. Finnis, *Natural Law and Natural Rights*, 245–46.

276. Ibid., 246.

277. See Aquinas, *De Regno* 1.6.

278. See Smith, *Law's Quandary*.

279. Vining, "Law's Ontology," 700 (referring to Smith, *Law's Quandary*, 47).

280. Ibid.

281. Moore, "Good without God," 234–35.

282. Brennan, "Are Legislation and Rules a Problem in Law?," 1214.

283. Ibid., 1210.

284. Ibid., 1207 (quoting Joseph Vining, *From Newton's Sleep*, 33–34).

285. It should be noted that failure to accept all that God reveals about himself and His law will lead to an incomplete and fractured account of natural law. Thus, although acceptance of the classical natural law thesis does not depend on the acceptance of all aspects of revealed theology but only natural theology, the result of failing to integrate revealed theology will be incomplete and imperfect.

286. Perry, "Political Authority and Political Obligation," 14–15.

287. Ibid., 12.

EIGHT.   Falling Off the Frame: The Limits of Legal Authority

1. Aquinas, *Summa Theologica* I-II, q. 96, a. 4.

2. Hart, *Concept of Law*, 65.

3. Raz, "Authority and Justification," 14.

4. Ibid., 15.

5. Ibid., 14.

6. Ibid., 15.

7. Hart, *Concept of Law*, 65.

8. Ibid.

9. Ibid., 72–73. Hart does allow for a variety of types of popular sovereignty. In the case of England, popular sovereignty is vested in the peers and the electorate; in the case of the United States it is the people at large.

10. Ibid., 71.

11. Suárez, *Selections from Three Works*, 368.

12. Ibid.

13. *Summa Theologica* I-II, q. 96, a. 4 (stating that laws are just "when, to wit, they are ordained to the common good—and from their author, that is to say, when the law that is made does not exceed the power of the lawgiver").

14. Porter, *Natural and Divine Law*, 250 (arguing that natural law does put restraints on otherwise legitimate forms of human institutions).

15. Crowe, "Clarifying the Natural Law Thesis," 160.

16. Ibid.

17. *Summa Theologica* II-II, q. 104, a. 5.

18. Ibid.

19. Ibid.

20. Ibid.

21. Porter, *Ministers of the Law*, 75. Unfortunately, Porter seems to forget or ignore this important point about the stringent restrictions imposed on possible determinations when she attempts to suggest that same-gender sexual relations might be capable of being a conventional specification of the natural law precepts regarding marriage (see, e.g., ibid., 119–28). Designating such as a conventional or particular determination of marriage is clearly outside the permissible determinations of the natural law as specifically revealed by the divine law contained in the scriptures; see, e.g., Gen. 19:5–8; Jude 7; Lev. 18:22–23; Lev. 20:13; 1 Cor. 6:9; 1 Tim. 1:9–10; Rom. 1:26–27. I believe that Porter would admit that such a determination would be inconceivable to the Scholastics she relies upon in developing her theoretical jurisprudence. It is unfortunate that this inconsistent practical conclusion detracts from her excellent theoretical work.

22. *Summa Theologica* I-II, q. 91, a. 3, reply to obj. 3.

23. Ibid., I-II, q. 96, a. 4.

24. Ibid., I-II, q. 95, a. 4.

25. Ibid.

26. Ibid.

27. Ibid.

28. Ibid., I-II, q. 95, a. 2.

29. Aristotle, *Nichomachean Ethics* 5.1.1129b11–14.

30. Ibid., 1129b14–25.

31. Aristotle, *Politics* 3.11.

32. Ibid., 3.15.1286a20–25.

33. *Summa Theologica* I-II, q. 95, a. 4.

34. Suárez, *Selections from Three Works*, 24–25.

35. See Pennington, "Lex Naturalis and Ius Naturale," 574.

36. See *Summa Theologica* II-II, q. 58, a. 1, quoting this definition. The topic of justice is much more complex and requires more distinctions and refinements, but this simple definition is sufficient for the purposes of the present discussion.

37. Cicero, *De Inventione*, in *The Orations of Marcus Tullius Cicero*, vol. 4, trans. C. D. Yonge (London: George Bell & Sons, 1888), 2.53.

38. Peter Abelard, *Sententiae Magistri Petri Abaelardi*, ed. David Luscombe et al. (Turnhout: Brepols, 2006), 134–35, translation quoted in Pennington, "Lex Naturalis and Ius Naturale," 575.

39. *Summa Theologica* I-II, q. 90, a. 2.

40. Aristotle, *Politics* 3.6.1279a17–19.

41. Ibid., 3.6.

42. *Summa Theologica* I-II, q. 96, a. 1.

43. See ibid., and I-II, q. 90, a. 2.

44. Ibid., I-II, q. 90, a. 2.

45. Ibid., I-II, q. 95, a. 2.

46. Ibid., I-II, q. 90, a. 2.

47. Bateman, "Sovereignty's Missing Moral Imperative," 33 (citing Plato, Aristotle, Socrates, Cicero, and Augustine).

48. This limitation, which requires that higher authorities not usurp the authority of lower orders, is often referred to as the "principle of subsidiarity." See, e.g., Pope Pius XI, *Quadragesimo Anno*, secs. 79–80.

49. Bateman, "Sovereignty's Missing Moral Imperative," 33–35, citing Aristotle, *Politics*, bk. 1; *Ethics*, bk. 10, last chapter; Plato, *Laws*, bk. 3; Cicero, *De Republica* 1.12, *De Inventione* 1.1, *De Legibus* 1.6.

50. Grenier, *Moral Philosophy*, 369.

51. Ibid.

52. Suárez, *Selections from Three Works*, 367.

53. Aristotle, *Nichomachean Ethics* 10.9.1180a.

54. Aristotle, *Politics* 7.2.1324b.

55. Ibid., 3.11.

56. Brian Tierney, quoted in Pennington, "Politics in Western Jurisprudence," 162.

57. Pennington, "Politics in Western Jurisprudence," 163.

58. Ibid., 165.

59. Ibid.

60. Quoted in Pennington, "Politics in Western Jurisprudence," 166.

61. *Summa Theologica* I-II, q. 94, a. 4.

62. Pennington, "Politics in Western Jurisprudence," 169.

63. Ibid.

64. Ibid., 166.

65. Quoted in Pennington, "Politics in Western Jurisprudence," 166.

66. Ibid., 162.

67. Cicero, *De Republica* 133–34.

68. Ibid., 134.

69. *Summa Theologica* I-II, q. 96, a. 4 (quoting Augustine).

70. Ibid.

71. Ibid.

72. Leo XIII, *Rerum Novarum*, sec. 52.

73. *Summa Theologica* I-II, q. 96, a. 1; see also Suárez, *Selections from Three Works*, 90 (stating that "it is inherent in the nature and essence of law, that it shall be enacted for the sake of the common good").

74. Suárez, *Selections from Three Works*, 91.

75. *Summa Theological* I-II, q. 96, a. 4.

76. Ibid.

77. Hart, *Concept of Law*, 97–107.

78. *Summa Theologica* I-II, q. 96, a. 4.

79. Mary M. Keys, *Aquinas, Aristotle, and the Promise of the Common Good* (Cambridge: Cambridge University Press, 2006), 213 (internal citations omitted).

80. Justinian, *Digest* 50.17.206, my translation of *iure naturae aequum est neminem cum alterius detrimento et iniuira fieri locupletiorem.*

81. *Summa Theologica* II-II, q. 77, a. 1.

82. John of Salisbury, *Policraticus*, ed. and trans. Cary J. Nederman (Cambridge: Cambridge University Press, 1990), 14.

83. *Summa Theologica* I-II, q. 96, a. 4.

84. Ibid.

85. Lewis and Short, *A Latin Dictionary*, s.v. "Legalis."

86. Moore, "Law as a Functional Kind," 200.

87. William Blackstone, *Commentaries on the Laws of England*, vol. 1 (Oxford: Clarendon Press, 1765–69), introduction, sec. 2.

88. Hart, *Concept of Law*, 6–7.

89. Aquinas uses the word *forte* ("perhaps") to describe the possibility of an obligation to conform to an illegal law; see *Summa Theologica* I-II, q. 96, a. 4.

90. See Perry, "Political Authority and Political Obligation," 4–5 (requiring a similar distinction between political authority and the obligation to obey laws, when he concludes "obligation to obey the law does not, in and of itself, entail legitimate political authority").

91. *Summa Theologica* I-II, q. 96, a. 4.

92. Gratian makes use of the phrase in a similar manner when he quotes Isidore dividing law into two categories, divine and human, including natural law in the first category (*Decretum* D.1, C.1).

93. Aquinas, *De Duobus Praeceptis* (my translation of *lex brevis, ut ab omnibus posset sciri*).

94. Sophocles, *Antigone*, trans. Robert Fagles (New York: Penguin, 1984), 503–5.

95. See Philip Soper, "In Defense of Classical Natural Law in Legal Theory," 219; Moore, "Law as a Functional Kind," 224.

96. *Summa Theological* I-II, q. 96, a. 4.

97. De Koninck, "On the Primacy of the Common Good," foreword and sec. 1, in *The Common Good and against Its Primacy* (quoting Aquinas, *Summa Contra Gentiles* 3.109).

98. Raz, *Authority of Law*, 272–75.

99. Ibid., 276.

100. *Summa Theologica* I-II, q. 96, a. 4.

101. See Newman, *Foundations in Justice*, 29: "Even if there were no State laws, the virtue which works for the common good of the state would . . . be legal justice because its acts would be commanded by the divine law."

102. *Summa Theologica* II-II, q. 104, a. 5, reply to obj. 2.

103. Ibid., I-II, q. 96, a. 4.

104. See, e.g., Raz, *Authority of Law*, 237; and Green, *Against Obligation*, 95.

105. Raz, *Authority of Law*, 130.

106. For an alternative explanation of the invalidation of human law that conflicts with natural law, see Budziszewski, *Natural Law for Lawyers*, 23–24.

107. J. Budziszewski, *Commentary on Thomas Aquinas's Treatise on Law* (Cambridge: Cambridge University Press, 2014), 192 (internal citations omitted).

108. Crowe, "Clarifying the Natural Law Thesis," 164.

109. Recall that although all authority comes from God, not every particular exercise of that God-given authority conforms to God's law. Legal authorities, like a gunman, may have the ability to enforce illegal commands, but the authority becomes authoritarian in such an instance. See chapter 7.

110. Martin Luther King, Jr., "Letter from a Birmingham Jail," April 16, 1963, http://www.africa.upenn.edu/Articles_Gen/Letter_Birmingham.html. In this letter, King quotes the same passages of Augustine and Aquinas to justify his refusal of unjust laws. Restricting one's movements to a cell is not a violation of the natural law (even though unnecessarily confining another to a cell would be). Thus, refusing an unjust law when, in King's words, "the cup runs over," may be permitted or even required by natural law; in other cases, when the cup does not run over, natural law would obligate us to drink the cup (so long as doing so does not violate the natural law) for the common good.

111. Finnis, *Natural Law and Natural Rights*, 364. In so defaming this ancient principle, Finnis joins company with the father of positivism, John Austin. See John Austin, *The Province of Jurisprudence Determined*, ed. Isaiah Berlin, Stuart Hampshire, and Richard Wollheim (New York: The Noonday Press, 1954), 185 (calling the principle "stark nonsense").

112. See Crowe, "Clarifying the Natural Law Thesis," 164.

113. Soper, "In Defense of Classical Natural Law in Legal Theory," 201, 202.

114. Finnis, *Natural Law and Natural Rights*, 359–61, 363–66.

115. Brennan, "Locating Authority in Law," 181.

116. Although it may be possible to defend the limitation on legal authority contained in the strong view of the principle, an unjust law is no law without

grounding it in the eternal law (see, e.g., Moore "Law as a Functional Kind," 198), such an approach lacks the deep ontological justification for legal authority in the first place.

117. Barnett, "Constitutional Legitimacy," 127.

118. Berman, *Law and Revolution*, 536.

119. Edmund S. Morgan, *Inventing the People: The Rise of Popular Sovereignty in England and America* (New York: W. W. Norton, 1988), 53.

120. Ibid., 82.

121. Henry Bracton, *De Legibus et Consuetudinibus Angliae*, 2:33, http://bracton.law.harvard.edu/Unframed/calendar.htm.

122. Leo XIII, *Libertas*, sec. 10.

123. See, e.g., Hart, *Concept of Law*, 205.

124. Ibid.

125. Ibid.

126. See, e.g., ibid., 167: "Yet the social morality of societies which have reached the stage where this can be distinguished from its law, always includes certain obligations and duties, requiring the sacrifice of private inclination or interest which is essential to the survival of any society, so long as men and the world in which they live retain some of their most familiar and obvious characteristics. Among such rules obviously required for social life are those forbidding, or at least restricting, the free use of violence, rules requiring certain forms of honesty and truthfulness in dealings with others, and rules forbidding the destruction of tangible things or their seizure from others." What evades Hart's analysis is that these core concepts "required for social life" are nothing other than principles of natural law used by individuals in making moral decisions and societies in making law.

127. See Justinian, *Digest* 1.1.9: "All nations who are ruled by law and customs make use partly of their own law, and partly of that which is common to all men. For whatever law any people has established for itself is peculiar to that State, and is called the Civil Law, as being the particular law of that State. But whatever natural reason has established among all men is equally observed by all mankind, and is called the Law of Nations, because it is the law which all nations employ."

128. See Hart, *Concept of Law*, 166.

129. Ibid., 167.

130. In chapter 9 we will consider this distinction in more depth, but, in general, the virtues other than justice have as their object the personal good; the virtue of justice, which is the object of law, has the common good as its object.

131. See chapter 6 and chapter 7.

132. Hart, *Concept of Law*, 179–80.

133. See chapter 4.

134. Leo XIII, *Rerum Novarum*, sec. 35.

135. See Hart, *Concept of Law*, 195 et seq.

136. Raz, *Authority of Law*, 112–14.

137. Ibid., 114–15.

138. Ibid., 115.

139. Porter makes a similar distinction, but she distinguishes between natural law on one hand and human law and shared moral determinations (or the mores of a community) on the other (see Porter, *Ministers of the Law*, 278–79). Yet, the mores of a community are merely the coinciding of moral determinations made by members of the same community.

140. Hart, *Concept of Law*, 206: "This sense, that there is something outside the official system, by reference to which in the last resort the individual must solve his problems of obedience, is surely more likely to be kept alive among those who are accustomed to think that rules of law may be iniquitous, than among those who think that nothing iniquitous can anywhere have the status of law."

141. See ibid., 195–205.

142. See Grenier, *Metaphysics*, 53–59. It is true that we have seen that laws do not need to be the best possible laws to be laws (see chapter 7). Yet, even such laws possess the transcendental property of goodness in that they are good to the extent they are in fact laws. Thus to say something that lacks an essential quality of law, justice, still exists as law undermines its transcendental goodness. The property of goodness requires that which is essential to exist as law must be present for the thing to exist. A law to be law must possess the perfections of law, that is, the essential qualities of law, even though it may not be a perfect law by lacking all accidental perfections, such as being the most efficient way to be such a law.

143. See the discussion in chapter 2 on the necessary connection between existence and goodness.

144. See Stanley Milgram, *Obedience to Authority: An Experimental View* (New York: Harper & Row, 1974); Milgram, "Behavioral Study of Obedience," *Journal of Abnormal and Social Psychology* 67 (October 1963): 371–78. In the experiment, subjects were commanded by the authority figure conducting the test to inflict increasing levels of electric shock on the other participant in the experiment when he or she answered questions incorrectly. In reality, the other person was an actor pretending to be hurt by the electric shock. Milgram found that despite expressing signs of discomfort with the order, 65 percent (26 of 40) of experiment participants administered the experiment's final massive 450-volt shock to the other person. See also Lynn Stout, *Cultivating Conscience: How Good Laws Make Good People* (Princeton, NJ: Princeton University Press, 2011), 102–6 (summarizing the consistent findings of those who have replicated the original experiment or performed similar ones).

145. Budziszewski, *Line through the Heart*, 152.

146. Ibid., 151, referring to Calder v. Bull, 3 U.S. 386 (1798).

147. *Summa Theologica* II-II, q. 60, a. 5.

148. Ibid.

149. See ibid., reply to obj. 1 (where Aquinas states that the only things made just or unjust solely by positive law, like driving on the right or left, are cases "where 'it matters not,' according to the natural right, 'whether a thing be done in one way or in another'").

150. Ibid.

151. Ibid.

152. Ibid., II-II, q. 67, a. 4.

153. Budziszewski, *Commentary on Thomas Aquinas's Treatise on Law*, 194.

154. Soper, "In Defense of Classical Natural Law in Legal Theory," 221.

155. See, e.g., Dworkin, *Law's Empire*, 255–56.

156. Gratian, *Decretum* D.4, C.2 and C.3; Aquinas addresses the same passage in Augustine in *Summa Theologica* I-II, q. 96, a. 6, obj. 1 and its reply. Aquinas distinguishes a case where one judges a situation contrary to a particular determination of human law by stating it is not legitimate to judge the law itself (disregard it) but that it is permissible to conclude that the human law does not apply to the particular contingent facts presented.

157. Soper, "In Defense of Classical Natural Law in Legal Theory," 221.

158. See Budziszewski, *Line through the Heart*, 151.

159. Hart, *Concept of Law*, 139–41 (using the contrast between a scorer applying a game rule and a scorer using complete scorer's discretion to illustrate that law is not the prediction of what decision a judge will make but the judge's decision).

160. See, e.g., Leo XIII, *Diuturnum*, sec. 7: "There is no question here respecting forms of government, for there is no reason why the Church should not approve of the chief power being held by one man or by more, provided only it be just, and that it tend to the common advantage. Wherefore, so long as justice be respected, the people are not hindered from choosing for themselves that form of government which suits best either their own disposition, or the institutions and customs of their ancestors."

161. Budziszewski, *Natural Law for Lawyers*, 63–67.

162. Ibid.

163. See *Calder*, 3 U.S. 386 (1798).

164. See *Summa Theologica* I-II, q. 96, a. 4.

165. *Papal Thought on the State: Excerpts from Encyclicals and Other Writings of Recent Popes*, ed. Gerard F. Yates, S. J. (New York: Appleton-Century-Crofts, 1958), 121.

NINE. The Point of the Structure: Justice and the Causes of Law

1. Ps. 18:9–10.

2. See Aristotle, *Physics*, in *The Complete Works of Aristotle*, Kindle ed. (Delphi Classics, 2013), 2.3; Grenier, *Metaphysics*, 210.

3. Grenier, *Metaphysics*, 212.

4. Ibid., 215.

5. See Aristotle, *Physics* 2.1 (Kindle 8471–72): "The form indeed is 'nature' rather than the matter; for a thing is more properly said to be what it is when it has attained to fulfilment than when it exists potentially."

6. Aquinas, *Summa Theologica* II-II, q. 57, a. 1, reply to obj. 2.

7. Grenier, *Metaphysics*, 219.

8. Ibid., 221.

9. Ibid., 220.

10. From the Latin *dicere* ("to speak") and *jus, juris* ("law").

11. Grenier, *Metaphysics*, 241.

12. Porter, *Ministers of the Law*, 87.

13. James Lennox, *Aristotle's Philosophy of Biology* (Cambridge: Cambridge University Press, 2001), 128.

14. Porter, *Ministers of the Law*, 86.

15. Author's translation of Bulgarus, *Materia Institutionum*, quoted in Stephan Kuttner, "A Forgotten Definition of Justice," in *The History of Ideas and Doctrines of Canon Law in the Middle Ages* (London: Variorum Reprints, 1980), V, 78: *Sicut dixi auctor iusticie deus est, iuris auctor homo est.*

16. Huguccio, *Summa Decretorum*, distinctiones I–XX, 19 (my translation).

17. Hart, *Concept of Law*, 86.

18. Aristotle, *Physics* 2.2.

19. MacIntyre, *After Virtue* (3rd ed.), 152.

20. Suárez, *Selections from Three Works*, 27–36. Suárez notes that there is disagreement regarding the order of etymology (Is *jus* derived from *justitia*, or vice versa?) and that some argue that *jus* is derived from *jubere*, "to command."

21. Pennington, "Lex Naturalis and Ius Naturale," 591.

22. Gratian, *Decretum* D.1, C.5.

23. Ibid., D.1., C.2.

24. As Suárez points out, the etymology of the word *jus* is disputed. It may derive from *jubere* or *justitia*. Yet, those, like Isidore, who argue that *jus* is derived from the words "just" or "justice" do so from the common understanding that law must be just to be law.

25. Huguccio, *Summa Decretorum*, 25, translation quoted in Pennington, "Lex Naturalis and Ius Naturale," 572.

26. Pennington, "Lex Naturalis and Ius Naturale," 573.

27. Tierney, *The Idea of Natural Rights*, 23.

28. *Summa Theologica* II-II, q. 57, a. 1.

29. Ibid., II-II, q. 57, a. 1, reply to obj. 1.

30. Isidore, *Etymologies* 5.2, quoted in *Summa Theologica* II-II, q. 57, a. 1.

31. Ibid.: *Sic igitur iustum dicitur aliquid, quasi habens rectitudinem iustitiae, ad quod terminatur actio iustitiae*, "A thing is said to be just, as having the rectitude of justice, when it is the term of an act of justice."

32. Ibid., II-II, q. 57, a. 2, reply to obj. 3.
33. Ibid., I-II, q. 49, a. 3.
34. Grenier, *Philosophy of Nature*, 144.
35. See *Summa Theologica* I-II, q. 49, a. 3.
36. See ibid.
37. Ibid., I-II, q. 49, a. 4.
38. Ibid., I-II, q. 71, a. 1.
39. Ibid.
40. Cicero, *De Inventione* 2.53: "Justice is a habit [*habitus*] of the mind that attributes its proper dignity to everything, preserving a due regard to the general welfare" (my translation).
41. *Summa Theologica* II-II, q. 58, a. 1.
42. Justinian, *Digest* 1.1.1.1.
43. *Summa Theologica* II-II, q. 58, a. 2.
44. Finnis, *Natural Law and Natural Rights*, 206.
45. *Summa Theologica* II-II, q. 57, a. 1, obj. 2.
46. Justinian, *Digest* 1.1.1.1.
47. *Summa Theologica* II-II, q. 57, a. 2, reply to obj. 1.
48. Ibid., II-II, q. 57, a. 1, reply to obj. 1.
49. Ibid.
50. Ibid., II-II, q. 57, a. 2, reply to obj. 2.
51. See Pennington, "Lex Naturalis and Ius Naturale," 573.
52. Anonymous Jurist (c. 1130?), to Cod. 1.13.2, s.v. *Que religiosa mente*, Paris, B. N. F. 4517, fol. 18r: (bottom margin); Vat. lat. 1427, fol. 22r (next to Cod. 1.12.6.6–9); translation quoted in Pennington, "Lex Naturalis and Ius Naturale," 574.
53. See Kuttner, "A Forgotten Definition of Justice," V.83 (my translation of *Differt a iustitia eo quod auctor iuris homo auctor iustitie Deus. Ideoque iustitia latius patet, multa sub se continens que necdum ius suis laqueis innodauit*).
54. Ibid.
55. See *Summa Theologica* II-II, q. 58, a. 8 and a. 10.
56. Ibid., II-II, q. 58, a. 11.
57. Aristotle, *Politics* 1.2.
58. Ibid.
59. See chapter 4 herein.
60. See Newman, *Foundations of Justice*, 27.
61. Joseph Pieper, *Justice*, trans. Lawrence E. Lynch (New York: Pantheon, 1955), 29.
62. See Pieper, *Justice*, 13; Aquinas, *Summa Contra Gentiles* 2.28.
63. See chapter 6.
64. Newman, *Foundations of Justice*, 70.
65. Ibid., 70–71.
66. MacIntyre, *After Virtue* (3rd ed.), 134.

67. See ibid.

68. In philosophical literature there has been a dispute over the meaning of the term "political justice" as it is used by Aristotle, with some arguing that it is synonymous with unqualified justice and others it is a type of particular justice, like commutative or distributive justice. See, e.g., Thornton C. Lockwood, Jr., "Ethical Justice and Political Justice," *Phronesis* 51, no. 1 (2006): 38–40 (he advocates a type of synonym between the two). In this section, I will argue that unqualified and political justice are categories of justice based upon their source, natural or political principles. Particular justice can thus derive from either unqualified or political justice.

69. See MacIntyre, *After Virtue* (3rd ed.), 139.

70. *Summa Theologica* II-II, q. 102, a. 2, reply to obj. 2.

71. Ibid.

72. Newman, *Foundations of Justice*, 73.

73. Aristotle, *Nicomachean Ethics* 5.7; and Newman, *Foundations of Justice*, 73.

74. Newman, *Foundations of Justice*, 74.

75. Kuttner, "A Forgotten Definition of Justice," V.87. According to Kuttner, this parallelism seems to echo an earlier statement of Hugh of St. Victor.

76. Pennington, "Lex Naturalis and Ius Naturale," 570.

77. See chapter 3.

78. Kuttner, "A Forgotten Definition of Justice," V. 84–85. The original definition read in the relevant part: *Iustitia est nature tacita conuentio in adiutorium multorum inuenta.* The words *in adiutorium multorum* were replaced by *cordibus hominum inspirata.*

79. Ibid., V.86.

80. Aristotle, *Nicomachean Ethics* 5.7.

81. Ibid.

82. Strauss, *Natural Right in History*, 125.

83. Ibid.

84. Aristotle, *Nicomachean Ethics* 5.7.

85. Ibid.

86. Strauss, *Natural Right in History*, 101–2.

87. *Summa Theologica* II-II, q. 57, a. 2, reply to obj. 2.

88. Newman, *Foundations of Justice*, 54.

89. Ibid.

90. See Aristotle, *Nichomachean Ethics* 5.3 and 5.8; Newman, *Foundations of Justice*, 72–73.

91. *Summa Theologica* II-II, q. 106, a. 1.

92. Pieper, *Justice*, 52–53.

93. *Summa Theologica* II-II, q. 61, a. 1–2.

94. Aristotle, *Nicomachean Ethics*, in Aquinas, *Commentary on the Ethics* 5.4.1131b32–1132a7 and 1132a14–19.

95. Ibid., 5.2.1130b30–33 and 5.51134a1–3 (stating that justice involves both equality in individual exchange and a proportionate [not necessarily equal] distribution of wealth among all in society).

96. James Gordley, "Equality in Exchange," *California Law Review* 69, no. 6 (1981): 1616. This equality in exchange does not mean that one party cannot use the thing received in exchange to make a profit, but this is not a gain from the exchange itself.

97. *Summa Theologica* II-II, q. 61, a. 1.

98. Grenier, *Moral Philosophy*, 199.

99. Pieper, *Justice*, 85.

100. Ibid., 88–89. For example, it would be unjust to distribute the tuition income of a university among professors on the basis of their personal wealth; a just principle would be to distribute it proportionately among the best scholars or teachers.

101. Ibid., 93–94.

102. *Summa Theologica* I, q. 65, a. 2, ad. 3.

103. Ibid., II-II, q. 61, a. 1.

104. See Aquinas, *Commentary on Aristotle's Nicomachean Ethics*, bk. 5, lecture 4, nos. 935–36.

105. Ibid.

106. Grenier, *Moral Philosophy*, 198, and Newman, *Foundations of Justice*, 90.

107. Newman, *Foundations of Justice*, 3.

108. *Summa Theologica* II-II, q. 58, a. 5.

109. Newman, *Foundations of Justice*, 98–99.

110. See Aristotle, *Politics* 3.4.

111. See Aristotle, *Nichomachean Ethics* 5.1.

112. See *Summa Theologica* I-II, q. 94, a. 3.

113. Ibid, I-II, q. 96, a. 2 and 3.

114. Ibid., II-II, q. 58, a. 6, reply to obj. 4.

115. Grenier, *Moral Philosophy*, 198.

116. *Summa Theologica* II-II, q. 58, a. 5.

117. Ibid., II-II, q. 79, a. 1.

118. Newman, *Foundations of Justice*, 49.

119. Ibid., 10, 12, and 13; and *Summa Theologica* II-II, q. 79, a. 1 and 3. Legal justice must be a habit of acting consistently with not only that which is legal under human law, political justice, but also that which is legal under the higher law, natural justice, because human law does not forbid all vice or require every virtue, but legal justice ordains all virtues to the common good and thus must have a domain broader than political justice. See Newman, *Foundations of Justice*, 10.

120. Newman, *Foundations of Justice*, 49.

121. Ibid., 6.

122. See Raz, *Authority of Law*, 42, 44.

123. See ibid., 105.

124. Porter, *Ministers of the Law*, 278–79.

125. Aquinas explains that although personal superiors like parents can issue commands that are analogous to laws, they are not strictly speaking laws because they lack promulgation by a public authority. See *Summa Theologica* I-II, q. 90, a. 3.

126. See Hart, *Concept of Law*, chap. 8.

127. Ibid., 151–54.

128. See ibid., chap. 8.

129. Ibid., 155.

130. Ibid., 153–54.

131. Rawls, *Theory of Justice*, 115.

132. Aristotle, *Nichomachean Ethics* 5.1.1129a31–1129b1.

133. *Summa Theologica* I-II, q. 94, a. 4.

134. Ibid.

135. Ibid.

136. Ibid., I-II, q. 94, a. 4.

137. Ibid., II-II, q. 120, a. 1.

138. Ibid., I-II, q. 94, a. 4.

139. Hittinger, *The First Grace*, 75.

140. *Summa Theologica* I-II, q. 94, a. 4.

141. Ibid., I-II, q. 96, a. 6.

142. Ibid.

143. See ibid., II-II, q. 120, a. 2, reply to obj. 1. See also Newman, *Foundations of Justice*, 63–64.

144. *Summa Theologica* II-II, q. 120, a. 1.

145. See Newman, *Foundations of Justice*, 62.

146. Archbishop Amleto Giovanni Cicognani, *Canon Law*, trans. Rev. Joseph M. O'Hara and Rev. Francis Brennan (Philadelphia: The Dolphin Press, 1934), 15.

147. Ibid., 15–16.

148. Suárez, *Selections from Three Works*, 317.

149. John Bouvier, *A Law Dictionary Adapted to the Constitution and Laws of the United States of America and of the Several States of the American Union with References to the Civil and Other Systems of Foreign Law*, 6th ed. (Philadelphia: Childs & Peterson, 1856).

150. See Porter, *Natural and Divine Law*, 154–55.

151. *Summa Theologica* II-II, q. 77, a. 1, reply to obj. 1.

152. Suárez, *Selections from Three Works*, 321–22.

153. Reinhard Zimmerman, *The Law of Obligations: Roman Foundations of the Civilian Tradition* (New York: Oxford University Press, 1996), 205.

154. See Pennington, "Lex Naturalis and Ius Naturale," 584 (explaining that contracts of *depositum* and *commodatum* were not "an absolute principle of natural law. Rather, they were an illustration of a precept of natural law").

155. Brennan, "Are Legislation and Rules a Problem in Law?," 1214.

156. Ibid., 1203.

157. See *Summa Theologica* II-II, q. 120, a. 1, and Newman, *Foundations of Justice*, 61.

158. *Summa Theologica* I-II, q. 96, a. 6; see also I-II, q. 97, a. 4.

159. P. Fenet, *Recueil complet des travaux préparatoires du code civil* (1827), 470, translation in Tunc, "Methodology of the Civil Law in France," 463.

160. Porter, *Natural and Divine Law*, 158.

161. See Newman, *Foundations of Justice*, 64.

162. L. J. Riley, *The History, Nature and Use of Epikeia in Moral Theology* (Washington, DC: Catholic University of America Press, 1948), 205 (quoting *Nicomachean Ethics* 5.7).

163. Hart, *Concept of Law*, 121–24.

164. Ibid., 124.

165. MacIntyre, *After Virtue* (3rd ed.), 187.

166. Ibid., 191.

167. Ibid., 172.

TEN. The Reality of the Art (Not the Science) of Law

1. Ps. 126:1.

2. MacIntyre, *After Virtue* (2nd ed.), 190.

3. Ibid.

4. Porter, *Natural and Divine Law*, 126.

5. Aristotle, *Nicomachean Ethics* 7.11.1152b19.

6. MacIntyre, *Three Rival Versions of Moral Enquiry*, 61–62.

7. Ibid., 64.

8. Ibid., 62.

9. Ibid.

10. Dominic Bourmaud, *One Hundred Years of Modernism: A Genealogy of the Principles of the Second Vatican Council* (Kansas City, MO: Angelus, 2006), 43.

11. MacIntyre, *Three Rival Versions of Moral Enquiry*, 63.

12. Aristotle, *Physics* 2.2.194a22.

13. Porter, *Natural and Divine Law*, 27–31, quoting Finnis, *Natural Law and Natural Rights*, 66 (emphasis added).

14. Ibid., 31. For example, she points out: "Even the traditional Catholic prohibition of the use of contraceptives is interpreted by them [Finnis and Grisez] as a sin against life, which represents the same stance of will as is present in murder, rather than as a violation of the natural processes of sexuality" (see ibid., 93).

15. Ibid., 93.

16. See, e.g., ibid., 226–33.

17. Ibid., 77.

18. Ibid.

19. Ibid., 77–78.

20. See ibid., 78–79.

21. Ibid., 77.

22. MacIntyre, *Three Rival Versions of Moral Enquiry*, 60.

23. Leo XIII, *Rerum Novarum*, sec. 21.

24. Porter, *Natural and Divine Law*, 306.

25. MacIntyre, *Three Rival Versions of Moral Enquiry*, 59.

26. Hittinger, *The First Grace*, 62.

27. Johnathan Crowe, "Five Questions for John Finnis," *Pandora's Box* 18 (2011): 11–12, http://ssrn.com/abstract=1943926.

28. Strauss, *Natural Right and History*, 7.

29. Ibid., 9–34.

30. Ibid., 37–38.

31. Ibid., 40.

32. I say "very simple state" because, contrary to the mythical creations of Hobbes, Locke, Rousseau, and others, there can be no such thing as a presocial man. Since sociability is part of man's nature, he can never be presocial. The practical manifestation of his social nature may be only weakly expressed in laws and institutions, but it is present nonetheless.

33. Cicero, *On the Laws* 132–33.

34. Strauss, *Natural Right and History*, 282.

35. Moore, "Good without God," 250.

36. Pieper, *Justice*, 21.

37. Hittinger, *The First Grace*, xx.

38. Aquinas, *Summa Theologica* I-II, q. 96, a. 4.

39. Moore, "Good without God," 235. In arguing that an act of God's will, promulgation, is unnecessary to recognize the objective, real goods of the natural law, he states: "Prescriptivity on this view is analyzed exclusively in terms of demands by one person on another. All that 'objective' prescriptions could be for such a view would be the demands of some Big Person on all of the rest of us. Thus, God. The reason why we have put this intuition aside is because of its denial of moral objectivity in any useful sense right from the start. Moral realism is the view that moral qualities give each of us objective, non-prudential reasons for action, and it will not do in asking how God helps in sustaining moral realism to deny the latter's truth. Moral realism is committed to the view that prescriptivity is to be taken as a feature of the world—objective reasons for action—so this direct route, from universally applicable prescriptions to Grand Prescriber, must be ruled out."

40. Finnis, *Natural Law and Natural Rights*, 44.

41. Rom. 2:14–15 (DV).

42. *Summa Theologica* I-II, q. 91, a. 2, reply to obj. 2.

43. Strauss, *Natural Right and History*, 164.

44. Ibid.

45. Hittinger, *The First Grace*, 21.

46. Harold J. Berman, *Faith and Order: The Reconciliation of Law and Religion* (Atlanta: Scholars Press, 1993), x.

47. Ibid., 4.

48. Budziszewski, *Line through the Heart*, 59.

49. *Summa Theologica* I-II, q. 62, a. 1.

50. Pope John Paul II, *Veritatis Splendor*, secs. 36–37.

51. See Newman, *Foundations of Justice*, 90–91.

52. Ibid., 93.

53. Ibid.

54. Hart, *Concept of Law*, 169–76.

55. Ibid., 169–71.

56. Ibid., 170–73.

57. Ibid., 171.

58. Ibid., 173–75.

59. Ibid., 174.

60. Ibid., 175–76.

61. Strauss, *Natural Right and History*, 279.

62. Cicero, *Treatise on the Laws*, in *The Political Works*.

63. Ibid.

64. Porter, *Natural and Divine Law*, 251.

65. Ibid.

66. MacIntyre, *After Virtue* (2nd ed.), 253.

67. Berman, *Faith and Order*, 5.

68. Ibid.

69. MacIntyre, *After Virtue* (2nd ed.), 253.

70. Berman, *Faith and Order*, 8.

71. Ibid.

72. Strauss, *Natural Right and History*, 134.

73. Newman, *Foundations of Justice*, 120.

74. Ibid., 18.

75. Porter, *Natural and Divine Law*, 250.

76. *Summa Theologica* I-II, q. 91, a. 2 (in the original Latin, the connection to justice is more evident than in English with the use of the word *debitum*, the same word to describe the "debt" due in justice).

77. John Dickinson, introduction to *The Statesman's Book of John of Salisbury: Being the Fourth, Fifth, and Sixth Books, and Selections from the Seventh and Eighth Books, of the Policraticus*, by John of Salisbury, Bishop of Chartres, trans. John Dickinson (New York: A. A. Knopf, 1927), xxviii.

78. Rémi Brague, *The Law of God: The Philosophical History of an Idea* (Chicago: University of Chicago Press, 2007), 238.

79. González, "Natural Law as a Limiting Concept," 24.

80. Aristotle, *Politics* 3.15.1286a5–10.

81. John Adams, "Letter to the Inhabitants of the Colony of Massachusetts-Bay," March 6, 1775, https://www.masshist.org/publications/apde2/view?&id=PJA02dg5.

82. MacIntyre, *After Virtue* (2nd ed.), 110–11.

SELECT BIBLIOGRAPHY

All quotations from the scriptures are from the Douay Rheims translation.

Aquinas, St. Thomas. *Commentary on Aristotle's Politics.* Translated by Richard J. Regan. Indianapolis: Hackett, 2007.

———. *Commentary on the Nichomachean Ethics.* Translated by C. I. Litzinger. Chicago: Henry Regnery, 1964.

———. *De Duobus Praeceptis Caritatis.* http://www.corpusthomisticum.org/cac.html.

———. *De Regimine Principum (De Regno).* In *Selected Political Writings,* edited by A. P. d'Entreves. Translated by J. G. Dawson. Oxford: Blackwell, 1959.

———. *De Veritate.* http://www.corpusthomisticum.org/iopera.html.

———. *De Veritate.* Translated by James V. McGlynn, S.J. Chicago: Henry Regnery, 1953.

———. *On Charity.* Translated by Lottie H. Kendzierski. Milwaukee: Marquette University Press, 1960.

———. *Summa Contra Gentiles.* http://www.corpusthomisticum.org/iopera.html.

———. *Summa Contra Gentiles.* Edited by Joseph Kenny, O.P. New York: Hanover House, 1955–57. http://www.dhspriory.org/thomas/english/ContraGentiles.htm.

———. *Summa Theologica.* Translated by Fathers of the English Dominican Province. New York: Benziger Brothers, 1947.

Aristotle. *Nicomachean Ethics.* In *The Basic Works of Aristotle,* edited by Richard McKeon. New York: Random House, 1941.

———. *Physics.* In *The Basic Works of Aristotle,* edited by Richard McKeon. New York: Random House, 1941.

———. *Politics.* In *The Basic Works of Aristotle,* edited by Richard McKeon. New York: Random House, 1941.

———. *The Politics of Aristotle.* Translated by Ernest Barker. Oxford: Oxford University Press, 1946.

Armstrong, R. A. *Primary and Secondary Precepts in Thomistic Natural Law Teaching.* The Hague: Martinus Nijhoff, 1966.

Aroney, Nicholas. "Subsidiarity, Federalism and the Best Constitution: Thomas Aquinas on City, Province and Empire." *Law and Philosophy* 26 (2007): 161–228.

Augustine. *Answer to Faustus, a Manichean.* Vol. 20, pt. 1 of *The Works of Saint Augustine: A Translation for the 21st Century*, edited by Boniface Ramsey. Translated by Roland Teske, S.J. Hyde Park, NY: New City Press, 2007.

———. *De Libero Arbitrio.* Edited by J. P. Migne. http://www.augustinus.it/latino/index.htm.

———. "The Problem of Free Choice." In *Ancient Christian Writers*, edited by Johannes Quasten and Joseph C. Plumpe. Mahwah, NJ: Paulist, 1955.

Austin, John. *The Province of Jurisprudence Determined and Uses of the Study of Jurisprudence.* New York: Noonday, 1954.

Barker, Ernest. Introduction to *Natural Law and the Theory of Society*, by Otto Gierke. Translated by Ernest Barker. Cambridge: Cambridge University Press, 1934.

Barnett, Randy E. "Constitutional Legitimacy." *Columbia Law Review* 103, no. 1 (2003): 111–48.

Barnhart, Robert. Note, "Principled Pragmatic *Stare Decisis* in Constitutional Cases." *Notre Dame Law Review* 80 (2005): 1911–27.

Bateman, C. G. "Sovereignty's Missing Moral Imperative." *International Zeitschrift* 8, no. 2 (2012): 30–41.

Benedict XVI, Pope. "Address to the International Congress on Natural Moral Law" (February 12, 2007). https://w2.vatican.va/content/benedict-xvi/en/speeches/2007/february/documents/hf_ben-xvi_spe_20070212_pul.html.

———. "Address to Members of the International Theological Commission" (October 5, 2007). https://w2.vatican.va/content/benedict-xvi/en/speeches/2007/october/documents/hf_ben-xvi_spe_20071005_cti.html.

———. "Message for the Celebration of the World Day of Peace" (January 1, 2008). http://w2.vatican.va/content/benedict-xvi/en/messages/peace/documents/hf_ben-xvi_mes_20071208_xli-world-day-peace.html.

Bentham, Jeremy. *"Legislator of the World": Writings on Codification, Law, and Education.* Edited by Philip Schofield and Jonathan Harris. Oxford: Clarendon, 2009.

———. *Of Laws in General.* Edited by H. L. A. Hart. London: University of London Press, Athlone Press, 1970.

Berkowitz, Roger. *The Gift of Science: Leibniz and the Modern Legal Tradition.* Cambridge, MA: Harvard University Press, 2005.

Berman, Harold J. "An Ecumenical Christian Jurisprudence." In *The Teachings of Modern Christianity on Law, Politics, and Nature*, vol. 1, edited by John Witte, Jr., and John S. Alexander, 752–64. New York: Columbia University Press, 2006.

———. *Faith and Order: The Reconciliation of Law and Religion.* Atlanta: Scholars, 1993.

———. *Law and Revolution: The Formation of the Western Legal Tradition.* Cambridge, MA: Harvard University Press, 1983.

Besselink, Leonard, Frans Pennings, and Sacha Prechal. "Introduction: Legality in Multiple Legal Orders." In *The Eclipse of the Legality Principle in the European Union*, edited by Leonard Besselink et al. Austin, TX: Wolters Kluwer Law & Business, 2011.

Bishop, Joel Prentiss. *Common Law and Codification, or, The Common Law as a System of Reasoning.* Chicago: T. H. Flood and Co., 1888.

Blackstone, William. *Commentaries on the Laws of England.* Vol. 1. Oxford: Clarendon, 1765–1769.

Bonaventure. *Itinerarium Mentis in Deum.* In *Works of Saint Bonaventure*, vol. 1, edited by Philotheus Boehner, OFM, and Sr. Frances Laughlin, SMIC. St. Bonaventure, NY: Saint Bonaventure University Press, 1956.

Bourke, Vernon. *History of Ethics.* New York: Doubleday, 1968.

Bourmaud, Dominic. *One Hundred Years of Modernism: A Genealogy of the Principles of the Second Vatican Council.* Kansas City, MO: Angelus, 2006.

Bouvier, John. *A Law Dictionary Adapted to the Constitution and Laws of the United States of America and of the Several States of the American Union with References to the Civil and Other Systems of Foreign Law.* 6th ed. Philadelphia: Childs & Peterson, 1856.

Bracton, Henry. *De Legibus et Consuetudinibus Angliae.* Bracton Online, 2:33. http://bracton.law.harvard.edu/Unframed/calendar.htm.

Brague, Rémi. *The Law of God: The Philosophical History of an Idea.* Chicago: University of Chicago Press, 2007.

Brennan, Patrick McKinley. "Are Legislation and Rules a Problem in Law? Thoughts on the Work of Joseph Vining." *Villanova Law Review* 55 (2010): 1191–1218.

———. "Locating Authority in Law." In *Civilizing Authority: Society, State, and Church*, edited by Patrick Brennan, 161–95. Lanham, MD: Lexington, 2007.

———. "Persons, Participating, and 'Higher Law.'" *Pepperdine Law Review* 36, no. 5 (2009): 475–90.

———. "The Place of 'Higher Law' in the Quotidian Practice of Law: Herein of Practical Reason, Natural Law, Natural Rights, and Sex Toys." *Georgetown Journal of Law & Public Policy* 7 (2009): 437–79.

Brown, Rebecca L. "How Constitutional Theory Found Its Soul: The Contributions of Ronald Dworkin." In *Exploring Law's Empire: The Jurisprudence of Ronald Dworkin*, edited by Scott Hershovitz, 41–67. Oxford: Oxford University Press, 2006.

Budziszewski, J. *Commentary on Thomas Aquinas's Treatise on Law.* Cambridge: Cambridge University Press, 2014.

———. *The Line through the Heart.* Wilmington, DE: ISI Books, 2009.

———. *Natural Law for Lawyers.* Nashville, TN: ACW Press, 2006.

Burdick, William L. *The Principles of Roman Law and Their Relation to Modern Law*. Clark, NJ: The Lawbook Exchange, 2004.

Cappalli, Richard B. "At the Point of Decision: The Common Law's Advantage over the Civil Law." *Temple International and Comparative Law Journal* 12, no. 1 (1998): 87–105.

Cardozo, Benjamin N. *The Nature of the Judicial Process*. New Haven, CT: Yale University Press, 2007.

Carl, Maria T. "The First Principles of Natural Law: A Study of the Moral Theories of Aristotle and Saint Thomas Aquinas." PhD diss., Marquette University, 1989. http://epublications.marquette.edu/dissertations/AAI9014051/.

Catechism of the Council of Trent. Translated by John A. McHugh, O.P., and Charles J. Callan, O.P. Rockford, IL: TAN, 1982.

The Catholic Encyclopedia. Vol. 6. New York: Robert Appleton Company, 1909.

Cicero, Marcus Tullius. *De Finibus Bonorum et Malorum*. 2nd ed. Translated by H. Rackham. New York: G. P. Putnam's Sons, 1921.

———. *De Inventione*. http://www.thelatinlibrary.com/cicero/inventione2.shtml.

———. *De Inventione*. In *The Orations of Marcus Tullius Cicero*, vol. 4, translated by C. D. Yonge. London: George Bell & Sons, 1888. http://classicpersuasion.org/pw/cicero/dnv2-8.htm#LII.

———. *De Officiis*. http://www.thelatinlibrary.com/cicero/off.shtml.

———. *Letters to Atticus*. http://www.thelatinlibrary.com/cicero/att1.shtml#6.

———. *On the Commonwealth [De Republica]*. In *On the Commonwealth and On the Laws*, edited by James E. G. Zetzel. Cambridge: Cambridge University Press, 1999.

———. *On the Laws [De Legibus]*. In *On the Commonwealth and On the Laws*, edited by James E. G. Zetzel. Cambridge: Cambridge University Press, 1999.

———. *Orationes: Cum Senatui gratias egit, Cum populo gratias egit, De domo sua, De haruspicum responso, Pro Sestio, In Vatinium, De provinciis consularibus, Pro Balbo*. Vol. 5. Edited by Albert Clark. Oxford: Clarendon, 1952.

———. *The Second Book of the Rhetoric, or of the Treatise on Rhetorical Invention, of M. T. Cicero*. In *Orations*, vol. 4, *The Fourteen Orations Against Marcus Antonius; To Which Are Appended the Treatise on Rhetorical Invention; the Orator; Topics; on Rhetorical Partitions, Etc*. Translated by C. D. Yonge. London: G. Bell and Sons, 1913–1921.

———. *Treatise on the Laws [De Legibus]*. In *The Political Works*, vol. 2, translated by Francis Barham. London: Edmund Spettigue, 1842. http://oll.libertyfund.org/index.php?option=com_staticxt&staticfile=show.php%3Ftitle=545&Itemid=99999999.

Cicognani, Amleto Giovanni. *Canon Law*. Translated by Rev. Joseph M. O'Hara and Rev. Francis Brennan. Philadelphia: The Dolphin Press, 1934.

Clarke, R. Floyd. *The Science of Law and Lawmaking: Being an Introduction to Law, a General View of Its Forms and Substance, and a Discussion of the Question of Codification*. New York: Macmillan, 1898.

Cohen, Jeremy. "Original Sin as the Evil Inclination: A Polemicist's Appreciation of Human Nature." *Harvard Theological Review* 73 (1980): 495–520.

"Corporate Crime and Abuse: Tracking the Problem." *Center for Corporate Policy*, 2003–2004. http://www.corporatepolicy.org/issues/crimedata.htm.

Corpus Juris Secundum. St. Paul, MN: West, 2013.

Cortest, Louis. *The Disfigured Face: Traditional Natural Law and Its Encounter with Modernity.* New York: Fordham University Press, 2008.

Crowe, Jonathan. "Clarifying the Natural Law Thesis." *Australian Journal of Legal Philosophy* 37 (2012): 159–81.

———. "Five Questions for John Finnis." *Pandora's Box* 18 (2011): 11–17. http://ssrn.com/abstract=1943926.

Curran, Vivian Grosswald. "Romantic Common Law, Enlightened Civil Law: Legal Uniformity and the Homogenization of the European Union." *Colombia Journal of European Law* 7 (2001): 63–126.

Cyr, Hugo. "Functional and Existential Authorities." *Canadian Journal of Law and Jurisprudence* 28, no. 2 (2015): 265–88.

Dante. *The Divine Comedy.* Vol. 3, *Paradiso.* Translated by John D. Sinclair. London: Oxford University Press, 1939.

D'Arcy, E. *Conscience and Its Right to Freedom.* New York: Sheed & Ward, 1961.

Davies, Sharon L. "The Jurisprudence of Willfulness: An Evolving Theory of Excusable Ignorance." *Duke Law Journal* 48, no. 3 (1998): 341–420.

Davis, Susan. "This Congress Could Be Least Productive since 1947." *USA Today*, August 15, 2012. http://usatoday30.usatoday.com/news/washington/story/2012-08-14/unproductive-congress-not-passing-bills/57060096/1.

Degraff, Thelma B. "Plato in Cicero." *Classical Philology* 35, no. 2 (1940): 143–53.

De Koninck, Charles. "On the Primacy of the Common Good: Against the Personalists and the Principle of the New Order." *The Aquinas Review* 4 (1997). http://ldataworks.com/aqr/V4_BC_text.html#BC_h003.

Denzinger, Henry. *The Sources of Catholic Dogma.* Translated by Roy J. Deferrari. Fitzwilliam, NH: Loreto, 2007.

Dickinson, John. Introduction to *The Statesman's Book of John of Salisbury: Being the Fourth, Fifth, and Sixth Books, and Selections from the Seventh and Eighth Books, of the Policraticus,* by John of Salisbury, Bishop of Chartres. Translated by John Dickinson. New York: A. A. Knopf, 1927.

Dworkin, Ronald. *Law's Empire.* Cambridge, MA: Harvard University Press, 1986.

Easterbrook, Frank H., and Daniel R. Fischel. "Antitrust Suits by Targets of Tender Offers." *Michigan Law Review* 80 (1982): 1155.

Fahey, Denis. *The Mystical Body of Christ in the Modern World.* 3rd ed. Palmdale, CA: The Christian Book Club of America, 1994.

Ferrara, Christopher A. *Liberty, the God That Failed: Policing the Sacred and Constructing the Myths of the Secular State, from Locke to Obama.* New York: Angelico, 2012.

Feser, Edward. *Neo-Scholastic Essays.* South Bend, IN: St. Augustine's Press, 2015.

Figgis, John Neville. *The Divine Right of Kings.* 2nd ed. Cambridge: Cambridge University Press, 1934.

Finnis, John. *Aquinas: Moral, Political, and Legal Theory.* Oxford: Oxford University Press, 1998.

———. *Natural Law and Natural Rights.* 2nd ed. Oxford: Oxford University Press, 2011.

———. "Reason, Revelation, Universality and Particularity in Ethics." *American Journal of Jurisprudence* 53 (2008): 23–48.

Flaccus, Gillian. "Calif. Man Gets 30 Years for Ponzi Scheme" *Washington Post,* May 27, 2006. http://www.washingtonpost.com/wp-dyn/content/article/2006/05/27/AR2006052700250.html.

Flathman, Richard. *Political Obligation.* New York: Atheneum, 1972.

Frederick II, Emperor. *The Liber Augustalis or Constitutions of Melfi Promulgated by the Emperor Frederick II for the Kingdom of Sicily in 1231.* Translated by James Powell. Syracuse, NY: Syracuse University Press, 1971.

Ghent, Henry of. *Quodlibet.* In *Opera Omnia,* vol. 10, edited by G. A. Wilson. Leiden: E. J. Brill, 1979.

Gilmore, Grant. *The Ages of American Law.* New Haven, CT: Yale University Press, 1977.

Goldsworthy, J. D. "God or Mackie? The Dilemma of Secular Moral Philosophy." *American Journal of Jurisprudence* 30 (1985): 43–77.

González, Ana Marta. "Natural Law as a Limiting Concept: A Reading of Thomas Aquinas." In *Contemporary Perspectives on Natural Law: Natural Law as a Limiting Concept,* edited by Ana Marta González, 11–25. Hampshire: Ashgate, 2008.

Gordley, James. "Equality in Exchange." *California Law Review* 69, no. 6 (1981): 1587–1656.

Gratian. *Concordia Discordantium Canonum [Decretum].* In *Corpus Iuris Canonici.* Graz: Akademische Druck-u. Verlagsanstalt, 1959. Electronic reproduction, vols. 1–2. New York: Columbia University Libraries, 2007. http://www.columbia.edu/cu/lweb/digital/collections/cul/texts/ldpd_6029936_001/pages/ldpd_6029936_001_00000059.html.

———. *The Treatise on Laws (Decretum DD. 1–20),* vol. 2. Translated by Augustine Thompson and James Gordley. Washington, DC: Catholic University of America Press, 1993.

Greene, Abner S. *Against Obligation: The Multiple Sources of Authority in a Liberal Democracy.* Cambridge, MA: Harvard University Press, 2012.

Greene, Robert A. "Instinct of Nature: Natural Law, Synderesis, and the Moral Sense." *Journal of the History of Ideas* 58, no. 2 (1997): 173–98.

Gregory the Great. "The Book of Pastoral Rule and Selected Epistles," translated by Rev. James Barmby. In *Nicene and Post-Nicene Fathers.* Vol. 12, *Leo the Great and Gregory the Great*, edited by Schaff and Wace. Grand Rapids, MI: Eerdmans, 1979.

Grenier, Henri. *Thomistic Philosophy*. Vol. 1, *General Introduction, Logic, and Philosophy of Nature*. Translated by J. P. E. O'Hanley. Charlottetown, PEI: St. Dunstan's University, 1948.

———. *Thomistic Philosophy*. Vol. 2, *Philosophy of Nature*. Translated by Rev. J. P. E. O'Hanley. Charlottetown, PEI: St. Dunstan's University Press, 1950.

———. *Thomistic Philosophy*. Vol. 3, *Metaphysics*. Translated by J. P. E. O'Hanley. Charlottetown, PEI: St. Dunstan's University, 1948.

———. *Thomistic Philosophy*. Vol. 4, *Moral Philosophy*. Translated by Rev. J. P. E. O'Hanley. Charlottetown, PEI: St. Dunstan's University, 1950.

Grisez, Germain. *The Way of the Lord*. Vol. 1. Quincy, IL: Franciscan Press, 1983.

Hart, H. L. A. *The Concept of Law*. New York: Oxford University Press, 1961.

Henle, Robert J. *Latin Grammar*. Chicago: Loyola University Press, 1958.

Henriques, Diana B. "Madoff Is Sentenced to 150 Years for Ponzi Scheme." *New York Times*, June 29, 2009, http://www.nytimes.com/2009/06/30/business/30madoff.html?pagewanted=all&_r=0.

Herstein, Ori J. "A Legal Right to Do Legal Wrong." *Oxford Journal of Legal Studies* 34, no. 1 (2014): 21–45.

Hill, John L. *After the Natural Law: How the Classical Worldview Supports Our Modern Moral and Political Values*. San Francisco: Ignatius, 2016.

Hittinger, Russell. *The First Grace: Rediscovering the Natural Law in a Post-Christian World*. Wilmington, DE: ISI Books, 2003.

Hobbes, Thomas. *De Homine*. Translated by Charles Wood, T. S. K. Scott-Craig, and Bernard Gert. Indianapolis: Hackett, 1991.

Holmes, Oliver Wendell. *The Common Law*. Clark, NJ: The Lawbook Exchange, 2005.

Hornick, Blake, and Arren Goldman. "Commentary: The End of the Reagan Era of Deregulation and Worship of the Free Markets." *Andrews Securities Litigation and Regulation Reporter* 14, no. 17 (2008).

Hudson, W. D. *The Is/Ought Question: A Collection of Papers on the Central Problems in Moral Philosophy*. London: Macmillan, 1969.

Huguccio Pisanus. *Summa Decretorum*. In *Monumenta Iuris Canonici Series A: Corpus Glossatorum*. Vol. 6. Edited by Oldřich Přerovský. Rome: Biblioteca Apostolica Vaticano, 2006.

Isidore of Seville. *Etymologiarum sive Originum*. Vol. 5. Edited by W. M. Lindsay. Oxford: Clarendon, 1911.

John Paul II. *Veritatis Splendor*. http://w2.vatican.va/content/john-paul-ii/en/encyclicals/documents/hf_jp-ii_enc_06081993_veritatis-splendor.html.

John of Salisbury. *Policraticus*. Edited and translated by Cary J. Nederman. Cambridge: Cambridge University Press, 1990.

Johnston, David. "The Jurists." In *The Cambridge History of Greek and Roman Political Thought*, edited by Christopher Rowe and Malcolm Schofield, 616–34. Cambridge: Cambridge University Press 2005.

Justinian. *Digest*. In *Corpus Iuris Civilis*, edited by Joannis L. G. Beck. Leipzig: Carolum Cnoblock, 1829. http://www.archive.org/stream/corpusiuriscivi00beck goog#page/n2/mode/2up.

———. *Digest*. Translated by S. P. Scott. Cincinnati: The Central Trust Company Executor of the Estate Samuel P. Scott, 1932.

———. *Institutes*. Translated by S. P. Scott. Cincinnati, OH: The Central Trust Company Executor of the Estate Samuel P. Scott, 1932.

Kahn, Paul W. *Political Theology*. New York: Columbia University Press, 2011.

Kelsen, Hans. *General Theory of Law and State*. Cambridge, MA: Harvard University Press, 1945.

Kennedy, John F. "Address to the Greater Houston Ministerial Association at the Rice Hotel in Houston, TX" (September 12, 1960). http://www.american rhetoric.com/speeches/jfkhoustonministers.html.

Kent, James. *Commentaries on American Law*. 12th ed. Edited by O. W. Holmes, Jr. Boston: Little, Brown, and Company, 1873.

Keys, Mary M. *Aquinas, Aristotle, and the Promise of the Common Good*. Cambridge: Cambridge University Press, 2006.

King, Martin Luther, Jr. "Letter from a Birmingham Jail" (April 16, 1963). http://www.africa.upenn.edu/Articles_Gen/Letter_Birmingham.html.

Kossel, Clifford. "Natural Law and Human Law." In *The Ethics of Aquinas*, edited by Stephen J. Pope, 169–93. Washington, DC: Georgetown University Press, 2002.

Kozinski, Thaddeus J. *The Political Problem of Religious Pluralism: And Why Philosophers Can't Solve It*. Lanham, MD: Lexington, 2013.

Kuttner, Stephan. "A Forgotten Definition of Justice." In *The History of Ideas and Doctrines of Canon Law in the Middle Ages*, 75–109. London: Variorum Reprints, 1980.

Langholm, Odd. *Economics in the Medieval Schools: Wealth, Exchange, Value, Money and Usury according to the Paris Theological Tradition 1200–1350*. Leiden: E. J. Brill, 1992.

La Porta, Rafael, Florencio Lopez-de-Silanes, and Andrei Shleifer. "The Economic Consequences of Legal Origins." *Journal of Economic Literature* 46, no. 2 (2008): 285–332.

Lennox, James. *Aristotle's Philosophy of Biology*. Cambridge: Cambridge University Press, 2001.

Leo XIII. *Arcanum Divinae Sapientiae* (February 10, 1880). http://www.vatican.va /holy_father/leo_xiii/encyclicals/documents/hf_l-xiii_enc_10021880_arcanum _en.html.

———. *Diuturnum*. https://w2.vatican.va/content/leo-xiii/en/encyclicals/documents /hf_l-xiii_enc_29061881_diuturnum.html.

————. *Immortale Dei* (November 1, 1885). http://w2.vatican.va/content/leo -xiii/it/encyclicals/documents/hf_l-xiii_enc_01111885_immortale-dei.html.

————. *Rerum Novarum.* http://w2.vatican.va/content/leo-xiii/en/encyclicals /documents/hf_l-xiii_enc_15051891_rerum-novarum.html.

Lewis, Charlton T. *An Elementary Latin Dictionary.* Oxford: Oxford University Press, 1999.

Lewis, Charlton T., et al. *A Latin Dictionary: Founded on Andrews' Edition of Freund's Latin Dictionary.* Oxford: Clarendon, 1879.

Lincoln, Abraham. "First Inaugural Address" (March 4, 1861). In *The Speeches of Abraham Lincoln.* London: Chesterfield Society, 1908.

Locke, John. "Of the Beginning of Political Societies," "Of Slavery," and "Of the State of Nature." In *Second Treatise of Government.* Indianapolis: Bobbs-Merrill, 1952.

Lockwood, Thornton C., Jr. "Ethical Justice and Political Justice." *Phronesis* 51, no. 1 (2006): 29–48.

MacIntyre, Alasdair. *After Virtue: A Study in Moral Theory.* 2nd ed. Notre Dame, IN: University of Notre Dame Press, 1984.

————. *After Virtue: A Study in Moral Theory.* 3rd ed. Notre Dame, IN: University of Notre Dame Press, 2007.

————. *Three Rival Versions of Moral Enquiry: Encyclopaedia, Genealogy, and Tradition: Being Gifford Lectures Delivered in the University of Edinburgh in 1988.* Notre Dame, IN: University of Notre Dame Press, 1990.

————. *Whose Justice? Which Rationality?* Notre Dame, IN: University of Notre Dame Press, 1988.

Mahoney, Paul G. "The Common Law and Economic Growth: Hayek Might Be Right." *Journal of Legal Studies* 30, no. 2 (2001): 503–24.

Maritain, Jacques. *The Rights of Man and Natural Law.* Translated by Doris Anson. New York: Scribner, 1943.

"Martha Stewart Convicted," *Time,* March 5, 2004. http://www.time.com/time /nation/article/0,8599,598286,00.html.

McCall, Brian M. "Can a Pluralistic Commonwealth Endure?" Review of *The Political Problem of Religious Pluralism and Why Philosophers Can't Solve It,* by Thaddeus J. Kozinski. *Georgetown Journal of Law and Public Policy* 11 (2013): 45–61.

————. *The Church and the Usurers: Unprofitable Lending for the Modern Economy.* Ave Maria, FL: Sapientia, 2013.

————. "Exploring the Foundations of Dworkin's Empire: The Discovery of an Underground Positivist." *Journal of Law, Philosophy and Culture* 4, no. 1 (2009): 195–208.

McInerny, Ralph. *St. Thomas Aquinas.* Notre Dame, IN: University of Notre Dame Press, 1982.

Merryman, John Henry. "The French Deviation." *American Journal of Comparative Law* 44, no. 1 (1996): 109–19.

Merryman, John Henry, and Rogelio Pérez-Perdomo. *The Civil Law Tradition: An Introduction to the Legal Systems of Western Europe and Latin America.* 3rd ed. Stanford, CA: Stanford University Press, 2007.

Milgram, Stanley. "Behavioral Study of Obedience." *Journal of Abnormal and Social Psychology* 67 (October 1963): 371.

————. *Obedience to Authority: An Experimental View.* New York: Harper & Row, 1974.

Miller, J. Bleecker. *Destruction of Our Natural Law by Codification.* New York: H. Cherouny, 1882.

Miller, Vaughne, and Claire Taylor. *The Treaty of Lisbon: Amendments to the Treaty on European Union.* House of Commons Research Paper No. 08/09, January 24, 2008. http://researchbriefings.files.parliament.uk/documents/RP08-09/RP08-09.pdf.

Modak-Truran, Mark C. "Beyond Theocracy and Secularism (Part I): Toward a New Paradigm for Law and Religion." *Mississippi College Law Review* 27, no. 1 (2007): 159–233.

Moore, Michael S. "Good without God." In *Natural Law, Liberalism, and Morality,* edited by Robert P. George, 221–70. Oxford: Clarendon, 2001.

————. "Law as a Functional Kind." In *Natural Law Theory: Contemporary Essays,* edited by Robert P. George, 188–242. Oxford: Oxford University Press, 1992.

Morgan, Edmund S. *Inventing the People: The Rise of Popular Sovereignty in England and America.* New York: W. W. Norton, 1988.

Mueller, Robert S., III. *Today's FBI: Facts and Figures 2010–2011.* Darby, PA: Diane Publishing, 2011.

Nelson, Benjamin Lee Samuel. "Unwritten Law: Three Selections from the History of Political Philosophy." Unpublished manuscript, May 19, 2012. http://ssrn.com/abstract=2062924 or http://dx.doi.org/10.2139/ssrn.2062924.

Newman, Jeremiah. *Foundations of Justice: A Historico-Critical Study in Thomism.* Cork: Cork University Press, 1954.

Nielson, Kai. "The Myth of Natural Law." *Law and Philosophy: A Symposium,* edited by Sidney Hook. New York: New York University Press, 1964.

Northrop, F. S. C. "Naturalistic and Cultural Foundations for a More Effective International Law." *Yale Law Journal* 59 (1950): 1430–50.

O'Keefe, Daniel M. "*Stare Decisis*: What Should the Supreme Court Do When Old Laws Are Not Necessarily Good Laws? A Comment on Justice Thomas' Call for Reassessment in the Supreme Court's Voting Rights Jurisprudence." *St. Louis University Law Journal* 40 (1996): 261–303.

Opolot, James S. E. *World Legal Traditions and Institutions.* Rev. ed. Jonesboro, TN: Pilgrimage, 1981.

Papal Thought on the State: Excerpts from Encyclicals and Other Writings of Recent Popes. Edited by Gerard F. Yates, S.J. New York: Appleton-Century-Crofts, 1958.

Patsuris, Penelope. "The Corporate Scandal Sheet." *Forbes*, August 26, 2002. http://www.forbes.com/2002/07/25/accountingtracker.html.

Pennington, Kenneth. "*Lex Naturalis* and *Ius Naturale*." *The Jurist* 68 (2008): 569–91.

———. "Politics in Western Jurisprudence." In *A Treatise of Philosophy and General Jurisprudence*. Vol. 7, *The Jurists' Philosophy of Law from Rome to the Seventeenth Century*, edited by Andrea Padovcani and Peter G. Stein, 157–211. Dordrecht: Springer, 2007.

———. "Representation in Medieval Canon Law." *The Jurist* 64 (2004): 361–83.

Perry, Stephen. "Political Authority and Political Obligation." In *Oxford Studies in Philosophy of Law*, vol. 2, edited by Leslie Green and Brian Leiter, 1–74. Oxford: Oxford University Press, 2013.

Pieper, Joseph. *Justice*. Translated by Lawrence E. Lynch. New York: Pantheon, 1955.

Pigden, Charles. "Logic and the Autonomy of Ethics." *Australasian Journal of Philosophy* 67, no. 2 (1989): 127–51.

———. "Naturalism." In *A Companion to Ethics*, edited by Peter Singer. Oxford: Wiley-Blackwell, 1993.

Pius IX, Pope. *Quadragesimo Anno*. https://w2.vatican.va/content/pius-xi/en/encyclicals/documents/hf_p-xi_enc_19310515_quadragesimo-anno.html.

———. *Qui pluribus: On Faith and Religion*. Edited by Padraig M. O'Cleirigh. Kansas City, MO: Angelus, 1996.

Plato. *Laws*. In *The Collected Dialogues*, edited by Edith Hamilton and Huntington Cairns. Princeton, NJ: Princeton University Press, 1961.

———. *Republic*. In *The Collected Dialogues of Plato*, edited by Edith Hamilton and Huntington Cairns. Princeton, NJ: Princeton University Press, 1961.

Pope, Alexander. "An Essay on Man." In *The Poems of Alexander Pope: A Reduced Version of the Twickenham Text*, edited by John Butt. New Haven, CT: Yale University Press, 1966.

Porter, Jean. *Ministers of the Law: A Natural Law Theory of Legal Authority*. Grand Rapids, MI: Eerdmans, 2010.

———. *Natural and Divine Law: Reclaiming the Tradition for Christian Ethics*. Grand Rapids, MI: Eerdmans, 1999.

Pound, Roscoe. "Common Law and Legislation." *Harvard Law Review* 21 (1908): 383–407.

"Q&A: The Lisbon Treaty." *BBC News*, January 17, 2011. http://news.bbc.co.uk/2/hi/europe/6901353.stm.

Rappaport, Aaron J. "On the Conceptual Confusions of Jurisprudence." *Washington University Jurisprudence Review* 7, no. 1 (2014): 77–106.

Rawls, John. *A Theory of Justice*. Rev. ed. Oxford: Oxford University Press, 1999.

Raz, Joseph. "Authority and Justification." *Philosophy & Public Affairs* 14, no. 1 (1985): 3–29.

———. *The Authority of Law: Essays on Law and Morality*. Oxford: Clarendon, 1979.

———. *The Morality of Freedom*. New York: Oxford University Press, 1986.

———. *Practical Reason and Norms*. London: Hutchinson, 1975.

———. *Practical Reason and Norms*. Oxford: Oxford University Press, 1999.

Reiman, Jeffrey. "The Constitution, Rights, and the Conditions of Legitimacy." In *Constitutionalism: The Philosophical Dimension*, edited by Alan S. Rosenbaum, 127–49. New York: Greenwood, 1988.

Rhonheimer, Martin. "Natural Law as a 'Work of Reason': Understanding the Metaphysics of Participated Theonomy." *American Journal of Jurisprudence* 55, no. 1 (2010): 41–77.

Riley, L. J. *The History, Nature and Use of Epikeia in Moral Theology*. Washington, DC: Catholic University of America Press, 1948.

Rommen, Heinrich A. *The Natural Law*. Translated by Thomas R. Hanley. New York: Arno Press, 1947.

Ross, W. D. Introduction to *Aristotle's Prior and Posterior Analytics*. Oxford: Oxford University Press, 2001.

Rousseau, Jean-Jacques. *The Social Contract*. Translated by Maurice Cranston. Harmondsworth: Penguin, 1968.

Rziha, John. *Perfecting Human Actions: St. Thomas Aquinas on Human Participation in Eternal Law*. Washington, DC: Catholic University of America Press, 2009.

Sapien, Brendan. "Financial Weapons of Mass Destruction: From Bucket Shops to Credit Default Swaps." *Southern California Interdisciplinary Law Journal* 19 (2010): 411–42.

Scanlon, Cora Carroll, and Charles L. Scanlon. *Second Latin*. Charlotte, NC: TAN, 1976.

Sciolino, Elaine. "French Voters Soundly Reject European Union Constitution." *New York Times*, May 30, 2005. http://www.nytimes.com/2005/05/30/world/europe/french-voters-soundly-reject-european-union-constitution.html?_r=0.

Simmons, A. John. "The Principle of Fair Play." In *The Duty to Obey the Law: Selected Philosophical Readings*, edited by Williamson A. Edmunson, 107–41. New York: Rowman & Littlefield, 1999.

———. "The Principle of Fair Play." *Philosophy & Public Affairs* 8, no. 4 (1979): 307–37.

Simons, Marlise. "Dutch Voters Solidly Reject New European Constitution." *New York Times*, June 2, 2005. http://www.nytimes.com/2005/06/02/world/europe/dutch-voters-solidly-reject-new-european-constitution.html.

Smith, Steven D. *Law's Quandary*. Cambridge, MA: Harvard University Press, 2004.

Soper, Philip. "In Defense of Classical Natural Law in Legal Theory: Why Unjust Law Is No Law at All." *Canadian Journal of Law and Jurisprudence* 20, no. 1 (2007): 201–23.

———. "Legal Theory and the Claim of Authority." *Philosophy & Public Affairs* 18, no. 3 (1989): 209–37.

Sophocles. *Antigone*. Translated by Robert Fagles. New York: Penguin, 1984.

Stout, Lynn. *Cultivating Conscience: How Good Laws Make Good People*. Princeton, NJ: Princeton University Press, 2011.

Strauss, Leo. *Natural Right and History*. Chicago: Chicago University Press, 1953.

Suárez, Francisco. *Selections from Three Works*. Vol. 2. Edited by James Brown Scott. Translated by G. L. Williams, Ammi Brown, John Waldron, and Henry Davis. Oxford: Clarendon, 1944.

Tatarkiewicz, Wladyslaw. "Paradoxes of Perfection." *Dialectics and Humanism* 7, no. 1 (1980): 77.

Te Velde, Rudy A. *Participation and Substantiality in Thomas Aquinas*. Leiden: E. J. Brill, 1995.

Tierney, Brian. *The Idea of Natural Rights: Studies on Natural Rights, Natural Law, and Church Law, 1150–1625*. Grand Rapids, MI: Eerdmans, 1997.

Tunc, André. "Methodology of the Civil Law in France." *Tulane Law Review* 50 (1976): 459–73.

Vining, Joseph. *The Authoritative and the Authoritarian*. Chicago: University of Chicago Press, 1986.

———. *From Newton's Sleep*. Princeton, NJ: Princeton University Press, 1995.

———. "Law's Own Ontology: A Comment on Law's Quandary." *Catholic University Law Review* 55 (2006): 695–710.

Warkentine, Edith R. "Beyond Unconscionability: The Case for Using 'Knowing Assent' as the Basis for Analyzing Unbargained-for Terms in Standard Form Contracts." *Seattle University Law Review* 31, no. 3 (2008): 469–547.

Washington, George. "Farewell Address" (September 17, 1796). In *Documents of American History*, vol. 1, 9th ed., edited by Henry Steele Commager. Englewood Cliffs, NJ: Prentice-Hall, 1973.

Weinreb, Lloyd L. "The Moral Point of View." In *Natural Law, Liberalism, and Morality: Contemporary Essays*, edited by Robert P. George, 195–212. Oxford: Oxford University Press, 2001.

Westerman, Pauline C. *The Disintegration of Natural Law Theory: Aquinas to Finnis*. Leiden: Brill, 1998.

"What's America's Real Crime Rate?" *Economist*, February 14, 2012. http://www.economist.com/blogs/democracyinamerica/2012/02/prisons-and-crime.

Whitman, James Q. *The Legacy of Roman Law in the German Romantic Era: Historical Vision and Legal Change*. Princeton, NJ: Princeton University Press, 1990.

Williston, Samuel. *A Treatise on the Law of Contracts*. 4th ed. Eagan, MN: Thomson/West, 2013.

"WorldCom Scandal One of Many." *CNN Money*, June 27, 2002. http://money.cnn.com/2002/06/26/news/companies/accounting_scandals/.

Yochum, Mark D. "Ignorance of the Law Is No Excuse Except for Tax Crimes."
    Duquesne Law Review 27, no. 2 (1989): 221–35.
Zimmerman, Reinhard. *The Law of Obligations: Roman Foundations of the Civilian Tradition.* New York: Oxford University Press, 1996.

U. S. Court Decisions

Brown v. Bd. of Educ., 347 U.S. 483 (1954)
Calder v. Bull, 3 U.S. 386 (1798)
Dred Scott v. Sandford, 60 U.S. 393 (1856)
Lambert v. California, 355 U.S. 225, 243 (1957)
Loving v. Virginia, 388 U.S. 1 (1967)
McCreary County v. ACLU of Ky., 545 U.S. 844 (2005)
Payne v. Tennessee, 501 U.S. 808 (1991)
Planned Parenthood of Se. Pa. v. Casey, 505 U.S. 833 (1992)
Schrenger v. Caesars Ind., 825 N. E.2d 879 (Ind. Ct. App. 2005)
Van Orden v. Perry, 545 U.S. 677 (2005)
W. Coast Hotel Co. v. Parrish, 300 U.S. 379 (1937)

BRIAN MCCALL

is associate dean for academic affairs and
the Orpha and Maurice Merrill Professor in Law
at the University of Oklahoma College of Law.